ACCLAIM FOR SHANE READ'S TEXTBOOKS

*S*hane Read is a bestselling and multiple award-winning author who also teaches highly acclaimed litigation courses throughout the United States. Two of his textbooks, *Winning at Deposition* and *Winning at Trial,* have won the highest award from the Association of Continuing Legal Education for a legal textbook. Read is the only author who has won this prestigious award twice.

In Read's latest textbook, *Turning Points at Trial,* he brings you the strategies and skills used by the greatest lawyers in the country in every phase of litigation, from deposition, to trial, to appellate oral argument.

TURNING POINTS AT TRIAL

"Required reading for trial lawyers, but also exceptionally informative for anyone interested in legal proceedings."

— *Kirkus Reviews*

"*Turning Points at Trial* kicks ass and takes names. It uses a unique and effective technique to teach trial skills. Shane Read has interviewed some of the best trial lawyers in America on topics from opening statement to final argument. From each legend Read has gleaned the "secrets" to their success and then uses actual trial transcripts to hammer home these "secrets." He wraps up each chapter with a checklist. *Turning Points at Trial* is one of the best trial advocacy books I have read in my 46 years of practicing law."

— Dicky Grigg, Past President, International Academy of Trial Lawyers

"I have seldom, if ever, been very impressed with any legal writing about trial skills or great trial lawyers as they are mostly dull and too elementary. Not any more — Read's book is the best I have ever read and is an amazing work which is interesting and fun to read with so many good ideas on every aspect of effective trial presentations."

— Lewis Sifford, Past President, American Board of Trial Advocates

WINNING AT DEPOSITION

*W*inner of the Association of Continuing Legal Education's highest honor for a legal textbook.

"The book is a triumph.... [I]t makes for gripping reading, made all the better by Read's focus on the missteps of the famous lawyers and litigants he studies."

— *The Vermont Bar Journal*

"In every respect, D. Shane Read's book skillfully summarizes the art and science of taking depositions. [It] is an excellent resource for attorneys of all experience levels and areas of practice. *Winning at Deposition* is arranged in cogent chapters addressing everything.... Given the book's almost encyclopedic treatment of deposition topics, it is difficult to imagine that anything significant is omitted."

—*The Colorado Lawyer*

WINNING AT CROSS-EXAMINATION

"This book is a wealth of well-presented information, accessible and intriguing to those with limited legal knowledge as well as more experienced litigators."

—*Kirkus Reviews*

"*Winning at Cross-Examination* is so full of so many wonderful things that it is almost impossible to do justice to it with simple descriptions..... The scholarship and analysis of the many legal writings and articles on the subject of cross-examination are very insightful and are presented in a very well organized and thoughtful way. No matter whether an attorney practices civil or criminal law, this book is a tremendous and indispensable resource."

—Lewis Sifford, Past President, American Board of Trial Advocates

"In this brilliant analysis of spectacular trial successes, Shane Read persuasively focuses on the pivotal role of a unifying theme, a carefully crafted bottom-line message, rooted in virtue and woven creatively into a compelling story. From that indispensable foundation, the trial lawyer's entire house — particularly the all-important role of effective cross-examination — is built. No courtroom "house builder" of our time is more skilled than Mark Lanier, the living embodiment of the author's 'how to' guidance, who repeatedly strides across the pages of this eminently readable, extraordinarily practical book."

—Ken Starr, Former U.S. Solicitor General

WINNING AT PERSUASION FOR LAWYERS

"Public speakers of all kinds—and especially courtroom lawyers—will find this book invaluable."

— *Kirkus Reviews* (starred review)

ACCLAIM FOR SHANE READ'S TRIAL CONSULTING AND TRAINING COURSES

"If you follow Shane's advice, he can turn you into a great trial lawyer and ensure you pick the best jury."

— Lisa Blue, Past President, The National Trial Lawyers and American Association of Justice, and National Trial Lawyer Hall of Fame Inductee (2015)

"Shane brings a career of studious dissection of what works in trial and what doesn't. Learn from Shane and kick your game way up!"

—Mark Lanier, recognized internationally as one of the top trial attorneys in the United States

"Shane Read is an immensely skilled teacher and storyteller. This is one of the best CLE programs of all time."

—Stacey Thomas, Program Manager, Pennsylvania Bar Institute

TURNING POINTS AT TRIAL

TURNING POINTS AT TRIAL

Great Lawyers Share Secrets, Strategies and Skills

SHANE READ

This book is sold with the understanding that neither the author nor the publisher is engaged in rendering legal advice. Every effort has been made to make this book as accurate as possible. However, there may be mistakes, both typographical and in content. Therefore, this text should be used only as a general guide and not as the ultimate source of litigation rules and practice. Readers are responsible for obtaining such advice from their own legal counsel.

The purpose of this book is to educate and entertain. Any forms and agreements herein are intended for educational and informational purposes only. The author and publisher shall have neither liability nor responsibility to any person or entity with respect to any loss or damage caused, or alleged to have been caused, directly or indirectly, by the information contained in this book.

The views expressed in this book are solely those of the author and do not reflect the views of the Department of Justice.

Cover design by George Foster
Interior design by Patricia LaCroix

Publisher Cataloging-in-Publication

Read, Shane
  Turning Points at Trial / Shane Read
   p. cm.
  ISBN: 978-0-9850271-1-7

   1. Trial Practice—United States. 1. Title

KF8915.R43 2016

Shane Read is available for training and continuing legal education programs for organizations and law firms. He also writes an email newsletter with litgiation tips. For more information, go to www.shaneread.com or contact him at shane@shaneread.com.

Discounts are available for bulk orders.
  Westway Publishing
  4516 Lovers Lane, Suite 182
  Dallas, TX 75225
  support@westwaypublishing.com
  (888) 992-9782

For Benjie
A beautiful brother and trial lawyer
(1958–2015)

ENHANCE YOUR JOURNEY AS YOU READ THIS BOOK

You can enhance your learning experience in two important ways as you read this book. First, watch the videos that are referenced in the book. You will find them immensely helpful in learning the principles discussed in the text. Second, sign up for Shane Read's free bi-monthly newsletter which contains Shane's latest ideas, tips from other thought leaders, and bonus material not contained in this book.

Access the videos and newsletter at: www.shaneread.com/newsletter.

SHANE READ'S TRIAL CONSULTING AND IN-HOUSE BOOT CAMPS

Shane Read is a nationally recognized expert who has helped thousands of attorneys throughout the USA and Europe transform their deposition, trial, and oral advocacy skills through his consultations, in-house training programs, and keynote speeches. For more information, go to www.shaneread.com.

CONTENTS

PART THREE
Cross-Examination

PART FOUR
Cross-Examination of the Expert Witness

PART FIVE
Closing Argument

PART SEVEN
Appellate Oral Argument

INTRODUCTION

*I*n my previous three textbooks, I have taken the lead to explain litigation skills. Here, like a good commentator at a championship game, I have let the great trial lawyers I interviewed take center stage.

As I wrote this book, I had one goal: I wanted this book to give readers access to specific trial strategies they could use that could not be found anywhere else. To that end, I did not want my subjects just to tell a bunch of war stories that were exciting but of no help to lawyers with more ordinary cases.

As a result, I required each of my interviewees to provide me with a transcript of a particular trial skill where there was a turning point that affected the trial's outcome. While all the transcripts were captivating, I analyzed them to confirm that they would reveal skills and strategies with wide applicability for all trial lawyers.

I then asked the lawyers to discuss, first, their trial strategies in general and then the specific skill from the transcript that resulted in the turning point for their trial. As the book evolved, I decided to include a section on depositions and appeals because many cases are won before or after a trial.

Learning trial skills from great lawyers in the context of these fascinating cases makes them easier to learn and more memorable. For example, the cases analyzed include the largest jury verdict against the Catholic Church for sex abuse by a priest, a $9 billion verdict against a pharmaceutical company for marketing a dangerous drug, a civil rights case against a police officer for falsely arresting a woman for murder, and the heart-wrenching case of a couple who fought for the return of their adopted daughter from her biological father who had obtained custody two years after the adoption.

This book also provides numerous links to related video and audio sources at www.TurningPointsatTrial.com for further study. In addition, each chapter has a checklist that summarizes the lawyer's strategies that are discussed in the chapter. This checklist provides a quick reference that ensures that the reader can remember the lessons learned. There is a wealth of strategies and skills taught in the book. In the checklists alone, there are 447 tips.

As you read the book, you will notice that the great lawyers who are profiled share common principles about trial strategy and the execution of trial skills. Unfortunately, these ideas and techniques are seldom taught in law schools nor practiced in most courtrooms. The good news is that no matter what type of trial practice you have, you can learn the right skills and strategies from reading this book and immediately become more successful.

Courtroom advocacy is also an art. You will see that each lawyer adapts the trial principles and skills to fit his or her personality. By learning from the wide variety of successful lawyers who are profiled in this book, you can benefit from determining which strategies will work best with your own personality and skills and make adjustments as necessary.

A question you may have before starting this journey is, "How were the lawyers chosen?" There is no definitive list of great trial lawyers. Also, fame can be very misleading. Some famous lawyers achieved their notoriety for a particular case whose outcome was not dependent on the lawyer at all, but because the overwhelming facts, mediocre opposing counsel, the law itself, or some other cause determined the outcome.

Other famous lawyers have achieved acclaim through aggressive self-promotion. On the other hand, there are many great trial lawyers who never receive national exposure because they never seek it. Indeed, "famous" and "great" are not synonymous when it comes to describing a lawyer.

Consequently, this book does not pretend to create the definitive list of the greatest trial lawyers. While some of the lawyers in this book are household names, they were not chosen for their fame. I chose all the lawyers because they are certainly among the best at their craft and were passionate about sharing secrets, strategies, and skills so others could be successful. I also wanted to share with you perspectives from all around the country. In that regard, I interviewed lawyers from New York, California, Washington, D.C., Chicago, Alabama, South Carolina, Missouri, and Texas. The interviews cover the entire spectrum of trial practice lawyers, from plaintiff's attorneys to defense attorneys, prosecutors to criminal defense attorneys, as well as appellate attorneys.

In my teaching and writings, I am a strong believer that "less is more." With that in mind, let's end the introduction and begin a fascinating journey to improve your trial skills by learning from the best lawyers in America.

PART ONE

———∞———

Opening Statement

INTRODUCTION

*A*n opening statement is a speech given by a lawyer at the start of the trial that explains to the jury what the evidence will prove. Too often, lawyers throw this presentation together at the last minute and hope that by the time closing arguments arrive, they will have a more-organized speech. The unprepared lawyer is comforted by the conventional wisdom that states that you should save your best ideas for closing arguments anyway. This "wisdom" is based on the belief that jurors will follow the court's instructions given at the trial's outset to keep an open mind until all the evidence is presented. If no one is jumping to conclusions, the lawyer believes he can wait until closing arguments to comfortably summarize for the jury what has occurred at trial.

In reality, nothing could be further from the truth. A widely cited study found that 80–90 percent of jurors come to a decision about the case during or immediately after opening statements.[1] Human nature confirms this fact. We make quick judgments about who is right or wrong in our everyday life. It is nearly impossible to turn this decision-making process off just because a judge tells us to do so.

Moreover, law schools teach that you need to pepper your opening statement with the phrase, "The evidence will show…" in order to comply with the assumed prohibition of making arguments in opening statements. The flawed logic is that by repeating the phrase, you will only present the facts and not venture into the prohibited waters of arguing what the facts will prove. Again, this advice is completely wrong.

You will see in the following chapters that the opening statement is an opportunity to powerfully argue your case to the jury. In Chapter One, Mark Lanier, who the *National Law Journal* described as one of the most influential lawyers of the first decade of this century, will explain and show why the conventional wisdom is wrong. In Chapter Two, Windle Turley will share the secrets and strategies that allowed him to obtain the largest jury verdict ever against the Catholic Church because of sex abuse by one of its priests. In Chapter Three, you will learn a formula to use in any of your upcoming trials from Bryan Stevenson, who also gave one of the best TED Talks ever recorded.

---

[1] Donald E. Vinson, *Jury Psychology and Antitrust Trial Strategy*, 55 Antitrust L.J. at 591 (1986) (Study based on 14,000 actual or surrogate jurors).

CHAPTER ONE

---⊗⊗⊗---

Mark Lanier

Create a Spellbinding Opening Statement

Lanier gave a frighteningly powerful and skillful opening statement. Speaking… without notes and in gloriously plain English, and accompanying nearly every point with imaginative… overhead projections, Lanier, a part-time Baptist preacher, took on Merck and its former CEO Ray Gilmartin with merciless, spellbinding savagery.

—Fortune, July 2005

---

*I*n 2015, *National Trial Lawyers* named Mark Lanier "Trial Lawyer of the Year." In 2010, the *National Law Journal* declared Lanier as "one of the decade's most influential lawyers." While he has had many trial successes, we are going to look at two of Lanier's national record-setting verdicts: one involving the drug Actos and the other involving the drug Vioxx—a verdict which *The New York Times* reported "cemented his place as one of the top civil trial lawyers in America."

Although a lot can be learned from examining Lanier's trial transcripts, he brings to the courtroom many intangibles that cannot be seen. Perhaps Lanier's most striking quality is his love of teaching. When you see him in trial, he enthusiastically presents evidence on direct examination and passionately cross-examines witnesses so that the jury stays extremely interested and understands what is happening. He is sincere and easy to follow. He always uses visual aids and chooses words that are descriptive and uncomplicated.

> **CHAPTER HIGHLIGHTS**
> - Create a memorable theme
> - Use descriptive phrases and analogies
> - Tell a story that covers the good, the bad, and the ugly

Although he has several lawyers and paralegals supporting him at trial, he examines all the witnesses himself.

He is also extremely likable and charismatic. He explains that when he was growing up, his parents were constantly moving all over the country. He learned to make new friends quickly and adapt to different cultures. In short, he learned how to fit in and be liked.

When I saw him in a recent trial, he was grilling an expert witness on cross-examination. The expert was battling back and would not give an inch. The expert sneezed; Lanier immediately interrupted his examination and said, "Bless you." I asked him how he could so quickly switch from an intense cross-examination to a kind gesture toward the witness. Lanier's answer reveals his courtroom demeanor and should be a model for others to follow:

> There is a difference between dealing with an issue and dealing with a person. If I've got an expert on the stand that I am cross-examining who I think is putting a bunch of hooey out there for the jury, well, I'm going to dissect the hooey, and I am going to try and force that witness to accept the fact that what he is saying is bogus.
>
> That doesn't change the fact that I care genuinely for each person. They've got to sneeze—well, "Bless you." It's not personal, it's business. Even if I think that they are selling their soul for money, that they are a testifying prostitute, a jukebox you just put your money in it and they'll sing any song you want them to sing, it's not going to cause me to wish them ill. I want them to be the best they can be. I want their life to be good. I hope that's part of being genuine.

Lanier has a very strong desire to win. He confesses that he is a "very poor loser." He tells his clients, "If we win, you're going to find me to be nice and convivial and excited and happy. If we lose, there is a chance I won't talk to you much for the next few weeks because I just get, really, really solemn and down over losing. I'm hypercompetitive."

Lanier's journey to becoming one of the most successful civil attorneys in the country was not without detours. He graduated from Lipscomp University with a B.A. in Biblical Languages. He wanted to become a preacher but realized that by becoming a lawyer he could pay for his love of preaching without the hassles of becoming a permanent preacher. He never had an overwhelming desire to become a lawyer and make a lot of money. Says Lanier, "The motivation in my life is teaching and preaching, and taking care of my family—and law is that third priority that funds me to do it. I just happen to be really efficient at being a lawyer in a way that my skill set…makes money."

Lanier recalls early in his career that a top lawyer in Texas called him into his office and gave him this advice: He told Lanier that while he was currently a B-plus lawyer, he had the skill set to be an A-plus lawyer. But he cautioned Lanier that he would never become an elite A-plus lawyer unless he fixed his problem. Lanier asked, "What's my problem?" The lawyer said, "You put your family above your job. My daughter is thirteen. I've never been to one of her birthday parties, because I'm taking depositions and I'm working. You go to your kids' birthday parties; you put your children and your wife above the practice of law. If you do that, you'll never be better than a B-plus lawyer. Do you understand?" Lanier replied, "Yes sir, I understand."

But Lanier was thinking, "Thank the Lord I can be a B-plus lawyer and put my family first. I'd be happy as a clam as a B-plus lawyer, putting my family first, putting my faith first and my ministry there, because I didn't get in this game to be an A-plus lawyer. I got into this as a way to fund my family and my faith."

Lanier's actions speak louder than his words. Even when he is in a multi-week trial out of town, he always flies home to teach his Sunday school class, which often numbers in excess of 800 people. He recently took his class on a two-year survey of the Old Testament while simultaneously winning the record-setting Actos verdict (discussion to follow) in a courtroom in Louisiana. To get a sense of the effort Lanier puts into his Sunday school class, you can find a link for a video at this book's website, www.TurningPointsatTrial.com.

He also built the Lanier Theological Library in Houston, Texas, which houses a collection of over 100,000 books, with topics ranging from Church History and Biblical Studies to Egyptology and Linguistics.

As for his family, Lanier is married with five children. His mother lives across the street, and his sister lives just a few blocks away. The families eat lunch together every Sunday after church.

> *To define success, you look back at the memories that you've got of your existence on this planet — the ones that give meaning and purpose to your life. That starts with [the questions], how have you taken care of your family, how have you taken care of your talents and your skill sets, how have you served? For me, it's not just service in the law, it's also just service in a more direct ministry of life.*
>
> *— Mark Lanier*

Lanier's story would not be complete without learning why he chose to become a plaintiff's lawyer. After graduating from law school at Texas Tech University, Lanier was a defense attorney at a large firm in Houston. He was in trial, defending a railroad company that was at fault against a badly injured plaintiff. Lanier thought he had figured out a way to win the case, so he took it to trial — but lost.

As he was driving home, he thought about having to tell his family about the loss. More important, he thought about the plaintiff who would be able to tell his wife they could now afford to keep their house, provide clothes for their kids, and have a life for their family. Lanier had what he called, in reference to St. Paul's vision of Christ and subsequent conversion, a "Damascus Road experience." He asked himself, "What am I doing? I thought I was going to win this case by lawyer's skill, even though the facts dictated I shouldn't." Lanier imagined a different outcome, where he would have gone home to "crow" about the fact that his legal skills produced an unjust triumph.

He left the big firm and joined a small plaintiff's firm before starting his own firm in 1990. Since then, Lanier has received every accolade possible for a trial attorney. Given his recognition as being one of the very best, I asked him what difference does the quality of the attorney make in a case's outcome. Perhaps he was being overly modest in his answer, but he believes that facts generally determine the outcome. He explains this further by presenting three distinct scenarios.

In scenario one, one side has an average lawyer with all the winning facts, and the other side has a brilliant lawyer. As long as the average lawyer does a good job, the facts will determine the outcome no matter how brilliant the other lawyer is.

> *Lawyers generally don't make a difference in winning the case. Lawyers make a difference in losing the case.*
> — Mark Lanier

In scenario two, the good facts are evenly divided between both sides: There is an average lawyer on one side and a great lawyer on the other side. Also, assume that neither lawyer makes big mistakes. The facts will determine the verdict, but the lawyers will influence its size.

As Lanier says, "Maybe the damages could be more with a great lawyer on the plaintiff's side, or the damages can be less with a great lawyer on the defense side, but generally the facts will dictate the outcome."

In scenario three, there is a great lawyer on one side and an average lawyer on the other. However, one of the lawyers makes a big mistake. If the great lawyer is the one to mess up, the average lawyer might win regardless of the facts, and vice versa. "Now here's where the difference falls," says Lanier. "Great lawyers don't tend to mess up; average lawyers are more likely to mess up." Lanier concludes that a lawyer's skill can make a difference, but "it's not as big a difference as a lot of people think."

Lanier's charm is that, despite all of his success, he is not arrogant. Many people who have seen him at trial (including myself) would say that he makes a very big difference in the cases he tries, no matter what the facts are.

1.1 THE BIGGEST MISTAKE LAWYERS MAKE IN THEIR OPENING STATEMENTS

Without hesitation, Lanier says the biggest mistake he sees trial lawyers make is "stretching the truth, trying to make something that it's not. Jurors smell that, and you lose credibility. When you lose credibility, you lose the ability to persuade."

Lanier "loves it" when other attorneys stretch the truth in their opening statement or during the trial. He doesn't object to improper questions at trial. Instead, he gets a real-time transcript of the testimony from the court reporter. He lets the opposing lawyer stretch the truth with the witness, so that the witness walks farther out on a limb. Then, on cross-examination, he uses the transcript to contrast the unreasonable things the witness had just said with the truth as shown by the evidence or other testimony.

When I saw Lanier in trial, he would crucify witnesses on cross-examination with the words used by their lawyer in the opening statement. Any exaggeration the defense attorney made in opening would come back to haunt the attorney, as Lanier would ask the witness, "Your attorney said 'X' in the opening statement. Now the truth is 'Y,' isn't it?"

1.2 CREATE A THEME FOR YOUR CASE

Months before a trial begins, Lanier thinks about an engaging theme for his case. It is a task that preoccupies him. He is not searching for a factual theme but a "story theme, a TV show, a movie." He recounts how he thought of the show *Crime Scene Investigation*—known as *CSI*—and related it to the jury that was deciding his first Vioxx trial. Although the Vioxx trial will be discussed in detail later, all you need to know now is that Lanier told the jurors in his opening statement that it was as if they were on a detective show called *CSI: Angleton* (Angleton is where the trial took place).

After he had won the initial Vioxx trial, there were two subsequent Vioxx trials where Lanier was not the lawyer. Lanier relates that the defense lawyers stole his theme and told the jurors in those trials that they were to act like detectives in a *CSI* show to prove that the plaintiff did not have a case. The next Vioxx trial where Lanier was the attorney took place in New Jersey. The defense filed a motion in limine that sought to prevent Lanier from making any reference to *CSI* until closing argument. But in New Jersey, the defense goes first in the closing argument instead of the plaintiff. Consequently, Lanier knew that the defense had made the motion so that it could use the *CSI* analogy in its closing as it had done in the previous trials and prevent Lanier from taking advantage of it.

Lanier was not that easily fooled. He prepared a different theme. He summarized for me the closing he gave in New Jersey:

> Ladies and gentlemen, we are here about Vioxx, and you've been sitting listening to this trial for the last eight weeks. It's a trial about a beating heart, and this, in fact, is something we all have in common. We would not be here if our heart was not beating. We have an expression about something being as serious as a heart attack, because when your heart stops beating, it's traumatic, and it's tragic, but here we are…and the bad guys on the other side have said that this is like the TV show *CSI*.
>
> I find that appalling and offensive that they would ever make that suggestion. No lawyer should suggest this is *CSI*. Do you know why? Because "CSI" stands for "crime scene investigation." Now the judge has told you about the burden of proof here. The judge has said it's the preponderance of the evidence, [but a criminal trial requires much greater proof]. It's beyond a reasonable doubt.
>
> This is not what the judge has told you in this case. You shouldn't be thinking of this as a crime scene investigation — like I've got to prove my case to a criminal burden of proof. That's deceptive, that's lawyer trickery, and that's not what it is. It's not even almost beyond a reasonable doubt. All I need is the greater weight of credible evidence.
>
> You can have 49 percent doubt and vote for my client. This is not *Crime Scene Investigation*. Shame on you [defense counsel] for even making that suggestion! Now, I'm not against the TV show. But here's the TV show for this case: It's called *Desperate Housewives*.
>
> But instead of *Desperate Housewives*, we'll call this *Desperate Executives*, and instead of starring these five lovely ladies in New Jersey, we'll star Regal Martin, David Anstas, Briggs Morrison, Elise Rayson, and Edward Scolnick.

When Lanier recited his closing for me, he showed me the PowerPoint slides he had presented to the jury. The first one was an advertisement for the TV program *Desperate Housewives*. His next slide was a modified version of the first slide with the heads of the Merck executives substituted for the TV stars. Then, he continued with his recitation about four episodes of *Desperate Executives*.

> Here is your first episode: "Shoot for the Moon." [Lanier explains that he then put relevant arguments into the first episode.] Now that's the end of the first episode. Before we go to the next episode, let's pause for a com-

mercial break. This is a real Vioxx commercial. You listen — do they give a warning? You won't hear one.

Lanier then explained the second episode and so on. If you want to see an excerpt of Lanier's closing argument, go to this book's website, www.TurningPointsatTrial.com.[1]

In our talks, I challenged Lanier to make a simple case interesting, because most lawyers don't have the life and death cases he has. He advised that in any trial, you need to tell the jurors that the verdict is their chance to make a statement. It is your job to tell them what the statement is and make it personal for them. For example, in a fender-bender case, you might say:

> Ladies and gentlemen, we should not have to do this when someone is at fault in a car wreck. We're not supposed to have to go through all of this. We're not supposed to have to file a lawsuit. We're not supposed to have to hire lawyers. This ought to be dealt with forthwith, straight away by responsible people. But here we are, and this is your chance to say, "Don't do this. If you're responsible for someone's wreck, don't do this."

1.3 HOW TO CHANGE BAD FACTS INTO GOOD FACTS

In addition to spending time on finding an engaging theme, Lanier tries "really, really hard to understand all of the facts... I divide them up into three categories: facts that are good for me, facts that are neutral — not good or bad — and then facts that are bad for me. Then I take all of the bad facts, and I figure out how in my story I can move them over into a different column and make them good."

Lanier practices what he preaches. In the courtroom, he is the most knowledgeable person there, whether those others are opposing counsel, the judge, or a witness. He not only has mastered the facts but has thought through them so many times that he can simply explain them to the jury.

He explained to me how he changes bad facts into good facts. In the first Vioxx trial (discussed later), Bob Ernst was in excellent health when he died from taking Vioxx. But in another trial, Lanier represented John McDarby, who was "one pork chop away from a heart attack. He had every risk factor there was. He was very old, he was obese, he was diabetic, he had a family history, and he had high cholesterol." People asked him how he could win with all those negatives. He replied, "I'm just going to turn them into positives."

He then demonstrated to me what he had explained to the jury:

> Look, we all live on a table or on flat land, but there's a table's edge or cliff, and that's the heart attack [Lanier points to the edge of a table in front of

---

[1] If you want to see Lanier discuss his strategies in detail for *Ernst v. Merck* and his second Vioxx trial, go to www.TurningPointsatTrial.com.

us]. It's the leading cause of death in America. Some of us live real close to the edge, and other people live far away. If you are a 17-year-old kid, you're far away from the edge, but as you get to be 75, you're closer. Male, closer, diabetic, closer, smoker, closer, and all of these things move you closer to the edge of the cliff. [As Lanier talks, he moves a Styrofoam cup from the center of the table, which represents the 17 year old, closer to the edge as he mentions the risk factors of "male, diabetic, and smoker" etc.]

> *Your story needs to be the full story. It needs to cover the good, the bad, and the ugly.*
> — Mark Lanier

Now let me tell you about Vioxx. Vioxx is a shove toward the cliff. [Lanier pushes the cup that is now at the edge of the table and knocks it off.] If you're a 17-year-old guy — girl, it doesn't matter — you probably could take all the Vioxx you wanted. It's not going to bother you: You can take that stuff, you can take that shove, but you take someone who's right up against the edge of the cliff, and Vioxx is the last thing in the world that person needs to be taking. I'll prove that to you, and I'll prove that Mr. McDarby was right up at the edge of the cliff, and he had no business being on that drug.

Lanier's use of the table as a visual aid perfectly demonstrates how to turn bad facts into good facts. As hard as Merck argues that McDarby's heart attack was caused by his other risk factors, Merck could not overcome this powerful image that McDarby was the last person in the world who should have taken Vioxx, given how close to the edge he was.

1.4 DON'T OVERSELL YOUR CASE

Lanier cautions that he tries very hard in his opening statement not to oversell. The reason is that the other side follows him, "and if you oversell an opening, the other side is going to get up, and they are going to tear up what you've said. Everything you say, you've got to be able to prove. Your opening needs to be thorough — you need to cover what the other side is going to say as well." For example, Lanier points out that in the example above, you have got to explain the weaknesses in your case. "Heaven forbid I try to make the McDarby case and not mention all of his risk factors."

By discussing the bad facts in his opening, the jury is primed for when the defense counsel highlights the plaintiff's bad health, suggesting those risk factors caused his death and not Vioxx.

However, don't misunderstand Lanier's advice "not to oversell" as a license to be overly cautious in your opening statement. As we will see, he argues passionately and vigorously. He does not deliver a meek opening in any shape or form. He argues powerfully with descriptive words and PowerPoint slides, but he is always grounded in the facts.

1.5 DELIVERING AN OPENING STATEMENT

When Lanier gives his opening statement, he has a PowerPoint slide that accompanies every topic he discusses. Although Lanier has a trial team of lawyers and paralegals, he creates his own PowerPoint slides. This control helps him create the exact visual aid he has in mind and helps him with his delivery. He does not need to memorize which slide is coming next or what argument goes with the slide because he already knows, having put in the time on the front end to create them.

When he first begins working on his opening statement, he writes an outline on paper. This outline develops into a story accompanied by PowerPoint slides. When Lanier walks into the courtroom, he leaves the written outline behind. Lanier believes it is better to have no notes and forget something, than to get up there and be wedded to a notebook where you are flipping through pages. If you do the latter, you are going to "lose eye contact with the jury and lose that connection."

As far as what Lanier would say to young lawyers who claim that they need an outline to speak in front of a jury, he explains that if they think they need notes, "They need to wean themselves away from it. They need to get into Toastmasters or go back to high school, and do high school debate. They need to do something to learn how to speak publicly without that."

Lanier then mentions the great plaintiff's lawyer, Gerry Spence. Lanier points out that Spence would instruct that if you have no notes, it will cause you to have this ache in your gut that you can channel into energy that makes you genuine. Spence would tell young lawyers that they should tell the jury the following:

> I'm really nervous that I'm going to forget something, but I want to be able to talk from my heart to you. Instead of just reading what I wrote, let me tell you what I think. If I'm a little nervous, it's because I'm afraid that I'm going to leave something out, but this is more than me reading a speech to you—this is me speaking to you about how I feel.

Lanier elaborates on why he uses themes, PowerPoint slides, and stories to communicate with the jury: First, you want to put your message in terms that make the most sense to people. Through visual aids and the words you use, you want to create a message the jury will understand. He mentions a study that states if you use a word someone doesn't understand, your audience will miss the next seven words you say while their brains try to assimilate

> **Practice Tip**
>
> The PowerPoint presentation for your opening statement does not need to be listed on your exhibit list. It is a demonstrative exhibit. Attorneys usually exchange them by agreement on the night before or the morning of the trial.

what you have just said. "You want to talk in a language they understand. You want to talk in metaphors that they can relate to, in images and pictures that are already anchored in their brain, so you're just tying onto something that is already anchored there." When he needs to educate the jury about a complicated scientific term that will be used in the trial, he introduces the word, pauses, and then explains what the word means.

Let's turn to Lanier's opening statement in his record-setting Vioxx trial.

1.6 *ERNST V. MERCK*

In 1999, Merck began selling a new drug, Vioxx, which it claimed would benefit arthritis sufferers. Its main competitor was Pfizer's drug Celebrex. Before these two drugs, arthritis sufferers had no choice but to take aspirin or Aleve. One problem with aspirin was that if you were elderly and took too much of it, it could cause dangerous bleeding in the stomach. Merck declared that Vioxx was revolutionary because it could inhibit pain like aspirin but avoid the side effect of stomach bleeding.

Vioxx quickly became immensely popular and profitable. By 2004, its worldwide sales were well over $11 billion. But shortly after Merck introduced Vioxx to the world, a study was released that showed that patients who took Vioxx instead of Aleve had a greater risk of heart problems because it would cause blood clots. While some doctors and patients believed this was proof that Vioxx was dangerous, Merck interpreted the study as showing that the only reason Vioxx patients suffered an increase in cardiac problems was because Aleve was uniquely able to protect against dangerous blood clots, not that Vioxx caused them. This study became known as the VIGOR study.

However, Merck's assessment changed in 2004. At that time, Merck concluded a study that sought to see if Vioxx would help prevent colon polyps. The study found that after 18 months of taking Vioxx, patients had an increased risk of heart attacks. With this information, Merck withdrew Vioxx from the market. While Merck claimed that it was withdrawing the drug out of an abundance of caution, David Graham, an FDA scientist, testified before the Senate Finance Committee that the FDA's failure to keep Vioxx off the market in the first place was "the single greatest drug catastrophe in the history of the world." An FDA study found that Vioxx may have caused an estimated 28,000 deaths between 1999 and 2003.

Mark Lanier was the first lawyer to take Merck to trial on a Vioxx claim, and his record verdict was heard around the country. The turning point in the trial was Lanier's opening statement. At the conclusion of the trial, the $253.5 million verdict was one of the largest ever awarded to a single plaintiff in any type of case. That verdict has since been surpassed by another of Lanier's verdicts in 2014, when his client received a $9 billion verdict for dangers related to the drug Actos.

Years after Lanier's historic Vioxx win, Merck agreed to pay a $950 million settlement to the U.S. government for illegally promoting the drug and deceiving the FDA about its safety. It also pled guilty to a criminal misdemeanor charge of introducing a misbranded Vioxx into interstate commerce.

While it is true that Lanier's historic Vioxx verdict was reversed on appeal — and his $9 billion Actos verdict may be reduced on appeal — those facts do not take away from the truth that Lanier's persuasive skills in a courtroom achieve unprecedented results from juries and, ultimately, enormous settlements from defendants. Moreover, the massive verdicts that Lanier obtains have a significant impact on corporate defendants. The negative press and decline in stock prices from such trial outcomes are wake-up calls to pharmaceutical companies and give Lanier leverage to settle the claims for his other clients. For example, years after the first Vioxx trial, Lanier settled 85 percent of all Vioxx lawsuits for $4.85 billion. When Lanier obtained a $9 billion Actos verdict against Takeda Pharmaceutical and Eli Lily, Takeda's stock fell 9 percent in one day after the verdict was announced.

Before examining the opening arguments in the Vioxx trial, let's take a closer look at the case. The plaintiff was Carol Ernst, the widow of Bob Ernst. Bob began taking Vioxx a year before he died in 2001 in his sleep. He was 59 years old. He was a marathon runner. He took Vioxx to treat tendonitis in his hand. The trial began in state court in Angleton, a small town in Texas (population 18,977), on July 14, 2005. Five weeks later, the jury returned a verdict of $24 million in compensatory damages and $229 million in punitive damages.

The trial had many significant challenges. Not only was it the first attempt to hold Merck accountable for Vioxx, the medical examiner in the case, Dr. Maria Araneta, had concluded in her autopsy report that Bob had died from an irregular heartbeat (arrhythmia), not a heart attack caused by blood clots. No study had ever found that Vioxx caused arrhythmia, but studies had shown Vioxx increased the risk of blood clots.

Lanier was not discouraged. He hired a private investigator to find Dr. Araneta, who had moved to Abu Dhabi. He convinced her to come to Texas and give a videotaped deposition, where she concluded that, upon closer examination, Bob had died of a heart attack in contrast to her autopsy finding. She explained in her deposition that her autopsy report did mention an emergency room note that Bob might have had a heart attack. She said, "Something blocked that artery that was already narrowed — either a clot, a fissure, block... but...these things could be dissolved. He was resuscitated very vigorously. [The clot] could have been dislodged, you know. And they fractured his ribs. They were pounding on his chest."

Lanier's charisma was immediately evident to the jurors and everyone in the courtroom. *Fortune's* description of Lanier's opening statement was used to begin this chapter but is repeated here for ease of reference:

> [Lanier] gave a frighteningly powerful and skillful opening statement. Speaking without notes and in gloriously plain English, and accompanying nearly every point with imaginative overhead projections, Lanier, a part-time Baptist preacher, took on Merck and its former CEO Ray Gilmartin with merciless, spellbinding savagery.

After Lanier's opening statement, Merck would never recover. *Fortune's* description sets forth the ideal opening statement that every lawyer should aspire to give. Lanier's presentation had the combination of a memorable story and creative visual aids. For example, when Lanier argued that Merck did not stop marketing the drug because "nothing could stop the Merck marketing machine" from making needed money for the company, he showed the jury a slide of a steamroller. When he discussed how Merck "duped the FDA," he showed a slide displaying a pair of hands hovering over three walnut shells. His mastery of storytelling continued as he showed pictures of Bob running in a race, competing in a tandem bicycle race with his wife, and posing with his wife on his wedding day. Lanier paused and said, "Then things changed," and Bob's photo was replaced by a silhouette. "Bob Ernst died." The argument was captivating and easily understood.

Contrast that ideal opening with the failing critique given to the defense counsel by *Fortune*.

> In Merck's opening statement, [the defense counsel] presented a thorough, meticulous, and seemingly plausible rebuttal of Lanier's contentions. But in contrast to Lanier, defense counsel spoke matter-of-factly of "NSAIDS" and "coxibs" and "cardiothromboembolic" events with only perfunctory stabs at translation. He seemed to read much of his presentation and illustrated it only with stodgy, corporate head shots of Merck officials or hard-to-read excerpts from documents with meanings shrouded in medical jargon.

Fortune said the winner was undisputed. "Lanier is inviting the jurors to join him on a bracing mission to catch a wrongdoer and bring him to justice. 'You've got to be the detectives here,' he told them. 'If this were TV, this would be *CSI: Angleton.'* Merck, in contrast, is asking the jurors to do something difficult and unpleasant like — well — taking medicine."

The defense team continued to make mistakes during the trial. For example, Lanier's direct questioning of Carol Ernst concluded before the lunch break.

Lanier predicted to a reporter for *Fortune* during the break that Merck's lawyer would conduct a disastrous cross-examination of Carol.

For 90 minutes, Merck's lawyer conducted a long-winded and disrespectful cross of Carol. At one point, she was asked about Bob's strained relationship with his adult children from a previous marriage.

Lanier said at the time, "The only reason for questions is a lawyer ego." The jury agreed. In post-trial interviews, jurors stated that they found Carol's cross-examination "insulting" and "disrespectful."

With this background, let's focus on the turning point in the trial.

> *The trial offers a stark choice between accepting Lanier's invitation to believe simple, alluring, and emotionally cathartic stories versus Merck's appeals to colorless, heavy-going, soporific reason.*
> — *Fortune*, commenting on *Ernst v. Merck* opening statements

1.7 LANIER'S OPENING STATEMENT

As we look at Lanier's opening statement, I have highlighted in bold several phrases that will be discussed. Lanier began by thanking the jury for their time and introduced his client, Carol Ernst, and her daughter to the jury. He then talked about how he would present evidence.

> There are a lot of Merck witnesses I want you to hear from. I'm not allowed to make them show up. So they won't be here because I can't bring them here. Merck has to voluntarily bring them in.
>
> There's one fella I'm allowed to force to show up because he lives within a hundred miles of the courthouse. But everybody else, if Merck will bring them, I'll put them on live so I don't have to show you movies. But if Merck won't bring them, we'll have to do them through the movies.

Lanier immediately puts Merck on the defensive. He suggests that Merck has something to hide by not bringing witnesses to testify live at trial. He further puts the fault on Merck if he has to show the jury "movies" of the depositions because Merck won't bring the witnesses to trial. These video depositions are, by their nature, not nearly so interesting as live testimony. As a result, Lanier lays the groundwork for the jury to believe that if there is a video deposition shown at trial, it is because Merck was scared to bring the witness to trial. The jury's boredom while watching the videos can also be blamed on Merck.

Lanier then spoke for a moment about how the evidence would be presented in the case and continued as follows:

> I appreciated [defense counsel] referencing yesterday [during voir dire] that I was supposed to turn this into entertainment. I don't know about that, but if I do put you to sleep, you're allowed to throw your steno pads at

me — because you've given up five weeks of your life, and I'm not going to put you to sleep. I want you awake, and I want you tuned into the evidence.

Throughout his opening, Lanier builds a bond with the jurors. Imagine if you were a juror. What a relief it would be to hear from a lawyer that the trial will be interesting! In order to make it interesting, Lanier shows several PowerPoint slides on a projection screen with photos of Bob and Carol living a happy life. As he talks to jurors in this next segment, the photo of Bob fades, leaving the outline of his body.

> They did get married after being together for a number of years. Interestingly enough, they were introduced over exercise. And you'll hear Carol talk about her other daughter, Kendra, being the matchmaker between Carol and Bob.
>
> They got married. They had a wonderful time together. But ultimately, ultimately, the picture starts to fade and things start to go different. And let me tell you why. [Photo of Bob on projector screen fades and is replaced by Bob's silhouette.]
>
> You see, Bob Ernst is dead today. **One of my witnesses that I want to bring in the case I cannot bring you. Bob Ernst cannot come in here today.**[2] He is no longer here. He didn't know he was going to need to be here. He didn't leave us anything in video. He didn't leave us anything in writing that would talk about the issues that we need to talk about.
>
> So what you'll have is, you'll have Carol and you'll have Bob. They had been married for 11 months. And Bob was only 59 years old when he died. Now, some who are younger, that may seem like real old — but I promise you, as you start getting up there, it gets younger the older you get.
>
> He was 59 years old when he died. And what you've got to do is, basically, be the detectives here. You've got to figure out why he died. That's your job: Figure out whether or not, of the reasons he died, Vioxx is one of those causes. And that's your job. This is — **if we were going to put it in to a TV show, this would be *CSI: Angleton* because this is your chance.**
>
> **And I think the way you do it is going to be real easy.**

Lanier is a master communicator. He explains that his best witness, Bob, is dead. So, Merck has deprived Lanier the ability to put on his best case. Lanier addresses a weakness in his case — Bob's age. He explains that while Bob may seem old at first glance, he really had a lot of life left to live. Then, he gives them an analogy to understand the case; they are going to be detectives like those in TV's most popular mystery series that takes place in different cities (i.e., *CSI: NY*). Lanier then explains the importance of their role as detectives.

> [Y]our job is to get us to justice. There isn't anybody else. The way our country is set up, there is no one else — no one else that can find out

---

[2] Throughout this book, words in the transcript have been put in bold to highlight the point being made in the discussion that follows.

> whether or not Merck is a cause but you. That's it. **That's the calling.** This is what's on your life right now. Nobody else has this power. A judge can't do it. This is not a bench trial. Judge can't do it. Politicians can't do it. Nobody else can do it. This is something you've got. This is where you can make a difference in the world, absolutely can....
>
> I'm going to show you the motive, and I'll prove it to you. And my burden is to prove it by 51 percent, but I got to tell you, I'll prove it to you. **There's not going to be that doubt in your mind.** You're going to see the motive. You're going to see it clear.

The key to telling a meaningful story is to relate why it matters. Lanier empowers the jury and explains that this is not just a trial, but a chance for the jurors to make a difference in the world. Second, Lanier does what so few lawyers do (but should). He takes on an additional burden of proof and promises that he will prove his case beyond any doubt. He is not going to hide behind the lessor proof of 51 percent. How comforting it must have been for the jurors to know that their decision will be easy because Lanier will bring overwhelming evidence of absolute proof. Lanier's approach is consistent with how we reach decisions anyway. Jurors decide who is right, not who is just barely right (51 percent). Judges can give the instruction that a plaintiff only needs to prove his case by 51 percent, but it can't overcome human nature.

> Let's start with motive. Merck had the motive. What was the motive? **The motive was money.** Don't get me wrong. I think it's fine for a corporation to exist to make money. That's how we have jobs. That's how we have products. I think that's a good thing. But what companies have to do is, they have to watch to make sure that money doesn't take a priority position over health and safety.
>
> Merck had new management that came into play in 1994, and this new management took the company and **they tried to turn Merck into an ATM machine**, a machine that's spitting out the money, a machine where they could punch the buttons and they could draw out all the cash they want and need....

Discusses weakness

Notice below how Lanier turns a weakness into a strength. He anticipates that the defense counsel will discuss all the good Merck has done. Lanier admits Merck was a great company in the past, but he will show that it is not anymore.

> See, the historical company Merck had been was a family-run company. It had been a good company. I'm going to tell you, the history of Merck before this is a good history. Founded by George Merck. They put out real nice books on it [indicating]. This was a company that was really working hard to find good drugs over the years.

This is a company that stumbled upon a drug that cured an African blindness — river blindness — and the people who could be cured with the drug didn't have money to buy it. They didn't have insurance. And so Merck gives it to them [for free] to try and take care [of the people].... They had been a good company run by scientists....

By discussing how good Merck used to be, Lanier actually reveals how bad the company has become. Read how he continues to truly turn a weakness into a strength:

In 1994, Merck broke with tradition and they hired a new CEO.... **the family is not running the company anymore. That's over.** This is now this big international concern. And what the board did is they chose to be a new kind of company in 1994. They hired Ray Gilmartin.

Now, you might be thinking, "All right. I wonder what kind of a guy Ray Gilmartin is. Was he a top-flight doctor? Was he ... like Dr. Vagelos ... one of the best doctors in the country?" No, he wasn't.

Well, if the board didn't turn to a doctor, maybe they turned to a chemist because they're doing chemistry, right? Maybe they turned to a chemist and got one of the best chemists in the world to help this company develop good chemicals. No, they didn't hire a chemist either.

Maybe they hired a pharmacist. It's a pharmacy company. Maybe they hired a pill expert, a drug expert. Maybe that's who Ray Gilmartin is. No, Ray Gilmartin is not any of those things. And those were not the priorities Ray Gilmartin brought to the company when he came.

What the company did is, they went and they hired Ray Gilmartin, and Ray Gilmartin is a Harvard-trained businessman, not a scientist. There's nothing wrong with a businessman running the company if he runs it right, but you're going to see what he did. If a Boy Scout has a compass or a Girl Scout has a compass and the needle is supposed to always point north, Ray Gilmartin took this company and made the needle always point to the dollar sign, and that's how they chose their direction.

> *If a Boy Scout has a compass or a Girl Scout has a compass and the needle is supposed to always point north, Ray Gilmartin took this company and made the needle always point to the dollar sign, and that's how they chose their direction.*
>
> — Mark Lanier, opening statement

Ray Gilmartin made it not science first, like it had always been, not health first, not medicine first, not drugs first. **Ray Gilmartin made it profit first. He turned a good drug company into a business-first company.**

And this is what I'm going to prove to you.... I'm going to give you chapter and verse on it.

The analogy of the Boy Scout and his compass and Girl Scout with her compass is perfect. Merck has lost its bearing, and that explains why it put a dangerous drug on the market.

Merck's motive

And Gilmartin comes in. He restructures everything. He does something that I'm calling it, at the risk of a bad pun, murky ethics, because he takes the scientists and the science teams that are supposed to be putting science first, and he puts the salespeople on the science teams. He takes the briefcases and laptop people and a PR-type guy and a sales-type guy, and he integrates them into the people who are supposed to be developing the drugs. They got the salesman at the front end trying to figure out how to write the drug and test the drug in a way the salesman can best sell the drug....

You say, "Oh, Lanier, how do you know?" You're going to see the evidence of it, because the FDA...finds a pattern and practice within Merck of misrepresenting the truth about the safety of their drugs. I've got to show you a letter we found.

Here is a letter we found...Is that big enough for you all to see? Can you all see that? [T]his is what the FDA says: "This letter is in reference to Merck & Company's submission of promotional materials....[The FDA] regards the promotional material [regarding the drug Trusopt] to be false and/or misleading."

False or misleading. Now, if I'm a drug company and I get a letter like this, my reaction is going to be, "OK. Who's responsible? Come into my office. We don't do that. We tell the truth. We tell nothing but the truth. Doesn't matter if you're a salesman. You don't go out there and give out false and misleading material. You do it again, you're going to be fired. Or the people under you who do it again, they're going to be gone. I'm not going to have people working for me who do this."

And I would love to tell you that that was done and this is the only letter I've been able to find from the FDA writing them up for their falsehoods and their misrepresentations, but it's not the only letter....

Notice that when Lanier shows the jury the letter on the projector screen, he is concerned whether the jury can see it. Great trial lawyers see their case through the jury's eyes. Lanier is not just presenting information. He wants it to be understood. He wants to make sure the jurors can see this important exhibit. If they can't, he will correct the problem. He is their friend, someone they can count on to present information that they can understand.

Oh, maybe they quit in July of '99...Oh, no. We can fast-forward to December of 1999. They're still getting letters from the FDA on Vioxx because their Vioxx ads are false, misleading, and contain misrepresentations of Vioxx's safety profile, unsubstantiated comparative claims, where they say Vioxx is better than these other drugs....

That's why I tell you, that's why the evidence is going to show you the FDA finds a corporate pattern. It was sales at all cost. It was not business as usual. See, the new management turned Merck into an ATM. The story doesn't end there....

Merck's financial problems

Because while they turned Merck into an ATM, the new management has, they got desperate. Gilmartin gets desperate because his ATM is set to run out of money starting in the year 2000/2001.

Lanier goes on to tell the jury that the patents on several Merck drugs are expiring. That means that Merck can no longer have exclusive control over the drugs. So, Merck needs a new drug to fill this void. Lanier argues that Gilmartin and others believed Vioxx would save the company. But there was a problem: The FDA had already approved a similar drug, Celebrex. Merck knew it had to rush to get Vioxx approved so it could catch up to Celebrex's head start.

Merck cuts corners

So Merck goes to the FDA. They say,...would you approve us on a faster basis? Treat this like an emergency cancer drug.... They get a six-month rush on the FDA [instead of the two-year process]. I got to tell you—just bluntly—Merck starts selling the drug Vioxx before they finished testing it....

Can you imagine if we stopped our studies and decided safety early? I want to measure safety. I'm going to tell Judge Hardin, "Judge Hardin, we're going to do a test. We're going to go out and measure safety. How safe is it to fall from a 100-story building?" Let's get some people who will do it for us, but I tell you what we're going to do.

Well, we don't want to hurt people. **We'll use watermelons. We're going to drop watermelons from a hundred-story building and see how they handle the fall. But let's measure the results—let's not wait until the end. Let's go down to the tenth floor, and let's just cut the study off a little early and measure the results there.**

Down come the watermelons. This one is OK. This one is OK. This one is OK. Man, these watermelons look great. There's no problem

> **dropping them from the hundredth floor if you measure them at the tenth floor.**
>
> You need to be on the sidewalk. You need to finish the test before you start selling the drug. Bottom line: Merck doesn't because Merck is in a hurry. This is the motive. Merck's got to have the money.
>
> New subject. Point Number 2. As you follow the focus of the evidence, look at the means. Let's look at whether or not Vioxx is, in fact, the means.

Lanier is the master of analogies. He uses another one to explain a complicated testing method: Watermelons dropping from a 100-story building. It is an image everyone can visualize easily. Moreover, the idea of testing a watermelon before it hits the ground is ridiculous, which is exactly Lanier's point.

Lanier then succinctly and clearly explains the risks to the heart associated with taking Vioxx.

Merck hides the ball

> Merck can choose any people they want to bring down to this courthouse to be the face of the company, to try to personalize the company so you don't think about the monstrous buildings they have all over the world. You think about the individual who comes into the courtroom. And that's their choice, and they get to pick that, however they want to do it.
>
> But I'll tell you who I hope they'll bring down, because I would like to put him on the witness stand…. I would put him on the witness stand Monday if they'll bring him down here. This man's name is David Anstice. And David Anstice is the president of Merck America—in essence, the American Merck company….
>
> They carefully pick what they give to the FDA. And then, what they also do is they dump hundreds of thousands of pages on the FDA when the FDA has got [a very small amount of time] to read them. Where's the best place to hide a leaf? It's in the forest. Where's the best place to hide water? In the ocean.

> *Where's the best place to hide a leaf? It's in the forest. Where's the best place to hide water? In the ocean.*
>
> — Mark Lanier, opening statement

Lanier paints a picture of Merck being an impersonal company that deceived the FDA. He knows that Merck is not going to bring Anstice to trial. While Merck may have legitimate business reasons for not bringing its head of the American division to testify, Lanier puts Merck on the defensive for not doing it. Then, he uses a wonderful analogy of leaves and water to explain Merck's deception to the FDA.

Lanier never passes an opportunity to use a familiar phrase or create a new one to convey his message. Here are two more:

> The first thing Merck does, **faced with the facts, [is that] they literally rewrite the book.**... And do you know what they do? They invent a story. They do what I like to say: **"They turned science into science fiction."**

Merck recruits and then threatens doctors

> Have you ever heard the expression about offering someone a carrot? I always think of the cartoon with the carrot out in front of the donkey, and the donkey is walking trying to get the carrot, and you try and move someone where you want them to go by putting a carrot out in front of them. That's what they do to the doctors. They offer them carrots. They offer them treats. They offer them things. They offer to — oh, all sorts of things.
>
> They'll go to doctors, and they'll say, "Doctor, we have this shiny nice brochure on Vioxx. It's got all of this wonderful information, and...we've worked really hard on it. And it's illegal for us to pay you to read this because we can't pay you to do that. Do you know what we could do? We could give you $500 and ask you to look at it and tell us if you think that that's a good color blue and do you think the print is big enough and do you think...you know, is it pretty? Does it communicate well? Understand, when we give you this $500, that's not for reading this. That's for giving us feedback." And they play these kinds of games.
>
> And they go to other doctors nationally.... They say, "Hey, if we give this doctor a $10,000 grant to study something, then this doctor will get on board and tell everybody Vioxx is safe."...
>
> Now, not all the doctors go along with it.... **I guess if the carrot doesn't work, they take a stick and start whacking the donkey to make it move....** And you're going to hear his testimony about a number of doctors that are saying, "Hey, we think Merck is the reason we lost our job."

Lanier frames almost all of his arguments with an analogy that is easy for the jurors to understand and visualize. Here, Lanier describes that Merck treats doctors as if they were donkeys who can be rewarded with carrots or punished with sticks.

Merck advertises Vioxx

> Do you know how much they spend to push their drug? Over $1 billion dollars. That's 1,000 million. A million dollars, that's a lot of money. You can line up a thousand people, a lot more than in here, and give every one of them a million dollars. That gets you to a billion.... They spend over a million dollars just at this party to launch it.

And then they put together the largest sales force in the history of any drug.... They had Dorothy Hamill do the figure-skating thing, and now she skates so much better because of Vioxx.... And please understand, none of us can go buy that drug. There's not one human being, unless you're a medical doctor and write your own prescription, who can go out and buy it. Why they're advertising to us is an issue, because they're trying to get you and me to go to our doctors and ask for Vioxx instead of Celebrex....

$161 million being spent at this time period to sell Vioxx to us.... That's more in that same time period than Pepsi spent selling Pepsi. That's more than Budweiser spent selling Budweiser. At least Budweiser and Pepsi are things people can go buy.... They're putting hundreds of millions in to seduce the doctors to prescribe it. They're sending doctors on all sorts of junkets.... Merck says it's a good company, but it's not a good company to me...[as they are] paying doctors by giving doctors take-home coupons to go to the nicest restaurants and get all this food to take home to their family.

Lanier never forgets his audience. He simplifies everything. He wants this complicated case to become straightforward. He doesn't just say how much money Merck spent; instead, he breaks it down to a figure that everyone can understand. And just to make sure, he compares that figure to the amount of money Pepsi spent on its product.

Merck v. Bob

So where are we so far? We got to move through — Merck had the motive: money. Merck had the means: Vioxx. And nothing is going to stop it from being out there. But when you put that together, **the motive** and **the means**, that's where you find the **death of Bob Ernst.** Let me bring it home now to Bob Ernst.

OK. Bob Ernst goes to his doctor. Do you know what he goes there for? Bob goes to Dr. Wallace because his hand hurts. He's got hand pain. He's been taking naproxen for his hand pain, but you have to take naproxen a couple of times a day. And Bob was excited because he had been told Vioxx is a once-a-day pill. He could just take it once a day. So Bob goes to his local doctor for hand pain...The doctor did a bunch of tests on him....

Is this a fella who's one pork chop away from a heart attack? No, he's not. He's in great shape. Bob goes in there, and they check his cholesterol. His total cholesterol is 169. That's a thumbs-up. His high-density cholesterol, his HDL, is 43. That's a thumbs-up. His pulse is 58. That's a thumbs-up. His blood pressure is 108 over 64. **This guy is the picture of health.**

> *Is this a fella who's one pork chop away from a heart attack?*
> — Mark Lanier,
> opening statement

All of his test results like that are in the safe range. He's in great shape. But his hand hurts. That's what started this whole thing. **That's why Carol doesn't have a husband now. He went to the doctor because his hand hurt.**

Bob exercised regularly. He ran. He biked. He was a weight lifter. He swam. He competed in triathlons.

After analyzing Lanier's opening, you forget that it is a mere negligence case. Lanier frames his story in so much bigger terms. It is framed as a murder case. He uses the words "motive," "means," and "death" to describe a monstrous company that knew its greed would kill people and never cared.

Lanier uses another analogy to describe Bob's health. Was he just one pork chop away from a heart attack? No, he was not. Bob's only problem was that his hand hurt. Then, Lanier summarizes his case: "That's why Carol doesn't have a husband now. He went to the doctor because his hand hurt."

Merck pressures Bob's doctor

Lanier contrasts Bob's health with Merck's marketing to Bob's doctor, Dr. Wallace. Dr. Wallace works in Cleburne, a small town in Texas. He's on Merck's "hit list." Read how Lanier chillingly describes Merck's actions:

They've got a bull's-eye on the back of Dr. Wallace. There it is. He's on [Merck's] hit list. They're monitoring every prescription he writes. Did you know they can do that? Merck has some way of finding out every prescription…that he writes. And they're doing it. Now, they've redacted some of this document, but you can see up at the top on their project "coffin nail." What a horrible thing to call it!

Here is their hit list for Vioxx, and here are the names of the doctors, and here is how much they're writing. And they've got Dr. Wallace from Cleburne, Texas, right there. And they're going to show you that…12.70 percent of [Dr. Wallace's] prescriptions are Vioxx. And Merck makes it a goal for those salespeople to get Dr. Wallace over 50 percent, and they start making sales calls [to] Dr. Wallace….

Merck is in Dr. Wallace's office constantly. Merck wines and dines Dr. Wallace, literally…they pay him to do things…So they go, "Dr. Wallace, here is the deal. We can't pay you to write a Vioxx prescription, but I'll tell you what we can do. We'll give you, say, $300 or so if you'll let our salesman come with you on your visit with the patient and stand there and watch you physically write the Vioxx prescription.

"We're not paying you to prescribe Vioxx. We're paying you because it educates our salesmen to be able to see the way you write a prescription…. We're not doing anything wrong. We're paying you for the educational aspect of it."

And I asked Dr. Wallace about this in his deposition, and I'm going to play it for you. I said, "Dr. Wallace, is there some magic about the way you write a prescription that that salesman is going to learn something from you that he hadn't learned from the thousand other doctors he's been paying money to stand and watch them write prescriptions?" He smiled and he said, "No, I don't do it any differently."

That's what they do. They wine him. They dine him. They take him to dinners. They pay him to watch and learn. And then they give him samples and samples and samples. They give him enough to where he's able to give Bob Ernst a couple months of samples.

Causation

So net result, when you bring all of this home to Bob Ernst, how does it play out? Bob Ernst goes to the doctor for hand pain. Merck has been in there working the doctor over. And as a result, Vioxx is a cause of Bob's death.

Now, Merck thinks that they can win this or anything else they ever come across because how am I going to prove to you that Vioxx was the cause. But that's not going to be the law. I don't care what [defense counsel] says. You can write it down, you can go to the bank on it. The Judge's instructions to you are going to say, specifically, there can be more than one cause, because there is in most anything in life.

Lanier then tells the jury that the only reason Bob, who was perfectly healthy before taking Vioxx, died from heart problems is because Vioxx caused his heart problems.

Conclusion

Lanier wrapped up his opening statement with one of his strongest arguments:

The last thing, Your Honor, before we break, I would like to talk about their alibis briefly. This is where they start pointing their finger everywhere.... They're going to say, "Well, we never really knew that Vioxx caused heart attacks."

Lanier then discusses the studies that Merck conducted. Some studies showed that if you took Vioxx for more than 18 months, your risk of heart problems increased. Lanier points out that Merck did everything it could to ignore the bad studies and embrace the good ones.

It's going to make you sick. It's going to make you sick, the way they maneuver their numbers and change this and move that over there and redefine things.... You need to hear Ray Gilmartin, who stands up and publicly tells the stock investors and the stockbrokers, "Oh, don't worry about all these rumors that our drug causes heart problems."

I took his deposition. I said, "How can you stand up there and say that? I don't care if they are investing in your company. How can you say that? I'm looking at the study. Out of a hundred people taking the sugar pill, you get one death. Out of the hundred people taking this dose of Vioxx, you got four deaths. Out of a hundred taking that dose, you got two. By either account, you got two to four times as many. How can you say there's no increase when there's one with the sugar pill and there's six with Vioxx?"

And he looks me in the eye and he says, "Well, that's not significant, the difference between one and six."

So, I did what you would do. I pulled out my wallet. I handed him a dollar. I said, "Would you give me six back? I'm glad to notice there's no difference here with you. I'll spend the rest of my time with you all day swapping money until you agree that there may be a difference here."

Because that's just wrong. It's wrong to stand up and say something that's not the truth. But they've done it, and they're going to do it here, and I'm going to prove it to you.

Lanier ends his opening with this crescendo.

They're going to blame the victims. "Oh, this must be because Bob, even though he exercised daily, even though he ate right, even though he wasn't overweight, even though he had his cholesterol checked, even though he was the picture of health in every area except his arthritic hands and low blood sugar, even though he's the picture of health, this must be his fault."

No, no. Here is what you have: The motive, the means, the death. You got alibis that are nothing more than finger-pointing, and it's wrong, because what it's left you with is, it's torn apart.... It's taken your soul mate, and you'll [looking at Bob's widow, Carol] get to explain that to the jury.

You'll hear from her. I have to ask her questions, and you're going to think, "Lanier, I thought you were a nice guy. Why are you making her say all that stuff?" I have to. We have to not only say it for you, but we have to put it on a cold record.... about the anguish and how hard this has been on her and what she lost....

But it's a sweet story. It's a touching story, and you'll love it. You'll love to hear about their first date and where it was. It's the same restaurant they went to the night Bob died. And it's a neat story.

And I know [looking at Bob's widow, Carol] you're thankful to God for every day you had with him.

But you'll get to hear about it. And the worst part is, is while there are some good people at Merck—and I'm sure they're going to bring good people in here—this didn't have to happen, because the real people, the management, the people I want in here, the people I challenge them to bring so I can put them on in evidence for you, are people who changed the lifelong slogan. Merck used to be, "Where patients come first." That's not where it ended up. Thank you, Your Honor.

Lanier comes full circle. He began his opening statement by showing the jury photos of Bob and Carol together. He described Bob's active lifestyle and his love for Carol. He also explained that he could not force Merck's top executives to attend the trial, but that he hoped they would come and answer his questions. He ended his opening the same way. He started and ended his opening with his best fact: a healthy man, who was loved by his wife, died of a heart attack after taking Vioxx. He then couples that fact with Merck's cowardice in not showing up for the trial.

Reflecting back on his opening statement, there are so many images and simple ideas that Lanier has created that bolster his argument. A full list is located in the Chapter Checklist at the end of this chapter. Here are just a few: 1) Bob and Carol were soul mates, 2) Bob was the picture of health, 3) the only problem Bob had before taking Vioxx was pain in his hand, 4) Merck is afraid to bring witnesses to trial, 5) Merck thinks that six deaths out of a hundred is the same as one death out of a hundred, but won't give Lanier six dollar bills for every one he gives them, 6) to study whether watermelons will explode on impact from a 100-story building, you need to let them fall to the ground instead of the 10th floor, and 7) Merck had the motive, means, and victim.

1.8 DEFENSE OPENING STATEMENT

There is no quicker way to lose a jury's attention than to read your opening statement. Your goal is to connect with them, and you do that by looking them in the eyes and saying something powerful at the very beginning to get their interest. We know from the *Fortune* account previously mentioned that Merck's attorney read much of his opening statement. But what *Fortune* did not mention was how badly he started.

Imagine if you were on the jury and had just heard Lanier give an opening statement that was spoken like a preacher with powerful PowerPoint slides. Would this be a good response?

May it please the Court.

Good afternoon, ladies and gentlemen. I'm pleased to speak with you this afternoon on behalf of Merck.

As you might imagine, we wouldn't be here today if there weren't two sides to this story. If it were an open and shut case, as plaintiffs have suggested, this case would have been over long ago. As Judge Hardin mentioned during jury selection, this will be a somewhat lengthy case — lots of evidence to be presented, documents, and witnesses, some live, and some who gave their sworn testimony before trial and videotape. You'll see both during this trial.

We appreciate the important job that each of you have ahead of you. It's a tough job to sort through and weigh all of the evidence — to tell the difference between allegations and proof—and we appreciate you undertaking that responsibility here.

We believe that at the end of this case, you will see that the scientists and leaders at Merck conducted themselves prudently and responsibly.

Who wants to hear that this will be a "lengthy case" with "lots of evidence." On top of that, defense counsel explains that the jurors have a "tough job." Instead of reading his opening statement, the defense counsel should have spoken passionately to the jurors and told them that he would make their job easy. He would make it easy, because he would prove that whatever smoke Lanier tried to create, there was no fire: Vioxx did not cause Bob Ernst's death. Instead of presenting lots of documents and witnesses, he would only need to show them the critical ones necessary to reach the obvious answer.

Finally, word choice is vital. The defense counsel was speaking to a jury that came from a very small town in Texas. Only someone who embodies the corporate world would use words like "the scientists and leaders at Merck conducted themselves prudently and responsibly." To connect with the jury, defense counsel needed to use words for jurors in Angleton, Texas, not some hearing before the FDA. Better words would have been, "the people at Merck knew what was right and did it."

How would you have started the opening if you represented Merck? As with any opening, you want to grab the jury's attention and start with your strongest point. Let's compare the defense counsel's opening statement with another lawyer who represented Merck in a similar case. That lawyer is Phillip Beck. Here is his approach:

> Thank you, your honor. Mr. Birchfield [plaintiff's counsel] talked for about 60 minutes. While he was talking, about 60 people across the United States died from exactly the same thing that caused Mr. Irvin's [plaintiff's] death, and not a single one of them was taking Vioxx.
>
> I'm going to talk for about 60 minutes, and while I'm talking, another 60 people across the United States will die of the same thing that caused Mr. Irvin's death, and not a single one of them is taking Vioxx. The reason is that the thing that caused Mr. Irvin's death is the leading cause of death in the United States of America. That was true before Vioxx ever came on the market, and that's true today after Vioxx is no longer being sold.

> Several hundred thousand people a year die from having arteries that are clogged up with plaque, then having a rupture in the plaque, and then having a blood clot form in the artery so that not enough blood gets to the heart. It's the leading cause of death in the United States.

Merck would get a hung jury in this trial and then win on the retrial. Notice how well Beck frames his argument. Unlike the defense counsel's view in Lanier's trial that it is going to be a long trial with a lot of evidence that presents a tough job for the jury, Beck says the case is simple: The plaintiff died from something that is very common in America; indeed, it is the leading cause of death, and it has nothing to do with Vioxx. Also, in contrast to the approach in Angleton that was defensive and apologetic, Beck came out swinging. Finally, instead of providing content that was bland, Beck provided the jury with a startling fact about the leading cause of death in the United States.

1.9 CHAPTER CHECKLIST ✏️

Lanier's philosophy about life and the practice of law

1. A great lawyer can influence the outcome of a case, but it is not so big a difference as people think. The key is that the average lawyer will make more mistakes than a great lawyer, and those mistakes can lose a case.

2. It is not worth being a great trial lawyer if you have to sacrifice your time with your family.

3. Success is when you reach the end of your life and looking back, you feel that you have taken care of your family, taken care of your talents, and have served.

4. "I have a limited number of days on this earth. I don't want to spend my efforts doing something I don't believe in."

5. When an expert is clearly lying on the stand, you should challenge the expert's conclusions but never make it personal.

6. The biggest mistake lawyers make is stretching the truth. Jurors smell that, and you lose credibility.

Lanier's strategies for a great opening statement

1. Long before the trial begins, think of a theme in the form of a story, TV show, or movie that applies to your case.

2. Look for ways to change bad facts into good facts.

3. Don't oversell your case.

4. To maintain credibility, your story needs to cover the good, the bad, and the ugly.

5. Even in a run-of-the-mill case, you need to make the case personal for the jury and explain to them why it is important.

6. Do not use notes. Instead, speak from the heart.

7. Use PowerPoint slides to communicate your story to the jury.

8. Use words the jurors will understand.

Tips learned from Lanier's opening statement

1. Speak in gloriously plain English.

2. Accompany every point with imaginative, easily understood visual aids.

3. Entertain the jury.

4. Tell the jury you will make their job easy.

5. Empower the jury.

> "If we were going to put it on a TV show, this would be *CSI: Angleton* because this is your chance."

> "The way our country is set up, there is no one else. No one else can find out whether or not Merck is a cause but you. That's it. That's the calling."

6. Take on a higher burden of proof. Even though Lanier only had to prove his case by 51 percent, he said, "I'll prove it to you. There's not going to be that doubt in your mind."

7. Discuss weaknesses to maintain credibility with jury and frame the argument before the other side does. "The history of Merck before this is a good company…. but the family is not running the company anymore."

Lanier's descriptive phrases and analogies

1. "If a Boy Scout has a compass and the needle is supposed to always point north, Ray Gilmartin took this company and made the needle always point to the dollar sign, and that's how they chose their direction."

2. "[The CEO] turned a good drug company into a business-first company."

3. "The new management turned Merck into an ATM."

4. "We're going to drop watermelons from a hundred-story building and see how they handle the fall. But let's measure the results — let's not wait until the end. Let's go down to the tenth floor, and let's just cut the study off a little early and measure the results there."

5. "Where's the best place to hide a leaf? It's in the forest. Where's the best place to hide water? In the ocean."

6. "Faced with facts, [Merck leaders] literally rewrote the book."

7. "[Merck] turned science into science fiction."

8. "I guess if the carrot doesn't work, they take a stick and start whacking the donkey to make it move."

9. "$161 million being spent at this time period to sell Vioxx to us…. That's more in that same time period than Pepsi spent selling Pepsi."

10. "Is this a fella [plaintiff] who's one pork chop away from a heart attack?"

11. "That's why Carol doesn't have a husband now. He went to the doctor because his hand hurt."

12. When Merck CEO said, no difference in studies that showed 6 out of 100 taking Vioxx died when compared to 1 out of a 100 who did not, Lanier said, "I'll spend the rest of my time with you [the Merck CEO] all day swapping money [one dollar for six dollars] until you agree that there may be a difference here."

13. Bob was the picture of health.

14. Carol lost her soul mate.

15. Merck is afraid to bring witnesses to trial.

16. Lanier described that Merck had the motive, means, and victim, which translated to greed, Vioxx, and Bob.

Lessons to learn from defendant's opening statement

1. Don't read the opening statement.

2. Don't use bland visual aids.

3. Don't show hard-to-read documents on projection screen.

4. Don't use complicated words.

CHAPTER TWO

Windle Turley

Connect with the Jurors

The main skills I have are a desire to figure out a way to help somebody and a compulsion to do that.

— Windle Turley

---

*W*indle Turley has obtained a wide variety of record-setting verdicts for plaintiffs both at the state and national level. In 1992, and again in 1997, his wins were recognized as among the ten largest jury verdicts in the nation. Not only is he a great trial lawyer, he is a mentor and teacher of the craft. He has written more than 50 legal articles on the preparation and trial of injury cases and two books, *Aviation Litigation* and *Firearms Litigation*.

Turley believes that opening statements are the most important part of a trial. Before learning his strategies, which you can use in your next opening, let's learn a little more about Turley to better understand his principles and beliefs about the art of trial.

Turley has always been passionate about helping people. While in college, he was a student pastor and preached at small Methodist churches near his school. He enrolled in seminary after college but soon gravitated instead toward law school; he felt he could make a greater impact on people's lives by trying to challenge and change laws that were unfair to most. Not surprisingly, he became, in his words, "a people's lawyer."

From the first moment Turley stepped into a courtroom, he was comfortable speaking before judges and juries. He combines this natural talent with, as Turley says, "an intense desire to make a difference to people who need some help." He laments that, for most attorneys, the practice of law is just a job. But Turley says, for

> **CHAPTER HIGHLIGHTS**
> - Be a witness for your entire case
> - Defuse your opponent's case
> - Bond with the jury

a good trial lawyer, "that is *never* enough, *never* enough, particularly on the plaintiff's side of the docket…you have to have your heart in it."

In 1972, Turley's compulsion to help his clients resulted in the first successful jury trial to establish that an airline manufacturer had to make planes crashworthy. The case involved two fathers and their six-year-old sons, who were passengers in a small Cessna plane. As the plane was about to take off, the pilot's door opened, and the plane ran off the runway. The plane's wheels came off, causing the plane to tip over. All would have been well enough except that the wing burst a fuel line when the plane tipped over, causing gasoline to flood the cockpit, cover the passengers, and then ignite. The fire killed the two young boys and one father, and badly burned the other.

After recovering on the claim against the pilot for negligence, Turley proceeded to trial against the airplane manufacturer on the innovative claim that a manufacturer had a duty to build a plane that was crashworthy. Turley not only won the case but recovered punitive damages. The lessons he learned in representing individuals against a large corporation on novel claims would serve him well later when he took on the Catholic Church.

2.1 TRIAL STRATEGIES

Turley's courtroom skills are self-learned. He has never had a mentor or been a second chair at trial. He was inspired by the great Melvin Belli, known as the King of Torts. He was particularly struck by Belli's philosophy that the plaintiff's case should be a "rush to disclosure." That means, as Turley explained, "don't hold back, don't hide, disclose your case as quickly as you can."

> *My experience has been that there is so much more to learn about every case, it doesn't make a difference if you disclose everything you've got [i.e., your strengths], you'll get more. You're just that much further down the road.*
>
> —Windle Turley

Regarding the risk of showing the opposing counsel your strengths early rather than surprising him later, Turley adamantly responds, "Hell no! They know [your strengths] anyway, or they're going to find out. If they don't know where I am by the time I go to trial, then shame on me, because that is why a case isn't going to settle."

A dilemma many lawyers face during discovery comes in a deposition when a witness for the other side testifies to something that you can prove is wrong. Pressed to reveal if there were ever a situation when he would not confront the witness and save the surprise for trial, Turley says, "If I got it, I go for it."

By applying this strategy consistently, Turley settles most of his cases on favorable terms before trial. Insurance adjusters and opposing counsel know the value of Turley's cases and the consequences of going to trial if they don't settle.

Perhaps Turley's greatest and most admirable trait is his soft-spoken temperament. It helps him connect with jurors. With all of his accolades, Turley is not arrogant or impatient. Instead, he is an unpretentious gentleman. Not surprisingly, his modesty outside the courtroom is proof that his demeanor in the courtroom is genuine. It is something he has worked very hard on over the years.

This characteristic not only benefits him in trial but also long before the trial begins, when dealing with opposing counsel in the heat of battle. Turley is convinced that whenever you are about to get into an argument with opposing counsel, you should "always speak softer than the other lawyer."

When lawyers become confrontational and start arguing, "the best move is to just be softer and softer and just try to settle things down." When Turley first started out, he was just the opposite. "I tried to out-loud them, out-argue them, and out-mean them." But he finally learned that such an attitude is counterproductive because it "just doesn't lead to anything good. You get back what you give." When questioned whether he felt other lawyers would get an advantage when they are loud and he doesn't return the anger, Turley replies, "Those people never intimidate me, and I don't know anyone that they do intimidate. I think most people look at that and say, 'that's just show.'" But Turley points out that sometimes, an aggressive and loud attorney can try to intimidate your witness at a deposition and, at that point, it is your job to intervene, take a break, and get things settled down.

2.2 OPENING STATEMENT STRATEGIES

Let's now turn to opening statements, specifically, the opening Turley gave in one of his most celebrated cases. Turley instructs that there are four ingredients every opening must have to be successful.

First, he says, "you have a great opportunity to draw attention to your case and, ultimately, if the jury doesn't think your case is extraordinarily important to somebody or to society, they're probably not going to do much for you."

Second, "here's your opportunity to tell the jury your entire story and for you to be a witness for your entire case."

Third, it "gives you the opportunity to defuse your opponent's case" or "to pop the defendant's bubble." You do that by telling the jury, "In a moment, defense counsel is going to tell you this, and this is why that is not true." As Turley says, "You knock him down on every point he or she is going to make."

Fourth, the opening statement is a chance for you to bond with the jury. Turley claims this comes through

> *If you pick the right phrases, you can embrace the ordinary juror. You become a common man with them.*
>
> — Windle Turley

"wordsmithing. You talk about the things they talk about around their breakfast table." For example, you can talk about "our community." This lets them know they are going to be in a position to be a decision-maker.

Many lawyers argue their case in voir dire, but Turley thinks this is a big mistake. First, he says, doing so wastes precious time needed to get information from jurors in order to strike them. Second, lawyers argue "half-ass" in voir dire and then give another "half-ass" argument during opening statements. Instead, Turley advises arguing a case in "one glorious sweep" when opening.

Once the trial begins, Turley likes to present his witnesses in a way that allows him to maintain as much total control of the case as possible. He does not put a witness that is impeachable or subject to a significant cross-examination on the stand early in a trial. For example, in the Kos trial to be discussed, by the time the defense got to any of Turley's witnesses that were impeachable, the case was already over.

Preparation and delivery

A few months before the start of a case, Turley creates a trial notebook that includes a section allowing for constant preparation of his opening statement. As he thinks of an idea, he jots it down in this section. At least two weeks before the trial, he begins earnestly working on his ultimate opening statement.

Then, several days before the trial, he writes it out word for word. Although he won't read it verbatim to the jury, he will paint a picture with the words he has written. "You have to make sure every sentence and every word counts," explains Turley. He works incessantly on "key phrases" to ensure delivering them correctly.

To avoid presenting a memorized speech, Turley goes to the podium with an outline containing just a few key parts written out word for word. When delivering the opening statement, he will only occasionally look at his outline.

Turley makes sure he keeps eye contact with the jurors and avoids pacing. He is also a big believer in using visual aids during his opening statement and throughout the trial.

As you will soon read, the Kos trial had very enticing facts that would naturally interest a jury. In explaining how a lawyer with a run-of-the-mill case could capture the jury's attention, Turley admits it is difficult but says it means that the lawyer just has to work harder. He used the example of a very simple — and, seemingly uninteresting — case: a plaintiff who suffers whiplash from a car wreck. The key is to communicate to the jury that such a case is really a "community issue." This is not just a fight between two drivers. As Turley says, "This is something that can involve every single one of us this afternoon. We should have the right to go home safely without someone slamming into the rear of our vehicle. You just have to broaden the issue and get it away from the defendant and the plaintiff."

2.3 THE RUDY KOS TRIAL

One of Turley's most challenging trials provides a perfect teaching tool for preparing an opening statement. That case involved ten former altar boys (and another who had committed suicide) who

> **Practice Tip**
> Early in his career, Turley would prepare his opening statement on the morning of the trial. After losing five cases in a row, he changed his philosophy forever.

were abused by Father Rudy Kos of the Dallas Catholic Diocese over a 15-year period. Turley represented seven of them, plus the parents of the deceased victim. Sylvia Demarest, a Turley protégé and former member of his firm, represented the other three.

When the abuse occurred (between 1977–1992), the victims were as young as nine years old. Kos would give the boys marijuana, alcohol, and sedatives to coerce them to engage in masturbation and oral sex. One of the victims, L.,[1] committed suicide when he was 20 years old.

For the most part, the diocese did not contest that abuse occurred but claimed that it was not negligent in its supervision of Kos nor involved in a cover-up of the abuse. Arguing its innocence, the diocese explained that it could not conduct an investigation without a direct complaint from a victim and that it suspended Kos in 1992 as soon as such a complaint was made. When indirect allegations were forthcoming, the diocese took reasonable steps based on the information it received. Even though it was shown in hindsight that Kos abused children, this did not take away the fact that church officials made reasonable decisions based on the information they had at the time.

> *Turley was the perfect advocate for the altar boys against the Church. He was very calm, persistent, and very well-prepared.*
>
> —Sylvia Demarest, attorney for three of the plaintiffs in the Kos trial

Turley's opening statement incorporates what I have found to be necessary ingredients for an opening statement. Those ingredients are based on the acronym STAPLE. Remembering this acronym is made easy by visualizing a staple holding your opening statement together (like it does for a stack of papers). Here are the STAPLE ingredients:

> **S**tart and end strong
>
> **T**ell a story
>
> **A**ddress weaknesses
>
> **P**icture/visual aid
>
> **L**aw: briefly discuss the law
>
> **E**ye contact/no notes

---

[1] Since the victims were minors when the abuse occurred, their names have not been used and have been replaced instead by their first initial to protect the victims' privacy.

With this foundation in mind, excerpts of Turley's opening statement are presented here, in the same order that Turley had originally delivered them during the trial.

2.4 TURLEY'S OPENING STATEMENT

Turley starts strong

Court: OK, plaintiffs, ready to begin with opening statements?

Turley: Plaintiff is ready.

Court: You may proceed.

Turley: Thank you, Your Honor.

Last week, in a city nearby here, a mother and father continued to grieve and hurt and cry as they asked themselves the same question that they've been asking for the last five years: "Was it something we did? Was it something that we did not do? Why is he dead? Why did our altar boy kill himself?"

In Dallas earlier this week, a young man came home from work, went to his apartment, started through his regular evening routine having the same feelings and experiences that he has felt for several years now — feelings of depression, unresolved anger, and hate, feelings of helplessness — all that had continued to plague him almost every day for five, six, seven years.

Across town last week, another young man went to a therapist he regularly goes to, and in the office, the young man recounted his recent thoughts of depression and suicide and shame and guilt. And in one way or another, ten young men and the loving parents of another continued to have disturbing images of scenes of sex and abuse in their childhood. These things will not leave their minds. Some of the children of the case have painful recall of hundreds of individual acts of sexual violation continuing over a period [of years]; for others, one in particular...wakes up and carries with him...a very vivid memory...that won't fade, and that is of a young boy who has passed out after consuming alcohol and drugs and...awakens to find that his penis is in the mouth of his priest.

It is critical to grab the jury's attention in the first moments of an opening statement. Jurors make snap decisions about the lawyer and the case. Notice how Turley has carefully selected four snapshots to begin his story. He starts with the most dramatic — the parents' grief over their son's suicide caused by the abuse — and ends with the most shocking, i.e., Kos' performance of oral sex on a minor. In between, we have a young man facing daily depression and one more seeing a therapist where he shares his feelings of shame and thoughts of suicide. Turley shows his mastery of the facts of the case by not just reciting what happened in the past before the lawsuit was filed, but instead how his clients are currently (i.e., "just last week") being harmed by the diocese's actions.

Notice how Turley does not begin his opening statement chronologically as most lawyers do. Instead, he immediately captures the jurors' attention by employing a wonderful technique that is rarely used: He explains what his clients are going through in the past few days. By doing so, Turley believes that jurors will compare their lives to the damaged lives of the plaintiffs and become motivated to seek justice for them.

Turley connects with jurors

> What caused all of this pain? How could this have been? Was it necessary? Was it preventable? What must now be done to help the victims and make certain that it never reoccurs? These are the questions, ladies and gentlemen, that we will explore with you in the next few weeks. And these are the questions that we will answer together as, at the end of the case, **we'll reason together** to try to see why did it happen and was it preventable.
>
> You know, we're starting down a long road here together. We're on a road where we're searching for truth. I'm an advocate of my clients, and I'm very proud of that. **I'm very proud to be an advocate for them. But I also want to be an advocate for you as we search together for the truth. This is a common mission that we share, to find the truth in this case.** At the same time that we do that, we will try to move this case along for you. There is a lot that we need to say. There is a lot that has to be done. But I promise you, and I make this promise to you now, **I'm going do my very best never to waste your time.** I'm going to share with you information that we think you need and have to have to make your decision, but I'm not going to share with you information that is just interesting.
>
> I'm not unmindful at all of how disruptive jury service can be to one's daily routine. I know it is. I thank you for being here, and my clients thank you for being here. We're very grateful for the attention that I know you're going to give to this case during the next few weeks....

One key to a successful opening statement is to connect with the jurors. Here, Turley readily admits that he is an advocate for his clients, but he then invites the jurors to join his search for the truth. Turley wants to "pull the jury in." He is not going to persuade them to decide something they are not interested in doing but, instead, he will work with them on an exciting journey to uncover the truth.

After introducing his clients, Turley continues.

Turley introduces themes: children's safety and trust

Let me talk to you about what this case is not about. This case is not about religion in the theological sense. It's not about a religious discussion and whose beliefs are more nearly correct than someone else's. We're not here to invade or discuss or study the theological basis of the Catholic Church. That's not what this case is about. What the case is about, I think, are two things: A common sense concern for the safety and welfare of children, common vigilance, common prudence, and common carefulness. And the case is also about, to a very great extent, trust.

> *What the case is about, I think, are two things: A common sense concern for the safety and welfare of children.... And the case is also about, to a very great extent, trust.*
> — Windle Turley, opening statement

You'll hear that word...a lot in this case. It's the profound, devoted trust that parents and their children have in the Catholic Church — the parents and children in this case. It's an ingrained trust. It's an ingrained religious faith that causes them and caused them, in many respects, to act the way they did over these years. It's...the kind of trust that transcends far above and rises far above suspicion of acts or words of an individual priest because the priest is the embodiment of their religious convictions.

Now why is this an important case? It's an important case not just because we're dealing with serious injuries and long-term damages to ten young men and a wrongful, unnecessary death to another one — it's important for those reasons, for sure — but the case **is also important for another reason, every day in this country ten million children are left in the care of other caretakers, a million of them outside of their homes are taken to be with somebody else to look after their welfare and their safety. They are our children, they're our grandchildren, they're our nieces and nephews, and our neighbors across the street. They are our children.**

That's why this case is important, because your mission in this case is to explore and understand; the part that you will take in the case is to identify what would have been a prudent and careful and safe standard of care for children entrusted to institutions like the defendant in this case, what would be a standard of prudent care to which these children should have been subjected.

And at the end of the case, the judge will ask you a lot of questions. It's not a guilty or not guilty kind of verdict you'll deliver; you'll answer fact questions. Those fact questions — some of them will deal with responsibility, and some of them will deal with the magnitude of the losses that are involved here and the damages. But basically they fall into two categories.

One set of questions will inquire, not in these words, but it will inquire whether the defendant's conduct permitted or allowed this abuse to take place. That's one area of the questioning, whether it was **careless or imprudent, whether it failed to be vigilant,** whether it failed to act on the signs and signals that were there. That is one area.

The other areas of questions that you'll be asked to answer will be this: What must now be done? What must now be done to take care of the victims, and what must now be done to make certain that there's not a recurrence? So, in a very simplified way, those are the two — two broad areas of inquiry that we'll look at.

Now, let's start by letting me share with you some information about the defendant in this case. This chart is not as complicated as it looks.

> **Practice Tip**
> Use understandable words such as "carelessness" and "vigilance" instead of legal words such as "negligence" when explaining legal concepts to jurors.

Turley explains that he wanted to make the jury a part of the trial. He wanted to show them that the issue involved is not one that just affects the plaintiffs, but that there is also a *community* sense of safety.

Turley says that words such as "careless," "imprudence," and "vigilance" are easier for the jury to understand. Jurors rarely understand the word "negligence" in a legal sense, so, he never uses that word.

Turley makes clear to the jury that he is not trying to put the Catholic religion on trial. The jurors may have friends who are Catholics or may rightly be sensitive to any attack on religious beliefs. Instead, Turley makes the issues in the case easy for anyone to relate to: the protection of children and the violation of their trust. But Turley goes a step further; he shows how this violation of trust is more serious in this case because there were religious figures in a position of spiritual authority who betrayed the plaintiffs.

When telling a story to jurors, the story needs to be framed around issues that involve important human truths so that jurors will be motivated to care about what you have to say. For example, what sounds more compelling to you: 1) this is a case about a failure of oversight by the diocese to supervise one of its employees, or 2) this is a case about the protection of children and the violation of their trust? Turley's insight and brilliance are on full display.

After this excerpt, Turley concludes this section by mentioning that the jury will need to decide actual damages, as well as how much punitive damages (damages intended to punish the defendant) will be necessary to send a message so that this abuse won't happen again. He then uses a chart to explain how the various people were involved with the Dallas Diocese and the three churches where Kos worked. After this explanation, he turns his attention to foreseeability.

Turley discusses foreseeability

Now, let me talk to you…about another part of this case, something called "foreseeability." Think about it for a moment, and you'll know how very important it really is because foreseeability is what alerts. Foreseeability is what puts us at a higher state of vigilance. Foreseeability ultimately is what determines whether we have breached our duty to other people. Foreseeability in this case is important, but it's pretty straightforward, and **I don't think it will be very disputed.** The Church family, this Church family, ladies and gentlemen, knew a whole lot about this problem of pedophile priests long before the public knew. The evidence will show in this case that this was not a new issue with the Church family. They knew about this problem before you and I ever heard about it.

The 10 years of sexual abuse [and] the chemical abuse that we're going to be talking about that one of their employees, **Father Kos, inflicted on these young men was not something that just dropped out of the sky.** This wasn't a first occurrence. It wasn't something new or unheard of to the defendant in this case. They were not ignorant of the risk of pedophile priests and sexual abuse of children in the Church. They were not ignorant of that risk. It had occurred before in this diocese.

And it occurred while Father Kos was abusing children in this diocese. And you're going to hear evidence about that. We're going to…bring you evidence and talk to you about that. Many of those instances occurred with priests stationed out here at All Saints, in addition to Father Kos.

Every bishop and vicar general, I think, of every diocese in this United States knew about this problem probably before we did. They all knew it by the early '80s, and in 1985, an explicit document was sent to Bishop Tschoepe here in Dallas describing the problem of pedophile priests and what needed to be done. That document came from a group of concerned leaders at the national level of the Catholic Church. They sent that document, and it will be discussed here in this trial.

No question that by then it was well understood, if not before, that this is something we must be vigilant about. It's foreseeable that we could have a problem here in the Dallas Diocese. So it's against this background of foreseeability, to be on the alert for a concept that had emerged in the preceding decade, that we start to look at what happened in this particular case.

Turley deftly challenges defense counsel to deny foreseeability. Although he knows it is the heart of the diocese's defense, he states that he doesn't think it will be "very disputed." Turley stated in his interview that for decades, the Catholic Church had defended its actions because it had always said that it had no prior knowledge of what its priests were doing.

But despite this history of denial, Turley knows he can prove that there is no evidence to support such an argument. In essence, Turley challenges defense counsel to go ahead and anger the jury by suggesting that Kos' abuse caught the diocese by surprise. If defense counsel does as Turley expects, Turley's proof to the contrary at trial will be all the more devastating after defense counsel's denial.

Turley explains witness order

> We're going to present this case to you, folks, inasmuch as we can, in a chronological sequence, because we're going to cover a time period that starts really back in about 1975 and comes up through 1992.... To make it faster and simpler for all of us, we're going to try to do this in a chronological way to make sense. But there is some problem with that. For example, sometimes if we follow chronologically, we're going to have periods where we're going to have to read to you testimony out of a deposition and then maybe show you a deposition on video, and then maybe read another one back-to-back. And we don't like to do that, but we're going to do it because we think it's the way that we need to do it in this particular case. And I just ask you to bear with us....
>
> I would like to tell you we're going to bring you a whiz-bang, exciting, stimulating witness that's going to blow your socks off, for the very first witness, but I can't. We can't do that and do it in chronological order. So bear with us as we start this evidence later today or tomorrow.

It is almost always best to start a presentation of proof with the best witness or, at least, one of the very best. After giving the opening statement, you want to build on that momentum and never let go. Hopefully, such a witness will be "exciting," but in this case, Turley could not do that.

Turley explains his reasoning as follows: He has a "strong, strong opinion that you never want to give up control of the ball." He suggests starting off with a witness that has information to give but who cannot be impeached. Turley usually does not start off with the plaintiff because he wants the jury in complete agreement with him before he gets to the plaintiff. In his experience, every plaintiff can be damaged on cross-examination. In the Kos trial, Turley did not want to risk putting on a plaintiff early and have the other side even come close to neutralizing him. He wanted to maintain momentum "as far down the road as possible" before putting anyone on the witness stand that the defense could "remotely touch." Having said that, Turley points out that the momentum from a powerful opening statement must be maintained by keeping a boring witness off the stand.

In this next excerpt, watch how Turley continues to create a bond with the jurors and works to earn their trust. Without trust, persuasion is difficult if not impossible to achieve. Aristotle explained that one of the three keys to persuasive public speaking was ethos, or the credibility of the speaker.

Turley builds trust with jurors

> We're going to bring you [red flags that put the diocese on notice about Kos' behavior], and you hold us to this proof. **You make me prove this to you. I will.** And at the end of this case, you call me to account, and you make me tell you whether I have proven these things because we will.

Turley tells the jurors not just to trust what he is saying but make him prove everything he is saying. In other words, "Don't believe me unless I prove it to you." This argument also anticipates the typical defense counsel argument that reminds a jury that the plaintiff has the burden of proof.

> **Practice Tip**
> Arrange to exchange with opposing counsel the PowerPoint slides to be used in the opening statement, so that any objections can be corrected before opening statements begin.

Turley told me that he uses a chart to show what his proof is going to be, and who is going to say it. Then, he tells the jurors to make sure he proves these facts to them because he is going to show them the same slides in his closing. Although such an approach is very powerful, Turley cautions, "you have *got* to deliver."

Turley then summarizes the red flags of Kos' predatory behavior that the diocese should have recognized. He starts with Kos' application to the Holy Trinity Seminary in Dallas.

Kos gets an annulment before entering seminary

> In September of 1975, Rudy Kos' ex-wife, when she is being interviewed by this gentleman right here (indicating), Father Duesman, who is with the Marriage Tribunal, she is talking to him on the phone, and she says to him, what we've printed here, "Rudy is gay, and he has problems with boys. And I've told the chaplain over at Carswell about it."... Father Duesman will acknowledge that that conversation took place.... he has notes to help him remember that that conversation took place. And down at the bottom of his notes he wrote, "Something is fishy. The petitioner, Kos, needs to level with us." That's the first sign, the first warning sign that we're going to deal with. It happened way back in 1975. In the diocese's file was evidence that Father Rudy Kos was a pedophile before he ever started day one in the seminary. I think that will be an undisputed fact in this case.
>
> *Defense Counsel: Objection. It is very much disputed.*
>
> *Court: So noted.*

Notice how Turley doesn't just recite important testimony he expects, but rather, he displays it so the jury can see it as well. Unlike a book where you can refer back to preceding pages if you either forget or miss something, in a presentation such as an opening statement, there is no going back. The lawyer, then, needs to repeat important information or display it to ensure that the jurors understand it. Moreover, an opposing counsel must choose objections very carefully. Here, defense counsel simply highlights how damaging Kos' ex-wife's warning is and the note of Father Duesman by vigorously objecting and having the court nonchalantly overrule it.

Kos' activities at St. Luke's church after seminary

At St. Luke's was Father Clayton. He was the pastor. Father Clayton, in December of '85, starts a series of reports on Rudy Kos, a lot of them. I've documented some of them here on this chart. [**Turley effectively uses a chart to help jury remember the number of reports.**] A lot of reports. And what is he saying? He is saying to Monsignor Rehkemper, second in command at the diocese, and to the Bishop, that Father Rudy Kos is having boys stay in the rectory with him overnight—not just one night, not just occasionally, but every night, boys are going and coming, lots of them, all of the time....

Then we go into January of early '86. Father Clayton starts to keep logs about the goings and comings of these young men. December 26, he sends another warning to the Bishop, "These young boys are still going. They're coming and they're staying overnight. This isn't right." May 5, he sends another warning to the diocese. Same thing. He does it again on July 21 and August 18, to the diocese, giving them the logs and specific names and the names of some of those young men sitting right out here, telling the diocese that these kids are being permitted by Father Kos to stay overnight over and over again in the rectory, and something is wrong.

OK, what happened? Nothing. In 1986, the diocese finally says to Father Kos, "Your conduct is imprudent. It could jeopardize the diocese." The conduct could jeopardize the diocese? They told him to stop doing it or he might be suspended.

In 1987, Clayton again warns the diocese. For two years, he has been giving warnings to the diocese. In 1987, the diocese is informed once more that Kos is still taking the boys away, this time overnight, taking them out of town to Disneyland, to Orlando, down in south Texas, to Houston, to Magnolia for overnights.

In 1987, Father Clayton finally, almost out of desperation, says to the diocese, "This is a crisis situation. Early intervention is needed."

Turley effectively uses an exhibit to list the multiple times the diocese was put on notice of Kos' behavior. Remember that Turley said that he believes word choice is important. Did you notice how he built a sense of urgency in recounting about Father Clayton's correspondence with the diocese. He built to a crescendo and stated that "finally...out of desperation" at the lack of the diocese's response, Father Clayton declares Kos' actions to be a "crisis situation."

In the next excerpt, Turley explains the other warning signs.

Kos' financial problems

....January '89. Now Father Kos has been transferred, and he has been made into the pastor—the pastor at a church that has a school with lots of little kids in Ennis, Texas, St. John's....

By August of 1991...the diocese is now being called upon by Father Kos to bail him out of his severe credit problems, to make him loans—a lot of loans, a lot of money. We're not sure of the exact amount, but we think the evidence will show that it may have been from 45 to 60 or even more than $60,000 that in 1991 the diocese firmed up in loans to Father Rudy Kos. That is a great big red warning signal.

What was this man doing with this money? Anybody who had an ounce of investigative thought would have known that all of the toys, all of the gifts, all of the clothes, all of the computers, and the computer games that he was buying and supplying to these kids had to be for something more than just out of the kindness of his heart....

Kos sleeps with boys

> *This isn't right. I have seen him sleeping with a boy in the bed.*
> —Windle Turley, quoting expected testimony

December 1991. Now somebody else is reporting on Kos. This time it's his assistant pastor, Father Williams, who has testified in the case. And he will come and testify here in trial. He starts to report, not knowing that Father Clayton had for almost two years when they were in Irving [Texas], he starts to report to the Bishop the same kind of things that Father Clayton had been reporting: "He is keeping kids overnight in the rectory, Bishop. Something needs to be done. This isn't right. I have seen him sleeping with a boy in the bed. This isn't right."

Turley methodically goes through each warning and the church's failure to respond. These warnings climax with the following passage.

Father Williams complains to diocese about Kos' behavior

[In] April 1992...I think in response to Father Williams, who is a psychologist, not a practicing psychologist, but has a degree in psychology...[the Church finally] said, "OK, we'll send [Kos] to get an independent examination." Well, they didn't send him; instead, they went. Father Williams and

Monsignor Rehkemper went. And they met with a well-known counselor [Brenda Keller] who has a lot of experience in sexual deviation, here in Dallas. They met with her and told her what the facts were that they could gather. And in about five minutes or less she said to them, "Sounds like a textbook pedophile."

....Still, in April of 1992 nothing was being done.

In June of 1992, Father Williams sends a 12-page summary, a letter recounting incident after incident after incident of Father Kos and these boys, including the one I mentioned to you about catching him in bed with one of them. He sends that to the diocese in June of 1992, and Father Kos keeps preaching. He isn't removed.

And finally, Sister Gardner, a principal at a school, private school, I think, in Waxahachie, as I recall, she writes to the Bishop, to the diocese, and says, "Somebody has to do something." But, you know, they didn't. They still didn't. And they didn't do anything until [victim] M. hired a lawyer and got ready to file a lawsuit. Then—then, for the first time, they suspended Kos.

Those are the red flags in this case, ladies and gentlemen, that indict the Dallas Diocese and make it responsible for what happened to those young men.

What did the Church know? Well, in addition to these things, it knew that Rudy Kos was a pied piper of children, boys. He was a pied piper to boys. [**great use of imagery**] That is a big sign and a big signal that you have to watch out for. The Church also knew that if it made the wrong decisions about Kos, that kids could be hurt. It made the wrong decision, and kids were hurt.

Turley explains that the image of a "pied piper" illustrates his belief that a lawyer needs to be a wordsmith. That is, use the right phrase to paint a picture with words that will ultimately persuade a jury.

Turley dramatically points out to the jury that even when an expert says that Kos was a pedophile, nothing was done until there was the threat of exposure with a lawsuit. He foreshadows his closing, where he will point out that the Church won't understand the need to change its ways unless the jury sends a message with punitive damages.

In the next excerpt, Turley discusses the diocese's fear of scandal. He also artfully addresses a potential weakness in his case.

Turley explains why the victims' stories are similar

But for most of [the victims], it was a long-term, intensive sexual and chemical abuse, sexual abuse which, let me just tell you, it was almost the same with every single one of them. When these young men came in and started hiring us to represent them, we were very careful not to ask them—or not to tell them what had happened or ask them if this is what happened. We asked for their story. Most of those young men, until a month ago when they got together for the first time, did not even know who the other plaintiffs in this lawsuit were. But they came in and, one after another, said the same story.

Turley deftly defuses any attempts by defense counsel to suggest that the boys are making up their stories. Instead of similar stories being evidence of a conspiracy to make up allegations, Turley hints that the similar stories will show Kos' pattern of abuse. Turley then explains the abuse in detail.

Turley describes sexual abuse

They relayed to us how Kos would offer to crack their toes there within the rectory. He would offer to pop their toes and massage their feet. He would massage their feet until they were comfortable, and their feet, with their socks on, would be in his crotch. And pretty soon the socks would be off. In the next session, the socks would be off, and he would be rubbing their feet against him.

And after they became more comfortable with this, finally, he would be masturbating himself regularly with their bare feet, first through his clothes and then with his penis out. And then after a few months or years of this, and **they seemed to experience this perhaps with less terror,** Kos entered into oral sex on almost all of them. Not all of them, but almost all of them. There are some exceptions.

One of the young men that I represent and Ms. Demarest [a lawyer who represents other plaintiffs in this case] can tell you about the experiences that [these] young men had. One of the young men that I represent, after he had passed out from the consumption of alcohol and drugs, went home with a bloody rectum. This was not casual fondling.

Isn't Turley's word choice effective? Kos was monitoring the boys "terror," and when it decreased, he would increase the abuse.

Turley then explains that sexual abuse is just part of the damage that the boys suffered. While some lawyers might have just focused on the obvious, Turley realized that the case was much more than one of sexual abuse. Read how he incorporates two more issues of damage to show how his clients were victims.

Turley describes chemical abuse

The chemical abuse is also a serious part of this case. We would be here on the chemical abuse even if there were no sexual abuse issues because Father Kos [gave] most of them the very first drink of alcohol they ever had.... J., when maybe he was nine or ten years old at a park over in Oak

Cliff with a friend of his, they drank beer and smoked marijuana. These other young men began to indulge more and more in alcohol that Father Rudy Kos gave them, not all them, but almost every one of them. In fact, maybe all of them did with alcohol, not all of them with drugs. Father Kos gave them Valium, gave them marijuana, gave them other drugs. We'll talk about what some of them were, to the extent they can remember. Some of these young men today suffer serious chemical addiction problems.

The betrayal of trust

But there is another area of damages that, to my mind, is much more difficult to explain but equally profound, and it is the massive betrayal of trust. One can see chemical abuse. One can understand sexual abuse. It's a little more difficult to understand how a young Catholic boy — 10 of the 11 were altar boys — how a young Catholic boy devoted to his faith and wanting to serve his religion, wanting to give his life to the Church for a while during his youth, wanting to be a good kid, wanting to be a good Catholic, loved Father Kos. Father Kos preyed on children that came, in some instances — not all — from dysfunctional families, single parent families, families in the midst of crisis. Kos reached out and grabbed those kids and **preyed on them like a vulture.**

Father Kos, to many of these young men, became not only their Father [as a] spiritual priest, but their surrogate, biological father. The relationship was intense. These young men believed their Church, they believed their priest. I think we can only imagine the intensity of that relationship that went on for so long.

Then Father Kos says to them, "You are special." You see, almost none of them knew this was happening with the others. A couple of them finally figured it out. Most of them didn't know. Father Kos says to them, "You're special. I love you. You're special. I'm giving you…this new leather jacket. You're special. I'm fixing your car for you because I love you," and then [the victims find] out that it wasn't just one, but there were many. And to find out that what he was doing to them was immoral, illegal, and just as wrong as it could be.

Understand that when this started, when these kids were twelve or thirteen years old, most of those boys didn't even understand what Kos was doing with their foot and his penis was necessarily wrong. I think they sensed it. And you can judge that for yourself when they testify. But it had to develop. And it was in later years that they came to finally figure out this is not right. This is wrong.

So it's that betrayal of trust that — that just wiped out, wiped out, in many instances, their religious faith. All of us have some kind of faith, something we believe in, you know, Baptist, Nazarene, Presbyterian, Episcopalian, Catholic, whatever, or something else, or nothing, we believe

> *...he abused their spirituality.*
> — Windle Turley, opening statement

in nothing. That is a belief. We all have a faith in something. This...predator not only abused them physically and with chemicals, but he abused their spirituality. He destroyed their spirituality, in many instances. And that is a life-long impairment.

Author Stephen King once said, "The trust of the innocent is the liar's greatest tool." Turley shows how Kos preyed on innocent children who believed his lies. Turley explains that our spiritual belief is most sacred, and Kos has forever taken that away from the boys he abused. Turley creates a haunting image of Kos as a vulture.

Next, Turley discusses the abuse of each particular boy. But before he does, he makes a brilliant move. Remember that the plaintiffs in the courtroom are now adults, some of them in their mid 20's. Turley wants to remind the jury of their innocence. So, he does the following:

> OK, on this chart we have collected the 11 victims in this case, the same thing we have on the screen, but you can't see it. We start, really, in 1981, although J.'s abuse probably commenced prior to that time when Father Kos had a hold of him and was taking care of him [and] letting him live with him.
>
> I hope you can see these pictures because these young ages, nine, 13, 15, seven, 11, 12, those are the faces of the victims. These faces that you see out here (indicating) of these fine, handsome young men today, those are not the kids and the children that were abused, these (indicating) are the people and the kids that were abused.

Turley uses the chart with pictures of the plaintiffs taken at the time when the abuse occurred to show how young and innocent each victim was. It is one thing to say a plaintiff was nine years old, but it is much more powerful to show a photo that captures that moment in time.

Turley then talks about each victim, as follows. (Space does not permit reference to all of the victims.)

Turley describes Kos' abuse of particular plaintiffs

> J. ...was the son of a single parent—in a single parent family. He was somewhat sick with a respiratory problem out at Methodist Hospital where Rudy Kos worked before he went to the seminary. And he struck up this friendship with Father Kos. He was only about five years old then. And Father Kos got close to...J.'s mother, built up her confidence and got her to agree to let him keep J. And he did, off and on, sometimes almost continuously for several years. And he kept him and did to him the same thing that he did to these other kids. J. and a young friend of his, he will testify,

were introduced to marijuana and beer, my recollection is, at about the age of ten, possibly eleven, at a park here in Oak Cliff. J. doesn't remember a whole lot about this. He remembers the foot masturbation. He thinks he remembers some other things. A lot of this is lost in his tortured memory, understandably.

Turley constantly makes an effort to maintain credibility with the jury. A great opening statement must address the weaknesses in your case. If the jurors find out the problems within a case from opposing counsel, then they will wonder why the lawyer was not up front with them. Such a deception will cause a breach of trust that can never be overcome.

Turley convincingly explains why J. does not remember everything. It is not that he is making things up; it is because his brain has protected him by diminishing painful memories. Again, notice the wonderful choice of words Turley uses. He doesn't just say that J. has a bad memory. He turns that weakness into a strength by using the words "tortured memory, understandably." That is, it is not the plaintiff's fault that his memory is bad, but Kos'.

W. also was first exposed to Kos at All Saints in 1982. His abuse was a little shorter than some of the others, lasting about three years. But it had a devastating effect because perhaps, among the victims here of the alcohol and the drugs, **W. continues to suffer deeply. He drank so much, he will testify, that he hardly remembers what all Kos did to him.** He says that… Kos introduced him to drink. And that he soon, as a young man, started drinking when he was only thirteen, this is like when he is thirteen, fourteen, fifteen years old. He would pass out every time, he will testify. And things happened to him while he was unconscious. He doesn't remember all of it. But today he has a very, very hard problem dealing with some of these issues. And he will testify that there haven't been very many months since then that he's been sober.

In almost every case, ladies and gentlemen, in almost every case, the evidence in this case will show that whatever they were going to be, **whoever they were going to become was altered by what happened to these young men during these ten, eleven years that Rudy Kos worked on them.**

Turley again addresses the weakness that the boys can't recall all of the abuse. But he turns that weakness into a strength. Kos knew that by getting the boys to drink he could make them compliant and also abuse them while they were passed out. In Turley's words, he "altered" what these boys had a right to become as adults as he systematically "worked on them."

> …whoever they were going to become was altered by what happened to these young men during these ten, eleven years that Rudy Kos worked on them.
> — Windle Turley, opening statement.

In another section, Turley points out:

> You cannot do that without leaving [the victim] filled with self-doubt and guilt and a loss of self-esteem.... For example, the evidence will show that one young man today, to this very day, is hesitant to put his little girl's shoes on her feet because of his identity with what Kos did with his own feet.
>
> Another one will testify, as to his children, that he is afraid to hug them freely.... [S]everal of them will testify about their problems with intimacy with their girlfriends or their spouses. These boys...were prisoners of their childhood. They had a maladjusted adolescence. They lost it. The most beautiful years in their life were taken from them....
>
> The evidence will show in the case that Father Kos wouldn't let them hang out with girls. Every time they mentioned a girl, he would say, "Bad. Men are here to serve God. Women are here to work. Don't have relationship with a girl." He would become very upset and jealous.

Turley articulates very well the different impacts the abuse had on the victims. But if this were not enough, Turley next points out one of the most unsettling consequences of abuse that the victims will endure for the rest of their lives.

Turley discusses lingering effects of abuse

> The risk of becoming...an abuser themselves. It is one of the known risks of sexual abuse. It's...something that worries [the victims]. They're all concerned about it. They shouldn't have to be, but they are: depression and suicidal thoughts, learned helplessness. Finally, after a long period of this kind of conduct, they start to feel helpless. It's one of the reasons that they remained more or less in bondage to Father Kos until some of them were in their early twenties. Distrust of others, anger and hostility, unresolved fears of intimacy, anxiety disorders, insecurity about their own masculinity and identity.

> **Practice Tip**
> Instead of waiting until the testimony begins, Turley puts every important fact in his opening statement to create momentum. He tells the jury that the plaintiffs have been sexually abused, chemically abused, robbed of their spirituality and youth, and are at risk of becoming abusers themselves.

Whenever he gets the chance, Turley weaves into his argument an explanation for a potential weakness in his case. If the defense counsel were to suggest that some of Kos' conduct was consensual, Turley heads that argument off at the pass and explains that Kos caused the victims to experience a feeling of helplessness, which prevented them from reporting the abuse.

Turley discusses boy's suicide

I want to visit with you for just a moment about L., the young man who committed suicide. The situation is only slightly different. It sounds enormously different in that he is dead and the others are here, but what led him to his death is the same identical thing that happened to these other young men. **He just happened to have experienced more pain, more terror, more hurt than he could tolerate.** There came that time, January 31, 1992, when he took a gun to his head and took his life. He can't testify about what Father Kos did to him, but others can testify what happened. You will hear evidence from other witnesses in this case that he was there with Father Kos in the rectory at All Saints. He was there with Father Kos in the rectory at St. Luke's in Irving. You'll hear evidence from witnesses in this case that will testify that if he was a young boy in the rectory, Father Kos was massaging his feet, that every young boy that was there, almost without exception, got a foot massage. And we know what that led to....

We think that the evidence will be that L. was certainly a troubled young man. He suffered a great deal. That's why he was easy prey for Father Kos. He was already hurting. That's why Father Kos could do him the way he did. And we're not saying and we will not say in this case that the only thing that killed L. was Father Rudy Kos and the Catholic Church, but what we are saying is that they were a cause, one of the causes of his tragic suicide. And that's the question you'll be asked at the end of this case, not whether they did it all, but whether they were a cause.

Again, Turley knows how important it is to maintain trust with the jury. He never hides that his clients might not be perfect. But he consistently turns every weakness into a strength by offering a very credible explanation. Turley gives the jury a haunting image that L. committed suicide because he could no longer "tolerate the hurt."

Turley explains that proving the suicide was caused by the abuse was one of the most difficult challenges of the trial. The victim obviously could not testify about it. Kos could not be cross-examined about it because he was not at the trial. There were no witnesses to any abuse, although there were witnesses to the foot massage.

In view of that, Turley established that Kos had a close relationship with the boy and that his pattern of contact was similar to that of the other abused boys. The decedent also wrote some very affectionate letters to Kos. Finally, Turley got an expert witness to conduct a psychological autopsy on the decedent. The psychologist took all the information and reached a conclusion that Kos had sexually abused the boy.

Another weakness Turley has hinted at, but next addresses head on, is why the boys continued to see Father Kos even after they became adults. Here is what he said.

Turley discusses why the boys continued to see Kos when grown

One might ask, one may say, "As these boys got older, why didn't they just cut it off? Why didn't they just walk away from Kos?" A couple did, but most of them didn't. You want an answer to that question. You need an answer to that question. And we're going to give it to you because there is a very clear answer. Why [can] a predator priest…seize a child and hold them in bondage until they're or eighteen or twenty or twenty-five, how can a predator priest do that?

Well, there is a very specific reason for it. You're going to hear from experts in the case, like Dr. Kliman and others, who will explain that there is a phenomenon that takes place called learned helplessness. It's also sometimes referred to as traumatic bonding. It's the same phenomenon that prevents an abused spouse from walking out. It's the same phenomenon that prevents an abused child from complaining to its parents that the other parent is abusing them. It's learned helplessness. It's traumatic bonding. It's a very complicated phenomenon. We're going to talk about it in this case.

And I think when it's over you'll see that Rudy Kos had a hold of these young men in such a way that they were his prisoners. They could not, for a long, long time, act. They could not act…. They felt loved. They felt like…it was a special relationship just between them and Father Kos and the Church.

Turley always tries to make his client's problem relatable to the jury. While all the jurors for this trial had probably never heard facts like these before, they would have known or heard of women in their lives who did not leave an abusive husband. Turley explains that the "learned helplessness" that an abused spouse feels is the same trauma the former altar boys experienced.

Perhaps the biggest concern Turley had in his lawsuit was the anticipated defense argument that if the victims' parents—many of whom knew Kos very well—were not aware of the abuse, how could the Church be aware? Turley does not gloss over this problem but instead, dissects it.

Were the parents to blame?

Now, about the parents, where were the parents when all of this was going on? Why didn't they do something about it? We need to answer that question for you, too. And we're going to. You're going to hear in this case instances of incredible, incredible trust the parents had and devotion they had to their Church and to their priest. Some of these parents trusted their Church. It was the most important thing in their life, outside of their children. All of these mothers and fathers, 11 sets of them, had trusted their most valuable thing, their child, to the Church and to Father Rudy Kos, an employee of the Church. [**Turley reminds jurors that the diocese is responsible for Kos.**]

For example, one mother will testify in this case that, when she found out something was going on, just a few months before all of this broke in 1992, she got together with Father Kos, the person whom she had invited to their family dinners over and over and over and [who had] stayed at their house, [whom] she had lent…money — closest relationship you can imagine between a parishioner and a priest…and said, "What is this sexual thing between you and my son?" And he said, "Well, it was several years ago. It was just one instance of masturbation, so I could teach him, therapeutically teach him, about sex. And it never happened again. It was just that one experience, and it's all over."

This woman, devoted as she was to her children and her Church, believed that [explanation] for three months before she finally got some other information and started blowing the whistle. I tell you that story because it's not unique. You're going to hear it probably from others in this case. It is an example of what this devout religious conviction and faith in the Church and faith in the priest do to a person's judgment.

You know, good people don't like to believe bad things about others. And…all of the people that I've met in this case were good people. One writer said, "Good people are rarely suspicious. They can't imagine doing things to others that they would be incapable of doing themselves."

I've got something else. You know, sometimes when people are victims of sexual abuse, sexual assault, rape, one of the favorite tactics of the defendant is to blame them somehow for their own situation. I had hoped that would not happen in this case, but I fear it may. Well, it's not going to be explicit. The diocese's attorney is not going to stand up here in front of you and say, "These young men were at fault. They're to blame." He is not going to stand up here and say, "The parents are at fault. They're to blame." He is going to be a little more subtle than that. It is going to be almost subliminal. And I want to talk to you about that, because it permeates through this whole case.

He is going to say to you not that they were blamed, but they were fooled. That's another way of saying they were dumb. That's another way of saying they're responsible. It's another way of saying they did something wrong. It's a back-handed way of blaming the victim. So when you hear somebody get up here and say, "They were fooled," just remember, in my judgment, it's a very subliminal way of saying, "It was the parents. It was the kids. They were the ones at fault in this case."

> *If it's one thing they don't need, it's another truck load of guilt. These parents have had guilt up to the eyebrows.... We don't need anybody saying, "Well, you got fooled."*
>
> — Windle Turley, opening statement

I want to tell you, folks, these young boys and these parents did not do one single thing wrong. They are faultless in this matter, topside and bottom, and there will be no evidence in this case, no evidence in this case to say otherwise. They do not need to have salt poured in their wounds by having somebody say, "Well, you were fooled because you were dumb. You are really to blame because you let this happen." If it's one thing they don't need, it's another truck load of guilt. These parents have had guilt up to the eyebrows. And the boys have had guilt up to the eyebrows. We don't need anybody saying, "Well, you got fooled."

Again, Turley's argument and word choice is masterful. "Good people are rarely suspicious" is an idea to which anyone can relate. Moreover, any attempt to argue that the parents were to blame will be just an attempt to give them a "truck load of guilt." It is the Church that created this atmosphere of trust, and the parents can't be blamed for their loyalty.

Did Kos fool the diocese?

....Hindsight. It was mentioned the other day (Do you remember?) when you all were selected to serve on this jury. Let me talk to you just a second about that. [Defense counsel] has suggested to you the other day that there is something wrong with looking at things in hindsight. Well, I want to tell you that every single lawsuit in this courthouse is almost, for certain, based on hindsight. If we didn't exercise hindsight we would never fix anything that was broken....

We have to exercise hindsight. And we're going to exercise that hindsight based on facts that were in existence that the diocese had available to it. We're not going to ask them to assume anything just on what was available to them at that time....

You know, we don't have to go to hindsight unless there has been a failure of foresight. So when somebody says we shouldn't exercise hindsight in this case because we're all smarter in hindsight, you just think to yourself, we're here to think in hindsight because somebody else didn't exercise foresight....

So, it's going to be suggested to you that the reason all of this happened was that Rudy Kos was just a really smart guy and that he tricked not only everybody around him, but he also tricked the psychologists and the psychiatrists that talked to him. Let me visit with you about that....

[The Church] had [Kos] see a doctor here, a psychiatrist by the name of Dr. Jaeckle. This was in 1992—started in late '91 [and ended in] early '92. He went to see Dr. Jaeckle. And Dr. Jaeckle talked to him, and he went back. He went for many sessions. Dr. Jaeckle never gave him a clean bill of health. And he testified about that, and he will testify from this witness stand, "I never gave him a clean bill of health." But, you know, they didn't tell Dr. Jaeckle about any of this (indicating on chart). They forgot to tell the psychiatrist that was evaluating him that Father Clayton, in 1985, had kept a year-long log of goings and comings of boys to his room. They forgot to tell him what Father Williams was saying about the same thing. And they didn't tell him about the letters that the parishioners had sent complaining about these same issues. And they didn't tell Dr. Jaeckle that they knew that he was—in their records—that he had problems with little boys way back when.

So Dr. Jaeckle never arrived at a definitive opinion. Was he tricked? Yes, Dr. Jaeckle was tricked by the diocese. That's where the trickery was. That's where the manipulation was. The one lady that they sent him to—that they went to and told what happened, she said, "A textbook pedophile." Then they sent him down to St. Luke's Institute in Maryland in the summer of 1992. We're near the end of all of this, and most of the damage has already been done. They sent him to St. Luke's. And there will be no evidence in the record that they shared any of these warning signs with St. Luke's Church.

What did St. Luke's say about him? St. Luke's said, "The working diagnosis is pedophile, but you need to have some tests conducted to make certain." And Bishop Grahmann nixed that. "We're not going to do any of those kinds of tests." And they didn't. Who was tricked? St. Luke's? Well, who did the tricking?

Let me just say that when you talk about trickery and manipulation, the evidence in this case is going to be quite clear that Rudy Kos never, never got a clean bill of health from any psychologist or any psychiatrist who saw him after he became a priest, not a one, not a one.

Turley is a master of turning the expected arguments of the defense counsel upside down so that they cannot hurt him. For example, it wasn't Kos who tricked the parents and the diocese, it was the diocese that tricked the psychiatrists by not giving them all the information they knew about Kos.

> *When somebody says we shouldn't exercise hindsight in this case because we're all smarter in hindsight, you just think to yourself, we're here to think in hindsight because somebody else didn't exercise foresight.*
> —Windle Turley, opening statement.

The final component to a winning opening statement is to end strong. Here, Turley ends with his theme: "The church hates scandal."

Turley concludes opening

....This is what I'm saying: That the Diocese withheld important information from the examiners. **If it had been a bank, [they] would go to jail.** They withheld important information from the examiners. Why in the world would they do that? Why would the diocese not want this understood? Because the Church didn't want to catch Kos. They really didn't, not very much. Maybe a few did, but not really. Why? Because the Church hates scandal. The Church hates scandal. Bad things will follow if Kos is a pedophile. Very bad things, the least of which would be to move him to a different parish, the most of which would be an unraveling and a coming forth of numerous victims that we have to accommodate, and possibly an unraveling of other pedophiles.

The Church knew that was going to happen. Brenda Keller told them that was probably what was going to happen. They knew it anyway because they had been through it before. Many victims will come forward. That's why the Church didn't really want to know. That's why they were not aggressive. That's why they didn't go out of their way to investigate this matter and determine what was really happening, because the church hates scandal.

Thank you ladies and gentlemen.

Turley's opening statement is a wonderful recipe to follow. Not only does Turley include all the ingredients of a successful opening statement, but he also puts the ingredients together perfectly. He starts and ends strong. He tells a story with descriptive images to make the information interesting. He addresses the weaknesses in his case, so when he sits down, he has no fear that the opposing counsel will say, "Let me talk about something Mr. Turley was afraid to discuss with you. And he was afraid to talk about it because he does not have a good answer for it." Turley also repeatedly used visual aids to make his opening statement more interesting and memorable.

Although this section focuses on the masterful skills Turley used in his opening statement, a few excerpts from the defendant's opening are provided so that you can see how the Church responded to Turley's argument.

2.5 DEFENDANT'S OPENING STATEMENT

Defense counsel begins opening statement

The defense counsel for the Catholic Diocese does not start strong. Instead of stopping the plaintiff's momentum with an image or facts to support his defense, he starts by introducing himself and members of the diocese that were in the courtroom to the jury. He then thanks the jury for their service and fore-warns them that it is going to be a "long trial" and virtually begs them not to jump to conclusions. He then states the following regarding the abuse:

> There isn't any practical dispute about what happened insofar as the abuse is concerned, with one exception, and that is—who is labeled L., the deceased boy. He didn't leave a suicide note. He didn't leave a diary or something indicating he had been abused. We don't know whether he was abused or not....
>
> Rudy Kos is not here denying it. It all happened in secret, behind closed doors, so there is no way for me to address it, one way or the other. The bottom line is that I think it happened. I think Rudy Kos did what he allegedly did.
>
> Now, I want to talk about a couple of things, kind of in reverse order here. First, what to expect. There are going to be a lot of witnesses.

Why not just come out and admit Kos' actions at the very beginning and say so with outrage? The defense attorney needed to gain the jury's trust immediately. No one on that jury cared about introductions. They wanted to know if the abuse had occurred and if the diocese could have done something to prevent it. Unfortunately for the defense, counsel qualifies an outright admission of abuse with the words "I think it happened" and there is "no way for me to address it, one way or the other." Turley says that he has no idea why the defense counsel would not just admit that the abuse occurred and defend the case on the Church's lack of knowledge regarding it.

After this failed argument, the defense counsel nonchalantly turns to an explanation of the way the trial will proceed. He points out that the leaders of the Catholic diocese had completely changed since the child abuse had been discovered. He then points to each plaintiff in the courtroom, summarizes the abuse they suffered, and states how much money they are seeking. Read on to decide if his tone and strategy were effective.

Defense counsel discusses abuse

> Let me talk about, for a minute, what really is alleged to have occurred here. And I don't think that's been addressed, really, as much as it should be. And then I want to come back and talk about Rudy Kos and a time-line, and how this occurred. Everybody naturally is pretty hesitant to talk about sexual matters. In this case, you're going to hear about a lot of things that you probably never dreamed, much less wanted to hear about. And so I apologize today, in advance, but it's important that you understand what happened, what they're suing for, and why it happened and when it happened....

[Counsel looks for M. in the courtroom in order to point him out to jury.] Where did you go, M.? Right there (indicating) with the short haircut, white shirt. M. is the individual who is designated as "John Doe I." M. knew Rudy Kos. M. was abused between about the ages of 13 and 17, according to — to all of the testimony that we're aware of. **Most of the conduct involved was Rudy Kos rubbing M.'s feet and then rubbing M.'s feet against his crotch. I mean, that — that's the bottom line. That's what most of it was.**

There were, in later years, two or three instances, according to M.'s testimony, of oral sex between the two of them. M. was never intoxicated during any of this. This drug and alcohol stuff, there is some of that involved, and you're going to hear some evidence about it, unbeknownst to the Church, but you're going to hear some evidence about it, and that's why I want to set that out individually with each.

That's the end of it with M. **That's the full nature and extent of the abuse,** according to M. M. is suing the diocese. Rudy Kos is being sued too, but he is not here. And I'll talk about him in a minute. But M. is suing my client for 10 million [in] dollars actual damages and an additional ten million dollars in punitive, for a total of 20 million, is what M. is suing for.

Now, S. is seated right next to M., in kind of the grayish suit. S., between the ages of 13 and 21, Kos did this same thing, rubbing S.'s feet and then rubbing them against his crotch. And that went on a number of times, all in private, never with anyone around to see it, **no one in any of this, let me add at the outset here, never saw any sex occur between anybody.**

That continued with S. between the ages of 13 and 21. After that time, there were apparently **some other occurrences that involved oral sex.** S. is suing the diocese for $5 million in actual damages and 10 million more in punitive, for a total of 15 million in damages.

Defense counsel continues to suggest that the abuse may not have occurred and then minimizes the abuse that may have occurred. For M., "most of it was" Kos rubbing his foot in his crotch. Then, there were only a couple of instances of oral sex and those situations never involved alcohol. "That's the full nature and extent of the abuse." Defense counsel then compares this minimal abuse to the greed of the plaintiff in seeking multi-million dollar damages.

Turley explains that at trial, his expert witness destroyed defense counsel's argument. The expert testified that "even slight abuse can have devastating effects." That is, just an improper touching of an adolescent can create a lifelong trauma that cannot be overcome — not to mention serious sexual abuse.

If you wanted to challenge the damages, a better argument would have been to fully admit the abuse, not contest how devastating it was to the victims, and then argue that despite their justified outrage, the damages they were seeking would be challenged at the trial.

Another lesson to learn is that the defense counsel makes a mistake of pointing to each plaintiff and then addressing him by his first name. Out of respect, the defense counsel should have referred to them as Mr. [last name]. A courtroom is a very formal place, and first names are rarely used with adversarial witnesses. Turley thought this was "disrespectful." Furthermore, as Turley pointed out in our interview, the defense counsel reinforces the image that the plaintiffs are children by calling them by their first name.

Moreover, after he identifies them, he proceeds to undercut their claims. He would have gained more credibility with the jury if he had identified them, sincerely apologized to them, and then explained to the jury that there were only two disagreements between the defense and the plaintiffs: 1) whether the diocese should have been aware of Kos' behavior and, if so, 2) the amount of damages.

The defense counsel continues with the discussion of the plaintiffs' claims and reaches a boy referred to here as T.

Discussion of T.'s claims

> T. is one of the nicest guys involved in all of this case, not to say anything negative about anybody else. T. is a nice guy. **And it's kind of a puzzle.** T., between the ages of fourteen and fifteen, was involved with this foot rubbing with Kos. At age sixteen there was apparently an occurrence of oral sex. And in between the ages of 18 and 20, **after the age of consent in Texas, which is 17,** if you didn't know that, between the ages of 18 and 20 met Rudy Kos, on a regular basis, at the Drury Inn over in Irving. **I can prove 19 occurrences. He actually says it was every week or so over a two-year period, as an adult.**
>
> After that, after Rudy Kos was caught, after Rudy Kos was fired, after he was sent to a psychiatric facility, he came back to Dallas when T. was 21. In 1992, on this timeline way over to the right, he picked him up at the airport. And on two occasions, apparently, picked him up after Kos had already been fired, and they went somewhere together and engaged in sex together again. T. is suing us, not just Kos. T. is suing the diocese for 8 million dollars in actual damages and $10 million in punitive damages.

The defense counsel calls T.'s claims a puzzle. The suggestion is that after he reached the age of consent, there was no longer any abuse, since T. willingly participated. He infers that because T. willingly had sex with Kos after Kos had been caught, that perhaps all of the encounters were voluntary. Ask yourself if defense counsel's discussion of all of the plaintiff's claims would lessen a jury's anger or give it additional ammunition in support of a finding that the church was in denial.

The defense counsel concludes his summary of the plaintiffs' claims with the following:

Defense concludes summary of claims

> Part of my point here is that when you add all of these up, if you didn't keep track of them in your head, I doubt you did, it comes out to one hundred and forty-six million five thousand dollars that the diocese is being sued for, and being sued for on a basis that we don't think we did in the first place.
>
> Now, **do we, as a diocese, have egg on our face today?** You bet we do. You bet. There isn't any doubt about it.

Is "egg on our face" an appropriate comparison? Or does it suggest a lack of understanding of the seriousness of the claims? The remainder of the opening statement is beyond the scope of this section, since we are focusing on Turley's skills. But remember that setting the tone is very important in your opening statement. The defense counsel may have had an impossible task in defending the diocese's actions and may have been hamstrung by arguing points his client was forcing him to present, but it is the lawyer's task to rein in his client and present only arguments that will be successful. When defending a client where it feels like representation of the captain of the Titanic, remember that a tone that rings true with the jury will certainly lessen the amount it awards.

2.6 REVIEW OF TURLEY'S OPENING

Did Turley incorporate the elements of the acronym STAPLE into his opening? Remember that STAPLE stands for:

> **S**tart and end strong
>
> **T**ell a story
>
> **A**ddress weaknesses
>
> **P**icture/visual aid
>
> **L**aw: briefly discuss the law
>
> **E**ye contact/no notes

He started strong by immediately telling the jurors about the grief stricken parents who asked, "Why did our altar boy kill himself?" Then, instead of just presenting bland information, he told a story about how each plaintiff met Father Kos, what Kos did, and how the plaintiff was currently suffering.

Throughout his presentation, Turley addressed possible weaknesses in his case from the virtually identical stories the boys told, to their lack of memory, to the parents' failure to suspect Kos of abuse. He gave credible explanations for each of these facts that made the jurors trust his presentation.

Whenever he could, Turley showed the jury pictures, a list of allegations that put the diocese on notice, or a chart explaining the structure of the diocese and the churches that Kos served in.

As for the law, Turley discussed the issue of foreseeability. It is a key element of the defense, that Kos' abuse was not foreseeable because the diocese was never put on notice of his abuse so that it could do something.

Finally, you need to deliver your opening without notes, or, at most, a one-page outline. By making eye contact with the jurors, you can connect with their emotions, see their reactions, and show them confidence in what you are saying.

2.7 THE VERDICT AND AFTERMATH

On July 25, 1997, after a two-and-a-half-month trial, the jury awarded $119 million ($101 million in compensatory damages and $18 million in punitive damages) to the plaintiffs for the diocese's gross negligence in allowing Father Kos to interact with children and, ultimately, to sexually abuse them. The jury apportioned the fault as 15 percent on Kos and 85 percent on the diocese. Prior to the Kos trial, the largest jury verdict against the Church was under $2 million.[2] To this day, it is the largest verdict ever awarded against the Catholic Church in a sexual abuse case. The case was later settled on appeal for $30.9 million.

The Church was in denial about its liability prior to trial. No settlement offer was made until the court ordered mediation shortly before trial. Only then did the Church make an offer: $1 million to be split among all 11 plaintiffs.

After the verdict, Monsignor Rehkemper—the number two official in charge of the Dallas diocese during the Kos' abuse—stated, "If [the parents] are not responsible, why is the diocese responsible?....It irks me that they should sue the diocese over something Kos did.... It is hard for me to believe that all 11 of them were so traumatized that they couldn't tell anyone. Ideally, it was their responsibility to tell someone about it.... They were not all infants; they were children growing up. They knew it was wrong."[3] He further declared, "Anybody who reaches the age of reason shares responsibility for what they do. So that makes all of us responsible after we reach the age of 6 or 7."[4]

[2] For a list of all the trials against the Church and their outcomes, go to http://www.bishop-accountability.org/legal/civil_trials.htm.
[3] Renae Merle, "Ex-official says parents share blame for sex abuse," *Amarillo Globe News,* August 9, 1997, http://amarillo.com/stories/080997/abuse.html.
[4] Ed Housewright, "Cleric quits after abuse comments," *Dallas Morning News,* August 19, 1997, page 1A.

But the plaintiffs had put on evidence at trial that the diocese should have done more. For example, Monsignor Rehkemper first met with a priest who was concerned about Kos' behavior with boys in 1986, six years before the first youth complained. Rehkemper explained that he did not act on the priest's concerns because there was no proof of abuse.

Rehkemper's beliefs shed a little light on why Kos would be allowed to continue to interact with boys despite evidence of abuse. Richard Swipe, a former priest who had treated hundreds of pedophile priests prior to 1997, concluded at the time of the trial that "bishops simply didn't consider molestation a major sin, even though they felt it needed to be concealed to protect the reputation and finances of the Catholic Church. After I was ordained in 1959, I learned that some priests had sex with adults and even minors, and to some degree, this was taken for granted by Church authorities."[5]

Turley states that the case settled on appeal because there was not enough insurance coverage for the large verdict. Moreover, the clients—despite the abuse—were empathetic with the Church and did not want to bankrupt the diocese. Furthermore, the three boys that were represented by Sylvia Demarest had already settled on appeal, and that put pressure on Turley's clients to settle instead of continuing the fight.

Terry Mckiernan, president of a research organization that maintains an Internet archive and database dedicated to transparency regarding clerical abuse in the Church (www.bishop-accountability.org), put the Kos trial in perspective. At the time of the trial, the Church had weathered several storms regarding allegations of sexual abuse and had the momentum on its side in its fight to defend allegations of clerical abuse. But the Kos trial was "the canary in the coal mine" for the Church. The enormous verdict, which was more than 100 times greater than any other before that time, "showed the Catholic Church that [clerical sexual abuse] would cost [it] in a way that would have been inconceivable earlier."

After the civil trial, Kos was convicted in 1998 in a criminal trial of three counts of aggravated sexual assault and was sentenced to life imprisonment.[6]

---

[5] Brooks Egerton, "Documents show bishops transferred known abuser Church officials say policies have since changed," *Dallas Morning News*, August 31, 1997, page 1A.

[6] As a side note, Turley explains that Kos had been on the run and his deposition was never taken nor was he at the civil trial. Eventually, some of Turley's investigators found out that Kos was working as a paralegal in San Diego. Turley and his investigators went to Kos' office in San Diego unannounced, and when Kos came out to the reception area, he turned completely white and almost fainted. They all went to the conference room. Turley asked to talk to him about his clients and then wanted to know if there were any other victims. Kos said a few things, thought better of it, and ended the conversation.

As it turns out, Turley explains that the fact that Kos was not at the trial worked to Turley's advantage. So many of the victims and their families had such anger toward Kos that his presence would have proven to be an emotional distraction that would have been overwhelming.

2.8 CHAPTER CHECKLIST

Turley's trial strategies

1. You have to have your heart in your case in order to win. Do not approach your case as just a job.

2. Turley describes his main skills as having a desire to figure out a way to help someone and a compulsion to do it.

3. During discovery, disclose your strengths as quickly as you can. It will force the other side to settle for a higher dollar amount prior to trial.

4. When there is a confrontation with another lawyer, "always speak softer than the other lawyer."

5. Don't argue your case to the jury panel in voir dire because you will waste precious time needed to get information from the jurors.

Turley's opening statement tips

1. Four ingredients for every opening: 1) draw attention to your case and convince the jury that your case is extraordinarily important to somebody or to society, 2) be a witness for your entire case, 3) defuse your opponent's case, and 4) bond with the jury.

2. Wordsmith your opening statement to use phrases that help you bond with the jury.

3. Talk about things jurors would discuss around the dinner table.

4. Get the jury on board with the issue in your case, and let them know they will get to be a decision-maker.

5. If you have a "boring" case, you have to work harder to make it matter to the jury. You can do this by making the issue larger than just the plaintiff's, but rather, one that matters to everyone.

6. Use visual aids in your opening statement and throughout trial.

7. Do not prepare your opening the day before or the morning of trial. Begin preparing months in advance and, in earnest, a couple of weeks before trial.

8. It is OK to use an outline but maintain eye contact with the jury.

9. Present your strongest witnesses first so that you maintain the momentum of your opening statement.

Fifteen memorable passages from Turley's opening statement

1. I'm very proud to be an advocate for them. But I also want to be an advocate for you as we search together for the truth. This is a common mission that we share, to find the truth in this case.

2. I'm going do my very best never to waste your time.

3. What the case is about, I think, are two things: A common sense concern for the safety and welfare of children.... And the case is also about, to a very great extent, trust.

4. This is an important case because every day in this country 10 million children are left in the care of other caretakers.

5. Every bishop and vicar general, I think, of every diocese in this United States knew about this problem probably before we did.

6. You make me prove this to you. I will.

7. He was a pied piper to boys.

8. He preyed on them like a vulture.

9. He abused their spirituality.

10. A lot of [details of the abuse] is lost in his tortured memory, understandably.

11. [The victim who committed suicide] just happened to have experienced more pain, more terror, more hurt than he could tolerate.

12. Good people are rarely suspicious [referring to the parents of the plaintiffs]. They can't imagine doing things to others that they would be incapable of doing themselves.

13. If it's one thing they don't need it's another truck load of guilt. These parents have had guilt up to the eyebrows.... We don't need anybody saying, "Well, you got fooled."

14. So when somebody [opposing counsel] says we shouldn't exercise hindsight in this case because we're all smarter in hindsight, you just think to yourself, we're here to think in hindsight because somebody else didn't exercise foresight.

15. If it had been a bank, [they] would go to jail.

Author's comments

Remember the acronym that holds the key to a successful opening statement: STAPLE. It is easy to remember that acronym by visualizing a staple that holds your opening statement together much like it does for a stack of papers:

Start and end strong

Tell a story

Address weaknesses

Picture/visual aid

Law: briefly discuss the law

Eye contact/no notes

CHAPTER THREE

⸻ ∞ ⸻

Bryan Stevenson

Speak from the Heart to Persuade

Bryan Stevenson is America's Nelson Mandela, a brilliant lawyer fighting with courage and conviction to guarantee justice for all.

— Desmond Tutu

---

*B*efore turning to direct examinations in the next section, it is important to first learn the essential public-speaking skills needed to deliver an effective opening statement—since it is often the turning point of a trial. While textbooks give this topic only cursory treatment, if at all, the delivery of the opening statement is in many ways the most important part of a trial's success. The Appeals section of this book examines in depth Bryan Stevenson's expertise and background. For now, all you need to know is that he is one of the country's preeminent civil rights attorneys who has received innumerable accolades for his legal work on behalf of death row inmates and those who are suffering from cruel and unusual punishment in prison.

I knew my book would not be complete without Stevenson when I saw the video of the TED talk that he gave in March 2012. For those unfamiliar with TED talks, the TED conference began in California in 1984 with a series of lectures covering innovative ideas in technology, education, and design (TED). The annual conference has grown, and its website, TED.com, which archives videos of TED talks, has reached more than one billion views.

> **CHAPTER HIGHLIGHTS**
> - Know your audience
> - Learn techniques to deliver a persuasive speech
> - Don't overwhelm your audience with facts

3.1 HOW TO DELIVER A WINNING ARGUMENT

Stevenson received one of the longest ovations in TED history, and his speech has been viewed more than 2,803,870 times. Not surprisingly, out of all the TED talks ever given, Stevenson's speech is featured as one of 11 must-see TED talks online. This chapter explores why he is such an effective speaker and reveals how to incorporate his ideas into an opening statement. Even though Stevenson did not present his argument to a jury, the fact that there is a video of this memorable speech allows an audience to both see and hear what makes a winning argument. His speech can be seen at www.TurningPointsatTrial.com. The time stamps in the discussion to come reference the appropriate portions of the video.

Stevenson's topic was the unjust incarceration of adults and juveniles, as well as the unfair treatment of minorities and the poor. As with any opening statement, the challenge of the speech was to present a message that would be both memorable and persuasive. This is the key to a winning opening statement, but lawyers almost never spend enough time thinking about the best way to frame their message.

Stevenson could have started his speech with compelling statistics about the number of children in prison or with a story of someone who had been wrongfully convicted. While those ideas might have been effective, he chose an even better way.

Stevenson says that, whether he is arguing to a jury, a panel of judges, or giving a speech, "I'm just a big fan of knowing the audience." For his TED talk, he was given only a few days' notice. It was scheduled during the same month that he had not one, but two Supreme Court arguments. He was not familiar with the TED talks and was about to decline the invitation, when his staff informed him how important the talks actually were. When he arrived at the conference, he realized that he was following lectures that were highly visual, including a talk by Andrew Stanton (director of the movie *Finding Nemo*), who had breathtaking video clips accompanying his lecture.

The bottom line was that the TED audience was very tech savvy and expected stunning visual aids for each speech. But Stevenson rarely uses visual aids in his speeches, nor did he have the time to put any together — even if he had wanted to do so. As a result, he had to find a way to grab the attention of this tech savvy group and keep them interested.

Whether or not he is speaking in court, Stevenson has the same challenge. He explains it as follows:

> I'm advocating for really "dis-favored" people. For people who are not well respected [or] well liked. They come into it with the burden of having been

convicted or condemned for doing something awful. They are not being judged neutrally or fairly; there's a presumption against them. For me as the advocate, the first thing I want to do is to just get people to step back from whatever hostility or animus they have brought into the space, based on what they know about the client or the topic or the issue. Narrative is a really useful way to do that because it distracts you from wherever you are.

3.2 CREATING A THEME FOR AN OPENING STATEMENT

Regarding the creation of his TED talk framework, which was built around the theme "identity," Stevenson says:

> The thing about identity for me in that talk was I need you all to not be afraid that I'm going to talk about things like the death penalty and jails and prisons and race, which can sometimes scare people or worry people. I want you to be willing to listen to me even though I do something that you don't necessarily have an intuitive enthusiasm for. I represent people convicted of murder. People convicted of serious crimes. People who are in jails and prisons. That doesn't by itself get you a lot of goodwill and credibility.
>
> The identity point was, basically, I need to share something about my identity, so you're not confused about who I am and what I'm trying to do, but I also want to remind you about your identity, and you all want to be fair people. You all want to be open minded. You all want to avoid being judgmental and biased, and that's something you can choose to be if we just talk or think for a second about our identity. For me, that's a pre-cursor to then making the substance point I want to make about this problem."

If you just make the substance point first, the people who came in hostile are going to be fighting you the whole time you're talking, but if you can get people to think about something that calms everything down and neutralizes the instinct to be oppositional, all of sudden they'll hear whatever substance argument you are making and the fact you are presenting it in a very different way.
— Bryan Stevenson

When specifically asked if this strategy applies to opening statement, Stevenson replies:

> I think that's true because there's a narrative that people are bringing into the courtroom about the case, and some of it has been shaped by what the other side has said. Some of it is shaped by the questions asked during voir dire. Voir dire can really terrify people. You are trying to test where their limits are on certain issues, but they're internalizing it. "Oh my God, this is somebody who's a serial killer," or "This is someone who put poison in the water." Because you're having to test whether they can still be fair under certain conditions…that can create a lot of anxiety.

I think the first objective is to get people back to a place where, if they are in a criminal case, there is a presumption of innocence, or in an environment like TED—a willingness to listen to someone who does something that they may not care that much about—or in an appellate argument, to take you seriously. You say something that allows them to see you as credible and reliable."

3.3 STEVENSON'S TED TALK

Opening remarks

Here are Stevenson's opening remarks for his TED talk, with the time stamps that reference the corresponding places on the video on www.TED.com.

> **0:13** Well, this is a really extraordinary honor for me. I spend most of my time in jails, in prisons, on death row. I spend most of my time in very low-income communities in the projects and places where there's a great deal of hopelessness. And being here at TED and seeing the stimulation, hearing it, has been very, very energizing to me. And one of the things that's emerged in my short time here is that TED has an identity. And you can actually say things here that have impacts around the world. And sometimes when it comes through TED, it has meaning and power that it doesn't have when it doesn't.

> **0:48** And I mention that because I think identity is really important. And we've had some fantastic presentations. And I think what we've learned is that, if you're a teacher your words can be meaningful, but if you're a compassionate teacher, they can be especially meaningful. If you're a doctor, you can do some good things, but if you're a caring doctor, you can do some other things. And so I want to talk about the power of identity. And I didn't learn about this actually practicing law and doing the work that I do. I actually learned about this from my grandmother.

Stevenson has not told his audience what he is going to talk about. He has only told them how he spends his time, that TED has an identity, and he wants to share with them where he got his identity. Stevenson's body language is relaxed. He doesn't begin his talk by pounding his fists on a podium (if there were one) or attacking his audience for their lack of engagement or ignorance. Stevenson calmly explains what he does and introduces his theme: identity.

Stevenson explains that his goal is never to come out arguing. Instead, he wants to get his audience, whether it is a jury or not, in a place where its members are willing to listen. Who would fight a speaker who wants to talk about how he learned his identity from his grandmother? Stevenson immediately pulls his audience in with a story, instead of confronting them with an argument.

The same holds true for an opening statement. While delivering an opening statement, it would be objectionable to talk about your identity in detail, since you are required to talk about what you expect the evidence to show. Your identity is not part of the trial. However, you could certainly talk about your client's identity. Whether representing an individual or a corporation, Stevenson's strategy is brilliant. In order to persuade a jury or an audience, its members need to care about the lawyer and the client being represented. Engage them immediately with a story.

Grandmother gave him his identity

1:18 I grew up in a house that was the traditional African-American home that was dominated by a matriarch, and that matriarch was my grandmother. She was tough, she was strong, she was powerful.... Her parents were born in slavery in Virginia in the 1840s. She was born in the 1880s, and the experience of slavery very much shaped the way she saw the world.

And my grandmother was tough, but she was also loving.... And she just had this quality that you always wanted to be near her.... And I remember, when I was about eight or nine years old, waking up one morning, going into the living room, and all of my cousins were running around.... And after about 15 or 20 minutes of this, she got up and she came across the room, and she took me by the hand, and she said, "Come on, Bryan. You and I are going to have a talk." And I remember this just like it happened yesterday. I never will forget it.

2:56 She took me out back, and she said, "Bryan, I'm going to tell you something, but you don't tell anybody what I tell you." I said, "OK, Mama." She said, "Now you make sure you don't do that." I said, "Sure." Then she sat me down, and she looked at me, and she said, "I want you to know I've been watching you." And she said, "I think you're special." She said, "I think you can do anything you want to do." I will never forget it.

And then she said, "I just need you to promise me three things, Bryan." I said, "OK, Mama." She said, "The first thing I want you to promise me is that you'll always love your mom." She said, "That's my baby girl, and you have to promise me now you'll always take care of her." Well, I adored my mom, so I said, "Yes, Mama. I'll do that." Then she said, "The second thing I want you to promise me is that you'll always do the right thing, even when the right thing is the hard thing." And I thought about it, and I said, "Yes, Mama. I'll do that." Then finally she said, "The third thing I want you to promise me is that you'll never drink alcohol." (Laughter) Well, I was nine years old, so I said, "Yes, Mama. I'll do that."

Family had history of alcoholism

3:59 I grew up in the country in the rural South, and I have a brother a year older than me and a sister a year younger. When I was about 14 or 15… One day my brother came home, and he had this six-pack of beer — I don't know where he got it — and he grabbed me and my sister, and we went out in the woods. And we were kind of just out there doing the stuff we crazily did. And he had a sip of this beer, and he gave some to my sister and she had some, and they offered it to me. I said, "No, no, no. That's OK. You all go ahead. I'm not going to have any beer." My brother said, "Come on. We're doing this today; you always do what we do. I had some, your sister had some. Have some beer." I said, "No, I don't feel right about that. Y'all go ahead. Y'all go ahead." And then my brother started staring at me. He said, "What's wrong with you? Have some beer." Then he looked at me real hard, and he said, "Oh, I hope you're not still hung up on that conversation Mama had with you." (Laughter) I said, "Well, what are you talking about?" He said, "Oh, Mama tells all the grandkids that they're special." (Laughter) I was devastated.

4:55 And I'm going to admit something to you. I'm going to tell you something I probably shouldn't. I know this might be broadcast broadly. But I'm 52 years old, and I'm going to admit to you that I've never had a drop of alcohol. (Applause) I don't say that because I think that's virtuous; I say that because there is power in identity.

> *There is power in identity.*
> — Bryan Stevenson

5:18 When we create the right kind of identity, we can say things to the world around us that they don't actually believe makes sense. We can get them to do things that they don't think they can do. When I thought about my grandmother, of course she would think all her grandkids were special. My grandfather was in prison during prohibition. My male uncles died of alcohol-related diseases. And these were the things she thought we needed to commit to.

For over five minutes of a 21-minute speech, Stevenson still has not told his audience what he is going to talk about. He is spending these important first few minutes connecting with his audience, grabbing their attention with a compelling story about his childhood and his identity, so its members will care about the message he is about to deliver. Likewise, you could deliver a winning opening statement, spending those precious first few minutes telling the jury about your client — not the reason for the lawsuit — but facts about your client that will motivate the jury to care.

If you have been watching the video, by now you have observed that Stevenson does not use notes. He makes constant eye contact with his audience. He speaks in a measured pace that is easy to follow. One of his great delivery skills is that he emphasizes at least one important word or phrase in most sentences. He also deemphasizes words (i.e. speaks them more softly than the other words) for dramatic effect. Listen to how he does this throughout his speech. By doing so, he makes it clear what is important. This emphasis also makes the idea more memorable. In addition, he pauses before he gets to an important point to emphasize it. In this next section only, I have highlighted in bold the words he emphasizes in his talk to show the effectiveness of this technique. In other sections, I have highlighted some parts that will be analyzed after the excerpt.

Stevenson also smiles a lot. The key is that his smile is never insincere. For example, he smiles when he says something self-deprecating or in response to the audience's laughter to confirm he is laughing at himself, too. He also might smile when he introduces a topic that he knows his audience might find hard to agree with at first. It is all part of his goal to have a sincere conversation, and he wants everyone to be comfortable. His smiles welcome the audience into his world.

But at the 5:16 mark, his tones and gestures pivot dramatically for a moment. He makes a fist and pumps it as he forcefully says, "There is power in identity." This will be the theme of his speech, and next, he will set forth facts to support it.

Mass incarceration has fundamentally changed the justice system

5:39 Well, I've been trying to say something about our criminal justice system. This country is **very** different today than it was 40 years ago. In 1972, there were 300,000 people in jails and prisons. Today, there are 2.3 **million**. The United States now has the **highest** rate of incarceration **in the world**. We have **seven million** people on probation and parole.

And **mass incarceration**, in my judgment, has **fundamentally** changed our world. In poor communities, in communities of color there **is this despair**, there is **this hopelessness**, that is being **shaped** by these outcomes. One out of three black men between the ages of 18 and 30 is in jail, in prison, on probation or parole. In urban communities across this country— Los Angeles, Philadelphia, Baltimore, Washington—**50 to 60 percent** of all young men of color are in jail or prison or on probation or parole.

Our system **isn't just being shaped** in these ways that seem to be distorting around race, they're also distorted by poverty. We have a system of justice in this country that treats you **much better** if you're **rich** and **guilty** than if you're **poor** and **innocent**. **Wealth, not culpability**, shapes outcomes. And yet, we seem to be **very comfortable**. The politics of fear and anger have made us believe that these are problems that are **not our problems**. We've been disconnected....

> 7:35 I represent **children**. A lot of my clients are very young. The United States is the only country in the world where we sentence **13-year-old children** to die in prison. We have life imprisonment without parole for kids in this country. And we're actually doing some litigation. **The only country in the world.**

Stevenson relates the statistics in such an easy manner. He doesn't look at notes. He emphasizes the important numbers. The key to his success is that he provides context for the statistics and explains why they matter. His statistics become persuasive when he shows how they affect neighborhoods in the United States and also when he highlights how out of line they are with the rest of the world.

Notice his hand gestures. He does not make the mistake of most lawyers who put their hands straight down to their side or clasped behind their back or in front of their body below their waist. When he declares that the politics of fear and anger have made us believe that "these problems are not our problems," both his hands are open and pushing away from his body to show that we keep the problems at a distance.

Next, Stevenson candidly discusses why supporters of the death penalty have a "sensible" argument but then offers a new way to look at the issue through this lens of identity. He knows to maintain credibility with his audience, he needs to recognize sound arguments that are against his point of view.

Death penalty is defined by error

> 7:51 I represent people on death row. It's interesting, this question of the death penalty. In many ways, we've been taught to think that the real question is, do people deserve to die for the crimes they've committed? And that's a very sensible question. But there's another way of thinking about where we are in our identity. The other way of thinking about it is not, do people deserve to die for the crimes they commit, but do we deserve to kill? I mean, it's fascinating.
>
> Death penalty in America is defined by error. For every nine people who have been executed, we've actually identified one innocent person who's been exonerated and released from death row. A kind of astonishing error rate — one out of nine people innocent. I mean, it's fascinating. In aviation, we would never let people fly on airplanes if for every nine planes that took off one would crash. But somehow we can insulate ourselves from this problem. **It's not our problem. It's not our burden. It's not our struggle.**

Stevenson slows down for emphasis as he speaks the last three sentences above in bold. His tone is not judgmental but one that encourages an awakening in his audience. Stevenson's entire speech is distinguished by succinctly stated ideas. While those against the death penalty might talk about its many problems and cite a bunch of statistics, Stevenson powerfully sums up the issue in one sentence: "Death penalty in America is defined by error." He uses an analogy of flying on airplanes to help the audience understand the error rate.

> *Death penalty in America is defined by error.*
> — Bryan Stevenson

Terrorism against blacks after reconstruction

> **8:49** I talk a lot about these issues. I talk about race and this question of whether we deserve to kill. And it's interesting, when I teach my students about African-American history, I tell them about slavery. I tell them about terrorism, the era that began at the end of reconstruction that went on to World War II. We don't really know very much about it. But for African-Americans in this country, that was an era defined by terror. In many communities, people had to worry about being lynched. They had to worry about being bombed. It was the threat of terror that shaped their lives. And these older people come up to me now and they say, "Mr. Stevenson, you give talks, you make speeches, you tell people to stop saying we're dealing with terrorism for the first time in our nation's history after 9/11." They tell me to say, "No, tell them that we grew up with that." And that era of terrorism, of course, was followed by segregation and decades of racial subordination and apartheid.
>
> **9:40** And yet, we have in this country this dynamic where we really don't like to talk about our problems. We don't like to talk about our history. And because of that, we really haven't understood what it's meant to do the things we've done historically. We're constantly running into each other. We're constantly creating tensions and conflicts. **We have a hard time talking about race, and I believe it's because we are unwilling to commit ourselves to a process of truth and reconciliation.** In South Africa, people understood that we couldn't overcome apartheid without a commitment to truth and reconciliation. In Rwanda, even after the genocide, there was this commitment, but in this country we haven't done that.

What if Stevenson had begun his talk with the thesis that America doesn't talk about race because it is unwilling to admit its mistakes and move forward? He would have immediately put his audience on the defensive. Instead, he waits patiently to make his point after he has engaged his audience. Stevenson knows he can persuade his audience only if its members are listening.

Is the death penalty fair if carried out disproportionately against blacks?

10:19 I was giving some lectures in Germany about the death penalty. It was fascinating because one of the scholars stood up after the presentation and said, "Well, you know, it's deeply troubling to hear what you're talking about." He said, "We don't have the death penalty in Germany. And of course, we can never have the death penalty in Germany." And the room got very quiet, and this woman said, "There's no way, with our history, we could ever engage in the systematic killing of human beings. It would be unconscionable for us to, in an intentional and deliberate way, set about executing people." And I thought about that. What would it feel like to be living in a world where the nation state of Germany was executing people, especially if they were disproportionately Jewish? I couldn't bear it. It would be unconscionable.

11:12 And yet, in this country, in the states of the Old South, we execute people — where you're 11 times more likely to get the death penalty if the victim is white than if the victim is black, 22 times more likely to get it if the defendant is black and the victim is white — in the very states where there are buried in the ground the bodies of people who were lynched. And yet, there is this disconnect.

Stevenson does not mention his theme of identity in this section, but it is certainly the undercurrent. He contrasts the morals of Germany with those of the United States. There would be an uproar in the United States if Germany were executing people who were disproportionately Jewish; yet, the United States takes the same actions against blacks, and there is silence. He ties in the idea of disproportion to the preceding passage, where he discussed the terrorism of lynching. The analogy to Germany is all the more compelling when Stevenson adds the context of the South's history of lynching.

Next, Stevenson discusses the consequences of our failure.

Our identity is at risk

11:34 Well I believe that our identity is at risk. That when we actually don't care about these difficult things, the positive and wonderful things are nonetheless implicated. We **love innovation**. We **love technology**. We **love creativity**. We **love entertainment**. But ultimately, those realities are **shadowed** by **suffering, abuse, degradation, marginalization**. And for me, it becomes necessary to integrate the two....

Stevenson emphasizes the word "love" and the word that follows, and then pauses for dramatic effect and says by what that love is "shadowed." His voice and gestures in the video, coupled with the words he has chosen, show he speaks from the heart. He next explains why the shadow exists.

12:35 You know, ultimately, we all have to believe things we haven't seen. We do. As rational as we are, as committed to intellect as we are. Innovation, creativity, development come not from the ideas in our mind alone. They come from the ideas in our mind that are also fueled by some conviction in our heart.

> *Ultimately, we all have to believe things we haven't seen.*
> — Bryan Stevenson

And it's that mind-heart connection that I believe compels us to not just be attentive to all the bright and dazzly things, but also the dark and difficult things. Vaclav Havel, the great Czech leader, talked about this. He said, "When we were in Eastern Europe and dealing with oppression, we wanted all kinds of things, but mostly what we needed was hope, an orientation of the spirit, a willingness to sometimes be in hopeless places and be a witness."

Stevenson supports his argument by using a quotation from a famous leader. This is a great technique to use in an opening statement. A quotation from a famous person, by someone history looks upon favorably, makes the point you are arguing more powerful and credible.

Next, he relates what that idea of having hope means to his audience.

To be fully human, we must pay attention...

13:24 Well, that orientation of the spirit is very much at the core of what I believe even TED communities have to be engaged in. There is no disconnect around technology and design that will allow us to be fully human until we pay attention to suffering, to poverty, to exclusion, to unfairness, to injustice. Now, I will warn you, that this kind of identity is a much more challenging identity than ones that don't pay attention to this. It will get to you.

Here, he challenges the audience but, with his facial expressions, you can easily see that he offers encouragement without judgment. In his gestures, it is clear that that there will be a reward for the audience if it undertakes the challenge.

13:56 I had the great privilege, when I was a young lawyer, of meeting Rosa Parks. And Ms. Parks used to come back to Montgomery every now and then, and she would get together with two of her dearest friends.... And one time, I was over there listening to these women talk, and after a couple of hours, Ms. Parks turned to me, and she said, "Now, Bryan, tell me what the 'Equal Justice Initiative' is. Tell me what you're trying to do." And I began giving her my rap. I said, "Well we're trying to challenge injustice. We're trying to help people who have been wrongly convicted. We're trying to confront bias and discrimination in the administration of criminal justice. We're trying to end life without parole sentences for children. We're trying to do something about the death penalty. We're trying to reduce the prison population. We're trying to end mass incarceration."

15:06 I gave her my whole rap, and when I finished, she looked at me and she said, "Mmm mmm mmm." She said, "That's going to make you tired, tired, tired." (Laughter) And that's when Ms. Carr [Rosa Parks' friend] leaned forward, she put her finger in my face, she said, "That's why you've got to be brave, brave, brave."

We need to be brave

15:24 And I actually believe that the TED community needs to be more courageous. We need to find ways to embrace these challenges, these problems, the suffering. Because, ultimately, our humanity depends on everyone's humanity. I've learned very simple things doing the work that I do. It's just taught me very simple things. I've come to understand and to believe that each of us is more than the worst thing we've ever done. I believe that for every person on the planet. I think if somebody tells a lie, they're not just a liar. I think if somebody takes something that doesn't belong to them, they're not just a thief. I think even if you kill someone, you're not just a killer. And because of that there's this basic human dignity that must be respected by law. I also believe that in many parts of this country, and certainly in many parts of this globe, that the opposite of poverty is not wealth. I don't believe that. I actually think, in too many places, the opposite of poverty is justice.

16:27 And finally, I believe that, despite the fact that it is so dramatic and so beautiful and so inspiring and so stimulating, we will ultimately not be judged by our technology, we won't be judged by our design, we won't be judged by our intellect and reason. Ultimately, you judge the character of a society, not by how they treat the rich and the powerful and the privileged, but by how they treat the poor, the condemned, the incarcerated. Because it's in that nexus that we actually begin to understand truly profound things about who we are.

This section of Stevenson's speech is full of memorable lines that would move anyone to act. (Attendees that day contributed $1,000,000 to Stevenson's Equal Justice Initiative). Some of those lines are: "Our humanity depends on everyone's humanity," "Each of us is more than the worst thing that we've ever done," "Human dignity must be respected by law," and "The opposite of poverty is not wealth, it is justice."

> *Each of us is more than the worst thing we have ever done.*
> — Bryan Stevenson

Imagine how ineffective this speech would have been if he had read it from behind a podium as most lawyers do in a courtroom. The powerful lines were not a matter of luck, but the result of carefully choosing descriptive words to convey his ideas. Great oratory takes a lot of time—but the payoff is worth it.

Keep your eyes on the prize, hold on

17:05 I sometimes get out of balance. I'll end with this story. I sometimes push too hard. I do get tired, as we all do. Sometimes those ideas get ahead of our thinking in ways that are important. And I've been representing these kids who have been sentenced to do these very harsh sentences. And I go to the jail, and I see my client who's 13 [or] 14, and he's been certified to stand trial as an adult. I start thinking, well, how did that happen? How can a judge turn you into something that you're not? And the judge has certified him as an adult, but I see this kid.

And I was up too late one night, and I starting thinking, well gosh, if the judge can turn you into something that you're not, the judge must have magic power. Yeah, Bryan, the judge has some magic power. You should ask for some of that. And because I was up too late, wasn't thinking real straight, I started working on a motion. And I had a client who was 14 years old, a young, poor black kid. And I started working on this motion, and the head of the motion was: "Motion to try my poor, 14-year-old black male client like a privileged, white 75-year-old corporate executive."

18:03 (Applause)

18:08 And I put in my motion that there was prosecutorial misconduct, and police misconduct, and judicial misconduct. There was a crazy line in there about how there's no conduct in this county, it's all misconduct. And the next morning, I woke up and I thought, now did I dream that crazy motion, or did I actually write it? And to my horror, not only had I written it, but I had sent it to court.

18:26 (Applause)

A couple months went by, and I had just forgotten all about it. And I finally decided, oh gosh, I've got to go to the court and do this crazy case…. And as I was walking up the steps of this courthouse, there was an older black man who was the janitor in this courthouse. When this man saw me, he came over to me, and he said, "Who are you?" I said, "I'm a lawyer." He said, "You're a lawyer?" I said, "Yes, sir." And this man came over to me and he hugged me. And he whispered in my ear. He said, "I'm so proud of you." And I have to tell you, it was energizing. It connected deeply with something in me about identity, about the capacity of every person to contribute to a community, to a perspective that is hopeful.

Well, I went into the courtroom. And as soon as I walked inside, the judge saw me coming in. He said, "Mr. Stevenson, did you write this crazy motion?" I said, "Yes, sir. I did." And we started arguing. And people start-

> *All our survival is tied to the survival of everyone.*
> — Bryan Stevenson

ed coming in because they were just outraged. I had written these crazy things. And police officers were coming in, and assistant prosecutors, and clerk workers. And before I knew it, the courtroom was filled with people angry that we were talking about race, that we were talking about poverty, that we were talking about inequality.

19:48 And out of the corner of my eye, I could see this janitor pacing back and forth. And he kept looking through the window, and he could hear all of this holler. He kept pacing back and forth. And finally, this older black man with this very worried look on his face came into the courtroom and sat down behind me, almost at counsel table. About 10 minutes later, the judge said we would take a break. And during the break, there was a deputy sheriff who was offended that the janitor had come into court. And this deputy jumped up and he ran over to this older black man. He said, "Jimmy, what are you doing in this courtroom?" And this older black man stood up, and he looked at that deputy and he looked at me, and he said, "I came into this courtroom to tell this young man, keep your eyes on the prize, hold on."

20:27 I've come to TED because I believe that many of you understand that the moral arc of the universe is long, but it bends toward justice. That we cannot be fully evolved human beings until we care about human rights and basic dignity. That all of our survival is tied to the survival of everyone. That our visions of technology and design, and entertainment and creativity have to be married with the visions of humanity, compassion, and justice. And more than anything, for those of you who share that, I've simply come to tell you to keep your eyes on the prize, hold on.

Thank you very much.

Stevenson ends with a second theme, "keep your eyes on the prize," that ties in with his opening theme of identity. He cites an adage that has been attributed to Martin Luther King, Jr. and others: "The moral arc of the universe is long, but it bends toward justice." His speech has evolved not just from a request to help those wrongfully in prison, but from a challenge that "our survival" is tied to helping those less fortunate than we are.

3.4 APPLY STEVENSON'S TALK TO YOUR NEXT OPENING STATEMENT

Consider incorporating Stevenson's outline and delivery skills into your next opening statement. Following is a summary of his speech, including ways to tailor his outline for your next opening.

When delivering your next opening statement, do not use any notes at all. Stevenson spoke for 21 minutes without them, and so can you. Begin, as Stevenson did, by talking about your client's identity before launching into the facts that support your argument. For example, if you represent a company, talk about the people running it so that jurors can emotionally connect with them.

After you portray your client as someone the jury can support, put forth your best facts to prove your case. Stevenson had a wealth of information about the death penalty and mass incarceration in his talk, but he chose only the most powerful facts to make his points. Less is more.

Stevenson candidly addressed a weakness in his argument regarding the death penalty. He realized that many people believe that someone who commits a heinous murder deserves death in return. Stevenson admitted that such a belief was "sensible" but then explained why it was not. He said that the real question was whether society deserved the right to kill. Likewise, you need to concede the good points the other side will make, but point out why the jury should still support your stand.

Stevenson connected the problems in prisons to human values to which we all can relate. For example, the death penalty was not unfair because a particular individual was wrongfully put to death, but because it was disproportionately applied to blacks. While he could have argued that mass incarceration of the poor and minorities was unfair to those groups, he made the problem larger by arguing that to be fully human, we must pay attention to suffering and injustice. Similarly, find the human values that are present in your case, such as right and wrong, reasonable expectations, fairness, or anything else to which jurors can relate. Don't focus only on any false accusations against your client or the wrong that your client has suffered.

Finally, as Stevenson did, end strongly. He began by talking about identity and ended with a call to action, "keep your eye on the prize, hold on." Don't just repeat in your conclusion the theme in your opening remarks. End with something new that gets the jury excited about your case.

3.5 CHAPTER CHECKLIST 🖉

Stevenson's tips for creating a presentation

1. Know your audience. Stevenson wants to see his judge in action or learn who is going to make up his audience, so he can learn how to connect with its members.

2. If your audience will be hostile to your client, distract its members with a story to get them to step back from any hostility.

3. Stevenson began his speech by discussing his identity, in order to make the audience non-judgmental.

4. Don't begin your presentation with your substantive point because the people who are hostile toward you will fight you the whole time.

5. The goal in the beginning of speech or opening statement is getting audience members or jurors in a place where they are willing to listen.

6. If you represent a defendant in a criminal case, your first task is to get the jury to a place where they believe in the presumption of innocence.

7. Stevenson uses quotations from famous people on whom history looks favorably to bolster his argument.

Lessons to Learn from Stevenson's Speaking Style

1. Do not use notes.

2. In most sentences, emphasize a key word or phrase.

3. Pause for dramatic effect.

4. Smile genuinely to put your audience at ease.

5. Don't overwhelm the audience with facts.

6. Tell a story.

7. Gesture broadly with your hands.

8. Don't pace back and forth.

9. Speak from the heart.

Ten Memorable Quotes from Stevenson's TED Talk

1. "There is power in identity." His grandmother made him promise her three things: 1) always love your mom, 2) always do the right thing even when the right thing is hard to do, and 3) never drink alcohol.

2. "The system of justice treats you much better if you are rich and guilty than if you are poor and innocent. Wealth, not culpability, shapes outcomes. And yet we seem to be very comfortable."

3. "I believe that our identity is at risk. That when we actually don't care about these difficult things, the positive and wonderful things are nonetheless implicated. We love innovation. We love technology. We love creativity. We love entertainment. But ultimately, those realities are shadowed by suffering, abuse, degradation, and marginalization."

4. "We have to believe things we haven't seen."

5. "I believe each of us is more than the worst thing we've ever done. I believe that for every person on the planet. I think if somebody tells a lie, they're not just a liar. I think if somebody takes something that doesn't belong to

them, they're not just a thief. I think even if you kill someone, you're not just a killer. And because of that, there's this basic human dignity that must be respected by law."

6. "I also believe that in many parts of this country, and certainly in many parts of this globe, that the opposite of poverty is not wealth. I don't believe that. I actually think, in too many places, the opposite of poverty is justice."

7. "Ultimately, you judge the character of a society, not by how they treat their rich and the powerful and the privileged, but by how they treat the poor, the condemned, the incarcerated. Because it's in that nexus that we actually begin to understand truly profound things about who we are."

8. "I've come to TED because I believe that many of you understand that the moral arc of the universe is long, but it bends towards justice. That we cannot be fully evolved human beings until we care about human rights and basic dignity. That all our survival is tied to the survival of everyone."

9. "Ultimately, our humanity depends on everyone's humanity."

10. "Keep your eyes on the prize, hold on."

PART TWO

Direct Examination

INTRODUCTION

$\mathcal{D}$irect examination is the part of a trial when an attorney asks witnesses (who are favorable or neutral) questions that can help prove his or her case. Most attorneys incorrectly assume this task is easy, and their lack of preparation shows.

One difficulty is that, unlike normal conversations between two people, the witness cannot ask the lawyer questions. As a result, the attorney must create a conversation with the witness. Because this is unlike any conversation in real life, I believe this is the hardest part of a trial, as it goes against our natural instincts.

Another difficulty is that the witness is scared to death. Gallup conducts a poll each year that asks Americans to identify their top fears. "Public speaking" is routinely number one. It beats out snakes, drowning, and even death. When the comedian Jerry Seinfeld heard about this poll, he joked that if you believed Gallup, it meant that the person at a funeral giving the eulogy would rather trade places with the person in the casket.

In addition, lawyers rarely empathize with their witnesses, and this failure to do so affects outcomes. Lawyers usually just tell their witnesses to walk into the courtroom, tell the truth, and don't worry about anything else. Then the witness gets on the stand, the lawyer says, "tell the jury what happened," and the train wreck begins. Not only is the person on the witness stand scared of speaking in public, but he or she is doing so in a courtroom—perhaps the most intimidating place anyone could try to tell one's story. A witness faces a daunting challenge because the setting is extremely formal, the witness is under oath, there is a judge sitting just a few feet from the witness, and there is a court reporter, who is recording every word the witness says. Finally, there is an opposing attorney who has spent weeks preparing for his chance to tear the witness' testimony apart.

While direct examinations are difficult, they are also extremely important. There is a Jewish proverb that declares, "The drunkard smells of whiskey—but so does the bartender." Your job on direct examination is to show the jurors that your witness is indeed the bartender. You want them to see that your witness is trustworthy, likeable, and sober. If you don't, the opposing counsel will certainly show them that your witness is a drunkard.

In the next two chapters, the secrets to direct examination that will forever change the way you ask questions will be covered. Ken McClain will show why leading questions are the essence of direct examination, despite what conventional wisdom says. He will also explain why, during direct examination, visual aids should be integrated with all your questions.

In Chapter Five, Maureen O'Brien will reveal how she got a very reluctant witness—specifically, a rape victim—to tell her traumatic story in a courtroom. Her tips for being successful with the extremely challenging witnesses she handles every day will make your task infinitely easier the next time you are in court.

Every witness has a story to tell. Read on to learn how to get each witness to share that story successfully with the jury.

CHAPTER FOUR

⸛

Ken McClain

Be the Truth Teller in the Courtroom

Eric was just trying to provide for his family, and he ends up needing a double lung transplant because he did his job well.

— Ken McClain, attorney for Eric Peoples

*K*en McClain has won several multimillion-dollar verdicts that have been recognized nationally by the *National Law Journal*, including a $90 million verdict in 2000. In 2010, he obtained two verdicts that were each over $30 million. One of his more recent high-profile cases involved representing former Kansas City Chief players in a lawsuit against their team for post-concussion syndrome and chronic traumatic encephalopathy.

McClain's law office, Humphrey, Farrington & McClain, P.C., is in Independence, Missouri, where he focuses on personal injury and toxic tort litigation. After graduating with honors from the University of Michigan Law School in 1982, McClain began his career at a defense firm. He soon realized that he did not get to try many cases as a defense lawyer. Since he had always wanted to be a trial lawyer, he knew he had to leave. He then became a plaintiff's lawyer and never looked back. At his first trial, he won a million-dollar verdict.

> **CHAPTER HIGHLIGHTS**
> - Do not use scripted testimony
> - Use leading questions to tell your story
> - Don't hide the blemishes in the witness' testimony

4.1 STRATEGIES FOR DIRECT EXAMINATION

Being good at direct examination is the most overlooked trial skill. Not surprisingly, due to this lack of focus, lawyers are not very good at it. In contrast, one reason McClain is so successful is because he is a master at telling a powerful story through direct examination. He knows that a well-executed direct examination can be a turning point at a trial.

He strongly believes that the biggest mistake lawyers make is not using leading questions during direct examinations. After you read his direct examination, which follows, you too will share his passion; that is, the use of leading questions is the best way to get a witness to tell his or her story.

First, let's examine what a "leading question" is. A leading question suggests the answer to the witness: "It rained last Tuesday, correct?" On the other hand, an example of a non-leading question would be, "What was the weather last Tuesday?"

Most lawyers are reluctant to ask leading questions on direct examination because they are under the mistaken belief that leading questions are only allowed on cross-examination. However, the federal rule (Fed. R. Evid. 611) and most state rules allow leading questions on direct examination, provided the questions further the examination. The only prohibition regards asking a leading question during the heart of the testimony. This is because the courts don't want attorneys suggesting key facts on main points that could affect a jury's decision.

McClain's trial experience has proven to him that the conventional wisdom that claims leading questions must be avoided is mistaken. "There's this whole belief by lawyers that jurors know the difference between leading questions and non-leading questions, or that jurors want to hear witnesses talk, as opposed to lawyers. My experience has been they just want the story. They don't know the difference, and most lawyers don't know the difference between a leading or a non-leading question either."

> *Lawyers should ask questions that tell the story and allow the story to be told in the most direct way possible. If there's an objection as to leading, then you just have to adjust. Most of the time, lawyers won't object to anything you want to do.*
>
> *— Ken McClain*

McClain has found that leading questions are in the eye of the beholder. Although some of his questions may, in fact, be defined by a textbook as leading, he will do a direct examination in the most effective way he can without regard to the artificial rules that would seem to prohibit such questioning. McClain says, when he tries a case before a judge who is overly strict about leading questions, "Even when [the judges] do get involved, most of the time it's a short-lived phenomenon, and they essentially just sit back and let you ask your questions."

But McClain did not always ask his questions this way. When he first began trying cases, he would write out every question in a non-leading format. Then, he found out how difficult it was to get lay witnesses to tell the story "in a direct way that was meaningful to the jury." Hence, he developed a style to help them, and over time, his role shifted to becoming the storyteller himself.

McClain is not wedded to notes during his examination. He has with him only a bullet outline with references to those exhibits he plans to use. Sometimes he will just have the documents that he wants to discuss. As you will see in the direct examination below, McClain often has exhibits that relate to the witness' testimony on a projector screen. It helps the witness tell his story and also serves as McClain's outline.

How does McClain prepare his witnesses for the courtroom? He has his associates do the majority of the preparation, but they are never working from a script of questions and expected answers. McClain is purposefully not involved. When he is at trial, he discusses the topics on the bullet-point outline that his associates have prepared, but he also wants to hear the witness's exact words for the first time. He wants to have an honest reaction to what the witness says. The "genuineness" of the witness' testimony only comes through to the jury if it is hearing unrehearsed answers.

In contrast to McClain's style, many lawyers want to rehearse every question and every answer multiple times. The reason for this is twofold. First, the lawyer wants to carefully craft answers in hopes of presenting the best ones at the trial. Second, the lawyer wants to make sure there are no surprises at trial, so every possible question that could occur during direct examination is covered. The result is a scripted testimony that has every answer included, down to the commas and periods. McClain laments that the result is "so boring."

McClain wants to hear the testimony in court just as the jury is hearing it—for the first time. The authenticity of an unrehearsed testimony is worth the trade-off of an occasional surprise. If a surprise arises, he says to "roll with it." For example, in a recent case, McClain was surprised when his expert witness at a trial answered that he was not board certified in rheumatology. Most lawyers would be scared to ask the reason if they did not already know the answer—but not McClain. He explains, "That's the part of being honest about the testimony [with the jury]." So, he asked the doctor, "Why not?" The doctor explained that he had been grandfathered in and that he actually had helped draft the certification test.

> If you only know generally what the testimony's going to be, that is helpful to you in terms of the jury believing they're having a true discovery process and not simply watching a play.
> — Ken McClain

Most lawyers try to hide all the warts of their witness. Lawyers fear that the blemishes will ruin their case. McClain has no such worries. He tells the witness, "We're not going to lie. We're not going to tell a story that's not true, so don't worry about it. There's nothing that you can screw up that I can't fix." As McClain has learned, "The little things that do occur simply make it a more genuine experience."

McClain's fundamental belief that the truth will prevail influences how he conducts voir dire. He points out that most lawyers will do anything to keep a juror who has declared favoritism for his side from being dismissed from jury service. McClain knows that such a practice is disingenuous and that the rest of the jurors on the panel will see the duplicity in such an approach.

For example, suppose a potential juror states that he has read a lot of articles about the issue in controversy and that he could never be fair to the defendant. That person would be a perfect juror for any plaintiff's attorneys. Most plaintiff's attorneys would try to rehabilitate the juror so the judge would not dismiss him for having an unfair bias toward the defense. For instance, a plaintiff's lawyer might ask these questions: "Could you put aside what you have read and be fair to the defendant? If the judge instructed you to keep an open mind, could you follow the judge's instruction?" Such questions are an attempt to talk the witness out of his bias and persuade him to be open-minded. Many jurors who initially say they can't be fair will state that they would follow the judge's instructions because they don't want to admit otherwise.

Instead of taking such a convoluted approach, McClain would rather say, "I appreciate your honesty, and I think it would be better for you to sit on another case, don't you?" McClain would give up the favorable juror, in order to show the remaining jurors that he wants no special advantages and is not afraid of the truth.

The case we are going to examine in this chapter involves a plaintiff who was injured in a popcorn manufacturing plant from exposure to diacetyl, an ingredient used to give popcorn its buttery flavor and aroma. No summary of the lawsuit is necessary, as the transcript itself illustrates how well McClain gets his witness to tell his story. It is this ability to create a powerful picture of the events for the jury that results in McCain's success.

> *The strategy throughout my entire presentation is that I'm going to be the truth teller in the courtroom.*
>
> — Ken McClain

For the moment, all that's necessary to know is that Eric Peoples sued two manufacturers of microwave butter flavoring: International Flavors & Fragrances (IFF), and Bush Boake Allen (a subsidiary of IFF). Peoples claimed that these manufacturers knew the flavoring was hazardous yet failed to warn the plant workers of its dangers and provided no safety instructions for using it in the manufacturing of microwave popcorn.

4.2 DIRECT EXAMINATION OF ERIC PEOPLES

In the following passages, Ken McClain is questioning Mr. Peoples. Key moments in the examination and testimony are set in bold type.

Background

Q. *Mr. Peoples, would you state your full name for us, please?*
A. Eric Marshall Peoples.

Q. *And is this your wife, Candy?*
A. Yes, it is.

Q. *And do you have two kids?*
A. Yes, I do.

Q. *What are their names?*
A. Adrianna Peoples and Brantley Peoples.

Q. *Have you grown up here and lived here most of your life?*
A. Yes, I have.

Q. *Mr. Peoples, just to let the jury know, is it difficult for you to talk for extended periods of time?*
A. Yes.

Q. *And you have asked us to break your testimony up so that you cannot get too worn out?*
A. Yes, I have....

Q. *So today **I just want to deal with just, you know, introducing the jury to your life before all this happened, and some of your life experiences, and what kind of things you like to do, and the way your life was before the popcorn plant, and what's happened to you.** And we're going to restrict it to that, and then we're going to let Mr. Patton [the opposing counsel] ask whatever questions he wants to ask about that subject and do some other things this morning. Is that all right?*
A. That's fine.

Q. ***We've selected some photographs that came from your family photo album to give the jury some sense of your life and your background....***

McClain sees his case through the jurors' eyes. He does not overwhelm them with information, or a "data dump." He presents the information within a framework and makes it interesting by using transition phrases. In short, he tells the jury — and the witness — what the subject is for each area of examination. For example, McClain informs the jury that he will ask the witness about his life experiences before he got injured. Now, the jury understands why he is asking questions about the witness' interests, relationships, and hobbies. McClain then tells the jury that he will not only ask questions, but he will also display photos from Eric's family photo album. Visual aids are crucial when developing a witness' story and making it interesting.

Notice that McClain does not refer to his client by his first name as most attorneys do but rather by his last name. He does this often because by using the first name, he says, "I feel you're being too familiar with the witness, and instead of looking like an officer of the court, you're really looking like a partisan in this deal. I want the jury to view me, in this case, as a truth teller, as an officer of the court, more than an ambulance chaser." Therefore, McClain prefers taking a neutral role, particularly when questioning his client as a witness.

Q. *Can you tell me, did you grow up in Joplin?*
A. I grew up in Carthage.

Q. *Did you go to school there?*
A. Yes, I did.

Q. *Let's look at some photographs of you as a child. Sports were a big part of your family life?*
A. Yes, it was.

Q. *This is Exhibit #41.1. And you were a Chiefs' fan from the beginning?*
A. From the beginning.

Q. *Still a Chiefs' fan?*
A. Very strongly.

Q. *All right. Here's a picture of you, Exhibit #44.2 on a three-wheel bike, like I kind of remember being around. How old were you in this picture?*
A. Approximately, one and a half or two....

Q. *What kind of town is Carthage to grow up in, Mr. Peoples?*
A. Oh, it was a wonderful town to grow up in. Very open community. It's one of those towns that you couldn't get away with anything; everybody knew everybody else.

Q. *And were you comfortable in that town?*
A. Yes.

Q. *Did you enjoy growing up in that town?*
A. Yes, I did.

McClain then has Eric discuss photos that depict him with friends at a Kansas City Royals baseball game and dying Easter eggs, as well as photos of his extended family, such as one of his grandmother and another of his father getting remarried. In contrast, most lawyers simply have their witnesses blandly discuss backgrounds and hobbies. McClain knows showing the jury photos that relate to the witness' testimony is much more interesting and memorable. McClain then asks about Eric's hobbies in high school.

Q. *Go on to the next slide. Now, tell us about yourself. We learned that you were a sports fan as a kid. What kind of things did you get involved in, in high school?*
A. When I was in high school, I got involved in the drama club. I loved to act and put on plays. I also was in what we called swing choir. We danced and sang to various

types of music. We toured. We went to competitions. I didn't sing too much in the group choir because it conflicted with my acting, but I was in swing choir.

Q. *This is you, here?*
A. Yes, it is....

Q. *Let's go to the next one. Is this the same era?*
A. Yes, it is.

Q. *You were very suave? Or so you thought?*
A. So I thought....

Q. *OK. Coming out of high school what did you decide to do?*
A. I joined the navy, got married to my first wife. It was not Candy. It was another wife.

Q. *How old were you when you got married?*
A. Eighteen.

Q. *Did that work out?*
A. No, it did not.

Q. *Let's look at the next photograph....*

McClain continues to make the testimony come alive through the use of photographs. He does not put the jurors to sleep with the monotonous background questions that most lawyers ask. Instead, he carefully selects photos to give the jury a picture of Eric's health, interests, friends, and character before the injury. He also is not afraid to bring out a possible weakness in his client's character. McClain lets the jury know through questioning that the witness' first marriage did not last. Later, McClain will ask more about why that marriage failed.

Health

Notice how McClain uses a transition phrase in the first question to indicate a new topic:

Q. ***Now, let's talk for a moment.*** *Were you generally a **healthy lad?***
A. Yes, I was.

Q. *[Did you] have any serious illnesses as you were growing up?*
A. When I was about two I had the croup, where I was put in a croup tent for a day. But that was cured and fine....

Q. *Now Mr. Patton [opposing counsel] said that this croup event was a whooping cough? Was it a whooping cough?*
A. No.

Discharge from Army

It is vital to bring out any weaknesses in a witness' story before cross-examination. Otherwise, when the opposing counsel starts questioning the witness on a blemish that had not been revealed, credibility can be lost with the jury. Once that trust is lost, it can never be gained back. Watch what McClain does in the following excerpt. Also notice that he uses a transition phrase—highlighted in bold—to let the jury know that 1) he is changing topics and 2) the witness is going to discuss an embarrassment. McClain also lets the jurors know—highlighted in bold—that neither McClain nor Peoples is hiding anything from them and, therefore, they both can be trusted.

Q. *All right. Go ahead to the next slide. Is this you in your army, I mean, navy—even I know better than that—navy uniform?*
A. Yes, it is.

Q. *All right.* ***Now, you've already introduced us a little bit, and I told the jury we're going to tell them the truth, the whole truth, and nothing but the truth?***
A. Yes.

Q. *Your navy service started out well, but your marriage didn't end up going very well?*
A. No, It did not.

Q. *And were the two interrelated: your navy service and your marriage?*
A. Yes, it was.

Q. *What happened?*
A. With the marriage, my wife was not able to handle me being gone as [I] needed to be to serve in the navy…. She filed for divorce. She just couldn't handle that.

Q. *And was that very stressful for you?*
A. Very stressful.

Q. *And was that at the end of your service?*
A. Yes, it was.

Q. *By the way, you served on a submarine?*
A. Yes, I did.

Q. *During the Gulf War?*
A. Yes, I did….

Q. *In the midst of this, did you get into an incident with an ensign?*
A. Yes, I did.

Q. *And tell the jury about that.*

McClain directs Eric to tell the jury the details of the incident. There is no reason to be afraid of the truth. Instead, the fear lies in hiding something from the jury that will later come out during cross-examination.

A. With everything that was going on, the ensign was dogging me for lack of a better word. I tried my best to maintain my composure, to treat him with the respect that he deserved being an officer. But anybody can only go so far, and my temper flared, and I hit him.

Q. *And are you sorry about that?*
A. I'm very sorry.

Q. *And did you meet with the captain about that?*
A. Yes, I did.

Q. *Was this at the end of your enlistment period?*
A. Yes.

Q. *You were set to be discharged?*
A. Yes.

Q. *How did your captain suggest to handle it?*
A. Due to witness statements and also his knowledge of what I was going through with the divorce and everything, he was sympathetic to my situation. He allowed me to be discharged with other than honorable, and it became honorable in six months. And so it was other than honorable because of this incident, but he said that it would become honorable after six months....

Q. **And you're not proud of this event, but that was what happened?**
A. **That is what happened.**

McClain always controls the examination. He does not rely solely on the witness to tell the story. Most witnesses are scared to death to testify, and the lawyer must ensure that the story is told well. Here, McClain emphasizes to the jury that Eric is not proud of his discharge from the navy, and in doing so, McClain has taken away any ammunition defense counsel might use on cross-examination.

> **Practice Tip**
> If a weakness is revealed during a direct examination, the cross-examiner will look foolish if he or she tries to cover the same ground.

According to McClain, the defense counsel made a strategic error in his closing argument regarding Eric's discharge. At the trial, McClain had put on evidence suggesting the defendants had lost a study that would have helped Eric prove his case. To counter this contention, defense counsel argued that Eric could not complain about the lost study, since he had himself lost the paperwork that could have proved that his discharge was not dishonorable (since it was the defendants' contention that the discharge was dishonorable).

McClain relates what happened next in his closing rebuttal argument: "Then I came back really softly on rebuttal and said to Eric, 'I'm sure sorry. I know that it's easy to get wound up during these arguments, and I'm sure that's what happened with [the defense counsel]. I know that if he had to think about it over again, he wouldn't have attacked you like that.'"

McClain could have raised his voice and attacked the defense counsel in his rebuttal, but he took a softer approach that is consistent with his belief that you should be a gentleman. In short, he minimized the hurtful words that the defense counsel had said to Eric in the heat of the moment.

Marriage and children

Most attorneys repeatedly ask the witness, "What happened next?" Such a question is so vague and broad that oftentimes the witness has no idea what is being asked of them. The witness will either look quizzically at the lawyer (and the question will have to be rephrased) or he or she will ramble on and on, hoping that somewhere in the long-winded answer is the requested information. Notice how McClain leads the witness from the discussion of the navy discharge to the witness' marriage and children.

Q. *All right. Go ahead, the next slide. Now, you got back and you decided I have to start over, right?*
A. Yes.

Q. *OK. And you met Candy?*
A. Yes.

Q. *And you two fell in love?*
A. Yes.

Q. *About when did you get married?*
A. We got married on December 4, 1992.

Q. *And at that point in time did you have a fixed idea of what your occupation was going to be?*
A. At that time when we were married, I was working at Leggett & Platt. But no, whatever came along, basically.

Q. *Your goal in life was to stay in Carthage and have your own family and raise them?*
A. Yes….

Q. *Let's look at the next slide. The children came along pretty quickly?*
A. Pretty quickly, yes.

Q. **Eric, do you feel like you found yourself in your marriage to Candy and your fatherhood?**
A. Yes.

Q. **And do you feel like that's the most important thing you do?**
A. Yes….

In these last two questions, not only does McClain ask leading questions, he asks very good ones. He frames the expected answer as he desires. He knows that he is more articulate than the witness, so he uses better phrases than the witness would. For example, most witnesses would simply say they love their spouse and children. McClain uses more powerful words: "Do you feel like you found yourself in your marriage to Candy and your fatherhood?" He then follows that question with one asking Eric if being a husband and father is the "most important thing" in his life.

Q. *And were you healthy?*
A. Yes, sir....

Q. *Any health problems at all since you married Candy and the kids came along?*
A. No, other than a common cold, my [minor] car accident with the nose, but other than that, no.

Q. *Did you enjoy playing with your children?*
A. Always.

Q. *Were you active with them?*
A. Constantly.

Q. *Tell the jury about that. What is it as a father you enjoyed doing? Some of us sit around and watch TV and let the children play around us, you know, unfortunately. What did you like to do?*
A. In my home, if you were on the floor you were fair game. They're just typical kids, they never stop. They would play, and we would wrestle. We would run and laugh and just cackle. I mean my daughter loves to be flipped upside down and held. Of course, I was very gentle with her. But they loved it from a very early age. We wrestled all the time....

Q. **And can you tell us, is this kind of an overview of who you were and what you were and how you were before all this happened?**
A. Yes, it is.

Q. **Mr. Peoples, would you give anything to be like that again?**
A. Yes, I would.

Q. *Is that the nature of or at least part of what you feel is your loss here?*
A. Yes.

Q. *Now, we're going to talk about going to work at the popcorn plant in another session, but I'm going [stop] because we're going to break this up, that's where I'm going to leave it for the morning. And let Mr. Patton [the defense counsel] ask whatever questions he would like to. OK?*
A. OK.

McClain signals to the jury—and the witness—that he will wrap up the health and family situation before the injury occurred. He then uses a leading question to frame his argument: "Would you give anything to be like that again?" The leading question allows McClain to describe the witness' emotions rather than risking a less powerful answer if McClain had asked a non-leading question, such as, "How do you feel now?"

> **Practice Tip**
> Use a leading question with a powerful description to frame the closing argument.

Given his poor health, the judge allowed Eric to testify in parts with long breaks in between and to be cross-examined on each section instead of all at once. Also, notice that McClain knows that the break is coming up, so he ends on powerful testimony. He makes it clear to the jury that there is no way to undo the injury and that there is no amount of money that can substitute for his inability to be healthy again.

After several witnesses, Eric was recalled. Observe how McClain summarizes Eric's previous testimony so the jury will remember what Eric has said and where he is in his story.

Eric begins work at the Jasper Popcorn Plant

Q. *We were just at the point in the story when you had gone to work at the popcorn plant or were about to. At that point in time you were **healthy, you had two small children, and your life looked like it was going pretty good?***

A. Yes.

Q. *All right. Pick up your story then…Can you tell us when you heard that you were going to go work at a popcorn packaging plant, how that impacted you? **What did you think about that?***

A. It's something that I hadn't ever done before…I mean the pay was very good for what we had to do…. I was looking for something steady…. I started out at seven dollars an hour to pick up bags of popcorn and put it in the cartoner [a machine that assembles cartons].

McClain never asks, "What happened next?" First, he summarizes previous testimony to remind jury of significant facts. Then, he directs the witness to important facts he wants the jury to hear, such as a man being excited about a minimum wage job.

Q. ***At some point in time** did you **desire to get a promotion** in the plant or how is it that you became a mixer?* [**This transition signals to the jury and witness that a new topic is going to be covered.**]

A. About a month after I started, I heard through the grapevine basically that we had an actual opening in the mixing room for my shift…. You're kind of like the chef of the plant, so to speak, because you're the one that makes what everybody likes and that's the butter flavor….

Q. *So you could set your own schedule and pace as long as you kept the butter flavor mixed, and it was working in the system, you were pretty well free to do whatever you wanted to do?* [**McClain summarizes the advantages of the new job for the witness so the witness only has to answer "yes."**]

A. That is correct.

Q. *So what would you do?…you'd go and check the butter flavor and make sure that there was enough of the mixture?*

A. Yes, make sure…the tanks…were at a decent level. I watched him make a batch until the salt addition, and they ran me out because I didn't have a mask….

Q. *Now you mentioned something,* **let me just stop you for a minute,** *so I don't forget it. There was a mask that was used on the salt?*
A. What we called a painter's mask.

McClain chooses the topics, and he interrupts the witness to discuss the mask. While the plant had painter's masks, other testimony will show that such protection was not nearly enough.

McClain says that Eric was "an excellent witness and very articulate. He came across as being very sincere and really was just an unassuming guy that had loved this job because it was a clean job and he'd been in so many dirty jobs, and he thought it was safe because he was making food."

Eric then discussed applying for a job opening at the plant. In the following excerpt, Eric relates what the job requirements were.

A. I had to be able to lift 30 to 35-pound buckets five feet to dump them into the mixing tank. I had to lift fifty-pound salt bags approximately four feet to be able to put them into the auger....

Q. *Now, let me ask you this. Were you able to lift five-pound buckets up over your head? I mean the five-gallon buckets, not five pounds. They're a lot heavier than five pounds?*
A. Thirty to 35 pounds.

Q. *Thirty to 35-pound buckets up over your head?*
A. Yes, without any trouble....

Q. **Were you in pretty good physical condition at that point in your life?**
A. I'd like to think so.

McClain specifically asks Eric about his strength so he can later contrast it with his present failing health. Watch how McClain emphasizes Eric's strength with the next series of questions regarding Eric's previous job.

Q. *Before you went to work at the Jasper plant, had you been working with automotive parts?*
A. ...[My friend and I] would take engine blocks, set them up on the table. . . .

Q. **But in other words,** *you could lift up engines and all kinds of things.* **You were a strong guy** *and when they said, you know, you got, 30-gallon buckets to lift every night over your head, 30 of them or so, you said, no sweat?*
A. No sweat.

Q. *So you got the job?*
A. Yes, I did....

Q. *As far as you know, was there a better job in the plant?*
A. I couldn't think of one except maybe in an air-conditioned office.

Q. *Like Jim Cook has?* **[Jim Cook was a supervisor.]**
A. Like Jim Cook has....

Q. Did the job have a wage differential?
A. Yes. My wage went up from the seven when I started to over $11 an hour....

Q. What did that do in your mind?
A. Oh, we were excited. That's more than I've ever made in, you know, for a forty hour-a-week job.... I became a jack-of-all-trades in the mixing shop.

*Q. **So you thought this kind of was preparing you for even further advancement because not only did you learn the mixing job, you learned every job in the plant?***
A. Yes.

Practice Tip

On occasion, summarize facts from previous answers to form part of the next question. This technique, known as looping, reminds jurors of previous testimony.

In the last question, McClain articulates Eric's hopes for the new job so he doesn't have to rely on Eric's description. McClain continually summarizes important information for the jury so that they will remember it. Notice how he does it in the next section with questions three, four, and five.

Q1. Did you like everybody?
A. I got along with everybody.

Q2. And did you have nice conversations with everybody as you'd go relieve them from one job to the other...
A. Sure. I mean it was a really good place to work; very nice people on the shift.... It got to a point some of us would go golfing after work in the mornings or we would go bowling and just hang out. It got to be almost like a second family so to speak. Several of them came over and met Candy and the kids.

*Q3. **So it was a good place to work not only because you were getting paid well, but they were nice people too?***
A. Yes, they were.

*Q4. **And it was good clean work?***
A. Good clean work.

*Q5. **And you thought there was a future there?***
A. I had no plans to going anywhere.

*Q6. **Now, let's talk about the kinds of products you used... [transition phrase to new topic]***

Artificial butter flavoring

Q. Tell the jury what was the artificial flavoring?
A. The artificial flavoring that we used was BBA.

Q. So BBA was artificial?
A. Yes.

Q. And what was the natural flavor?
A. The Scisorek....

Q. *Was there a distinction in your mind about the aroma of the two products?*

A. ....The first time I opened the artificial, the BBA, it was very, very potent. And he [the coworker] warned me that it would be very potent. He said, "It's a very strong, almost overpowering flavor." It would make your eyes water, it would make your nose run. But as far as any pain, there was no pain in the lungs or the nose or anything like that.

Q. **Was Dr. Egilman right? It's like cutting an onion?**

A. Yes.

Q. **It's the same kind of reaction?**

A. Just like cutting an onion. Your nose would run, and your eyes would water but there was no pain in inhaling it.

McClain connects Eric's testimony with what the plaintiff's expert witness had said earlier in the trial about the symptoms from inhaling BBA's aroma.

Q. *OK. Now tell the jury how much of each [butter flavoring] you used?*

A. ....I would use anywhere between 25 and 30 buckets [of BBA] a night ....

Q. *Would you use the BBA every night?*

A. Every night.

Q. *So you'd use between twenty-five and thirty buckets of BBA every night?*

A. That's correct.

Rabbi visits plant

Q. *Did you ever see anything on here [labels] that alarmed you?*

A. No.

Q. *Did you take note that it was kosher?* [**McClain directs the witness to the specific topic he wants to discuss.**]

A. Yes.

Q. *Tell the jury what made you think about it?*

A. To me, when you hear the word "kosher," that means that it's, well, for one to say for the Jewish people to have in their diet, which in my personal understanding, made it safe for all people. That nobody is harmed in any way, shape, or form by this product. And as far as I know, the Haubeins, who owned Jasper Popcorn at the same time I was there, was Jewish as well, and their product was kosher when it came out—the popcorn that came out of the line was kosher.

Q. *And in fact, did the rabbi visit the plant?* [**short specific question**]

A. Yes. We had a rabbi visit quite often—normally on the day shift so it was strictly hearsay that he was there. But you could always tell when he was coming. Extra little polish was put on everything, and stuff was buffed up a little bit. He did come one time on the night shift to meet us. He hadn't met the night shift, and he came and was just a wonderful gentleman to me. I mean, just a great guy. He walked through the entire plant with his little ceremony that he does, you know, to the mixing room, up on the mezzanine, and then, of course, we lost track of him when he went back in the warehouse. And then he left from there.

Q. *So not only did the label say that it was safe, it was blessed?* [McClain makes his point for the jury in the form of a question to the witness.]
A. Yes.

Q. *So Eric, did you have any sense when you were doing any of this, that there were any risks associated with working with this product?*
A. No.

Q. *Or that you were taking any kind of health risk?*
A. No.

Q. *Would you have ever worked with it had you known that there was any risk to your health?*
A. No....

Q. *Did you ever refuse to follow directions about how to work around this material?*
A. No, I did not.

Q. *Ever take any shortcuts?*
A. No, I did not.

Q. *You followed it **to the letter**, about what ought to be done?*
A. The way Bart [coworker] trained me is the way I did it.

McClain highlights that Eric always followed orders "to the letter" and never took shortcuts. He further highlights the irony that a Rabbi blessed a product that is dangerous to make.

Health problems begin

Q. *Now, tell us then, what your first indication was that somehow you were not as healthy or you were having some kind of lung problem?*
A. Just about a year after I was at the plant.... we noticed that at first it came on almost like cold symptoms and almost overnight.... I got to work, I started to have chills. I was becoming nauseous.... My sinuses went berserk. I attempted to treat it with over-the-counter medication for the rest of that month. Nothing would help.... and I went to the ER.

Q. *Did [the ER doctors] think that it was anything but a cold?*
A. They told me they believed it was the beginning of pneumonia... [The doctor] did not want me around this popcorn.

Q. *Then what happened?*
A. The majority of everything let up.... but I was still having severe shortness of breath ....One tragedy of the medical condition is how suddenly it appeared with no warning signs. The symptoms did not start out small and grow. Instead, all of a sudden, you would feel incredibly weak as if you were out of shape.

Labels

Q. So, other people around in the plant were getting sick?
A. Or had been previously, yes.

Q. And so you started asking yourself — what?
A. Just what in the world was going on? You know was it something I was using? Was it something else from the plant? You know, just trying to find out what the bases were here. [*sic*]

Q. At that point did you read the labels on the packages? [**short specific question directs the witness**]
A. Yes. I went back on every package that I handled, and I looked at the labels to see if there was any type of warnings on anything.

BY MCCLAIN: Let's put the labels up there, Scott.
(By McClain) You looked at this label? [**McClain shows exhibits on a projection screen so the jury can see and hear important information about labels.**]
A. Yes, I did.

Q. And you saw that it was generally recognized as safe on the FEMA GRAS[1] list?
A. Yes.

Q. And all flavor ingredients contained were approved for use in a regulation of Food and Drug Administration?
A. Yes.

Q. And the kosher symbol? And did you say, well, aha! This must be the culprit?
A. No, sir. I dismissed it.

Q. You thought this can't be the culprit?
A. That can't be it.

Bringing out weaknesses

Eric's doctor had told him not to return to work, but Eric refused his recommendation. McClain did not shy away from this possible weakness in Eric's testimony. That is, Eric might be accused on cross-examination of not following his doctor's orders that would have improved his condition. Instead of waiting for a potentially damaging cross-examination, McClain took the ammunition away in the following excerpt:

Q. Why did you go back [to work]?
A. It was my job. I had to have a paycheck, you know.

*Q. **Trying to support two little kids?***
A. Yes.

McClain emphasizes that Eric went back to work not to satisfy a greed for money, but because he had to support his two young children.

> **Practice Tip**
> Prevent a damaging cross-examination by being the first attorney to bring out bad information about a witness and control how it is presented to the jury.

---

[1] The FEMA GRAS is a list of generally recognized safe flavorings that is published by the Flavor and Extract Manufacturers Association.

Diagnosis

McClain guides Eric through his six-month struggle to get a diagnosis for his debilitating shortness of breath. It concludes with this testimony:

A. At that time they came in and they told us that they diagnosed me with bronchiectasis, with obstructive lung disease, and I was being placed on a double lung transplant list.

Clarifying questions

As mentioned earlier, due to Eric's health, the court allowed his testimony to be broken up into parts. Consequently, McClain would conduct a portion of the direct followed by a cross on that particular portion. Then, other witnesses would testify, and Eric would resume his testimony. The following excerpt shows McClain tackling head on an issue that was raised on cross-examination. In a few short specific questions, he clarifies any possible confusion created by cross-examination.

Q. *There's one point that Mr. Patton [the defense counsel] asked you about at the end of the day on Friday that I want to clarify. In Dr. Scacewater's[2] note, there was a note [that you had told him you had worn a respirator while at work]. Is that right?*
A. Yes.

Q. *Now you did wear a mask when working around the salt?*
A. That is correct.

Q. *But it wasn't the double cartridge mask, was it?*
A. No.

Q. *It wasn't the canister respirator, right? You didn't wear that?*
A. No, I did not.

Q. *And no one told you that you ought to?*
A. No.

Q. *Were you here when Mr. Ewing said that even if you'd worn that, that wouldn't have had any impact on the butter because that was for dust not for vapors?*
A. Yes, I was.

Q. *So it doesn't have anything to do with this lawsuit?*
A. It has nothing at all.

All seven of these questions were leading. Remember, a leading question suggests the answer to the witness. On redirect examination, courts liberally allow leading questions, even when they go to the heart of the testimony. In the hands of a great lawyer, they are an efficient and powerful way to clear up an opposing attorney's attempts on cross-examination to confuse the jury.

---

[2] Dr. Scacewater had treated Peoples and others who had worked at the plant. According to Eric, the doctor had mistakenly written in his treatment note that Eric had told him that he had worn a respirator while at the plant.

McClain effectively clarifies the facts and undercuts defense counsel's credibility when he points out in his last question that defense counsel's line of questioning has nothing to do with the lawsuit.

Precautions taken at other plants

In order to highlight the failures of the Jasper Popcorn Plant, McClain compared it to others, such as the Bush Boake Allen plant.

Q. *Now, Mr. Peoples, let me just ask you a question before we talk about the rest of this. You've been here throughout all the testimonies except for Dr. Trulock and the visualization of what's going to happen —*
A. That's correct.

Q. *— in your double lung transplant. Have you heard about all of these respirators that were used at the Bush Boake Allen plant?*
A. Yes, I have.

Q. *And all the precautions?*
A. Yes, I have.

Q. *And all the ventilation?*
A. Yes.

Q. *And did you hear Mr. Cook [a manager at Eric's plant] say that if he'd known about any of this stuff, he would have taken the same precautions in your plant?*
A. Yes.

Q. *Mr. Peoples, if you had known that the people making this butter flavor were wearing respirators even after they enclosed the system and had vent hoods and air monitoring going on all the time, would you have worn such a respirator?*
A. Yes, I would.

Q. *You weren't a risk taker?*
A. No, I wasn't.

Q. *You would have taken the precautions that they recommended?*
A. If the people making this product wore this in their precautions, then to me that would be sense enough for everyone that worked with it to wear it.

McClain highlights the issue of negligence by comparing the Jasper plant to the precautions taken by the maker of the artificial butter flavoring at its own plant. He then further points out that Eric was not a risk taker who would have ignored safety guidance if it had been given to him.

Double lung transplant

Q. *Now at this point in time [when he first learned about the diagnosis], did you think that a lung transplant.... **was like getting two new tires?***
A. Something to that effect, yes....

Q. What did you [later] find out?

A. That, well, first off that the surgery itself, which we were ecstatic to hear had a 98 percent survival rate…dropped to fifty percent [after five years]…. I know it's coming. It's going to have to or else I won't be here at all. But everything that is involved with it from the anti-rejection medicines, to the physical therapy, to once again, I will have to literally make myself cough. And they told me that I will probably have what they call a vibrating vest, which will vibrate my upper chest to make me spit this mucus up….

Q. Is that because with a transplanted lung they can't attach the nerves so you can't feel when you have to cough?

A. That's correct.

Q. So you've got to wear a vest that vibrates just so that you can do what we normally do to get stuff out of our lungs?

A. [Yes.]

Notice the imagery McClain uses in the first question. He makes sure the jury understands that getting a lung transplant is nothing like getting a set of new tires. He ends his questioning by bringing out more details about the vibrating vest so the jury understands how awful it is to wear one.

> **Practice Tip**
>
> Use descriptive words and imagery in your questions to make them memorable for the jury. For example, McClain asks: "Did you think a lung transplant was like getting two new tires?"

Q. Now, Mr. Peoples, knowing what you know in terms of what your odds are with the lung transplant, tell the jury what this does to your mental state on a daily basis?

A. I feel like I'm sentenced to death row. My prison cell is my lungs. I can't maneuver very much or go very far…. I mean, and I understand that we're all going to die eventually, but they don't even think I'll make it to 50….

Pain and suffering

McClain created a chart regarding Eric's emotional damages. It was a very good visual aid for the jury and also provided a memory aid for the witness so that he would not forget to discuss an area of damages.

Q. We've made some boards up. In terms of emotional damages, you said you feel fear. **Well, what are you afraid of? [McClain has a down to earth conversational style.]**

A. Every night after I've kissed the kids good night, Candy and I would go in the bedroom. And when I lay down to go to sleep and I close my eyes, the first thing that goes through my mind is whether or not I'm going to wake up in the morning. With 20 percent lung capacity, I mean it's better than it was, but they told me that any obstruction almost…I wouldn't make it to the hospital to get the obstruction cleared. So, I guess if you had to classify it, it would be almost a fear of death at this age.

I mean, you know, you hear stories about how people live long healthy lives. My grandfather is 80 years old. My great-grandmother was 98. My great-grandmother on my mom's side was 95. I mean, you know, and the things that they got to see and the changes that they experienced. You know, living that long and to know that I may not even make it to fifty. I mean it just it scares me.

Q. *Anger?*

A. .... I would get mad at things that I couldn't do. You know, the main one of course is playing with my children. And I get so angry because it used to be nothing, just part of life to roll around on the floor for hours until Dad was just so tired, you know. You know kids, they just never run out of energy, and... Dad would have to finally have to say, OK, I've got to rest. Now I can't even do that.

I get angry because I can't help like I used to.... My brother took over mowing the yard for me when I first got sick. Never asked any questions, he just said, "When you need it, give me a call."

Q. *Now, he's in Tulsa?*

A. Now, he's in Tulsa....

Q. *I was thinking about that this weekend. I got to coach my two daughters' basketball games on Saturday. Tell the jury about what you wanted to do in that regard for your kids?* [**McClain always makes sure the testimony connects with the jury. He empathizes with Eric's injuries and now wants him to explain them in terms anyone could understand.**]

A. I wanted to coach them. My daughter always was an athletic little girl. She loved to run and play, and I looked forward to coaching soccer, or softball, or volleyball—whatever it is that they wanted to do, both of them. As was mentioned, the sore spot is Brandon and I were never able to play football. But we always said when Adri was born that if she wanted to play, we would do everything possible to make sure she played.

You know, and I looked forward to doing that. I looked forward to teaching them how to shoot if they showed interest in hunting. Teaching them how to fish and how to look for the spots like my dad did, and to share with them the wading the creek that meant so much to my father and I because that was our time, and I wanted it to be my time with my kids also. Now I can hardly even cheer at a soccer game. I go, and I just sit. I try to cheer, but I have to carry this thing around with me, and the other parents, you know, they just don't seem to understand. You know, I get looks, I get glares.

Q. *Is that the embarrassment point you've got here [on the board]?*

A. That is an embarrassing point, yes. The embarrassment that I can't be a typical father like I want to be, you know. To carry this around with me—even not to have this, and to go to Wal-Mart and have to use an electric cart. I'm 32 years old. I shouldn't have to use an electric cart. I don't have any casts on my ankles or anything on my legs. I shouldn't have to use that at 32 years old.

McClain then took Eric through a detailed list of emotional damages listed on the board including depression, anxiety, despair, back pain, cold chest, dizziness, numbness, drainage, night sweats, sinus pain, sexual difficulties, headaches, bronchitis, drug side effects, steroid use, jitteriness, nasal drying, sleeplessness, changing the oxygen pack, bone marrow cancer test, severe dry mouth, and physical therapy.

McClain gave the jury an organized and thorough presentation of Eric's significant damages for pain and suffering. He never spent too long on one issue. It never seemed like endless piling on but rather a coherent description of Eric's problems.

Physical therapy

McClain used a video of Eric's physical therapy to show his frustrations and physical weakness. Below is an excerpt from that testimony.

Q. *Describe for the jury your physical therapy on a daily basis?*
A. All right. At first I would go to what we call the Rehab Center.... [then I joined] the YMCA in Carthage. That way we could go as a family, and Candy and I could walk or play with the weights, or whatever....

Q. *Now, did we film you in one of these daily workouts that you —*
A. Yes.

Q. *Would it be helpful in showing the jury the difficulty that you have?*
A. I think so.

(Direct examination continues during the viewing of the video of Mr. Peoples going to the YMCA.)

Q. *Is this the outside of the Y?*
A. Yes.

Q. *This was three weeks ago?*
A. Yes.

Q. *A little bit cold?*
A. It was a little cooler. The mask, as I said, that the cold air hurts, so the mask helped to keep the air warm that I breathe in so I'm not breathing that harsh, cold air....

Q. *Are you catching your breath here?*
A. Yes.

Q. *And coughing?*
A. And coughing. . . .

Q. *So, what you're trying to do is get inside out of the cold?*
A. Get inside first, yes.

Q. *And you tried to push yourself and all of a sudden you had a coughing spasm?*
A. Yes. . . .

Q. *Now does walking into the workout gym with an oxygen tank on, is that part of your embarrassment?*

A. Part of it, yes. You get a lot of stares....

Q. *How long do you generally walk?*

A. Between five and seven minutes is usually about as long as I can go. . . .

Q. *Now sometimes you know, when I push myself, well, you can see that I haven't done much working out lately. But I think that if I just push myself, I'll get in better shape. Does that work for you?*

A. No, all it does is wear me down even more.

Q. *So this isn't really to increase your lung capacity, it's just to stay even?*

A. Just to maintain what I have, yes. Also, when we went up for the transplant [consultation], we were warned at that time that if I wasn't in physical condition to survive it, they wouldn't even consider it.

Q. *So after you're done riding the bike—how long will it take you to recover?*

A. I have to go home and lay down before I'm able to actually function again.

Q. *So the drill is every morning get up, take the kids to school?*

A. Uh-huh.

Q. *Take your medicines?*

A. Yes.

Q. *Then go workout. And this ten minutes will take how much time out of your day?*

A. Altogether it will take, with the resting afterwards, probably four to five hours if not more.

Q. *So this is your job every day?*

A. Pretty much. It's about the only thing that I have as far as getting out and doing that I have to look forward to.

Conclusion

Q. *Now, let me just ask you a philosophical question. You heard me say to the jury in opening and in voir dire this business about emotion injury and pain and suffering, are you asking the jury to award you damages for emotion injury and pain and suffering?*

A. Yes, I am.

Q. *For the items that we talked about?*

A. For everything that I go through every day.

Q. *And if they award you money for your economic loss, how much you've lost in wages and paid medical bills, why is it that you think that pain and suffering damages and emotional injury damages are appropriate here? Why do you want them to award them to you?*

A. Because I want somebody, somebody out there somewhere to say that my life is worth something. That everything that I've missed out on and am going to miss out on in the future means something. And that's why I ask that.

Q. *Mr. Peoples, can you think of anything more important than the joy of life that you're now missing?*
A. No.

Q. **Now that it's been taken away from you, is its absence all the more sweet in your memory and all the more bitter in fact not to have it?**
A. Every day....

Q. *Mr. Peoples, do you believe that these things that you're missing out on are very important to the quality of life of any individual?*
A. Yes.

Q. *And to you particularly?*
A. Yes.

By McClain: *I don't have any further questions.*

McClain ends strongly. Notice how he summarizes the impact of the entire damages argument in one question: "Now that it's been taken away…" He compares the sweet memory of good health to the bitter reality of not having it. It is a torture that no one would want to have to deal with on a daily basis. It is also the perfect way for McClain to end his direct examination.

4.3 VERDICT AND AFTERMATH

On March 14, 2004, after three hours of deliberations, the jury awarded $18 million to Eric and $2 million to his wife — a verdict which made national news. In 2012, Eric and his wife again made national headlines when they filed for bankruptcy.

4.4 BIGGEST MISTAKES LAWYERS MAKE

Regarding the biggest mistake lawyers make on direct examination, McClain responds, "Lawyers tend to just want to get the story out because they feel like I've got to get through this. I've got to [prove the elements of my case] and go over every small point to be sure that I've dotted every 'I' and crossed every 'T,' which of course, they do." While it is obviously important to put on evidence to prove your case, the lawyers, McClain says, "make the direct part of their case so boring that they lose the jury before they get into the second half [when the defense puts on its case]."

> *My cross-examination demeanor and my direct-examination demeanor are equally high energy. I have felt like most lawyers are sleepwalking through their directs.*
>
> — Ken McClain

But McClain has learned from experience that such a strategy is a big error. He explains:

Lots of lawyers think that they can make it up in cross-examination. That's what I used to think, and it'll work if you've got some really exciting cross-examinations.

On the other hand, why not make your directs very interesting? Why not make them very animated? Why not make it exciting for the jury because they're hearing something new. Certainly don't fall into the trap of simply going through the motions and losing your jury before you're ever able to win the case on cross.

Follow McClain's advice—make direct examinations compelling and memorable—and win more cases.

4.5 CHAPTER CHECKLIST 🖊

McClain's Advice for Direct Examination

1. If you don't use leading questions, it is very difficult for lay witnesses to tell their story.

2. The conventional wisdom that says jurors want to hear the witness tell the story is wrong; they just want to hear the story. So, don't be afraid to use leading questions.

3. Objections to leading questions are a short-lived phenomenon at trials.

4. Lawyers should ask questions that tell the story and allow the story to be told in the most direct way possible.

5. Do not use a detailed outline. Use an outline with bullet points that refers to exhibits.

6. Do not use scripted testimony at a trial. Don't force jurors to watch a play.

7. McClain has associates prepare the witness for trial testimony so that he can hear the testimony fresh in court, just like the jury hears it.

8. The biggest mistake lawyers make is they dot every "I" and cross every "T." By doing so, they bore the jurors and lose them.

9. McClain's strategy throughout his entire presentation is that he will be the truth teller in the courtroom.

10. Most lawyers try to hide the blemishes in their witness' testimony. McClain tells his witness, "We're not going to lie. There's nothing you can screw up that I can't fix." These blemishes make testimonies "a more genuine experience."

11. McClain's cross-examination demeanor and direct examination demeanor both have a lot of energy. Most lawyers sleepwalk through their directs.

Tips to Learn from McClain's Direct Examination of Eric Peoples

1. Use transitions to notify the jury of the new topic you are going to discuss.

2. Show the jury photos that relate to the witness' background and hobbies.

3. To maintain credibility with the jury and prevent an ambush on cross-examination, don't hide the weaknesses in your witness' testimony.

4. Most witnesses are petrified to testify in court.

5. Do not rely on the witness to tell his story. You must get the details you need through your questioning.

6. Use leading questions to frame your themes for the jury and to get the answers you need from the witness.

7. Summarize previous testimony in the form of a question to remind jury of important facts.

8. Look for opportunities to connect the similarities of your witness' testimony with a previous witness in order to corroborate facts.

9. Ask short, specific questions with one fact to direct the witness to the exact information you need.

10. Use imagery in your questioning to keep your themes before the jury (i.e., "Is getting a lung transplant like getting a new set of tires?")

11. On redirect, use precise leading questions to clarify confusion created by cross-examination.

12. Use an easel or PowerPoint slide to list damages so the witness won't forget a topic and so the jury can actually see the damages in addition to hearing testimony about them.

13. Use a video to show a day in the life of your client.

14. Conclude testimony with your strongest point.

CHAPTER FIVE

---∞∞∞---

Maureen O'Brien

Telling the Story with a Reluctant Witness

He mouthed "sorry" to me.

— Victim tells jury what she saw when she looked at
one gunman while she was being raped by another.

---

aureen O'Brien recently retired from one of the largest District
Attorney's offices in the country, the Cook County State's Attorney's Office,
which oversees Chicago and its surrounding municipalities. While there, she
distinguished herself as an outstanding trial attorney.

She also supervised several felony trial courtrooms that maintained
caseloads of 500 active cases. She gave final approval regarding murder investigations and evaluated all major cases for plea offers. With over 115 jury trials
and 1,000 bench trials to her name, she has seen it all. Her most challenging—and rewarding—cases were sex offense cases. She liked them because
they combined compelling testimony with scientific evidence. But the cases
were often fraught with the difficulties of having a reluctant and traumatized
witness and needing to explain scientific evidence to a jury. Sometimes, when
the witnesses were weak, the challenge was to show how the testimony was corroborated by the physical evidence.

5.1 TECHNIQUES

It is misguided to think that direct examination is easy for either the lawyer or
the witness. It is exceedingly difficult. In the preceding chapter, Ken McClain
revealed the importance
of using PowerPoint
slides, leading ques-
tions, and a command
of the examination to

> **CHAPTER HIGHLIGHTS**
> - Prepare the fearful witness for trial
> - Avoid the most common mistakes of direct examination
> - Get the jury to cheer for your witness on cross

tell his client's story to the jury in a civil case. His techniques result in compelling stories for the juries and very large verdicts for his clients.

In this chapter, we examine how a prosecutor accomplishes that task with one of the most difficult categories of witnesses: the rape victim. Rape victims are perhaps the most challenging witnesses because the horrific trauma they have suffered adds a huge layer of complexity to the witness' ability to be comfortable on the witness stand and tell the jury about the unimaginable suffering. By looking at strategies O'Brien uses to get her witness in the case below to tell her traumatic story, we can apply those techniques with confidence to any of our witnesses — no matter how difficult they might be — and be assured of success. But before we examine O'Brien's particular strategies, let's examine the basic techniques of direct examination.

There are a number of different types of questions to use on direct. Your goal should be not to rely solely on one type but rather to use a variety so that the examination is interesting, unpredictable, and memorable. Leading questions were discussed in the previous chapter and are the bread and butter of a great lawyer, despite the conventional wisdom to the contrary. In criminal trials, a judge may be less willing to allow leading questions when the testimony gets to the heart of the disputed issue. But whether it is a civil or criminal trial, here are the other types of questions needed when necessary: 1) specific non-leading, 2) looping, 3) transitions, and 4) commands.

From the previous chapter, we learned that a leading question is one that suggests the answer to the witness, either through the words chosen, or the tone of voice of the questioner. Here is a quick review.

Example: Leading questions

Q. The traffic light was red, wasn't it?
Q. You began work on Monday, January 15?
Q. When you were robbed, the robber was wearing a red sweatshirt?

In the first question, the ending phrase "wasn't it" suggests to the witness that the traffic light was red. In the second question, the words refer to a specific date which implies that the questioner knows the witness started work on Monday, January 15, and that the witness should agree with that specific fact. In the third example, the questioner suggests the color of the sweatshirt — and the type of upper body clothing — to the witness.

Example: Non-leading questions

Next are the same questions, which are now composed so that they are non-leading.

Q. What color was the traffic light?
Q. What day did you begin work?
Q. What was the robber wearing?

To give the witness more help, provide the witness several choices in your question. I call such a question a specific non-leading question.

Examples: Specific non-leading questions

Q. Was the traffic light red, yellow, or green for cars going in your direction?
Q. Did you begin work on a Monday or Wednesday?
Q. Was the robber wearing a t-shirt, long-sleeve shirt, or sweatshirt?

These questions direct the witness to the information you need without leading him. The witness is given reasonable choices that do not suggest the answer. These questions are necessary to move the testimony along.

In addition to freely using leading questions to develop testimony and mixing in specific non-leading questions to keep the examination interesting, here are some additional ideas to use during direct.

Looping is the technique of repeating a portion of the witness' previous answer in your next question. The reason to loop the witness' answer into your next question is to remind the jury of the answer and build on it for the next question. Unlike a book where you can refer back to a previous page if you forget something, there is no such luxury in live testimony. So, you want to loop important answers so the jury can remember them by hearing them a second time. The following is a very simple example which shows how to loop a witness' answer.

Example: Looping

Q. What color was the car that hit you?
A. **Red**.

*Q. Was the **red** car going fast or slow?*
A. **Very fast**.

*Q. Which direction did this **very fast** car come from?*
A. From my left.

Here, each answer (in bold) is repeated in the following question (in bold).

In addition to looping, it is essential to use transition phrases to guide the witness and the jury to the topics you want to discuss. Anytime you want to change a topic, use a transition phrase to signal to everyone where you are going.

Example: Transition phrases

Q. *Let me turn your attention to the night of the accident.* Where were you driving?

Q. *Let's fast forward a moment.* What pain are you feeling as you sit in this courtroom today?

Q. *Now that we've discussed your injuries, I want to back up for a minute and cover what job you had before the accident.* Where were you working?

Each of the transition phrases is in italics. The point is to carry on a conversation with the witness. She is looking to you for guidance. Give it to her. Tell her and the jury what your next set of questions is going to cover. It gives everyone a frame of reference. Imagine if you read a book with no chapters. It is the same concept.

Example: Commands

Q. *Let me stop you right there, what did you mean by excruciating pain?*

Q. *You said that it was dark, describe for the ladies and gentleman of the jury how dark it was?*

Q. *Explain in more detail your decision to have surgery.*

So, as you can see, a command is a direction to the witness on how better to answer the question you have previously asked or are going to ask. It is your chance to bring out as many details as you need to paint a memorable picture for the jury. Don't feel that you are stuck with the witness' initial answer. It is your job to ask as many follow-up questions as necessary to get the information the jury needs.

5.2 WITNESS PREPARATION

This chapter focuses on what O'Brien says was one of her most satisfying cases — satisfying because of the verdict and the unimaginably brutal nature of the crime. When O'Brien first gets a case, she talks to the victims so she can get a feel for who they are and what their family is like, and then she sizes up what kind of witnesses they would be. O'Brien recalls that one of the victims in the case, Robin, was "very, very shy." Another victim, Mary, was gregarious and chatty.[1]

> *I don't want a lot of emotion in my office. I want it to be saved for the stand.*
> —Maureen O'Brien

O'Brien was the senior attorney on her trial team. Her office requires that all prosecutions have a team of two prosecutors in court. One of the benefits of this policy occurs when the team is composed of attorneys with different styles, which was the case for O'Brien and her younger partner, Bonnie Greenstein. By dividing up the direct

---

[1] The names of the victims have been changed to protect their identities.

examination of witnesses between lawyers, O'Brien believes that a jury stays more interested in a case because of the differing styles of each lawyer asking questions.

Due to the vicious facts in the case, O'Brien did not want to offer the defendants a plea deal that would allow them to serve less time in jail than the maximum sentence permitted by law. The turning point in the trial would occur if she could get the victims to tell the jury about the horrific things that happened to them. It is common in sex crime cases that the victims do not want to have to relive the crime by talking about it, particularly when they have to reveal details about it in a courtroom. There is also the added emotional factor of parents not wanting their children to have to go through the pain of testifying in court. Finally, victims often do not want to testify about the crime in front of their parents — whether they do it during witness preparation or the trial itself.

Obviously, getting a sex crime victim to tell the jury about the crime is a very difficult challenge in and of itself. In this particular trial, another concern O'Brien had was that there was no DNA evidence linking one of the three defendants, Timothy Moore, to the crime (the details of the crime are discussed later in this chapter). Consequently, O'Brien decided to offer defendant Christopher Pittmon a plea bargain that would reduce the charge to armed robbery with a prison sentence of 35 years. She rarely tries to "flip" a defendant to testify for the government by offering him a plea to a lessor charge or sentence but, in this case, she felt she needed Pittmon's testimony to make sure Moore was convicted.

To prepare a witness for trial, O'Brien will informally meet with her witness a couple of months before trial. But she doesn't want to meet so many times that the witness becomes like a robot that matter-of-factly recounts what happened before the jury. She also wants to build a strong emotional bond with the witness. She provides guidance to many of her witnesses not only for the trial itself, but also — in conjunction with other specialists — for coping with the trauma they have been through. To avoid distractions, she likes to meet with witnesses in her office on Saturdays when the office is quiet, and when there are few, if any, interruptions.

In her witness prep, O'Brien gave Mary and Robin some tough love instructions. After reviewing the police reports and one of the statements a defendant had given, there was a suggestion that Mary and Robin had tried to buy weed. As mentioned above, it is often difficult for rape victims to talk about their assaults. It is also difficult for any witness to admit that she may have made some mistakes. O'Brien lectured Mary and Robin, "Listen, guys. Here's how this is going to go. If you lie about a discussion to buy pot, if you lie about a stupid little thing, the jury is not going to believe you about anything else. Anything!" It is a similar lecture she gives to all her witnesses. They must completely tell the truth, or their credibility will be destroyed.

O'Brien preaches that it is essential that the witness be believable and likable. Once that is accomplished, the physical evidence can be used to fill in gaps or corroborate the story.

For the first few sessions, O'Brien talked to Robin about everything but the sex acts. She wanted to learn all the facts surrounding the sex acts, but not get her witness numb to the emotions of the rape by having her repeat the story. O'Brien's goal is not necessarily to get the witness to cry on the stand, but she wants the witness to temporarily relive the experience and convey to the jury the drama of the horrific crime.

She instructs her witnesses to "replay it like a TV program in your head. You only have to do it one more time [in court]." O'Brien comforts and coaxes them through this difficult process. Not only is the event difficult for witnesses to tell, but they have pushed the awful details to the back of their mind so they can move forward with their lives. Naturally, they resist wanting to talk about them.

5.3 THE BIGGEST MISTAKES LAWYERS MAKE

When asked to list the biggest mistakes attorneys and prosecutors make, O'Brien says the first mistake prosecutors make is they don't read the police reports and the defense expert's reports, "I mean *really* read them." O'Brien scours the reports. She knows "all the paper," as she refers to it. "For example, the labs, medical records, supplemental evidence, and technician reports."

She wants to read all of the documents in her case because she wants to know what the defense will use during cross-examination of her witnesses. She wants to prepare her witness for potential accusations by defense counsel, such as what the witness left out in his or her account to the police or what is inconsistent with the police report.

When she prepares a witness for trial, the witness always asks her, "What is the defense going to ask me?" O'Brien can anticipate the cross because she knows the "paper," and with years of trial experience, she can predict the lines of attack.

In this chapter's case study, one problem was that the victims did not give many details to the police at the crime scene or at the hospital that night. O'Brien wanted to prepare her witnesses for the potential theme on cross-examination that they were making up facts which they failed to tell the police. During witness preparation, O'Brien got the explanation she needed: The witnesses were so distraught after the crime that they were vomiting and screaming at the crime scene. In that condition, they could not tell the police many facts.

O'Brien believes a second mistake prosecutors make is that they don't prepare cases well. Not only does this include not knowing the "paper," but it encompasses not meeting with the witnesses enough. Even when prosecutors meet with the victims enough, they neglect to prepare their other witnesses to the same degree. Her advice also applies to lawyers who are not prosecutors. Preparation is the key to success no matter what the case is.

Third, lawyers don't spend enough time thinking about the order of witnesses at trial. O'Brien wants to have a good framework to tell her story to the jury. Unlike most lawyers, she spends a lot of time thinking who would be the best witness to start the trial with.

Fourth, she finds that some prosecutors don't care if they win or lose and some don't like being in trial. "You have to really want to win. If the crime itself isn't motivating enough, find something about the victim that you like."

> *Find a hook about the case that makes it interesting to you and then use that hook to persuade the jurors.*
> —Maureen O'Brien

5.4 TRIAL STRATEGIES

For direct examination, O'Brien instructs lawyers that they need to not only prepare their witnesses for direct examination but also for cross-examination. In rape cases, it is important to know the physical evidence because that can determine the questions for cross-examination. For example, if there is no DNA evidence left inside the female victim and none was collected from the sexual assault kit, the cross-examiner may use that lack of evidence to argue that there was no intercourse. But the truth may be — as it was in this case — that the male was interrupted by the police before he could ejaculate inside the victim. While defense attorneys may use this lack of DNA evidence as a strategy, O'Brien points out that it is not the victim's fault that there isn't any physical evidence from the sexual assault kit. Instead, there may be other evidence such as ripped clothing, bite marks, or fingerprints.

The order of your witnesses can have a big impact on whether you keep the jury's interest and tell them a compelling story. In the case discussed in this chapter, the officer who first responded to the scene was unavailable to testify. O'Brien could have set the scene with the victims, but she wanted the jury to hear it from a responding officer's point of view first. So, she interviewed a paramedic from the fire station. While others might think this effort was a waste of time, O'Brien knows the importance of setting the scene properly. She believes the scene needs to be described by a person with no material stake in the outcome.

At trial, the paramedic did not wear his work uniform but wore his formal dress uniform, which made him look like a police officer from early England. His uniform grabbed the jury's attention with its air of authority. His testimony was no less compelling. O'Brien came close to tears as the paramedic described what he saw when he first arrived. He cared about the girls and it showed.

O'Brien also put on the witness stand the two nurses who examined Mary and Robin. Prosecutors often stipulate to medical testimony or lab results instead of calling a witness in order to save time and effort. O'Brien thinks this common practice does a disservice to the client's case unless the witness is unavailable. O'Brien wanted the nurses to testify how a rape examination is done to illustrate the humiliation the girls had to go through after the attack.

In Illinois, a podium is in the middle of the courtroom where the lawyer conducts witness examination. O'Brien moves the podium closer to the jury box—to the end of the jury box furthest from the witness stand. She wants to make sure the jury pays attention to the witness instead of focusing on her while she is at the podium.

This also forces the witness to look in the direction of the jurors, since O'Brien is near them, which causes the jurors to become more engaged with the witness. O'Brien wants jurors to "feel the victim's pain. I want them to focus on her."

By having the podium at the far end of the jury box, it also forces the witness to speak loudly. If necessary, O'Brien will tell the witness that she can't hear her, and the witness will realize she has to really speak up since O'Brien is so far away.

O'Brien is always aware of the witness' needs—from the simple to the problematic. She is attuned to whether the witness needs a break to get her composure or is distracted or intimidated by someone in the courtroom, such as a defendant or someone in the audience.

As for notes, O'Brien does not always rely on them but has them at the podium. She does not write out her questions but writes out the facts based on her witness preparation. If you truly know the facts of your case, you don't need to rely on your notes. Yet, the notes can help to make sure you have covered all the facts necessary to establish the elements of the crimes.

O'Brien is a big believer in listening to the witness. O'Brien has seen too many lawyers who are

---

Practice Tip

When a witness gets flustered and starts to cry, O'Brien walks right up to the witness stand to comfort him or her. This act reassures the witness and shows the jury that O'Brien cares about the witness. O'Brien has seen many attorneys make the callous mistake of simply waiting for their witness to stop crying and then they continue on with the direct matter-of-factly as if nothing ever happened.

concerned with asking the next question instead of listening to the answer while the witness is giving it. The witness may not answer the question, may go off track, or be visibly nervous, and you will miss all of these problems if you are looking at your notes in anticipation of asking your next question.

Here is a final tip that relates to exhibits: O'Brien stages and lines them up in the order she is going to ask the witness about them. This tactic reminds her which exhibits to discuss with the witness and gives her a framework for the order in which to ask them. Also, she does not waste the jury's time by marking the exhibits with stickers or taking them out of their bags or containers while the jury is in the courtroom. This is done beforehand.

5.5 *STATE OF ILLINOIS V. TIMOTHY MOORE AND CORTEZ LYONS*

At 11:00 p.m. on Tuesday, November 21, 2006, three high school friends, Robin, Mary, and Eddie, got in Mary's car to go get some cigarettes. Mary and Robin had been best friends since they were four years old. Robin was 17 years old and a senior in high school. They were out late because it was the beginning of Thanksgiving break.

In the next section, we inspect O'Brien's direct examination of Robin. Robin was very shy. Like many witnesses, and particularly those witnesses who are victims of sexual assault, the challenge for the attorney is to get the witness to tell the jury a coherent story about what happened. There is a lot to learn from O'Brien's deft skill in getting Robin to tell her harrowing story.

5.6 DIRECT EXAMINATION OF ROBIN

Background questions

O'Brien began by asking Robin some basic background questions and then more specific questions about her studies in college and goals in life. O'Brien has seen too many lawyers just gloss over background questions in a rush to ask the witness about the crime. This is a mistake. "You have a small window of opportunity for the jury to get to know your victim, to identify with her, and to like her." By getting the jurors to care about the witness, the jurors will root for the victim on cross-examination to "say the right thing or hold her own with the defense attorney."

Q. *All right. And, specifically, what is your career goal?*
A. Communications is very broad. So I'm not really sure what I want to do with it yet. And I'm also getting my American language interpreting.

Q. *I'm sorry? Can you —*
A. I'm also getting my American sign language interpreting.

Q. And what are you going to do with your American sign language interpreting?
A. Be an interpreter hopefully.

Q. All right. Is there any particular reason why you're going into that field?
A. My mom is deaf.

The Night of the Attack

Q. I'm going to direct your attention now to November 21, 2006, right around 11:00 p.m. Do you recall where you were?
A. Yes.

Q. Where were you?
A. We were at a gas station.

*Q. **Let me stop you there**. Before you went to a gas station, where were you?*
A. My house.

Q. Who were you with at your house?
A. Mary.

Q. What were you guys doing?
A. Just hanging out. Nothing.

Q. At some point did you and Mary make plans to do something?
A. Yes.

Q. What were you going to do?
A. We were going to pick up Eddie, and our plan was to eventually buy weed and just hang out at Eddie's house.

There are two lessons to learn from this exchange. First, O'Brien immediately demonstrates her control of the witness in the courtroom. When she asks, "Where were you?", she does not get the answer she wants. Second, she commands, "Let me stop you there," to make Robin talk about what happened before they arrived at the gas station. Her reason for doing this is because of the importance of what happened before they arrived at the gas station. O'Brien wants the jury to hear from Robin on direct—not cross—that Robin and her friends were going to buy marijuana, not just cigarettes.

In her closing argument, O'Brien will admit that the friends made several mistakes that night, but none that justified the crime that was committed. Their first mistake was trying to buy illegal drugs.

O'Brien then needs to set two scenes for the jury: the first is at the gas station, the second is where the crime occurred.

Events at the gas station

Q. Did you go to Eddie's house?
A. Yes.

Q. How did you get there?
A. Mary's car.

Q. Do you recall what kind of car it was or what it looked —
A. Yes. It was a black Pontiac G6.

Q. And so, when you left your house, who was driving?
A. Mary.

Q. Where were you in the car?
A. Passenger's seat.

Q. Did Eddie live far away from your house?
A. No. Maybe four blocks....

Q. Did he get in the car?
A. Yes.

Q. And where in the car did he enter?
A. He approached the passenger — the passenger rear seat, and sat like in the middle of the backseat.

Q. All right. And you indicated earlier that you then went to a gas station?
A. Yes.

The seating arrangements (Mary in the driver's seat, Robin in the passenger's seat, and Eddie in the back seat) become important later when O'Brien develops how the crime occurred. She next discusses why the friends went to this particular gas station.

Q. And for what purpose were you going to a gas station?
A. To buy cigarettes.

Q. Now, who smoked?
A. All three of us....

Q. Is there something special about that gas station that you go there to buy cigarettes?
A. They would never ID us, and we were under 18.

Q. OK. So you would go there because you wouldn't get carded?
A. Uh-huh.

Buying cigarettes illegally and marijuana may not be the biggest crimes, but O'Brien wants Robin to be truthful about everything that happened that night. O'Brien knows that once a witness loses credibility, it is lost forever.

Robin then explains that when they got to the gas station, Mary went inside and she and Eddie stayed in the car.

Q. Did you notice anything unusual during the five-minute wait while Robin — or, excuse me, while Mary was in the gas station?
A. There was a group of guys near the front of the gas station hanging out and talking and kind of looking at Mary's car.

Q. So, they were looking in your direction?
A. Yes.... A man approached the car, and he walked to the driver's side rear door and kind of — and tapped on the window.

Q. All right. ***So you say that a man approached, and he went to the driver's side rear door. And, as he approached your vehicle,*** *did you watch him walk toward the car?*
A. Yes.

The bold text shows where O'Brien loops the previous answer into her next question. Lawyers often effectively use this looping technique, which is used to remind jurors of the previous answer by repeating it in the first part of a subsequent question. It is a very effective tool for lawyers, because jurors might miss a significant fact when hearing oral testimony, whereas they can always read it when given a document to refer to.

[O'Brien asked Robin if she saw that person in the courtroom, and Robin identified Lyons.]

Q. When Lyons tapped on the window, what, if anything, did you or Eddie do?
A. Eddie leaned over and like cracked the window about an inch.

Q. And did either Eddie or the defendant say anything?
A. He asked if Eddie wanted to buy drugs.

Q. When you say he, you mean the defendant Lyons? [**O'Brien makes it clear for the jury whom Robin is referring to.**]
A. Lyons.

Q. He was speaking to him through this cracked window?
A. Yes.

Q. Did he talk about what kind of drugs?
A. I don't remember what all the drugs were that he named off, but Eddie just kept telling him no. And then, when he mentioned the weed, Eddie said OK.... Lyons says let me in the car and we'll do the deal. So Eddie opened the door, and he got in the car right as Mary was coming out —

Q. Now —
A. (Continuing) — and approaching —

Q. I'm sorry. I didn't let you finish. I'm sorry. Please say it again. [**O'Brien realizes she has unnecessarily interrupted the witness. She encourages the witness to continue with her train of thought.**]

———&&&———

Q. What did Mary do?
A. Mary was very confused. So she got in her car, and she said, "What's going on?" And Lyons said, "I'm just here to sell your boy some weed." And Mary said, "OK, well, you have to do it quick because the gas station attendant is calling the cops." And

Lyons said, "yeah, that's my cousin in there messing around. So, if we just drive to my house, I can — we can just make the exchange over there."

Mary drives into an alley

On the way to Lyons' home, Lyons asks Eddie if he was in a gang and "strapped" with a gun. Eddie said "no" to both questions. O'Brien now sets the scene for the crimes in the alley that is just a few blocks from the gas station.

Q. *And what was going through your mind at that moment?*
A. When we approached the alley?

Q. *Yes.*
A. Really dumb idea.

Q. *OK. Did you say anything to Mary?*
A. No. Mary got very nervous, and she was — are you sure we're turning? He's like, yeah, it's fine, just turn in here.

Q. *Did he tell you why you were pulling into this alley?*
A. So he could run inside and get his weed.

Q. *Did he say where he was going like to run inside and get **his weed**?* [**O'Brien loops "his weed" from previous answer.**]
A. His house....

Q. *How far down the alley, once Mary turned into the alley — did she stop at the mouth of the alley, or did she continue to drive down the alley?*
A. She drove down the alley....

Q. *Did he tell her where to drive?*
A. Yes.

Q. *What did he say about that?* [**Whenever the witness fails to give important details, O'Brien asks a follow up question as she does here.**]
A. He said it's a little bit further down. And then, when we reached the parking spot, he told us right here, just to pull in here....

Q. *Would you say that you were at the beginning, the middle or the end of the alley when Mary stopped the car?* [**O'Brien wants more details to show the jury that the friends were trapped.**]
A. Close to the end....

Q. ***Did Mary just pull into a parking spot, or did Lyons tell her to pull into one?*** [**O'Brien provides the witness a choice of answers**]
A. Lyons told her to pull into one.

Practice Tip

In this section, O'Brien (1) loops, (2) seeks out details when needed, and (3) gives the witness a choice of two options to focus the witness on the answer needed. These three skills are the essence of successfully formulating questions for direct examination.

In the following sections, O'Brien presents the jury with details of the crime and shows how Robin had the opportunity to identify the defendants.

Lyons pulls out a gun

Q. After the defendant Lyons said, "I'm just going to go run in and get it," what did he do?
A. He opened his door and like stepped one foot out of the car. And, as he turned around, he pulled the gun out and sat back in the car and rested it on his lap.

Q. Did you see him pull the gun out?
A. Yes....

Q. When he opened the door were you looking at him?
A. I was looking at him.

Q. So did you have to turn around to do that?
A. Yes. [**O'Brien has witness explain how she was able to see Lyons if he was in the backseat.**]

Q. What happened when he opened the door with respect to the car?
A. The dome light turned on. [**O'Brien brings out the important detail that there was lighting inside the car.**]

Q. Was there lighting in the alley, if you recall?
A. Yes.

Q. Where was that lighting coming from?
A. There were streetlights, and I believe there was an apartment a little bit down that had its back porch light on.

Q. So, regardless of the dome light, would you say that there was lighting there?
A. Yes.

Q. And, when the car door opened and the dome light went on, you had additional light; is that correct? [**O'Brien emphasizes that the dome light provided additional lighting.**]
A. Yes....

Q. Do you know what it [the gun] looked like?
A. Yes. [**Here, the witness does not describe the gun, so O'Brien makes sure to ask a follow-up question to get the details.**]

Q. What did it look like?
A. It was silver — I believe it's called a revolver. It kind of spins. It had a wooden handle.

Q. Where did you see Lyons pull this gun from?
A. Like his pants. **Like the inside of his pants (indicating).**

Q. All right. Indicating for the record the front waist area of his pants. [**"Indicating for the record" means the appellate record which is based on the transcript the court reporter produces. O'Brien uses this phrase not only to explain what gesture the**

witness made to the appellate judges who might read the transcript later, but it also gives her a chance to remind the jury what the witness has just shown them.]

Q. *So it came from the waist area, not like a pocket or anything?* **[O'Brien loops again and rules out any other possibilities. These questions solidify the fact that Robin got a good look not only at Lyons but also the gun he used.]**

A. No.

Q. *When you saw him put the gun on his lap, what did you do?*
A. I turned around and I—I think I said, "Oh, shit."

Q. *What did Lyons say?*
A. He said I need your—or give me your cell phones.

Q. *That's the first thing he said?*
A. Yes….

Q. *Why did you give it to him?* **[The answer may be obvious, but O'Brien wants the jury to hear Robin say it in her own words.]**
A. I was scared for my life.

Eddie and Mary each gave their cell phones to Lyons. Then, Lyons asked for anything else he thought they might have, such as Mary's purse, Robin's wristlet, Eddie's necklace and Eddie's coat. But O'Brien wants to paint a picture for the jury so that they understand how frightening this was. Watch how she accomplishes this by eliciting details from the witness:

Q. *Now, when he said this, can you tell the ladies and gentlemen of the jury when he asked for your additional things what kind—***what tone of voice he was using?*** **[O'Brien gets details.]**
A. Firm and loud.

Q. *What were the words that he said?* **[Gets details]**
A. Do you think this is a fucking joke? Give me everything—like give me all your shit.

Q. *What was going through your mind at that point?*
A. I was terrified.

Q. *Did you see the gun at that time, if you recall?*
A. Yes.

Q. *And where was the gun with Lyons at that moment when he was saying those things?*
A. In his hand and up to Eddie's temple.

Q. *So now you said the gun is in his hand, and where exactly on Eddie's —***could you demonstrate how the defendant held the gun at Eddie's temple?*** **[More details]**
A. To my own temple?

Q. *If you don't mind.*
A. His left temple (indicating).

O'Brien: Judge, indicating for the record that the witness has indicated in court her finger is extended to her left temple. [**O'Brien builds the appellate record and reminds jury of the demonstration.**]
Court: The record will so reflect.

In the previous two sections, O'Brien elicits important details about lighting to show that Robin was able to see Lyons and the gun he used. All the witness wants to do is get her testimony over with. She wants to talk about the attack and get off the witness stand. But O'Brien knows that she needs to be in charge of what facts are told to the jury. She makes sure to ask the witness about important details and uses the looping technique to remind the jury of previous answers.

Two other assailants arrive

Q. While this was going on, did something else happen?
A. Yes.

Q. What happened?
A. Two other men approached from like the end of the alley, and he [**Lyons**] said, "My boys are here to back me up."

Q. Now, prior to him saying my boys are here to back me up, you say that two men came from the end of the alley. My question is: Is it the mouth of the alley or the end of the alley where you were located? [**Looping**]
A. The end of the alley where I was located.

Q1. When these two men came there, what did they do?
A. One of them opened Eddie's door, and the other one opened my door, and they were just screaming.

Q2. What kind of things were they screaming? [**O'Brien gets more details**]
A. I remember, "give me what you have," things like that. But a lot of it was just noise because I was so scared....

Q3. I'd like to start with the rear passenger guy. What did he specifically say or do when he opened the car door?
A. He opened the door and started punching Eddie.

Q4. And did you turn around to watch this, or did—were you just hearing it?
A. I turned around for a quick second.

Q5. Did you notice anything else aside from the guy punching Eddie?
A. He had a gun.

If O'Brien had not asked any follow up questions to Q1, all the jury would know is that two men opened the car doors and started screaming. But O'Brien asks short specific questions to get the details that she needs. We learn that one man was punching Eddie and had a gun. In other questioning not shown here, we learn that Lyons is now by the hood of the car. We also learn that the man who opens the back door and punches Eddie is Christopher Pittmon.

Pittmon and the other man, Timothy Moore, had been in the gas station with Lyons. They knew to meet Lyons in the alley a few blocks from the gas station once Lyons got into Mary's car at the gas station. Although the robbery was clearly planned, O'Brien believes the rapes were also. She believes this because of the identical manner in which the rapes occurred (see below). If it had been spontaneous, the sex acts would have occurred differently.

Q. What did you notice about the person who opened your door?
A. He had a gun. I know he had a gray sweater on.

Q. What, if anything, did he do with that gun when he opened the door?
A. He put it to my right temple (indicating) [**and rifled through the glove box**].

O'Brien: Judge, indicating for the record that the witness extended her index finger to her right temple.
Court: The record will so reflect.

Q. What was going through your mind?
A. I thought I was going to die....

Q. What was Lyons saying when he was at the front with Mary?
A. If you tell anybody what happened, we'll find you, we'll kill you.

Q. And what about the guy who's got the gun to your head? What's he saying about those kind of things? Like after he got the CDs, he didn't run away, did he?
A. No.

Q. Did he ask for anything else?
A. **I was very nervous. I — I said, "You can have the car. We'll walk. Or, you know, you can have anything you want." And he said, "We can have anything we want?"....**

Q. Why did you say "take whatever you want, take the car, take anything"? What were you trying to accomplish?
A. I was trying to get out of there alive.

Q. Now, you said "take whatever you want, you can have whatever you want." And you said someone said what? [**Looping**]
A. "Oh, we can have anything we want?"

Q. Was that the guy who had the gun to your head?
A. Yes.

The man who had initially approached Robin's door would later be identified as Timothy Moore. Robin testified that when the three men were searching the glove box and car, they were moving all around the car. She would testify that Moore was the man who said, "Anything we want?" When Moore spoke those words, he had moved to the driver's side of the car and Lyons had come over to Robin's side of the car and put a gun to her head.

After the trial, Robin would write a victim impact statement for the sentencing hearing where she told the court that she had a lot of guilt for uttering the words, "You can have anything you want." She mistakenly felt that those words invited the men to do what happened next. But her fate was sealed when Lyons was let in the car at the gas station.

Robin explains what Lyons does next when he hears Moore repeat Robin's words, "We can have anything we want."

The sexual assaults

Q. What does Lyons say to you next, or what does he do?
A. He put the gun to my head, told me you know what to do. He put his hand on the back of my head and motioned my head towards his penis (indicating).

In the witness preparation sessions, Robin used slang to refer to body parts and the sex acts. O'Brien told her she needed to use the more formal words that would be used in the jury instructions to describe the elements of the crime. O'Brien also did not want the slang to offend the jurors. Robin followed O'Brien's instructions and used formal words such as "penis."

Throughout this part of the examination, O'Brien had to draw details from the witness to prove the elements of the crime and to build a record to show how horrible the crime was—not only to get a conviction, but also because the details could help justify a maximum prison sentence if there were a conviction. There is no need to show all of the details here, but a few examples are necessary to show the difficulty the witness had in recounting such a horrifying event and how O'Brien helped the witness tell her harrowing tale.

Q. Did the defendant put his penis inside of your mouth?
A. Yes.

Q. Did he say anything at the moment that that was occurring?
A. Don't mess up....

Q. During the time that this happened, could you feel the gun to your head the entire time?
A. Yes.

Q. How were you wearing your hair that night?
A. In a bun.

Q. And while you had the defendant Lyons' penis in your mouth, what, if anything, was he doing with respect to your hair?
A. He would pull on my bun (indicating).

Q. And can you just describe that a little bit more when you say he's pulling? What's he doing?
A. He is pulling my bun, you know, back and forth, motioning my head what to do (indicating).

Q. So is it fair to say that he is pulling you up and down — your mouth up and down on his penis by pulling your hair?
A. Yes.

Q. At some point does this act stop?
A. Yes.

Q. And who stops it?
A. The guy who was by Mary's door [Moore].

Q. And was something said?
A. He said, "Do you want to come and get some of this?"

Q. When he stopped, did he — did Lyons stay on the passenger's side with you, or did he go somewhere?
A. He walked to Mary's door.

Q. Now, when Lyons walked to Mary's door, did he walk behind the car or in front of the car?
A. In front of the car.

Q. And did you watch him as he walked in front of the car?
A. Yes....

Q. What about the other guy who was initially with Mary? What did you see him do?
A. He walked in front of the car to my side of the car.

Q. And you were able to see him at that point as well?
A. Yes.

Q. And that was the same person who initially opened up your car door and put the gun to your head?
A. Yes.

Q. And was that the same person who riffled the CDs?
A. Yes.

O'Brien knows that Robin and the other victims' ability to identify the defendants is critical to her case. Whenever there is an opportunity to show the jury the details of what Robin saw relating to her identification of the defendants, O'Brien provides those facts to the jury.

Q. Where was Pittmon during this time?
A. Outside of the rear passenger door.

Q. Did you at some point notice what he was doing or saying?
A. He was holding a gun to Eddie's head....

Q. Did he remain with Eddie the entire time?
A. Yes.

———∝∞∝———

Q. Once they switched sides…what did [Moore] say or do at that point?
A. He grabbed my waist and pulled me out of the car and positioned me to bend over.

Q. Did he have a gun in his hand?
A. Yes.

Q. Did you get a look at that gun?
A. Yes.

Q. And what kind of gun was it, or what did it look like?
A. Black.

Q. Did you recognize his voice when he spoke to you?
A. Yes.

Q. Did you recognize it as the same voice of the same person that you—who was on your side earlier who opened your door?
A. Yes.

Q. Was he wearing the same gray jacket that the guy who opened your door initially was wearing?
A. Yes.

O'Brien continues to elicit details about Moore's voice and clothing so the jury realizes the man (Moore) that initially opened Robin's door and rifled through the glove box is the same person who is about to rape her. It was also important because although Robin could not identify Moore after the crime, the clothing description she provided matched those of the clothes worn by Moore when he was caught on videotape at the gas station when the crime began.

Q. When he pulled you out of the car, where did he pull the gun on you?
A. My left temple.

Q. What did he say to you?
A. He tried to unbutton my pants but couldn't do it. So he told me to unbutton them…

Q. What was going through your mind?
A. I—I was scared. I knew what was about to happen. I thought I was going to die…. **[He was behind me and I was standing outside the passenger door.]** He told me to bend over, he took the gun and hit me in the back, and then guided me to bend over. And I had my hands placed on the passenger's seat.

O'Brien asks more details about how Robin's clothes were taken off and the position of their bodies. Then, she builds to the dramatic moment shown next.

Q. When you bent over the seat, did you see anything in the car?
A. Mary was in the —

Q. It's OK. Take a couple seconds. OK?
A. (Nodding head.) Can I have like one minute?

Q. Of course. Let me know when you're ready.
A. OK.

Q. All right.
A. She was in the same position I was, facing me.

Q. All right. Could you see, other than her face, what was happening over there with her?
A. Yes.

Q. And what did you see?
A. He was putting his penis inside her.

Notice how O'Brien's eyes are not buried in her notes. She intently listens to her witness. Because she does, she notices that the witness is crying and needs some time to regroup. O'Brien recalls that she walked up to Robin, gave her a tissue and a cup of water, did not make a big deal of it, and through her actions reassured Robin.

O'Brien then continues to elicit details of Lyons's rape of Mary, and Moore's rape of Robin. As dramatic and horrific as the testimony was, O'Brien does not forget to have the witness implicate Pittmon, who was in the backseat during the rapes.

Q. Did you continue to be face to face with Mary while this was happening?
A. Yes.

Q. Were you able to see in the backseat at this time?
A. Yes.

Q. Do you remember what, if anything, you saw in the back seat?
A. Eddie was sitting there with a gun to his head and was forced to watch. Pittman was saying, "We're fucking your bitches." Things like that.

O'Brien ends strongly

These horrible assaults ended when a neighbor called 911 and a police car arrived in the alley, which caused Pittmon, Moore, and Lyons to run away. After showing Robin some photos and other pieces of evidence to identify, O'Brien concluded her direct on a powerful note. One of O'Brien's witnesses in the trial was Pittmon, a defendant who had agreed to testify against his codefendants for a reduced sentence. O'Brien needed his testimony to ensure that Moore was positively identified because Robin and Mary were unable to do so in a lineup.

A great direct examination always ends strongly. You want to have a lot of momentum when you end so that the cross-examination never gets off the ground. Here, to show the jury that Pittmon had at least a shred of remorse once he saw the rapes taking place, O'Brien asked Robin if Pittmon said anything else while he was in the backseat with a gun being held to Eddie's head.

Q. What did Pittmon say or do to you during these attacks?
A. He mouthed "sorry" to me.

Q. And at what point — what was happening with you when he did that?
A. The other guy was inserting his penis in my vagina….

O'Brien: Nothing further.

Pittmon would later testify at trial. O'Brien points out that the crimes were so horrific that Pittmon, who originally participated in the crimes, regretted being a part of them once he saw them being carried out to completion.

5.7 DIRECT EXAMINATION OF CHRISTOPHER PITTMON

After the assaults, Eddie, Mary, and Robin had varying degrees of success in identifying the assailants from photographs and lineups. As a result, O'Brien needed to resolve any questions before trial. She decided to offer a plea to Pittmon. In exchange for pleading guilty to the count of armed robbery and receiving a sentence that was less than the maximum allowed, Pittmon would not be charged with aggravated criminal sexual assault if he agreed to testify at trial.

Bring out weaknesses

Q. Do you have a 2005 felony conviction for the offense of unlawful use of a weapon?
A. Yes.

Q. Do you also have a 2006 conviction for burglary?
A. Yes.

Q. You are testifying under a plea agreement; isn't that right?
A. Yes.

Q. You are testifying in exchange for a term of years being offered by the State's Attorney's Office if the judge goes along with it; isn't that right?
A. Yes.

Q. And how much time are you anticipating getting on the charge of armed robbery?
A. According to my plea agreement?

Q. Yes.
A. 35 years.

O'Brien does not want the jury to hear for the first time on cross-examination that her witness is a two-time convicted felon or that he has entered into a plea agreement with the state in order to get a reduced sentence. An attorney always needs to keep the jury's trust and should reveal the bad facts about her witness before the other attorney highlights them on cross-examination.

Lyons and Moore are Pittmon's good friends

In the excerpt below, O'Brien shows the jury through the use of very specific questions that Pittmon knew Lyons and Moore very well in order to bolster his identification of them.

Q. Do you know a person by the name of Cortez Lyons?
A. Yes.

Q. How do you know him?
A. Grew up in the same neighborhood.

Q. How long have you known him?
A. Maybe '97, '98.

Q. When you say the same neighborhood, what neighborhood are you talking about?
A. Where I live. Around Lexington and Fifth. Around there.

Q. Where did Cortez Lyons live in 2006?
A. Sixth and Fillmore. I'm not sure of the address.

Q. Do you know a person by the name of Timothy Moore?
A. Yes.

Q. How do you know him?
A. He stayed next door to me. Grew up.

Q. When you say he stayed next door to you, do you mean in Maywood?
A. Yes....

Q. Does he live directly next door to you?
A. Yes.

Q. How long have you known him?
A. Probably 12 years.

The assaults

Pittmon described the assaults from his vantage point in the backseat of the car. Those descriptions are very graphic and do not need to be repeated here, but note how O'Brien skillfully gets the witness to corroborate the details Robin testified to.

In the excerpt below, we see a challenge most attorneys face when their witness hides his mistakes. No one likes to admit at trial that they made a mistake, much less participated in a rape. Watch how O'Brien does not give an inch when Pittmon tries to hedge and minimize what he did. This excerpt begins at the point where Pittmon has just testified that he arrived in the alley with Moore to meet Lyons. He gets in the backseat next to Eddie and is watching Moore and Lyons force the girls to perform oral sex.

Q. Well, did anybody say anything to you?
A. Yes.

Q. What did they say?
A. Moore asked me if I wanted some, if I wanted to participate, if I wanted some....

Q. But he probably didn't say do you want to participate, did he? [**By listening, O'Brien realizes that the witness has softened what was actually said, and she makes the witness use the actual words.**]
A. No.

Q. What are his exact words that he said to you?
A. Do you want some of this shit? Do you want some of this shit?

Q. And what did you say?
A. No.

Q. And you stayed there though; isn't that right? [**O'Brien makes the witness admit that he did nothing to stop the crimes or leave.**]
A. Yes.

Q. And did you have contact with the guy in the backseat?
A. Yes.

Q. What did you do to him?
A. I was basically watching him.

Q. And what were you watching him for?
A. Kind of like, you know—I kind of felt, you know…Lyons handed me his gun and told me to watch him. And at the time I kind of felt like, you know, as if I was—I don't know if I was trying to uphold an image or, you know, not wanting to be labeled, you know, to be scary or whatever the case may have been. But—you know, so I was kind of, you know, partially in. I had one foot in, one foot out....

Q. You mean you mean one foot in, one foot out of the crime. Is that what you're saying?
A. Yeah. Like, you know, I felt—I felt that I had—I had to do this, you know, but at the same time I didn't really want to—I didn't really want to be there. Do you know what I mean?

*Q. **Yeah. Well, you were there; isn't that right?***
A. **Yeah.**

*Q. **And you had a gun. You had your own gun?***
A. **Yes.**

Pittmon tries to tell the jury that he used a gun on Eddie because Lyons had given him one. He also suggests that he really did not want to be there. O'Brien does not let the witness hedge about what happened to the girls or Pittmon's role in it. By forcing the witness to be truthful, O'Brien maintains the jury's trust in her. The jury sees O'Brien as someone who is going to get to the truth without shading it in any way.

5.8 AFTERMATH OF THE TRIAL

The jury convicted Lyons and Moore of multiple counts of aggravated criminal sexual assault and armed robbery. They each received 120 years in prison. Essentially, this was a life sentence since they are not eligible for parole until they have served 85 percent of the sentence. As mentioned earlier, Pittmon pled guilty to armed robbery and received 35 years in prison. He will probably serve half that sentence before being eligible for release.

As she always does after a trial, O'Brien spoke with the jury. The jurors believed Robin and Mary, but getting to hear from Pittmon was "very helpful." Their comments validated O'Brien's decision to use Pittmon as a cooperating witness. The crimes were too vicious to risk an acquittal pertaining to Moore. Unlike Lyons, who had three people identify him, had confessed to the crimes, and had his DNA recovered from a sexual assault kit, the case against Moore was not nearly so strong.

Before the sentencing hearing for the defendants, Robin submitted two letters to the court. Such letters are commonly referred to as victim impact statements. One letter discussed Pittmon, the other discussed Lyons and Moore. As for Pittmon, she explained, "Thank you for testifying on our behalf.... I am grateful you did not participate, but I also do not understand why you did nothing to stop it. I've thought a lot about it, and I can honestly say that I am 100 percent positive that I would try to stop two men from sexually assaulting two girls. I would never stand there like a coward as you did. That is what you are, a coward."

She also wrote a letter regarding Lyons and Moore. "That night when I arrived at the hospital the first thing I had to do was call my house, and my dad picked up, it was one of the hardest things to do to have to tell my dad that I had been raped. I've been through pain, sadness, hurt and confusion and, at the end of the day, I can push through and be a survivor, but I will always be angry. The memory of that night will be forever with me."

5.9 CHAPTER CHECKLIST ✎

Preparing the witness

1. Divide direct examinations with co-counsel so the jury sees a variety of courtroom styles and stays interested in the case.

2. Know the entire case file before meeting with the witness.

3. Meet with each witness several times before trial.

4. Find a place and time with no interruptions for witness prep.

5. Build an emotional bond with the witness.

6. At trial, be aware of the witness' emotions. If the witness cries, don't be afraid to approach the witness stand and comfort the witness.

7. If your witness has an emotional story to tell, don't have him or her repeat it in the witness prep sessions. Save the drama for the trial.

8. Tell your witness to replay her story for the jury as if she were describing events in a TV show.

9. Prepare your witness for the questions he or she will face on cross-examination. It is the one fear all witnesses share.

Trial tips

1. Your first witness needs to set a compelling scene for the jury.

2. If possible, move near the jury box when examining the witness so the jury is between you and the witness. This forces the witness to look at the jury and speak loudly enough for the jury to hear her.

3. Be aware of the witness' simple needs, such as a break for water, as well as his or her more complex needs, such as positioning your body so the witness cannot see the defendant at counsel table.

4. Only rely on notes to make sure you have covered everything.

5. Be relaxed and in command.

6. Do not write out the questions you are going to ask, but instead write out topics and facts you need.

7. Listen to the witness' answers.

8. Have exhibits marked and placed in the order you will use them in your examination.

9. O'Brien loops, seeks out details when needed, and gives the witness a choice of two options to focus the witness on the answer needed. These three skills are the essence of a successful direct examination.

10. Ask specific background questions so the jury can connect with your witness.

11. Ask questions so the jury will root for your witness to say the right answers on cross, causing the witness to "stick it" to opposing counsel.

12. End your direct examination on a memorable point. O'Brien ends Robin's direct with her testimony that she saw one of the assailants mouth "sorry" as she was being raped at gun point by one of the other assailants.

13. Bring out the weaknesses in your witness' testimony on direct.

Most important mistakes lawyers make

1. Not knowing all the documents in their case.

2. Not taking the time to decide which witnesses are important.

3. Not taking the time to prepare their witnesses.

4. Not thinking about the order of witnesses and the framework that provides for telling a story.

5. Not having exhibits organized in front of jury.

6. Not caring enough to win the case.

PART THREE

Cross-Examination

INTRODUCTION

Cross-examination is the questioning of an adverse or hostile witness. While I believe direct examination is the most difficult part of a trial, I also believe that cross-examination is the scariest. How do you prove to the jury that the witness who has just helped the opposing side on direct examination is really not that helpful or should not be believed?

The reason cross-examinations are usually disasters is that attorneys believe in the myth created by Hollywood that an attorney should be able to get a witness to confess to lying. For this reason, cross-examinations are often more suicidal than homicidal. Why? No witness is ever going to confess that he or she is a liar. Consequently, your goal should not be to get the witness to admit that he or she is a liar; your goal should be to *prove* to the jury that the witness is untrustworthy.

Cross-examinations are very intimidating, not only because attorneys are under the mistaken belief that they should get confessions as those seen on TV or in movies, but also because of attorneys' very real fear that witnesses won't answer their questions or that witnesses will hurt their case by repeating damaging testimony from the direct examination.

Not to worry. In the next two chapters, two excellent attorneys reveal their proven techniques to succeed every time. In Chapter Six, Alan Dershowitz will show how his preparation, creativity, and bluffing caused a turning point when he was defending a terrorist. In Chapter Seven, David Bernick, one of the most respected civil defense attorneys, will take us behind the scenes to show how he developed clear themes and controlled an extremely difficult witness in a trial that made national headlines.

CHAPTER SIX

⚬⚬⚬

Alan Dershowitz

The Creative Cross-Examination

It's so often just not carefully thought through strategically what the purpose of the cross-examination is, and, indeed, whether the witness ought to be cross-examined, or if he ought to be cross-examined at length.

— Alan Dershowitz

Alan Dershowitz has been called the nation's "most distinguished defender of individual rights." He joined the Harvard Law School faculty at age 28 and became the youngest full-time professor in its history. He has taught and lectured on a wide variety of topics, including criminal law, constitutional law, history, philosophy, psychology, and theology. He has written more than 1,000 articles, and his books, including *Taking the Stand: My Life in the Law, The Best Defense,* and *Chutzpah,* have sold more than 1,000,000 copies worldwide. In 1983, the Anti-Defamation League of the B'nai B'rith presented him with the William O. Douglas First Amendment Award for his "compassionate eloquent leadership and persistent advocacy in the struggle for civil and human rights."

He has been the lead attorney or part of the defense team for innumerable famous cases, including those representing Bill Clinton, O.J. Simpson, Claus von Bulow, Patty Hearst, Mike Tyson, and Julian Assange. After attending Brooklyn College, he graduated from Yale Law School at the top of his class and was editor in chief of the *Yale Law Journal*. He was a clerk for Associate Justice Arthur Goldberg of the United States Supreme Court, before eventually becoming a professor at Harvard Law School.

CHAPTER HIGHLIGHTS

- Develop a plan and execute it
- Become an advocate for your client on cross-examination
- Ethically bluff the witness

We are going to look at one of Dershowitz's first and most fascinating cases, one that involved a conspiracy of terrorist bombers who gained international attention. The turning point came when Dershowitz cross-examined the lead investigator and destroyed his credibility to the degree that his guilty client walked out of the courtroom a free man. Not only was his cross-examination brilliant, but it can also teach us the foundations of conducting a successful cross-examination. We can also learn how far one can go when bluffing a witness about the evidence you have. But before we do, let's learn Dershowitz's secrets about trial strategies and, more specifically, cross-examination.

6.1 TRIAL STRATEGIES

I asked Dershowitz how important a lawyer's skills are in affecting a case's outcome. He explained:

> Lawyers can lose almost any case. A bad lawyer can lose almost any good case. There's no set of facts that precludes a bad lawyer from screwing it up. I've seen that. I think O.J. Simpson's probably the best example of that, of bad lawyers losing what appears to be an airtight case. Any first year law student should have been able to win that case. In terms of lawyers turning around a losing case and winning it, I've certainly seen it done. I think I've done it in a couple of cases. Not all that many, but in a few cases you can really make the difference. I had a judge tell me once, a First Circuit judge, that the case was lost. Then, I did my rebuttal argument [at oral argument], and we won it on rebuttal.
>
> I've seen just too many cases of bad lawyers just taking good cases and destroying them by lack of preparation, by falling into traps of the other side. I think lawyers can make a considerable difference.

> Given a choice between having the facts on my side and a good lawyer, I think I'd always take the facts.
> —Alan Dershowitz

Dershowitz supports his conclusion by recalling what he has seen in his own cases and in his review of hundreds and hundreds of trial transcripts where he has been hired as an appellate lawyer. He points out, "I do the autopsies on the trials, and I just hang my head. I just can't believe how bad some of the trial lawyers are in failing to preserve issues and walking into traps."

Another mistake lawyers make is undervaluing the importance of the opening statement. Dershowitz explains that most lawyers simply neglect it. Instead, they "save everything for the close, by which time the jury has often decided."

I asked Dershowitz about a complaint I often hear from attorneys: "All my cases are boring." They wish they had some high-profile cases to spend time on and make their work more interesting and rewarding. Dershowitz related the story Judge Benjamin Cardozo told while on the New York Court of Appeals before he became a Supreme Court Justice. Someone asked Judge Cardozo, "How come you get all the interesting cases?" He said, "Are you kidding? They're the most boring cases in the world until I get them, and I make them interesting." Dershowitz agrees. "That's what you have to do. Every case has to be the most important case." For example, Dershowitz suggests that when you work on a simple case, you need to declare, "This case will challenge the way in which tickets are written in the city of...."

The obvious exception to this guidance is when you want to make the case unimportant so it will go away. Otherwise, "if the case is going to trial, you have to figure out a way of making it fascinating for the jury and interesting for you too."

6.2 RULES OF THE JUSTICE GAME

Dershowitz is well known for his "Rules of the Justice Game." He discerned the rules from the cases he litigated, his teaching, and the process of writing his book, *The Best Defense*.

I asked him about the reaction he has received from these rules that some find very provocative. "I've gotten a lot of judges telling me off the record that they agree. I've had some judges get really angry with me." Here they are with some slight amendments made by Dershowitz due to subsequent experience since writing *The Best Defense*:

Rule I: Most criminal defendants are, in fact, guilty.

Rule II: All criminal defense lawyers, prosecutors, and judges understand and believe Rule I.

Rule III: It is generally easier to convict guilty defendants by violating the Constitution than by complying with it, and in some cases it is impossible to convict guilty defendants without violating the Constitution.

Rule IV: In order to convict guilty defendants, many police witnesses lie about whether they violated the Constitution.

Rule V: All prosecutors, judges, and defense attorneys are aware of Rule IV.

Rule VI: In order to convict guilty defendants, many prosecutors implicitly encourage the police to lie about whether they violated the Constitution.

Rule VII: All judges are aware of Rule VI.

Rule VIII: Many trial judges pretend to believe police officers who they know are lying.

Rule IX: All appellate judges are aware of Rule VIII, yet many pretend to believe the trial judges who pretend to believe the lying police officers.

Rule X: Many judges claim to disbelieve defendants about whether their constitutional rights have been violated, even if they are telling the truth.

Rule XI: Most judges and prosecutors would not knowingly convict a defendant they believe to be innocent of the crime charged (or a closely related crime).

Rule XII: Rule XI does not apply to members of organized crime, drug dealers, career criminals, terrorists, or potential informers.

Rule XIII: Almost nobody really wants justice.

6.3 HIGH PROFILE CASES

Although Dershowitz has one of the most interesting legal practices of any lawyer, he is modest in explaining the rewards of working with a celebrity client. He points out, "Celebrities will almost always disappoint you. Most are boring, banal, and self-centered. Working on a high-profile case is a decidedly mixed bag. If you never have a celebrity case during your career, you haven't missed anything."

6.4 OBSERVATIONS ON CROSS-EXAMINATION

In reviewing hundreds and hundreds of transcripts, Dershowitz has noticed that many lawyers use the same cross-examination tactic no matter who the witness is. Lawyers do not adjust their cross-examination styles to the witnesses who are on the stand. He points out, "I sometimes follow a lawyer in four or five cases because I read four or five of their transcripts. Cross-examination is always the same, and it never works."

A second complaint Dershowitz has is that "lawyers feel they have to cross-examine every witness, and they often don't have a very clear strategy as to what they intend to achieve by the cross-examination." Without a clear strategy, lawyers do not know whether they're going to try to make the witness their witness and thereby enhance the witness's credibility or whether they're going to try to destroy the witness's credibility.

I wondered if Dershowitz would agree with what I have often observed in courtrooms. I have seen plenty of lawyers try to destroy a witness's credibility on one topic and then try to use the witness to support their case on another topic. If the tactics are done in the wrong order, nothing good is accomplished. For example, a witness may have good testimony that will help your case, as well as damaging testimony that will hurt your case. If you try to destroy the witness's credibility first and then try to ask questions to elicit answers that will support your case, there is little reason those "good" facts will help you because you have previously destroyed the witness's credibility. Dershowitz strongly agrees that you need to elicit favorable facts before you attack the witness's credibility.

Dershowitz emphasizes that you need to have a purpose and execute it. For example, your goal might be simply to conduct a 30-minute cross with the sole purpose of getting one answer that you're going to use in your closing argument.

Dershowitz also points out that to be an effective advocate in the courtroom, whether it's on cross-examination or during another aspect of trial, you need to work closely with your client. He believes lawyers continually neglect this strategy. The key is to develop a relationship in which your client tells you both the bad and good about the witness you are cross-examining. While the client is all too willing to tell you the bad things about the witness, you must get your client to tell you the good things about the witness as well. Oftentimes, the client "won't tell you the positive things because he thinks that's going to hurt your case. But, he or she is not in the position to make that judgment. They have to tell you everything."

The length of a cross-examination obviously varies, but Dershowitz thinks both directs and crosses often go on far too long, and that this has significant consequences for their cases. "I think prosecutors lose more cases by over-trying them. I think some defendants also lose their cases by having overly long cross-examinations. I've read cross-examinations that go on four or five days and there's ten minutes that's worthwhile."

However, Dershowitz points out that a long cross can have a benefit. For example, one strategy is to ask numerous non-confrontational questions to lull the witness into a sense of complacency and then ask the question that is going to make the difference.

Nonetheless, too often a cross-examination is conducted by a lawyer who, with a paralegal or law student sitting next to him or her, listens to the entire direct examination and then goes through the direct point by point on cross, thereby making the witness reiterate everything. "That's just a terrible cross-examination. I see that so often."

Criminal defense attorneys often argue to juries the presumption of innocence for their clients. Instead, defense attorneys should challenge what Dershowitz calls "the presumption of regularity." Juries have the mindset that since someone's been indicted, he's probably done it, so let's just go along and do what juries are supposed to do. Let's listen and find him guilty.

But Dershowitz explains that "the presumption of regularity, the assumption that everything is routine

> *I've seen so many cases reading transcripts where the only result of cross-examination is to take very bad testimony on direct, that is very damaging testimony on direct, and make it even more damaging because you've now re-elicited it on cross. The jury's saying to itself, "Oh my God, he did it the same way on direct and on cross. It must be true. It must be important."*
> —Alan Dershowitz

and this case is routine like everything else, almost always leads to bad results." Consequently, the defense lawyer's challenge is to "make it untrue." You have to show the jury that it "really is better for ten guilty to go free than for one innocent to be wrongly accused."

As for delivery, Dershowitz never uses notes. This is true whether he is making an opening statement, conducting a cross-examination, or arguing an appeal at oral argument. Likewise, when opposing counsel conducts direct examination, Dershowitz does not take notes. He believes it is critical to listen, and you cannot listen effectively if you are taking notes. He believes in this skill so strongly that he does not let his students take notes for the first two weeks of class. He wants them to listen and focus on how important that skill is.

6.5 THE MURDER OF IRIS KONES

Dershowitz points out that there is a widespread myth that guilty clients will confide their guilt to their trusted lawyers. But the reality is that guilty clients don't trust lawyers with their dark secrets. Most guilty defendants believe that their lawyers will work harder for innocent defendants than for guilty ones. Only one client who was accused of a killing admitted to Dershowitz that he was guilty — but he really had no choice.

Iris Kones was a 27-year-old Jewish woman who was an assistant to Sol Hurok in his accounting department. Hurok emigrated from Russia in 1905 and produced numerous shows in New York City that featured Russian artists and their works. Among other firsts, he introduced the Bolshoi Ballet to the United States. His venue in New York City had the marquee: "Sol Hurok Presents." On a Wednesday afternoon in January 1972, he made final arrangements for the American premiere of Russia's Osipov Balalaika Orchestra.

But he was concerned about threats that had been made by the Jewish Defense League (JDL). By way of background, the JDL was started by Rabbi Meir Kahane in New York City in 1968. Dershowitz explains that the JDL was a Jewish self-help organization whose primary purpose — initially — was to protect elderly Jews from assaults in New York City. But its focus soon turned to international issues, and its method of activism turned from self-defense to premeditated use of guns and bombs. The JDL began to target Arab diplomats, activists, and others because of their countries' war against Israel, and Russia for its repression of Jewish religious practices and its opposition to Jewish emigration to Israel.

At Sol's performance hall, the then recent disruptions by the JDL included the planting of smoke bombs and the release of live mice. So, he met with security to ensure that extra measures were in place. On this Wednesday afternoon in January 1972, two well-dressed young men asked the receptionist at the concert hall about an upcoming concert. While the receptionist looked for the information they had requested, the men left the reception area but left behind a leather briefcase with a bomb inside.

At the same time, another young man targeted the New York City office of Columbia Artists Management that arranged for Russian artists to perform in the United States, leaving a similar briefcase in its office. After the men left, both briefcases exploded and filled the offices with billowing smoke. Iris Kones tried to escape Hurok's offices but could not. Instead, she lay on the ground trying to escape the smoke and breathe. She died of asphyxiation.

Soon after the bombs exploded, the Associated Press received an anonymous call: "Soviet culture is responsible for the deaths and imprisonment of Soviet Jews." The calls ended with the JDL motto: "Never again." Although the JDL had made bomb threats and committed other terrorist threats against targets in Russia in the name of defending Jewish rights, ironically, the first death it caused was that of a Jewish woman, Iris Kones.

On June 16, 1972, Sheldon Seigel, Stuart Cohen, and Sheldon Davis were arrested for committing Kones' murder. The federal statute under which they were charged provided that if a murder was committed in connection with the commission of a felony (i.e., planting a bomb), the defendant could be charged with felony murder, with the death penalty as a possible punishment.

When Dershowitz took the case, Seigel, a childhood friend of Dershowitz's, and his two codefendants proclaimed their innocence and suggested the bombing was the work of another Jewish militant organization (Betar). As part of his investigation, Dershowitz considered the possibility that the government had planted an informant within the JDL to gain access to the defendants' trial strategies.

Dershowitz's suspicions grew when the government admitted it had no fingerprints or eyewitnesses linking the defendants to the bombing. Then, Dershowitz's attention turned to Sheldon's codefendants. Could one of them be the informant? That would explain why no one was taking any plea offers. After exhaustive research, he concluded it was his own client. I asked Dershowitz why the prosecutors did not inform him that his client was the one cooperating. He said that he learned later that the prosecutors believed the defense lawyers were so intertwined with the JDL that they could not be trusted.

He confronted Seigel, who then admitted his involvement. Dershowitz was furious over having been tricked by his client and having spent months trying to defend someone who actually had been cooperating with the government, and who would never face a murder conviction because the government would offer him immunity in exchange for his testimony.

> *Thank God you know, I've wanted to tell you a hundred times, but I was sure you'd hate me and abandon me. Please help me get out of this mess.*
> — Sheldon Seigel

How Seigel became an informant is important to understanding Dershowitz's trial strategy to prevent Seigel from testifying against his friends, about which Seigel was adamant. Seigel was very good with electronics and soon became involved with building bombs for JDL. He built a couple of bombs that were planted in a building where Amtorg, the Soviet trade mission to the United States, was located. An anonymous caller warned of the bombs and ended his warning with the JDL motto: "Never again." The building was cleared and the bombs were defused. The police investigation was led by Santo Parola, who was able to trace some of the electronics for the bomb to a Radio Shack, where it was determined that Seigel had made the purchases.

The police then followed Seigel and searched his car without a warrant when he was not in it. They found an array of bombing materials. When Seigel returned to the car, he was arrested. Parola sought to make Seigel an informant. He told Seigel that the police could link him to the Amtorg bombs and that, since the car he was driving was his brother's, the police might bring his brother into the case. He also threatened to kill Seigel if he did not cooperate because the Amtorg bombs had almost killed several police officers when they had rushed to defuse the bombs.

Seigel did not want to tell on his friends. Parola said he would not have to. Instead, all Seigel had to do was give the police enough warning so they could disarm bombs in the future. After deciding to help, Seigel was released, and he later called a special number at the police department and warned of a bomb that had been planted at a Soviet estate in Glen Cove, Long Island. The police were able to disarm the bomb.

But that was not enough for Parola; he now wanted names of participants, not just a warning. He again threatened Seigel with the evidence he had against him for the Amtorg bombing. Seigel wanted assurances that if he did give names, no one would know that he was the source. Parola agreed and also told him that since he had never read Seigel his Miranda rights, nothing Seigel told Parola could be used as evidence against him. Seigel also met with a prosecutor who wrote a handwritten statement that said: "It is the intention of the U.S. Attorney's office to apply for a grant of immunity for Mr. Sheldon Seigel concerning the...bombing of Amtorg and the attempted bombing at Glen Cove."

After these assurances, Seigel testified before a grand jury about the Amtorg and Glen Cove crimes. But Parola would change the terms once again. A few weeks later, a sniper shot at four children who were in a bedroom inside the Soviet mission to the United Nations located near Park Avenue in Manhattan. Seigel had not provided any warning. There was international and national pressure for the New York City police to make an arrest. Seigel refused to provide any names about the sniper attack. Notwithstanding prior promises, Parola said that Seigel would now have to testify publicly at the trial in the Amtorg and Glen Cove bombings.

Seigel felt trapped and started to make recordings of his conversations with Parola. He rigged his car so that his leg could trip a switch to start a cassette recorder when Parola was in the car where they often would have their discussions.

Seigel told Parola about several upcoming assassinations and bombings that the police were subsequently able to prevent. But the Hurok and Columbia Artists bombings mentioned earlier, where Iris Kones was killed, had occurred without any notice. When Parola asked Seigel about the events, he denied that the JDL was involved. Parola put $5,000 cash on the front seat of his car, where they were talking, and Seigel still refused to cooperate. The police chief authorized Parola to make the ultimate offer: If Seigel revealed who was involved in the Hurok and Columbia bombings, he would never be revealed as the informant at any trial and would not be prosecuted for the Hurok and Columbia crimes.

With this assurance, Seigel disclosed who was involved and that he had made the bomb. Unfortunately for Seigel, this most important conversation was not captured on tape because the recorder had been broken that day.

At a pretrial hearing for the trial of the Hurok and Columbia bombings, the prosecution moved to sever (separate) the trials of the three defendants so Seigel could be given immunity from prosecution in order to testify against his codefendants. The prosecution wanted separate trials because judges won't allow defendants to testify against another defendant at the same trial.

By giving Seigel immunity, the prosecution believed Seigel could be forced to testify against his codefendants at a separate trial because he had no legal reason to refuse to testify for fear of self-incrimination (i.e., take the Fifth). In other words, even if the trials were separate, Seigel could refuse to testify if his testimony that implicated his codefendants in a crime would also implicate himself. But with the prosecution's immunity promise, Seigel had no legal excuse not to testify. Yet, Seigel did not want to testify against his friends even with immunity.

By means of a novel legal theory, which is set forth in detail in his book *The Best Defense,* Dershowitz objected to the severance and immunity offer because he believed the government could not compel Seigel's testimony—even if he were offered immunity—since the government's proof of Seigel's involvement in the Hurok and Columbia bombings had been obtained from three improper sources: 1) illegal wiretaps of the JDL that initially alerted the police to Seigel's illegal activities, 2) an illegal search of Seigel's car (where the bomb materials had been found), and 3) Parola's promise to Seigel that he would never be called as a witness.

In short, Dershowitz argued that the government could not prosecute Seigel because it had violated his Constitutional rights in obtaining evidence against him, and this tainted evidence could not be used in a trial against Seigel.

Consequently, Dershowitz argued, it was disingenuous for the government to give Seigel immunity from prosecution when the government could not proceed with the prosecution because of the tainted evidence.

The court ordered a hearing on Dershowitz's motion. This chapter focuses on Dershowitz's cross-examination of Parola on the issue of Parola's promise to Seigel that he would never be called as a witness. Before we look at Dershowitz's cross, let's look at a sample of the threats and promises Parola made to see the pressure he was applying on Seigel.

Here is a transcript of a recording where Parola asked Seigel about the name of the sniper who fired on the Soviet mission at the United Nations.

> **Parola:** Just the fucking name of the guy. They can't use you for anything. I can't possibly produce you, I can't. All I want to know is one thing: you don't have to tell me nothin' else after that, do you know or don't ya?
>
> **Seigel:** *No.*
>
> **Parola:** That's the God's honest truth. Or don't make any fuckin' answers at all, and I'll draw my own conclusion. You hear me? 'Cause all I'm askin' for is a crummy, fuckin' favor, that's all. I told ya, I can't hurt the guy, I can't do nothin' to the people that're involved. I probably pick'm up, I'll probably harass the shit out of 'em a little bit, but that's about as far as I can go with it, 'cause I can't use you, I could break the fuckin' people's balls is all I can do, just break their balls....
>
> **Seigel:** *Uh, huh.*
>
> **Parola:** Just mention a nice name to me so that I could get into the good graces downtown again, huh. So's maybe I can get promoted.

Other times, Parola threatened Seigel with violence.

> **Parola:** You're not going to jail on either one of them [Amtorg or Glen Cove bombings]. And if…you ever say that I said it, I'm gonna deny it, and I'm gonna meet ya some fuckin' night, and I'm gonna run ya over with a truck. [Y]ou…ever rat on me, boy, I'll fuckin' brain ya that I told ya. If you can't help me, you're no fuckin' good to me, Shel, I'll have to run you over next time I see you…. Did you hear what I said, you fuck, don't play games with me.

Another time, Parola insisted that Seigel might have to testify if he stopped providing information:

> **Parola:** What did you tell the guy, that you would testify as a last resort, didn't you?
>
> **Seigel:** *Except I knew I wasn't.*

Parola: What makes you think I can't convince a federal jury that this is the truth? You don't think I can twist a jury's fuckin' head? Hey, when I testify, I'm not the same guy sitting in this car, you know.

Seigel: *Neither am I.*

Parola: I don't curse.

6.6 TECHNIQUES

Now, let's quickly review the keys to a successful cross and then study Dershowitz in action. First, you need to pick a topic that you can win on. This is crucial to effective cross-examination and something that most lawyers don't give enough thought to. Only pick a topic where your success is assured.

Once you pick a topic, the vast majority of your questions should be leading. A leading question suggests the answer to the witness. To make the question crystal clear, it should only have one fact in it so that the witness has to answer "yes" or "no" to the one fact you have asserted in your question. To force the witness to answer "yes," you can begin your questions with the phrases "Isn't it a fact" or "Isn't it true." After you have mastered that technique, you can drop those phrases which can become distracting after multiple questions and simply assert with an authoritative tone of voice the statement you want the witness to agree to. This technique turns the question into a declaration.

Examples of leading question with one fact

Q. Isn't it a fact that the traffic light was red?

Q. Isn't it a fact it was raining at the time of the accident?

Example of declaratory statement

Q. The traffic light was red. (strongly delivered with no rise in pitch at the end)

6.7 CROSS-EXAMINATION OF PAROLA

Now, let's turn to the hearing where Dershowitz had to prove that Parola had promised Seigel that he would never have to testify, understanding that because the equipment had been broken the day of the conversation, Dershowitz did not have any recording to back up this conversation. Dershowitz's strategy was to conduct the cross-examination in four parts, or phases. In the first phase, Parola would be asked questions about statements he made to Seigel that Seigel had recorded. Since Parola did not know Seigel had made any recordings, Dershowitz would coax Parola into lying about those conversations. In Parola's mind, there was no risk to lying because it was his word, as a police officer, against a suspected bomber's.

Phase two of the cross-examination would involve questions that incorporated Parola's verbatim statements to Seigel which would plant in his mind the idea that there might be tape recordings.

Phase three would involve questions from a "transcript" that was recreated from Seigel's memory but for which there was no tape recording. The fourth phase would involve playing the recordings for the court to show which questions were supported by recordings and which were not.

Phase One

Q. *Did you ever tell [Seigel] that the reason you did not advise him of his rights [was] so that the information he gave you could never be used in evidence against him?*
A. No, sir, I did not.

Q. *Did you ever have such a discussion with him?*
A. No, sir, I did not.

Q. *Did you ever promise him that he would never have to be publicly revealed if he gave you the information in the Amtorg case?*
A. No, sir.

Q. *In regard to information that you were seeking from Mr. Seigel relative to a shooting into the Soviet Mission, did you at any point tell him that if he gave you information about that, that you would never call upon him to testify at any trial or ever reveal him as an informant?*
A. Oddly enough, Mr. Seigel volunteered that information to me.

Notice how each question contains one fact. While most questions should be leading in that they suggest to the witness what the answer should be because it's true, Dershowitz does not want to suggest the answer in phase one. Indeed, he wants the witness to lie.

All these answers were in complete contradiction to the recordings Seigel had made where Parola stated the opposite. In short, Parola had lied, and Dershowitz would be able to prove it through objective evidence — the tape recordings — not just Seigel's testimony.

Phase Two

Now, Dershowitz incorporates verbatim language from the tape recordings he has:

Q. *Did you ever have the following conversation with Mr. Sheldon Seigel? "You're not going to jail on either one of them, and if you ever say that I said it, I'm gonna deny it and I'm gonna meet you some fuckin' night, and I'm gonna run you over with a truck."*
A. No, sir, I deny that.

Q. You are certain that you never said anything about running him over with a truck?
A. I never said anything like that.

Q. Have you ever made the following statement: "You ever fuck me up like that when I tell
you something, you ever rat on me, I will fuckin' brain you."
A. I don't believe I made that statement.

Again, notice how each question contains only one fact. Dershowitz remembers that Parola slowly became very nervous, asked for a glass of water and almost dropped it with his shaking hands. Dershowitz relates that Parola's confident answers turned into evasive and forgetful ones. As Dershowitz continued to read him alleged statements he had made, he would answer with "I would have said something like that to keep rapport with the informer," and "I don't remember but it sounds familiar." Parola could see the noose tightening around his neck and the prosecution could see its case slipping away.

Phase Three

In this phase, Dershowitz's plan was to act as if he were reading from an actual transcript when in reality he was reading from a transcript recreated by Seigel. Dershowitz asked Seigel to write down as best he could remember the conversation he had with Parola about the Hurok bombing. Although this attempt was a good starting point, it would not be good enough to trick Parola. So, Dershowitz, who had grown up in the same neighborhood as Parola, added phrases and changed the syntax of certain sentences so that it would sound authentic.

Q. Did you have the following conversation with Sheldon Seigel:

> **Parola:** Hey, where you been?
>
> *Seigel: What do you mean?*
>
> **Parola:** I told you two o'clock, didn't I?
>
> *Seigel: No. You told me between two and two-fifteen.*
>
> **Parola:** Hey, don't get cute. Hey, look, you got to do us a favor. If you can help us on the Hurok thing I would appreciate it. I promise you, Shelley, just give us the names and leave the rest to us. If we can't prove it without ya, then we can't prove it.

A. In substance, I could have had that conversation.

Dershowitz continued to read from the "transcript."

> **Parola:** Once we know who did it, you don't think we can turn these guys? Are ya kidding? We'll get it out of them. I'm tellin' ya, we can do it.

Seigel: What if someone finds out?

Parola: No one's going to find out. You won't even have to go to the grand jury in this one. We can do this whole shmeer without even using you.

A. It sounds familiar.

The prosecutor was growing nervous. He asked the judge to require the defense to turn over to the prosecution any transcripts or recordings it may have. The judge took a recess to consider the request, with the success of Dershowitz's cross hanging in the balance. If the judge required Dershowitz to turn over the recordings, Parola would soon realize that Dershowitz was limited in proving the answers to certain questions he posed. Here is the court's ruling:

> **Court:** *[Professor Dershowitz is] entitled to examine this witness as to his credibility and as to the substantive facts. Now, he may do it by playing the tape for him, or he may do it in his own way.... Go ahead.*

When Parola responded to another part of the "transcript" with an equivocation, "I possibly would say something like that," the judge responded, "What do you mean possibly? Did you or didn't you?" The judge started interjecting more questions, particularly after the prosecution objected to Dershowitz's dramatic reading of the "transcript." The judge said, "I understand your pain, but it is pretty exciting stuff."

Dershowitz knew the cross-examination was going well when the Court all but took over the cross.

> **Court:** *Take it sentence by sentence.*
>
> **Dershowitz:** *[Reading]* "Look, just tell me who did the Hurok thing. Just give me their fucking names."
>
> **Court:** *In March of 1972 did you have such a conversation with Mr. Seigel?*
>
> **Parola:** Yes, I could have had that conversation relative to Hurok, your Honor.
>
> **Dershowitz:** *[Reading]* "We will never use you as a witness, we will build the case around you. We will use your leads."
>
> **Court:** *Did you say to him in that conversation — and don't tell me you could or couldn't have — I want to know did you or didn't you?*
>
> **Parola:** I believe I have testified on the record, your Honor, that I did, in fact, say to Mr. Seigel that we could build a case around him.
>
> **Dershowitz:** *[Reading]* "We ain't going to use you. We just ain't going to, won't have to, we can make the case without you."

Court: Did you say that?

Parola: In those exact words, I don't recall, your Honor.

Dershowitz: Did you give the substance of that statement to Mr. Seigel?

Parola: In substance, I would say yes.

Court: Then it is a fact, isn't it, that at some point in time you said to Seigel: "We will never use you." Is that correct?

Parola: My conversations, your Honor, with Seigel: "We would never use you if we can build a case around you."

Court: I didn't put that "if" part in. I am asking you whether you ever told it to him without the "if." Read that language, Professor, please. The last few lines of that.

Dershowitz: *[Reading]* "We ain't going to use you. We just ain't. We won't have to. We can make the case without you."

Court: Did you say that to him?

Parola: That sounds familiar to me, your Honor. I don't recall exactly if those words are the words.

Court [shouting in anger]: Just don't interrupt me. I take it when you say, "that sounds familiar," that that means that you recollect that in substance, if not in those words?

Parola: In substance, sir.

Court: Yes.

Dershowitz had achieved his turning point. Parola had admitted that he had promised Seigel he would not be used as a witness in the Hurok case. Parola had admitted the authenticity of the conversations which Dershowitz did not have on tape but had only recreated. Parola left the stand without his credibility.

I asked Dershowitz how he felt during the cross. He said, "It was exhilarating to be able to trap somebody." He also became nervous when the judge started asking questions because he did not want the judge to take over for him.

Phase Four

It was nearing the end of the day, and Dershowitz wanted to play for the judge the portions of the tapes that corroborated the transcript. But the prosecution wanted to get possession of the tapes so it could authenticate them and create transcripts. The court agreed with the request and adjourned for the day. In hindsight, Dershowitz wishes he had informed the court at that point that the crucial part of the admission he obtained from Parola was achieved by reading from a "transcript" that was not supported by a recording. Instead, the prosecution took the offensive by later pointing out the trick to the court.

At a hearing in chambers, the judge's anger at Dershowitz was obvious:

Court: Now, I want to suggest to you, sir, that in this court, at least, one expects lawyers to keep their punches above the belt...

Dershowitz: Your Honor, I do not think there were any punches below the belt.

Court: You and I then, sir, have two different ideas of the level at which one practices law....

Dershowitz: I just don't understand your argument, your Honor.

Court: Don't get the idea I am arguing with you, sir. I am expressing the opinion of the Court.

Dershowitz: If, in fact, he testified one way, thinking there were not tapes, and testified another, thinking there were tapes, I don't understand how anything but truth has been searched [out].

Court: Is it your view that you can ask questions that were, in fact, taken from a wiretap or a tape recording and in the middle of real questions, for instance, make up a little question, which you slip in there, which never existed....

Dershowitz: When you say never existed, are you suggesting made up?

Court: Yes.

Dershowitz: No, that would not be proper. If you are asking whether it would be proper in the middle of conversations, which the witness assumed were on tape, to ask him about conversations which we believe occurred, but which were not recorded on tape, most affirmatively yes.

Court: Indicating by your actions, mannerisms, readings and other attitudes in the courtroom that it was on tape?

Dershowitz: By all means, yes.

Court: You and I have a diametrically different view.

Dershowitz: I guess we do, your Honor.

Court: I regard it as a reprehensible practice.

Dershowitz: If you would explain to me —

Court: I am not in the business of answering questions. You do understand that, don't you.

Dershowitz: I do not understand what is wrong with that in any way.

Court: I can't help you, then…. I authorize and direct that those questions and answers be stricken from his testimony. Is that, as the expression goes, perfectly clear?

After more testimony was given on the allegedly illegal wiretaps of the JDL and the search of Seigel's car, the court ruled that the prosecution could compel Seigel to testify at the trial against the other two suspects. At the first of those two trials, Seigel was called to the witness stand with a grant of immunity, but he refused to testify and was held in contempt of court.

Dershowitz appealed this ruling. The appellate court found that the wiretaps had been illegal and that Seigel could not be forced to testify or prosecuted for the Amtorg or Glen Cove bombings or the explosives found in his car. The end result was that Seigel was a free man who could not be compelled to testify in any of the cases against the JDL. The cases against the two codefendants collapsed without Seigel's testimony.

While not directly addressing the ethics of Dershowitz's cross that the trial court found offensive, the appellate court did praise "counsel for Seigel [who] explored complex factual and legal issues competitively yet courteously and always in the pursuit of the truth." Even if the ethics had been directly discussed, Dershowitz would have won. In post-hearing briefing, he had provided several legal authorities declaring that it "has long been regarded as the essence of effective cross-examination, especially of a lying witness, to convey the impression that the cross-examiner has more, less, or different evidence than he actually has."

Dershowitz even mentioned in his brief that Abraham Lincoln was known to have used a similar tactic. Lincoln was defending a man charged with murder. A witness claimed to have seen Lincoln's client commit the crime "by moonlight." Lincoln, suspecting that the witness had not seen the murder, cross-examined the witness with an almanac. Lincoln suggested to the witness that the almanac proved that the moon was only in the first quarter on the night of the murder and thus not very bright and had disappeared entirely by the time of the murder.

The witness was discredited, and the defendant was acquitted.

There are two competing stories regarding the precise technique Lincoln used to achieve his success. In one account, Lincoln bluffed the witness with an almanac from a different year that supported the facts in Lincoln's questions. In another account, Lincoln bluffed the witness, and the witness would have won the battle if he had been shown the real almanac. But since the witness knew he was lying, he assumed the almanac must have been correct and never denied the truth of Lincoln's questions.

As Dershowitz told me with a smile, it is very helpful when you have Abe Lincoln on your side.

I asked Dershowitz if he felt any sympathy for Parola, who had done a lot to save innocent people's lives from the JDL's activities. Dershowitz quickly replied, "Of course. That's why after it was over I went over to him and I told him what a good cop he was, what a great investigator he was. I was not on the side of the JDL, I was on the side of the cops, but you have to do your job."

6.8 EPILOGUE

After the trial, Dershowitz taught this cross-examination in his ethics classes at Harvard Law School for many years. One question that often arose is whether it is fair for the judge to intervene and ask questions, since to do so will intimidate a witness to answer "yes" to a judge despite what the truth may be. Dershowitz has no problem with such an intervention. The reason is that if Parola had not made the promise to Seigel, he simply would have related that fact to the judge. In short, Dershowitz believes that neither the judge nor he could scare Parola into admitting to something that was not true.

But Dershowitz also likes to raise broader issues with his students. For example, he wants his students to experience what it feels like to get a client off for the murder of a young woman who is in the prime of her life. He has them read the trial judge's comments spoken in the courtroom as he was forced to dismiss the case against Seigel and his codefendants:

> Do you know who isn't in court today? Iris Kones. Someone has committed a dastardly, vicious, unforgiveable, unforgettable crime; someone is frustrating the administration of justice in a case that, in my mind, involves murder. People who deliberately do so will learn the power of the law even if there are those who have literally gotten away with murder.

Dershowitz explains that while "enunciating these final words, Judge Bauman turned his eyes from the defendants and focused them on me, almost as if to say, 'And you, Dershowitz, are the one responsible for frustrating justice and allowing guilty murderers to go free.'"

Dershowitz admits that his "look pained me, because he was right…. I've thought of Iris Kones often, and of other victims of my clients who have gone free because of my legal arguments and my investigative work. I think especially of Iris Kones because she is the only homicide victim who was killed by someone I defended who I know for sure was guilty and went free."

Dershowitz adds that he often thinks of Iris Kones because her family is active in Jewish causes and with Harvard University, where he is constantly reminded of his role in freeing her murderers. He concludes with this thought: "Although I don't believe in divine justice, it is true that Sheldon Seigel died at a very young age after an unsuccessful heart transplant. His premature death didn't make me feel any less responsible for the morally unjust, but legally proper, result I helped produce in his case."

6.9 CHAPTER CHECKLIST

Dershowitz's Trial Guidelines

1. A bad lawyer can lose almost any good case.

2. Occasionally, a great lawyer can turn a losing case into a winning case.

3. "Given a choice between having the facts on my side and a good lawyer, I think I'd always take the facts."

4. Lawyers undervalue the importance of the opening statement.

5. By the time that closing arguments occur in the trial, the jury has often already decided the case.

6. Every case you take to trial has to be your most important case. Someone once asked Judge Cardozo, "How come you get all the interesting cases?" He said, "Are you kidding? They're the most boring cases in the world until I get them, and I make them interesting."

7. Criminal defense attorneys assert the presumption of innocence when they should challenge the presumption of regularity (the assumption that everything is routine and leads to conviction).

8. Be aware of the Rules of the Justice Game (set forth in full at the beginning of this chapter).

9. "If you never have a celebrity case during your career, you haven't missed anything."

10. There is a widespread myth that guilty clients will confide their guilt to their trusted lawyers. The truth is guilty clients don't trust lawyers with their dark secrets. Most believe that their lawyer will work harder for innocent defendants than guilty ones.

11. A legally proper trial strategy may result in a murderer being freed, but the emotional consequence for the lawyer is that he knows that an innocent victim will never receive legal justice.

Dershowitz's Cross-examination Insights

1. Many lawyers use the same cross-examination tactic no matter who the witness is.

2. Lawyers mistakenly feel they have to cross-examine every witness.

3. Lawyers do not have a clear strategy as to what they intend to achieve on cross.

4. You need to have a plan and execute it.

5. Many lawyers make damaging testimony on direct even more damaging by having the witness repeat it on cross.

6. To be an effective advocate on cross, you need to work closely with your client to get all of both the helpful and the hurtful information about the witness.

7. Many lawyers have overly long crosses. Dershowitz has seen examinations go on for four or five days when they should have lasted only ten minutes.

8. A long cross can have a benefit if you lull the witness into a sense of complacency and then slip in an important question.

9. Don't make the mistake of having an assistant take notes of the direct examination and then use those notes on cross-examination. You need to create your own outline that focuses on the priorities to bring out on cross.

10. Whether it is opening statement or cross, don't use notes.

11. It is critical to focus on listening to answers during cross-examination.

12. A question is proper if you have a good-faith belief in asking it.

13. An approved tactic, especially when cross-examining a lying witness, is to convey the impression that you have more, less, or different evidence than you actually have.

14. It is hard for anyone to complain of your tactic if Abe Lincoln used it.

CHAPTER SEVEN

⟨⟨⟨

David Bernick

Beating the Evasive Witness

Science was the plaintiffs' Achilles' heel. Bernick's cross-examination of one doctor was so devastating that the man's career as an expert witness abruptly ended.

— *Fortune* (October 30, 1995)

David Bernick is a litigation partner at Paul, Weiss in New York City. He also practiced law at Kirkland & Ellis LLP for over 30 years and was general counsel of Philip Morris International from 2010–2012. He has a long list of acknowledgements, including: 1) recognition by clients and peers as one of "America's Leading Lawyers for Business — General Commercial Litigation and Products Liability," *Chambers USA*; 2) recognition by peers as one of the Best Lawyers in America for Business Litigation, "Best Lawyers in America," *Woodward & White*; 3) recognition by clients and peers as one of the "World's Leading Lawyers for Business," *Chambers Global*; and 4) recipient of the prestigious Learned Hand Award from the Chicago Chapter of the American Jewish Committee.

Bernick has defended corporations in a variety of complex litigation. For example, in 1985, he won a defense verdict for Dow Chemical, when grain workers claimed Dow's chemical fumigant "Agent Green" caused them debilitating neurological damage. In the early 1990's, many states began to file suits, seeking to recover from tobacco companies the medical costs that states had paid for the treatment of tobacco-related diseases. Bernick successfully represented the tobacco company Brown & Williamson in these cases. Some were favorably settled prior to their trials, while others were settled during

> ### CHAPTER HIGHLIGHTS
> - How to win against very bad facts
> - Avoid the mistakes most lawyers make on cross
> - Unique techniques to control the most difficult witnesses

the course of the trials. After the state recovery cases were settled nationally through a master agreement, Bernick won a defense verdict when Ohio iron-workers brought their own lawsuit.

He has also successfully litigated complex cases for Apple in a class action concerning the iPod, for Phillip Morris USA in a class action involving "light" cigarettes, and for Abbott Laboratories in weight-loss drug cases. At the time of this book's publication, Bernick was the lead attorney representing the defense in the AndroGel testosterone replacement gel multi-district litigation, which had more than 1,000 cases.

Despite Bernick's extraordinary success, his road to becoming a lawyer was not a straight one. He went to college with the desire to study physics but soon became interested in philosophy and intellectual history instead. He graduated early from the University of Chicago in 1974 and then pursued a master's degree in philosophy from Yale University. After graduating from Yale, he went to law school with the goal to get "back into the mainstream," when he realized academe was not for him. After graduating in 1978 from the University of Chicago Law School, he soon learned that he was good on his feet in a courtroom and loved working on complex, intellectually stimulating cases. Says Bernick, "All in all, it seemed very unpredictable at the time, but the goodness of the fit says to me now that I could have predicted it myself if I had had a better sense of what made me tick."

In this chapter, Bernick's most recent trial victories — including a landmark trial — will be examined, with particular focus on cross-examination. You will see that many of his trials require him to explain complicated science so the lay people on the jury can understand it. Most lawyers are either afraid to do this or fail miserably in their attempt. After Bernick shares with us his secrets about handling a scientific case and other trial strategies, we will examine in-depth a cross-examination he conducted where he constantly had to control an evasive witness. The tools he used were extremely effective and are ones that you can use with any witness who dodges questions.

In the cross-examination we will analyze below, Bernick was asked by W.R. Grace & Co. to take over its criminal defense six months prior to its trial. Bernick got an acquittal in the largest criminal environmental prosecution brought by the federal government. He proved that the trial skills he developed in the civil arena handling the defense of corporations in complex litigation were equally as effective in a criminal court. Before diving into this fascinating trial, let's look at some of Bernick's trial strategies and then see how he used them to defend Grace.

> *You can't let the plaintiff get ahead of you when he puts on his case. You need to win your case on the cross-examination of the plaintiff's witnesses.*
> —David Bernick

7.1 MOST COMMON MISTAKES LAWYERS MAKE

In regards to the most common mistakes he sees lawyers make, Bernick used as an example the trial of Michael Jackson's doctor, Dr. Conrad Murray, for involuntary manslaughter. A jury had convicted Dr. Murray of involuntary manslaughter when prosecutors proved that Dr. Murray had given Jackson nightly doses of propofol to help him sleep. Propofol is a strong sedative that is only used in hospital settings. But Jackson was not in a hospital and had hired Dr. Murray for $150,000 a month to be his personal physician as he prepared to make a comeback concert tour. Jackson had several ongoing ailments, one of which was insomnia, and Jackson soon died after Dr. Murray administered one of his nightly doses to him at his home. It was the classic mistake of defending the case by trying to create a reasonable doubt instead of presenting a strong case. In doing so, it was a death by a thousand cuts.

Another mistake Bernick sees is that in the civil context, defense attorneys let plaintiff's lawyers become the storytellers and then refuse to tell a story themselves. But a great defense attorney will take the plaintiff's story, accept an enormous amount of it, but then "show how there is a whole storyline that the plaintiff has missed. That's a winning equation." Bernick insists that the defense attorney must be just as much a storyteller as the plaintiff's attorney—and be just as passionate. As he says, "I never tried a case that I didn't believe in, and when I believe in it, there is no question that my audience knows that I believe in it. No question at all."

Bernick added that the plaintiff's attorney has a real advantage: He does not have to win the "science battle" as long as he comes close. If he does, sympathy for the plaintiff will get him to the finish line. Jurors want to give an injured plaintiff *something*. Bernick states that he has to win the science battle and have that become the benchmark that shows the company acted responsibly. "People don't like zinging a company that's tried to do the right thing." Bernick's goal is to tell a story with values such as responsibility, fairness, good intentions, and good people.

> *I am an enormous believer in fighting the plaintiff on his own turf. Defense by denial is a losing game.*
> —David Bernick

7.2 VOIR DIRE STRATEGIES

In jurisdictions such as Texas, there are very few limits as to what an attorney can discuss with jurors during jury selection (voir dire). In such a jurisdiction, Bernick believes voir dire is a powerful tool in relaying a story. He recounts part of the jury selection strategy he used in Texas when representing a company being sued for making allegedly dangerous silicone breast implants. During voir dire, one of the potential jurors asked Bernick why a company would ever make breast implants and why would anyone ever buy them? The man was implying that getting an implant was foolish and maybe even immoral. The man asked, "Why can't the plaintiff just be happy with what God gave her?"

Bernick took advantage of the question to argue his case to the jury panel by framing his story. He did not shy away from the question or get defensive. First, he explained to the potential juror that breast implants were not just used by the woman who wants to be bigger and look more attractive. Bernick asked the man, "What if you were to learn that women who have breast cancer sometimes will not have surgery because they don't want to change their look. But if they know they can get the implant, they will have the surgery. Do you think that's OK?" The man replied, "Oh, well, of course, that makes sense. All the sense."

Bernick continued, "Now, let's talk about a woman who never had cancer, but there are some women when they develop, they develop on one side and they don't develop on the other side. It is something that just happened to them, and there's nothing they can do about it. Do you believe that a woman should have a choice of whether she can make herself whole on both sides?" The man answered, "Yeah, I can see that. That's probably OK."

Bernick then addressed the potential juror's first questions. He knew it would be challenging based on the man's viewpoint. "Let's go to the last person. We sell these implants to all these different kinds of women. I want to ask you about this girl who grows up, and all the other girls are developing, and she just doesn't develop, and she is totally embarrassed. She won't even go to the beach, and she lives with it—lives with it but she gets married. She has kids and she just says all my life I have always wanted to look good in clothes and to go to the beach, and I am going to do this for myself now. Do you think she ought to be able to make that choice?" The man answered, "Yeah, I can understand that."

In sum, Bernick believes voir dire affords this unique ability to interact one-on-one with eventual jurors on core issues in a non-threatening way that reveals to them a bigger picture for the case.

7.3 OPENING STATEMENT

When Bernick first gets a case, he goes through an exercise he calls "Swallowing the Whale." By that he means, learning as much as possible as early as possible, and then thinking about the legal structure. This is critical because, ideally, you don't want the case to go to trial. But if it does go to trial, the underlying question of "Was my client right or wrong?" gives to a lawyer a focus and a real understanding of what actually occurred, which provides a powerful touchstone of relevance. Your storyline that explains why your client was right begins during the opening statement and never stops. As Bernick says, "You tell the story at the beginning, you tell the story on cross, and you tell the story in closing."

Bernick believes opening statements are "totally important, *totally important.*" As a result, a lawyer needs to spend time in discovery to find out just what is important for the storyline, as well as getting the admissions which need to become the pillars of any cross-examination. By doing so, the opening statement tells the jury that a witness will admit a particular fact during the trial because you have already gotten the admission in discovery.

Science is an important tool for the defense because jurors trust it. In their everyday lives, jurors go to doctors and rely on science. Explain scientific evidence in the opening statement, and further develop it with the relevant witnesses. It is a tremendously powerful tool.

Some lawyers challenge Bernick on this point because they believe jurors can't understand science. When asked if he simplifies science for the jury, Bernick's answer might be surprising: "Most of science really isn't that esoteric…. The basic concepts of science are not like rocket science." Bernick concedes that some science, such as the theory of general relativity, is not easy to wrap one's mind around. Luckily, most people don't have to litigate general relativity. But Bernick says that he has litigated cases involving corrosion science, economics, statistics, and nuclear weapons science, just to name a few. The key is to get the jury to understand enough so that they believe what's being said. Then, if on cross-examination the lawyer is able to make believable points about the science, the jury will agree.

Most stories for corporations are hugely scientific stories. In the Grace case, one issue was, what amount of asbestos exposure would cause harm to people? Bernick had to explain to jurors the epidemiological studies that showed whether a certain dose was low enough that it did not cause a problem or vice versa. Bernick states that if the company is a scientific organization, the jury cannot judge it unless the jurors understand the science, which then becomes a part of the company's personality. That personality and the people's conduct provide a fabric for the storyline. But he cautions, science can't be faked: One must know and understand the studies to genuinely and effectively explain them to a jury.

7.4 MAINTAIN CONTROL OF WITNESS ON CROSS-EXAMINATION

One key of cross-examination, says Bernick, is to maintain control of the witness (which he repeats a second time, slowly, for emphasis). It is the focus of this chapter. When a witness doesn't answer a question, Bernick will repeat the question until he gets a response. After several attempts, if the witness still won't answer the question, that is fine with Bernick. He has made his point, and in return, the jury will see the witness's lack of candor. Bernick very rarely asks the judge for help when the witness won't answer. On occasion, he will ask for help if the witness is being repetitively obstructive and impairing his ability to progress through the examination.

Experts can be the worst at not answering questions. As Bernick has learned, an expert can "be evasive till the cows come home." In such a situation, fight for an answer, and if they still are evasive, be ready to switch gears. Bernick will let the witness know that he is content with such evasiveness. He will say something like, "If that's what your answer is, if that is the best you can do, that's fine. Let me ask you this." When an expert realizes that you are going to move on, he or she starts to worry that maybe the evasiveness has gone a little too far, and as a result, the expert will give in on the next question. Bernick's strategy works because evasive witnesses are insecure; otherwise, they would not be evading the question in the first place.

On the other hand, Bernick believes that the most powerful witnesses are the ones who directly answer your questions because they are so confident in their answers. In addition, their demeanor does not change from direct examination to cross-examination.

One of the mistakes Bernick sees lawyers commit on cross-examination is that they ask questions whose answers they don't themselves know. Bernick notes that in a criminal case, such a technique might be necessary because the lawyer did not gain all the facts from civil discovery. However, this becomes a mistake to be avoided in a civil case.

Another problem on cross-examination occurs if the deposition of the witness on the stand has not been taken personally by the lawyer, and the person who actually took the deposition did not focus on the key issues of the case. In that situation, the deposition is useless because it does not contain relevant testimony that may be inconsistent with the trial testimony. Consequently, you must use the primary source documents to cross-examine the witness on inconsistent facts contained in the documents. This circumstance requires a lawyer to have a lot of facts at his or her fingertips to build arguments. The preferable method is to have a deposition that has been taken with focus and contains inconsistent statements that are readily available.

Another key is that a lawyer must have an endpoint that is, as Bernick emphasizes, "pay dirt." He has no patience for attorneys who conduct a cross-examination to elicit subtle answers that can be referred to in closing argument. "That is a joke," he says. "No one is going to sit there and say, 'Oh well, I am going to remember that.'" Nonetheless, many attorneys will tell the jury in closing argument, "Remember when he said this? Many of you may not have thought that was important, but I am going to tell you how it is the key to the case."

> *You have got to win your case on cross. If all you are doing is establishing points for an argument in closing, closing is way too late.*
>
> —David Bernick

If cross-examinations have not put a lawyer ahead in the jury's eyes by the end of the plaintiff's case, that's a problem. Cross-examinations must be successful. Bernick explains further that this does not mean that the jurors necessarily believe you have the stronger argument, but they do sense that this is a horse race. If the defense doesn't succeed on cross-examination, the jury will get conditioned to believe the plaintiff's evidence first.

Finally, a basic strategy on cross-examination is to end on an important point with a witness before a break or at the end of the day. This technique creates drama and makes the testimony more memorable.

7.5 CROSS-EXAMINATION OF EXPERTS

There is a belief among some trial lawyers that a lawyer should never battle an expert on his or her turf. The rationale is that the expert is more knowledgeable about this subject than the lawyer could ever possibly be. As a result, lawyers focus on questions that force the witness to answer without relying on expertise. For example, a lawyer might attack an expert's credibility by pointing out to the jury that the expert has a bias for the side for which he or she is testifying or that the expert has made inconsistent statements within the trial.

However, Bernick is not afraid to cross-examine experts on their own subject matters. He maintains, "It is not like they are geniuses that you can't understand." One key in doing so is preparation. He reads all the articles that will support and have formed the expert's opinions. Bernick becomes familiar with the data. He learns the underlying science—whether there are exposure levels, such as in the Grace case, or autoimmunity and related issues when defending companies from silicone breast implant litigation. As Bernick succinctly puts it, he could never have developed the theory of autoimmunity in a million years, but he can certainly understand it.

7.6 USE CHARTS ON CROSS-EXAMINATION

Bernick believes charts are essential to a successful cross-examination. These are not charts projected via a PowerPoint slide that can't be physically marked. Instead, these charts should be mounted on a board that you put on an easel or displayed by overhead projector, both of which will allow for the marking of the charts. The key is to be able to interact with the charts by physically writing on them.

A chart has many benefits. First, a chart can help organize the examination so the jury can see where an argument is going. If the chart has already been seen during the opening statement or with another witness, that helps as well.

Second, a chart can help control the witness so that he or she can't evade your questions. By pointing at a question on the chart, you can force the witness to answer yes or no. When the witness tries to dodge the question, a lawyer can say, "No, no, stop at *this* one." Then, not another question is asked until the witness answers, and the lawyer writes either "yes" or "no" for that question on the chart.

Third, a chart gives the jury a focal point. It becomes part of the dialogue. It helps to be demonstrative, giving every spoken word added emphasis.

Bernick emphasizes that the "ability to interact with the chart is a very, very powerful tool. It is unbelievable." The jury will become trained to anticipate what will be written when the lawyer takes out a pen and goes to the chart. The jury knows that an important question has just been asked and is anxiously waiting to learn what answer will be written on the chart.

For his closing argument, Bernick will use the charts to remind the jury of the damaging admissions that the witness made on cross-examination.

7.7 CLOSING ARGUMENT STRATEGIES

The first thing Bernick does in his closing argument is stand in front of the jury with his forearms at a 90-degree angle to his body, facing up with the palms of his hands open to the jury. The gesture means, "Here we are," and "I'm not any different from the person you have just seen in the trial."

> *Closing argument is victory lap time.*
> —David Bernick

He then tells the jury, "You know what my story is, and I am going to review it. I am going to tell it to you again, and you are going to know it is absolutely right because you have already heard it, and that's the whole deal."

7.8 DO NOT USE NOTES

Bernick does not use notes for opening statement. In his mind, he pictures what he wants to tell the jury. This picture might be a timeline or the building blocks of his story. Then, he has visual aids that he will show the jury. But the slides are not scripts of a written opening statement. Instead, they are diagrams with a minimal amount of text, emphasizing a picture that communicates his ideas to the jury.

Bernick explains that he does not rely on assistants to create his visual aids. He draws all his slides by hand and then gives them to a graphic designer to replicate. He wants the slides to convey the precise image he has in his mind for the point he is making. It is not a task you can delegate to others.

On cross-examination, Bernick does not use notes. Instead he often uses an overhead projector to show the witness documents that can serve as an outline. In addition, he can zoom in when necessary or highlight documents with a marker when appropriate. He will also have one or two easels with charts mounted on boards to show the witness. On the boards, he will write the witnesses' answers or check off boxes, depending on the design of the chart.

7.9 INSIGHTS FROM THE GRACE TRIAL

Here are some helpful background facts to understand the challenge Bernick faced at the Grace trial. Grace operated a vermiculite mine in Libby—a picturesque small town of 2,600 people in northwestern Montana. Grace bought the Libby mine from Zonolite Co. in 1963 and closed it in 1990. Vermiculite is a mineral that is often used to aerate the soil in gardens and in attic insulation. The vermiculite was contaminated with asbestos, and over the years, mine workers and people living in the community were exposed to the asbestos dust that came from the operation of the mine and the asbestos that was contained in the vermiculite which was used in consumer products.

Estimates vary, but the EPA declared that asbestos exposure at the Libby mine caused over 200 deaths and illnesses in 1,800 workers and residents. The asbestos contained microscopic needle like fibers that could become airborne and lodge in lungs and cause cancer, breathing problems, and death. The illnesses and deaths occurred because in the past, the government standards for asbestos control grossly underestimated the risk of exposure at Libby and at other mines throughout the country. Because of the way exposure to harmful amounts of asbestos affects the body, people became sick or died many years after the exposure. Consequently, the danger to exposure was not known at the time people were first exposed.

As a result of the asbestos problems at the Libby mine, the EPA forced Grace to clean up its mine so that there would be no further risk of asbestos exposure. In civil litigation, Grace challenged in court the extent to which the EPA required it to clean up the mine and lost. In 2008 Grace paid $250 million to pay for Libby's cleanup.

The judge who ruled against Grace was the same judge who would hear the criminal jury trial to be discussed in this chapter which began in February 2009. Six months before Grace was set for the criminal trial, Bernick was called to lead the defense. Bernick describes his challenge: The government had won on the cleanup and "won completely in the court of public opinion, but the final chapter was to make the people of Grace pay [in a criminal trial]."

The government brought the criminal charges against Grace and five of its officers for violating the Clean Air Act. The government alleged that the Defendants obstructed the EPA's investigation of and access to clean up the mine and community from 1999 forward, and were guilty of criminal endangerment through the release of asbestos into the air from 1999 forward, and conspired to violate the Clean Air Act in 1976–77 with additional acts in furtherance of the conspiracy after 1990. Grace faced a $280 million fine, and its officers faced prison time. After a seven-week trial, Grace and all the individual defendants were acquitted (some individuals had their charges dismissed by the court before the verdict).

Listening to Bernick's explanation that Grace had acted reasonably, his reasoning makes perfect sense. Bernick speaks in a measured pace with a down-to-earth conversational tone. He effortlessly uses logic that is easy to follow, emphasizing a key word in each sentence to make his points interesting and memorable.

But when you are sitting in his comfortable conference room overlooking the Manhattan skyline in New York City, it is easy to forget the hostile atmosphere Bernick experienced during this trial, as well as the overwhelming challenge he faced, no matter how brilliant his persuasive skills. The local newspaper in Missoula, Montana, where the trial was held printed these front page headlines, among others: "Death in the Air" and "Civil Suits Have Been in the Courts for Decades." In addition, Libby had been declared a Superfund area (polluted land identified by EPA as needing long-term clean up) by the federal government which had spent 14 years and $400 million trying to remove the deadly asbestos fibers from the town, including a total of 1,890 homes.

In such a hostile atmosphere, where the jurors knew people who had suffered asbestos-related illnesses and death, Bernick points out that many attorneys would mistakenly defend the case on the grounds that the government could not meet its burden of proof. By making nitpicky attacks on the government's proof, the hope would be that jurors who believed Grace was guilty would nonetheless not vote guilty because the government failed to prove its case beyond a reasonable doubt.

> *Most of my cases have been cases that don't sound good to the jury to begin with. But it is like a karate move where all that weight is coming against you. If you are successful in creating the key inflexion points, the case can move in your direction. Then the jurors say, "Hey, it is not right if I come out the way that the newspapers want me to."*
>
> —David Bernick

But Bernick is an enormous believer in the amazing and unappreciated ability of jurors to focus on doing their jobs in a high-profile case. Jurors want to show the public that they have done a good job. Consequently, he rejects the aforementioned approach to challenge whether or not the government had met its burden of proof. He feels the only way to have won the Grace case was to "tell the much broader story of what actually happened, and to step up to all of the problems that were there, and to say, "absolutely…. There are all these problems. Let me tell you why they happened and to be completely forthright about all that, but then to say this case focuses on a different period of time, and let's now talk about why all that happened, which really was long before Grace was even there."

Bernick wanted to explain to the jury that the reason the illnesses in the past occurred was because science was behind the times. As the science regarding the understanding of the harms caused by asbestos exposure improved, so did Grace's response. In short, Grace was relying on the best scientific information available, which is all anyone could expect. Bernick believes jurors "generally will look at science if they understand it enough as being something that you can't fudge about because you will be exposed. If you are scientifically correct, then the jury has a basis for saying, "How can I fight that?"

But Bernick cautions that a corporate defendant cannot fight the prosecution on science alone. If it does, the jurors will still be hesitant to acquit bad defendants. Likewise, if you try to paint the defendants only as good people but have nothing independent to back up your claims, jurors will vote against you. Consequently, Bernick adds, "If you fight the battle of establishing the full story about who did what, and you accept responsibility, then you may not cause the jury to believe at the end of the day that you are free of fault, but they will listen to you then about the science, and so it's within the science that creates the platform for giving the jury something serious to consider."

> *Science ultimately is one of the few predicates or levers that a corporate defendant has.*
> —David Bernick

Bernick adds that just like a civil case where the plaintiff walks into the courtroom with the benefit of the doubt against a corporate defendant, in a criminal prosecution, "the government will always have enormous credibility and authority, but if it oversteps, if it goes too far or it has been less than completely [right] as a government should be, then it flips and then, [the jury asks,] 'Why did the government do that?'"

The key, Bernick insists, is to build from an acceptance of responsibility for what you really can't deny happened in the past, and add transparency and understanding to it. Then, you explain to the jurors that the allegations of recent violations of the Clean Air Act are not justified. Consequently, the question becomes, "Why is the government really doing this?" This question is addressed as the last part of your defense. If you ask that question too early, as Bernick explains, "and you do it without having built all that architecture, it looks like you are just trying to blame it on the government, which a company cannot do."

Bernick points out that the hardest part about this case was not the individual defendants; it was the company. He knew that it would be very difficult for the jury to feel sorry for a corporate defendant. In his closing argument, he argued, "This is a case that's not stronger or weaker with respect to individuals or the company. It is not a good case." He added, "Make your verdict totally clear, and the test of its clarity is acquitting the company. That's the only way your verdict will be clear is if you acquit the company."

Another factor for a corporate defendant is the trial judge. It is critical that in a high-profile case, where there has been bad publicity for the corporate defendant, the judge maintains decorum and integrity during the proceedings. If the judge does his part, then all the lawyer has to do is systematically tell a story. Bernick likes to turn a bad atmosphere into his advantage. For example, when the government is the heavy favorite, one can highlight what the government has not done but should have. There is no excuse for the government not doing its job right. When everything is laid out in front of the government, Bernick argues that the question becomes, "Why *didn't* they do these things?"

7.10 EXCERPTS FROM THE OPENING STATEMENT IN *UNITED STATES V. W.R. GRACE & CO.*

In the prosecution's opening statement, the government told the jury that Grace exposed hundreds of Libby residents to the dangers of asbestos when materials from its mine wound up in local running tracks, baseball fields, and school grounds. The government also declared that Grace hid the risks from the residents and government regulators.

As mentioned earlier, Bernick believes you should set out a storyline in the opening statement, use themes from it on cross-examination, and then remind the jury about that storyline in the closing argument. Since this chapter focuses on Bernick's cross-examination skills, his entire opening statement will not be examined. But it helps to see how he sets forth his themes during the opening statement and later uses them again in his cross-examination:

> My name is David Bernick, and I'm from Chicago, and I represent W.R. Grace. And before I do anything else, I want to make sure that I mind my manners, express the deep appreciation that all of the parties to this case, and all the lawyers in this courtroom, and all the clients, and indeed, everybody who is sitting here has for your willingness and resolve to listen to all the evidence in this very, very important case. We want to thank you in advance. I can tell already, not much time has passed, but you are forward in your chairs, and you are focused, and you are taking notes, and that's absolutely terrific, that's what the case is about. I hope you'll feel that same degree of interest and attention as the days wind on and as this case winds on, but I'm very, very confident that you will.

Bernick immediately builds a bond with the jury by sincerely thanking them for their service and promising the jury that he is "very confident" that they will find this to be a very interesting trial. That is just what the jurors want to hear. Bernick appreciates their time, and he is going to make it exciting.

Next, he will discuss the natural emotions of the jurors, who know that people have suffered from asbestos exposure, but he points out that a different case is before the jury:

> This is not a case that's being prosecuted by any individuals who have been injured as a result of conduct at the Libby mine, nor is it being conducted on their behalf. This is not a case that's being brought by the Town of Libby, nor is it being conducted on the behalf of people at the Town of Libby. It is purely and simply a case brought by the government against Grace and, indeed, it focuses on the relationship between the government and Grace.
>
> So these [claims] all have to do with the relationship between Grace and the government. And, of course, relationship is a two-way street, so the focus not only is on Grace, but it's also on the government. The government's proceeding that they say was obstructed, the government's knowledge as to which they say there was a conspiracy to defraud.

Throughout his opening, Bernick would remind the jury, "Keep your eye on the ball." He urged the jury to focus on what the government knew about asbestos exposure and what the government was alleging that Grace did that was criminally wrong. He used PowerPoint slides to show that Grace did not hide anything from the government. He also candidly told the jury that Grace was not perfect.

> Circumstances, though, were not rosy. I've showed you a little bit ago about how the air exposure measurements came down. I do not want to leave you with the impression that, oh, gee, Grace just did a great job, all is well. That's not the case. There were problems. There continued to be problems at Libby. Progress was made. It was made too slowly. We're not going to argue that proposition here. It's not part of the case, but I don't mean to wrap Grace in a cloak of having done a great job in the 1960s. That is not our position. That is not a fact. There were continuing problems. But the broader problem that was out there, it wasn't confined to Libby, was that the government was finding out, because there was published science that the old standards that had been used to set what was OK were wrong, grossly wrong. They didn't protect workers. And this became known through scientific studies. And as a consequence, as you get into the early 1970s, there were a whole series of new organizations, new regulatory organizations that were created by the federal government.

Bernick concedes that mistakes were made and builds his credibility with the jury by being honest.

Throughout his opening, Bernick used PowerPoint slides to visually communicate his ideas to the jury. The slides were clean, crisp, and not overloaded with text. They reassured the jury that what Bernick was saying made sense.

Bernick concluded with a series of slides that showed the current illnesses were caused by exposure long before the conduct the government alleged was criminal.

> Could we shift to the Libby community disease slide? I don't know where that is. Here we go. These very specific claims, charges, are what the case is about. But at the end of the day, what I think the government's remarks this morning in comments in opening statement illustrates, is this case... is never taken away too far from that dark pall that is the disease at Libby. And that's something, again, you are going to have to work very, very hard to decide, is that really relevant and if so, in what respect? But you've heard that the government is going to offer evidence that falls right into that category. It's going to offer evidence that says that the people of the Libby community are now getting sick with asbestos-related disease at an alarming rate. And even this week, you are going to hear testimony from witnesses who will talk about the fact that they have lived in Libby and that they are getting sick. Witness after witness after witness. And the effect of that, of seeing all those witnesses line up, will obviously be to invoke the pall. Obviously to invoke the question of people getting hurt.
>
> Will it really be relevant to any of these different theories, any of these different charges? You will have to decide that. But you are going to hear about it.... We don't believe it's relevant, but we also do not believe that it's true. I want to take you through a couple concepts to leave in your mind as you think about the evidence that you hear from the stand, because science has a way of clarifying and de-emotionalizing these very important claims that are being made. They cannot be decided on the basis of emotion. They have to be decided on the basis of science. And you will have the opportunity to see this science, and what you will see, you will see that there is this concept called "latency." ...

> *Science has a way of clarifying and de-emotionalizing these very important claims that are being made. They cannot be decided on the basis of emotion. They have to be decided on the basis of science.*
>
> —David Bernick, opening statement.

Bernick ends with his strongest point. The science is on his side, not the government's. As he instructed in the trial strategies section presented earlier, science is one of the only levers a corporate defendant has. He plays his card well. He knows that in a high-profile case, jurors want to be seen as doing a thorough investigation and coming to the right decision. If he can prove that science is on his side, he will win.

7.11 CROSS-EXAMINATION OF ROBERT LOCKE

Having glimpsed Bernick's skills from his opening statement, let's focus now on his cross-examination skills. The following is an analysis of the turning point in the trial: Bernick's cross-examination of the prosecution's star witness, Robert Locke. Locke began working for Grace in 1974 and finished his career there as a global vice president and chief technical officer. During his tenure at Grace, he had overseen the company's safety and environmental policies.

He had vast knowledge of Grace's operations. In 1998, he left Grace and filed a lawsuit against Grace for wrongful termination because he claimed that his job had been restructured and that he had been forced out. His role on direct examination was to take the jury behind the company's walls and relive what happened there. For example, he testified on direct examination that executives at Grace had known of the asbestos dangers and had covered them up.

His direct testimony revealed that he was in management, was very knowledgeable about claims that Grace had made inadequate responses to asbestos concerns, and he had knowledge of very specific events. He also claimed that he was not anxious to testify, he had no axe to grind with Grace, was doing the right thing, and had not been promised anything from the government in exchange for his testimony.

As you read the following transcript, notice how clearly Bernick establishes two large themes on cross-examination. The first theme was that Locke was not the neutral witness portrayed on direct examination but a man with a deep grudge against Grace who began plotting his revenge for his alleged wrongful termination as soon as he left Grace.

Bernick's second theme was to show that Locke was a well-educated businessman who had to admit certain facts that proved Grace's innocence. Those themes became even stronger when Locke does not answer simple questions and becomes evasive. The more evasive Locke becomes, the more his claims to be a neutral fact witness are undercut and his bias against Grace shows through. Here are just a few of the points you will see Bernick make below:

1. Locke was upset when he left Grace.

2. Locke took documents from Grace without permission that were unrelated to his termination which suggest he wanted revenge against Grace for his termination.

3. Locke at first denies he ever tried to talk to Grace's general counsel about his wrongful termination lawsuit, but then admits that he did.

4. Locke denies threatening Grace's general counsel to testify against Grace in ongoing civil lawsuits against Grace for asbestos illnesses if Grace does not settle his wrongful termination lawsuit. Locke's claim is contradicted by the general counsel's contemporaneous notes.

5. Despite a court order requiring the production of calendars, thirty days before trial, Locke destroyed his personal calendars from 1998–1999 that

related to his termination, but he kept all of his other calendars which dated back to 1976.

6. Locke never went to the government with documents he took from Grace that allegedly showed criminal conduct, which suggests there was no criminal conduct.

7. When the government approached Locke about Grace's actions, Locke at first denies that the prosecutor told Locke and the investigators to have "some fun" with the documents Locke took from Grace, but then he admits the conversation took place when Bernick confronts him with Locke's sworn testimony.

8. Locke denies he is testifying in support of the government's case against Grace despite appearances to the contrary.

9. Locke admits that asbestos was widely used in the mid 1970s and the government was having problems determining how to regulate it. This is inconsistent with Locke's and the government's claim that Grace violated clearly established government guidelines set by the government.

10. Locke denies volunteering to the government that he made disparaging remarks about valued Grace employees that even he respected and then admits that he did volunteer the information.

11. Locke becomes evasive when Bernick challenges Locke's testimony given during direct examination that despite his efforts, others at Grace delayed safety studies. Locke then admits that he was the cause of the delay because he was "kicking up his heels."

In addition to the concessions Bernick gets from Locke, pay close attention to the techniques Bernick uses to force Locke to answer his questions when Locke is evasive. The techniques are explained after each excerpt and are summarized at the end of this section. It is a unique opportunity to see a great lawyer battle a very smart witness and win. The skills Bernick uses are successful ones—but rarely seen—that you can use in your next trial.

Locke's lawsuit is unrelated to government's claims

Q1. Good morning, Mr. Locke. My name is David Bernick, and I represent Grace. I don't think we've met before, have we?
A.   No, sir, we haven't. Good day, how are you?

Q2. Good morning, ladies and gentlemen. I'm sorry?
A.   I say good day, how are you?

Q3. I'm fine. All right. I want to begin where you just left off in your examination with [**the prosecutor**] *for a moment and talk about the claim that you have. I'm not going to get into the substance of what the claim is, maybe others will. I want to ask* *you some questions, first of all, about what **the claim that you have against Grace personally is not**. [Bernick highlights for jury his first theme.]*

*Is it true, Mr. Locke, that this is a claim that you have, your personal claim, that is **not a claim** about what happened in 1976 or 1977 or 1978, while you were working at Grace? Isn't that true?*

A. I believe it's a wrongful termination claim.

*Q4. OK. Just bear with me. Just be clear. Again, I'm not going to get into the substance of what the claim is, I'm trying to get us reading off the same page in terms of what relationship it has or does not have to the offense that you've testified about at some length over the last two days. And so to be clear, your claim, your personal claim is **not a claim** that has to do with what happened in 1976 or 1977 or 1978, true or not?*

A. I believe that's essentially true.

*Q5. Thank you. Is it also true that this **is a claim that doesn't have to do with** the vermiculite business, true or not?*

A. That's correct.

*Q6. Is it true that this claim **doesn't have anything to do with** that hamster study; is that true?*

A. Maybe there's some connection, but I can't think of what it is.

*Q7. You don't have to speculate, just tell me whether it's true or not. That's the way that this goes. So you showed some decision trees. Your claim **doesn't have anything to do with** any kind of decision trees, right?*

A. I don't believe so.

Bernick starts his cross-examination with a strong theme. He makes it clear to the witness and jury what line of questioning he is going to pursue: "I want to ask you some questions, first of all, about what the claim that you have against Grace personally is not [about]." Notice how there is no warm-up with the witness. The witness has been testifying for two days. The jury is ready to see if Locke will be challenged, and Bernick does not disappoint.

With only the first few questions, Bernick gets important facts that support his first theme. He establishes that Locke's personal lawsuit against Grace has nothing to do with 1) what happened between 1976 to 1978, 2) the vermiculite business, 3) the hamster study, or 4) decision trees. This line of questions sets up his next set of questions that follow below. Bernick will make the point that in contrast to his claim on direct to being a neutral witness without a grudge, Locke took documents related to what happened in 1976–78 and various scientific studies that showed that he wanted to use those documents as revenge against Grace for his alleged wrongful termination.

As you will see throughout the cross, Bernick does not ask questions unless he can force the witness to answer the way he wants. He can do this because he is a master of the facts in this case and can use the witness' deposition testimony or documents to prove the witness wrong if he doesn't answer correctly.

> *Just tell me whether it's true or not. That's the way that this goes.*
> —David Bernick reminds witness who is in control.

Bernick also teaches us the importance of controlling the witness. In the third question (Q3), the witness does not answer the question. Bernick immediately signals to the witness and the jury that he is in control of the examination, and if the witness fails to answer a simple question, he is going to remind the witness and the jury of the evasive answer.

Without permission, Locke selects documents unrelated to his lawsuit

Q. Now...I guess it's 1998, when you were in the process of leaving W.R. Grace, you've told us that you took the time to go through some old document files. Do you recall **that**?
A. Yes, I did.

Q. And when you went through those old document files, is it true that you made a **selection of certain documents** to take with you? [**Bernick's second topic**]
A. That is correct.

Q. And is it true that when you made that **selection** and you took those documents with you, you knew that you were going to be leaving Grace at that time, correct?
A. Oh, yeah, I was on my way out.

Q. And you **were a very unhappy person** when it came to Grace, correct?
A. I—I—I was not a happy camper.

Q. And when you decided to make that **selection**, the **selection** that you made back in 1998, when you were leaving the company, was a selection that didn't have to do with your termination, it was a **selection** that had to do with 1976, with the vermiculite business, with the hamster study and with decision trees, correct?
A. I was very concerned about my liability—

Q. I just asked you whether the **selection** that you made was a **selection** that wasn't related to your termination; rather, it was related to the subjects that I've just listed here. Is that true?
A. I appreciate that you're attempting to get a flat yes and no answer.

Q. Yes, that is most desirable. This is cross-examination.
A. Yeah.

Q. **And if you can respond to the question factually, yes or no, that will greatly expedite the circumstance. I will try to ask you questions that ask for a yes or a no. I ask you the question again.** Isn't it true that when you made your **selection** of documents in 1998, when you were an unhappy person leaving Grace, the documents that you **selected** did not relate to your termination; rather, they related to the subjects that I've listed here, 1976, the vermiculite business, the hamster study, and decision trees, true or not?
A. I'm afraid I can't answer that question without delivering an explanation with it, sir. I'm sorry.

[The witness has evaded answering a simple question, but Bernick has made his point to the jury. He will move on and hammer the witness the next time he tries to dodge a question.]

Q. *All right. That's fine. We'll go on to another question. Isn't it true that when you left in 1998,* **you did not get permission** *from your boss to take those documents with you?*
A. I was told by the person who—

Q. **Did you get permission** *from your boss or not, Mr. Locke?*
A. I was not required to obtain permission.

Bernick: I move to strike, Your Honor. Could we have an instruction for the witness to be responsive to the questions that are being asked?

Court: Mr. Locke, I think you're going to have to respond to the question that is put to you. If you can't answer them, say, I can't answer it.
   You may proceed.

Bernick: Thank you.

Q. *(By Bernick) Is it true* **you did not obtain permission** *from your boss to take those documents with you?*
A. I can't answer that question without giving a misimpression.

Q. *OK. That's fine. You don't have to give any misimpressions. Can you answer the question, did you or did you not get permission from your boss to take those documents with you? Asks for a very simple fact.* **Did you get that permission or not?**
A. No, I didn't.

By using clear themes and concise questioning that calls for simple "yes" or "no" answers, Bernick immediately turns the tables on the witness after two days of direct examination. He establishes the following: 1) Locke took documents from Grace without permission that related to studies done in 1976–78 that had nothing to do with his alleged wrongful termination, and 3) he was not happy with Grace. Bernick implies through his questioning that it might be understandable for Locke to take documents related to his alleged wrongful termination, but the fact that he took unrelated documents without permission shows a bias to twist the information in those documents in order to win concessions from Grace in his personal lawsuit.

   More important, Bernick establishes control of the witness by repeating simple questions when the witness tries to dodge them. The court's intervention and instruction to the witness intimidates the witness and shows the jury that the judge believes the witness is not forthcoming. When you are trying to attack a witness's credibility as Bernick is, you could not hope for anything more in the first few minutes of cross.

> **Practice Tip**
> On cross, maintain control by being patient and persistent. Bernick repeats the same question, "Did you get that permission or not?" four times until he gets the witness to answer.

Denies meeting with Grace's general counsel

Q. *Let's talk about what you did with those documents.* [**Bernick introduces another topic for the jury.**] *You had the documents in your possession and during the period of time that followed your decision to leave, during that period of time, you retained an attorney and you filed a lawsuit against W.R. Grace, correct?*
A. That's correct.

Q. *And isn't it true that after you filed the lawsuit against W.R. Grace, you decided to make a call on folks at Grace to talk about your lawsuit?*
A. That's such a general question. **I don't know.**

Q. *It is a general question. After you filed the lawsuit, did you make a call on people at Grace to talk about your lawsuit?* [**Bernick doesn't give an inch. He simply repeats the question and makes it more forceful by repeating the witness' disingenuous answer that he cannot answer because it is such a "general question."**]
A. I may have. I don't know exactly where.

Q. *Isn't it a fact, Mr. Locke, that actually, your lawyer gave written permission for you to go down to Boca Raton, Florida, and talk about your lawsuit with the general counsel of Grace, David Siegel?*
A. Oh, I couldn't think of his name. Yes, yes. [**Later in the cross, Locke will admit that he has known David Seigel for years.**]

Q. *So you did remember the fact that you talked with somebody, correct?*
A. Well, you know, I talked with Mike Peergrossi (phonetic) after I left. I mean, I talked with people after I left. [**Locke now admits he spoke with people when moments earlier he said, "I don't know."**]

Q. *So how many people did you talk with about your lawsuit?*
A. About the lawsuit?

Q. *At Grace. That's my question that I asked you about, Mr. Locke.*
A. OK. That would only have been Dave can, can —

Q. *Let me finish the question so we can be completely clear.*
A. Yeah, I'm trying to.

Q. *How many people at Grace did you discuss your lawsuit with after you left?*
A. How many people at Grace did I discuss it with? I guess only the lawyer at corporate, **Dave Siegel**. I can't think of anyone else right now.

Q. *So this is not some happenstance, casual conversation. You traveled all the way down to Boca Raton, Florida, to talk with the general counsel of Grace about your lawsuit, true or not?*
A. Yes, I did.

Bernick shows the jury that Locke is evasive in his answer when he claims at first that he did not talk to anyone at Grace about his lawsuit, when the truth is that he traveled to Florida to meet with the head lawyer for the company.

Q. *And you know that the general counsel is the number one lawyer at the company, correct?*

A. I've known Dave Siegel for years and I don't know — I don't recollect right now and I don't know that I knew at the time exactly what his position was on the legal staff at W.R. Grace.

Locke's answer is disingenuous. If he had known Siegel for years, he would certainly know what job he had and that the general counsel for the company is the head of the legal department.

Locke destroys calendars before trial begins

Q. *Well, do you remember, one way or another, if it was the back end of 1999? Not asking you to speculate. You testified for two days about all kinds of dates and times. Just asking you whether it squares with your recollection that you met with him [David Siegel] in December 1999?*

A. I don't know that it was December '99.

Q. *We've asked, and I believe the Court has issued an order, that asks for your calendars for 1999, 1998. You have all these little calendars in your cigar boxes. Do you have a calendar for 1998, and 1999, and 2000?*

A. No, I don't.

Q. *You don't have those anymore?*

A. No, I don't.

Q. *So you kept all the old calendars that go way, way back [30 years], but you haven't kept any of the new calendars?*

A. Again, in order to answer your question, I'm going to have to give an explanation.

Q. *Well, I'll put my question real simply.* [**Bernick has trained the witness from his prior repetition of questions that he doesn't even need to repeat this one before the witness answers.**]

A. I don't have them.

Q. *You don't have them. When did you last have them?*

A. Back around Christmas.

Q. *Of when?*

A. No, maybe even January of this year, January of 2009. I was cleaning them out.

Q. *So January of 2009, that's about 30 days before this trial…. And then at some point after January, or from that point forward to this trial, I take it that you disposed of all the other calendars other than the ones the Department of Justice had, correct?*

A. That's correct. I'd be able — I'd be glad to explain why, but — I don't know that that's required as an answer to your question.

Q. *I'm just asking whether you got rid of them?*

A. Yes, I did.

Q. *Didn't you understand that your calendars relating to 1998 and 1999 would be relevant to the litigation that you've got pending against Grace?*

A. No, I guess not….

Q. *So if someone were to try to refresh your recollection about your personal claim against Grace, like your recollection has been refreshed here over these days by the calendars back in the late '70s and early '80s, no one would be able to refresh your recollection what happened in 1998 or 1999 from your calendars because you threw them out, right?*

A. You're implying a causal relationship.

Q. *I'm not implying anything. I'm asking you for a fact.* [**Bernick does not argue with witness. He simply repeats his question.**] *The fact is that if someone wanted to refresh your recollection of what actually happened when you took those documents, and what you did with them, in 1998 and 1999, and what you did between the time of your leaving and the time of this trial here, nobody would be able to refresh your recollection because the calendars are not available, true or not?*

A. The answer will be that I couldn't use the calendars to refresh my recollection.

Q. *Now, did you tell the Department of Justice that you were throwing all those calendars out?*

A. No, I didn't.

Q. *Who did you tell that you were throwing them out?*

A. Nobody.

Q. *Tell your—*

A. Oh, nobody except my wife.

Q. *What about your personal attorney? Did you let him know that you were throwing out the evidence?*

A. Throwing out the evidence?

Q. *Sure, the evidence of what happened in 1998 and 1999 in connection with your resignation.*

A. This — this — I considered this stuff to be trash that I — and no longer had any reason to retain…. **I was just cleaning out, that's all.**

Q. *Just cleaning out, that's all?* [**Bernick repeats the disingenuous answer to highlight it for the jury.**]

A. Yeah. Why was I keeping a box full of all my cancelled checks from 1958? I mean, I just got rid of everything.

Q. *For the same reason that you had kept them for each and every year since 1958, all the way before, 30 days before this trial took place, you kept them every single year, correct?*

A. **It's just a habit.**

Q. *Just a habit.* [**Bernick repeats another disingenuous answer.**]

A. You're making some kind of big deal out of this.

Q. *I'm not making a big deal out of anything. I'm just asking you factual questions, Mr. Locke. Let's go back to the meeting with Mr. Siegel....*

The trial took place in March 2009, and Locke has destroyed calendars just a month before trial. Notice how Bernick shows the jury that Locke kept the ones related to events from 30 years ago but has selectively destroyed ones helpful to the defense regarding his claimed wrongful termination. Moreover, Bernick highlights not only that the calendars were destroyed but that Locke did not tell the Department of Justice or his personal attorney about it. Locke knew the calendars were important because he relied on the older ones during his direct examination to refresh his memory about events at Grace. It could not have been lost on the jury why Locke would destroy only a very small selection of calendars out of all the ones he had kept for decades.

Locke denies and then admits he met with Grace's general counsel

Q. *And when you went down to talk with Mr. Siegel and you were interested in getting a settlement, a monetary settlement for your case, you told Mr. Siegel that you had been working with one of the Boston newspapers and with a plaintiffs' law firm on actions against Grace involving the asbestos content of Zonolite Attic Fill insulation and other products, didn't you tell that to Mr. Siegel?*

A. I certainly didn't say things like that, but that may be what Dave—

Q. *Didn't ask you to speculate. I'm asking you whether you told Mr. Siegel that you had been working with a plaintiffs' law firm on litigation against Grace involving the vermiculite business. Did you tell him that—*

A. No.

Q. *—or not?*

A. Yeah, please let me try to answer your question.

Q. *I want to know, Mr. Locke, whether you told him those words?*

A. I did not tell him—I did not tell him those words. That would sound like a threat. I was not mentioning a threat, I was just telling him I didn't want to be involved in this crap and yet I didn't want to sign the separation and release agreement. We just settled this darn thing.

Q. *Do you remember telling him that you had to decide whether you would approach your testimony as friend or foe to Grace? Did you tell Mr. Siegel that?*
A. I don't believe I would have.

Q. *Just asking you whether you did or not.*
A. No, no. Gee whiz.

Q. *Gee whiz. The answer is, "No, I didn't tell him that." Is that what you're saying?*
A. I wouldn't have said something like that. That sounds like—

Q. *I didn't ask you what you would have said. This is very simple. I have a conversation, I have a conversation that Mr. Siegel has written down words about. He will be here to testify about it, and the jury will then be able to hear it, if it is permitted and it happens.*
A. No.

Q. *I'm saying, are you saying you did not tell Mr. Siegel that you had to decide whether you were going to be friend or foe? Are you denying that?*
A. I don't—no, I don't remember saying anything like that.

Practice Tip

Whenever the witness answers "may," "could have," or "guesses," Bernick fires back, "I did not ask you to speculate." Bernick's response forces the witness to directly answer the question.

The fact that Locke denies the conversation does not matter. Siegel will testify later in the trial about what Locke said and will have contemporaneous notes to corroborate that Locke said he had to decide whether he would be friend or foe. The lesson is that Bernick has boxed the witness in to a denial that can be contradicted by another witness.

Never went to government with revealing documents

Q. *In 1999 and in 2000, government was sitting there, you never gave the government those documents, correct?*
A. Well, no, I was—

Q. *Did you give the government the documents or not?*
A. No, I didn't.

Q. *Did you call the government to say that you had important documents that related to potential criminal conduct and that they ought to be aware of them? Did you make that telephone call?*
A. No, I didn't.

Q. *2001?*
A. No, I did not.

Q. *2002?*
A. No, I did not.

Q. *Well, you may find it uninteresting, Mr. Locke, but the fact is you sat there, with all these documents that you say you thought bore upon criminal conduct, and you never once picked up the telephone to alert any of the authorities, correct?*
A. That is correct.

Q. *But the government ultimately decided to come to you, right?*
A. That's correct.

Q. *And I think you described how the black Crown Victoria pulled up.*
A. I may have used those words, yes.

Q. *Well, you just used those words under oath before the jury two days ago. You don't remember that?*
A. OK. All right. Fine, yes.

Q. *It was news to me.*
A. I remember the day vividly.

Q. *OK. And you remember the car pulls up, and the feds are there, and you become very concerned about what's going to unfold, correct?*
A. They sure got my attention, yes.

Q. *Sure got your attention. And you decided to conduct an initial interview with the government, right, for two or three hours that night?*
A. I talked with them—well, I think it was in the afternoon. I think I answered their questions for, I don't know, an hour, hour and a half, or something....

Q. *And not only did you give the interview, but you also turned over to the government all these documents that you had in your basement, right?*
A. Ah, that was later.

Q. *That was later. Did they subpoena those documents or did you voluntarily produce all those documents?*
A. I voluntarily produced them.

Q. *And then you all sat around in a conference room and went through all those documents and, boy, you folks sat down and you just had some fun, right?* **You just had some fun with those documents, right?**
A. **I wouldn't characterize that as fun.** This was a—

Q. *Isn't that exactly what the prosecutor told you? He said, I'm going to be gone for an hour. But if I'm not back, you folks should just continue on, talking about you and Mr. Cassidy. "Kevin, you can take this seat and have fun with these documents." Wasn't that said to you during the course of that interview?*
A. I don't remember it.

Q. *I'm going to show you page 6938.141. Look at the top of the page. It says, "I'm going to be gone an hour. But if I'm not back, you folks should just continue on. Kevin, you can take this seat and have fun with these documents." Does that refresh your recollection of the conversation that you had?*
A. **Ah, not a great deal. This is page 141 of something. What is it?**

Q. *It is the transcript of your sworn testimony in the interview that was conducted here in Missoula. That's what it is.*
A. OK. In December of?

Q. *December of 2004.*
A. Of 2004. OK.

Q. *And you don't remember sitting around and the prosecutor talking about having fun with the documents?*
A. I don't remember him talking about having fun, no. I think he was just being jocular.

Q. *Just being jocular. Just chose to say that.*

Bernick reveals to the jury Locke's grudge toward Grace when he gets Locke to admit that he was told to have "fun" with certain Grace documents, but it was not an easy admission to get which further confirmed Locke's grudge and his desire to hide it. As the transcript reveals, Locke at first denies that he was ever told to have "fun" with the documents by the government. When shown a transcript of his prior sworn statement where he specifically mentions it, he at first says, "Ah, not a great deal. This is page 141 of something." He tries to discount the contradiction contained in the prior sworn statement. Bernick doesn't stand for it. He punches back, "It is the transcript of your sworn testimony…That's what it is."

Judge scolds Locke for not answering

Bernick introduces another theme for the jury: Locke was a central advocate for the government in its criminal prosecution against Grace. Locke is smart (has a Harvard MBA), had inside information, and held a high management position at Grace. When asked about his role, Locke dodges several questions and answers that all he was doing was trying to "stand up and do what was right." Let's pick up the examination where Locke continues to evade the questions.

Q. *I didn't ask you that. I said you voluntarily turned over—did you turn over the evidence because you thought it was just the right thing or did you turn over evidence because you were an un-indicted co-conspirator at the time?*
A. I didn't know I was an un-indicted co-conspirator. I was trying to do the right thing.

Q. *Trying to do the right thing. The Crown Vic pulls up, and you cooperate, and you voluntarily produce evidence, and you don't think that somehow you're not fostering a prosecution against W.R. Grace? You are, aren't you?*
A. This is a criminal investigation, and they're requesting—

Q. *It's a criminal investigation, Mr. Locke, where you are here to support the government in its case against W.R. Grace, correct?*
A. I'm doing what is—

Q. Mr. Locke, please answer the question.

Prosecutor: Your Honor, he's interrupting; that's the third time.

Mr. Bernick: I'd like not to —

The Court: Now, there's three of you talking. But if you'll all listen to what I have to say, **the question can be answered yes or no. He's not answering the questions. Please, answer the question.**

The witness: OK, sir.

The Court: As I said before, if you can't answer them, say, "I cannot answer that question."

The witness: OK. Thank you.

Mr. Bernick: Yes, I'll wind up very quickly, because I know we're approaching noon, Your Honor.

Q. Mr. Locke, the fact of the matter is you are testifying on behalf, in support of the government's case against your former employer, true or not?
A. Not true.

Q. Not true. And at the same time you're prosecuting your own personal litigation that you feel very, very strongly against W.R. Grace, true or not?
A. Not true.

Bernick asks the witness if he is fostering a prosecution against Grace. The witness does not answer yes or no. Instead, he tries to provide an explanation. Bernick hits gold when the judge overrules the prosecutor who is trying to protect the witness with his objection. The judge sympathizes with Bernick and sternly tells the witness, "Please, answer the question." Now Bernick has gotten the jury to see that the judge believes the witness is being evasive. That is the definition of a devastating cross.

Locke admits asbestos was widely used in 1970s

Most attorneys forget to get helpful information from a witness that the witness will readily agree to give. Watch how Bernick establishes the wide use of asbestos in the 1970s to show that Grace was not doing anything unusual compared to other businesses.

Q. Be fair to say, were you knowledgeable about the fact that in the early 1970s at that point in time, asbestos had been used commercially literally for decades in the United States?
A. Oh, yes, yes.

Q. And, in fact, as of the 1970s, we wouldn't think about it today, but if you heard this figure—did you hear the figure that something like a million tons of asbestos were used in the manufacturing processing in the United States annually?
A. A million tons?

Q. *A million tons a year.*
A. I guess I could believe that.

Q. *Were you familiar with the fact that asbestos appeared, that is was used, in literally hundreds of commercial products and processes in the early 1970s when you became involved?*
A. Depending on how you count products; probably, yes.

Q. *They were in brake linings, correct?*
A. Uh-huh.

Q. *You have to respond orally for the court reporter.*
A. Oh, I'm sorry. Yeah, I know it was used in brake linings. Friction materials.

Q. *Floor tiles?*
A. Sure.

Q. *Insulation?*
A. Yes.

Q. *Roofing?*
A. Yes.

Q. *Gaskets?*
A. Yes.

Q. *Literally hundreds, if not thousands, of products. Correct?*
A. Yes.

> **Practice Tip**
> Don't forget to get helpful information from the witness on cross-examination that he or she will readily agree to give.

Q. *The problem of regulating asbestos was a big problem throughout the United States in the early 1970s, correct?*
A. I only knew about it from my point of view.

Q. *Well, even from your own point of view, the regulations—let's just talk about the regulations. There were a whole series of regulations that related to exposure. The effort of the Government was to try to reduce exposures to the workplace, right?*
A. Yeah, that would be OSHA.

Locke relates unfavorable opinion of good coworkers to prosecution

In Locke's interview with the government, he volunteered some unflattering opinions about his coworkers that showed a bias against them. His bias was highlighted on cross-examination when he at first refused to admit he ever had made the embarrassing statements. During this examination, the term tremolite is used. Tremolite is a form of asbestos that was associated with the mining of vermiculite at Grace's mine in Libby.

Q. *Now, I notice in the course of looking through your interview with the government that you have formed some pretty distinctive views with respect to people* [at Grace] *you've had contact with on tremolite.*
A. Yes.

Q. *Some of them, colorful views. Let's talk about Dr. Yang. You had pretty significant views with respect to Dr. Yang, didn't you?*
A. Yes....

Q. *Did you think that she was fair and truthful, or were you concerned that she didn't tend to tell the whole truth?*
A. Truthful, fair. Sometimes I think that she was not always as direct as she could have been under the circumstances.... [**Bernick gets the witness to admit that Yang was at least fair and truthful, but the witness maintains that she was not direct.**]

Q. *Isn't it true that you actually **volunteered** to the government during the course of your interview, just as an aside, that when you took over research as one of your responsibilities, you rapidly checked the payroll records to see whether certain people were still working there, and you were very happy to see that Julie Yang did not. Isn't that what you told the government?*
A. I think that's correct.

Q. *Pretty harsh judgment about Dr. Yang, right?*
A. Well, **it was a very private judgment.**

Q. ***It wasn't a private judgment.*** *You shared it under oath with the government.*
A. **I was being interrogated on the record, and I was asked a question.**

Q. ***No, no, you volunteered this.***
A. I didn't tell this to the world.

Q. *No, you volunteered that. Let's just take a look at 6938.23. This is when you were having fun with the documents, and you happened to be...going through the hamster study.... And then you just actually go on and, just on your own, you do kind of a drive-by on Dr. Yang.* **You say, "Just as an aside, many years later, I took over research as one of my responsibilities, and I rapidly checked the payroll records to see whether certain people still worked there, and I was very happy to see that Julie Yang did not."** *You weren't asked that. You just volunteered it, right?*
A. **I guess you are right.**

By listening intently to the answers, Bernick reveals to the jury the times when the witness has tried to evade questions and, as a result, continues to undercut the witness. While most lawyers have their heads buried in their notes thinking of the next question to ask while the witness is answering the previous question, Bernick focuses intently on each answer and how he can follow up on it.

> **Practice Tip**
>
> When the witness does not answer the question, cut him off in mid-sentence and repeat the question.

Here, Bernick gets the witness to admit that he was not being interrogated as he first states but instead, volunteered his opinion.

Bernick next turns his attention to Locke's opinion of Dr. Dement.

Q. Now, Dr. Dement, who was the NIOSH [National Institute of Safety and Health] researcher who first became involved in the epidemiological study—the proposed epidemiological study of the Grace miners. You remember Dr. Dement, right?
A. Yes, I do.

*Q. And you told the Government that as far as you were concerned, **he was a miserable little guy.***
A. Well, that's a pretty harsh assessment but — [**Like so many times before, the witness does not answer the question. Bernick cuts him off and forces him to answer.**]

Q. Well, that's the assessment you gave.
A. —if you say I said that, I said that.

Q. Sorry?
A. That's a harsh assessment, to be gratuitous, but if you say I said that, I'm sure I did.

Q. Are you denying that you said that?
A. No, I'm not denying that.

Q. You told the government that all on your own without any kind of prompting, right?
A. OK, yes. OK, yes.

Q. Well, I don't want you to say yes just to—I do want you to say yes or no. I would rather have you say yes. But I want to make sure it is a fact that that is the opinion that you expressed, a fact that that is the opinion that you expressed to the government in this case. Right?
A. Yes.

Bernick never lets the witness waffle. "OK, yes" is not the absolute answer Bernick wants. He can force the witness to answer definitively because he has the prior sworn statement where the witness made the unequivocal assessment of Dr. Dement.

Locke admits that he is the reason that study was delayed

Earlier in the cross-examination (not shown here), Bernick forced Locke to admit that Elwood Wood, nicknamed "The Chipper," was a good analyst at Grace who was very explicit about what he wanted done. In addition, he was responsible and a product steward. Wood was in charge of handling the tremolite issue for Grace. Below, Bernick asks Locke about his testimony on direct examination where he told the jury that Grace delayed a request by the National

Institute of Safety and Health (NIOSH) for Grace to conduct an epidemiological study of tremolite.

Q. *Now, at the time that [NIOSH] came in [with a proposal], you've told us an account ... during your direct examination, right?*
A. Yes.

Q. *And in connection with this proposal, your basic story was that NIOSH wanted to do—September of 1980, NIOSH wants to do a study of tremolite, right?*
A. I think it was November of 1980....

Q. **And you're saying that Grace basically delayed that process until July of 1981**, *when Chip Wood gave the okay for a tremolite study...that's the story that you told the jury, right?*
A. It didn't start for some period of time. I think it was later than '81, when it started.... **[Witness dodges the question. Bernick asks if Grace delayed that process, not when it began. Bernick repeats the question.]**

Q. **Your story was Grace delayed it** *when it was proposed and delayed it after it was accepted, right?*
A. That's right, that was our practice.

Q. *And in support of that, you talked a lot about a memo that you wrote, that laid out the strategy, or potential strategies. And the memo is dated November 26. I want to show you Exhibit 239. Do you remember talking about this memo* **[on direct]** *that you wrote?*
A. Yes....

Q. *This was the memo where you went through the different options that you wrote down for how Grace could proceed [in response to the NIOSH request].*
A. Yes.

Q. *And those options included delay, right?*
A. Yes.

Q. **And the essence of what your testimony was, was the proposals were made in 1980, you laid out a bunch of options, and the company went down the road of delay, right?**
A. There was delay, yes. **[Again, the witness dodges the question as to whether Grace caused the delay. Bernick repeats question.]**

Q. *Well, no, the thrust of your testimony—I listened to it. The way I took it was not that there was delay, but that Grace produced the delay.*
A. Yeah, it was a result of Grace actions, yes.

Q. *And they produced the delay, in your inference, only just because they didn't like the study, right?*
A. We wanted to delay it, the commencement, as long as possible.

Q. *You've just reiterated that now. Now,* **you didn't tell the jury what actually was behind these different options, did you?**
A. Discussions among us inside Grace. **[Witness does not answer question. Bernick repeats it.]**

Q. *Yeah, you didn't talk about what the actual motive was for these options, why you proposed them, did you?*

A. I guess not. I don't understand your question. It reflects our internal discussion as to what we could do to delay or turn it off.

Q. *Isn't it true that you told the government why you proposed these options?....*

A. I think that I—I—I recognized more fully today, than I did at the time of my initial interrogation by the government, that I really was a member of the conspiracy at that time. And I realize that today, better than I did then. [**Witness does not answer question.**]

Bernick: Move to strike.

> ## Practice Tip
> Always have the witness' prior statements readily available so if he testifies inconsistently at trial, you can quickly show the jury the inconsistent statement to prove your point.

Court: Yes, ladies and gentlemen, you will disregard what he said. At the end of the case you will get an instruction on how you can judge the credibility of witnesses. One of them being a factor, Mr. Locke, as to how the witness behaves on the stand. You may proceed.

Bernick achieves the ultimate success. Earlier in the cross-examination, we saw the judge instruct the witness to answer the question when he was frustrated by the witness' evasiveness. Here, he goes a step further. First, the judge agrees with Bernick that the witness has not answered the question and tells the jury to disregard the response. Second, he scolds the witness and reminds him and the jury that the jury can judge his credibility by the way he "behaves on the stand." He might as well have told the jury: "I don't believe this witness, and neither should you."

Q. *In fact, you told the government that when you made these proposed options, you were out of the area of tremolite and you were kicking up your heels. Didn't you tell the government that?*

A. I may have. We can refer to the transcript.

Q. *I'll be happy to. I want to show you 6938.289, line 11. "Why do I think I did it?...I think I was getting kind of frustrated at this point. I had been dealing—it is like how long we were in World War II. Like over three years. I have been dealing in this tremolite jazz for now over four years. I am now out of finance, and I am in manufacturing and all of manufacturing that is not vermiculite. I'm in the best of all possible worlds. I still get my paycheck, but I'm not involved in any way with vermiculite. I guess I was kicking up my heels a little bit, saying one of our options was A or B." Do you remember stating that?*

A. Yes, I do.

Q. *So you told the government you're kind of kicking up your heels, fair?*

A. Yes, that's what I said. Yes. [**Witness finally admits that reason he suggested delay was because he did not want to put in the effort.**]

Q. *Now, the government, in this direct examination, didn't ask you to recite these reasons, correct?*

A. No, I was volunteering them. [**Witness does not answer question. Bernick repeats question.**]

Q. *The government, when you showed up and testified to the jury on direct examination, they didn't ask you about the reasons that you gave, when you talked with them, did they?*

A. I guess not.

Q. *And as a result of your direct examination, you didn't tell the jury any of that stuff, did you?*

A. No, I didn't.

Q. *You told the government that this memo, and the options, was also sarcastic. Didn't you tell them that?*

A. I may have. [**Witness does not answer question. Bernick impeaches witness with prior sworn statement.**]

Q. *I want to direct your attention to 6938.297. That's at line 17. Mr. Cassidy is saying, "That's why I'm surprised when you say you cooked these options up. Were these things that you saw going on, you didn't just"—Answer, "No, I am describing the way we ran the business." Ms. Kato [**says**], "Sardonic?" Answer, "I'm being sarcastic."*

And continue on to make sure we get the last of it. Top two lines. "Sarcastic, yes. Maybe I was tired. I don't know." Did you tell the government that during the interview?

A. No, I wasn't asked. [**Witness does not answer question. Bernick repeats it.**]

Q. *Did you tell the government that during the interview in 2004?*

A. Oh, I got—apparently I did, yes.

Q. *Government didn't ask you about that in direct examination, and you didn't share that with the jury in your direct examination, did you?*

A. No, I couldn't have. No.

Q. ***Not you couldn't have, you didn't.***

A. No, I didn't, no.

Q. *Now, I want to pick out something else. I can't read this, and now I'll shift this over a little bit. Three, you have testified a lot about, we did this and we did that. We, we, we. Do you remember in your testimony sometimes people [objecting] and saying, "No... it's not we, it's Mr. Locke"? Do you remember that?*

A. Yes, I do.

Q. *Well, when it came to these options, we didn't develop these options, you cooked up these options on your own, correct?*

A. No, I think they reflected the business—

Q. *You cooked up these options by yourself, true or not?*
A. Not true.

Q. *I'm going to direct your attention to what you told the government. At page 6938.293, [the] government's asking questions at lines 18 through 21. Ms. Kato asked you, "How did you come up with the options? Where did you?" And we see in your answer—we don't see any "we's." You say, "I just cooked them up. I didn't get them from anybody. I just cooked them up myself." Was that your testimony under oath to the government back when you talked with them in December of 2004?*
A. Yes, it is.

Q. *[The] government didn't ask you to share that on direct examination either, did it?*
A. No.

Q. *And, in fact, isn't it true that you got some reaction to these options from a person named Chip Wood, who convened a meeting to express his displeasure with this memo?*
A. I didn't remember that. No, I don't remember that.

Q. *But you told the government that shortly after this memo was done, you became suddenly much less involved in tremolite matters than you had been before the memo, correct?*
A. Well, yeah, over the passage of time I did, yes.

Q. *Not passage of time. You told the government that—well, let's just show you. 6938.292,19. Mr. Horgan asked you, "Did anybody come back and comment about any of these two?"*

And your answer was, "No, but I think I got a lot less involvement in tremolite matters after I wrote this memo than prior to it." It's not just the passage of time, you were being asked specifically to comment, the reaction that people had. And the reaction that people had was to reduce your involvement in tremolite matters, correct?
A. That's what I—the words say what they say. I'm saying I got a lot less involvement after this time than prior to it.

Q. *And you said that in specific response to the question of whether there was some reaction to the memo, correct?*
A. Yes.

Q. *Now, let's bring ourselves to July of 1981. And July of 1981, Mr. Wood OK'd the idea of going forward with the tremolite study, correct?*
A. I believe so.

The witness's credibility diminishes every time Bernick shows the jury that the witness has not answered his simple questions. The jury naturally believes that the witness either is hiding something or favoring the government; otherwise, why wouldn't he answer the questions?

Bernick always has the line and page number of Locke's prior statement to show him if the witness' answer at trial is different from his prior testimony.

There is no delay or fumbling to find the transcript. Rhythm is vital in maintaining control of the examination. Bernick is teaching the jury that if the witness does not tell the truth, he will quickly prove it to them.

Grace was not hiding danger from government

The government charged in its indictment that Grace committed fraud by hiding the dangers of asbestos. Through a series of precise questions, Bernick makes it clear that the government was well aware of the asbestos dangers. A technical term, "friability" (i.e., the ability to be easily crumbled) is also discussed.

Q. *There was no secret about friability, was there?*
A. I—I don't know what all these government agencies knew and how specific it was.

Q. *There was no secret. In your experience at Grace, there was no deep dark secret about friability, was there?*
A. Ah, I was there and you weren't. [**This snide remark by the witness will not serve him well.**]

Q. *That is certainly true. And you're on the stand, under oath, and you're supposed to be supplying facts. And the fact is that there was no deep dark secret about friability. It was because of friability, friability that consumer products gave off fibers and that Grace had to do the testing, right?*
A. I guess so, yes.

Q. *Well, it was. And the testing was no secret. Everybody knew about the testing. Grace relied upon the testing. Grace talked about friability and talked about—**they're not going to help you [prosecutors]. If you look over at them, they're not going to help.** Question is, the fact is that Grace told the government about friability every time it talked about fiber concentrations in the air, correct?*
A. Yes.

Q. *There was no secret about friability, correct? No secret. It was at the heart of the air concentration issue, true or not?*
A. I guess it was known in some parts of government.

Bernick concluded his cross-examination (not shown here) by getting Locke to admit that Chipper Wood had put a written plan in place describing how Grace would handle the safety issues related to tremolite. His point—which was not lost on the jury—was that Grace could not have been involved in a conspiracy to hide information from the government, evidenced by the fact that the company had put its entire plan in writing for everyone to see.

Bernick's techniques to force witness to answer questions

1. Ask simple questions.

2. Listen to make sure the witness has answered the question.

3. Repeat the question if the witness doesn't answer.

4. Sometimes, cut the witness off in mid-sentence to repeat a question if the witness continues to be difficult.

5. If the witness suggests you are implying something, fire back by saying, "I'm asking you for a fact."

6. When the witness gives a ridiculous answer, repeat the answer sarcastically to highlight the unresponsive answer. For example, when Locke admitted to destroying personal calendars a month before trial that he was ordered to turn over because "I was just cleaning out, that's all." Bernick responds, "Just cleaning out, that's all?"

7. When the witness does not answer a question, respond by saying, 1) "I didn't ask you that," 2) "Please answer the question," 3) "I'm not asking you to speculate. Answer yes or no," or 4) "I didn't ask you for that. It's just so simple."

8. Have ready any statements the witness has previously made so you can immediately confront inconsistencies with the witness during cross-examination.

7.12 CROSS-EXAMINATION OF INVESTIGATOR

After Locke's cross-examination, the defense became aware for the first time of four years of emails between the government's lead agent and Locke. Bernick argued that the government should have turned over these documents long before the trial started under the Brady doctrine. (The Brady doctrine requires the prosecution to turn over evidence or information favorable to the defense.)

At the defense's request, the court conducted a hearing, where Bernick called the government's lead investigator as a witness to ask him why these documents had not been turned over. The court would ultimately rule that the prosecutors should have turned over the documents but that its conduct was not intentional. The court allowed Bernick to recall Locke to the stand, instructed the jury to view Locke's testimony with skepticism, did not allow the government to conduct a re-direct examination of Locke, and informed the jury of the government's failure to turn over documents to the defense, which it was required to do under the Constitution. Next, you will see Bernick's cross-examination of the investigation before the jury.

While reading the following excerpts, focus on how Bernick forces the government's investigator to answer his questions.

Bernick's cross-examination

Q. Let's talk a little bit about Mr. Locke. The government needs—fair to say, as you understood it—the government stands in urgent need at the end of 2004 to get somebody from Grace who was there to talk about the conspiracy to defraud that took place at the end of the 1970s, correct? [The] government needed it.
A. We investigated it as well as the information provided, yes.

Q. Well, the government need, that was an urgent need that the government had, fair?
A. You say "need." I'm saying we're doing fact-finding and that was the information provided.

In earlier questions, Bernick made it clear to the jury that the government needed to begin a formal prosecution immediately because the time to bring charges was running out very quickly. The witness disagrees with Bernick's use of the word "urgent," but the point is clear to the jury, and Bernick moves on to the bigger battle with the witness.

Q. Fine. If the government were to charge the case they were investigating, they would need evidence from somebody who was there and, in that area, the government did not have a witness, correct?
A. That would be correct, yeah.

*Q. So let's talk about Mr. Locke and how Mr. Locke squared off against the government's needs. It's true that Mr. Locke was a **Harvard MBA**, correct?*
A. Yes.

*Q. It's true that Mr. Locke was a member of Grace's **senior management** for many, many years, correct?*
A. Yes.

*Q. It's true that Mr. Locke was **deeply involved**, deeply involved in the events that the government thought reflected a conspiracy to defraud in the late 1970s, correct?*
A. He was dealing exclusively with the tremolite issue.

*Q. **Can you just answer the question?** The question is not whether he was exclusively involved with the tremolite issue. The question was, wasn't Mr. Locke deeply involved with the events that the government was investigating as reflecting a conspiracy to defraud? Deeply involved.*
A. Yes.

In just a few short questions, Bernick establishes that Locke was extremely smart, held a high-level position in management, and was "deeply involved" in the matters the government was investigating. When the witness hedges and does not answer the second to last question, Bernick asks incredulously, "Can you just answer the question?" By carefully listening to the witness' answer, Bernick forces a "yes" answer by simply repeating his question.

Q. *Is it true that not only was he highly qualified, a member of senior management, and deeply involved in those events, he was an individual who was **very hostile to Grace**?*
A. I believe he was **hostile** to Grace, yes.

Q. *Hostile to Grace? **That's it?** Is it true that he had been passed over for years for senior positions that he wanted?*

Bernick has a unique and devastating style of questioning. When a witness doesn't answer his question, he responds sarcastically and summarizes the answer. Here, when the witness does not admit that Locke was "very" hostile, he asks sarcastically, "That's it?" Then, in the next series of questions he establishes that Locke was indeed very hostile. Read how Bernick succeeds in doing so:

Q. *Hostile to Grace? **That's it?** Is it true that he had been passed over for years for senior positions that he wanted?*
A. My understanding is he finished as a global vice president.

Q. *Is it true that he was passed over for years for positions that he wanted? That's what he testified to on the stand, right?* [**Bernick repeats question when witness doesn't answer.**]
A. Yes.

Q. *Is it true that he was **demoted** at the end of his career, demoted, in his own view, and in his own view he was demoted due to his disability?*
A. Yes.

Q. *Let's quit playing. You dealt with Mr. Locke for years, correct?*
A. Yes, I did.

Q. ***You cultivated him as a witness**, correct?*
A. That's correct.

Q. *This is a man who was seething with rage, in large part, because of how he had been treated at Grace and, in particular, that he had a disability that he thought led to his being demoted, true or not?*
A. Yes, I believe he felt he was wronged.

Q. ***Deeply wronged.***
A. Deeply wronged.

Q. *He **walked off in his last days on the job with his personal files** to use for his personal purposes, correct?*
A. That's my understanding.

Q. *He **filed suit against Grace**, correct?*
A. Yes.

Q. *He used the knowledge that he had of Grace files to tell Grace that if they didn't resolve his lawsuit, he would cooperate and **assist plaintiff's lawyers** who were suing Grace. Isn't that true?*

A. There is a document that states that.

Q. *Well, that is a fact as you understood it, correct?*

A. (No response.)

Q. *As you understood it, he sought to use his documents and his knowledge and his documents at the company to get leverage over Grace by saying if they didn't settle his personal lawsuit that he would help the plaintiffs' bar sue Grace, correct?*

A. I believe that's what that document says that we turned over to you in discovery.

Bernick methodically gets the witness to admit the following about Locke: 1) He was passed over for positions, 2) he was demoted, 3) the investigator cultivated him as a witness, 4) Locke felt he had been deeply wronged, 5) Locke took files from office when he left, 6) Locke wanted to assist plaintiff's lawyers who were suing Grace, and 7) Locke wanted to get leverage over Grace to settle his personal lawsuit.

Q. *Locke wanted to play a role as a witness. He wanted to do that. He wanted to be a key witness, correct?*

A. I don't know.

Q. *You didn't drag Mr. Locke in struggling against you to the courtroom; he was looking forward to it, correct?*

A. You mean in 2004 or now?

Q. *As it developed, between 2004, yeah, and 2006, he became a guy who wanted to play a key role as a witness, correct?*

A. I think once he went on the record, he understood.

Q. ***Didn't ask you for that. It's just so simple.***

A. OK.

Q. *Isn't it a fact that Mr. Locke was not simply a dispassionate, "I'll do it if you want witness," he wanted to play a key role in the trial?*

A. He was willing to cooperate.

Q. *That's not an answer to my question.*

A. I don't know the answer to that.

Q. *You just don't—you dealt with him for two years between 2004 and 2006, and you had no sense about whether the guy wanted to play a key role at the trial?*

A. No. In fact, I think he wanted the trial to go away.

Q. *Oh, he wanted it to go away. He didn't want to testify, is that what you're saying?* [**Bernick asks sarcastically.**]

A. I don't think he wanted to go through and testify.

Q. *Did that change? Or did he never want to go through and testify?*

A. (No response.)

Q. *We've got all the emails here.* [**Bernick knows emails will prove his point.**]
A. I understand that. You're asking me what he knows or what he thinks?

Q. *I'm asking you what your understanding was. This is all about the conduct—not of Mr. Locke here—it's about the conduct of the prosecution team, and that's why I'm asking you questions. I'm asking for your understanding. Was it your understanding that Mr. Locke wanted to play a role as being a key witness in this case, true or not?*
A. True.

Q. *Is it true that Mr. Locke wanted to be part of the team?*

Prosecutor: Your Honor, I'm going to object to this as speculation.

Court: It isn't, if you've read those emails. Overruled. [**The court scolds prosecutor for objecting.**]

Q. *Isn't it true that your understanding was that Mr. Locke wanted to be part of your team?*
A. I think he wanted to cooperate with our investigation, yes. [**Witness hedges answer.**]

Q. *Didn't ask you that. Lots of people cooperate with investigation, and they don't sit there and write emails providing information on briefs and giving you Internet research results that relate to the people who are being prosecuted, right?*
A. That's correct.

Q. ***He wanted to be part of your team***, *he wanted to belong, and be active in your team, correct?*
A. **Yes.**

If the witness had never given the final "yes" answer, Bernick could have ultimately shown the emails that Locke exchanged with the witness. Those emails give Bernick the leverage to force the witness to answer his questions.

Every time Bernick has to repeat a simple question because the witness does not answer a question, Bernick's credibility with the judge and jury goes up. Let's look at one more exchange:

Q. *Now, these were all of the things that Mr. Locke wanted, and he got them all as a result of the relationship that he had with you and with others on the prosecution team, correct? He got a special letter, his own tailored letter, right? He got special treatment, special input. Special, special, special. He had a special relationship, did he not? With you and other members of the prosecution team.*
A. A significant relationship with me, yes.

Q. *Not a significant* [**one**], *a special one. It was special to the point—*
A. Special, yes.

Q. *You've never had, you've never even been told of a relationship that was as unique as this relationship, correct?*
A. Yes.

Bernick uses a wonderful technique in this line of questioning. He summarizes all the things Locke received from the government and uses them to confront the witness with the logical conclusion that if Locke received all of these unique benefits from the government that other witnesses do not receive, a special relationship had been created. For example, although Locke had testified that he had turned down a grant of immunity from the prosecution, Bernick learned of evidence that he believed showed Locke was assured he would not be prosecuted even though he was not given a formal grant of immunity. The lack of a "formal" grant of immunity prevented the defense from using this agreement with the government to show his bias. Moreover, the emails sent between Locke and the government's lead agent and the agent's notes showed that Locke had a much closer relationship with the prosecution than Locke testified to.

So, when the witness hedges by saying it was "significant" instead of "special" as Bernick asked, Bernick just repeats the question again until he gets the answer he wants. He knows that the documents he has support the answer he wants and can confront the witness with them if the witness continues to answer incorrectly.

7.13 THEME IN CLOSING ARGUMENT

Let's take a quick look at Bernick's closing argument. He starts strong and gets to the point. As he instructed us earlier in this chapter, closing arguments are a victory lap. After his devastating cross-examinations of Locke and the government investigator, he takes his.

> I want to start out with one word, one word: credibility. The whole truth. Credibility. In this case, if you read the Court's — when you read the Court's instructions or I should say reread the Court's instructions, you'll see and come to understand that credibility is almost the very first thing you have to consider. You have the latitude as part of your decision-making power to decide whether any and all evidence that's been presented by either side through any witness is credible.
>
> And if you decide that that evidence is not worthy of your belief as jurors, you can completely disregard it. That's what the instruction says, that's what the law says.
>
> And, therefore, credibility in any case is an important critical determination that is left solely to your decision making. The Court doesn't decide it. Nobody decides it. You decide what's credible.
>
> And the easiest way that — the instruction that the Court has goes through many things that you can consider. But I put up on the board the whole truth, because you all know that when any witness takes the stand, they take an oath, and without that oath their testimony wouldn't have the kind of reliability that's necessary to warrant your consideration.
>
> And when they take that oath, they swear to tell the whole truth. Not a part of it. Not a spin. The whole truth. Unfortunately, in this case credibility

is not simply an important issue, it is almost the entire issue in the entire case. Credibility problems have cast a dark shadow, a pall, of doubt over this entire case from the very beginning.

Bernick then walked the jury through several slides and discussed how the government's case and its witnesses, such as Locke, lacked credibility. He then concluded by confronting head-on the issue, facing his client:

> And, finally, I want to talk about my client specifically and raise with you what I think is something tough. My client's a company. A company's comprised of people. They are not going to go to jail, the people at Grace. They will—if we're found guilty, there will be a penalty.
>
> And most of all, the company will be a convicted criminal, which has a profound impact on the people of Grace. But in a sense it's more difficult. It's more difficult to justify in your own minds, rather than individuals, a company, to be able to say, well, what's the big deal? How can we let off a company, to say nothing of a company that at least in this part of the country does not enjoy a high reputation?
>
> And we understand that, and we understand that history. But that is why it's particularly important that you focus on Grace, because Grace is a true test of your deliberations and whether this process produces justice based upon the facts. It is Grace. It is the determination with respect to Grace. It is the ultimate way to make sure that the message that your verdict reflects has clarity to it.
>
> So it is not only important to my client, the company, and the people that work there. It is of vital importance to establish that this system in fact works in a highly controversial case for a company that many people would say, "Well, I read in the newspapers it's a bad company." So what if they get convicted? So we really ask you to treat the company the same way that you would treat an individual and give us the same clarity of your determination. Thank you very much for your attention. Thank you very much.

Unlike most attorneys who make the mistake of reminding jurors of their promise in voir dire to treat a company like an individual and not show favoritism toward an individual, Bernick does not patronize the jury about their previous promise. Instead, he gives a candid assessment of the challenge the jurors and his company face. By speaking the truth, instead of shying away from it or trying to spin it, he gains credibility.

7.14 AFTERMATH OF TRIAL

After seven weeks of testimony, the jury deliberated little more than a day to acquit Grace and three former executives of all charges (the government had dismissed charges against two other Grace employees during trial). It was a remarkable victory for a company that the EPA had accused of operating a mine contaminated with asbestos that killed more than 200 people and caused serious illness in another 1,800 people over several decades.

7.15 CHAPTER CHECKLIST

Bernick's trial strategies for defense attorneys

General trial strategies

1. When Bernick first gets a case, he "swallows the whale" to learn everything he can about the case and form a legal architecture for it. But at a trial, the focus must be on following a powerful storyline from the beginning of opening statement and throughout the trial.

2. In a hostile environment, be aware that a good judge is essential and factor who your judge is into how you present your case.

3. Spend time in discovery getting what is important for the storyline to be told at the trial.

4. Science is an important tool for the defense because the jurors trust it.

5. Tell the story at the beginning, tell the story on cross, and tell the story in closing.

Voir dire

1. Jurors have an amazing ability in high-profile cases to focus on doing their jobs.

2. Tell the client's story in voir dire.

3. Don't shy away from the potential jurors' answers or questions that highlight the weaknesses in the case.

4. Voir dire is a unique opportunity for a lawyer to interact with potential jurors and address any skepticism, show them a "bigger picture" of the case, and cultivate favorable views of you as a lawyer and person.

Opening statement

1. It is vitally important.

2. The jury must come to know that there are two sides to the story.

3. In a hostile atmosphere in a criminal case, do not nitpick on the prosecution's burden of proof.

4. Face up to your client's weaknesses and tell the broader story.

5. If a lawyer's case is scientifically correct, jurors will believe the lawyer if they hear the full story.

6. The key is to build from an acceptance of responsibility and bring transparency to a client's actions.

7. A company cannot blame the government without first applying Point 6.

8. When the government is a heavy favorite, highlight what the government has *not* done.

9. Show the jury the storyline that the plaintiff has missed.

10. Tell a story with values such as responsibility, fairness, good intentions, and good people.

11. Do not use notes.

12. Any slides shown to the jury should have a minimal amount of text.

Cross-examination

1. Don't let the plaintiff get ahead when presenting his or her case.

2. Win the case on the cross-examination of the plaintiff's witnesses.

3. Don't be afraid to battle an expert in his area of expertise. Learn the underlying science of the expert's opinion.

4. Use charts on cross-examination either on a board or displayed on an overhead projector. The key is to physically interact with the chart.

5. A chart organizes the examination so the jury can see where the arguments are going.

6. A chart reminds the jury of the storyline that has been used with previous witnesses.

7. A chart controls a witness as it allows a lawyer to point to a question or information on the chart to emphasize a point.

8. The chart gives the jury a focal point.

9. Emphasize an important point with the witness before a break so the jury will remember it better.

10. When a witness does not answer a question, repeat it until he or she does.

11. After several attempts at repeating a question, if the witness does not answer it, the jury will get your message. There is no need to ask the judge to instruct the witness to answer at this point.

12. Sarcastically repeat an evasive answer to show the witness and the jury how disingenuous it was.

13. The most truthful witnesses are the ones who directly answer questions because they are confident in their answers.

14. Do not elicit subtle answers with the hope of connecting the dots in closing. The jury will not remember such subtle answers.

15. Have an endpoint that is "pay dirt."

Direct examination

1. When it is your turn to put on witnesses, keep it short.

2. Fill in only the necessary gaps in the evidence.

Closing argument

1. Trials are not won here.

2. Remind the jury you have proven everything you promised in opening statement.

3. "Closing arguments are victory lap time."

Common mistakes lawyers make

1. Defense lawyers let plaintiff's lawyers monopolize the storytelling.

2. In criminal cases, the defense of trying to create a reasonable doubt is a death by a thousand cuts for the defense.

3. Lawyers get caught up in legal issues and rules of evidence instead of realizing that great drama wins cases.

4. Lawyers mistakenly ask questions on cross-examination to which they don't know the answers and get burned by them.

Analysis of Grace trial

Opening statement

1. Bernick starts by thanking jurors for their sacrifice and promises that he will make it a very interesting trial.

2. Next, he concedes that jurors have a natural inclination to be emotional but argues the case is about the relationship between Grace and the government, not individuals.

3. Bernick used PowerPoint slides that were clear and persuasive.

4. Bernick tells the jury, "Keep your eye on the ball." Focus on what the government alleges Grace did criminally wrong.

5. Bernick candidly admits Grace had made slow progress in dealing with asbestos problems.

6. Bernick declared, "Science has a way of clarifying and de-emotionalizing these very important claims that are being made [by the government]. They have to be decided on the basis of science."

Cross-examination tips

1. Bernick is a master of the facts.

2. He listens intently to answers.

3. He asks simple questions and repeats them when the witness doesn't answer.

4. Sometimes, if the witness is being very difficult, Bernick cuts the witness off in mid-sentence and repeats the question.

5. He starts each cross-examination by telling the jury and the witness what the topic is. For example, he says, "Let's talk about [the topic]."

6. When the witness answers that Bernick is implying something, Bernick fires back, "I'm asking you for a fact."

7. When the witness gives a ridiculous answer, Bernick responds sarcastically to highlight the unresponsive answer. For example, Locke admitted to destroying personal calendars a month before trial that he was ordered to turn over because "I was just cleaning out, that's all." Bernick responds, "Just cleaning out, that's all?"

8. When the witness does not answer a question, Bernick responds by saying, 1) "I didn't ask you that," 2) "Please answer the question," 3) "I'm not asking you to speculate. Answer yes or no," or 4) "I didn't ask you for that. It's just so simple."

9. Unlike many attorneys who only try to undercut witness's credibility, Bernick also gets helpful information.

10. Bernick has ready any statements the witness has previously made so he can immediately confront inconsistencies during cross-examination.

11. Bernick gets the witness to admit leaving out important facts during direct testimony.

PART FOUR

Cross-Examination of the Expert Witness

INTRODUCTION

*P*art Four teaches how to cross-examine an expert witness. The challenges are many. First, unlike most witnesses, expert witnesses have testified regularly in court. Consequently, the environment does not scare them. Second, they have been challenged many times by opposing counsel. As a result, they are battle tested and have refined their answers to best argue their position in response to a lawyer's questions. In addition, experts have unique knowledge about their area of expertise that is hard for you to acquire.

But don't be discouraged. We are going to look at very smart experts and learn techniques from brilliant lawyers that you can use on your next cross-examination. You may be surprised to find that many of the skills used in cross-examining a regular witness will also work against experts. The trick is that there is less room for error in your execution.

Part Four of this book builds on what we have learned in Part Three, but it also teaches the specific techniques to use with an expert witness. The challenge for the attorney is to undermine an expert's credibility even though the witness has an expertise in a particular field that the attorney does not. Most trials have a "battle of the experts," and you cannot afford to be on the losing end.

In Chapter Eight, Robert Bennett shows us fail-safe tips to win every time. His examination relates to the John F. Kennedy assassination and how society values unique artifacts. In Chapter Nine, Frank Branson provides us with the tools to use to cross-examine the hired gun for the other side and prevail every time.

CHAPTER EIGHT

Robert S. Bennett

Wage Guerrilla Warfare with the Expert

I look at cross-examination as if you're a guerrilla fighter. You're in and you're out. You know what points you want to make; you jump in, you get them, and you get out.

— Robert S. Bennett

---

*R*obert S. Bennett is one of the country's finest criminal defense attorneys and crisis management lawyers for corporations. In his career, he has represented President Bill Clinton, Secretaries of Defense Clark Clifford and Caspar Weinberger, former World Bank President Paul Wolfowitz, and New York Times reporter Judith Miller.

He first realized he had the interest and skills to be a trial lawyer when he was in college at Georgetown University. While there, he became the coach for the debate team at Gonzaga College High School. His coaching skills drew upon his accomplishments as a debater for his high school at Brooklyn Prep. Although you might think his interest in debate was the genesis of his desire to become a lawyer, he actually wanted to become a doctor and enrolled in Georgetown's pre-med program. But, while in college, he met a prosecutor for the United States Attorney's Office for the District of Columbia who invited him to visit his office and the courthouse.

After this meeting, Bennett found himself spending many afternoons watching trials. Seeing these lawyers in action made Bennett realize he wanted to be a trial lawyer. He would later graduate from Georgetown University Law Center and get a Master's of Law from Harvard. Not surprisingly, he began his career as an Assistant U.S. Attorney for the District of Columbia.

CHAPTER HIGHLIGHTS

- Set up cross in your opening statement
- Thoroughly investigate an opposing expert
- Know the weaknesses of your case and how to overcome them

8.1 *ZAPRUDER V. UNITED STATES*

Many of Bennett's famous cases are examined in his memoir, *In the Ring* (Three Rivers Press, 2008). One case is intimately intertwined with U.S. history and perfectly illustrates skills all lawyers can use to cross-examine expert witnesses. Bennett's cross-examinations were the turning point in the trial and merit a closer look so we can gain valuable insights from Bennett's techniques.

The case involved President John F. Kennedy's assassination and Abraham Zapruder, a Dallas businessman and amateur photographer, who had his 8 mm movie camera with him that day as the president's motorcade passed by.

For 19 seconds on November 22, 1963, Zapruder captured the motorcade in the moments before, during, and after the assassination. Although other people were filming that day, his film was the only one to capture all of these key moments. Devastated by what he had seen, he returned to his office, put his movie camera in his office safe, and notified the Secret Service. Once the movie's existence became known, he received multiple financial offers for it. But he did not want the movie to be misused for many reasons, not the least of which was his concern for the Kennedy family.

> *I saw his head explode. I have a film of the assassination. I saw the President shot down in the street, in the presence of Mrs. Kennedy.*
> — Abraham Zapruder's response to his son's hope that Kennedy had only been injured

He did not try to find the highest bidder but instead decided to sell the film to Time/Life because he believed the publishing company would respect what was captured on the film. Time/Life agreed to pay Zapruder $150,000 in several installments. Zapruder donated the first installment of $25,000 to the widow of Officer J.D. Tippit. Lee Harvey Oswald had killed Officer Tippit shortly after the assassination. Zapruder made the donation out of sympathy and also to quell public resentment that he might be trying to profit from the tragedy.

In 1975, Time-Life sold the film back to Zapruder's widow (Abraham had died in 1970) and the Zapruders' two children for $1. The price was so low because Time-Life had grown weary of handling the numerous requests to view the film and wanted to be relieved of this burden. The Zapruder family transferred the film to the National Archives and Records Administration for safekeeping and consciously decided not to profit from those wanting to use the film for advertising.

On April 24, 1997, after conducting hearings, the John F. Kennedy Assassination Records Review Board (ARRB) determined that the Zapruder film should be owned by the government and stored permanently in the Records Collections of the National Archives. After seizing the Zapruder film, the government and the Zapruders could not reach an agreement on what would be fair compensation.

Interestingly, despite the government's seizure, the Zapruders still owned the copyright to the film. The Zapruders had made a high-quality copy of the film because the original film, although in excellent condition, would be better preserved if it were no longer viewed through a projector. So, the family could still make money by selling copies or still photographs of the film or by licensing its use.

The only thing the government seized was the original film. Consequently, its value was what a buyer would be willing to pay to possess the original film without the benefit of owning the copyright to it. The question was how to value an iconic film which could no longer be viewed through a projector. That is, the value was whatever it had to an owner who could only mount it in a display case or have the privilege to say, "I own the original."

The government's best offer was $750,000, but some experts believed that at auction the film could sell for $25,000,000. The parties agreed to arbitrate the dispute before a three-person panel on May 25, 1999.

8.2 BENNETT SETS UP CROSS-EXAMINATIONS DURING THE OPENING STATEMENT

Notice how well in his opening statement Bennett foreshadows the points he will be making during the cross-examinations of the government's experts.

> **Bennett:** Good morning, Judge Adams, Mr. Dellinger, Mr. Fineberg. My name is Robert Bennett, and I have the privilege of representing the Zapruder family in this proceeding.... Here with me today are Mr. Henry Zapruder and Mrs. Myrna Reese, who are representatives of the family.... It is particularly appropriate that Mr. Zapruder is here today, because he was there at the beginning of the tragic saga that brings us here. He's part of the story.
>
> On November 22, 1963, he was a young attorney at the United States Department of Justice, and shortly after returning from lunch, he, like so many of us, heard a news report about an attempt on the life of President John F. Kennedy. And, shortly after that — after he came back from lunch and heard this troublesome report — he received a call from his father, Abraham Zapruder, who was in tears. He told Henry that the president was dead, but Henry, having just heard a news report, protested and said, "No, Dad, I just heard the report that they've taken the president to the hospital."
>
> The elder Mr. Zapruder then spoke words [that] Henry and his family have never forgotten. He said, "Henry, that's not right. I saw his head ex-

---

Practice Tip

The keys to a powerful opening statement are to start strong and tell a compelling story. Bennett does both.

---

plode. I have a film of the assassination. I saw the president shot down in the street, in the presence of Mrs. Kennedy."

The elder Mr. Zapruder, a dedicated photographer, never again looked through the lens of a camera, but his film, known as the Zapruder film, has achieved worldwide fame. It is currently at the National Archives. It has been taken by the government, and the issue before this distinguished panel is how much the government must pay the Zapruder family as just compensation for the taking of this unique and important piece of history.

Without wasting time on background facts, Bennett immediately gets to the heart of the matter as explained through Abraham Zapruder's chilling and mournful words: "The president is dead.... I saw his head explode. I have a film of the assassination."

Bennett then sets forth the issues before the court: why arbitration was necessary and how to value the film. As we see in the next excerpt, Bennett employed a great tactic for use in any opening statement: He used the opposing party's statements to damage its case. For example, at the AARB hearing, the government's own witnesses testified regarding the need to seize the film from the Zapruders.

> Bennett: Mr. Gunn [General Counsel for the Board] says that the original Zapruder film possesses an intrinsic historical value such that the Review Board should take action to insure that the original is kept at the National Archives, **regardless of the cost**.... I should underscore that repeatedly the government has spurned the offers of the Zapruder family to have copies, to have advanced copies, to have the most sophisticated copies available, at no charge.... The government insisted that it have this piece of history.

Bennett then focused on three of the many experts who testified at that Commission's hearing regarding the film's value.

> Bennett: Dr. Kermit Holl, Dean, College of Humanities and Professor of History at Ohio State, said **the Zapruder film is a trophy**. It's not a piece of evidence, it's a trophy. And, Art Simon, a Professor of English, Assistant Professor at Montclair State College and author of the JFK book...titled *Dangerous Knowledge*, said, "What, then, is the status of the original film? **I would suggest to you that it is a secular relic,** a material of the past and, for reasons that are either psychological or, for some, perhaps spiritual, individuals and nations hold onto such relics." And, he emphasized the importance of originals.
>
> He pointed out in his testimony that thousands upon thousands of constitutions are in people's pockets in pamphlet form, but there's only one

original. And, Richard Trask, who testified before the Commission, an author and historian and archivist, who wrote a book called *Pictures of Pain*, said, "To call the film remarkable is an exaggerated understatement." He said, **"This film, in my opinion, is the most important surviving document of the President Kennedy assassination."** And, he interestingly noted, **"I believe on the open market, something like that Zapruder film would be in the tens of millions of dollars."**

Now, perhaps, members of the panel, I'm too much of a cynic. And, while I do very much appreciate the professionalism that has been shown to us by the representatives of the government, I must, in all candor, say, and perhaps I'm too cynical, but it appears that when the Assassination Review Board, speaking for the government, wanted the original, when they took the original, when they made the record for having the original, this original film was an icon, a trophy, a unique piece of history. **But, now that the day has come to pay for it, I expect we're going to hear it is not very valuable after all.**

Bennett brilliantly highlights the inconsistent position the government has taken. He logically argues, how can the government claim now that the film is not worth much when its previous witnesses have testified that the film is a "secular relic" that is worth "tens of millions of dollars"?

8.3 CROSS-EXAMINATION PRINCIPLES

Before looking at Bennett's cross-examinations in the Zapruder case, let's explore his principles for cross-examination. When asked what he thought was the biggest mistake lawyers made on cross-examination, Bennett responds, "They don't seem to have a real focus on what they want to get out of the witness. Anytime I cross-examine a witness, I know the one or two points I want to get out of that witness. What I find is that a lot of lawyers are just sort of all over the place." If you were to study Bennett's cross-examinations, you would find that his points—or themes—are very easy to find, and he never takes an unfocused examination.

Bennett goes on to explain that the second biggest mistake lawyers make happens with expert witnesses. "[L]awyers have big egos, especially trial lawyers, and they just love the idea of taking on an expert. Generally, I'm not sure that's a very good idea because no matter how smart you are, or how good you are, or how prepared you are, you're taking on somebody who has spent their whole life in that field." Bennett gives as an example the futile attempt to try to cross-examine a doctor on the intricacies of a medical device or pro-

> *I always ask myself, "Where are the weak spots of the witness," whether it's a lay witness or an expert—a weak spot that a jury would be able to understand.*
> —Robert S. Bennett

cedure. In his pragmatic approach to trying a case, Bennett said, "Sometimes that's necessary, but most of the time it's not." In short, Bennett cautions not to give an expert an opportunity to show how brilliant he or she is.

Notice that Bennett's strategy not to take on the expert on his or her turf is different from David Bernick's discussion in section 7.5. My advice is to try both and see which works best for you. In my practice, I have found Bennett's approach the one that best fits my skill set. You may come to a different conclusion.

As for Bennett's strategies for cross-examination, he said it should be obvious that leading questions are your primary tool.

A leading question, as defined in Chapter Six, is a question that suggests the answer to the witness. For example, "The traffic light was green, wasn't it?" The answer can also be suggested by ending your question on the same pitch or a lower pitch. Try this experiment. Say out loud the following question and use a higher pitch on the last word "green:" "The traffic light was green?" By using a higher pitch on the last word, the listener hears your doubt about the color of the traffic light. Now, say the same question but use a slightly lower pitch on the last word than the rest of the question. By using a lower pitch, you suggest the answer green and really turn a question into a statement of fact that indicates to the witness that he should agree with your statement.

Bennett shared another tip. "I always know what I want to get out of a particular witness, and then I listen very carefully to their direct testimony because very often, they'll say something that gives me an opportunity."

Bennett's tip requires you to think on your feet and quickly adjust your planned cross-examination by adding a new line of questioning based on what you hear on direct examination. Begin developing this skill at your first trial.

Consequently, don't have a rigid outline. There is always something the witness will say on direct examination that you can add to your outline. When you hear a mistake on direct examination that fits into the themes of your case, don't miss an opportunity to seize upon it simply because, instead of listening intently to the direct examination, your head is buried in your notes and you are thinking about your upcoming cross-examination.

Bennett also believes you should start your cross-examination by eliciting favorable information from the witness before attacking him or her. There are several examples of this in the Zapruder case, which will be discussed later in this chapter.

Bennett adds that the atmosphere you create on cross-examination is critical. "There is nothing worse than having a whole bunch of binders and papers. It breaks the flow. I would rather lose something than create that kind of a climate…. I might have one binder that would have some key things in it but not much more than that.

"You always think in terms of your closing. What I'm thinking about is, at the end of the day, what am I going to say to that jury?"

Bennett agrees with my trial philosophy that "less is more" and points out that he tries cases in about half as much time now as when he began as a lawyer. "I think it's a matter of, as you get older, you have more confidence in yourself. I think young lawyers are afraid that they'll miss something; whereas, I think as you get older, you pick a couple [of points] and you go with your strengths." His tactic succeeds with juries. He believes it builds confidence with the jury that says you are not going to waste their time but instead get right to the point.

> **Practice Tip**
>
> To truly prepare for a trial, you must know the weaknesses of your case and how to overcome them. Too many lawyers are one-sided and never take a hard look at their own case. Bennett cautions, "You've got to put 20 minutes of every hour of preparation…. [by standing] in the other guy's shoes."

Yet he adds that his motto for "less is more" is, "You over prepare and you under try." I like his principle because it asserts that it takes a lot of effort to make "less is more" successful. It would be an unforgivable mistake if a lawyer were to interpret "less is more" to mean that you could "wing it" at a trial and do just the minimum amount of work. Bennett reveals that from the first day he gets a case, he thinks about his closing argument. He asks himself, "What are the points I could make that I think could convince this jury to acquit my client." He cautions that you can't put it in concrete because you don't have all the evidence, so you need to stay flexible. The worst thing you can do is use tunnel vision.

In regards to expert witnesses, Bennett always thinks in terms of how he can get the witness to look weak or not knowledgeable. To do this, he always tries to ask some questions to which he knows the answer will be "no." He points out that all the experts will have fabulous qualifications. "Their resumes are all good. I don't mess around with that, but what I do is try to get them to say, 'I don't know.'" Similarly, Bennett believes too many lawyers waste time trying to prove their expert is smarter than the opposing expert. This exercise is lost on juries who don't care about the alleged subtle differences between the experts' educations. "To most jurors, whether you go to Harvard or Stanford, or whether you go to some other place, everybody's resume looks pretty much the same."

Another mistake lawyers make, Bennett says, is that they try to demonstrate that they are smarter than the expert. This always fails. Instead, he advises, "It's easy to show that an expert on the other side has not done something. I always ask the question whenever I know there's going to be an expert on the other side, what hasn't that expert done? What has he failed to do? Maybe [there's something] he didn't have the opportunity [to investigate]."

For an expert witness, Bennett will track down everything the witness has written and the transcript of every testimony he has given. He is looking for a "nugget of gold" he can use in a cross-examination.

A good example of this occurred when Bennett was appointed special counsel for the Keating Five in 1989. This was the most difficult case of his career. Charles Keating's Lincoln Savings and Loan in California had a financial collapse that was one of the great scandals of all time. Five senators received more than $1,000,000 from Charles Keating or his associates while the senators were trying to persuade government regulators to pull back on their oversight of Keating's Savings and Loan. When Keating's Savings and Loan collapsed, ethics complaints were filed against the senators involved, and they became known as the Keating Five. One of those senators was Dennis DeConcini of Arizona.

At the Senate hearing (which was televised nationally for 26 days), Senator DeConcini called former U.S. Attorney General Griffin Bell to testify to his good character and actions. Bell was a powerful witness who would be very difficult to cross-examine. But Bennett was aware of a passage from Bell's book, *Taking Care of the Law*.

On cross-examination, Bennett asked Bell about his own words from his book:

> Q. *I would like to read a passage from your book…. [you stated that there is] "rampant self-dealing…operating on Capitol Hill. By self-dealing, I mean a member of Congress attempting to influence a government decision to reward himself indirectly by winning benefits for a valued constituent…. The propriety of such a contact comes into question if it is something more than a neutral request for information…." Do you remember writing that?*
>
> A. Yes.
>
> Q. *What did you mean when you say, "more than a neutral request for information," if you recall?*
>
> A. ….you ought to be careful to avoid self-interests, not only not to be in a self-interest position, but to avoid the appearance of it. That was what I had in mind.

Practice Tip

Investigate an opposing expert by doing the following:

1. Search for transcripts, verdicts, disqualifications, and settlements involving experts through Westlaw and LexisNexis.

2. Examine the expert's website, Facebook page, and scour the Internet for information.

3. Search databases of litigation groups such as DRI and AAJ.

4. Contact other attorneys to get their opinion of the expert and copies of prior depositions that have been disclosed under Federal Rule 26.

5. Search for any prior statements the expert has made in his writings.

This point that Bennett brought out on cross-examination was exactly the standard that Senator DeConcini presently opposed and that Bennett believed applied: Senators should not engage in activity that is improper or has the appearance of impropriety.

Your strategies for cross-examination will only be successful if your own expert survives your opponent's cross-examination. When Bennett hires an expert, he finds out who has the most expertise in the particular field. He researches who has written peer-reviewed articles in the subject matter, gets recommendations from his client, and surveys the Internet. Once you find an expert, you need to determine if they have any interest in your case. Some stay away from litigation completely.

Bennett shared some unique strategies to make sure your decision to hire an expert for your case is sound. Bennett believes there is no substitute for an in-person interview of the expert before you hire him. You cannot determine an expert's jury appeal over the phone—although that is how most attorneys make their decision.

At the meeting, he never asks, "Will you be a witness for me in this case?" The reason is that the expert doesn't know what all the facts are. Bennett wants to make sure the expert is familiar and comfortable with the facts before agreeing to provide an opinion. In contrast, Bennett has seen other lawyers make "a big mistake" because they hire somebody to be an expert and then, after they sign a fee agreement with them, they send them the material. The fee agreement will state how much the witness will be paid for his time to testify at a deposition and at a trial.

When this happens, on cross-examination, Bennett will use this line of attack: "So, doctor or Mr. So-and-so, you agreed to be a witness in this case before you ever even saw a piece of paper, before you knew what the facts were." Bennett explains, "It suggests that they're a whore." He points out that this happens a lot because experts are very busy people, and due to a lack of time, they often sign the fee agreement before looking over the case. When an expert signs a fee arrangement letter before he knows anything about the case, it can be "very devastating."

When Bennett interviews an expert, he hires him or her first as a consultant who may not be used at the trial, saying, "I just want your honest opinion on Mr. X. Why don't we just work together and if you are in a position at the end of the day where you're comfortable with our position, then maybe you will be used at trial."

8.4 ZAPRUDER ARBITRATION TRIAL

To win the Zapruder arbitration, Bennett knew it would come down to the experts. So, he found the best and developed a strategy to demolish the government's experts. His experts included Dr. Jerry Patterson, a senior vice-president at Sotheby's and a world-renowned independent appraiser, and William Landes, an economics and law professor with a subspecialty in art and collectibles at the University of Chicago Law School.

The legal issue in the arbitration was, on its face, simple. Under the Fifth Amendment, the government cannot take private property for public use from a person without paying a fair market price for the property it takes. The fair market value is what a willing buyer would pay a willing seller, and this fair market value is to be determined at the time of the taking — August 1, 1998.

The challenge for Bennett was to prove the fair market value of something as unique as the Zapruder film. Bennett's experts chose to value what the Zapruder film would sell for at auction for two reasons: 1) this is where the Zapruders would have sold the film if it had not been seized by the government, and 2) it was the fairest way to determine the value for a unique collectible.

On the other hand, the government's experts used two different — and inconsistent — formulas. One expert, Cameron Macauley, took the price paid by Life Magazine in 1963 ($150,000) and then applied a very low rate of return that applied to goods such as bread and butter (the Consumer Price Index). He valued the film at $780,000. The second expert, John Staszyn, concluded the film was worth $1,000,000 in his initial expert report but then reduced it to $400,000 in his supplemental report. He used a market comparison approach, where he tried to compare the film's value to other similar objects.

Let's look at Bennett's cross-examinations of the government's two experts.

8.5 CROSS-EXAMINATION OF CAMERON MACAULEY

Comparing Zapruder film to imaginary Lincoln assassination film

On direct examination, the government attorney asked Macauley about the size of the Zapruder film. The witness reached into his pocket and took out a blank Kodak 8 mm film that was similar in size to the Zapruder film (about 6 feet long). Indeed, it fit into the government's theme that the Zapruder film was neither unique nor valuable. Bennett felt the point of the demonstration was to trivialize the importance of the Zapruder film by comparing it to an ordinary 8 mm film.

Practice Tip

You must listen intently on direct examination for new opportunities to pursue on cross-examination.

When Bennett saw what he called a "hokey" demonstration, he knew he had a new line for cross. Bennett explains, "I had no idea that they would pull that stunt, and it just gave me the best opportunity that I had, and he made my case for me."

Q. Good morning. My name is Robert Bennett, and I represent the Zapruder family.
    Let me show you this 8 mm film that you were shown by counsel. When you appraise something, you are kind of predicting the future sometimes, right? If somebody comes in and shows you something and they say "If I were to sell this what could I get?" or if it is an auction process, "What is likely someone would bid?", is that a fair statement?
A. Yes.

Q. You are rewinding that. Let's not look to the future. Let's look to the past a little bit. Let's say by some miracle what you were winding there was the assassination footage of Abraham Lincoln.
A. I wouldn't be treating it this way.

Q. Of course, you would not be. That would be very, very valuable, would it not?
A. Yes.

Q. Getting to the bottom line, there is just absolutely no doubt, is there, based on your expert opinion that if that was an Abraham Lincoln assassination film similar in all respects to the Zapruder film, it would be an exceedingly rare, unique, valuable item? Is that not a fair statement?
A Yes, just as if there had been one of Garfield and McKinley.

Comparing Zapruder film to other collectibles

Q. Yes. Now let me show you a baseball. I will represent to you that we bought that baseball for $10. It is an official Major League baseball. You are aware, sir, because you keep track of sales and auctions, that the **Mark McGwire baseball sold recently at auction for $3,000,000.** *Is that correct?* [McGwire broke the season record for home runs with that ball.]
A. Correct.

Q. Would you agree with me that it is probably a fair assumption since that baseball has not been hit by anybody, much less Mark McGwire, that that is probably in better shape than the Mark McGwire baseball? Would you agree with me?
A. Let's call it mint shape.

Q. Mint shape. How do you explain that I could pick that little ball up for $10, but the Mark McGwire baseball went for $3,000,000?
A. Well, we're comparing apples and oranges here.

Q. No. We are comparing two baseballs: that baseball and the $3,000,000 baseball. How do you explain that?
A. Of course, it's the aura of his having hit it.

Q. It is associated with him.
A. Yes.

Q. **It is associated with an important event,** *of a baseball record. Is that right?*
A. Nobody has denied that. Yes.

Q. *And yet you are testifying today before this panel that the Zapruder film, which you have said in your report and which you have repeated here again today, is probably one of the most valuable films ever.* **You are saying that film is worth a third or a quarter of Mark McGwire's baseball?**

A. Yes, I am, because I am not comparing it with the baseball.

Q. *You have read our reports? Is that correct?*

A. Yes, I have.

Q. *You are aware of the fact, are you not, that the golf woods of President Kennedy's sold at auction? The hammer price* [**auction price**] *was $772,500. Is that correct?*

A. That's correct.

Q. **So you basically say that the value of the Zapruder film is about the same price, based on your analysis, as the golf clubs?**

A. **Yes, but I didn't compare it or derive our value from that.**

Q. *No, but collectors who are interested in golf, collectors who are interested in baseball, are paying staggering sums of money for things that they want to own for whatever reason. Is that correct?*

A. Collectors will pay anything for something if they want it badly enough. Of course.

Q. *Well, now, if you were running an auction of the Zapruder film, you would not, would you, say the only people who are permitted to come here and bid are lovers of film, people who are artists who appreciate the aestheticism of the film, would you?*

A. Have I ever said that?

Q. *No, sir. I am asking you. You would not say it?*

A. No.

Q. *You would want everybody imaginable to come in, the people who would want it because it is art, because it is history, because it is unique, because it is Kennedy. Is that not a fair statement?*

A. Yes. Auctions are open to the public.

Bennett does not argue with the expert on his turf, but gets him to compare the Zapruder film to items everyone can understand. As an aside, here is the context for the Mark McGwire home run baseball that sold for $3,000,000. In 1927, Babe Ruth set a single-season record for home runs by hitting 60 homers. In 1961, another New York Yankee, Roger Maris, broke the record with 61 home runs. Maris's record was thought to be unbreakable. On September 8, 1998, McGwire hit his 62nd home run of the season over the left field wall at St. Louis' Busch Stadium against the Chicago Cubs. He finished the season with 70 home runs. Barry Bonds now holds the record with 73 home runs.

Bennett's point is that, although McGwire's baseball has great significance in baseball, it seems unreasonable to suggest that a film of Kennedy's assassination could be appraised at a third of the value of McGwire's baseball. Bennett further drives home his point when he asks the expert to explain how he can give the same value to the Zapruder film as that paid at auction for Kennedy's golf clubs.

The expert admits the CPI rate of return compares different items

Q. Now, when we get to the bottom line of your analysis, what you essentially say, as I understand it, what you essentially say is I cannot find anything, and so what I am going to do is I am going to take the $150,000 price paid by Time-Life in 1963, and I am going to apply the CPI rate of return. Is that correct?
A. That's correct.

Q. Now, one thing I do not understand. On your direct examination and even on the beginning of my cross, you suggested that you kind of have to compare things with other things just like it. Is that right?
A. If possible, yes.

Q. Yes. And yet you use a rate of return, a CPI rate, which on your direct examination includes housing, cars, education, and entertainment. Is that correct?
A. That's correct. I think that has integrity.

Q. Now, you are not an economist, are you?
A. No, sir.

Q. Have you read the economist report of Professor Doctor Landes at the University of Chicago?
A. Yes, and I think it's full of contradictions.

*Q. **Well, I will tell him that,** but you do know that in his rate of return he sort of does something like what you are doing, isn't it? He is taking a rate of return. He is comparing oranges with oranges. He is saying these are the rates of returns of collectibles over a period of time. Is that not what he did?*
A. Yes, and that's in direct contrast with other authorities of his stature.

Q. Who?
A. Oh, I wish I had that.

*Q. **Well, if you think about it you can remind me before I close.***

Q. You are aware, are you not, of the da Vinci Codex?
A. I've examined every page of it myself personally.

Q. OK. Then you are aware that in 1980 it sold for $5.1 million. Is that correct?
A. Yes, but it was expected that $15 million would be the price of it at that sale.

*Q. **That is not my question, but I appreciate you adding that.** It sold for $5.1 million in 1980, right?*
A. Correct.

Again, Bennett never argues with the expert on his turf. Instead, he asks simple questions that any layperson can understand. When the expert fails to answer simple questions by dodging the question

---

Practice Tip

When an expert does not answer a question and instead provides an argumentative response, Bennett fires back, "That is not my question," and then repeats the original question until the witness gives a direct answer.

or adding more to his answer than a simple "yes" or "no," he shows his bias for the side that hired him. For example, to the simple question, "Have you read Professor Landes' report?", the witness answers "yes" and gratuitously adds that it is full of contradictions. Bennett reminds the witness that he only asked him if he had read it. Likewise, in the last question in this excerpt, the witness fails to answer a simple question and adds more information to his answer. Bennett sarcastically responds, "I appreciate your adding that."

You'll notice that Bennett refers to the da Vinci Codex. That is the item that Bennett's experts thought the Zapruder film was most comparable to. It is a fascinating historical document. The da Vinci Codex was the name used at trial to reference the Codex Leicester, which is one of Leonardo da Vinci's 30 scientific journals. The Codex Leicester was purchased by Bill Gates at Christie's auction house in 1994 for $30,802,500. The codex was an 18-page compilation of da Vinci's drawings and writings in Italian on topics that included astronomy and the properties of water, air, and light. (Da Vinci wrote the codex using mirror writing, which allows one to read the text only if you hold the manuscript before a mirror. The reasons why Da Vinci wrote the manuscript in this manner remain unclear.)

The Codex Leicester proved that there were wealthy people, such as Bill Gates, who would pay huge sums for an item of great historical significance.

Admits plaintiff's experts are very well qualified in their field

Q. *So, then you would agree that our experts, who you heard testify, Dr. Patterson and Ms. Warren, are very well-qualified experts in their field?*
A. Their field, yes.

Q. *All right. And part of their field is the auction market, is it not?*
A. Yes.

Q. *And you would agree your qualifications do not match theirs in that area of expertise?*
A. No, **and that area of expertise is pure speculation. Ours is not.**

Here, the witness again gratuitously adds information in his answer to a very simple question. Bennett's point is that his witnesses are experts in auction sales, and the government's expert is not.

Admits Steve Johnson is an expert

What happens next does not happen on many cross-examinations, but we can learn from Bennett how to make the most of an advantage when it is given. Just before the trial, Bennett got a call from his own expert, Steve Johnson, who mentioned that Macauley had recently hired him to appraise one of his films. When Bennett heard this news, his "eyes were coming out of his head."

Bennett then got an affidavit from Steve Johnson regarding what happened. He developed a plan to get Macauley to admit to Johnson's expertise and if he denied it, Bennett would then surprise him with the affidavit. But even Bennett could not believe what happened next:

Q. *I see. What about Mr. Johnson? You have read his report? Steve Johnson.*
A. Yes, I have.

Q. *He is a film man, is he not?*
A. **With limitations he is.** I know him very well.

Q. *You know him very well. He is an expert in film, is he not?*
A. **He's not an expert** from a technological point of view at all nor from a production point of view. He has been in the audio-visual—he was in the audio-visual department at Indiana University when I first met him, and he got an education degree in audio-visual education, an ADD, but he **hasn't had the depth of experience of hands-on knowledge of motion pictures.**

Q. *You agree that he is an expert appraiser of films?*
A. He's highly qualified.

Macauley has fought Bennett with every answer. He states that the government's expert has limitations, is "not an expert" in certain areas, and hasn't had in-depth experience in motion pictures. He only grudgingly admits he is highly qualified, but won't admit he is an expert.

As Bennett explains, the better course for Macauley would have been to say, "Yes, he's a great expert that I just disagree with." Instead, he said in substance, "Well, he's not as good as me." Bennett could not believe what he was hearing because he knew Macauley had "hired my guy to evaluate his own stuff."

Q. *And you are aware that he valued this film at $33 million?*
A. Yes, I am aware of that.

Q. ***In fact, Dr. Johnson is such a good expert you hired him last week to appraise a film of yours. Is that not correct?***
A. I did?

Q. *Did you not?*
A. **This is news to me.**

Bennett could not believe what was happening. He originally thought he would simply show that Macauley thought Dr. Johnson was an expert who he trusted to appraise one of his own films. "Now, I had a witness who was lying [about ever hiring him]." It was the turning point in the trial.

> *Now I was hitting gold.…. You should have seen the faces of the three arbitrators.*
> —Robert S. Bennett

Q. I have an affidavit here, Mr. Macauley. Let me read it to you.
A. Please do.

Now, Bennett warns the witness that he has an affidavit, and Bennett cannot believe that instead of "folding," the witness continues with the lie.

Q. Because if this affidavit is wrong, Dr. Johnson is going to have some difficulty. "Steve Johnson, being duly sworn, deposes and says: '1) In late 1998 or early January 1999, C. Cameron Macauley telephoned me and asked me if I would appraise for donation purposes some films that he owned."' Is that correct?
A. Films. We've discussed off and on the possibility of exchanging work, but I'm not sure what this film refers to.

Q. The first paragraph. You deny that in late 1998 or early 1999 you asked him if he would appraise for donation purposes some films?
A. I have generally talked to him about that. I don't recall the time or the details of it.

Q. So you do not dispute then it was 1998 or early January 1999?
A. All right.

Q. Let me go to the second paragraph.
A. All right.

Q. "On Sunday, May 16," that is 10 days ago, "Mr. Macauley again telephoned me." Did you talk to him 10 days ago?
A. Yes.

Q. "—to ask me if I would appraise for donation purposes a vintage film that he owns about a rare bird."
A. Oh, yes. Uh-huh. **I don't own it. I co-own it.**

Bennett could not believe the witness was still trying to lie. Here, he gives the disingenuous answer that he co-owns it. Bennett goes in for the kill.

Q. I did not ask you about owning it. I asked you is that a true affidavit?
A. Yes, that is correct.

Q. So you thought he was pretty good to appraise this film for you?
A. Oh, yes. Yes. I think he would do a good job.

Bennett points out that the lesson from this series of questions is that he did not immediately confront the witness with the affidavit. Instead, he drew the witness out by asking him questions that he knew he could prove were lies by using the affidavit if necessary. That way, if the witness lied, he could highlight the witness' lack of credibility. Imagine how less effective the cross-examination would have been if Bennett had skipped all the buildup and just asked the last question in this fashion: "I have an affidavit from Dr. Johnson that says, quote, 'Dr. Macauley hired me to appraise one of his films 10 days ago.'"

Reliance on Trask's claim that the film "falls short"

Q. Now, do you have your report with you?
A. Yes, I do, sir.

Q. Would you be kind enough to turn to page 27 in your initial report?
A. Yes.

Q. You make reference to a research historian who you indicate that you have spoken to, Richard Trask. Did you speak to Richard Trask?
A. Yes, by phone I have.

Q. Pardon me?
A. By phone, I have spoken to him.

Q. In Paragraph 4, the following appears [a quote from Trask]: "It is perhaps the best evidence of what happened to the President," referring to the Zapruder film, "but even as the best evidence, it falls short of our learning or being able to comprehend exactly what happened and who did it."
A. That's right.

Q. Why is that in the report? What is the significance of what Trask says?
A. Well, he's an authority on the Zapruder film. He devotes a whole chapter in his book about it.

Q. What is the point you are trying to make here?
A. That it is—let's see. That it has exhausted its evidentiary value for one thing, that the Warren Commission examined it very carefully, and all of the scientific studies since. I think that's what he's saying here.

Q. Have you read the record of the Assassinations Records Review Board?
A. Not completely.

Q. You say not completely. Did you read what Mr. Trask had to say?
A. I saw the television version.

Q. Well, when you talked to Mr. Trask, when was it that you talked to Mr. Trask?
A. Oh, maybe two years ago.

Q. Did Mr. Trask tell you what he told the Board, that this film was an icon?
A. I don't think he did.

Q. Did he tell you what he told the Board, that this film was a trophy?
A. No, I don't think he told me that.

Q. Did he tell you what he told the Board, that this film might go for tens of millions of dollars?
A. We didn't have that kind of a discussion. No.

Claim that Getty Museum has no interest

Q. *Would you look to the second to the last paragraph [of the rebuttal report] and let me read it to you as the predicate for my question?*
A. Uh-huh.

Q. *It says, "The LMH team,"—that's us—"takes for granted an assumption that numerous wealthy individuals and institutions would have vigorously competed with one another for the right to own the Zapruder film had it ever been placed up for auction. "The Getty Center in West Los Angeles, one of the world's most prestigious and unquestionably the world's wealthiest museums, is the home of what many would agree is one of the finest extant collections of important photographic works. A discussion with the director of the Getty Center's renowned photography section on 10-28-98 confirmed that the Getty had no interest in acquiring the film despite its characterization by LMH appraisers as the most important and valuable photographic masterpiece that has ever existed." Do you see that?*
A. Yes.

Q. *Why did you put in the report and emphasize in bold print that the Getty had no interest in acquiring the film?*
A. Well, this was not my personal conversation, but Mr. Neff, as I understand—

Q. *You did not talk to him?*
A. No, I did not.

Q. *But this is in your report?*
A. Yes.

Q. *Are you aware of the fact that Mr. Neff has written a letter?*
A. It's a part of our addenda.

Q. *No, not the letter I am talking about. I am referring to Exhibit Z-24, if you please. Let me read something to you.*
A. This may be new to me. I don't know.

Q. *It may be new to you. It is a letter, Exhibit Z-24. It is dated March 24, 1999. I am going to read a portion to you, and then I am going to ask you one or two questions, and then I am going to sit down. It is written to my colleague, Mr. Manhardt. He says in relevant part—well, let me read the whole letter. It is pretty brief. "In the fall of 1998, I received a telephone call from Dr. Ernest Rose, who identified himself as a consultant to the Department of Justice." Now, Dr. Rose is your colleague?*
A. That's correct.

Q. *The gentleman sitting in the courtroom? Is that correct?*
A. Yes, sir.

Q. *Let me just skip to the relevant parts. Referring to your report, he says, "In this testimony," referring to your report, which I just read to you, "I am quoted as saying that the J.*

Paul Getty Museum 'had no interest in acquiring the film despite its characterization by LMH appraisers as the most important and valuable photographic masterpiece that has ever existed.' This representation of my views is misleading, and I am writing to correct it. It is true that I told Dr. Rose that the J. Paul Getty Museum had no interest in acquiring the film, but I also told him, **which he fails to bring before the arbitrators,** *that we have no interest in such an acquisition, not because we question the value of the film, but because the Getty does not collect films or motion pictures.*

Moreover, I told Dr. Rose that in my personal opinion the film has **substantial cultural, artistic, and monetary value and might be of interest to a number of museums whose acquisition objectives include the collection of films.** *I compared it to Andy Warhol's painting of Campbell's Soup cans containing, like the Zapruder film, a series of images that are sequential in nature and look similar, but are each quite different. The Warhol painting is generally viewed today as a work of art.*

Q. Had you seen this letter before?
A. Yes, I have.

Q. By the way, you agree that he is a world-class expert in what he does, right?
A. I don't know that much about his reputation, frankly. He has a prestigious position, I admit.

Cross-examination to support case

Q. *You would agree that the Zapruder film is very unique and is very, very valuable?*
A. No. I would agree that the Zapruder film is unique in many of its characteristics, but not in others because there were two other films and many photographs. Well, there are not only two other films. There were 26 or 36 other films.

> **Practice Tip**
>
> Check the facts of the expert witness' report. Go through each line. You are bound to find inconsistencies or even, in situations like this, downright misleading statements.

Q. *You will agree it is one of the most valuable films of all time? Is that correct?*
A. Yes, I would.

Q. *In fact, that is what you say in your report. Would you turn to page 29, please?*
A. OK. The main report, right?

Q. *Of the direct report.*
A. Yes. OK.

Q. *Would you read the last paragraph, the last four lines, to the panel, please?*
A. This is Defining Comparability?

Q. *Defining Comparability.*
A. Comparability. Yes. "No short piece of motion picture film ever taken has become as famous and perhaps, given its length, none as valuable as the Zapruder film, nor has a comparable film blessed with fortunate circumstances and notoriety ever been sold in any marketplace. Therefore, it seems reasonable to conclude that no other known motion picture exists that can be considered fully comparable."

Q. *Now, when you wrote that, how valuable it was, how incomparable it was, you believed you were telling the truth to this panel. Is that not correct?*
A. Absolutely.

Q. *And you stand by that statement today you just read?*
A. I do, in combination with our appraisal.

Q. *Thank you. I have nothing else.*

A neglected strategy on cross-examination is to elicit information from the witness that supports your case. That is, instead of trying to destroy the witness' credibility, oftentimes, there are opportunities to get information from the witness that supports your case. Bennett does exactly that. Not only do most lawyers never take advantage of this strategy, but the few that do feel that they can't get favorable information from a witness and also try to destroy the witness's credibility. Both can be accomplished.

Here is the trick. When trying to get favorable information and also attempting to attack the witness's integrity, it is generally better to get the favorable information first. The reason is obvious: The witness is more likely to be forthcoming and agreeable before a series of questions is asked that are designed to attack his truthfulness or expertise.

But there is an exception to this order of questioning, and Bennett takes full advantage of it. When a witness has made statements prior to a trial (in an expert report or deposition), confidently attack the witness's methodology, expertise, and/or truthfulness before asking questions that support your case to which a reasonable witness would agree. The reason Bennett waits until the end of his cross-examination is because he knows, if the witness does not agree with him, he can point the witness to the expert's report, where the information has already been presented in black and white.

8.6 OPPOSING COUNSEL'S DIRECT EXAMINATION OF JOHN STASZYN

John Staszyn was the government's other expert. In his initial expert report he appraised the film at approximately $1,000,000. In his rebuttal report he lowered the valuation to $400,000.

Staszyn mistakes photo of Akron dirigible for photo of Hindenburg

To fully appreciate how devastating Bennett's cross was on this point, we need to see Staszyn's testimony on direct examination. He discussed the limited value of the Zapruder film and compared it to famous photographs of disasters. One such photograph was the Hindenburg explosion. He was dead certain about the Hindenburg photograph, its value, and who took it.

The Hindenburg was one of many luxury zeppelins that carried passengers from Europe to the U.S. in half the time of ocean liners, and its crash was one of the most famous air transportation disasters in the world.

After traveling from Europe, the Hindenburg attempted to land at Lakehurst, New Jersey, on May 6, 1937. A spark ignited a leak in the dirigible's hydrogen container that held 7,000,000 cubic feet of hydrogen. It caused the Hindenburg to burn in 32 seconds. The explosion killed 35 out of 97 passengers and crew. The disaster was so tragic that it brought an end to passenger travel on commercial zeppelins, after more than 30 years and 2,000 successful flights.

On the other hand, the Akron dirigible crashed in 1933. Although 73 of the 76 people on board were killed, the crash is much less famous—perhaps because it crashed at sea but, more likely, because it was not caught on film and seen by millions of people when the narrator of the Hindenburg disaster proclaimed, "Oh, the humanity!" As a sidenote, airplane travel was about to overtake the dirigibles in any case. In 1935, Pan Am completed its first successful flight from San Francisco to Hawaii and ushered in commercial aviation.

Here is the direct examination.

Direct examination

Q. *I guess one of the examples that has come up in the course of these proceedings about tragic photos that are well known, one example mentioned was the Hindenburg disaster. As I understand it, there are both motion pictures of that and still photos of that. Is that correct?*
A. Yes.

Q. *Are you familiar with the trade in those?*
A. Well, I'm familiar with Margaret Bourke-White's photograph of the Hindenburg.

Q. *Why are you familiar with that one in particular? Why is that notable?*
A. Because it comes to auction.

Q. **You have to forgive us, Mr. Staszyn. Not everyone is as familiar with these famous photographers as you are.** *I take it Margaret Bourke-White is a famous photographer. Is that right?*
A. Yes. Yes. She's a famous photographer known for, you know, her work.

Q. *And so how do her pictures of the Hindenburg sell relative to the many other news photos and other photographers who were there that day?*
A. Well, **her photographs of the Hindenburg are the most valuable.**

Q. *And about what do they sell for?*
A. Less than $60,000.

8.7 BENNETT'S CROSS-EXAMINATION OF STASZYN

Notice below how prepared Bennett is. He realizes two things: 1) the government's expert has made a mistake regarding the origins of the Hindenburg photograph, and 2) the government has emphasized the witness' expertise in this area.

Expert admits mistake about photo

> **Practice Tip**
> There is always something to gain from a witness's direct examination that is not in your intended cross-examination outline.

Bennett employs one of his important principles of cross-examination: Listen intently to the direct examination. Let's watch what Bennett does:

Q. *Now, you testified in your field of expertise, and if I heard you correctly you were describing a photograph of the Hindenburg by Margaret Bourke-White.*
A. Yes.

Q. *Are you sure she did a photograph of the Hindenburg?*
A. The Hindenburg.

Q. *She never did the Hindenburg, did she? I thought you testified about Bourke-White. Look, I do not want to play games with you. Let me show you the Sotheby's photograph book in New York. There is a Margaret Bourke-White [photograph] of a dirigible, but—*
A. Yes.

Q. *This is what you were talking about?*
A. This is what I'm referring to. Correct.

Q. *And that is not the Hindenburg?*
A. No.

Q. *You were mistaken?*
A. Yes.

Q. *That is the Akron?*
A. Correct.

Bennett challenges Staszyn's expertise

To fully appreciate Bennett's success on this theme, one would need to read the portion of the direct examination that built up the expert's qualifications in photography, but such an endeavor would take too long because so much time was spent on it. Staszyn was asked every imaginable question about the number of photographs he had appraised or matted in his career. Unfortunately for the government, he got confused about the Hindenburg photograph. Next, he would have to admit his lack of expertise regarding motion pictures:

Q. *Looking at your resume, which is part of the material, you view yourself as essentially an expert in photography. Is that right?*
A. And photographic materials.

Q. And photographic material. While you deal occasionally with film, you do not hold yourself in your resume out as an expert in films. Is that a fair statement?
A. Moving film?

Q. Yes.
A. No.

So, the entire build up on the direct examination was undercut by a few precise questions. Then Bennett used Staszyn's lack of expertise with auctions to show how much better Bennett's undisputed auction experts were.

Q. Now, you testified on direct that you do matting. You have a company that does matting?
A. Yes. I do archival matting and framing of photographs, animation cells, paper — usually paper material.

Q. Is that a significant part of your business?
A. At some points of the year it's significant, yes.

Q. And you heard our witness, our expert witness, Ms. Warren, yesterday say that she had actually hired you to do some matting for Sotheby's?
A. Correct.

Q. OK. Have you ever headed a department at Sotheby's?
A. No.

Q. Have you ever been employed by any of the major auction houses as an employee of the auction house, not as an independent contractor?
A. No.

Q. Have you ever had responsibility for taking a valuable collectible and seeing that it was marketed and auctioned off properly?
A. I've taken material for clients to auction, yes.

Q. No, no. I mean for an auction house.
A. No.

Q. Would you agree with me that it is a fair statement to say that Mr. Patterson and Ms. Warren [the plaintiff's experts] have far more expertise than you in the auction business? Is that a fair statement?
A. As working for an auction house, yes.

Q. Knowledge of the auction process?
A. Correct.

Bennett exposes government experts' inconsistent methodology

You never want to find yourself in the position that your own experts disagree with each other. Such was the predicament the government was in. Macauley used the Consumer Price Index to determine the value of the Zapruder film, while Staszyn used a comparative approach that is the approach Bennett's expert's used. Bennett highlights this important inconsistency.

Q. *By the way, during direct examination, counsel for the government asked you your methodology, and the sum and substance of it was that you made a number of comparisons. You took a market comparison approach. Is that correct?*
A. Yes.

Q. *And you compared the film to things other than film?*
A. Yes.

Q. *Do you really feel that is a legitimate way to do it?*
A. Yes.

Q. *And that is the way Ms. Warren did it and Mr. Patterson did it? Is that not correct?*
A. I don't think it was a thorough job.

Q. *You think you did a more thorough job than they did?*
A. Yes, because I considered more markets.

Q. *Do you know—*
A. Would the codex fall in the photography market? No.

Q. **This may be unfair, but for the moment I am asking the questions. You agree that a comparative approach is the right approach? [Bennett never lets the witness get control of the cross-examination.]**
A. Correct.

Q. *And you agree that you looked at things outside the film?*
A. Yes. I was forced to.

Q. *And you agree that Ms. Warren and Mr. Patterson likewise followed a comparative approach? Is that correct?*
A. Yes.

Q. *So when Mr. Macauley testified earlier today that you do not go to the comparative approach but you go by taking $150,000 and adding to it a rate of return of the general CPI [Consumer Price Index], you do not agree with his approach, do you?*
A. I didn't use that approach.

Q. *I did not ask you if you used it. I read your report. You did not use it. Do you agree with that approach, yes or no?* **[Bennett listens carefully and when witness doesn't answer question, he repeats question.]**
A. I am not sure whether that is the proper approach.

Q. *You do not think—*
A. I am not sure.

Q. *You do not think it is, do you?*
A. I'm not sure.

Practice Tip

You can never get a witness to admit that he is a liar, but you can *prove* the witness is a liar.

Bennett shows that Staszyn does not agree with the analysis of the other government witness. If you are the government and the two experts you are paying to testify can't agree on the methodology to use, you are in trouble. Moreover, if one of your experts is using the same methodology as your opponent (comparative approach), the one (Macauley) using the consumer price index to arrive at a value of the film has lost all credibility.

Bennett gets expert to admit there is an international market for film

Q. But there would be, in your view, a market for this film?
A. Yes.

Q. Both national and international?
A. Yes, perhaps. Yes. International, I'm not so sure about. You know, I don't know why someone in Italy would buy it, to tell you the truth. Nationally, yes.

Q. Well, you put in your report, and let me read page eight of your report so we are clear about it. I do not want there to be any misunderstanding. You say, "Foreign assets in America should be considered. These assets may be more expendable in America than in your own country by avoiding taxation and accountability. Such assets could seek out the rare and valuable and the nationally significant." Do you remember saying that?
A. Yes, I said that.

Q. Okay. So you feel that —
A. Yes. I believe that, yes. It could happen.

Q. You thought it was likely enough to happen that you put it in—
A. I had to —

Q. Let me finish. It would be in the report, right?
A. Yes.

Having looked at two of Bennett's cross-examinations, don't think that you have to wait for the trial of your career to use his techniques. Everything he did can be used in almost any cross-examination. Let's break it down and see what he did.

First, he doesn't try to get the witness to admit that he is not qualified or has made incorrect conclusions. I believe that is the greatest mistake lawyers make on cross-examination. Lawyers are under the mistaken belief that if they argue with a witness long enough, like the dramatic moment in a TV show or Hollywood movie, the witness will confess that he is wrong.

In the Zapruder case, neither of the government's experts was ever going to admit he had incorrectly valued the Zapruder film or that he was not qualified to appraise it. No witness is going to admit these failings on the stand. A lawyer's goal on cross-examination is to prove that only his or her expert witnesses are the ones that should be believed.

Let's break down what Bennett did with these two witnesses. For the cross-examination of Cameron Macauley, Bennett had three areas of attack. First, Bennett showed that Macauley's testimony was inconsistent with statements he made prior to the trial, such as those within his expert report. This is a strategy you can use for any witness. Almost every witness testifies inconsistently with prior statements.

For example, Macauley claimed in his report that another expert (Trask) said the Zapruder film did not have a lot of value and that the Getty Museum did not want the film. Those prior claims were undercut by the fact that Trask had actually said the film could sell for "tens of millions of dollars." Also, the Getty Museum said that it would want the film but did not collect motion pictures.

The second area of Bennett's cross-examination attacked the expert's valuation of the film. Every expert witness makes certain assumptions to arrive at a conclusion. Bennett attacked those assumptions by asking the witness to compare the value of the Zapruder film to an imaginary one of Lincoln's assassination. He then made the witness compare the low value he gave to the Zapruder film to other collectibles that had sold at auction, such as Mark McGwire's record-breaking home run baseball and Kennedy's golf clubs. Moreover, Bennett attacked the witness' use of the consumer price index to value a very unique and highly collectible item.

> **Practice Tip**
>
> You can cross almost every witness with questions that don't attack him but rather seek answers that will support your case. Don't forget this often neglected strategy.

The third area Bennett used for his cross-examination was to get the expert to support Bennett's case. He did this by getting Macauley to admit that Bennett's experts were well qualified. Then, he showed Macauley where he stated in his own expert report that the Zapruder film was so unique, it was incomparable.

Two of these same areas of cross-examination were used for the government's second expert. Bennett showed that Staszyn had made an incorrect statement in his expert report, and at trial, Bennett compared the Zapruder film to a photo Staszyn initially believed was of the Hindenburg, but later conceded was actually of a different dirigible.

Bennett also got Staszyn to admit that Macauley's use of the consumer price index to value the film was not sound.

And the last area on which Bennett cross-examined Staszyn was his credibility. Bennett did this by showing the arbitration panel that while Staszyn was an expert in photos, he had no expertise in motion pictures nor in auction houses, which Bennett's experts said the Zapruder film would have the best chance of being valued fairly.

8.8 THE ARBITRATORS' QUESTIONS

At the close of evidence, the arbitrators asked questions of counsel before closing arguments. Read how quickly Bennett comes up with a powerful response that directly answers the question for Bennett:

> *Dellinger: My only other question is for Mr. Bennett. I think you may know what it is. Let me just play, the way I have seen some questioners do, sort of devil's advocate. Let me give you the hardest view of this that a camera original is virtually worthless…. There is a whole universe out there of films of historically important events…. Just to mention one we have not mentioned yet, the shooting, the assassination of Lee Harvey Oswald by Jack Ruby, which may have been on television and not on film, but even in recent years there are simply scores of historic events, which have been captured on film.*
>
> *Those films are quite valuable as a copyright as part of an archives, but, as Staszyn said at page 6, this appraiser has found no other film of importance without a copyrighted public sale; that the object here, a camera original strip of film, has just never been considered of any value, that there would be a market if they were of any value at all, and if we had some kind of market, if anybody ever thought that freed from the copyright the camera original copy of the scene of the burning of Atlanta from Gone With the Wind or the raising of the flag at Iwo Jima, if those had had some value, then we could argue about what multiple of that kind of value would be appropriate for this particular strip of film….*
>
> *You lose your case because you cannot show that anybody has ever considered this kind of item to have any value before and that is what you do in the absence of evidence here. That is my honest, best shot.*

Bennett: Well, if that were true, we would be in Alice in Wonderland, with all due respect. You know the great story about Alice going to the party. She looks, and everybody is standing on their head. That would mean that the rarest of things have no value because some lawyer cannot come into a courtroom and say, you know, there have been five or six others kind of like it in the past, so that is my first point….

Point number two is the best I can do is to bring forth experts who give you judgment. The best I can do is go out and find the best experts I can find that appreciate the issue you just raised with me and come in and say look, here is the best I can do.

We brought two people here who have 62 years of combined experience at two of the world's greatest auction houses, Sotheby's and Christie's. You heard their testimony. You heard them on cross. They wore two hats, to use Arbitrator Fineberg's words, one a business hat, and another I think Arbitrator Fineberg labeled it as the aesthetic hat. They said we are confident, way above the threshold of the law....

Another answer to you is nobody disputes that if there had been an assassination film of Lincoln that that would be incredibly valuable. I mean, we just cannot do any better than what we have done.... The final answer to the question is where we start. These two days are a lot different than what happened before the Assassination Review Board. I again ask you to go back and look at what those people said why they were taking the film from my clients.

Bennett told me that he always tries to work the Alice in Wonderland analogy into his closing arguments. "It humanizes you, me, the lawyer. It tells the jury I'm a father. Now, it tells the jury, I'm a grandfather. Totally irrelevant, but it humanizes you. It's a graphic that they can understand."

Although the story he uses is not precisely the one from Alice in Wonderland, it is a spin-off that he has read before, although the origin of the spin-off is unknown. Bennett explains the story in more detail: "Alice is this cute little girl, and she's walking down, and she falls in a rabbit hole. She twirls down, and she hits the bottom ... and you can see a jury just saying, 'Where the hell is he going with this?' Everything is upside-down. There's even an animal holding a goldfish bowl upside down, but somehow the fish doesn't fall out of it. I say, 'I think of that in this case here. Here [substitute prosecution or plaintiff's claims, i.e., the prosecution is basing its case on the testimony of a man with five felonies.] This is upside-down.'"

8.9 BENNETT'S CLOSING ARGUMENT STRATEGIES

Another theme he uses often in closing statements is to explain to the jury what the case is not about. For example, in one of his earlier cases that proved to be significant for his career, he represented Dominic Paolucci. Paolucci was a navy officer who, among other things in his distinguished career, took part in the U.S. landing on Omaha Beach in 1944. In 1970, he became president of a firm that had contracts with the U.S. military. Paolucci was indicted in a criminal conspiracy that alleged he defrauded the government by persuading it to enter into a naval contract to train the Iranian army. The fraud was allegedly committed when a retired admiral and captain negotiated the contract on behalf of Paolucci's company in return for being hired by the same company.

In his closing statement, Bennett argued, "Before talking about what this case is, let me just talk briefly about what the case is not.... We are not talking about mistakes. We are not talking about poor judgment. We are not talking about the most perfect of all [the science of hindsight]. We are talking about these men getting together and deciding to break the law of the United States of America…. Paolucci is not charged with bribery…not charged with conflict of [interest], not charged with any of that. So, this mountain of government testimony is a molehill."

Bennett's client was acquitted.

Here is another analogy he uses in defending criminal prosecutions. Often the government will argue in its closing statement that the nature of the crime forced it to rely on bad people or people to whom it had to give favorable pleas in return for their testimony. So, the prosecutor argues, "Look, this is the defendant's guy, he didn't hang out with honest people but bad people." Second, the prosecutor argues, "Look, just believe him to the extent we've corroborated the evidence." The prosecutor continues. "Let's look at the other pieces of evidence."

To counter this argument, Bennett argues, "Let's say you're in a restaurant, and you ordered a beef stew, and you get it, and you notice there are these green rotten pieces of meat, and you call the waiter, he says, 'Oh gee, I'm sorry,' and he picks out the rotten pieces of meat, and he says, 'That's OK now.' That's what the prosecution is asking you to do."

8.10 ZAPRUDER VERDICT

On July 19, 1999, the arbitrators ruled two to one in favor of the Zapruder family. They awarded $16,000,000 in damages plus $1,000,000 in interest. This was more than 17 times what the government had offered to settle the case for and argued for valuation at trial.

8.11 CHAPTER CHECKLIST ✏

Bennett's trial strategies

1. Over prepare and under try your case.

2. When first getting a case, think about the closing argument. What are the points that can be made that would convince a jury to rule favorably?

3. For every hour preparing a case, spend 20 minutes thinking about the case by being in the opponent's shoes in order to understand one's own weaknesses.

Bennett's tips for cross-examination

1. Be a guerrilla fighter: Know the one or two points to make on cross-examination and get out.

2. Listen carefully on direct examination for the witness to create an opening for a new topic on cross-examination.

3. When preparing topics for cross-examinations, think of weak spots that a jury would understand.

4. When eliciting information on cross-examinations, think how these answers could be used in the closing argument.

5. Start a cross-examination by eliciting favorable information before attacking the witness.

6. Atmosphere is critical. There is nothing worse than conducting a cross-examination with a bunch of binders and notes.

7. Use leading questions.

Bennett's strategies for cross-examination of expert witnesses

1. Think of topics that will make the witness look weak or not knowledgeable.

2. In order to make the witness look weak, ask questions to which he will answer, "I don't know."

3. Don't take on the expert in his area of expertise.

4. Don't try to prove your expert has a better resume than your opponent's unless the differences are very important. Jurors don't care about minor differences.

5. Get all of the opposing expert's prior testimonies and writings. Scour them for "nuggets of gold" to help in your cross-examination.

Bennett's insights for hiring expert witnesses

1. Investigate literature and other sources to determine who is the best in the field.

2. To best determine the expert's credibility, there is no substitute for an in-person interview.

3. Don't have the expert sign a fee agreement to testify at the trial until he or she has reviewed the case. You don't want your expert impeached at trial because he or she got paid before ever looking at the case.

Summary of cross of Macauley

1. Bennett makes the expert compare Zapruder film to imaginary film of Lincoln's assassination.

2. Bennett forces the expert to compare film to other collectibles, such as McGwire's baseball.

3. The expert admits that the CPI rate of return compares different items rather than unique collectibles.

4. The government expert admits the plaintiff's experts are very well qualified.

5. The expert admits mistaken reliance on another's authority (Trask) that the Zapruder film "falls short."

6. Bennett attacks the expert's unfounded claim that Getty Museum has no interest in film.

7. The expert admits he has hired the plaintiff's expert to appraise one of his own films.

8. Bennett gets the expert to admit that no film is so valuable as the Zapruder film.

Summary of the cross-examination of Staszyn

1. Bennett proves that Staszyn mistakes the photo of the Akron for the photo of the Hindenburg.

2. Bennett highlights Staszyn's lack of expertise in film and auction houses.

3. Bennett exposes the government experts' inconsistent methodology.

4. Bennett gets the expert to admit there is an international market for film.

Bennett's advice for closing argument

1. Use the *Alice in Wonderland* analogy to explain to a jury that believing the other side's case would be the same as believing that it is normal when "everything is upside-down."

2. An effective argument is to tell the jury what the case is not about. For example, it is not about making mistakes or bad judgment. The prosecution has to prove a crime occurred.

CHAPTER NINE

Frank Branson

The Art of Undermining the Expert Witness

You see things in the witness's eyes. You see things in the witness's conduct that leads you to believe, I need to go here, rather than where we are in the paper.

— Frank Branson

Frank Branson grew up in White Settlement, Texas. While in law school, he worked as an insurance adjustor. When he saw how people he grew up with were treated by insurance companies, he knew it wasn't right. He became a plaintiff's lawyer and never looked back.

Frank Branson has received numerous honors. The Law Offices of Frank Branson was selected by *U.S. News and World Report* as one of the best law firms in the country in 2013. The *National Law Journal* selected him as one of the top 50 "Elite Trial Lawyers for Plaintiffs" in the United States in 2014. He represents both individuals and families in everything from workplace catastrophes to defective products and high-stakes business disputes.

His passion to help the less fortunate is guided by the values his father instilled in him. His father was a high school football coach who had an "overwhelming desire to win." But his father also believed that winning was only worthwhile if it was done within the rules. His father also preached, "Don't ever quit."

As a result, Branson uses his immense trial skills to create a level playing field for his clients in their battles with large corporations such as Ford Motor Company. Branson gets personal satisfaction from helping a client take on a huge company and winning, because he forces the company to play by the rules. Let's learn his secrets to successful cross-examination.

CHAPTER HIGHLIGHTS
- Learn the art of crossing an expert
- Learn to recognize where the witness is weak
- Expose the expert's bias

9.1 *SIMO V. MITSUBISHI*

In this chapter, we will examine Branson's cross-examination of the key expert witness in *Simo v. Mitsubishi*, which was a case that involved a tragic car wreck. The plaintiff, Chefik Simo, was a passenger in a 2000 Mitsubishi P45 Montero Sport. In the early morning hours of October 11, 2002, the driver of the Montero Sport suddenly steered left to avoid another car and then he attempted to get back into his original lane by quickly turning back to the right. The Montero Sport rolled over, and while it was on its side, the SUV was hit by a Federal Express tractor-trailer.

Simo was a star freshman soccer player for Furman University in Greenville, South Carolina. He was one of the best soccer players in the United States and had already been recruited to play professional soccer. He suffered severe injuries from the accident and underwent several surgeries. He incurred $277,000 in medical bills and was unable to play soccer again.

At trial, Simo claimed that the Montero Sport was unreasonably dangerous because its center of gravity was too high, which caused it to roll over on flat, dry pavement (i.e., to roll over "untripped"). The jury returned a verdict for Simo of $7,000,000. The turning point in the trial was Branson's cross-examination of the defendant's star expert, Don Tandy.

9.2 CROSS-EXAMINATION STRATEGIES

Before turning to the specific lessons we can learn from Branson's cross, let's first study Branson's general strategies for cross-examination. When he cross-examines, he doesn't do it from a list of questions that he has written down. He explains, "I have questions I've written out, and I make sure I've covered them before I sit down, but it's pretty extemporaneous. The reason is, I take the cross where I think the witness is going." He wants to catch the witness in an exaggeration, a lie, or an admission.

I asked him how he knows which line of questions to ask a witness. He then explained by using the example of properly riding a horse: "I don't ride horses, but I have friends who ride horses. They insist that you steer a horse, not with the reins, but with your knees.... You get inside the witness's head, and it happens." Branson further explained, "You look for body language, you look for inflections and voice changes.... It's the way the witness says things, or the looks."

Just as we have seen with the other great trial lawyers in this book, Branson makes it clear that you cannot conduct a cross-examination if your head is buried in your notes. A series of questions read from an outline, even if it is a good series, is like directing a horse with the reins and not your knees. You won't get anywhere.

Branson further explains that you need to remember the courtroom's dynamics. The witness is in a less protected position, both physically and psychologically. The judge's chair is higher than the witness's, the jurors are staring at the witness, and the witness is being questioned by a lawyer who has spent weeks and weeks preparing for this moment. The witness is trying to guess what the ultimate point of your questions is and how to avoid the outcome. In that state of fear, the witness will often inflate the truth or try to distract you from a weakness in his testimony. Only by looking at the witness constantly can you perceive when these moments occur. This advice also applies when you are questioning a seasoned expert witness who is motivated by money to testify the way his client wants him to.

Branson believes a lawyer's attitude is extremely important when cross-examining a witness. He tries not to be rude or curt in his cross-examinations. However, he is very firm. For example, Branson once took the deposition of the former president of Ford Motor Company, Jacques Nasser, for a case in which Branson's clients alleged that the defective tires on new cars made the cars defective. As always, Branson made complicated issues simple for the jury. He asked Nasser if he had started his career in sales. The former president of Ford replied, "yes." The following exchange then took place:

Branson: "When you were in sales, did you ever have anybody come in and say, 'I'd like five Firestone tires and, by the way, throw in an SUV?'"
Nasser: "No."

Branson: "They come in, buy the car, and the tires that are on it."
Nasser: "Yes."

Branson: "If the tires are defective, the car is defective."
Nasser: "Yes."

With that exchange, Branson made his case for product defect against Ford Motor Co. But Branson had gained so much respect from Nasser through his questioning that, at the end of the deposition, Nasser offered Branson a box of cigars. Not many lawyers can get a witness to concede liability and have the witness offer a gift as a sign of respect at the end of the battle.

To lay the groundwork for a successful cross-examination, Branson often employs a "report card" as a tactic during his depositions.... First, he will get the exact definition of the important jury instructions he will use at trial. In the example he shared with me, the definitions were for negligence and gross negligence. From those definitions, he creates a chart that lists the

> *In a deposition, you can develop a relationship [with the witness]. I wasn't rude to him. I wasn't curt with him, but I made him admit a lot of things that were true.*
> —Frank Branson

facts that support plaintiff's claims for each definition. Then, he asks the witness to grade the company he or she works at (or worked at) or a codefendant's actions concerning each fact.

For example, he might ask a witness who is in management to grade on a scale of A to F whether there was any operator error. Branson has found that all jurors can relate to the report card. Branson points out that a report card can also be very effective when there are codefendants and the defendant grades his codefendant more harshly than his own company. "The jury gets angry if they give themselves real high marks when the evidence shows otherwise. They also get angry if they turn on their codefendants."

I asked Branson how often he gets objections to what I call the "report card cross." He pointed out that sometimes the attorney will object at the deposition or at trial, but judges have almost always allowed him to present such a cross-examination.

To see a video of Branson in action, go to www.TurningPointsatTrial.com and click on the video "Nasser." You will find a video excerpt of Branson taking the deposition of Nasser. He asks Nasser to grade Firestone's conduct regarding the defective tires it provided for Ford's vehicles. He asks such questions as, "Did Firestone adequately manufacture tires at its plant?" Nasser writes an "F" on the chart for Firestone's grade. Nasser gives Firestone the same grade for whether it adequately investigated dangers to U.S. customers regarding the tires.

You will notice from the deposition that Branson is extremely knowledgeable about the facts of his case. He is polite and firm with the witness, and he builds a rapport with him. At the end of the clip, you can see that Nasser has graded his codefendant a lot harsher than he graded Ford. The report card is a wonderful visual that explains very powerfully the negligent conduct of Firestone.

On the same website, there is a video clip of the deposition of William Ford, Jr., then current chairman and CEO of Ford. By using Ford's own commercial, Branson gets the president of Ford to admit, in so many words, that the commercial is deceptive advertising. During the deposition, the deceptive ad is contrasted with an ad that shows Ford's noble beginnings. You can see the concern and regret on the witness's face as Branson gets him to admit that a teenager should never drive a truck as aggressively as shown in the commercial. Branson's technique here teaches us a valuable lesson: a simple question combined with a powerful exhibit will force the witness to answer truthfully. If the witness does not answer truthfully, his only other option is to give an outrageous answer that no one would believe.

Branson shared a final thought about cross-examination. Thirty years ago, he conducted long cross-examinations. He would make notes as the witness was testifying on direct, and then cross-examine the witness on each of these topics. He found that such a tactic "offends the jury time-wise."

> **Practice Tip**
> Don't waste the jury's time. Branson suggests that you should limit your cross to 45 minutes to an hour and a half at most.

9.3 CROSS-EXAMINATION OF EXPERT WITNESS FOR MITSUBISHI MOTORS

Let's turn our attention to Mitsubishi's expert in the Simo trial. Branson explained that he had a day's worth of ammunition to cross-examine the witness with, but tried to limit his cross to 90 minutes. As auto manufacturers are apt to do, they put on a "real dog and pony show. They pick their key expert, and they use high, glossy boards and videos and animations, and they have one knight in shining armor, if you will, and if you can pierce the armor of that knight, you go a long way towards winning."

Branson stated that after direct examination, the jury seemed to believe the expert. He was "crème de la crème." He had worked at Ford Motor Company. He's an engineer. He's defending truth and justice.

Let's learn from a master by taking an in-depth look at Branson's cross-examination of Mitsubishi's expert witness.

Witness's expert fees

*Q. In your answers on direct examination, you referred to what **real automotive engineers do**. Remember that question and answer?*
A. Talking about some of the work that I had done and other engineers I knew, yes.

Q. Yes. And in fact from 1986 to 1995 you worked in the capacity as a real automotive engineer —
A. Well, I worked —

Q. — at Ford Motor Company?
A. At Ford Motor Company, yes.

Branson: *Could I ask the witness to help me with a chart for just a moment?*
Court: Sure.

*Q. If you will put on the chart what you made in your last year at Ford Motor Company as a **real automotive engineer**.*
A. Personal salary?

Q. Yes, sir.
A. If I can remember the range.

Q. It would have been a specific number.
A. Somewhere in that range.

Q. *It was the year 1995, did you make 130 or 140 [thousand dollars]?*
A. I just don't remember.

Q. *OK. That's fine. And were you a **good automotive engineer**?*
A. Yes.

Q. *Was that a good salary for an automotive engineer?*
A. Yes.

Q. *Now, when you left Ford Motor Company—when you were there, was your job to testify about Ford products?*
A. No, I didn't testify, didn't get deposed and things like that but I was working on products.

Q. *Your primary job was to work on automobiles, was it not?*
A. Yes.

Q. *And that's a reasonable salary for what an automotive engineer should make?*
A. I guess at the time.

Q. *The first time you were put forward as an expert witness was when you left and went to work for Carr Engineers?*
A. Yes.

Q. *When you went to work for Carr Engineering in 1995, write down if you would what they paid you to become an expert witness.*
A. Depends on the year.

Q. *Let's start with the first year.*
A. It was around the same range in the first year, then it increased.

--------- ✦ ---------

Q. *Your last year at Carr Engineering—you were there for six and a half years?*
A. Yes.

Q. *Your last full year what did you make?*
A. Last full year I would have made over a million dollars.

Q. *So from going from a real automotive engineer to being an expert witness in six and a half years, you raised your income from 130 or 40 to over a million dollars?*
A. Yes, sir.

Q. *Would you write that down for us? That would have been 2002.*
A. (The witness complied.)

In just a few questions, Branson establishes his first theme for cross. The Defendant's expert witness has increased his income tenfold to become an expert witness instead of a "real automotive engineer." This point is made all the more dramatic because opposing counsel did not bring this issue out on direct. It is critical to discuss the weaknesses in your witness's testimony on direct so that you don't lose trust with the jury by having it uncovered on cross by opposing counsel.

Q. *You testified before this jury yesterday that mostly what you do is litigation for lawyers that represent automotive carriers, insurance companies and the motor carriers themselves, is that true?*
A. Yes.

Q. *And by litigation you are talking about doing testing to support the defenses. You are talking about teaching lawyers like [defense counsel] all the things he asked you about in this case. So you do litigation support in that you say here's our strong points, here's our weak points, here's how we prove them. That's part of what you do as an expert witness, isn't it?*
A. Not really. I do testing and I do analyze crashes and I determine what happens. And I tell lawyers like [defense counsel] what my findings were. But I don't tell him really about his case.

Q. *Well, has [defense counsel], for example, called you during this trial to ask you some questions?*
A. Yes.

Q. *A number of times?*
A. I think twice.

Q. *And that would be part of litigation support for [defense counsel], wouldn't it, in this case?*
A. Yeah, in fact the second time was you've got to get to Greenville now.

Q. *Well, I can see where he probably needed help. Write down this number for me if you will, $22,281,978.23. And write the year, put an arrow from January 2002 to October of 2005.*
A. (The witness complied.)

Q. *Now, I have asked you whether you testified in October of 2005 that between the time you started your company in January of 2002 and that trial you had earned — you had been paid from Ford Motor Company alone $22,281,978.23.*
A. That's what the company had been paid according to Ford's report.

Q. *Would you put a dollar sign by that number, please.*
A. (The witness complied.)

> **Practice Tip**
> The greater the percentage of annual income that an expert witness makes from testifying in court, the easier it is to show his bias. Branson constantly compares what the expert did as a "real automotive engineer" when he worked at Ford to what he now does in his new job as a highly paid expert for car companies.

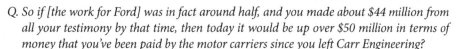

Q. *So if [the work for Ford] was in fact around half, and you made about $44 million from all your testimony by that time, then today it would be up over $50 million in terms of money that you've been paid by the motor carriers since you left Carr Engineering?*
A. With all your assumptions, that's possible.

Q. And you are not standing here to tell this jury under oath that that's not possible, are you?
A. I think that would be high, but I can't give you an exact number.

Expert's bias toward Mitsubishi

Q. Now, this is not your first rodeo with Mitsubishi, is it?
A. Rodeo, you mean case?

Q. Yes.
A. Yes, sir.

Q. In fact, I think you testified that at the very minimum you've been involved in over twenty Mitsubishi cases?
A. It's probably a best guess, yes.

Q. And [defense counsel] and you have worked together a lot?
A. Several occasions, yes.

Q. Not only with Mitsubishi but with Ford and with other manufacturers?
A. Yes, that's true....

Q. But how many times for 44 and $50 million have you actually come down here and said to a jury, "I don't care how narrow it is or how tall it is or what the injuries were when it rolled over, this SUV is not defective?" How many times have you done that since January of '02 to earn all this money?
A. Cases that go to trial, I wouldn't have that testimony.

Q. Pardon?
A. The cases that go to trial would be ones where I did an evaluation and found the vehicle to be reasonably safe.

Q. Well, in fact, let's be honest with the jury, you have never testified that any vehicle you've ever reviewed was too narrow and had a low stability to roll over and was defective, have you, sir?
A. Well, too narrow, it's true. What were the others?

Q. Have you ever testified that any company that hires you to come down and tell the jury [that]...they've manufactured and sold unreasonably dangerous and unsafe vehicles?
A. Not one that's come to trial, correct....

Q. Have you ever testified that Mitsubishi manufactured and sold to the American public a defective vehicle?
A. Not the ones I analyzed, no....

Q. Have you ever testified in any case that you have earned all this money at, that you never tipped up a production model sport utility vehicle?
A. That I have never tipped up a production model?

Q. Done for litigation testing.
A. Probably true, yes, that's true.

After focusing on the fact that the expert has testified exclusively for defendants and has never wavered in his conclusion that the SUVs were not defective, watch how Branson hammers home the point.

> *How many times for $44 and $50 million have you actually come down here and said to a jury…this SUV is not defective?*
> —Frank Branson, during cross-examination of expert witness.

Q. *You grew up in Ohio, went to Ohio State?*
A. I went to Ohio State but I'm an Army brat so different parts of the world.

Q. *But you have lived in Texas since you went to work for Lee Carr?*
A. Yes, I have.

Q. **Did you ever hear in Texas the phrase that you need to dance with them that brung you?**
A. **Did I ever hear what?**

Q. *Dance with them that brung you.*
A. Dance with what?

Q. *Dance with them that brung you?*
A. Dance with them that brung you? No, I haven't.

Q. *Well, it's kind of one of the things we do in the South of making examples. I think it came out back when young ladies would go with young men to dances. And the fellow would kind of expect the young lady to dance with him. Now, these automobile manufacturers kind of expect you to dance with them since they brought you to this dance, don't they?*
A. I haven't seen that, not at all. In fact, I have found that if there is an issue with the vehicle they want to know soon.

Q. *Let me ask you a question. What do you think would happen to your gravy train if you turned to this jury and said, "you know, I have really looked at Mr. Bilek's testing and that it truly limits testing. And, you know, I think that is an unreasonably dangerous and defective vehicle."* **What would happen to the gravy train you have got with these automobile makers if you gave such testimony under oath?**
Defense Counsel: **Judge, this is just argumentative.**
Court: **Overruled.**
Witness: **I really couldn't tell you.**

Branson is well aware that the jury is from South Carolina, and the expert is not. He asks the expert about a phrase everyone in the South knows, "You dance with the girl that brung you [brought you to the dance]." When the witness admits he doesn't know it, the answer reminds the jury that the witness is *not* a local person, while the plaintiff *is*.

Branson then asks questions about the "gravy train." The impact of the question is doubled when defense counsel highlights its damage by objecting and then getting overruled by the judge.

Practice Tip

Use objections very sparingly. Don't object to a question just because the answer to it hurts your client. If you do, your objection will only highlight the bad answer if the judge overrules you.

Branson knows the witness is not going to confess that yes, his gravy train would stop, but Branson's question makes it clear to the jury what a truthful answer would be. That is all Branson needs. Moreover, the witness looks even more biased because he won't admit that he relies on the car companies for all of his income and that the opinions he gives favor them. A better answer would have been, "I always tell the truth so I would not testify for Mitsubishi unless that is what the facts revealed."

Next, Branson turns his attention to the fact that Mitsubishi must have known that people would drive its cars above 75 miles per hour and need to use accident avoidance maneuvers on the highway. Watch how he makes a complex issue very simple by using the car's speedometer.

Speedometer limit on Montero Sport

Q. *Can we agree that real automotive engineers working for real car companies know more about what makes a car stable to drive than those of us who go into dealerships and buy them?*

A. It just depends on the person, but in a general sense I would believe that to be true. **[The expert cannot even answer a simple question without qualifying his answer.]**

Q. *Now, can you understand how those of us who don't have the benefit of a master's degree in engineering and may be a little bit mechanically challenged believe we could rely on the automobile manufacturers to fully test the vehicles and design them so that they can be safely driven in foreseeable uses?*

A. Reasonable uses, yes. **[Branson continually paints the picture of his client's right to rely on the fact that the car he bought is not defective.]**

Q. *And you know that since the early 70's the automobile manufacturers have been able to foresee that people take their vehicles, whether they are pickup trucks or whether they are small sports cars or whether they are SUVs, and they drive them out on highways in road conditions.... And in accident avoidance maneuvers at highway speeds?*

A. That can happen, yes.

Q. *Well, it's foreseeable.* **In fact, you've made 40 — between 40 and $50 million testifying in cases.** **[Branson continually reminds the jury how much money the expert has made.]** *Certainly at this point to you it's foreseeable that there are going to be accident avoidance maneuvers on the highway, isn't it, sir?*

A. It can happen, sure, I agree.

Q. *Would you think that's something the design engineers need to look at when they put a vehicle out on the road?*
A. Yeah, and they do. [**Watch how Branson simplifies the issue for the jury in the next series of questions.**]

Q. *In that regard, let me just show you — we put the speed limit sign — do you know how many states in this country have speed limits of 75 miles an hour for passenger cars and for heavy trucks?*
A. I have never counted that.

Q. *I'll represent to you that these are the states: Arizona has a 75-mile-an-hour heavy truck and 75-mile-a-hour car speed limit…. In Wyoming it's the same. Do you see that, sir?*
A. Yes.

Q. *I think that's about 13 states…. Now, is it foreseeable that the drivers in those states will drive the speed limit?*
A. Yes.

Q. *And is it foreseeable that drivers will get a few miles over the speed limit even at 75?*
A. That's something that can happen.

Q. *Well, to your knowledge, Mitsubishi doesn't prohibit the sale of the Sport Montero in these 13 states, does it?*
A. No.

Q. *So when they design it and sell it in the United States, they expect normal driving conditions for this to be 75 miles an hour and sometimes more, don't they, sir?*
A. On some roads, yes.

Q. *Well, sir, in fact, tell the jury how high the speedometer goes on a Sports Montero?*
A. I don't know. I haven't memorized that. I would have to look at some pictures.

Q. *You mean, after all that money you don't know how high the speedometer goes?*
A. That's not something I memorized.

Q. *Would it be a hundred miles an hour maybe?*
A. Could be.

Q. *Could it be a 120 miles an hour?*
A. I just don't know.

An expert who has made over $44 million to testify about the safe driving speeds of SUVs ought to know what the speedometer on the SUV shows. Branson's disbelief at the expert's lack of knowledge probably mirrors the jurors' feelings. Branson then goes in for the kill with his next question.

> *You mean, after all that money, you don't know how high the speedometer goes?*
> —Frank Branson
> (He highlights for the jury the lack of preparation and the amount of money made by the defense's star witness.)

Q. *Now, let me ask you a question. Why would a manufacturer make a car with a speedometer up to 120 miles an hour if they didn't expect somebody to drive it that fast?*
A. I have never looked into that.

Q. *You told us that you designed vehicles. You reckon you could design a car so it only went 65 miles an hour?*

A. You can.

Q. *OK. And in that case, if it only went 65 miles an hour, you'd just need to put the speedometer up to 65, wouldn't you?*

A. I guess.

Q. *Let's go back for a moment and is **it reasonable for us to assume as consumers that Mitsubishi will design and test its vehicle to leave a margin of safety between its maximum capacity and the kind of steering inputs that will be put in by drivers in accident avoidance maneuvers?***

A. It depends. In reasonable maneuvers, yes. But like any vehicle, you can achieve something and put a vehicle out of control. So not in every possible situation.

Q. *I know that on direct examination from [defense counsel], he didn't necessarily want you just to answer the question he was asking you. He was using you as a teaching tool. **On cross, I have the right to ask you to answer my questions directly. Is it reasonable for us as consumers to believe that the auto manufacturers would build in a margin of safety when they design and test the vehicles?***

A. **Yes.**

Experts love to qualify their answers. They are afraid to give an inch for fear they will then have to give in more. Branson takes advantage of this strategy. In the last question, he repeats his previous question and highlights for the jury that the expert hasn't answered a straightforward question with a simple answer.

Next, we will see Branson attack the expert's testimony on direct that he had never heard of a guideline that required a car manufacturer to make a car that would slide at high speeds (i.e., skid while maintaining all four wheels on the ground) and thus not roll over.

Car design and knee pants

Q. *Prior to your joining Ford, Ford engineers wrote the following: "Passenger cars must be forgiving in all manner of unskilled driver situations that precipitate wild, panicked, motivated, evasive maneuvers of drivers of widening, varying abilities. Ford passenger cars are designed to slide out rather than roll over on flat, level pavement." You are aware of that, that's [exhibit] 73-10?*

A. Yes

Q. *And that was a guideline as far back as the early '70s for Ford on their passenger cars?*

A. Under a specific context, yes.

Q. *And you testified here that you have never heard about a guideline that required a vehicle to slide out rather than roll over?*

A. Under any possible circumstances, that's correct.

Q. *But that concept has been in Ford Motor Company's engineering department since 13 years before you — in fact,* **you were probably in knee pants when Ford Motor Company put that in their guidelines?**
A. I was in what?

Q. **Knee pants. Did you ever see a child that had on pants that didn't go past their knees?**
A. Oh, shorts.

Q. *I guess that would be them.*
A. I'm sure I had shorts in 1973?

Q. *You were — 13 years before you joined Ford, how old would you have been?*
A. I was 10 years old at that time.

This trial occurred in Greenville, S.C. If you had grown up in the South, you would know what knee pants were. Branson remembers that this exchange caused great laughter from the jury.

> ## Practice Tip
> Remind the jury that the expert is a hired gun. Branson continually contrasts the expert as being out of touch with people like those on this Southern jury.

Q. *At the time you were ten years old, Ford Motor Company already had design engineers dealing with the concept of when its vehicles got to capacity they wanted them to slide out rather than roll over in untripped rolls, didn't they?*
A. In their specific test procedures, that's true.

Another line of questioning for an expert is to get him or her to agree with issues your expert has resolved. Watch what Branson does.

Expert agrees with some of plaintiff's expert's conclusions

Q. *Now, let's get one thing specific. You are not contending that any obstacle caused this Sports Montero to roll over?*
A. You mean like a sliding into a curb or something? You are correct.

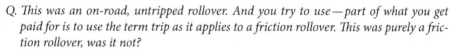

Q. *This was an on-road, untripped rollover. And you try to use — part of what you get paid for is to use the term trip as it applies to a friction rollover. This was purely a friction rollover, was it not?*
A. It was a friction rollover, yes.

Q. *Not tripped by anything?*
A. No pothole, no curb, anything like that, correct.

Q. *And Mr. Germane, the reconstruction expert upon whom you based your testimony, Mr. Gilbert who did the accident reconstruction for us, all agree this rollover began on dry, flat pavement where it slid out — where it started sliding and rather than slide out or spin out it rolled over?*
A. It overturned by sliding on the pavement, yes.

Now that Branson gets the expert to admit that there was nothing in the road that caused the SUV to roll over, Branson returns to the document at Ford that discusses Ford's safety standards.

Ford's safety standards versus Mitsubishi's

Q. *Now, in 1986 when you joined Ford, Ford engineers were saying that trucks including SUVs must be designed to be safe and predictable even in the most severe accident avoidance situations. That's true, isn't it?*
A. Yes.

Q. *And in fact, that was the department you were in, light trucks?*
A. I later went in, yes.

Q. *And is it your testimony before this jury that that's not what a motor carrier should do, that they must be designed to be safe and predictable even in the most severe accident avoidance situations?*
A. Well, in the context that document was written, I agree with it.

Q. *The context that document is written is here's what our SUVs need to be designed to do, wasn't it, sir?*
A. Yes.

Q. *In 1986, over 20 years ago.*
A. Correct. And that document talks about the various test procedures and how they are run.

The expert is never going to admit that the Mitsubishi SUV is unsafe. But he cannot deny the document written by Ford 20 years earlier that sets its standards. Branson has made his point. If Ford believes it should make an SUV that does not roll over, why doesn't Mitsubishi?

Q. *At the break I wrote out beside your numbers here you were an auto engineer at Ford, you were an expert at Carr, and you were an expert with your own company. Is that correct?*
A. I was an expert working in those areas.

Branson: *At this time, Your Honor, we would offer Exhibit 1127 as summary of his testimony in that regard.*
Court: All right. (Plaintiff's Exhibit No. 1127 was marked for identification and received into evidence.)

This exhibit was introduced into evidence after a lunch break. It refers to the witness's earlier testimony regarding how much money he has made as an expert witness, a point that Branson wants to emphasize. Not many lawyers are savvy and smart enough to create a chart that incorporates the witness's testimony and then move it into evidence as an exhibit so that the jury can look at it during deliberations.

Branson continues on this theme of a biased witness with the following line of questions:

Q. *And part of what you do as an expert is you try to put your company's best foot forward, isn't it?*
A. Try to do what now?

Q. *You try to put the company's best foot forward, you try to put things in such a manner that it helps out the people that hired you?*
A. Not necessarily. What you do is you go investigate a crash. If you are reconstructing a crash, it doesn't matter who really retains you. The crash is the crash and same with the testing.

Q. *And some of the things you can do can make how a crash looks or how the recreation looks or sounds look more dramatic than it would be if you did it different ways?*
A. That would be true for anything.

Q. *Let's look at Plaintiff's Exhibit 1118. Do you recognize that?*
A. Yes.

Q. *Is that one of your devices?*
A. That's a microphone.

Q. *And it's a microphone that's attached to the wheel of an automobile?*
A. Yes.

Q. *And when you attach it to the wheel of an automobile and you make a turn, whether it is a sharp turn or not so sharp a turn, if the tires squeal, this enhances that sound so that to people like us you make it sound a little more dramatic maybe than it would be if you didn't have a microphone attached?*
A. **Well, this is a microphone for that camera underneath. This isn't attached to the spinning wheel. This is the spare wheel underneath.**

Q. *I know. But the squeal comes out of that tire, doesn't it?*
A. **Yes. Yes, it does.**

End strong

Q. *In all these cases that you come down here and shared your wisdom with juries on behalf of automobile manufacturers you have told them the same thing, and that is in looking at an accident you look at three things. You look at the vehicle in the upper left-hand corner [of the exhibit]. You look at the driver in the upper right-hand corner. And you look at the environment in the — on the bottom. Now, isn't it true that during all these years you have done this **for all this money**, the number of times that you have found that the vehicle was unreasonably dangerous and defective in all your looking is zero, isn't that true?*
A. That's correct.

Q. *And then in each of those hundreds of cases that you have acknowledged, you then pointed the finger at the driver and the environment and generally at the driver?*
A. It wouldn't be hundreds of cases. But the majority would be the driver and some would be the environment.

Q. *So even though you acknowledge there are three things you look at, you appear to turn a blind eye to the vehicle and always point the finger at the driver if they are using accident avoidance maneuvers at the time of the accident?*
A. Not necessarily, just cases where I have testified at trials.

Q. *Just turns out that way?*
A. **Based on my analysis.**

Branson: *I may not have invited you to this dance but I appreciate your coming. No more questions, Your Honor.*
Witness: Thank you, sir.

Branson ends his cross with a summary of his key themes. For all the millions of dollars the expert has been paid, he has never found fault with the car. As Branson skeptically asks in his question, "It just turns out that way?"

Summary of Branson's themes on cross

1. Large income from testifying as expert.

2. Expert testifies solely for car companies.

3. Expert never testified that the SUV was unsafe.

4. Expert is unprepared. He does not know maximum speed on speedometer.

5. Mitsubishi has lower safety standards than Ford.

6. Expert used microphones to exaggerate sound of squealing tires during a turn.

7. Expert always blames the driver and not the car.

9.4 CHAPTER CHECKLIST ✎

Branson's advice for cross-examination

1. Don't use written questions.

2. Take the cross where the witness is going.

3. Look for areas to attack by observing the witness's body language and changes in tone of voice.

4. Like riding a horse, a successful cross-examination is accomplished by feel. You don't direct a horse by yanking on the reins but rather by using your knees.

5. Try not to be rude or curt.

6. Use a report card and have the witness grade his actions or a codefendant's. Juries get angry when the grades don't match up with the facts.

7. Do not conduct long cross-examinations. Even if direct examination lasts for an entire day, limit your cross to as close to an hour and a half as you can.

Lessons learned from Branson's cross of expert witness

1. Branson showed the expert's huge increase in salary he made once he left his real job at Ford as an engineer and became a professional expert witness.

2. Branson attacked expert's objectivity by showing that expert had made millions of dollars by testifying solely for car manufacturers and never for plaintiffs.

3. Branson points out expert has never concluded that Mitsubishi was at fault for a rollover accident.

4. Branson frames questions with regional folk sayings that the out-of-state expert does not understand to highlight the expert's disconnect with the jury.

5. When witness qualifies an answer, Branson simply asks his question again until he gets a simple "yes."

6. Branson uses simple imagery that the jury can relate to. For example, if the car's speedometer goes to 120 m.p.h., shouldn't the car be designed to drive safely at that speed?

7. Branson uses a document from Ford to get witness to admit that Ford has a higher standard for safety than Mitsubishi. Branson then implies that Mitsubishi fails for not having the same standard.

8. Through his questioning, Branson points out that expert witness's "gravy train" would stop if he ever concluded Mitsubishi was at fault.

PART FIVE

Closing Argument

INTRODUCTION

*A*fter both sides have put on their witnesses and submitted their exhibits into evidence, it is time for what conventional wisdom says is the climax of the trial. But as we learned in Part One, jurors are making up their minds quickly and not waiting until closing arguments, despite the judge's instructions to do so. As Mark Lanier instructs in the next chapter, you can't convince the unconvinced jurors about the merits of your case, but you can arm the jurors on your side with the testimony and evidence to persuade other jurors during deliberations.

There are three significant differences between opening statement and closing argument. First, while attorneys are not allowed to discuss in detail the jury instructions in opening statement, they are allowed to in closing argument. Consequently, great trial lawyers will focus on the two or three most important jury instructions in their closing argument and explain how the evidence relates to the instructions. Jury instructions contain a lot of complicated legal terms and the jury needs guidance how to apply them correctly to the facts of the case. For example, in a negligence case, there will be an instruction defining what negligence is, and it is the lawyer's task to explain it clearly to the jury and to show why the facts prove that there was or was not any negligence.

Second, if you are a plaintiff's attorney or prosecutor, you get to give a rebuttal argument after the defense attorney has presented his or her closing argument. Courts allow for a rebuttal argument because it is an attempt to level the playing field since the plaintiff or prosecutor has the burden of proof.

Third, unlike an opening statement, a closing argument is not a prediction of what the evidence will prove but a recitation of what actually happened at trial. The attorney must highlight for the jury the important testimony and evidence that has been presented.

Part Five analyzes closing arguments in three civil trials. In all three chapters, you will find that each of the the great trial lawyers profiled embody a principle that was related by Ralph Waldo Emerson over 100 years ago. Emerson wrote, "I have heard an experienced counselor say that he never feared the effect upon a jury of a lawyer who does not believe in his heart that his client ought to have a verdict. If he does not believe it, his unbelief will appear to the jury, despite all his protestations, and will become their unbelief."

Now that we have come to the end of the trial, let's bring the jury in and watch how a closing argument should be delivered.

CHAPTER TEN

‹‹∞›

Mark Lanier

Empower the Jury to Change the World

I have a limited number of days on this earth. I don't want to spend my efforts doing something I don't believe in.

—Mark Lanier

---

ark Lanier's opening statement tips were discussed in Chapter One. Let's now focus on two of his most famous closing arguments.

10.1 LANIER'S CLOSING ARGUMENT STRATEGIES

Lanier believes that the opening statement is vital. By the time he delivers his closing, he realizes that he is not going to "convince those unconvinced" because the jurors have already chosen sides. But the closing argument still has value. His goal in closing argument is to "arm jurors [on his side] with the evidence they need to go back and argue against the other side's jurors in the jury room."

As we will see below, Lanier continues to display the same mastery of communication and persuasion in his closing arguments as we saw him do in his opening statements (Chapter 1). Most lawyers would have spent only a few hours late at night after the close of evidence to organize their closing argument for the following day. Being exhausted from the trial and rushed for time, the lawyers would neither have the time nor energy to create an imaginative closing. Even if they had the time, most lawyers would simply rehash their opening with a few tweaks to account for the evidence that came in at trial.

Not Lanier. His closing arguments are the result of a lot of hard work done each evening during trial. Lanier's technique cannot be emphasized enough. The only way to create a successful closing

> **CHAPTER HIGHLIGHTS**
> - The art of a powerful closing
> - How to convince the unconvinced jurors
> - How to get record-setting verdicts

argument is to spend some time on it during trial at the end of each day. That is when the testimony is still fresh in your mind. If you wait even a day to recall the highlights of the testimony from the previous day, they will be too difficult to remember. Such a practice takes a lot of discipline. It is hard to spend time each day on a far-off event like your closing when there are so many immediate demands on your time, such as preparing for the next day of trial. But the time spent will pay huge dividends in your closing argument.

In addition, if you spend time on your closing each day, it will help keep you focused on the controlling themes of your case. You will be continually reminded of the evidence you need to bring out the next day at trial to support your themes.

Lanier adds new ideas and new analogies to his closing to keep the jury interested. But there is another reason why he makes his closing different from his opening: he is always afraid that the other side is going to take the idea he used in his opening and "blow it out of the water." Lanier used to play chess at a high level, and that experience taught him to look at his case from his opponent's point of view—just as you would do in a chess game.

> **Practice Tip**
>
> Much like when playing chess, Lanier looks for those arguments the other side can make that will beat him if he makes a certain argument. This concern drives him to think ahead and always be several moves ahead of his opponent, whether it is in a game of chess or at trial.

I asked Lanier why he begins his closing arguments by thanking the jury instead of just launching into a dramatic theme to grab the jurors' attention. He referred me to a study that was done using waiters at restaurants to determine if the manner in which they presented the bill would effect the amount of their tip. It revealed that the waiter's interaction could raise the tip by 24 percent. When each waiter brought the bill to a table (and did nothing else), the tip received—whatever it was—became the study's baseline tip. Then the study's same waiters, when bringing the bill, included a mint for each of the table's patrons, so for a four-top table, one mint per patron was provided with the bill. The tips went up four percent. (That is, if a waiter had earned $100 that night without delivering mints, he now earned a four percent increase, which totaled $104.)

Then, the same wait staff provided two mints per patron when they dropped off the bill. The tips rose 13 percent. Then they took the same wait staff, had them give the mints, two per patron, but in the following manner: lay down the bill with one mint per patron, turn and take one or two steps away, turn back and say, "You guys have been such a great table. I am going to give you all some extra mints" and then leave the second mint per patron.

The tips increased 24 percent from the baseline. You've almost doubled the tip (13 percent) with the same number of mints because it became unexpected, and the customers were shown true appreciation by the waiter.

Lanier explains how he applies the waiter study to his closing arguments. The best way is to try to have breakfast or a meeting with your clients before the closing argument. He then tells the jury:

> This morning I had breakfast with my clients and I told them, 'This is my last chance to talk to you, I don't get another chance. Is there anything I have left out, anything I haven't said, anything I need to tell this jury as your lawyer, as your spokesperson, because this is it? I do it today or I don't get to.' They said, 'Yes, there is. Would you please tell that jury thank you very much, you took time away from your lives, time away from your work, time away from your home, and we've watched you and we really, really appreciate it,' so on behalf of my clients I want to say thank you.

Lanier instructs that that's giving them the two mints with the step away. "I think it's powerful. I think it's effective." Lanier adds that he has used this formula dozens of times. An objection to it as not being evidence has only been sustained once. Lanier warns that the "thank you" has got to be genuine. So, he has to have had time to eat with the plaintiff and carry on the conversation he later will report to the jury.

Another tip Lanier shared is that he is not afraid to speak in the first person and give his opinion. You will see in the excerpts below that Lanier uses phrases such as "I feel," "I think," and "I believe this with every shred of my being." Some trial technique textbooks instruct students to avoid using the word "I" in a closing argument because a lawyer is not allowed to express his opinion of the evidence or the credibility of the witnesses. Instead, a lawyer is only allowed to argue why a witness or evidence should not be believed. Such instruction, while technically correct, is not practical. Whether you speak in the first person or third person, you are still giving your opinion. An objection has never been upheld after Lanier has offered his opinion in closing argument.

> **Practice Tip**
> To make deliberations easier for the jury, Lanier puts his exhibits on his exhibit list in their numerical order of importance. For example, exhibit number one is his most important exhibit, exhibit number two is his second most important exhibit, and so on. By listing the exhibits this way, it is easy for the jurors to find the important exhibits among the hundreds that will go back to the jury room.

There is another reason Lanier prefers to say "I don't believe witness X" instead of putting it in the third person, such as "Witness X is not believable." He realizes that not all the jurors may be on his side. He does not want to create an additional barrier between the skeptical juror and himself by using the third person voice when speaking. By using the word "I", Lanier does not further offend the skeptical juror by forcing his opinion on him or her, but instead allows that juror to see that Lanier is just expressing his opinion. Lanier will rely on the jurors that are already on his side to persuade the skeptical juror during deliberations.

We will look at Lanier's closing arguments from two of his most famous cases. Let's first examine *Ernst v. Merck*. In Chapter One, we analyzed Lanier's opening statement in that case. You may remember that Lanier sued Merck alleging that its painkiller, Vioxx, caused Bob Ernst to have a heart attack when Merck knew the drug was dangerous.

10.2 LANIER'S CLOSING ARGUMENT IN *ERNST V. MERCK*

Lanier: Thank you, Judge.
Good Morning.

Jury: Good morning.

Lanier: Almost six weeks. It's been a long time. Y'all have been very gracious. Yesterday afternoon, after we ended court, **we had tuna fish sandwiches in the courtroom next door.** And I've had a chance to visit with Carol Ernst, and I told Mrs. Ernst I said, "This is my last chance to talk to the jury. Is there anything I forgot to say? Can you tell me something I need to tell them from you?"

And she did. she said, "Yeah. I really wanted to say at the end of my testimony, but I was afraid I'd get in trouble if I said it" — which she would not have. **But she wanted to say "thank you."** She recognizes you've taken time away from work. You've taken time away from your families. You've made a commitment to put up with a lot of people, to put up with me. You've waited out in the halls while we fuss and fight over things, and she really appreciates it. Thank you very much.

Many lawyers thank the jury at the beginning of their closing. It often comes across as perfunctory. Other times, it seems like just a way to warm up before a lawyer gets to the heart of his closing. Lanier does it better than anyone. He does not thank the jury, but his client does. What a powerful image of the widow eating a simple tuna fish sandwich in the courtroom next door, wanting to make sure the jury knows how grateful she is.

After the section above, Lanier begins to discuss the jury charge. He told the jury that he wanted to discuss the charge to give them a framework for his argument. The first section he discusses is the burden of proof.

Burden of proof

I want to start talking to you for a moment about this term, "preponderance of the evidence," which means the greater weight and degree of credible evidence admitted in this case.

That's an important term for you because — and as a lawyer, it's real funny how I look at that. That means just the greater weight, what weighs more — which is, if you put it in the scales, what's 51 percent? You know, **if you put 500 sheets of paper on each side of the scales and you take one extra sheet of paper and add it, that's extra.**

And it's hard for a lawyer, for me, to argue about this, in a way, **because I think I've proven my case by a much greater burden.** I mean, I think — I'm a believer in this. **I am a firm believer in this with every shred of my being,** and I feel like I should never have to stand up and say "it's just a preponderance of the evidence". And I think some of you will go back in the jury room and agree with me and say, "You know, I'm pretty convinced about this. This is very convincing to me. I believe this is what happened."

But some of you may not be so convinced, and the law has set up where we don't have a jury of one because the law recognizes we need balance. And so, the law, also, for 200 years now, has had this in it, you know, our American civil system because some people are going to go back there and say, "well, you know, I've still got a lot of doubt." And so, for those people the law is you don't have to make the decision, like in a criminal case where it's beyond your reasonable doubt. It's just got to be 51 percent.

Lanier explains two things to the jurors: what the legal burden is, and how he has exceeded that burden. Lessor lawyers often make the mistake of telling the jury, "I *only* have to prove that it is more likely than not that the events happened the way I say they did." Great lawyers prove their cases beyond 51 percent. Why? Because jurors want certainty.

Lanier then discussed the causation instruction. He points out that Vioxx does not have to be *the* cause of death, just *a* cause of death. Lanier then explained to the jury that in a case like this, it would be impossible to prove it with direct evidence, so circumstantial evidence is allowed.

David v. Goliath

After discussing the charge, Lanier turned to the subject of Carol Ernst. This was a new analogy that he did not use in his opening.

So, with that in hand [the jury charge], I want to talk to you for a moment. I want to talk to you about Carol and Bob Ernst. Carol is not here alone today. She does have Kendra, who introduced them, to her left. She's got Tim to her right, **sitting next to actually the Judge's wife. "Hello, Sue."**

And then if you drop back a row, we've got Shawna, with her husband, Duane; and we've got Bethany, with her husband, Alan, immediately behind. And they are allowed to be in for closing argument, and it's a delight to have them here today.

This is an important case. OK? It's a very important case. Everybody wants to look. When David fought Goliath, there were two armies that watched because it's something to see. And everybody's wondering, first of all, does Carol have the courage to go forward with the case?

> *Everybody wants to look. When David fought Goliath, there were two armies that watched because it's something to see.*
>
> —Mark Lanier, closing argument

She came to us—we filed this almost three years ago now. It's been a long three years. It takes a long time to get these to court. It takes a long time to read seven million documents....

I practice law up on [highway] 1960, 20 miles northwest of Houston.... I grew up in Lubbock, Texas.... But it's not just something that takes intestinal fortitude on our part to go fight this fight. It takes it on your part, too, because the media, the people, the victims, the companies want to know if someone would really step up and say, "Time out. Don't do business this way." Because it takes courage to do that, and I—I'm glad you're here, and I'm glad you've got the chance to do it.

When I opened to you, I suggested this was going to be like "CSI Angleton" because this is your opportunity to investigate the scene and figure out what happened.... And what I'd like to do now is take a step back and look at the journey we've been on for the last six weeks.

Merck knew it was in deep trouble at this point. Lanier, in this short span of time, has cemented his bond with the jury. It is Carol Courage against Goliath, and everyone has come to watch. When the judge's wife is sitting with the plaintiff's family, the defendant is in for big trouble. Not that anything unethical has happened, but everyone wants to be with a winner. It is clear to the jury that everyone, including the judge's wife, wants Lanier to win. In the afternoon, the judge's wife will sit with the Merck supporters, and defense counsel will point that out to the jurors. But by then, the damage has already been done. What a strong first impression it is for the plaintiff to have the judge's wife sitting on her side of the courtroom during Lanier's closing.

I asked Lanier if he had planned on mentioning that the Judge's wife was sitting with the plaintiff's family to the jury. He said that it was spontaneous. He looked out into the audience and just saw her there. And while the image was powerful, he admits the only brilliance he displayed was seizing the moment.

He then mentioned another time at this trial (during his opening statement) when he spontaneously seized the moment. Lanier had forgotten to turn his cellphone off, and it rang from his briefcase under counsel table. Lanier was stunned and said, "Your Honor, I am so sorry," and as he reached down and turned it off, the Judge said, "You might want to check who it is." They chuckled and Lanier said, "No, it's not my mom because she is in the courtroom, so after that I am OK," and everybody chuckled. In his next trial, defense counsel filed a motion with the court asking that Lanier be prohibited from having his phone ring and saying that the caller was not his mother because she was in the courtroom.

Returning to our analysis of Lanier's closing, Lanier creates an apt analogy of David versus Goliath and a wonderful synonym for Carol: courage. Finally, Lanier builds on the theme of David. Not only does Carol have courage, but Lanier has the courage to use his small law office to take on Merck's lawyers. Most important, he empowers the jury to have the courage to take on Merck with its verdict. Lanier is always connecting with the jury. Carol and Lanier need the jury's help to win, and he is going to make sure he helps the jury by clearly presenting the evidence and his arguments.

Denial, deception, and damage

Always mindful of the jury, Lanier frames his argument in themes. He adds three other themes to David versus Goliath.

> So, during this decade, **we've seen a decade of denial [first theme] by Merck. And that's going to be the first point I talk to you about,** the denial. But we've not just seen denial. **The dots connect from denial to deception [second theme].**
>
> And **I think the deception, you've seen part of it in this courtroom.** And I want to underscore it, and I want a chance to convince you of it, if I haven't already. **Not just deception, but the dots connect [to] the damage [third theme],** and the damage flows far beyond just the Ernst family. And we'll talk about that. But very directly the damage flows to the Ernsts themselves....
>
> Let's talk about who they brought, first. They brought **Dr. Reicin, the Vioxx defender.** This is a woman whose job ostensibly is to handle clinical trials.... She defends quite well. But we got her early email.... Dr. Reicin writes the following: (reading from email shown on projection screen to jury) The possibility of increased heart events, CV, cardiovascular events, is of great concern.... I just can't wait to be the one to present those results to senior management, exclamation mark. That's her exclamation mark, not mine. So, (reading) the expected results can kill, Vioxx. That's what she

says. She knows it from the very beginning. They haven't started selling the drug yet.

Dr. Reicin is the perfect example for Lanier's argument. He uses an email to prove Merck's deception. Lanier masterfully uses labels and descriptive language. Here, Dr. Reicin is not just a witness, but the "Vioxx defender." It is a label that defines the doctor as not someone who is an objective professional, but a biased promoter.

> **Practice Tip**
> Notice the alliteration Lanier uses in creating three interwoven themes: denial, deception, and damages. The fact that each word has three syllables also makes them memorable.

In the next section, Lanier looks at Merck's clinical Vioxx studies. He argues that Merck is concerned that one of its studies shows that there is an increase of heart problems for Vioxx users. So, Merck combines that study with other studies to water down the results. Look at the analogy that Lanier uses:

And this is where they go to the schoolyard and they get the kids **and they want to try and figure out how many kids have beards.** They take studies that are—are people on Vioxx for one day because they had a root canal from a dentist. And after you take Vioxx for one day from a root canal from a dentist, they see if the people taking Vioxx for one day had more heart attacks than the people who didn't.

Well, that's no study to be—that's mixing apples and oranges. That doesn't need to be combined, but that's what they choose to do.

Summarizes exhibits

Interesting here, I went back and I looked at the documents last night; and we've got an exhibit now, these exhibits will have different numbers on them. You've got two sets of stickers on some of ours because we've tried to renumber some critical exhibits and make them the top 20 exhibits for you, 20 or 30—I don't remember the exact number—but you'll get these exhibits back there.

Most lawyers are so focused about getting exhibits admitted at trial, they never consider whether the jury will be able to understand them. At the end of most trials, there are thousands of pages for the jury to sort through. Unfortunately, lawyers spend no time thinking about the needs of the jurors. Not Lanier. How grateful the jury must have been.

Merck rushes Vioxx to market

> They rushed this drug to market. The value of beating Celebrex to market, Merck figured out, is $611 million.... They figured out how to give the FDA one year of data instead of two years of data, like the FDA normally requires.... That's not right. That's not right. **Right and wrong doesn't change based on how much money's involved.** Right and wrong's right and wrong, and we know that.

As with Lanier's opening, he uses numerous memorable phrases. Here is one that sums up his theme of deception: "Right and wrong doesn't change based on how much money's involved."

Defense counsel's deception

> And then they come in here and they try and deceive you over the difference between something being "a" cause and something being "the" cause. And it started in voir dire. It started in jury selection: "Mr. Lanier's got to prove to you that Vioxx was the cause."
>
>   And that's not what the judge said. They're not the judge. They don't write the law, and they don't teach you the law; the judge does. He doesn't say "the". It's got to be "a" cause because there's no way anybody ever beats Merck. No one takes down Goliath if you believe that. If you believe them on that, no one can win. It can't be done, and they know that and that's what they're relying on.

Lanier includes Merck's trial lawyers in this theme of Merck's deception. It is important for your credibility to put on believable witnesses and exhibits. But your own words can undercut your credibility if you are not accurate. Lanier takes advantage of defense counsel's mistakes.

Fishing analogy

Lanier continues with his theme of deception when he talks about Merck's argument that since Bob's autopsy did not reveal a blood clot, Vioxx could not have caused his death. Lanier explains that often times when someone has a heart arrhythmia, there is no evidence of a clot. Here is how Lanier refuted the testimony of a Merck witness.

> Some clots are too small to be seen. They're microemboli. And the only thing that Merck's got in their defense is they bring the doctor who's the prostrate cancer specialist who says, "I looked at **one out of 150,000 slides,** and in that **one slide** I didn't see a clot."

And that is no different than my Rebecca Jane [Lanier's young daughter] telling me after five minutes of fishing in Lake Conroe, **"Dad, the lake doesn't have any fish. Let's go home."**

Add this analogy to Lanier's long list of effective comparisons. Doesn't his analogy convey how ridiculous the witness's assertion is?

Cause of death

Merck argued at trial that Bob died from atherosclerosis, which is a narrowing of the arteries that puts blood flow to the heart at risk. Merck claimed that Bob's arteries were 50 to 75 percent closed. Here is what Lanier pointed out.

> Merck deceives by claiming that atherosclerosis is the only reason Bob Ernst died. Now think about this for a minute. "50 to 75 percent closed" means that it's 50 to 25 percent open. And if we're to believe their expert, the pathologist guy, the prostate guy, he says that it was like a lead pipe. So, it's not like that vessel's just going to be clamping down on its own.
>
> But it's 25 to 50 percent open, and that's enough blood flow for Bob Ernst to run marathons. That's enough blood flow for Bob Ernst to ride a bike for 62 miles the week before. Dr. Rubin, he doesn't have a dog in the fight. And I used this early enough in the trial while they were still in their case. Don't you know if they could find one piece of medical evidence anywhere in the literature in the history of the human race to dispute this, they would have? But there isn't any because it's dead right-on.
>
> Dr. Rubin's book says for you to die a sudden death from atherosclerosis alone, at rest, you've got to have more than 90 percent occluded (blockage)....
>
> So, it's not the atherosclerosis that kills him. So, then they've got to have another trigger. So, here's where they come in with sleep apnea. Do you remember that from their pathologist? "Well, the trigger, it must have been sleep apnea that stressed the heart. Sleep apnea can stress the heart."
>
> **Now, what's harder, snoring or running 26 miles? Which one's going to take more oxygen for the heart? Or maybe if it wasn't sleep apnea, maybe it was bad dreams.**
>
> OK. What's harder, the nightmare or riding a bike 62 miles? You've got enough oxygen and blood flow to run a marathon and ride a bike for 62 miles, but you just don't have enough to make it through that bad dream.

> *Now, what's harder, snoring or running 26 miles? Which one's going to take more oxygen for the heart? Or maybe if it wasn't sleep apnea, maybe it was bad dreams.*
> —Mark Lanier mocks defendant's theory that plaintiff's sleep apnea caused his death.

Now let me ask this: If they really want to stick with the evidence, how much evidence have they given you that shows there was any sleep apnea? None.

How much evidence have they given you that said Bob had a nightmare? None.

Lanier turns Merck's argument on its head by arguing the opposite. Bob's arteries were 25–50 percent *open*. Lanier's exceptional use of comparisons continues when he contrasts the difficulty of running a marathon with having a bad dream.

Defense Counsel's Objection

There is always the danger when you make an objection that you will highlight for the jury the fact you are objecting to. Defense counsel should have learned that Lanier can brilliantly turn any weakness into a strength. Watch what happens in this exchange. Does Lanier flinch or keep on the attack? Which attorney appears weak and which attorney appears strong?

> They deceived you when they tell that 300,000 people die of this every year and everybody's got to die of something. This was just Bob Ernst's day. That's wrong. What you need to know is according to Graham, Dr. Graham with the FDA, 88,000 to 144,000 excess cases of heart disease occurred in the U.S. because of Vioxx.
>
> *Defense Counsel: Objection, Your Honor. You told the jury this didn't come in for the truth. That was just a notice document.*
>
> *Court: Yeah. The jury will follow any instructions I've given you.*
>
> Lanier: Yeah. **I'd take notice of it. I think they should have taken notice of it. I think everybody should.** This has been a decade of denial, this has been a decade of deception, and it's been a decade of damage.
>
> Let me move through damage quickly. Bob's body was damaged. That's obvious. This was a cause of his death. That's what the 51 percent of the evidence surely shows.

Usually, the judge will respond to an objection as he did here. He does not sustain the objection even if it has merit because he has already instructed the jurors that the arguments of counsel are not evidence. Judges have the attitude that the lawyers should be able to argue their case, and they don't want to play referee over objections when the jury has already been instructed that closing arguments are not evidence.

In this case, defense counsel should have known the result of her objection because the judge had given the same response to earlier objections. The objection just threw gasoline on the fire that Lanier was building.

10.3 DEFENDANT'S CLOSING

Only a few excerpts are presented here because the focus of this section is on Lanier's skills. The excerpts provide context for Lanier's rebuttal and show the contrast in executing a closing argument.

Jurors' promises

Time and again, lawyers make the mistake of reminding jurors of the promises the jurors made during jury selection to be "fair" and to "keep an open mind." What happens is that in jury selection, jurors take an oath to be fair and impartial and then a lawyer will ask the entire panel of potential jurors something to the effect: 1) "Do you promise to be fair in this case?" and 2) "Do you promise to keep an open mind?" The jurors all will nod their heads in agreement. The naive lawyer now thinks he has their assurance that they will resist every natural human temptation to form a quick opinion and will somehow keep a completely open mind until the moment deliberations begin after closing argument.

Where the genesis of such a strategy comes from is impossible to know, but many lawyers mistakenly use it. The lawyers' request is like asking jurors to watch a movie and wait until the credits roll to decide whether or not they liked it. Also, it is a sign of weakness to ask someone to be fair and open minded. If you have to ask someone that, are you showing confidence? Are you building a relationship with the jurors? Are you telling them you trust them? Watch how defense counsel begins her closing.

> Remember that when we were in voir dire, before you were selected for this jury, I talked to you about how jury service, I believe, is a sacred trust. And it's that sacred trust that protects the system of justice that we have in this country. It's a system of justice unlike anywhere else in the world, and it's worked for us for over 200 years.
>
> And that system of justice protects us. It protects all of us, because it makes sure that cases aren't decided by the press and they aren't decided by politicians and they aren't even decided by lawyers.
>
> Disputes, cases like this, are decided by a group of 12 people from the community, people like you guys who came in here and worked hard and listened to the evidence....
>
> You make a promise to come into the courtroom and decide this case not based on bias or emotion or anything like that but to commit yourselves to deciding the case based only on the evidence. And we appreciate

that commitment. Our system of justice depends on that commitment that each of you made.

Our system of fair and impartial justice asks that you give a company like Merck the same fair and impartial treatment that you would give to Mrs. Ernst, and **we know that each of you will do that because you promised to do that before you sat in those chairs**.

Carrying out the promise of being a juror is not easy. You're told that you're not supposed to be swayed by what the lawyers say, what their arguments are, that you're only supposed to listen to the evidence that's presented. Sometimes that's hard. That's not always an easy thing to do. But we know that you took an oath to do this — to do that in this case, and we know that we **can hold you to that oath.**

You're told that you're only supposed to look at the evidence that came in from the witness chair and the documents that you've seen and you'll get to take back with you. But sometimes that's easier said than done. **I trust, though, that each and every one of you who have made the commitment to do that will carry out that commitment in this case.** And that commitment means giving Merck the same consideration, even though it's a company, that you give Mrs. Ernst....

Please don't believe that because we're here telling you that Vioxx did not cause Mr. Ernst's death that we don't have sympathy for her and that we don't feel for her loss. We do.

But each and every one of us are governed by the system of justice in this country that requires we put that aside and look at the evidence and make a fair judgment of the evidence.

Now, I know that each of you committed to do that before you were selected to sit in those chairs, and I'm going to hold you to that obligation to be as fair and impartial as you can be in judging the evidence in this case.

The lawyer patronizes the jury. She repeatedly warns that she is going to "hold you to that obligation" and "we know that we can hold you to that oath." Not only do such admonitions reveal your fear that the jury will vote against you, it demeans them. No one likes being scolded or reminded that they have to be honest. She does not build a bond with the jury.

Now, in another section of the closing, defense counsel suggested the following to the jury:

> Now, Mrs. Ernst, when she testified, told you that she feels tremendous guilt because she recommended that her husband go and ask about Vioxx. And I'm sure that guilt hasn't been lessened in this case by all these lawyers telling her that Vioxx killed her husband. **But you have a chance to do**

> **Practice Tip**
> Don't talk down to jurors by telling them that you will hold them to the promise they made in voir dire to be fair. Jurors resent such a reminder.

the right thing, and that is to release Mrs. Ernst from that guilt, to tell her the truth, which is that Vioxx had nothing to do with her husband's death. What caused her husband's death was something that started long before she ever even met Mr. Ernst, and you have a chance in this case to tell her that and send her that message and relieve her of that guilt that she feels so she can go on with her life. Don't let her continue to carry this wrong impression with her.

Could anything be more tone deaf and paternalistic? This passage embodies Merck's lack of compassion and inability to see the case from the jury's perspective. Unless Carol Ernst was extremely unlikeable — which she wasn't — why would the jury want to send her a message. Second, it is beyond the realm of common sense that the jury would be doing her a favor by ruling against her. By contrast, Lanier on his worst day would not suggest that a verdict against Merck would be doing Merck a favor.

Lanier told me that when defense counsel said this to the jury, "It was a gift!" His first thought about defense counsel was: *Whatever you do, don't throw me into the briar patch* (from the story of Brer Rabbit as told by Uncle Remus). Lanier also remembers that defense counsel read her closing argument word for word. At one point she lost her place and it took her 27 seconds to find it again and continue reading her closing.

Defense counsel then briefly spoke about the damages to consider if the jury were to reach that question on the verdict form.

> And we haven't heard from Mr. Lanier exactly how much money he's going to ask you to award, but I would just ask you to use your common sense and your own judgment. You'll have to decide for yourself the value, if you get to this question, of what Mrs. Ernst has lost.
>
> And I think if you consider the circumstances of their relationship and the length of marriage and relationship, I think you can make that decision on your own using your good common sense.

Now, let's see how Lanier deals with these issues in his rebuttal.

10.4 LANIER'S REBUTTAL ARGUMENT

Lanier: No break needed?

Court: No, sir. Go ahead.

Lanier: Ladies and gentlemen, if you don't mind us moving a little bit while I do this, it will make it go a little bit quicker. So I'm going to let Dara [co-counsel] distract for a moment. I do want to take your attention away from what's been said for just a moment because it bothers me. I'm bothered by a lot that's been said.... I'm bothered because we've hit a point now where it's not just discredit the doctors. And Dr. Egilman, you can handle this. You've had them at your doorstep before. Dr. Lucchesi, he can handle it.

I got really miffed when they went after Mrs. Ernst, and I got miffed when they did it again today because that's not right. **For them to have the audacity to stand up here and say, please vote for Merck for Carol Ernst's sake, so Carol Ernst can go away from here knowing she's guilt free, that's bad. That's bad.**

The — to stand up here and to put stuff on there about her husband — oh, we heard that the son is going to testify that the husband smoked ten years ago — no, we never heard that testimony, because it's not true. We heard countless things from them that aren't true.

And to have the audacity to stand up here and say, "Oh, your husband was a drinker and a smoker 20 years ago. That must be what did it. Oh, your husband — you, Carol Ernst — **if you get to the damage question, please don't give it a lot of thought because they were only married for a year and only together for four or five, and they only probably had 20 to 30 years in the future. That's just not very important."** See, that — it's **subliminal.**

Raymond Gilmartin [CEO of Merck] is so important they can pay him $20–$30 million a year, but don't you even begin — even come close to thinking that a year in her life is important. Oh, Vioxx is so important they can spend a million dollars on a day for a launch party, **but don't think Merck numbers when you think about ordinary people. Merck numbers are reserved for Merck people.** Merck is the company that's allowed to give $380,000 a year plus stock bonuses to a woman whose job it is to defend Vioxx.

Those are Merck numbers. But don't think that way when it comes to ordinary people because people that are ordinary, everyday people — and I promise it could happen to you, and it could happen to me, and it could happen to anybody — and normal people just aren't worth that much.

It is obviously difficult to put a dollar figure on a human life. But Lanier sees an opening based on defense counsel's mistake, and he doesn't waste time capitalizing on it. He highlights how callous and illogical defense counsel's argument was that the jury should "help" Carol with her "guilt" over having encouraged her husband to take Vioxx.

This tone deafness was also present during the trial. At a lunch break during the trial after Carol testified on direct, Lanier predicted that Merck's counsel would decide to conduct a cross-examination and that it would fail terribly. Lanier said, "The only reason for questions is lawyer ego." Indeed, the cross-examination lasted an hour and a half. Merck's counsel questioned Carol about Bob's bad relationships with his adult children, whom Carol did not even know. After the trial, jurors commented that the questions were "disrespectful and insulting."

Lanier then expertly contrasts the money Merck has lavishly spent with the dollar value of Bob's life. The launch party refers to the approximately $1,000,000 spent by Merck one evening on a party to celebrate the launch of Vioxx's sale to the public. Lanier continued to discuss the damages as follows:

> Loss of companionship in the past, in the future. Well, let's see. He died. And it's been how many years, Carol? Four years? I would love for you to — think in Merck terms. OK? If the launch party is worth a million bucks, let Merck think that…each year of his life is worth a day of a launch party. Let them think — think in Merck terms and put 4 million.
>
> Loss in the future? He's got a 20-year life expectancy? I don't know. Sixteen years at the time he died, because it's been four years. Put 16 down there. Let them know you can think Merck Money.
>
> If you think, "That's a lot of money. I'm not going to be a part of that. That's a big verdict, that's fine. Cut it back. I'm not here for the greed factor. I promise you that.
>
> Don't get me wrong. This is not a cheap thing to do. But that's not what this is. You make the decision. I'm suggesting to you to let them know that you can think like Merck. I'd do the same thing on mental anguish. **I'd say every year she lives without Bob Ernst is worth one launch party.** I would say every year in the future is worth one launch party. **I'll bet you he meant more to her every year than that launch party meant to Merck in a day.**

> *Let them know you can think Merck Money.*
> —Mark Lanier,
> closing argument

Lanier expertly uses the label "Merck Money" and compares the money spent on a launch party to the value of someone's life to help the jury determine a dollar figure for the damages. It is truly impossible to put a dollar amount on a human life, but Lanier gets very close to accomplishing it with his comparison.

Punitive damages

In this section, Lanier discusses punitive damages. In Merck's closing, defense counsel kept reminding the jury not to be biased because Merck was a big company, and she pleaded with the jurors to treat Merck like a person. Lanier picks up on her request and turns it against Merck.

> Punitive damages. Now, with due respect to [defense counsel], [defense counsel] said, on punitive damages, that Merck was not malicious. And I'm going to agree, because what she's done is just changed what the Judge has told you.

Malice. Malice means an extreme degree of risk that you're aware of, but you proceed nonetheless. It doesn't mean our English word "malicious." Here's the deal. If you or I go do something like this, they're going to throw the book at us. We get in trouble for doing small things. OK? We get hauled out—and they want to be treated like a person. Remember that. They've told you that; treat us like a person.

Well, what do you think would happen if you or I went out there and we purposefully sold some stuff that we knew would likely kill some people? Oh, we don't know which ones. It's a shame. It will be a low incidence. But we still think it, and we do it anyway because we figure we can make a few hundred million dollars doing it, or a few billion in this case. They're pulling in two and a half billion a year off this drug. And it will affect our bonuses. It will affect our stock options. It will affect—

What do you think would happen to you and me? We would get the book thrown at us. They want to be treated like a person? Treat them like a person. Tell them no, we won't allow it. Tell them no, it can't be allowed....

I was taught that the Declaration of Independence with John Hancock's name down there front and center in big letters—I was taught that when he signed it, it was treason and it would cause—if we didn't win the war, it would cause him to lose his life. It would cause his family to lose their life. Everybody would be hung for treason, and all his property forfeited to the king.

And nobody wanted to sign it, and John Hancock picks up the pen, and he signs it front and center in nice, clear, legible writing, big letters. We've got the same. Get your John Hancock and put it here. OK?

John Hancock was asked, "Why did you do it that way?" And his answer was, "I want the King of England to be able to read it without putting his glasses on."

There are times and opportunities—and not everybody gets it—where you can stand up and make a statement. **And as a practical matter, does any of this money ever get paid? Does any of this money ever go—what happens for the next five years on appeal? What happens with everything? We've got no clue. Does the Judge even let the award stand, or does he have to cut it back—**

Defense Counsel: Your Honor, this is improper, I'll object.

Lanier: I'm just telling you, I'll do it this way, Your Honor. I'm just telling you this: You put down something that commands the attention of Merck and commands the attention of everybody else and says, no, we don't allow that. Don't think you can make $229 million by putting off your warning for four months. We'll take that away from you. We'll write it down. Don't think you can get however many millions you can by getting this thing to market. We're not going to do that. We won't allow it. We will stand up with a voice and say, "No." And you can't come into the courtroom and discredit me and discredit Carol and discredit Shauna and discredit all of the witnesses that testify. And then go back singing, **we won't allow it; that's not the way we do business....**

But I will tell you this: If you don't think they deserve punishing, then don't award the numbers. But if you do think they deserve it, **please don't let them off light. Give it to them right.** That's all I'm asking. If you don't think she deserves the numbers, don't give them to her. But please, please, please, give her what you think is right. Do what's right. **Let your voice be heard so we can fight another day.**

Thank you. Thank you, Your Honor.

> *Please don't let them off light. Give it to them right.*
> —Mark Lanier,
> closing argument

Lanier continually repeats his theme: The jurors should think in terms of Merck Money when it comes to damages. It is a very effective way to establish a benchmark for what should be paid. Most lawyers have a fixed rebuttal argument that is written in stone. They are really not rebutting what opposing counsel has said but are, instead, using arguments that they have saved for last and that they anticipate will respond to opposing counsel's closing.

Lanier's rebuttal is very effective because he has listened intently to opposing counsel's argument and is going to respond directly if necessary. When defense counsel pleads with the jury to treat Merck like a person and not a corporation, Lanier pounces on the argument and explains to the jury that if Merck were like a person, it would be in jail.

Then, he links the theme of thinking in terms of Merck Money with the analogy to John Hancock. Hancock was fighting for justice, and so is the jury. Lanier also makes effective use of rhymes. Such a technique makes a phrase memorable. He urges them, "Please don't let them off light. Give it to them right." Finally, he ends with a battle cry, "Let your voice be heard so we can fight another day."

I asked Lanier about the objection that was made when he discussed whether or not the judgment will get paid or that it might get reduced on appeal. Many lawyers would feel that Lanier's argument was improper because it was not discussing the evidence but legal procedures outside of what was proven at trial. Lanier agrees that at first it seems objectionable, but he doesn't know what the objection is. Lanier points out that all he was really saying is that the jury should base its verdict on the facts, and not base it on their thoughts of can the defendant pay or will it enrich the plaintiff too much. The jury's job is to base it on the facts, not whether it gets appealed or not or whether the judge might reduce it or not. That is the judge's job.

The jury returned a verdict of $253.5 million.

Let's look at one more of Lanier's closing arguments. This one involves the drug Actos.

10.5 *ALLEN V. TAKEDA*

Actos was a diabetes drug produced by Takeda Pharmaceutical in Japan and co-marketed by Eli Lilly from 1999 to 2006. Since 1999, Actos has generated $16 billion in sales. Terence Allen's doctor prescribed Actos to treat Allen's Type 2 Diabetes Mellitus. He took Actos from 2004 until January 2011 when he was diagnosed with bladder cancer.

In 2011, The FDA declared that extended use of Actos for more than a year could increase the risk of bladder cancer. Allen asserted many claims but, in short, he claimed that Takeda knew that Actos caused an increased risk of bladder cancer, failed to warn doctors of this risk, and put a dangerous drug on the market. Allen's wife, Susan, was also a plaintiff and sued for loss of companionship during his medical treatment. At the time of trial, Allen was cancer free but had a 40 percent chance of a relapse. Eli Lilly was a co-defendant because it also sold Actos in the United States.

In addition, Lanier alleged that "Takeda officials intentionally destroyed documents about the development, marketing and sales of Actos.... The company ditched files of 46 former and current employees, including those of top executives in Japan and U.S. sales representatives." In a pretrial ruling, the trial judge found that "[t]he breadth of Takeda leadership whose files have been lost, deleted or destroyed is, in and of itself, disturbing." Lanier obtained an instruction to the jury that the destroyed documents could be used as proof that they would have supported the plaintiffs' claims.

In this section, we will examine Lanier's punitive damages argument. At trial, the jury first returned a verdict on liability after deliberating for an hour and ten minutes, and then the lawyers argued the issue of punitive damages. Prior to the arguments, the judge gave the jury instructions on how to decide punitive damages, and the parties read an agreement to the jury about the defendants' net worth and profits.

Court's punitive damages instruction

The judge instructed the jury as follows:

> **Court:** *Punitive damages are designed to punish the defendants for wanton and reckless, outrageous conduct and thereby punish Takeda and Lilly and thereby discourage the defendants and other companies from acting in a similar way in the future. You must now decide the amount of punitive damages to be awarded. In deciding upon that amount, you should consider...*

the character of the wrongdoing you have found occurred in this case. For instance, the degree to which the defendants' conduct demonstrated an indifference to or a reckless disregard of the health, safety, or rights of others.... The degree to which the act or acts constituted outrageous or oppressive intentional misconduct....

Although you may consider harm to individuals or entities other than Terrence Allen in determining the degree to which the defendants', again, plural, conduct was reprehensible, you may not add a specific amount to your punitive damages award to punish Takeda and Lilly for any harm they might have caused to others who are not parties in this case.... The amount of punitive damages that you award must be both reasonable and proportionate to the actual and potential harm suffered by Terrence Allen and to the compensatory damages you awarded Terrence Allen.

Here are some of the key figures that were read to the jury. In 2013, Takeda's net worth was $23,652,755,000, and Eli Lilly's net worth was $17,631,000,000. Actos' net sales in the United States between 1999 and 2012 were $24 billion. The total number of patients that were prescribed Actos as of June 15, 2011, was more than 10 million.

The jury deliberated on punitive damages for 45 minutes.

10.6 STRATEGIES FOR PUNITIVE DAMAGES ARGUMENT

Lanier told me why his punitive damages argument achieved a $9 billion verdict. He wanted to empower the jury and convey that it was a part of something greater than Lafayette, Louisiana (where the trial took place), and the Terry Allen family (plaintiffs). He wanted them to know that they could "change the world." He wanted to make them realize the unique opportunity in front of them. "Whoever dreamed that those nine people when they woke up that day (for the punitive damages argument) would get to talk to Osaka, Japan, not indirectly, but directly?" Lanier explained to the jury that their actual words were going to be relayed to the boardroom of one of the largest pharmaceutical companies in the world within 30 seconds of being spoken. "That's so empowering to a jury, and that's giving them responsibility. It's an amazing thing, and you're letting them know they have their hand on the launch codes, the red button."

I asked Lanier how he decides how much to ask a jury to award a plaintiff or whether he asks for a specific amount at all. He said it depends on how you think the case is going. He has no specific rule that he follows. You have to rely on your gut. For this particular case, he was worried the jury would only return $750 million.

The key is that "you've got to be able to say it with a straight face." He explained how he once failed to follow his own advice, and it cost him.

First time I got a punitive award for 100 million was in 1998. It was an asbestos case. I am walking out of the courthouse with Dr. Bob, my lawyer psychologist, trial scientist, jury picker, best friend, and he is pouting.

I said, "Bob, we just got the largest asbestos verdict in history, why are you pouting?" He said, "Because you should have gotten a billion dollars if you hadn't stuttered when you asked for it, you would have gotten them." I said, "I just couldn't bring myself to say a billion!"

Lanier then summarized for me his punitive argument in that case. He gave it at a time when President Clinton had just launched an airstrike against Iraq in 1998. Here is what Lanier told the jury:

You know right now the U.S. Air Force is conducting air strikes against Iraq because we *think*, we don't know, we *think* they might have weapons of mass destruction. We *know* this company had a weapon of mass destruction and they used it for profit. We can't do air strikes against Carborundum, so what are we going to do? All you can do is fine them. You need to put down something real. Put down a...a billion [Lanier stutters] dollars.

10.7 LANIER'S PUNITIVE DAMAGES ARGUMENT

Lanier framed his argument around each of the factors the judge said the jurors could consider in awarding punitive damages. He would first state the factor and give the best example of the evidence that proved that factor. It was a simple, persuasive, and empowering argument that took less than ten minutes. Some excerpts are below.

Lanier: Thank you guys, thank you very, very much. Now at this point we've got a little bit left, a little bit of work left to do. I was listening to Her Honor read her instructions and y'all have got a copy of them. On the second page, I was struck by this language. If I could go to the ELMO please. You may also consider Takeda's and Lilly's financial condition and the impact your punitive damages award will have on Takeda and Lilly.

How do you have an impact on these companies? How do you get—right now it's 14 hours later in Osaka, Japan. So it's 9:00 o'clock on Tuesday morning. And they didn't come here to testify, but I promise you **they are by their cell phones and they are waiting to hear** because the message you proclaim, **what you say from Lafayette, Louisiana, is going to reach all the way around the world,** and they are going to get a call and they will either be trying to digest things, maybe popping champagne corks, or they are going to be trying to figure out whose head rolls and how to do business differently.

> *What you say from Lafayette, Louisiana, is going to reach all the way around the world.*
> —Mark Lanier, damages argument

> **You [change] the world. This is where you change it. This is where you do it. You make the difference.** It's not just that company. It's the other companies that watch, too. It's not just Takeda. It's not just Lilly. Everybody will watch what you do today.

Like he did in the Vioxx trial, Lanier empowers the jury. This is not just another case with an injured plaintiff. It is a unique opportunity for the jury to "make the difference." Notice how he plays on the fact that Takeda's headquarters are in Japan. Since its leaders are not at trial, Lanier argues that the jury will have to award a lot of money, or Takeda won't even notice. In reality it doesn't matter whether the headquarters are in New Orleans or Japan, but Lanier uses the geographical distance as an analogy to create a striking picture that Takeda's leaders are detached, far away, and not paying attention to the damage that Actos has caused.

> These bullet points [on the projector] say the degree to which the defendants' conduct demonstrated an indifference to or a reckless disregard of others' health and safety. What more can you say other than the kids' study. And that they'd go over to Europe to do it because they can't get permission to do it in the U.S. If that's not a reckless disregard, I don't know what is.
>
> I'm still offended by the fat lady San Francisco stupid comment. Lilly [said] "hey, these people that are diabetics are just fat, stupid, and lazy. We don't care."
>
> [Bullet point showing judge's instruction]: The degree to which the act constituted outrageous or oppressive intentional misconduct. This is the document destruction, and Her Honor made very specific findings that still apply here. Where are the documents that would allow us to really go back and examine what was going on in the higher chambers?
>
> [Another bullet point says] the degree to which the defendants were aware of what harm the conduct caused. They did the Proactive study. They can do the math. There are 10 million users of Actos. If there are 10 million people using Actos, you've got over 9,000 at that point. Now you're looking at 90,000 bladder cancers.
>
> [Another bullet point says] whether the harm caused was physical as opposed to economic. Yeah, this isn't **"gee, they cheated us out of a half cent at the gas pump."** This is very real. These are people with cancer. This is physical harm.

Lanier emphasizes how important this case is. It is not a fight about money and compensation. It's getting justice for being physically harmed and having your health taken away.

> [Another bullet point says] the degree of concealment and covering up. They weren't up front with the FDA...when they didn't give them

meta-analysis. They weren't up front with the FDA. They weren't up front with the medical community…when they ghostwrote and published a bunch of articles under people who didn't write them. They weren't up front with the doctors on the sales calls. They concealed that as well.…

In my last four minutes I'll make the following suggestion. I would suggest you send some kind of a message that basically says to Japan and to Lilly, "no way, absolutely no way." And it takes a lot of conviction. It takes courage. **It takes creativity. It takes a lot to do it.** Because you got a company, if they are going to make 20 or $30 billion off this product, do we honestly think fining them a few million here or there is going to do anything at all.

I mean, if they have got 23 billion as a net worth right now, how do you fine someone for doing this. That's the punishment. This is the punishment, this is the punishment. How do you — all you can do is fine them. You can't lock them up in jail. You can't take away their homes and possessions. **All you can do is speak the language of money and fine them.** So how do you do that?

$23 billion is too hard to wrap my head around — if I've got $23 [billion] in my pocket and you wanted to fine me for causing 9,000 cancers a year. **If you fine me a dollar and I got 23 and I peel off a George Washington and I give it to you and say "hey sorry," and I go skipping down the sidewalk because I made [22] bucks off the deal. That's what happens if you put one billion down there.…**

Do you put two and a half billion dollars down there? Do you put a billion down? Do you say "hey that's a lot of money I'm going to cut them back a little?"

Lanier makes complicated ideas seem simple. How can you visualize $23 billion dollars and determine an appropriate fine for a company that is worth that amount? By converting $23 billion to $23 that will fit in your pocket, he makes a $9 billion verdict seem very reasonable.

⸺ ∞ ⸺

Risk-benefit analysis is supposed to happen with every drug. The doctor said this. Here's the benefit, here's the risk. The problem is the way Takeda and Lilly do business, **they have changed that risk benefit formula. Now, it's we'll get the benefit and give you the risk.** That's what they have really tried to do here. The company didn't take any risk in putting this drug out there. Mr. Allen, Terry took the risk. Sue took the risk. We take the risk. And they have got the benefit. We've got to stop the madness at some point.

And the final point that I have is this.… It's up to you. You guys, when you're done, if we get to visit with you and you choose to visit with us, we're going to be thanking you sincerely. My clients are going to be hugging your neck. **I just want that phone ringing in Japan.**

After 45 minutes, the jury returned a record-setting verdict: $6 billion against Takeda and $3 billion against Lilly. While the verdict may be reduced on appeal, the phones were certainly ringing in Japan. Takeda's stock fell in Tokyo trading approximately 5.2 percent. The total loss to the company on that one-day stock slide was approximately $4 billion.

10.8 CHAPTER CHECKLIST

Lanier's strategies for closing argument

1. You can't convince the unconvinced jurors. Instead, arm the jurors on your side with evidence they need to persuade opposing jurors during deliberations.

2. Work on your closing after each day of trial. Don't wait until the end of trial.

3. Create new themes for closing. That way, if your opponent steals your theme from opening statement, you will have a new theme to argue.

4. Sincerely thank the jury on behalf of your client.

5. List exhibits in their numerical order of importance so the jury can easily find them.

6. Speak in the first person and don't be afraid to give your opinion about the evidence.

Tips from Lanier's Vioxx closing argument

1. Make your client real through use of visually descriptive language. For example, "After we ended court, Carol and I had tuna fish sandwiches in the courtroom next door.... She wanted me to tell you, 'thank you.'"

2. Take on a greater burden of proof than required. "If you put 500 sheets of paper on each side of the scales and you take one extra sheet of paper and add it, that's extra.... I think I've proven my case by a much greater burden."

Use powerful themes

1. "Everybody wants to look. When David fought Goliath, there were two armies that watched because it's something to see."

2. Alliteration makes themes memorable. Lanier spoke about Merck's denial, deception, and damages.

Memorable phrases

1. When speaking about Merck's insincerity in its clinical studies, Lanier compared it to going to an elementary school to "try to figure out how many kids have beards."

2. Merck deceived the FDA. "Right and wrong doesn't change based on how much money's involved."

3. Criticizing a Merck scientist who claimed Bob did not have a blood clot, after looking at only 1 out of 150,000 slides, Lanier compared it to his daughter who, after fishing for 5 minutes on Lake Conroe, said, "Dad, the lake doesn't have any fish. Let's go home."

4. When Merck contended Bob's heart failure was caused by snoring or bad dreams, Lanier countered, "What's harder, snoring or running 26 miles? What's harder, the nightmare or riding a bike 62 miles?"

Defendant's closing

1. Don't patronize and demean jurors by reminding them of their promise in jury selection to keep an open mind and to be fair. Defense counsel said, "I'm going to hold you to that obligation to be as fair and impartial as you can be in judging the evidence in this case."

2. Don't be tone deaf. Defense counsel argued that jurors could do Carol a favor by sending her a message that Vioxx did not kill her husband. Such a message would relieve her of the guilt she had been carrying, since she had recommended that Bob take Vioxx for his arthritis.

Listen carefully to opponent's argument and turn their words against them

1. Lanier referenced an FDA letter to Merck that Vioxx had caused about 144,000 deaths in the United States. Opposing counsel objected to that letter "as just a notice document." Lanier responded, "I'd take notice of it. I think they should have taken notice of it. I think everybody should."

2. "For them to have the audacity to stand up here and say, 'please vote for Merck for Carol Ernst's sake, so Carol Ernst can go away from here knowing she's guilt free,' that's bad. That's bad."

Damages argument in rebuttal

1. Lanier argued that Merck wants you to believe that its lavish spending on employees and parties is irrelevant. Lanier tells the jury that Merck believes that "those are Merck numbers…and normal people just aren't worth that much."

2. Merck spent $1,000,000 on a launch party for Vioxx. Lanier argued, "I'd say every year she lives without Bob Ernst is worth one launch party."

3. Lanier uses rhymes to make a memorable point. "Please don't let them off light. Give it to them right."

4. "Put down something that commands the attention of Merck…. You [Merck] can't discredit Carol…and then go back singing. We [the jury] won't allow it."

5. "Let your voice be heard so we can fight another day."

Memorable arguments from Lanier's Actos closing argument on punitive damages

1. "Right now it's 14 hours later in Osaka, Japan…. They didn't come to testify, but I promise you they are by their cell phones and they are waiting to hear because the message you proclaim, what you say from Lafayette, Louisiana, is going to reach all the way around the world."

2. "You change the world. This is where you change it. This is where you do it. You make the difference."

3. This is more than a case of "Gee, they cheated us out of a half cent at the gas pump."

4. "All you can do is speak the language of money and fine them."

5. "$23 billion is too hard to wrap my head around — if I've got $23 [billion] in my pocket and you wanted to fine me for causing 9,000 cancers a year. If you fine me a dollar and I got 23 and I peel off a George Washington and I give it to you and say 'hey sorry,' and I go skipping down the sidewalk because I made [22] bucks off the deal. That's what happens if you put one billion down there…."

6. "[Takeda and Lilly] have changed that risk-benefit formula. Now, it's we'll get the benefit and give you the risk."

7. "I just want the phone ringing in Japan."

CHAPTER ELEVEN

Tom Girardi

The Passionate Closing Argument

Tom, we want our son to have the same heart you have. So, we have named him Girard.

—From a letter (with photo of the newborn child) written by a client Tom Girardi represented against a large corporation

*T*om Girardi is a partner in Girardi Keese and has been practicing law since 1965. His career has many firsts. He was the first lawyer in California to win a million dollar verdict in a medical malpractice case. He was the youngest member ever to be admitted to the International Academy of Trial Lawyers, an organization limited to 500 lawyers in the world. In addition, he is a member of the Inner Circle of Advocates, an organization limited to 100 lawyers who have obtained the largest verdicts in the United States.

Girardi was inducted into the Trial Lawyer Hall of Fame by the California State Bar in 2003. In a recent survey of 65,000 lawyers to determine the finest lawyer in California, he received the most votes. He was the 2015 president of the Litigation Counsel of America and the former president of the American Board of Trial Advocates. In April 2014, he was inducted into the American Trial Lawyers Hall of Fame.

He has had many record-setting verdicts but is most famous for *Anderson v. Pacific Gas & Electric*. There were two trials lasting over seven months that resulted in $131,000,000 for 40 plaintiffs. These verdicts caused an eventual settlement of the entire litigation for $333,000,000. The litigation became immortalized in the movie *Erin Brockovich*. In addition to his unrivaled legal career, he is a Trustee of the Library of Congress

> **CHAPTER HIGHLIGHTS**
> - Frame your closing with a powerful theme
> - Use the jury instructions to your advantage
> - Express candor about weaknesses in your case

and the host of the weekly radio show, "Champions of Justice," which is broadcast on both coasts.

11.1 TRIAL TRENDS

> *You're in the persuasion business, and you can never forget that.*
> —Tom Girardi

Girardi started our interview by explaining how much trial practice has changed. He had his staff conduct a review of the cases that were tried in the 1980s compared to the cases being tried now. Although it was not a scientific survey, it was a thorough one. He found that in the 1980s, juries were deciding facts in about 80 percent of the cases. Currently, jurors are deciding facts in only about 20 percent of the cases.

Girardi elaborated that in the 1980s, jurors in a slip and fall case would decide the fact of how long ice cream had been on the floor before a customer slipped. Or in an automobile accident case, the jury would decide the fact of who ran the red light. Now, the parties agree on the facts, and the jurors only decide the ultimate legal question: Who was negligent? In short, juries are now deciding cases based on their philosophical viewpoint (i.e., was there negligence or bad faith), instead of resolving disputed facts as they did in the past.

Girardi also said that in the 1980s, a case would go to trial because the insurance company would force you to go to trial. "It was easier to get large verdicts." Now, the case where the drunk truck driver runs over a kid on the sidewalk gets settled by the insurance company before going to trial. In the 1980s the insurance company would offer $25,000 on a policy that had $1,000,000 coverage and force you to go to trial, whereas now the insurance company offers $650,000 and makes the choice to go to trial a lot more difficult.

11.2 SELECTING JURORS

Girardi believes that the "four strongest jurors" decide each case, even though there are twelve in the jury box. "The nice little lady in the back, just sitting there kind of looking at things, she probably doesn't have a voice." During voir dire or once the trial begins, one way to identify the leaders is to notice during breaks who leads the others to get coffee or lunch.

During voir dire, you can identify plaintiff and defense jurors by the way they answer this question: "What do you think of the jury system?" If a juror answers, "Oh, you have a right to trial by jury," you know he is a plaintiff's juror. "The reason we know that is because the only thing that's ever reported in the press is jury awards and some huge number." On the other hand, if you ask the same question in voir dire and the juror answers, "I don't know. I suppose if we can't find a better way to do things, this isn't a bad way to do it," you have identified a defense juror. The juror's uncertainty about the jury system is based on what he or she has read in the media. Girardi instructs that such a response reveals "three or four negatives about the jury system…. Deep down inside, the juror's [biased] inner thoughts are preventing the juror from saying [the truth]: 'You have a right to trial by jury.'"

For the case we will discuss below about the San Francisco Giants fan who was attacked in a parking lot at an L.A. Dodgers game, Girardi used several mock juries prior to trial, perhaps as many as 100 jurors in various aspects of trial preparation. For example, he would give opening statements and then question the mock jurors. To his surprise, he learned that the more Dodgers games the mock jurors had been to, the more likely they were to be a plaintiff's juror. This conclusion was very surprising and shows how important mock jurors are. Girardi found out that even though jurors who went to a lot of games were obviously Dodger fans, they were also aware of the unruly behavior and the fights that would break out in the stands.

I asked Girardi if one were to go to a Dodgers game today, would one notice bad behavior by the fans? He was quick to point out that the bad atmosphere occurred when Frank McCourt was the owner, not the new ownership group led by Magic Johnson. He did not shy away from his opinion of McCourt as an owner. "He was terrible. There used to be a watchtower in the parking lot because when everybody walks in the parking lot, an officer can't really see what's going on. So, he had these towers built. However, he decided they didn't need to have people in them. At the very place that the assaults took place, there's a tower 10 feet away. Of course, there's nobody in the tower to see the assaults that were taking place before Brian (the plaintiff) got hit.

It wasn't like somebody came out of the woods and knocked Brian. They were assaulting people before [they assaulted Brian]." In addition, to save money, McCourt used private security guards, who wore T-shirts, instead of uniformed police officers. This change had a big impact in failing to deter bad behavior.

11.3 YOU MUST CARE ABOUT YOUR CLIENT

There can be no doubt that Girardi is passionate about his clients. He once represented a woman who was burned badly while using a Coleman lantern during a campout. While the man and his wife were sleeping, the lantern "starts leaking white hot gas, burning Mrs. Espinoza on the face. When we go to trial, she's seven months pregnant.

"During the trial, it was proved fairly convincingly that the problem wasn't the Coleman lantern, but the way in which Mr. Espinoza had set it up. We lost the case. When the jurors came out, five were crying as they entered a defense verdict. About two and a half months later, I got a little note from Mrs. Espinoza with a picture of the baby that she had delivered. She said, 'Tom, I want you to know something. We want our son to have the same heart that you have. So, we have named him Girard.'"

I asked Girardi if he could ever have been a defense lawyer. His reply was quick. "I couldn't do it." He then explained how closely knit his office is and how much everyone cares about its cases. He related how he went down to the office on President's Day to pick up a file, and "all the secretaries are there. I said, 'What are you guys doing here? Are you trying to set me up on a wage an hour case or something?' They laughed and said, 'No, Tom. You know, we talked about it and, quite honestly, this isn't that big of a holiday, and we could come in, no phones, get all caught up. So, that's what we're doing.' I think the loyalty of those people, in part, is because of the cases we have. I don't think they'd be doing that if we represented AIG Insurance Company. You know what I mean? I think their heart goes out to these people."

Girardi gave another example where his being on the right side of a case motivated someone to do something extraordinary. He was representing numerous plaintiffs who had died from heart attacks after taking the drug Vioxx, a painkiller. Girardi was having a difficult time proving that the manufacturer, Merck, knew that its drug would cause blood clots that would lead to heart failure.

Out of the blue, Girardi received an envelope with no return address. Inside was "a memo from the Chief Medical Officer of Merck to the Executive Vice President. February 1st, 2001, when they're taking Vioxx into the clinical trials. It says, 'Are we going to give people Aspirin with the Vioxx? If we don't, we'll have so many heart attacks, it'll kill the drug.' These dirty bastards knew. Once that surfaced, that was…. Once I had it, that was the reason the cases settled."

More recently, Girardi related another incident involving an unsolicited document he received. He represented plaintiffs who had taken a diabetic drug, Avandia, which caused heart attacks despite the fact there was no warning on the drug's label. "In the mail one day, we get this…. It's a little report of the first time Avandia was given to people, as opposed to animals. They had two heart attacks. [An executive] writes in the margin, 'This will never see the light of day.' That's mailed to me. So, we asked them to produce the first disk, they sent it, but it didn't have that writing on it. I said, 'Listen, you guys. I don't want to get too picky here, but could you re-do it again, and I'd like the word day to appear in the left column.' Then they call back and said, 'OK, Tom. Let's sit down on this.' That's what settled that case."

11.4 CANDOR IN CLOSING ARGUMENT

Girardi emphatically declares, "I think the most important fact is candor in closing arguments.... Now, you have to say things like, 'You know, they brought that Dr. Hansen in. Weren't you impressed? I was impressed. The only little part that I want you to consider.... Dr. Hansen never saw those medical records of a year before, when he testified, that would have given him the reason why, in fact, [plaintiff's argument is right]. So, I want you to consider that.'" Girardi adds that if you don't concede your bad aspect of the case and explain it, then the jury "will go into the jury room and say, 'Oh that Hansen, he nailed them.'"

I asked Girardi how important he thought closing arguments were. He recounted a time when he was in front of a friendly judge with a defense counsel he knew. They were trying two cases. The judge allowed the lawyers to ask the jurors to vote after voir dire, opening statement, close of plaintiff's case, the close of defendant's case, and after the verdict. Only three jurors out of 24 voted differently from their initial vote after voir dire. That means that 88 percent of the jurors never changed their minds after their initial impression of the case. Girardi took from this admittedly unscientific experiment the lessons that the "philosophical bent in jurors when you select them is crucial and those initial stages [of trial] are extremely important."

For his closing argument, Girardi always begins by thanking the jury. A typical argument would go like this. "Let me tell you something. Every single one of you, you know, we know what you do, we know the kids you're taking care of, we know the jobs you have. You don't need this. Every single one of you, when you got that notice that you had to appear for a jury selection, no one in the world has ever said "Oh, great. I get to serve on a jury." None of you did, did you? But you know what? This case is going to be over once you're through the deciding. You know what you're going to say to yourself? This was really great. We had the chance to make things right. I'm counting on you."

> For a lawyer to get up there and simply address the good aspects of the case and to kiss off the bad aspects of the case is totally stupid.
> —Tom Girardi

11.5 HOW TO DISCUSS JURY INSTRUCTIONS

In his closing argument, Girardi focuses on the two or three most important instructions. They are the "whole ballgame." He doesn't want the jurors to hear the instructions for the first time when the judge "mumbles them" after closing arguments. In fact, Girardi uses words from the instructions during voir dire, in his opening statement, and throughout the trial. Girard points out that you can't recite the instructions verbatim until closing argument, but you can plant the seed in the jurors' minds so that they don't hear something for the first time after closing argument when the judge reads the instructions.

For example, in the Stow case discussed below, there was an instruction on causation that was favorable to his client. It stated that there could be more than one cause of an injury as long as it was a "substantial" cause. As a result, in voir dire, opening statement, and with his expert witness, he would discuss the fact that there was a cause of the plaintiff's injury other than the two felons who assaulted him — the Dodgers' lack of security at the game.

11.6 AN ARGUMENT TO MAKE WHEN JURORS FAVOR CORPORATIONS

Girardi shared an argument he uses whenever some jurors have a philosophical bent that favors corporations. Here is what he told the jury: "You know, in this case, if you belong to a good company, if you're part of a good company, there's no way in the world that you can compete with a company that cuts corners. You can't do it. If some company is out there cutting corners, and putting their product out, doing those sorts of things, and you're doing the right thing, testing the thing properly, proper warnings, there's no way you can compete. So, I think you better come in favor of the plaintiff in this case because the plaintiff deserves it. More importantly, you have to come in favor of the plaintiff to say good companies should not be punished."

11.7 HOW TO MAKE A DAMAGES ARGUMENT

Girardi instructs that if it's an "open-and-shut case," you should ask for a specific amount of damages in your closing. As he puts it, "you can really pound the money." On the other hand, if it is a close case, "and the Stow case is a close case…I mean, the Dodgers didn't beat the guy up, the two felons did. Then, you don't want to lose anybody by overreaching. So, you've got to keep your cards a little bit more covered."

He continued, "I have said things like, 'You know, it's a good thing I'm not a juror here. I know what I would do. I mean, I'd be in the 50 million dollar range. That would be me, and here I am. You are the people who decide that. You're in charge of that. Not some lawyer up here. That's your responsibility.' So, you maybe throw out a little number, not that they should come in that way, matter-of-factly telling them they shouldn't. I'm too involved, blah, blah, blah. So, at least you get a big number working. I think you have to be a little bit more careful when the facts are not necessarily open-and-shut."

> *Closing argument is huge in the damage arena. If you've lost the case, though, on liability, you're toast.*
>
> —Tom Girardi

Getting a large damage award depends on many factors, but I asked Girardi how a lawyer can make a difference in closing argument. He replied, "Somehow, without saying so, you have to get them in the shoes of your client. So, you can't tell the jury, 'What if you were a quadriplegic, what would you want?' You can kind of hint at it in a different way. It's like, wow, you know? What a terrible thing that's happened, huh? To this person. You can't treat *him* as if he's your family. You've got to be impartial. The translation is, 'What would you do if this were your family?'"

11.8 PUT IN THE HARD WORK

I wanted to ask Girardi the question I get asked a lot that goes something like this: "Why should I take the time and effort to create a powerful theme or a memorable opening statement when my cases are small and/or boring?" Girardi told me about one of his first cases, a car wreck case where his client had a soft-tissue injury to her neck. Girardi explained, "How do you ever go from Keck versus Higgs to Stow versus the Dodgers? Without Keck versus Higgs, and without all of these other little things, you can't do it. You can't walk into court for the first trial of a multi-million dollar case that could go either way. You're not going to be hired for that. You need a track record."

Girardi added that getting a good verdict never gets old. "It's so damned exciting. They buzz three times [to indicate] they have a verdict. I don't care if it's over 25 grand, over 10 billion, it's pretty exciting to get your report card, baby."

I asked Girardi what effect a lawyer has on the outcome of a civil case. He said it was "off the charts." When he returns to the office after a good trial, he will proclaim, "'I won the case.' Or you go back to the office and say, 'I lost the case.' You're telling the truth because the lawyer wins the case or the lawyer loses the case."

11.9 DELIVERY

When you meet Girardi, it is obvious that he is at ease with people and has a lot of charisma. I asked him for his view on using notes during a closing argument. He said, "I think you do need a couple of notes, just so you don't, in the heat of the moment, pass things over. I sneak the notes. So, if I want to cover seven topics, I'll put seven words down. I'll make sure that little thing is on the [podium] before I start my argument. Then, as I'm finishing up one point, I may kind of steal a glance. Oh yes, make sure we talk about that. Let's go into that point. So it looks like it's without any note or anything like that, but it's definitely.... You don't want to forget, sit down and say, 'Oh my god, I forgot to talk about such and such.'"

> **Practice Tip**
> Girardi rhetorically asks, "Would you read your marriage proposal to your significant other?" He advises that the same is true with closing argument. Whether you read your closing argument or not makes all the difference in the world in how you connect with your audience.

11.10 GET THE TRIAL TRANSCRIPT

Girardi likes to get a daily transcript of the trial proceedings. But even if he doesn't get a daily transcript, he makes sure to get a transcript of opposing counsel's opening statement. In his closing, he wants to "throw it up on the wall and say, 'Look what he said. Did that happen? You know, we're supposed to be honest about this stuff. This opening statement is what we're going to prove. Look at this. Did he prove that?'"

11.11 USE VISUAL AIDS

Girardi believes visual aids are important, but you cannot rely on them too much. Many lawyers make the mistake of giving them too much focus, and then the jury becomes distracted by the exhibit, instead of paying attention to what you are saying in your argument.

11.12 HOW TO ARGUE AGAINST A LIKABLE OPPOSING LAWYER

I asked Girardi how far he goes in using sarcasm in his closing argument. "In trying cases against nice guys, I say, 'Ladies and gentlemen, you have to understand one thing. This case is not a case that's decided by who has the better lawyer, who has the nicer person, or we're toast.'" Girardi always displays candor in the courtroom. He is not afraid to admit it if opposing counsel is likable or very good. As a result, he gains even more credibility with the jury by being sincere and gets it to focus on the facts of the case and not opposing counsel. Girardi adds that "when the other guy's been a jerk, you can be a little bit more feisty."

11.13 *STOW V. LOS ANGELES DODGERS*

Before we look at Girardi's closing argument, let's familiarize ourselves with the main facts in the case because doing so will help to put the closing argument in context.

On March 31, 2011, Bryan Stow and his friends went to Dodger Stadium on opening day. He and his friends were San Francisco Giants' fans and were wearing Giants clothing. As Stow was leaving the game, he was assaulted in the parking lot by Louis Sanchez and Marvin Norwood. The attack caused massive brain damage that would leave Stow wheelchair-bound and prevent him from ever working or living independently again.

At trial, Girardi had to prove that the Dodgers failed to use reasonable care to protect their customers. Girardi contended that the Dodgers tried to blame everyone but themselves for Stow's beating. This included blaming the LAPD, the fans in Sanchez and Norwood's section who failed to report the duo's conduct to ballpark security, and, of course, Bryan and his friends.

Amazingly, for all the security for opening day, there was none after the game in parking Lot 2 where the assault took place. Also, there were no officers in the Loge section where Louis Sanchez was visibly intoxicated, verbally assaulting others, throwing things at Giants fans, and starting fights in clear violation of the Dodgers' own policies and procedures. For example, no security guard or usher was assigned to work in the section where Sanchez and Norwood were sitting throughout the game. Moreover, while two security guards were deployed to Lot 2 after the game, they arrived approximately 20 minutes after the end of the game and after Bryan was attacked. The Dodgers attempted to paint the picture of a drunk Bryan Stow who shared blame for the fate he met on that evening.

Upon arriving at the Dodgers game, Bryan and his friends came across a Dodgers security guard, who told them "look at these fucking idiots" while looking directly at the Stow group. This was the Stow groups' first interaction with anyone at Dodger Stadium.

Others continued the heckling. While some fans were engaging in good-natured fun, others were out to harass, intimidate, and make Giants fans feel as uncomfortable as possible. Unfortunately for the Stow group, the Dodger fans they ran into fell into the latter category. Even though they did encounter some rough fans, the Stow group made it through the game without any major incidents. That is because Norwood and Sanchez were on the other side of the stadium.

Marvin Norwood and Louis Sanchez arrived at the game with Dorene Sanchez (Louis's sister and Marvin's fiancée), and Louis's son, Louie. Upon arriving at Dodger Stadium, Norwood and Louis Sanchez drank beer in the parking lot. This violated Dodger policy that prohibited alcohol consumption in the parking lot and was grounds for ejection from the premises. Marvin Norwood and Louis Sanchez purchased beers shortly after entering the stadium. Soon Sanchez began heckling Giants fans in their area, Loge 149. The heckling progressed to vulgarity. Sanchez began yelling, "Fuck the Giants" at the top of his lungs. Sanchez was directing his statements at the two Giants fans seated in his section. The Dodger Fan Code of Conduct explicitly prohibits "foul/abusive language or obscene gestures." Sanchez's actions also violated another code which provides "our fans' experience will not be disrupted by unruly actions or behavior."

Sanchez and Norwood consumed approximately six to ten 16-ounce beers during the game. One fan seated in section Loge 149 stated that Sanchez "was so drunk, he couldn't even walk…he was like wobbly." The Dodger Fan Code of Conduct provides "fans will consume alcoholic beverages in a responsible manner. Intervention with impaired, intoxicated, or underage guests will be handled in a prompt and safe manner. Those appearing intoxicated will be denied entry or will be subject to ejection from the stadium."

Soon thereafter, Sanchez began throwing food at the same Giants fans. He even hollered, "You're next" to Griffith McDaniel after a fight broke out in the Loge area. Because there was no security to report his behavior to, Grif McDaniel and Katie Gillespie hoped it would defuse on its own. Because Sanchez did not have his own sunflower seeds, he began taking them out of another fan's purse without her permission. Again, when throwing food was not causing enough of a ruckus, Sanchez switched to even more outrageous behavior.

Sanchez decided to throw a soda at two Giants fans he had been harassing all day, Gillespie and McDaniel. Sanchez took a soda, shook it, and released the cap causing liquid to squirt all over the two Giants fans. In shock, Katie and Grif stood up immediately. Then, Sanchez stood as if to provoke a fight. Grif, Katie's boyfriend, stood there staring at Sanchez; the two men were engaged in a standoff, and a crowd gathered. Then, Norwood intervened, pulling Sanchez back. Security never responded to the altercation. Throughout the entire game, Katie and Grif looked for security or an usher that they could report Sanchez's behavior to, but they never saw any Dodger personnel. Following the altercation, the Sanchez group then went toward the exit of the stadium; Katie and Grif went the other direction.

Upon reaching the parking lot, Sanchez and Norwood decided to smoke marijuana, a violation of Dodger policy, as well as a violation of state and federal law. But, again security did not respond to their behavior.

Prior to encountering Bryan Stow and his friends in Lot 2, Sanchez and Norwood encountered a group of young Giants fans as they were leaving the stadium. Sanchez ran toward the teenagers, began punching them, and said, "Fuck the Giants." The young men were stunned by the behavior. The young men just kept walking away, and Sanchez and Norwood retreated. Sanchez and Norwood began yelling slurs and profanity at the other Giants fans that would walk by their vehicle. They were saying, "Fuck the Giants," "Giants Suck," and other profanity.

Following the game, Bryan and his friends arrived at Lot 2. Since they had arrived by taxi, they planned to leave the same way. Due to the length of the cab line and the heavy traffic, the Stow group decided to try to catch a cab as it was about to enter the stadium, rather than one already stuck in stadium traffic. It was during this process that Bryan encountered Sanchez and Norwood.

Sanchez and Norwood were in the parking lot getting high. When Bryan walked by Sanchez and Norwood, Sanchez began yelling "Fuck the Giants," "Fucking faggots," and started harassing him. In response to Sanchez's harassment, Bryan said something to the effect of "It's not that serious. It's not like a heart attack. You know what a heart attack is?" Bryan and his friends continued to walk away. Upon hearing Bryan's statement, Dorene Sanchez told Louis Sanchez that Bryan was "talking shit." In response, Louis Sanchez took off looking for Bryan. Norwood followed.

Louis Sanchez yelled, "What the fuck did you say, homey?" Then he pushed Bryan, causing Bryan to fall into his friends' arms. Bryan and his friends continued walking through the parking lot away from Sanchez and Norwood. A few minutes passed. Then Bryan was punched from behind by Sanchez, and Bryan fell to the ground unconscious. Then Sanchez and Norwood began kicking Bryan in the head repeatedly. Corey, Bryan's friend, ran over to Bryan, threw his body on top of Bryan's, and yelled, "You've already knocked him out. Leave him alone!" Then, Sanchez and Norwood ran off.

Sanchez and Norwood ran back to Dorene Sanchez's vehicle yelling, "Drive, drive, drive," and "Get in the fucking car, drive." The group then drove off. As Sanchez and Norwood fled, Bryan lay unconscious in Lot 2 waiting for help. Approximately eight minutes after Bryan was knocked unconscious, an ambulance still had not arrived at the scene.

Bryan suffered a traumatic brain injury and now has heterotopic ossification, a common but very painful complication where bone grows in abnormal places such as soft tissue, as well as severe cognitive defects. Bryan requires 24-hour attendant care. He cannot walk more than a few feet even when aided by a walker. He has difficulty engaging in everyday activities and requires assistance in most basic activities, such as bathing.

At trial, Girardi presented evidence that there were previous incidents of fan violence at Dodger Stadium. For example, on September 19, 2003, during a Giants-Dodgers game, there was a shooting in the parking lot at Dodger Stadium resulting in a fatality. On July 17, 2005, during another Giants game at Dodger Stadium, there was a brutal assault on Maria Helenius resulting in three facial fractures and the permanent loss of sight in one eye. It was also known that there was a higher incidence of violence when the Dodgers were playing the Giants, especially on Opening Day. In addition, in 2009, uniformed LAPD officers were no longer allowed inside the stadium.

One of the Dodgers' primary defenses was that it had plenty of security on Opening Day. The Dodgers claimed that 223 Dodger personnel were on duty with 67 of them in the 27 parking lots. There were also FBI agents and 195 LAPD officers.

At trial, Girardi pointed out that the FBI was deployed to prevent terrorism, and of the 195 LAPD officers, more than half were patrolling areas outside of Dodger property, such as the exterior streets and Elysian Park. In fact, only the

Parking Lot Group, which was comprised of 54 officers, was dedicated solely to monitoring the parking lots at Dodger Stadium. Based on these figures, there was approximately one LAPD or Security Guard for every 455 fans. Each of the 121 LAPD/ LAD security was responsible for several acres of parking lot, as the Dodger Stadium property is comprised of 330 acres.

In particular, the two Los Angeles Dodger employees assigned to patrol Lot 2 following the game, Bryan Hill and Bryan Hines, made it to their designated post well after the beating of Bryan Stow and at least 20 minutes after the game had ended. According to the eyewitnesses who were present at the scene of the incident, there was no security in sight when Sanchez and Norwood were stalking Bryan Stow and his friends through the parking lots. There also was no security in sight when Stow was attacked and repeatedly kicked in the head, and no security was present when Sanchez and Norwood fled the scene.

11.14 GIRARDI'S CLOSING ARGUMENT

Girardi began by thanking the jurors for the time they had devoted to listening to the evidence. Then, he told them the important job they had.

> I think you'll have an opportunity to say, you know, we showed some real fairness in a court in Los Angeles. We devoted a lot of time, and fairness took place. I think that our little firm has worked hard for Bryan. I don't know if I've ever represented a nicer person than he.
>
> I've never seen a family like this. His mom and dad and his sisters have devoted their lives to taking him out of bed and rolling him over and everything else ever since this occurred. You know, that kind of unbelievable dedication is really cool.
>
> So here we are hoping that we can get justice out of this, and it's all in your hands.

Girardi empowers the jury. This is not just a case about a plaintiff suing for money. It is a chance for the jury to ensure that fairness takes place. He also points out that not only is the plaintiff a special person, but so is his family. Notice how Girardi hints of a David versus Goliath theme when he explains, "our little firm has worked hard for Bryan." By highlighting the contrast between the plaintiff and his small resources and the big corporation of the L.A. Dodgers, Girardi emphasizes that he needs the jurors' help to bring the defendants to justice.

Discusses jury instructions

What Girardi does next is masterful and rarely attempted: He simplifies the jury instructions for the jury, but his explanation is brilliant because he states that the instructions were written with Stow in mind. So, this is just not another case of an injured plaintiff seeking money. Instead, it is a situation where the laws were written specifically with someone such as Stow in mind.

> Now then, I'll tell you this. This is really great. **You know what the biggest help to us in this case is? It's the law. I think when they wrote the law, I think they were thinking in terms of Bryan in this case....**
>
> So what did we hear in this case? **There is a huge defense in this case, and it's the ABMD defense, anybody but McCourt Dodgers — right? — the LAPD, the CHP, the FBI, fans, et cetera.**
>
> However, jury instruction number 1, just a couple of sentences, "One who owns, controls, and/or manages property has an affirmative duty to exercise reasonable care for the protection of the individuals coming onto the property. The duty is non-delegable. A landowner cannot avoid that duty by designating it to another party." OK?
>
> The FBI had a presence there. That was because Major League Baseball was concerned about terrorism. They weren't concerned about assaults in the parking lot and drunken people yelling obscenities and so forth.
>
> The CHP [California Highway Patrol], they didn't get inside the parking lot. They were outside.
>
> LAPD was there, 65 of them across the street in the park, but they had no — they were just backup. And the law says that you have to follow — no kidding on this one. He can't delegate — the owner of this property can't delegate it to anybody else. It's his ballgame. He has to keep that property safe.
>
> And we'll see exactly what they did with that, and, of course, they didn't. So that's a pretty good help.
>
> Now, then, the law isn't finished helping Bryan.
>
> **Honest to God, the whole law was meant so that people like Bryan could make a recovery and hopefully get enough money for medical care and so forth to last him.** Because we have an issue here, don't we?
>
> We have these guys who assaulted him in the lot. That's certainly a factor, isn't it? And if I were a juror, I would say, gee, that's a factor.

> **Practice Tip**
> Girardi masterfully tells the jury that the law was written with his client in mind. The argument creates a sense of duty for the jury to carry out the law's intent. Try Girardi's unique strategy in your next closing.

Girardi succinctly — and sarcastically — sums up the defense. He calls it the ABMD defense. He mockingly states that it stands for Anyone But the McCourt (the Dodgers' owner) Dodgers are responsible.

Dodgers' claim that Sanchez and Norwood are solely responsible

Next, Girardi addresses one of the Defendant's main arguments during trial, that the culprits of the assault are the only ones responsible.

So, how about this. Jury instruction 431, this is a little bit longer, but I won't bore you too bad.

"A person's negligence may combine with another factor to cause harm. If you find that the Los Angeles Dodgers LLC and Frank McCourt's negligence was a substantial factor in causing Bryan Michael Stow's harm, then Los Angeles Dodgers LLC and Frank McCourt are responsible for the harm.

"If you find that Louis Sanchez and Marvin Norwood's conduct was a substantial factor in causing Bryan Stow's harm, then Louis Sanchez and Marvin Norwood are responsible for the harm.

"If you find Bryan Michael Stow's negligence was a substantial factor in causing Bryan Stow's harm, then Bryan Michael Stow is responsible for the harm."

Here's the key. "No party can avoid responsibility just because some other person, condition, or event was also a substantial factor in causing Bryan Michael Stow's harm."

So I think those two instructions…tell us what this whole thing is about.

Girardi emphasizes the most important part of the instruction. The Dodgers cannot escape responsibility by arguing that another person was substantially responsible for Stow's injuries if the Dodgers were also substantially responsible.

Sanchez and Norwood's heckling during the game

Next, he describes Louis Sanchez and Marvin Norwood's actions before the assault in the parking lot. Two of their targets in the Loge area during the game were Katie and her boyfriend Grif. Both were wearing San Francisco Giants jerseys and caps.

All right. We'll start with the Loge section. You know, I think one of the greatest exhibits that came in yesterday were the pictures of Sanchez and the other guy [Norwood].

Can you imagine those people for three hours, two hours and 40 minutes, were in this section wreaking havoc, standing up yelling foul things, you know, "F" the Giants, throwing peanuts, harassing people. This went on from the second inning to the end of the game, and then it didn't get better; it got worse.

One of the people [Katie] said she tried to shut him up ten times, et cetera, and it got worse….

Then as if that isn't enough, in, I think, the fourth or fifth inning, there's a fight that breaks out, and the accusation is made by Sanchez, "you're next." So now he's threatening this physical violence.

> Then, not satisfied with that, towards the ninth inning, he throws all the Coke on her [Katie], dousing her with the Coke, disgusting…. So, here now for two and a half hours, this guy is behaving this way, and nobody does anything about it.

Remember, one of Girardi's main themes is that the Dodgers were substantially responsible. So, he turns the jury's attention away from the Loge to the stadium in general.

> You know, the place was a mess. Dodger Stadium had gotten to a place where it was a total mess. Can you imagine they threw 93 people out that day, arrested one?
>
> You saw the one fight. I won't bore you and show it again. Here's this fight that goes on. Where was the security there? There was no security….
>
> You know, there's a culture of violence to the place. That's all there is to it.
>
> Beer sales were off the chart, and the victims were the people like Katie and her [boyfriend] who escaped, as you know.

Girardi discusses lack of spending on security

Girardi then returns to the ABMD defense, the Anyone But the McCourt Dodgers defense. The Dodgers had presented evidence at trial that fans did not report incidents to security. One way to do that was to send a text message to a Dodger phone number or call on the emergency line. Watch how Girardi responds.

> In the entire 2010 season, do you know how many emergency calls they got for the whole season? They got one.
>
> Then with respect to the text messages that the fans could use if there is any violence and so forth, they got two for the whole season. So this wasn't exactly a protectorate for the people, you know, for the people that were there.
>
> And, once again, jury instruction number 1 says, you can't delegate the responsibility to anybody, huh? You have to accept that responsibility yourself, Dodgers and McCourt.

Girardi points out that the ushers in each section did not have walkie-talkies or any means to communicate with security. He then bluntly argues why there was not more security.

> The Dodgers own pocketbook prevented them from providing a safe place. That's all there is to it. Why have gaps in any of these sections? I'm going to jump on to something because that reminds me.
>
> Their budget for security was $2 million for the five years. Sometimes it was a million-nine, 2.1. It was about $2 million.

They had about — we figured out, I think, it was about 64 cents a person for security for people coming to Dodger Stadium. Here these people are coming there, moms with their kids, et cetera, the Katies of the world, et cetera, going to this place, and the budget basically is 64 cents per every person that comes in there.

The beer is 10 bucks. It costs $10 to park your car, 15 if you get a better spot. I think the parking was about $240,000 the night of this game. And they said, gee, we spent more than ever. We spent 60 grand.

> **Practice Tip**
> Look for a memorable comparison that highlights your opponent's weakness. Girardi points out, "A beer is 10 bucks. The Dodgers spent 64 cents a person for security."

They spent 25 percent of what they got on parking to protect the people, and then they had all these outbreaks, and nobody did anything about it, huh? Did you properly take care of the people? Did you make sure the premises were reasonably safe?

After discussing the Dodgers' unwillingness to spend money on security, he describes the staffing of security in the parking lots after the game. The Dodgers had stated that as soon as the last pitch was thrown, the protocol was for two security officers to be in each parking lot.

Lot 2 held a thousand cars. I'm assuming about 2,000 people, then, would be going to lot 2, right? A couple people per car, I would assume. I don't know if there are too many loners. Some cars maybe got three, whatever.

And the game is over. Now, then, the Dodgers knew that you have to have some security in Lot 2, and, in fact, they assigned two people, didn't they, Hines and Hill? They were going to be in Lot 2.

Girardi then points out that the two security guards never got there because they got tied up with other matters in the left field section where they were stationed during the game.

Girardi addresses a weakness in his case

Girardi also knows that in order to maintain his credibility with the jury, he needs to discuss any significant weaknesses within his case. He does that next and then contrasts it with Stow's actions.

Because in a situation like this, you know, the big deal, you can't prevent 100 percent of the [bad behavior] — no. I think that's probably true [**addresses weakness**]. But can you do something about somebody in the Loge being a jerk for seven innings and assaulting other people....

The only thing that Bryan was doing wrong is wearing a jersey, a black one that said Giants. He wasn't assaulting anybody.

Girardi then mentions that Sanchez assaults several people in the parking lot before he reaches Stow who is walking through Lot 2 to get to a taxi. He takes on the Dodgers' argument in opening statement that they could not have prevented Sanchez's sudden attack because it was not foreseeable.

> You know, the idea was that this was a testosterone thing that happened in a second. Remember that stuff from opening statement? Well, it didn't happen in a second. It happened for three and a half hours — two and a half hours in the game. Then it happened in Lot 2 with four assaults and then yet another assault on Bryan that did him in.
>
> So this was not like this, who could have possibly stopped it. They could have stopped it when they should have thrown them out. They should have stopped it when the first assaults were taking place.
>
> There was also some pushing by Sanchez in the escalator going down, but they could have stopped it there. They didn't do doodley-squat. **The reason they didn't do doodley-squat was, man, because they wanted to watch the old budget.**
>
> And then look at the harm that took place here. You know, there's $4,700,000 of medical bills to date. That's an agreement by everybody. The guy can never work again. And for what? For going to a game, huh? For going to a game that he thought would be reasonably safe.
>
> How about — were you blown away by the testimony that they knew they had a gang problem in the stadium?
>
> Let's suppose this is your stadium, and let's suppose you find out that you have a gang problem there. Let's suppose you have drunkenness galore and fights galore. Do you think just maybe to be fair to the people that are coming there that you do something about it?

Girardi then attacks defendant's opening statement, in which it was said that security was reasonable, by pointing out the honest admission that a security guard made.

> So one problem my colleagues have is the honesty, integrity of their employees that night, Bryan Hill and Bryan Hines.
>
> Hines testified under oath that the only way to provide proper security was to have more security in Lot 2. That was the guy that couldn't get there because they had him over in the stands someplace, and he was trying to get back....
>
> **Security is not just numbers. It's having the people doing the right job.** [a powerful theme] That's important, too. It doesn't matter if there were a hundred security people if they are all sitting in one corner. You have to have the security people in the right places....

> *The reason they didn't do doodley-squat was, man, because they wanted to watch the old budget.*
> —Tom Girardi,
> closing argument

Our best expert, I think, was their guy Squires. Squires said that it met protocol to assign these two people to Lot 2, but apparently you didn't actually have to have the people there [said with sarcasm]. You just had to assign them there, and then that's all you had to do, and then we've done what we should do.

You see, assigning people to Lot 2 doesn't do anybody in Lot 2 too much protection unless you actually go to Lot 2.

I want to talk about the uniformed police issue. As you know, there was an issue about uniformed police officers being there on security.

And there was a cost item. So I think they're five-hour shifts. And if you have a T-shirt on, you only get 30 bucks [per hour]. If you have the full uniform on, you get 50 bucks [per hour]. There's a 20-buck difference. That would be a hundred bucks per police officer.

So if you had a hundred police officers as opposed to polo shirts but in uniform, that would be a substantial amount of money. That would cost about $10,000 per game. If you had 80 games, that would be about $800,000.

Well, the total budget they had was 2 million.... So this would bring up the budget to almost 3 million bucks.

And the evidence was pretty clear, especially when you have gang problems, just maybe the appearance of the man in blue would stop some of the nonsense.

Do you think Sanchez would have been yelling those obscenities for five innings if, in fact, a few rows up was a person in blue watching it?

Do you think he would have been thrown out of the game immediately when he was doing those sorts of things, throwing beer, charging for a fight, et cetera?

Defense counsel's misleading comments in opening statement

Girardi points out another inconsistency between what defense counsel said in opening statement and the evidence at trial.

I suppose I should talk a little bit about the conduct of Bryan Stow because he's accused of being negligent in this particular case.

As a matter of fact, a lawyer in this case said to you at the beginning of the case that we're going to call Jesus Hernandez who will say that Bryan Stow had his hands up and turned around and had his hands up.

I guess the idea there was that, therefore, Bryan Stow was instigating some sort of bad activity, and a lawyer told you that at the beginning of this case....

Girardi then points out that two police officers investigated Hernandez's account and accompanied him to Lot 2 after the incident and had him explain what he had seen. Hernandez said that the man initiating the fight wore a gray jersey and a hat. Stow was wearing a black jersey and did not have a hat. The two police officers interviewed six other witnesses who said that Stow was walking with his hands to his side. The officers concluded in their report that Hernandez was mistaken and that the other six witnesses were correct.

> Now, then, let's suppose you're a lawyer and you don't know about that testimony of the two police officers and you say something like, and then Jesus Hernandez will come here and — well, you would be negligent, wouldn't you? **We're supposed to be fair to you guys. That's our job. On the other hand, what if you knew that?**
>
> See all those boxes over — oh, they're gone. All those boxes over there, **everybody had the testimony. Everybody knew what those police officers were going to say. Everybody knew the police officers, independent people, said this guy** [Hernandez] **doesn't have it right.**
>
> And yet the statement is made to you....

Stow drinks beers at game

Girardi then attacked another claim the Dodgers made: Stow's abuse of alcohol led to the assault. The lesson to learn is that you should not make disparaging remarks about an opposing party unless they are reasonable and you can back them up. As a lawyer, your client may pressure you to take such a jab but only do so if it is warranted. As you will see, defense counsel's strategy backfires because Girardi masterfully turns the argument around and fires right back.

> The reason this is kind of important [the issue of whether Stow started the fight] is because you have to decide if, in fact, Bryan Stow was negligent and what percentage of fault he had. And I really think that although maybe there could be some issues on some other matters, I don't really think there could possibly be an issue on this, you know, because there is no evidence here that is credible before you that he did anything wrong.
>
> You know, once again, talking about the law protecting us here, "A person is not necessarily negligent just because he or she used alcohol; however, people who drink alcohol must act as carefully as those who do not." OK?
>
> So, in other words, this whole thing, they went on and on for two days, the alcohol level and blah, blah, blah and all that stuff. It doesn't mean doodley-squat if all Bryan was doing was walking in a nice manner trying to get out to Sunset Boulevard or someplace to get a cab back.

> **Practice Tip**
>
> Listen for inconsistencies between the promises made by opposing counsel in opening statement and the proof that is actually produced at trial. Girardi hammers opposing counsel in his closing argument for such broken promises.

When we're talking about responsibility, how about this? These four guys, San Francisco, big Giant fans, and they're going to go to the game. It's opening game. It's going to be great. They were the champs last year.

They are four paramedics. They spend their lives actually helping people, sometimes out of dangerous situations. And they decide to go to the game.

Punitive damages

Now, then, but there's another part of this case that says if it's more than that, if there was a willful disregard of the fans' safety, if there was fraud, oppression, or malice, all of these defaults here took place because they wanted to protect their pocketbook and not have the thing properly safe for everybody, if all of them realized we had all these other incidents in the past, if all of them realized that this was going to be a game that there's going to be a lot of drunkenness, and there is rowdiness and so forth and we're not going to do doodley-squat about it....

So one of the instructions you're going to be given is whether or not the Dodgers were guilty of more than just 'whoops'; if they were guilty about absolutely, positively, without a doubt knowing about a serious problem where some guy could end up with $4,700,000 in medical bills and not do anything about it. Isn't it disgusting?...

As Dr. Fried, Gil Fried, said, they had serious incidents in 2005, 2006, 2007, 2008, 2009, 2010. Just maybe you're on notice; just maybe you better do something about it.

Now, then, here's what you get to do. You get to check that box where they're guilty of malice, oppression, et cetera, massively important. And that's far beyond importance for just Bryan. That would be you as members of the community saying, hey, stadiums, you've got to do the right thing. That would be really great, huh?

You realize what a great feeling you would have if you impacted not just the unfortunate life of Bryan but impacted the lives of safety around, huh? That's your job, and I think you're going to say yes.

Dodger management reaction

The best one, though, Peter Wilhelm. How about this. He's the CFO. He's the main money guy of the company. I want you to see this first quote. Maybe I'll—"Major League Baseball determined the security at Dodger Stadium on March 31, 2011, was inadequate."

> **Practice Tip**
>
> Explain the important jury instructions in clear language that the jurors can understand. For the instruction on punitive damages, Girardi tells them, "So one of the instructions you're going to be given is whether or not the Dodgers were guilty of more than just 'whoops'."

OK. Now, then, do you remember the next question that was asked I think by his lawyer? "And did you agree with that?" "No, I didn't." Can you imagine, you're a baseball team. You're part of Major League Baseball. Major League Baseball comes down with a decision like this that says, 'hey, man, your security is bad'. And instead of saying 'I disagree,' wouldn't you say, 'man, how can we do better? Where are we lacking?'....

Better yet is their owner. When did you find out that there was no security in Lot 2 after Bryan Stow was harmed? About a year later. Are you ready for that?

Here you own this team. Something terrible is happening, and you're so callous about the whole thing, you find out a year later that there was nobody guarding Lot 2.

I think it's disgusting.

Girardi points out that when management does not understand the problem, only the jury can wake it up with a large punitive damages award. The "willful disregard" necessary to prove punitive damages is shown by the CFO's disagreement with Major League Baseball's assessment of the security at the stadium. This "willful disregard" is further evidenced by the owner's failure to ask any questions about Stow's assault until a year after the incident.

Stow's damages

There's another issue, obviously, which is a very important one to us, and that's an issue of damages in the case. I have to do that, too.

Now, the bad part about this case is that it's going to cost so much to take care of him. You know, I don't think jurors like to bring in huge awards and so forth just for nothing, but here you have a situation that we know there's — it will be filled out on the verdict form because the parties have stipulated the $4,700,000 in past medical. That's in agreement so you're bound by that.

Then there's also an agreement about $300,000, give or take. That will be on the jury form, his loss of earnings from the time of the accident up until now, so things start at $5 million as the floor.

Girardi then spoke about Stow's future lost earnings and his future medical expenses. The defendant's expert testified that the future medicals would be $12,000,000. While that sounds like a lot of money, Girardi shows the jury why it is not.

I divided his life expectancy for the number of hours he has to live according to the life expectancy, and under their plan he gets $16.72 an hour.

Now, the problem is he needs 24-hour care. 24-hour care costs $25 an hour. Then he needs all these surgeries. He needs all these other procedures.

He needs all these doctors that their doctor agreed with…. I don't think it would be fair to Bryan, I don't think it would be fair to his family if you don't follow the very precise numbers that were given with respect to our experts.

> **You understand Bryan did not ask for any of this. He got all this by going to a stupid baseball game. And, therefore, I think that the very minimum to let him roll out of bed and be walked to the bathroom is not what we're after. I think we have to try to make his life as good as he can make it, huh?**

It's terrible without a doubt, but, nonetheless, it can be better. The occupational therapy, the physical therapy, you know, all of those things that the doctor said he needs we have to have….

> **Practice Tip**
> Girardi breaks the seemingly large sum the Dodgers suggested for medical care down to an hourly rate to show how inadequate the "large" number actually is.

Home care option, $26 million, $25 million, et cetera. That's what you need right now to be able to do this, huh?…This money here, the $25 million, that didn't go to this guy. That goes to the doctors to treat him. You know what I mean?

This isn't, oh, man, he's a millionaire now. Look at him. Things are great. This is what we have to pay out. This is what we have to pay out to take some of the burden off his mom and dad and his sisters who are awesome.

Girardi reminds the jury that the money for future medical goes to health care professionals and not to line the plaintiff's pockets. Girardi then concludes with a discussion of damages for pain and suffering.

Pain and suffering

Plaintiff's attorneys always struggle with the decision of whether to give the jury an exact amount to award, a range, or none at all. Let's see how Girardi navigates this difficult choice.

> The other money that compensates him is for his pain and suffering. You can imagine, you can't even turn over, you have a heck of a time getting to the bathroom, and you can't handle yourself once you're in the bathroom and all those sorts of things. So under the law he's also entitled to reasonable compensation for those numbers.
>
> I think it's a good idea that I'm not in the jury box because I think I'd probably give more than you would. I wouldn't mind duplicating that, and maybe that's too much.
>
> Listen. I'm not—certain things you've got to do. You've got to hold them liable because they're liable. You've got to hold them that they're

guilty more of negligence because of this massive stupid way in which they tried to protect the people. You've got to do that....

With respect to what is fair personal injury compensation for the rest of this man's life, that's up to you.

You know what? I know one thing. You're going to do the right thing.

On behalf of my client, I thank you very much from the bottom of my heart.

11.15 DEFENSE CLOSING

Let's look at a few defense closing highlights. Some are presented here to show good or bad lawyering skills. Others are shown because they either address important issues Girardi raised in his opening summation or that he will respond to in rebuttal. As an aside, Girardi remembers that defense counsel was often turning pages and reading his closing as he delivered it.

May it please the Court, counsel. Good morning, ladies and gentlemen....

I'm going to start by taking you back to jury selection. You came in, you filled out a questionnaire, and then the next day you answered a lot of questions from us lawyers. As others were answering questions, you listened to answers, and then eventually you saw some people who were excused from the jury service, and those people were not the right fit for this case. Then the 16 of you were the right fit for this case, and suddenly you were standing up. You were raising your right hand, and you were taking an oath.

And your first thought was, 'Wow, I've been picked for this jury," and then the second thought was what about work, my kids, my family, how is this going to affect my schedule, things like that.

And that oath that you took probably went by you very quickly because things were happening fast and it's a pretty quick oath, but that oath is the dividing line between the 16 of you and everybody else in the world who's ever heard about this case. Nobody else who's ever heard about this case or has an opinion about this case has taken that oath and has to follow that oath.

That oath that you took is the bedrock for jury service. It's the playbook that tells you how you reach a verdict in a case like this.

Because it's so fundamentally important, because it went by so fast, I want to show you what that oath is. Let me just put it up on the screen.

This is the oath you took. "Do you and each of you solemnly swear that you will well and truly try the cause now before this Court and a true verdict therein render according only to the evidence and instructions of the Court?"

That was the oath. I've highlighted two parts of it because it tells you when you're deliberating what you can consider in reaching your verdict. It's the evidence and the law. That's it.

It is always a sign of weakness to talk about the oath. The weakness is highlighted when you start your closing with it and further exacerbated when you put it on a projector screen for the jurors to see.

The reason is that everyone thinks of himself as honest. It is an insult to remind someone that he has to be honest because he took an oath. When I asked Girardi about defense counsel's argument, he agreed it was patronizing. But I think there is another implication made by reminding jurors of the oath. The lawyer unintentionally implies that the oath is going to force you to do something against your common sense and against what you think is the right thing to do.

In short, you are not building rapport with the jury when you use the oath as a sort of "gotcha" to force the jury to deliberate in a certain narrow way that the attorney thinks is the only way he or she can win.

What the attorney implies by starting off this way is the following:

> Ladies and gentlemen, the plaintiff is very sympathetic and anyone in his right mind would vote for him and give him a lot of money. But you can't do that. I'm going to tell you why you can't do justice in this case. You took an oath to follow the law, and I'm about to give you a bunch of legal reasons that will prevent you from doing what you think is right in this case.

Instead of this contorted reasoning that makes no sense, the defense should have started with what he said next.

> There are a lot of gray areas in this case. There are a lot of disputed issues. But there are a few undeniable truths in this case.
>
> Number one, the only people that hit and physically injured Mr. Stow were Sanchez and Norwood. They're the only two. Nobody else lays a hand on them. OK?
>
> If they don't do what they did that night, none of us are here. Mr. Stow does not suffer these terrible life-changing injuries but for those two. Take them out of the equation, and we're not here.

Later, defense counsel makes another good point. But if he had put it at the beginning of his closing, he would have had a strong one-two punch to counter Girardi. Instead, both ideas got watered down because they followed the discussion of the oath.

> You know, you have to step back and not lose the trees here. As a society, we've made a choice. We don't want to live in a police state. We don't want

to live in martial law. We don't want to be surrounded everywhere we go by police and security. We just don't. That's not the society we want to live in. We want a free society.

But when you make a decision to live in a free society, which is the only way we should be living, there are risks that come with it. There are risks, and crime is one of those risks. And you can take reasonable steps and reasonable cautions, and crime is going to occur.

Sadly we saw it last year at the Boston Marathon, an organized sports event. Police all over, the police all over the place, and a bomb went off and caused terror.

Number of security personnel

Now, Professor Fried [Plaintiff's expert] walked in here and criticized Dodger management, but Professor Fried from the University of New Haven has never managed a baseball stadium or any sports facility.

Now, I've got—I think the world of teachers and professors, and it's wonderful the work they do, but you're going to walk into a courtroom and criticize a stadium when you've never been in those issues? You've never tackled the issues of running a stadium?

You have no credibility. You've got none because you haven't done it. You haven't been in the job. He criticized security, but he's never been a director of security. Professor Fried criticized stadium operations but has never operated a stadium.

He criticized training, but he's never trained a single usher or security guard in a stadium, and he's never developed training for a stadium. How do you come in and criticize training when you've never done it? Last, he criticized the training manual itself, but he's never implemented or written one.

Professor Fried told you there's no clear-cut standard for determining the number of security personnel needed to staff the event. He couldn't tell you the number. They can't tell you the number.

But here was his testimony, and this is where his causation argument—where he just dropped the ball. (Reading:)

"Professor, you're critical that the Dodgers should have had more security, but you don't know how many more security personnel it would have taken to prevent this fight and, in turn, Sanchez and Norwood from injuring Mr. Stow. You don't know, do you?"

"As I testified to earlier, it's not all about the numbers. I can't give a specific number."

OK. Stop. You need to come in and say if they had had ten more in parking Lot No. 2 or five more or if you had six or you put three here and three here, fine. Come in and tell me that. He doesn't even know, so how is it you can say the Dodgers dropped the ball when he can't tell you what they should have done?

I'll come back and talk about something for a second. The plaintiffs have two theories of what the Dodgers should have done, and in theory that would have prevented Mr. Stow from being injured. It's sheer speculation.

You kind of look at the definition of speculation. I looked at the dictionary online. Speculation is guessing. It's guessing about something unknown. You just don't know. You have to take a wild guess. All right.

The first theory, their first theory is Mr. [Sanchez] should have been ejected.

I asked Professor Fried, 'When? What inning?' 'I don't know. I don't have an inning. I don't know.' So what inning does he leave, and where does he go, and how do we know where he goes?

Ms. Burge, Geraldine Burge, gave us some interesting testimony on this. (Reading:)

"Let me ask you this. You sat in the row behind Mr. Sanchez the entire game. At any time during the game, ma'am, did you ever seek out security or other personnel within the Dodger Stadium to complain?

"No.... "

The bottom line is you can't say or know what would have happened if he gets ejected without speculating.

Speculation number two, if Hill and Hines [the Dodger security officers assigned to Lot 2] had been in the parking lot, this wouldn't have happened. That's their claim.

Interesting thing about Professor Fried, he said if Hill and Hines had been in the parking lot but in a different location — right? — different location before Mr. Stow was injured, patrolling in a different area, then the Dodgers fulfilled their obligations, no negligence. That's what he said.

So if they're 50 feet or 50 yards away or somewhere else patrolling, looking around for things and something happens back here, no negligence. That's what he said.

He also said — I remember I asked this question standing right up in here. I said, "suppose you've got the Sanchez and Norwood group over there and you've got the Stow group walking away, you're somewhere in that five-minute window, and Hill and Hines arrive and they come up, they look right, they see nothing going on, they look left and just see some guys walking away, two minutes into the five minutes, you would expect them to keep patrolling?"

He said, "true."

If they kept patrolling and then this attack occurred, then there wouldn't be any negligence?

He said, "I agree. I agree."

So this is all sheer speculation to say what would happen if they were there at the time because we don't know where they would have been. It also assumes they would have been deterred.

Stow's conduct

Mr. Stow's responsibility. I told you in my opening statement there were three parties responsible for Mr. Stow's injuries, Sanchez, Norwood, and I said, look. Unfortunately and sadly, Mr. Stow himself.

We make choices as adults. We take personal responsibility, and we sometimes make bad choices, and with bad choices come consequences. The punishment sometimes like in this case does not fit the crime, but there were things Mr. Stow did that put these events into action.

The definition of negligence also applies to Mr. Stow. Negligence is the failure to use reasonable care to prevent harm to one's self. A person is negligent if he does something that a reasonably careful person would not do. You must decide how a reasonably careful person would have acted in Mr. Stow's situation. So here's the evidence.

Now, I listened to Mr. Girardi very carefully about alcohol. I wanted to hear what he was going to do with this. It's a very bad fact for them. It's a very bad fact for them to deal with, and I listened carefully, and he spent three seconds on it.

His statement was "Alcohol is irrelevant, who cares?" He has a legal blood alcohol more than twice the legal limit, and you're just going to wave your hands at it and say it doesn't matter?

It explains some of the behavior. It explains what's going on out there. Hey, look. I have no problem going to a ballgame and having a beer or two. That's fine. But don't get yourself this drunk and then say I share no responsibility for what happened.

Anticipation of rebuttal

Now, as I said, Mr. Girardi gets to give a rebuttal. He gets to get up here and talk some more. I don't. So I would just ask you to do me a favor. Keep these four things in mind, four questions in mind as he's giving you his rebuttal argument.

Number one, is there evidence to back that up, what he's saying?

Number two, is that consistent with the law that we've been given by Judge Chavez?

Number three, is that a play to my emotions? Is that an emotion play?

Number four, if [I] could get back up here and respond, what would [I] say? What's the counter point, the counter evidence to that point?

And if you'll go through that as you're listening to him, I would certainly appreciate it because I don't get a chance to get back up here.

So I'm going to conclude with this. On behalf of my colleagues, I want to thank you, and on behalf of the Dodgers and Mr. McCourt, we appreciate the five weeks you've given us and the really hard work you're about to do, and we appreciate your assisting us in resolving this matter.

Thank you very much. Thank you, your Honor.

11.16 GIRARDI'S REBUTTAL ARGUMENT

> **Practice Tip**
>
> In rebuttal, do not get defensive and try to respond to all of opposing counsel's arguments. Instead, watch how Girardi comes out swinging and never lets up.

Court: Mr. Girardi?

Girardi: I won't have more than two hours, maybe two hours and 15 minutes, and that's it. Just kidding. Gosh, you know what? This is really interesting. How stupid is it to have safety people in the parking lot, right? You don't need any, right? Because, after all, there was no need to have any people in the parking lot because how could you tell if they would stop it?

Can you imagine that? It's disgusting. You see, here is — go back to rule number one. OK? "One who owns, controls, and manages property has an affirmative duty to exercise reasonable care for the protection of individuals coming onto the property." That's it.

So what is reasonable care? You have to do something to keep the people reasonably safe, don't you? Having nobody there, is that your idea of being reasonably safe? Nobody in Lot 2?

So you're supposed to go out now with this instruction that comes from him, and this is what you've got to decide. Did you keep it reasonably safe by having nobody there?

It gets better. Their Bill Squires guy, their big-time expert, they would have been negligent if they had not scheduled somebody to be in Lot 2. Well, nobody was in Lot 2.

We heard, gee, this was just a matter of seconds. Well, it wasn't a matter of seconds. There were four assaults that took place, and then somebody walked, you know, a hundred yards before yet a fifth assault took place.

And we're saying, 'gee whiz, had there been people there, security people there, there's no way this would have been averted.'

You see, they started this case by saying this was the testosterone, two-second hit, and it wasn't. It was a period of conduct. They can't get around that in any way, shape, or form....

I was going to say more about Gil Fried [plaintiff's expert]. God, he was terrible, wasn't he? [said with sarcasm] He wrote the book on security. As a matter of fact, he held up the book, the 600 pages of it, that's used all over the country on how to manage security.

I don't think Francine had written such a book. His expert hadn't written such a book, and these are guidelines.

But you know what? Quite honestly, I think if any of us would run Dodger Stadium, I think we would say to ourselves, 'You know what? We should have some security out there, especially in these lots when this game is over, especially when we looked at all the terrible problems that happened in the past.'

Just with our layperson's knowledge…we would say, 'Boy, you better have somebody there,' don't you think? Don't you think?…

You know what would really be great? "Ladies and gentlemen, we did the wrong thing. We had an obligation. This is an obligation here that we have to keep the premises reasonably safe, and, you know, we didn't have our people there. We've learned a lot by this. We have to do the right thing now by Bryan Stow. Wouldn't that be great?"

Instead they have the same arrogance that they had before the game started. That's what they've got, the same arrogance saying we don't have to keep it reasonably safe or how can you say security would even help. Then why have security anywhere, right? It's kind of disappointing.

You know, at this stage of life, you know, you would prefer people—first of all, we all make mistakes in life. I'm not going to talk about you. I'm talking about me. I know I have. And how you're judged as a person is not necessarily that you made a mistake, but how you're judged as a person, what did I do after I made the mistake.

We shouldn't even be here. The Dodgers should be paying the medical expenses for this man and his family right now. "Hey, man, we made a mistake. We're so sorry. How do we do this? Let's get all these doctors, all their bills. It's going to cost us a lot, but we got to do it, and we have to do the right thing with respect to this family for pain and suffering."

Wouldn't that be great? Wouldn't that be great? You would say, "Boy, the Dodgers, they're pretty good. There was a screw-up, but by golly, you made things great."

Instead you come in here, and you deny what the law is. You deny you have any ability to keep the place safe.

People get hurt. Too bad.… They came onto your property. They paid to be there. They paid for the tickets. They paid for beer. They paid for parking. They paid for everything and now too bad. We don't have to do our side of it. They're disgusting.

And as I told you, I didn't tell anyone that you should award double that amount for pain and suffering, did I? I said it's a good thing I'm not there because I would.

I know him [Stow] better. I know what he goes through every second. I've seen the involuntary tears come to his eyes when he moves so I'm much more torn by that. I'm much more emotional. You're not supposed to be emotional, but honest to God, you have to do the right thing here.

They did the wrong thing. You got to make it right. I wouldn't take a penny off the $25 million. That would be insanity. We need that….

You know, there was one more little issue on this punitive damage issue. I should tell you that — once again, you have this jury instruction. It considers several ways in which you come on to punitive damages.

One way is willful misconduct. "Willful and knowingly disregard the rights or safety of another person." OK?

This wasn't a whoops…. Dodgers, you had a knowledge that serious things could happen. You didn't do a darn thing about it. That's what that is. That's what that check mark means.

You know what? You're going to do the right thing. I know you will.

Girardi makes very succinct and persuasive points. First, he sarcastically mocks the defense argument that even if there had been security in the parking lot, there is no guarantee that they would have prevented the assault. The defense's own argument is undercut by the fact that two people had been assigned to Lot 2 to prevent such assaults but failed to get to their posts after the game.

Girardi then compares his expert — who defense counsel had attacked — to the defense's expert and points out how his expert is vastly more qualified. But he also deftly argues that you don't need an expert to understand that there should be security in a parking lot after a game — especially when there have been previous instances of violence.

Finally, Girardi focuses on a point that he thinks will motivate the jurors to vote for his client: Why didn't the Dodgers do the right thing and take responsibility? Moreover, why didn't they do anything to prevent the tragedy when they knew fans had been hurt before?

11.17 AFTERMATH

The jury returned a verdict of $17,914,238 for Bryan Stow. It assigned a percentage of negligence to the following: 25 percent for the Dodgers, 37.5 percent for Louis Sanchez, 37.5 percent for Marvin Norwood, and 0 percent for Stow. The verdict had a wide-ranging impact in addition to the money awarded to Stow. Girardi related that three large law firms that represent stadium owners wanted to learn from him what the stadium owners should do to prevent tragedies like the Stow case. Major League Baseball also interviewed Girardi to learn what the problems were. The results have been—among other things—that some stadiums have cut down on drinking by fans outside the stadiums before they enter, made it more difficult to sneak alcohol into games, and tightened security.

In a criminal proceeding, Louis Sanchez pled guilty to mayhem, and Marvin Norwood pled guilty to assault by means likely to produce great bodily injury. Sanchez and Norwood were sentenced to 8 years and 4 years in prison, respectively. At the sentencing hearing (an excerpt can be seen at www. TurningPointsatTrial.com), Stow's father spoke about the pain Sanchez and Norwood had caused, and Bonnie Stow, Bryan's sister, said, "I envy those people who can forgive others who commit crimes against their loved ones. I'm not one of those people."

As Judge George Lomeli delivered the sentence, Sanchez chuckled, which drew further ire from the judge. "Rarely, do I comment, but this is the kind of case that demands it. Even now, with your smirks, you show no remorse. Not only did you blindside Mr. Stow, you continued to hit him on the head and kick him in the head. You're complete cowards."

11.18 CHAPTER CHECKLIST ✏️

Girardi's Closing Argument Tips

1. A jury is usually led by its four strongest members.

2. You must be passionate about your client's case.

3. The most important quality to have in closing argument is candor, particularly about the weaknesses in your case.

4. When delivering your closing, make eye contact with jurors. At most, Girardi has a notecard with one word for each topic he wants to cover. Girardi rhetorically asks, "Would you read your marriage proposal to your significant other?"

5. Discuss the two or three jury instructions that are "the whole ballgame."

6. Don't let the jury hear instructions for the first time by the judge as he "mumbles" them after closing argument.

7. If you are a plaintiff's lawyer, and you have an open-and-shut case on liability, ask for a specific amount of damages. Otherwise, you need to be more careful in what you ask for.

8. In a civil case, a lawyer's impact on the outcome is "off the charts."

9. You should try your hardest on even the smallest cases, or you will never be prepared for the big ones.

10. Get a daily transcript of the trial so you can specifically argue in closing what the other side has failed to prove.

11. If you use too many visual aids, the jury will be distracted from what you are saying.

12. When arguing against a likable opposing counsel, admit this point to the jurors but remind them that the case is about the facts, not the lawyers.

Summary of Girardi's Closing

Here is a summary that outlines Girardi's closing argument. The bold topic headings can be used successfully in any type of closing no matter who you represent. After each bold heading, the specific argument Girardi made in the Stow case is described.

1. **Thank jury.** Girardi thanks jury for their month-long service.

2. **Empower jury.** Girardi connects with jury and makes it feel it can do something really special when he says, "You'll have an opportunity to say we did some real fairness…."

3. **Briefly mention client's good qualities.** Girardi highlights Bryan Stow's devoted family.

4. **Bottom line message.** Have a theme for your closing. Girardi frames the Dodgers' defense. He calls it ABMD: "Anyone But McCourt Dodgers."

5. **Discusses most important jury instructions.** Here, Girardi succinctly explains landowner's duty toward customers and that Dodgers only needed to be a "substantial factor" in cause of Bryan's injury. Explain instructions in simple terms jury will understand.

6. **Summarize good facts of your case.** Girardi describes the details of Sanchez and Norwood's harassment of Giants fans in the Loge section during the game.

7. **Address weaknesses in your case.** Girardi admits that no one can prevent every potential assault but argues that Bryan's assault was preventable. Another weakness is the fact that Bryan had been drinking, and a witness claimed Bryan had started another fight before he was assaulted. Girardi explains that Bryan was not involved in another fight and that defense counsel was negligent in making such a statement in its opening statement without facts to support it. As for Bryan's drinking, Girardi argues that common sense and a jury instruction declaring you can drink as long as you act responsibly protect Bryan.

8. **Highlight opposing counsel's inconsistent statements.** Point out to the jury promises that opposing counsel made in opening statement that did not come true at trial.

9. **Analyze damages.** Girardi details the medical costs, lost wages and punitive damages. He concludes his argument with a discussion of pain and suffering damages.

10. **End Strongly.** Girardi reminds the jury that Bryan is so incapacitated that he needs help to go to the bathroom and is in constant pain. He tells the jurors that Bryan is counting on them to help him get justice.

11. **Rebut only strongest arguments.** Girardi does not respond to every argument opposing counsel makes. He only addresses the important ones. He does not get defensive. Instead, he quickly attacks and drives home his points.

Memorable Quotes from Girardi's Closing

"Honest to God, the whole law was meant so that people like Bryan could make a recovery and hopefully get enough money for medical care and so forth to last him."

"A beer is 10 bucks. The Dodgers spent 64 cents a person for security."

"Security is not just numbers. It's having the people doing the right job."

"The only thing that Bryan was doing wrong is wearing a jersey, a black one that said 'Giants.'"

"The reason they didn't do doodley-squat was, man, because they wanted to watch the old budget."

"Our best expert was their guy."

"We're supposed to be fair to you guys. That's our job. On the other hand, what if defense counsel told you something he knew was not true? And yet the statement is made to you."

"So one of the instructions you're going to be given is whether or not the Dodgers were guilty of more than just 'whoops'; if they were guilty about absolutely, positively, without a doubt knowing about a serious problem where some guy could end up with $4,700,000 in medical bills and not do anything about it. Isn't it disgusting?"

"You understand Bryan did not ask for any of this. He got all this by going to a stupid baseball game. And, therefore, I think that the very minimum to let him roll out of bed and be walked to the bathroom is not what we're after. I think we have to try to make his life as good as he can make it, huh?"

"Wouldn't that be great [if the Dodgers admitted a mistake]? Wouldn't that be great? You would say, boy, the Dodgers, they're pretty good. There was a screw-up, but by golly, you made things great. Instead you come in here, and you deny what the law is. You deny you have any ability to keep the place safe."

CHAPTER TWELVE

⊶⊷

Frank Branson

The Closing Argument Built on Credibility

Credibility is where the game is played in a courtroom. If you don't have it, you ain't going to win. If you have it, you may not win, but if you have it and can put it all together, you can win and win big.

— Frank Branson

---

*B*ranson's accolades were discussed in Chapter 9. For this chapter, suffice it to say that The Law Offices of Frank L. Branson was selected by *U.S. News and World Report* as one of the best law firms in the country in 2012, and that Branson is one of the most respected plaintiff's attorneys in the country.

12.1 INTRODUCTION

We are going to look at the depositions and closing arguments of one of Branson's more difficult wins, *Bohne v. Enviroclean*. The estate of Robert Bohne and his widow sued Enviroclean Management Services, Inc., and Turner Yarbrough, a driver whom Enviroclean employed. Yarbrough caused a traffic accident that led to Bohne's death. The challenge was to prove how much a 76-year-old's life was worth. The turning point at trial came when Branson argued for damages using real-world analogies in his closing argument to the jury. Branson's victory was highlighted as a Top 100 verdict in 2007 by the *National Law Journal.*

CHAPTER HIGHLIGHTS
• Keys to maintaining credibility in the courtroom
• A closing argument is built on facts elicited during trial
• Empower jurors by emphasizing importance of their decision

12.2 *BOHNE V. ENVIROCLEAN MANAGEMENT SERVICES, INC. AND YARBROUGH*

This trial began in 2007. A few years earlier, Robert Bohne had been driving on a highway when his car was hit in a chain reaction caused by Turner Yarbrough.

Yarbrough was driving a tractor-trailer containing hazardous waste for Enviroclean Management Services, Inc.

While driving his 18-wheeler on the highway, Yarbrough plowed into a long line of cars, causing a chain reaction that ultimately led to one of the cars hitting Bohne's car. Bohne's car then rolled over and went off the road.

Bohne suffered several broken ribs, a traumatic brain injury, a broken vertebra, a collapsed lung, and several other internal injuries. He was hospitalized and spent the next 161 days in the hospital before he died.

Branson presented evidence that Yarbrough had a history of cocaine use, tested positive for cocaine after the accident, and was sleep deprived when the accident occurred. Branson also argued that Enviroclean did not investigate Yarbrough's background before hiring him. Such an investigation would have revealed that Yarbrough had been in rehabilitation for drug addiction, and his driver's license had been suspended. In addition, Yarbrough was hired as a warehouse worker, and Enviroclean did not properly qualify him to drive a tractor-trailer.

Enviroclean said that the safety director of the company at the time of the accident had since resigned from the company and was presently in the northern edge of Canada or Alaska, and therefore was unavailable to be deposed. Branson's investigators were unable to find him. The man who hired the driver (Yarbrough) for Enviroclean said that the Department of Transportation file for him was missing. In addition, a former manager had left because he was tired of putting profit over safety. The current safety director couldn't even approximate how much time he spent on safety.

The defense contended that another truck was involved in the accident and said that that truck interrupted the chain reaction started by Yarbrough, hit Bohne's car, and then fled the scene. The defense claimed that an alleged 911 call proved this theory, but the call was not allowed into evidence because the defense could not authenticate its accuracy.

The settlement attempts in this case reveal mistakes the defense made and provide insights into the confidence Branson has in his trial skills. At the mediation, Branson presented medical bills of $600,000 in addition to economic and mental damages. The defendant offered $300,000. Branson countered with a nickel below the insurance policy limit of $5,500,000. I asked Branson what was the point of demanding a nickel less than the policy limit, and Branson said with a wry smile that the mediator had wanted him to negotiate, so that was his negotiation.

The defendant got frustrated with the negotiations and demanded to speak to the plaintiff. The mediator called Ms. Bohne and Branson into the conference room. The defendant's lawyer told Ms. Bohne that the defendant had paid everyone else in this wreck except her and her husband. The reason was that another truck had been involved in the chain reaction of car wrecks, and it was *that* truck that had hit her husband.

During this second meeting, Branson met with Ms. Bohne and the insurance carriers. Branson knew she had a sense of humor, and told her in their presence, "If this defendant has the testicular fortitude to offer this phantom truck that they say they've got as a defense in this case, you have my word I'm going to stick it where the sun don't shine." She laughed and that ended the negotiations.

Just before trial, the defendant offered $1 million to settle the case. With Ms. Bohne's permission, Branson did not respond. Two days before closing arguments, the defendant raised its offer to $2 million and wanted to meet for negotiations. At Branson's office, the defendant offered $3,000,000 and said it would never offer a penny more. Branson countered with $5,300,000, which the defendant rejected.

Before looking at the closing arguments in this case, let's look at excerpts of the key depositions. Although Branson is a master at trial, he understands that a good deposition is often essential to winning at trial.

12.3 THE TRUCK DRIVER'S DEPOSITION (YARBROUGH)

Yarbrough was the warehouse workman who was asked to drive the tractor-trailer because he had a commercial driver's license. Branson asks him about his mental state prior to the accident.

Lack of sleep and drug use

Q. *You went to work and drove two hours after you'd taken your last dose of cocaine?*
A. Yes, sir.

Q. *How long did you smoke?*
A. Probably about six hours.

Q. *So you smoked for six hours, had three hours sleep, and then drove from 5:00 a.m. until 4:00 in the afternoon.*
A. Yes, sir. Well, I didn't say I slept.

Q. ***So you didn't sleep.***
A. I didn't say I slept.

Q. *So you smoke for six hours, what did you do for the other three hours?*
A. **I just kind of chilled** and then went on to work.

Notice how Branson listens to every word. When Yarbrough mentions that he did not go to sleep — which would have made him at least a bit rested — after smoking crack, Branson pounces on the answer to ask him what he did instead of sleep. "I just kind of chilled" is a terrible fact for the defendant's case, coming from a witness who then got behind the steering wheel of a tractor-trailer.

Work history

Q. *What happened between January 2001 when you left DART [Dallas Area Rapid Transit] and March 2003 when you went to work for Adventure Express.*
A. **I don't remember.**

Q. ***Think back for a minute now.*** *You worked between June of 2000 and January of 2001 for DART.*
A. Uh-huh.

Q. *And the next time you record having a job is March of 2003. Now that's over two years.*
A. Oh, OK. Well, I had spent like six months in state jail.

Q. *Tell me your recollection of when you've been in jail for what? When was the first time you were ever in jail?*
A. When was the first thing I ever did?

Q. *Well when was the first time you were ever arrested for something.*
A. **Well, I have a long history of arrests, sir.**

> **Practice Tip**
>
> When you get a vague answer such as "I don't know," don't move on to your next question. Instead, repeat your question until you get the answer you need. Branson persists, follows up, and gets an important admission.

Job application

Q. *At the time you applied for that job in 2004, you had been to the penitentiary for passing a forged check; you had been arrested six times for having a suspended driver's license; you had been convicted in 2003 for possession of marijuana while in a vehicle; you had been convicted for theft by check; you had had an accident where you were at DART driving a DART bus where someone said they were injured and you were under the influence of cocaine. All of that occurred prior to the time you were hired by Enviroclean Management Services. Is that true, sir?*
A. Yes.

Branson asks all of the questions that any employer should have asked when hiring Yarbrough. Notice how Branson asks a question with five sets of facts. Such a question only works if you are accurate with *all* of your facts. For example, if Branson were wrong on a year or any of the circumstances, the witness would have answered, "no," and Branson would not have known what was wrong with his question.

To correct the problem, Branson could have done two things, only one of which would have worked. First, he could have asked the witness why he said, "no." It is unlikely a hostile witness is going to help that much. Second, Branson could break down his five sets of facts into five separate parts and ask the witness if each one were correct. The result would not be nearly so effective as putting them all together as Branson did and getting a clean admission to all the facts. The lesson to learn is that by mastering the facts, Branson has a single devastating admission from Yarbrough that shows how unfit he was to be driving a commercial truck.

> **Practice Tip**
>
> Branson demonstrates that a summarizing question that contains favorable facts for your client and forces the hostile witness to answer "yes" is only effective if you painstakingly summarize the facts correctly.

12.4 THE SAFETY DIRECTOR'S DEPOSITION (LAROSEE)

Branson took the deposition of Alan Larosee, the safety director for Enviroclean at the time of the deposition. He was not the safety director at the time the accident occurred or when Yarbrough was hired. Branson recalls that he had planned for an associate to take the deposition. Instead, at the last minute, he changed his mind and took over. Below is a classic example of a witness giving outrageous answers, usually in the form of "I don't know," to questions which he should certainly know the answers. See if you agree.

Q. *The federal department of transportation regulates the interstate transportation of biohazardous waste among other hazardous materials, doesn't it?*
A. **I don't know.**

Q. *That's your job to know?*
A. Uh-huh. **I don't know.**

Q. *What percentage of the work you do involves safety?*
A. **I don't know.** I'd have to think about it.

Q. *Who within your company would you expect to be the person we should ask how a driver got hired with the history of drugs and other criminal violations and a bad driving record, how he didn't get tested for drugs while he was there, how he had an accident involving a fatality with crack cocaine in his system, and how all his records have now been destroyed or lost. Explain to the jury how that can occur in your company.*
A. **I don't know.**

Q. *Do you really care?*
A. What's the question?

Q. *I'm asking this question.*
A. Yes. I care.

Q. *Do you care as a safety director for this company?*
A. Of course I care.

Q. **OK. If you care so much tell us what you've done to find out how it happened and what was done about it by your company?**
A. **What have I done? Nothing.**

Q. *Tell the jury what you're going to do about it now that you know.*
A. **Nothing.**

Q. *Why?*
A. What's to be done?

At trial, Branson played excerpts of Larosee's video deposition for the jury. They were so powerful that defense counsel had this to say about the deposition while arguing against punitive damages in his closing argument:

> [Branson] played Mr. Larosee's deposition for you for an hour. Mr. Larosee doesn't know anything about this accident. All he has is here's what's in place at this time. And, yeah, he acted unprofessional in that video, but he came here hat in hand and apologized and told you, look, there's a system in place.

When defense counsel has to admit in closing that his client's safety director acted unprofessionally at a deposition, you know that the deposition was a home run.

12.5 WILLIAMS' DEPOSITION (THE MAN WHO HIRED THE DRIVER)

Stacy Williams hired Yarbrough as a waste handler and decided to make him a driver because he had a commercial driver's license. Williams later left the company because he was tired of Enviroclean's philosophy to put profit over safety.

Practice Tip

At a deposition, an outrageous answer that is not believable is as good as a confession. When the witness gives a ludicrous, insincere answer, the jury may choose not to believe anything else the witness says.

Enviroclean was grossly negligent

Q. *Would you say that Enviroclean was grossly negligent in hiring Mr. Yarbrough?*
A. Yes.

Q. *And would you say within that definition they are or are not guilty of gross negligence in allowing him to drive under the influence of drugs on the date of this accident?*
A. They are.

Q. *And would you say based on your experience as a regional manager for them that their gross negligence in hiring and turning Mr. Yarbrough loose with the truck was foreseeably going to cause someone to get hurt?*
A. Yes.

Q. *And based on what you saw and heard at the meeting a month after this, and your experience and training as a regional manager, would you or would you not say that the gross negligence you described of Enviroclean was a cause of Mr. Bohne's injuries and death?*
A. Yes.

Q. So is there any question in your mind that given a decision that would affect their bottom line and involve safety, that they would put their bottom line above safety, in nearly every instance when you were manager for them?

A. Yes.

Q. Is that true, sir?

A. Yes.

12.6 CLOSING ARGUMENT AND TRIAL STRATEGIES

Before we examine Branson's closing argument, let's learn his tips for trials and, in particular, for closing argument. Branson uses notes in his closing argument but cautions as follows: "The more information I've got before me, the more inclined I am to look at it." When he writes his closing, he creates an outline with paragraphs in it. By the time he delivers his closing in court, he has winnowed his detailed outline to a topical outline with two or three words for each topic.

For the opening part of his summation, he likes to use PowerPoint presentations when discussing the jury charge. He will discuss the two or three witnesses or pieces of evidence that prove each point of the charge. The charge provides a good outline and keeps him focused on his argument.

I asked Branson to reveal his most important tip for closing argument. He said that you have to believe everything you tell the jury. Some defense attorneys do this, but "they are few and far between." Branson explains that he is on a crusade. In the weeks before trial, he is working 12–14 hour days and constantly over the weekend.

Another mistake lawyers make is that they "are not able to adjust to what's happening" during a trial. As Muhammad Ali said, "You have to be able to float like a butterfly and sting like a bee." Instead of following Ali's advice, lawyers examine witnesses with a list of questions. No matter what the answer is, the lawyer just goes down his list of questions. They don't watch the witness. They're not aware of their surroundings.

In this case, Branson immediately noticed that Mrs. Bohne was having trouble hearing his questions on direct examination. He also realized that she was not opening up to the jury as he wanted her to. So, Branson

> *Awareness of what's going on around you in a courtroom is very material. If you've got a jury that's fussy about something, you need to know about it and do whatever you can to relieve their tension.*
>
> — Frank Branson

adapted. He moved over to the edge of the jury box near the witness stand, and "we had a conversation." Branson knew she was special, and he made sure that came across to the jury. "If that woman hadn't been such a truly unique, wonderful lady, and had a great relationship, you couldn't have had a [large verdict] no matter how bad the defendant's conduct was."

Being aware of the jury affects your courtroom demeanor. Branson points out that you can show anger toward the defendant, but not until the jury wants you to. Early in his career, Branson would have knock-down, drag-out fights with very difficult opposing counsel. Inevitably, he would come to trial angry. Not anymore. Branson soon learned that "angry lawyers don't get very far. Juries don't like you to come in angry."

Another lesson that Branson has learned is that less is more. It took him a long time to figure out the importance of the big picture. He now realizes that there is no point in cross-examining a witness for a day and a half. He did that as a young lawyer and "eked out modest verdicts, but the jury gets angry. They're uncomfortable. They want out of there. They've heard it. The old advice that you need to say it, you need to say it, and you say it again is not true."

Many lawyers do not realize how important their credibility with the jury is. Branson points out that maintaining your credibility begins in voir dire. He sees lawyers "harp" on the fact to the venire (panel of prospective jurors) that "all I want is twelve fair and impartial jurors." But at the first inkling that a juror might be biased for his client, the lawyer will do everything he can "to restore the juror to a more neutral position. Branson often does just the opposite. If it appears a juror will be biased in favor of his own client, he will move to strike the juror for cause. By doing so, he has shown the remaining jurors on the panel that he is really sincere in seeking twelve impartial jurors.

Another mistake Branson sees lawyers make is how they answer when the court asks them how much longer it will take to examine the witness. The lawyer will say, "Fifteen minutes." An hour later, the lawyer is still questioning the witness. "That jury is angry. You've told them, you've told this judge you'll be through in 15 minutes. I don't really care what's happening, in 15 minutes you've got to stop."

Practice Tip

Branson believes the conventional wisdom that you should try your case as if the jury had the education of sixth graders is wrong. Instead, he believes juries are really smart. "They may miss something every now and then, but if you talk down to them, they get really offended."

The jury remembers your broken promise about estimating the length of an examination, but also sees any disparity between how you act when you think the jury is present and when you think it isn't. Branson remembers a trial where opposing counsel had been "sugar and spice" throughout the trial but when a paralegal made a mistake, "He gave her an ass chewing of first order at a break." What the lawyer did not know was that a juror had stepped into the back of the courtroom and saw the scolding. The juror had seen that the lawyer was two-faced. "When he would try to snuggle up to the jury after that, they were cold. They share everything."

How important are closing arguments? Branson believes that jurors may have decided "who's right and who's wrong, but I don't think they've decided what they're going to do about it." Branson is passionate about how important closings are. He explains:

> As long as juries are made up of ordinary people, and as long as ordinary people cry at birthings and funerals and weddings, as long as they learn as children from stories told by their parents or grandparents at bedtime, as long as people will die for such concepts as love and war and hate, as long as women rouge their faces for men and men pull out chairs and open doors for women, there's a place for persuasion in a courtroom.

One of the most difficult decisions a plaintiff's attorney has to make is deciding whether or not to tell the jurors how much money to award the plaintiff in its verdict. If you don't give them a specific number, they won't have any idea how much you think the case is worth. But if you do give them a specific number, you run the risk that you undervalue your case by giving them a much lower number than they are considering. On the other hand, if the number is too high, you will lose your credibility with the jury because you have overvalued your case.

The Bohne case presented a particularly difficult problem. How do you put a price on an elderly man's life? Bohne was on his first marriage and had no children. He obviously had already lived most of his life. He had reached the U.S. national average for life expectancy, which is 76 years. In short, his time was up. So, how do you overcome statistics and common sense that Bohne had lived a very full life but was living on borrowed time? Moreover, Branson explains that jurors have a hard time putting a money value on pain and suffering.

Branson believed that he needed to show that not only do we value our citizens, but our special citizens such as Bohne, who had fought in the Korean War. He also had a special relationship with his wife. They went dancing twice a month, and he drew her a bath every night. He truly cared for her and was in love. Also, as a result of the accident, Bohne spent the last 5½ months of his life living in a hospital drowning in his own secretions before he died.

12.7 DEFENSE CLOSING ARGUMENT

Before we get to Branson's rebuttal argument where he argues damages to the jury, let's see how defense counsel addresses the issue and Mr. Branson's presentation of the evidence:

Defense Counsel: And I just want to close with this isn't about whether Mr. Bohne was a bad person. **I don't have any opinion that he was a bad person.** It's not about Enviroclean not valuing life. It's not about Ms. —I like Ms. Bohne. I thought she was very delightful on the stand, **at least**

from an entertainment standpoint. More informative and entertaining parts of the trial for me personally to listen to, because it's new information I didn't know. But as I was listening to her, I was thinking, you know, a lot of folks leave this world at a lot younger age, and I'm sorry that she had her loss. But Mr. Bohne—they did get to travel a lot and they got to do a lot of things. Look at those pictures. You can tell by the pictures.

And I noticed a white belt he's wearing. I remember those back in the '70s. If you look at the pictures and the time frame that they were taken, **he did get to live a life. They had a good life together. He wasn't taken from this earth when he was 35 years old with two kids and a wife, so they did get to spend time together.**

How long Mr. Bohne would live, if they want to base that on a chart, how about how long Ms. Bohne would live? I don't know. You don't know. All I can tell you is, is that no one on our side of the fence has any disrespect for the Bohnes or Mr. Bohne's loss of life. We take that very seriously.

Defense counsel makes some tactical mistakes. When he says that he does not have an opinion that Bohne was a "bad person," it sounds defensive and implies that he does not have an opinion—or at least not a very strong one—that Bohne is a good person. He should have just admitted that Bohne was a very good person and a loving husband because that is what the evidence undoubtedly showed. He compounds the mistake when he argues that because Bohne was old, he "did get to live a life," and "wasn't taken from this earth when he was 35 years old," and thus his life had less value.

Such an argument is very difficult to articulate well, and should not be taken on unless you are sure you can pull it off. The reason for this is because anyone who has lost a parent almost never thinks the time was right. Whether someone is 65, 75, or 84, death always seems much too soon. The void from the loss of life is huge and permanent. Defense counsel would have been better off not going into the details and simply saying—as he did at the end of the excerpt—that Enviroclean takes life very seriously.

A third mistake was defense counsel's discussion that he found Ms. Bohne's testimony entertaining. While he may have meant that he felt compassion for her, his word choice of "entertaining" made light of the gravity of the situation. A widow's testimony about the loss of her husband due to the alleged wrongdoing by another should never be considered "entertaining." Unfortunately for defense counsel, Branson was listening intently and would pounce on the poor word choice in his rebuttal.

In other parts of his closing, defense counsel became too defensive and highlighted his own weak argument when he said, "Mr. Branson, he's a good talker, good storyteller." Another time he said, "It's not what I believe or Mr. Branson believes. So—and it's not what's put up on a PowerPoint presentation. It's the evidence in the case. Lawyer talk does not equal evidence." Other times defense counsel would say, "You can throw big PowerPoint presentations up and you can do all that at the end of the day...."

Fearful of another visual aid, defense counsel pleaded with the jurors: "It's real important, because when Mr. Branson — he's got his big diagram and he'll have on there, you'll see it, it says brain injury, traumatic brain injury. Well, that's why I'm telling you, you got to look at the evidence, not the diagram that Mr. Branson made. Look at the evidence." At another point, he urges, "Now, when you compare that again to the chart Mr. Branson's made with an artist.... The actual objective test, the CAT scan of the head, is normal."

Defense counsel went on to say the following:

> I also told you the Court would instruct you not to let bias, prejudice, or sympathy enter in your deliberations. You've already seen some of that. Mr. Branson has attempted to elicit sympathy from you to decide this case in favor of Ms. Bohne. **You gave us your word** when you were sworn in that you would decide the case based upon the evidence, and that's what you believe; and as a jury, once you consider the evidence and discussed what you believe the greater weight and credible degree of the evidence is.

Like we saw in the defense counsels' arguments in Chapters 10 and 11, it is a real sign of weakness when you talk down to a jury and remind them of a promise they made to you in voir dire. Who wants to be warned that they need to follow the law? The lesson is that if you are so fearful of losing that you feel the need to remind the jury to be fair, there is no point because you have already lost.

12.8 BRANSON'S REBUTTAL ARGUMENT

> **Branson:** Let's talk for a minute about an issue that's important in this lawsuit, and that's pain and suffering and mental anguish. Over the years that I've tried these lawsuits — and one of the things I find is that it's really hard in talking to jurors after the lawsuit is over, to get any of us to open our mind to physical pain and suffering and mental anguish. We don't like to think about it for ourselves or our family and we certainly don't like to think about it for other people, for the same reasons we don't like to think about our mortality or somebody else's mortality. **These are unpleasant tasks.**
>
> But what I've seen over the years is when a jury will force themselves to steel up against our natural reaction. And our reaction is if we worried about our mortality and all these things happening to us, it would be hard for us to get by every day. So we put a block up. But I'm going to ask you on behalf of Robert Bohne to open that block and think about what — the

pain you've heard in this courtroom would have done to Robert Bohne during all those days in the hospital, **3,864 hours** in that hospital.

Branson confronts the first obstacle, that people don't like to think about their own death or the pain and suffering of others. If we did, it would be hard to get through each day. To emphasize how long Bohne was in the hospital, Branson converts the 161 days of hospitalization into hours. He next confronts notes in the medical records and statements Bohne made in the hospital when he said that he was doing OK.

> And yeah, I'm sure he told some people, from time to time, "I feel well" — that was Robert Bohne — or "I'm having a good day." But you heard the testimony from everybody that was there, from his doctors to his family.
>
> When you have **broken bones pressing on your spinal cord, it hurts.** And it eventually gets you to where you're not wanting to walk again and maybe not ever be able to live independently at home again. **When it hurts every time you breathe in and out, that's a whole lot of pain this man lived with for a long time.**
>
> And you now have taken on the task and have taken an oath to evaluate of that 3,864 hours of pain every minute, which is 60 minutes in each of those hours, and every second, and **each of those seconds would have been full hard seconds** for Bob Bohne in that hospital. And I think when you do and when we get through, there will be a way that **Enviroclean, the fastest growing hazardous transport and treatment company in the Southwest, will understand that we place a high value on our citizens.** And we place a real high value on people like Bob Bohne and his wife Kathleen.

Branson's argument is so successful because he gained the jurors trust immediately in jury selection and never let them down throughout the entire trial. If a lawyer had no credibility, these arguments would be nothing more than words without meaning. But when you have gained the trust of the jury, you can argue very persuasively in closing argument. Branson has an enormous reservoir of trust as a base to masterfully argue his case.

In the above excerpt, Branson creates even greater emphasis on the duration of pain and suffering by dividing the hours into minutes and then seconds. He also uses very descriptive words to show the jury the pain Bohne was feeling, such as the broken bones that were "pressing on [his] spinal cord." To highlight the constant pain, Branson brilliantly relates that Bohne had pain with every breath he took, since he felt his broken ribs every time his lungs filled with or expelled air. Next, Branson responds to a weakness in defense counsel's argument.

And so there's no misunderstanding, **Kathleen Bohne wasn't on the witness stand for defense counsel's entertainment, and it was not an entertaining process for her.** This has been hard on Kathleen and it's been hard to listen to the evidence. We're not here voluntarily. Nobody here stood and said I'd like to be in court. We're here because they took away a very precious life and a very precious part of Kathleen Bohne's existence. And we are forced here, and there is no testimony we did anything to cause ourselves to be here.

And until somebody gets Enviroclean's attention, they're going to keep coming into courtrooms like this and saying, "Oh, Mr. Yarbrough just fell through the cracks;" "Oh, Mr. Welsh just fell through the crack." That crack on August the 12th, 2004, was as big as the Grand Canyon when it came to testing their drivers for drugs. It wasn't happening. And under Mr. Larosee, it's not going to happen unless you as a jury weld together and say Bob Bohne was a unique man. We have a right to put a value on his life and on what's happened to him, and we're going to do it.

When you look at the pain-and-suffering issue, pain and death are partners. They're allies in the chief enemies of mankind. And this company, through its hiring practices, through its ignoring the DOT [Department of Transportation] and the minimum safety requirements of it, and Mr. Yarbrough's cocaine addiction, have deprived Kathleen Bohne of her future and they deprived Robert Bohne of what I think was the life of an uncommon, common man.

> *When you look at the pain-and-suffering issue, pain and death are partners. They're allies in the chief enemies of mankind.*
> — Frank Branson, closing argument

This is a man who didn't cause trouble in his life. When the country asked him—there's an exhibit in here I want you to look at it. It's Exhibit Number 22. In April of 1951, the UN forces and the American forces and Korea are making counter insurgencies responding to the Chinese, who have come in and gotten nearly to the South Korean capital of Seoul. When they [the Bohne family] ordered the flag [for Bohne's service], they sent with it two citations. One is the Korean service medal, and there's another for fighting in that battle.

This is a man who, when asked, stood up for his responsibility. And he's in his mid-to-late 30s when he meets this wonderful British widow with four children. He didn't have to leave being a bachelor, which he'd done all his life. **He didn't have to take on the responsibility of four children. He did it the way it should be done, until Enviroclean took that away from both of them.**

Branson attacks defense counsel's characterization that Kathleen's testimony was "entertaining." Branson scolds defense counsel and takes the opportunity to highlight for the jury that Kathleen did not want to be in court and how difficult it was for her to listen to the evidence. Here, he reminds the jury that Enviroclean interrupted Bohne's life of service and selflessness.

It is important to note that Branson's persuasive description of Bohne never would have taken place if he had not gotten these facts from Kathleen and other witnesses and exhibits during the trial. During trial, a great trial lawyer always thinks about the key facts and testimony he will need to elicit so he can argue them in closing. By eliciting helpful testimony at trial, Branson can paint a compelling picture of Bohne during the closing.

> When you evaluate pain and suffering, **there's an old English proverb that says an hour of pain is longer than a day of pleasure.** Now, all you have to do is think about that. If you've had a toothache, if you've had a headache, if you've had a sharp pain of some kind, it's intense and it seems like it hurts for a long time. If you've got a doctor's appointment and you think it'll take it away, think about how long that hour was before you could get there to get that away.
>
> Compare it to a day where you're having a good time. If you're fishing, you're out with your family, you're on the golf course, you're doing whatever you enjoy doing, those days go just like that.
>
> But an hour worth of pain, the English would write, probably is longer than a day of pleasure. When you look at how you evaluate that, you might want to think about how we evaluate our pleasure.

> *When you evaluate pain and suffering, there's an old English proverb that says an hour of pain is longer than a day of pleasure.*
>
> — Frank Branson, closing argument

Branson's use of the English proverb is the perfect backdrop to discuss how difficult pain can be. Famous quotations or proverbs that have stood the test of time add credibility to your argument. By stating that an hour of pain is "longer than a day of pleasure," Branson now has the jury thinking of pain in a much more realistic way, and he has given the jury a better way to measure constant pain than just the fact that Bohne was hospitalized for 161 days.

> Very recently, there was a boxing match. Oscar De La Hoya fought a fellow named Mayweather. And because we value, as a society, watching that boxing match, Mr. De La Hoya, who lost the fight, made $42 million for that fight. Mr. Mayweather, who won the fight, only won 20. But as a society we evaluated those two boxers' time for that short time in the ring with those kinds of numbers.

Branson knows his case is not worth $42 million, but he encourages the jury to broaden its consideration of how much society—without too much consideration—values someone's time. Then, by comparison, Branson can show how much society could value an individual's pain and suffering.

Branson explained to me that it is a difficult decision to choose between giving the jury a specific dollar amount for damages or giving them a range. He has done it both ways. "You've got to be careful not to offend the jury and let them think you're greedy…. When the numbers are big, it's easier."

In this case, Branson admitted that there were no lost wages and no children who would have gotten money from Mr. Bohne. But Branson had something that would overcome this obstacle. His case "had an absolutely invaluable relationship, a lot of love. I needed to empower them to be willing to give those big numbers, and I didn't want them to think that Ms. Bohne and I were greedy, so I gave them a range."

> Give you another example. We all—if you watch basketball at all, you watch Shaquille O'Neal. And whether you like the [Miami] Heat or you don't like the Heat, it's hard not to really have great admiration for Shaq on the basketball court. Now, we evaluate that as a society enough that Shaq gets paid $20 million [a year] to play basketball. That works out to $54,795 for every day of the year, whether Shaq is on the basketball court that day or not.
>
> One way to evaluate the pain and suffering that Mr. Bohne went through is to say whether one of those days in the trap he was in would be worth a day of Shaq's time. If you did, that would work out to about $9 million. That works out to each day, a day of Shaq O'Neal's—of Shaq's time that would work out to about, those 161 days [that Bohne spent in the hospital], about $9 million. You say, well, maybe it's only worth half a day of pay for Shaq O'Neal. That would be worth $4.5 million.
>
> And again, you're the sole judges of what's fair, of what this unique man's life is worth. And by giving your time for that evaluation, I believe you can prevent other people from coming down here and falling into the same trap.

As he mentioned to the jurors at the outset, thinking about pain and death is difficult and not something people often do. So, Branson gives the jurors many different comparisons to consider.

Branson now turns his attention to the punitive damages.

> And I know I've heard that from a man who created and sold maybe twelve or fifteen companies before or at the time he had this one going on that he doesn't think this [Enviroclean] is doing very well. I didn't see any evidence of that. In fact, they got a new fleet of Peterbilts [trucks], as best I can tell. They say they lease it.
>
> And at some point when you're back there—sometimes—I don't always share with a jury what I think is fair in a case because it truly is your decision. And whatever I say, please take it. And if you want to know, use it; and if you don't, you don't.

I think a fair way to evaluate this is put whatever punishment you think is appropriate under punitive damages over here. And when you look at the value of this man's life and the value of what they put him through **I would consider the 25 million pounds of hazardous wastes that they transported last year, and I would consider some 50 cents a pound for that. But still I suspect, from what I see, Mr. Fleeger leaves him a healthy profit. But just 50 cents a pound I believe would make them understand that we value human life. Now that's my opinion.**

Somebody may say, "Well, a dollar a pound would be fair." Some people may say less. I don't have to make that decision. And in just a few minutes I'm going to transfer that decision to each of your shoulders. And all I ask is that each one of you evaluate the evidence.

Branson gives the jury a concrete way of coming up with a dollar amount for punitive damages (damages to punish a defendant for its conduct). Always vigilant that jurors might want to award more damages than the figure he arrives at, he gives the jury some wiggle room to come up with a higher figure.

And please use your common sense, because the answer is pretty clear in this case when you do it. And do what you think is fair and give Robert Bohne and his wife a full and fair measure of damage. And please do it in such a manner that these defendants will understand. **Your verdict here, when you all affirm, will go in the permanent records of Dallas County and it will be a permanent record for Dallas and for the state of Texas.**

What I'd like for you to do when you get back there is do something that you can bring your children and even grandchildren at some point to the courthouse in the future and say, "I served as a part of a jury that righted wrong. I served as a part of a jury that made our highways safer. As a part of a six-person jury, I helped teach a hazardous waste company that was growing mighty fast that you've got to understand and appreciate the value of human life." And your verdict will stand. It will stand the test of time.

The key to persuading jurors is to make them feel they are involved in something special. The more important they see the cause, the more motivated they will be to rule in your favor. Here, Branson tells them that this is not just a wrongful death case, but a chance for the jury to do something that will last forever. How often do people get a chance to take part in history. A small jury award is not going to "right a wrong." Branson wants them to make history with a verdict that will get the defendant's attention and show future generations the importance with which we value a single human life.

And I was a little bit surprised when Matthew Fleeger [the president of Enviroclean] got on the witness stand and said, "Whatever you do, I will certainly abide by." I don't think he had very much option but to abide by whatever you do. That's the law of this land, fortunately. I'm going to tell you one more story.

Court: You've got about four minutes.

Branson: Thank you. And I'm going to hopefully get through it within my four minutes. There was a teenager walking down a beach early one morning, and an old man is walking the other way. And it's right after a big storm. And the teenager sees the old man picking up starfish that were blowing in from the ocean and throwing them back in the water.

And he comes up and he says, "Old man, what are you doing?" And he says, "Well, there was a big storm last night and the starfish all blew in. And when the sun comes up and gets hot they're all going to die if I don't put them back." And he said, "Old man, look, you've got a whole beach of hundreds of thousands of these starfish. It's not going to make any difference." And the old man held up the starfish and he said, "It will make all the difference in the world to this one," and threw him back.

Your decision is going to make all the difference in the world to this one, and I suspect to all of us. **David and Kathleen and my crew will stand here and shake your hand when you come back.** Thank you.

Court: Thank you.

Branson ends with the tale of the starfish. It is the perfect analogy for what Branson wants the jury to do: to make a difference.

I asked Branson why he tells the jury he will shake their hands after the verdict. He explained, "The jury needs to understand, this is important. I'm not going to make this argument after a two and a half week trial and leave. I want them to know that the client and I will be there to greet them." He pointed out that it is important to "empower the jury."

> *When the jury sees good and evil in the same courtroom, and the good is really good, and the evil is very evil, these kind of results occur.*
>
> — Frank Branson

The verdict

The jury awarded a verdict of $20,793,297. Kathleen Bohne was given $5,100,000. The estate of Robert Bohne was awarded $4,000,000 for pain and mental anguish, $690,297 for medical expenses, and $3,000 for funeral and burial. The jury awarded punitive damages of $1,000,000 against Yarbrough and $10,000,000 against Enviroclean.

12.9 CHAPTER CHECKLIST ✏️

Lessons learned from Branson's depositions

1. Don't ask questions from a checklist. Instead, listen to the answers, so you can attack weaknesses.

2. When the witness answers, "I don't know," repeat the question until you get an answer or the witness sticks by his disingenuous answer.

3. A summary question which contains favorable facts for your client that forces the hostile witness to answer "yes" is only effective if you painstakingly summarize the facts correctly.

4. At a deposition, an outrageous answer that is not believable is as good as a confession. Once the jury believes the witness is lying, nothing else the witness says will be believed.

Branson's trial tips

1. Adjust to what is happening at trial. Don't just ask a list of questions during an examination.

2. There is no need to cross-examine a witness for a day and a half. The jurors have heard it and want to get out of there.

3. You can't be two-faced. You must treat your staff with the same deference you show the jury.

4. Credibility is where the game is played in the courtroom.

5. For your closing, use a topic outline with only two or three words. The more information you put in your outline, the more likely you are to look at it too much.

6. Use the jury charge as a guide for your argument.

7. You must believe everything you tell the jury.

8. The conventional wisdom that you should try your case to the jury as if they were in sixth grade is wrong. You will offend jurors. Instead, Branson believes that juries are really smart.

9. Whether you give the jury a specific number for damages or a range depends on the trial. The key is not to appear greedy.

Lessons learned from Branson's closing

1. Listen intently to opposing counsel's argument, so you can pounce on a weak argument in your response.

2. The persuasiveness of your closing is built on the facts elicited at trial. During trial, think ahead to the key facts you will need to elicit, so you can argue them in closing.

3. Famous quotations or proverbs that have stood the test of time add credibility to your argument.

4. Analogies that jurors can relate to are essential to a persuasive argument.

5. Empower the jurors by emphasizing to them the importance of their decision. (e.g., "This is your chance to right a wrong," or "This is your chance to make history.")

Branson's powerful images used in closing argument

1. Bohne's 161 days in the hospital equal 3,864 hours.

2. A professional boxer was paid $42 million for one fight. How much is a human life worth?

3. A professional athlete is paid $9 million for the amount of time that Bohne spent in the hospital.

4. One way to calculate punitive damages is to award $1.00 for every pound of hazardous waste the defendant transported last year (which was 25 million pounds).

Branson's memorable quotes from closing argument

1. "[W]e don't like to think about our mortality or somebody else's mortality. These are unpleasant tasks."

2. "[Enviroclean won't change] unless you as a jury weld together and say Bob Bohne was a unique man. We have a right to put a value on his life and on what's happened to him, and we're going to do it."

3. "But I'm going to ask you on behalf of Robert Bohne to open that block [on thinking about pain and mortality] and think about what — the pain you've heard in this courtroom would have done to Robert Bohne during all those days in the hospital, 3,864 hours in that hospital."

4. "That crack on August the 12th, 2004, was as big as the Grand Canyon when it came to testing their drivers for drugs."

5. "Pain and death are partners. They're allies in the chief enemies of mankind."

6. "There's an old English proverb that says an hour of pain is longer than a day of pleasure."

7. "And I think when you do [consider Bohne's suffering and death] and when we get through, there will be a way that Enviroclean, the fastest growing hazardous transport and treatment company in the Southwest, will understand that we place a high value on our citizens. And we place a real high value on people like Bob Bohne and his wife Kathleen."

8. "What I'd like for you to do when you get back there is do something that you can bring your children and even grandchildren at some point to the courthouse in the future and say, I served as a part of a jury that righted wrong. I served as a part of a jury that made our highways safer."

9. "There was a teenager walking down a beach early one morning, and an old man is walking the other way. And it's right after a big storm. And the teenager sees the old man picking up starfish that were blowing in from the ocean and throwing them back in the water. And he comes up and he says, 'old man, what are you doing?' And he says, 'Well, there was a big storm last night and the starfish all blew in. And when the sun comes up and gets hot they're all going to die if I don't put them back.'

And he said, 'Old man, look, you've got a whole beach of hundreds of thousands of these starfish. It's not going to make any difference.' And the old man held up the starfish and he said, 'It will make all the difference in the world to this one,' and threw him back. Your decision is going to make all the difference in the world to this one, and I suspect to all of us."

10. "David and Kathleen and my crew will stand here and shake your hand when you come back [with your verdict]."

PART SIX

Deposition

INTRODUCTION

*I*n contrast to a few decades ago when trials were common, studies show that over 90 percent of all lawsuits are settled before trial. For those cases that settle, the deposition is very often the event that becomes the turning point. It is the time when you force the opposing witness to collapse, or when your witness falters irreparably. Consequently, the deposition becomes the event where one side realizes it cannot recover, and the case needs to be settled.

As an aside for the non-lawyers reading this book, a deposition is the sworn testimony of a witness that is taken after a lawsuit is filed but before trial. It occurs during the discovery period when each side collects documents and asks witnesses questions to determine the strengths and weaknesses of the case. The judge is not present, but there is a court reporter who takes down the testimony, and lawyers from each side are there to ask questions and assert objections to the questions.

Despite the critical importance of depositions, most lawyers do not take them seriously enough—whether they are asking the questions (known as taking the deposition) or asserting objections when their client's deposition is being taken (known as defending the deposition).

When a lawyer is defending a deposition, he incorrectly believes that any mistakes his witness makes can be corrected later. Such conventional wisdom could not be more wrong. While it is true that the witness can make changes to the deposition transcript after the deposition, any substantive changes can be used against the witness with devastating effect at trial. For example, at trial, opposing counsel could accuse the witness thusly, "You changed your sworn deposition only after you consulted with your lawyer after the deposition and realized that what you said the first time would really hurt your case." In short, for all intents and purposes, deposition testimony is trial testimony. A bad deposition cannot be fixed and can ruin a case.

Likewise, most lawyers taking a deposition are unprepared. They spend little time learning the law or reviewing documents before questioning the witness. The main reason for this lackadaisical attitude is that the attorney mistakenly believes that he can get prepared when it counts at trial. But since over 90 percent of the cases settle, such a belief is misplaced.

In the chapters that follow, you will see what a difference it makes when the lawyers know the law and facts inside and out when they take a deposition.

In chapter thirteen, Michael Brickman demonstrates how his preparation and persistence in forcing the witness to answer his questions resulted in an immediate settlement after the deposition. In chapter fourteen, Don Tittle explains how the answers he obtained at a deposition became the foundation for the turning point that decided the outcome later at trial.

As you read the fascinating cases in the next two chapters, remember two things: First, deposition testimony is really trial testimony and should be treated more seriously than lawyers currently treat it. Second, as Michael Brickman so aptly declares at the beginning of the next chapter, "[T]he best lawyers are not the smartest, but they are the ones that are best prepared, work the hardest, and put in the time."

CHAPTER THIRTEEN

⸻ ⬤⬤⬤ ⸻

Michael Brickman

Win at Deposition through Relentless Preparation

I find that the best lawyers are not the smartest, but they are the ones that are best prepared, work the hardest, and put in the time.

—Michael Brickman

---

*I*magine for a moment that a widow came to your office and told you this story about how her husband had died. John[1] was 41 years old with failing kidneys and heart problems. He was on dialysis for his kidneys and desperately needed a transplant. But he could not even get on the kidney transplant list because of his failing heart condition. During dialysis treatment he developed severe skin rashes all over his body and went to a dermatologist who gave him a prescription for Methotrexate. He died a few weeks later after taking this new medication.

In listening to the case, one calculation you might make is that there may not be much money to recover for a man who had serious kidney problems as well as other life-threatening complications. Assume you have never handled a medical malpractice case. To have any chance of success you would have to spend a tremendous amount of time getting up to speed on an unfamiliar area.

Moreover, a third problem is that the doctor who prescribed the Methotrexate had done so in similar doses for years. The odds, then, are that the prescription was reasonable. A fourth problem is that John had taken the prescription to a pharmacy that fulfilled it exactly as the doctor prescribed. So, there are no apparent mistakes on the part of the doctor or the pharmacy. Fifth, one defendant, the pharmacy, is part of a large American corporation with unlimited resources to fight the case.

> **CHAPTER HIGHLIGHTS**
> - Ask precise and simple questions
> - Know the law and facts better than the witness
> - Treat deposition testimony as trial testimony

---

[1] The names in this lawsuit have been changed and are fictitious.

Sixth, assume that you have a thriving law practice, and the demands for your time are already enormous. Given this situation, most attorneys would express sympathy to the widow but move on to more pressing and profitable matters.

Not Michael Brickman. When he met Sharon, he sensed that a wrong had been committed. He felt compassion for her and her young children and got

> *The only lawyers that don't lose are those who don't try any cases.*
> —Michael Brickman

excited about the challenge of trying something new with difficult odds. He thought, "It won't be the first time I lose, but it's worth the shot." He took the case and began his journey on the road to justice. But before we get to the three depositions which were turning points in this litigation, let's get some insight into what makes

Brickman such an extremely successful trial attorney and then learn how to apply his strategies to our own cases.

Brickman comes from a family of lawyers. His father was a lawyer, and all five brothers and sisters became lawyers. To say the law is in his blood is an understatement. He learned his most important lesson for being a great trial attorney shortly after law school. He was working for his father's firm in Charleston, South Carolina, when his father asked him to handle a small matter before a Master in Equity. His father used to joke that the firm's motto became "nothing is too small to handle now that Michael is here."

His father gave him the case file and told him to ask the co-counsel on the case—who was a friend of Brickman's father—to help him with the hearing. The co-counsel gave Brickman some easy questions to ask, and Brickman—with a nervous, squeaky voice—got through the questions. He was so focused on asking the questions correctly that he had no idea what the witness answered, but he felt that he had survived. He patted himself on the back and thought, "Oh, I'm a lawyer, I can do this."

But then the unexpected happened. The mentor had to leave the courtroom and was replaced by a new associate who was just as inexperienced as Brickman. When Brickman tried to cross-examine the next witness, it became clear to the judge that he knew nothing about the law or the facts. The judge called Brickman up to the bench, confirmed his suspicions and decided to postpone the hearing.

This would be Brickman's last humiliating experience: Brickman vowed he would never be unprepared again.

Brickman's law firm, Richardson, Patrick, Westbrook & Brickman, handles a wide variety of cases, but he often gets hired by other firms to try complicated cases. Some of those cases are class-action lawsuits or other types of complex litigation. Brickman's guiding principle is that he wants to be on the right side of the case, and the case needs to be interesting. Two of his biggest cases involved obtaining a multi-billion dollar verdict against Phillip Morris for false advertising about the safety of light cigarettes, and a $250 million verdict against U.S. Steel for causing an asbestos-related illness in a 70-year-old man. It is the largest asbestos-related verdict for a single plaintiff.

Given Brickman's "be prepared" mantra, it is not surprising to see the extraordinary effort he puts into a deposition. He commented that he is continually amazed at the number of attorneys who come to take a deposition with just a blank legal pad of paper. "I don't care how smart you are, you are not off the top of your head going to do a good job. You may do an OK job, you may get the general points, but you're not going to do a really good job."

13.1 DEPOSITION STRATEGIES

I asked Brickman to provide the specific steps he takes to get ready for a deposition. First, he gets as many documents as he can before taking a deposition. But, he cautions, there is a balancing act. He points out that you also "have to move quickly because you don't want the defense lawyer or the defendant to fully understand where you're going." When deciding how much pre-deposition discovery is enough, Brickman concedes it is a judgment call but, in the end, "you try to go [and take the deposition] as quickly as possible."

Second, you should have your theory down before you take the deposition. Obviously, as you gather more facts, your theory may need some adjusting, but "I have a theory of what I'm going to try to prove, what I'm going to try to get out of this deposition, and what I need to convince a jury that I have a meritorious case."

Third, your case theory will necessarily rely on expert witness testimony for the subject matter of your case. Brickman doesn't file a case without getting advice from the best experts in the field regarding the strengths of his case and how the defense is going to defend it. Brickman believes you don't just hire an expert who will tell you what you want to hear. Instead, "you go to the top guy in the field. The last thing you want is somebody who's the proverbial 'whore.'" You hire those "who are good people who have an interest in what you're doing."

Brickman instructs that to find an expert, start by researching those who have written on your topic in peer-reviewed publications. If they won't be your expert, get a recommendation from them until you find a highly respected individual who will give you the "real picture" about your case.

Fourth, by the time the deposition starts, Brickman knows the law and is thinking about three things: 1) What do I have to prove? 2) What do I want to get out of the witness to make my case? and 3) What areas do I need to avoid to prevent the witness from hurting my case?

> *The day of discovery depositions is long gone. So, as much as you can, you prepare for depositions as if they're going to be presented to juries.*
>
> —Michael Brickman

For example, for the dermatologist's deposition discussed below, Brickman was worried that the doctor would say that he knew about the risks of giving Methotrexate to someone on dialysis but, based on his prior experience, the rash was so severe that Methotrexate had to be prescribed in order to provide much needed relief to John.

So Brickman thought, "All right, if that's the worst excuse that would hurt me, how am I going to deal with that? That's how you prepare for the deposition. You think what do I have to prove, and where are they going to try to hurt me, and how do I beat them trying to hurt me?"

When you craft your questions, your goal is to "trap him into either telling you he didn't comply with the law or that he ignored the law or he doesn't know the law." Brickman takes a topic outline to the deposition. For some topics, he includes several questions beneath the headings, in case he needs a very specific answer. Otherwise, he stays focused on his topics and keeps the goals mentioned above in mind.

In my discussions with Brickman, I wanted to get his view on one of the most difficult strategy decisions a lawyer must make at a deposition: deciding whether or not to impeach a witness at the deposition by using statements or presenting documents that will prove the witness is lying. In Part One, "Opening Statements," you may remember that Windle Turley strongly believes in a "rush to disclosure." He is never afraid to show defense counsel the cards in his hand because he believes it increases the value of his case for settlement when his opponent knows how strong his case is. Also, even if opposing counsel recovers from the surprise impeachment, Turley believes there is always more to discover, so the impeachment just gets you further down the road toward victory.

Brickman does not share this philosophy. He sometimes follows it but points out that "the real issue is where do you think the case is going? You make a judgment call and hope you're right. Is this case very likely to settle? If so, I'm going to push as hard as I can, A, to show them they really should settle and B, to raise my settlement value because if I hide something, I won't get value for it in any settlement discussions."

On the other hand, Brickman advises, "If you think a case is going to trial, you have to assume the defense attorney is going to be smart enough to put in some evidence or testimony to recover from whatever was said in a deposition. So, I hold back if I think a case is going to trial. I'll have one or two surprises that I hope they won't be prepared for, and that I hold back from using in the deposition."

Which strategy should you follow? It is hard to argue with either Turley's or Brickman's reasoning, since they are both extremely successful trial lawyers. This is a situation where trial advocacy becomes an art and not a science. You must decide which strategy works best for your practice. If you polled lawyers, it would be hard to get a consensus. I am biased towards Brickman's strategy because the majority of my cases go to trial, and I am always looking for ammunition that I can use as a surprise when it counts most before a jury. However, if the vast majority of my cases settled, it would make sense to adopt Turley's tactics.

13.2 STYLE OF QUESTIONS

Now that we have seen how Brickman prepares for a deposition, let's examine his style of questioning, Brickman is a gentleman, but he can be tough if necessary. At the start of the deposition, he always gives the witness the benefit of the doubt. But, usually, "at some point, you end up having to display righteous indignation at what is said." It is paramount that you show the witness you are in control. One way to do that is to show the witness that you know more about the case than he does and that the deposition is your domain, not his.

In some situations, Brickman states that you have to raise your voice and tell the witness that you know he is playing games with you. Then, you tell the witness that you are going to let the jury know the witness is playing games. For example, Brickman might say, "If you think that's the way the jury is going to appreciate [what you said], you go right ahead and [say] it, but we'll see because I'm going to tell you, my experience is they're going to think you're lying." After hearing this, the witness realizes that he is not just in a quiet room with a couple of attorneys and a court reporter, but what he is saying will be put in front of a jury in a very public courtroom.

13.3 MEDICAL MALPRACTICE DEPOSITIONS

Below are the three key depositions in the medical malpractice case mentioned earlier. Although a brief summary was already given, we need a few more background facts to understand the depositions. When John developed chronic and acute skin rashes while on kidney dialysis, the dialysis clinic referred him to Dr.

Smith, a dermatologist. Dr. Smith gave him two steroid shots and prescribed Methotrexate for his condition. He ordered John to take a dosage of two 2.5 mg. tablets. John went to dialysis three times a week. Dr. Smith prescribed that John take the Methotrexate on those days when he was not going to dialysis.

John took the prescription to his local pharmacy where he got all his medicines, including those for his kidney condition. The pharmacy filled the prescription exactly as Dr. Smith wrote it, and John began taking the medicine exactly as prescribed. Seven days later, John had to be hospitalized for weakness and an inability to take in food.

Nineteen painful days later, John's body shut down, and he died of Methotrexate toxicity. His impaired kidneys could not eliminate the prescribed Methotrexate from his body. Dr. Smith responded to his alleged wrongdoing by pointing out that he had given a proper dose, that hundreds of others had been given the same medicine in the same dosage without adverse reactions, and that the dialysis clinic should have monitored John's blood levels to determine if there was any problem.

The pharmacy cautioned Brickman that a lawsuit would be a waste of time because its pharmacists had filled a valid prescription sent in by a qualified doctor and that it had no liability for correctly following a doctor's prescription.

Faced with these obstacles, let's see if Brickman can pull off an upset. The first deposition is that of the dermatologist, Dr. Smith; the second is that of the pharmacist; and the third is that of the pharmacist's supervisor.

The most striking characteristic of Brickman's depositions is that they read like extremely well executed cross-examinations at trial instead of the typical rambling depositions that dominate litigation. There are no wasted questions. His topics are well organized. He displays a mastery of the facts. By knowing the case better than the witness, Brickman can challenge the witness when necessary, instead of accepting the witness's answer at face value. Also, by listening intently, he can follow-up appropriately when a witness fails to answer a question.

As you see Brickman's great skills in action, notice also how the witness answers. When a witness knows a truthful answer will hurt his cause, I have found that he avoids questions with what I call one of two D's: 1) Dodge and 2) Doesn't answer. One key to being a great trial lawyer is recognizing when a witness is using one of these strategies and then using the proper technique to counter it. If you are not listening carefully, it often appears the witness has answered the question when, in fact, the witness has only partially answered it or answered a question you never asked. We will see how Brickman overcomes the difficult witness every time.

13.4 THE DERMATOLOGIST'S DEPOSITION

Brickman establishes doctor's knowledge of patient's medical history

Q. *Did you know anything about John's medical history when you saw him on July 22nd, 2010?*
A. I knew he was a dialysis patient, and I knew he was a diabetic.

Q. *How did you know he was a dialysis patient and how did you know he was diabetic?*
A. Because he had an active shunt, and he told me. (Indicating)

Q. *That was not noted in any way in your record?*
A. No.

Q. *Is it a mistake it's not noted?*
A. Yes. Normally we would put that in, the patient is a dialysis patient.

Notice how Brickman clearly establishes that Dr. Smith knew that John was on dialysis. This fact will become very important in establishing Dr. Smith's negligence. In addition, he gets the doctor to admit that it was a "mistake" not to put that information in the medical record. The doctor could excuse this mistake as a harmless notation error, since he knew that John was on dialysis and treated him accordingly. But Brickman knows that getting a doctor to admit even a simple mistake is not easy, and it will give him leverage as he tries to get him to admit more important mistakes later.

Lack of time to see patients

Q. *You appear to have a successful practice. Do you consider that to be the case?*
A. Yes.

Q. *And Ms. White (Dr. Smith's assistant) seemed to think that you see somewhere in the range of I think 45 to 50 patients a day?*
A. Yes….

Q. *And as I understand, you schedule your patients for 10 minutes in the office except for new patients, which are 15 minutes?*
A. That's correct.

Brickman establishes that Dr. Smith does not spend much time with his patients, a fact which dovetails with the doctor's admission above that he did not note in the medical records the significant piece of medical history that John was on dialysis.

Skin problems and dosage

Q. Are you able today to tell us the extent or severity of any of those three conditions [plaintiff's skin lesions, rash, and itching]?
A. I can only hypothesize that because of the dosage of Methotrexate I gave him that it may have been very severe. Because normally I would have started at a 1.25 dosage rather than at a 2.5. [**The doctor prescribed 2.5 milligrams because of the plaintiff's severe skin condition.**]

Q. And when you say 1.25, you talk about 1.25 milligrams of Methotrexate—
A. Milligrams of Methotrexate.

Q. Two times a day?
A. No.

Q. 1.25 only?
A. 1.25 Monday, Wednesday, Friday. In his case I think it was Tuesday, Thursday, Saturday.

Q. And why did you do it Tuesday, Thursday, Saturday?
A. Because he had dialysis on Monday, Wednesday and Friday and I didn't want the Methotrexate to wash out of his system.

Q. And you were worried that the dialysis would take the Methotrexate out?
A. That's correct.

Q. Did you tell him to take the medicine that day he picked it up?
A. I don't recall what day of the week that was but I explained to him the regimen, I'm sure, to take it on the days he doesn't have dialysis.

Q. If, in fact, July 22 was a Thursday, would he then have been supposed to have taken the medicine that day?
A. If he got that from the pharmacy that day I probably would have told him to take the dosage.

> **Practice Tip**
> A successful deposition depends on gaining the witness' respect. Knowledge is power. When the lawyer is better prepared than the witness, it gives him leverage and puts the witness on the defensive.

Brickman shows the doctor that he is very well prepared. The doctor may not know what day of the week it was, but Brickman has researched it because it is important to establish what day John started taking the medication.

Failure to monitor drug levels in blood

Q. Did you do any blood work on John or have any blood work done on John?
A. No.

Q. *Any particular reason you didn't do any blood work on him before giving him any of these medicines?*

A. On certain patients we start on Methotrexate we will give prior labs. Most of the time I would say no, we don't do that. But if a patient is taking hepatotoxic medication already, then we would do a baseline. In this case, because he was receiving so many blood tests every week because of the dialysis, I didn't feel it necessary.

Most lawyers would just accept the doctor's answer that the clinic was conducting the appropriate blood tests. After all, the doctor is the expert. He does this all the time. At face value, his answer makes perfect sense. Why put John through the aggravation of duplicate blood tests? Indeed, by not giving him repetitive tests, the doctor appears to being doing John a favor.

This is a perfect example of the difference between typical trial lawyers and great trial lawyers. While the ordinary lawyer would accept the answer and move on to another topic, Brickman knows better because he is prepared and knows how patients should be monitored. Watch how Brickman follows up:

Q. *What blood tests was he receiving every week?*

A. When I worked a dialysis unit we did CBC, electrolytes and liver function studies and renal tests.

Q. *I'm sorry. I missed the third one. You said CBC, electrolyte, the last one was renal test. What was the third one?*

A. LFTs.

Q. *LFTs. And was it your understanding that he was receiving all of these tests — excuse me — on a weekly basis?*

A. If it was a standard renal lab, yes.

Q. *Have you made any check to see if that is what the standard is at the [John's clinic]?* **[By carefully listening, Brickman realizes that Dr. Smith does not have specific knowledge about the clinic's practices but was making an assumption based on his past experience.]**

A. No.

Q. *Do you have any information with regard to John to know whether they were doing* these tests on a weekly basis?

A. No. **[Now, Brickman has established that Dr. Smith does not know what the standard tests are and how often they are given.]**

Q. *Were you counting on the clinic in any way to catch any toxic effects from the Methotrexate?*

A. Well, I'm sure they would have informed me of it. **[Witness deflects attention. It is the first evasive answer.]**

Q. *Were you relying on them to monitor him instead of you for any toxic effects of the Methotrexate?* **[Brickman repeats question.]**

A. I would have probably started monitoring at a month out, which is what I usually do. **[Witness distracts from question and gives his second evasive answer.]**

Q. **That's not my question.** *My question to you is, were you relying on the clinic to monitor John for any toxic effects from the Methotrexate as opposed to you?*
A. Yes.

Brickman has to repeat the same question three times in order to force the doctor to answer a simple question: Was the doctor relying on the clinic to monitor the toxic effects of Methotrexate? He finally gets a straight answer. Brickman shows us that when a witness deflects a question or tries to distract your attention by pretending to answer the question, you need to do two things. First, listen carefully so that you will realize there is an evasive answer. Second, ask the question repeatedly until you get a straight answer.

In addition, having completed the line of inquiry, most lawyers would have moved onto another topic and not uncovered another key mistake Dr. Smith made. Brickman does not change topics. Instead, he presses full steam ahead. He knows there is a crack in the doctor's defense because he knows more facts about the case than the doctor. Let's watch the pursuit.

Q. *Did you contact the clinic to let them know they needed to monitor him for Methotrexate toxicity?*
A. **I don't recall. [Witness uses the "doesn't answer" strategy.]**

Q. *Do you have any record indicating you contacted them?*
A. No.

Q. *Was that — would that be something you would note in your records?*
A. The nurses would usually note that because they would be the one to contact them.

Q. *Does that then mean since there is no such record or no such mention in your records that, in all likelihood, you did not contact the clinic?*
A. **I have to assume that.**

Brickman knows blood monitoring is a fundamental issue in the case. If Dr. Smith is counting on the clinic to monitor the drug level, then it may bear responsibility if he informed the clinic of the need to conduct certain tests. Brickman makes sure he gets a better answer than "I don't recall."

Lawyers and doctors often argue that if something is in the medical records, "It must have occurred," and if something is not in the medical records, "It did not occur." Whatever the truth really is, the side whose position is corroborated by the medical records has a great advantage in proving the particular fact. Through Brickman's persistence, the doctor changes his answer from "I don't recall" to having to "assume" that the clinic was never alerted to the need for monitoring, since there is no documentation in the medical records.

> **Practice Tip**
>
> When a witness answers a simple question with "I don't recall," don't accept it at face value.

Q. What tests would indicate whether somebody is having Methotrexate toxicity?
A. Normally the AST and the ALT would be quite elevated.

Q. Would that be specific to Methotrexate?
A. No.

Q. What else could cause that to happen?
A. Many medications can, alcohol intoxication.

Q. So unless you know you're looking for Methotrexate, that wouldn't necessarily tell a doctor who sees elevated levels, gee, this is Methotrexate toxicity; is that correct?
A. Correct.

Because Brickman knows that the tests can be elevated for a variety of reasons, he does not accept the doctor's initial explanation that the tests can effectively monitor Methotrexate toxicity.

Let's stop for a moment and see how Brickman's preparation and tenacity have changed the deposition's course. If he had not known the case inside and out, he would have been left with the doctor's initial explanation that the dialysis clinic was in the best position to monitor Methotrexate toxicity and that tests such as AST and ALT were effective in accomplishing this goal.

Perhaps months later in the discovery process the unprepared lawyer could have recovered somewhat if he were to learn from the clinic that it did not give effective tests, but then it would be too late to confront the doctor and prove he should have been aware of his failings.

Q. And unless a doctor knows somebody is taking Methotrexate, he won't necessarily think that Methotrexate could be causing those changes in those levels?
A. Possible. [Witness dodges question by answering with the word "possible."]

Q. Is that correct?
A. Yeah.

Q. Not just possibly, probably, isn't it?
A. Probably.

Q. Isn't there, in fact, a specific test that will find out if somebody has Methotrexate toxicity?
A. I'm not certain. [Witness again tries to dodge question.]

Q. Do you know if there's a test to find out the level of Methotrexate —
A. Of course.

Q. — in a person's body?
A. Well, of course. You can get to a level in the blood, Methotrexate level.

Once again, Brickman changes a vague answer into a helpful admission. He does this twice in this short segment. He achieves it the first time through use of the facts he has already obtained from the witness in the previous section. The doctor earlier admits that alcohol and many medications other than Methotrexate can cause elevated blood tests. So, it is disingenuous to now say that it is only "possible" a doctor won't consider that the elevated levels were caused by Methotrexate. Indeed, it is "probable" as the doctor finally admits, that an unsuspecting dialysis clinic would think there were many causes *other* than Methotrexate for high levels in tests.

More important, this section shows that Brickman is the expert, not the dodging doctor. At first the doctor claims that he "is not certain" if there is a specific test for Methotrexate. But when confronted again—by Brickman who knows the answer—the doctor admits there is such a test.

Imagine how nervous the witness must be getting. He walks into the deposition thinking one of two things: either he did nothing wrong or the deposing attorney won't find out that he did something wrong. But now, Brickman has obtained key admissions that 1) Dr. Smith was relying on the dialysis clinic to monitor Methotrexate toxicity and 2) the clinic was unaware Smith's patient was taking Methotrexate. Those admissions have cornered the witness with no way to escape.

Q. *Do you agree with me that somebody on Methotrexate should be monitored?*
A. Yes. [**Witness has to answer yes based on prior testimony.**]

Q. *And do you agree with me that typically the person that monitors a person on Methotrexate is the doctor that prescribed the Methotrexate for them?* [**Brickman knows this is the standard of care, and the doctor must now admit it**]
A. Yes.

Q. *And are you aware of anybody else prescribing Methotrexate for John other than you?*
A. No.

Q. *Would you also agree that in order for a doctor to know whether to monitor somebody for a medicine like Methotrexate they have to know the patient is taking Methotrexate?*
A. Yes. [**The "probably" answer from the earlier section now becomes a definite "yes."**]

Q. *And as far as you know nobody from the dermatology office, including you or any of your assistants, notified any of John's other doctors or clinics he was going to that he was taking Methotrexate; correct?*
A. Correct.

Q. ***Do you believe that to be a mistake?***
A. **Yes.**

Brickman gets this admission because his methodical approach forces the witness to answer this way or risk giving an outrageous answer that won't be believed by anyone. Imagine if he had answered it wasn't a mistake, given all his previous answers.

Practice Tip

You win if the witness gives a disingenuous answer to a simple question. The goal is to get an admission or an answer that is so incredible that the witness will lose all credibility.

Consequences of Methotrexate toxicity

Q. *Do you agree that Methotrexate toxicity can cause severe ulcerative esophagitis?*
A. Yes.

Q. *And Methotrexate toxicity can cause severe thrombocytopenia; correct?*
A. Yes.

Q. *Methotrexate toxicity can cause persistent metabolic encephalopathy; correct?*
A. Yes.

Q. *Methotrexate toxicity can cause Hepatitis; correct?*
A. Yes.

Q. *Methotrexate toxicity can cause arythia multiforme?*
A. Erythema multiforme, yes.

Q. *Erythema multiforme; correct?*
A. Yes.

Q. *And Methotrexate toxicity can cause severe pancotype —*
A. Panctyopenia.

Q. *Thank you.*
A. Yes.

Q. *Correct? All right. And were you aware that Methotrexate can cause all the things we just went over prior to prescribing it for John?*
A. Yeah.

Once again, Brickman's preparation pays off. He recites a litany of medical terms that help him prove the doctor's negligence. The doctor realizes that Brickman is very knowledgeable about the drug in question and understands any disingenuous answers will be met with a series of follow-up questions.

Dosage

Q. *You didn't give him a reduced dose, did you?*
A. I gave him the dose that I thought would be appropriate. [**Witness dodges question.**]

Q. ***That's not my question.*** *Did you give him a reduced dose as you defined it earlier for me?*
A. No.

Q. **Did you give him a dose that's recommended by the manufacturer of the Methotrexate?**
A. **Yes.**

Q. *And where did you find that recommended dosage?*
A. In the *PDR* [*Physicians' Desk Reference*].

Q. *And if the* PDR *says that's not a recommended dosage, then did you make a mistake?*
A. I—I don't think I made a mistake based on the clinical presentation. [**Witness dodges question.**]

Q. *That's not my question. If, in fact, you did not follow the recommended dosage in pre-scribing Methotrexate to John according to the* PDR, *did you make a mistake?*

A. Yes.

Q. *And if, in fact, John died from Methotrexate toxicity because you did not follow the recommended dosage, did you violate the standards of care with regard to John?*

A. Yes.

Q. *Well, let's go right to the* PDR *if we could. Let's mark — let's just mark what you sent us at the time.* [**Brickman now has the witness up against the wall and continues the attack.**]

Brickman uses the *Physicians' Desk Reference* as leverage to show that what Dr. Smith prescribed is not consistent with its guidelines for doctors. The *PDR* is the authoritative source on drug information, interactions, warnings, and dosages.

<table>
<tr><td>

Practice Tip

Whenever a witness gives an evasive answer, Brickman immediately reprimands the witness by saying, "That's not my question" and repeating the original question. He sends a clear signal to the witness that he knows the witness is not being candid and that he won't move on until he gets an answer.

</td><td>

Q. *And are you aware that the longer duration that some-body's given Methotrexate, the more likely they are to have toxic effects as opposed to being given a single dose?*

A. Yes.

Q. *So you did not follow the recommended dosage [in the* **PDR**] *in prescribing Methotrexate for John, did you?*

A. **No.**

Q. *You gave him a dosage more than double what's the recommended dosage; correct?*

A. No. Double there.

Q. *Double, but with more potential toxic effects because it stretched over time; correct?*

A. Well, yes, but that's a person who's not on dialysis.

</td></tr>
</table>

Q. *OK.*

A. You make a point for a person who's going to dialyze out a certain percentage of that.

Q. *But you specifically told him to take the medicine on days he wasn't going to dialysis because of the fact you didn't want that to happen; correct?*

A. I wanted him to maintain a concentration that would then, the next day, be driven out.

Q. *Now —*

A. It's almost like starting a new dose every time.

Q. *And when he takes the pill on Saturday, he doesn't get dialysis on Sunday, does he?*

A. **No.**

Q. *So it stays in his body until the Monday or Monday afternoon he takes it again; correct?*

A. Correct.

Q. *So you're giving him more than double the recommended dosage; correct?*
A. Correct.

Q. And is there anywhere in the electronic PDR that says you can give somebody with renal impairment a higher dosage—
A. No.

Q. *—than recommended?*
A. No.

Q. *You made a mistake, didn't you?*
A. Yes.

Q. *And that's what caused Methotrexate toxicity in John, isn't it?*
A. I assume so.

Q. *And that's your responsibility?*
A. Yes.

Without knowing the *PDR*, Brickman could not have proven his point. Did you notice how Brickman cut off the doctor's escape route. The doctor explains that it was acceptable to deviate from the *PDR* guidelines because John was on dialysis which would drain the drug from his system. As the doctor reasons, the double dose is OK because the dialysis will flush it out of his system the following day. But Brickman listens intently and knows that the reasoning makes no sense because John did not have dialysis on the weekend.

It is the turning point in the deposition. It sets up the confession in the next and final excerpt.

> **Practice Tip**
> Unless you are fairly certain the case is going to trial, use your weapons at the deposition to prove the witness wrong. The admissions gained are essential during settlement negotiations. There is no point in saving your ammunition for a trial that won't occur.

Doctor admits negligence

Q. *Do you know, as you sit here today or recall, how you came up with the dosing scheme of three days a week?*
A. Originally it was used by some of my professors at—where I trained. [**Brickman won't accept a vague answer.**]

Q. *Which professor?*
A. I can't really remember which one specifically, but several of them used the three-day—the three-day Monday, Wednesday, Friday dosing because they found that it caused fewer side effects. More common side effects like gastritis and ulceration in the mouth.

Q. *But have you come to learn that three times a week causes more serious toxic effects as opposed to giving it in a single dose or in a divided dose over 24 hours?*
A. Yes.

Q. *When did you come to learn that?*
A. Today. [**Brickman has forced witness to admit his "professors" were wrong.**]

Q. *And even though you came to learn it today, is this something you should have known before you prescribed it to John?*
A. Probably, yes. [**Witness dodges with the word "probably" and Brickman keeps pressing.**]

Q. *And by not knowing it, you violated medical standards of care?*
A. Yes.

Q. *And by not knowing it you violated medical safety rules for the care of your patients?*
A. Yes.

In this deposition, the doctor presumably thought he could simply stand behind his judgment and assumption that what he had always done was the correct treatment. It is very rare for a witness to admit negligence or confess to making a critical mistake. Often lawyers get into fruitless arguments with witnesses because they try to get them to "tell the truth." But witnesses are motivated by self-preservation to dodge the question, deflect attention, answer a different question, or not answer at all (i.e., "I don't know" or "I don't recall.")

Brickman explained that his biggest concern going into the doctor's deposition was that the doctor would say he used his judgment to prescribe the particular medicine and dosage based on his examination of John and the advanced state of John's condition. That might have resonated with a jury, even though factually Brickman did not believe it to be true. Here Brickman was so well prepared, and the logic of his questions was so sound that the witness had to tell the truth or look ridiculous.

After taking the doctor's deposition, Brickman focused on the pharmacy's liability for fulfilling a deadly prescription. Below are the depositions of the pharmacist, Kay Kimball, and her supervisor, Scott Robson.[2] Let's observe how Brickman builds his case by eliciting one devastating admission after another.

13.5 THE PHARMACIST'S DEPOSITION (KAY KIMBALL)

Pharmacist's duty to warn customer of drug disease interaction

Q. *And is that same basic theory true for drug disease interactions?*
A. Yes.

Q. *And let's just make sure we're clear. Such that if you believe there is a drug disease interaction with regard to a medicine about to be given to a patient, the pharmacist has a duty to do something at that point; correct?*
A. Well, the pharmacist's duty is to refer to the physician and make sure that the physician is aware of the issue and that the physician is aware that there, you know, could potentially be a problem. And then the physician would do the monitoring and

---

[2] The names in this lawsuit have been changed and are fictitious.

make sure that, you know, the dosage that they have prescribed is what they would like to continue with. [**The witness has not answered the question completely. Brickman makes sure she does.**]

Q. *And if there is a drug disease interaction potential that could put a patient in jeopardy and the pharmacist then checks with the prescribing doctor and he says go ahead and give it,* **is it still the pharmacist's duty to discuss the potential jeopardy that drug disease interaction could cause with the patient?**
A. Yes. [**Admission number one**]

The "drug disease interaction" mentioned above refers to the possibility that a prescribed drug to help with one disease may hurt the patient if he is compromised by another disease that interacts badly with the prescribed drug. By repeatedly probing until he gets the answer he needs, Brickman gets his first key admission from the pharmacist: She had a duty to warn a patient if the prescribed drug could interact with the patient's unrelated disease and put him in jeopardy.

Pharmacist lacks information during counseling session

Q. *Do you look at* [**the customer's**] *personal records at that time in any way before the consultation?*
A. No.

Q. *At—so that when you give the consultation your—you don't have the information regarding his drug history or personal file for disease history; correct?*
A. Correct. [**Admission number two**]

Q. *And is that the case for all the pharmacists as far as you know?*
A. As far as I know.

After establishing that the pharmacist has a duty to counsel the customer, Brickman gets the witness to admit that none of the pharmacists have information regarding a patient's medical history when they conduct the counseling. All they have is information generated by the computer as will be discussed in the next section.

SCOREBOARD
Brickman 2   Defendant 0

---

1. Pharmacist has duty to discuss adverse drug disease interactions with customer.

2. Pharmacist lacks customer's personal medical history when discussing interactions.

Pharmacist checks for drug disease interaction

Q. *And even if the pharmacy computer doesn't show any drug-drug or drug-disease interactions, you do your own search on **every occasion**?*
A. I do....

Q. *And does that search also allow you to determine if there is any drug-disease interaction?*
A. No.

Q. *Does anybody do any drug-disease interaction search?*
A. I can't speak for anybody, but I know that when I fill the prescriptions I look at what they've had previously. And based on what medications they've had previously, I can kind of determine what illnesses that they possibly do have.

Q. *Certain medicines are specific —*
A. For certain diseases.

Q. *Could you tell from looking at the [medications listed in John's] personal profile whether he had any medical conditions?*
A. Yes.

Q. *What medical conditions could you tell from looking at his profile that he had?*
A. That he was on dialysis. [**Third admission**]

Q. *Prior to this lawsuit did you expect that computer system to be able to put into his personal profile he was on dialysis or had a kidney disorder based on his taking medicine such as Eliphos, Phoslo, and Ren — what was it?*
A. Renvela.

Q. *Renvela, yes.*
A. Right.

Q. *That was your understanding prior thereto?*
A. Right.

Q. *Now, you have subsequent to this lawsuit checked and found that the computer did not put that in his personal profile, that he was on dialysis and had a kidney disorder; correct?*
A. Correct.

Q. *Do you know why it didn't do it?*
A. I do not know why. [**Fourth admission**]

The witness admits that she expects that the computer would list a customer's medical condition and is surprised to learn that the computer program does not do that.

> **SCOREBOARD**
> **Brickman 4   Defendant 0**
>
> 3. Prior prescriptions filled at pharmacy revealed John had kidney disease.
>
> 4. Despite prescriptions for kidney disease, John's profile on computer should show he suffers from kidney disease but does not.

Dosage

Q. And did you learn [from reading Dr. Smith's deposition] that Dr. Smith now believes that the dosage of Methotrexate for John was too high?
A. I did read that in the deposition....

Q. Do you know, then, why Dr. Smith was of the opinion that the dosage he put on the script for John was outside the manufacturer's recommended dosage?
A. I don't know why Dr. Smith said that, no. Dr. Smith — we get prescriptions from him for that same medication at that same dosage lots of times. So he prescribes it quite often and that's the dosage that he prescribes. Sometimes even more.

Q. Do you still get prescriptions from Dr. Smith with that dosage? [**A brilliant question. Brickman explores every important possibility and decides that Dr. Smith may still prescribe the wrong dosage even after his deposition.**]
A. I have seen a prescription from Dr. Smith with that dosage, yes.

Q. Recently?
A. Yes.

Q. How recently?
A. Within the last two weeks, maybe—two to three weeks. [**Fifth admission**]

Q. Did the Facts & Comparisons [in the Physicians' Desk Reference*] tell you how frequently that medication was to be given?*
A. It said weekly. [**Sixth admission**]

Q. And did you note that that was not the case for the Methotrexate prescription given to John?
A. I did note that. And all the prescriptions from Dr. Smith that we ever get are dosed exactly the same. [**Witness deflects question by explaining that it is not her fault.**]

Q. Wrong, you mean?
A. Were wrong, that's how they were dosed. He — that's how he writes the prescriptions —

Q. Right.
A. —on Tuesdays, Thursdays, Saturday or either Monday, Wednesday, Friday.

———— ⚬⚭⚬ ————

Q. Why didn't the computer pick up that the frequency of dosage was in error?
A. The computer did not pick that up because the computer does not look at what's taken on a daily basis.

Q. What do you mean? I don't understand.
A. The computer doesn't look at what med—the computer doesn't look at the frequency of the medication.

Q. So that if a medicine like Methotrexate is only supposed to be taken once a week and the prescription doesn't say wait a week for the second dose, that's not something the computer will catch—
A. No. [**Seventh admission**]

Amazingly, the computer will not alert anyone if the doctor mistakenly prescribes too many pills at one time. It is set up so it merely counts the total dosage of the medicine and divides it by the days the prescription is good for. In other words, if the doctor incorrectly wrote to take all the pills in one day, but the prescription was a 30-day prescription, the computer would have taken the number of pills, multiplied it by the strength of the pill, and divided it by 30 and if that average number was acceptable, it would not set off any alarm. Unfortunately, the pharmacist did not fully comprehend this problem with the system.

When the pharmacist said that Dr. Smith was still prescribing improper dosages even after his deposition, Brickman told me it was like receiving "manna from heaven." Brickman was in disbelief. First, how could the doctor still prescribe the improper dosage after admitting in his deposition that it was a mistake. Second, how could the pharmacist continue to fill the prescriptions knowing that a couple of weeks earlier Smith had admitted it was the wrong dose, and the pharmacist had since read the deposition. Brickman said it was all the proof he needed for punitive damages (i.e., damages based on willful or malicious conduct.)

SCOREBOARD
Brickman 7   Defendant 0

5. Dr. Smith continues to submit prescriptions for doses outside recommended guidelines.

6. Recommended dosage for Methotrexate is once per week.

7. Computer can't warn if prescription incorrectly instructs to take medication more often than recommended.

Q. Do you know if anybody told John that the frequency for the medication — the Metho-
trexate prescribed by Dr. Smith was contraindicated? [**Contraindicated means that a**
drug could harm a patient if it is not monitored.]
A. Not to my knowledge.

Q. Is that information he should have had?

Defense Counsel: Object to the form of the question.

Witness: I would think that he should have had — gotten that from his physician.

By Brickman:
Q. Should he have also gotten that from the pharmacy that gave him the medicine?
A. No, I — I don't think so.

Q. So that even though the dosage was wrong, according to Facts & Comparisons and
according to the PDR, and it's your job as a pharmacist to check the dosage, **you don't**
think you needed to tell that to John?
A. I didn't see anything wrong with — with the dosage —

Q. You know —
A. —as I filled it.

Q. You know now it's wrong, don't you?
A. Well, I know now, but I did not see anything wrong because we got — like I said,
we've gotten prescriptions from Dr. Smith and that's how he prescribes that particular medication. And I didn't see anything out of the ordinary about that prescription.

Q. Had you checked Methotrexate, looked it up, you would have found out Dr. Smith's
prescription was wrong; correct?

Defense Counsel: Object to the form.

Witness: Again, specifically we're talking about Dr. Smith writing that particular
prescription. **But physicians write prescriptions all the time that are not based**
on how the manufacturer says they should be prescribed.

By Brickman:
Q. And on those occasions it's the pharmacist's duty to check with the prescribing
physician to see if that's what he deliberately wants to do; correct?
A. Right. And the reason why he was not checked at that point is because we get the
prescriptions all the time written exactly like that, two tablets three times a week.

The above excerpt shows how a disingenuous answer is as good as an admission. The witness denies she has a duty to warn John that he should only be
taking the dose once per week as recommended by medical literature instead
of the three times a week as prescribed by the doctor. Her explanation is that
even though the dosage was incorrect, she had no duty because the doctor had
always prescribed it that way. Does that make sense? Of course not. Brickman
wins again.

Leaflet warns of danger

Q. *Let me show you what we have marked as Exhibit 2* [**leaflet about Methotrexate**]. *My first question is going to be is just what, in general, this is. But, again, if you need to look through it take your time.*

A. (Reading.) This is the leaflet that's given to—they're given with their prescription of Methotrexate....

Q. *Near the bottom of the first paragraph under Methotrexate 2.5 milligram tab, do you see where it says: Use of this medicine is not recommended if you have moderate or severe kidney problems? Do you see that now?*

A. Yes, I do.

Q. *Do you disagree with that?*

A. I don't disagree that it's not recommended. [**Admission number eight**]

Q. *Would you agree with me in light of what you now know about your own computer system and Methotrexate that when you filled the prescription for John you should have called Dr. Smith?*

A. Yes.

Pharmacists missed opportunities to document kidney disease

Q. *Do you know what a nephrologist is?*

A. Yes.

Q. *What is a nephrologist?*

A. That is a kidney doctor.

Q. *And on the medications for the Phoslo and the Eliphos and the Renvela, did you note that those came from nephrologists?*

A. Correct.

Q. *So that would have been an additional indication to the pharmacist filling those prescriptions that this person had kidney problems, kidney disorders; correct?*

A. Correct.

Q. *And all of—I think. I believe all the prescriptions for the Phoslo, the Eliphos and the Renvela came from nephrologists or nephrology clinics; correct?*

A. Correct.

Q. *So that every time somebody filled one of those prescriptions the staff pharmacist would have noted, one, the medication is for somebody with a kidney disorder on dialysis; correct?*

A. Correct.

Q. Two, it came from a nephrologist, somebody who treats people with kidney disorders; correct?

A. Correct.

Q. And those were filled a number of times by the pharmacy; correct?

A. Correct.

Q. So on each of those occasions that would have been another reminder to the pharmacy this was a person with kidney disorders because he's getting a kidney disorder medication or dialysis medication and—from somebody treating kidney disorders?

A. Correct. [**Admission number nine**]

Has not made changes

Q. Is there any new policy at the pharmacy dealing with Methotrexate to your knowledge?

A. No, not that I know.

Q. Has anything changed since this lawsuit as to how Methotrexate is—a prescription is inputted?

A. Not that I'm aware of, no. [Admission number 10]

Q. Has anything changed as to the need to call the prescribing physician about a dosage since this lawsuit?

A. No.

Q. Has anything changed about what needs to be told to a patient since this lawsuit—who's getting Methotrexate, that is?

A. No.

Q. If tomorrow Dr. Smith—if Dr. Smith does another prescription for Methotrexate with the inappropriate frequency of dosage, are you going to call him?

A. Yes.

Q. OK. And that's something you should have done when John got his medication?

A. In hindsight, yes.

Q. But everything in hindsight you knew at the time—everything you know now you knew at the time John got his medicine; correct?

Defense Counsel: Object to the form.

By Brickman:

Q. Correct?

A. That's correct. But these were prescriptions—or this wasn't a prescription that was, you know, unlike any others that he had sent to us. So it wasn't anything that—like a red flag that stuck out about it because this is how he would prescribe that particular medication, so....

Q. *Even though you knew the frequency of dosage was inappropriate?*

A. Even though. We had filled, you know, many prescriptions with the same frequency for him.

Q. *Is the only reason, then, you didn't take any other steps, even though you knew the frequency was wrong and you knew John was on dialysis, was simply because you had done it before for Dr. Smith?*

A. Yes.

Q. *No other reason?*

A. No other reason.

FINAL SCORE
Brickman 10   Defendant 0

1. Pharmacist must discuss adverse drug disease interactions.

2. Pharmacist lacks patient's personal medical history for discussion.

3. Prior prescriptions revealed John's kidney disease.

4. Despite prior prescriptions for kidney disease, John's profile does not show kidney disease.

5. Dr. Smith continues to submit wrong prescriptions to pharmacy.

6. Methotrexate should be taken once per week.

7. Pharmacy computer can't warn if prescription incorrectly instructs to take medication more often than recommended.

8. Pharmacy leaflet warns that Methotrexate should not be taken if kidney disease exists.

9. Pharmacy missed multiple chances to document John's kidney disease.

10. Pharmacy has not made any changes despite its failings.

The last deposition we will examine is that of Scott Robson, the pharmacy supervisor.

13.6 THE PHARMACY SUPERVISOR'S DEPOSITION

Normal dosage for Methotrexate

Q. *So prior to the lawsuit, you knew the frequency for Methotrexate was typically or generally or always once a week. You may not have known why, but you knew that's how it was particularly prescribed?*

A. Typically, the prescriptions I've seen have been anywhere from three to ten [tablets], once a week.

Robson admits that Methotrexate is given in one dose per week as opposed to the multiple doses Dr. Smith prescribed.

South Carolina regulations require consultation

Q. Do you agree that South Carolina requires that pharmacists consult with their patients and let them know of any side effects that could occur that they should be aware of for their safety?
A. No.

Q. You disagree with that?
A. I disagree that we go through all the interactions. Yes.

Q. Do you disagree that South Carolina requires that?
A. I don't know about that.

Q. You don't know whether they do require that or not?
A. All the interactions, I don't know that.

Q. Do you agree that failure to let patients know of any side effects that could occur is against the law and is pharmacy malpractice?
A. No, I don't know that.

Q. You do agree that the South Carolina Board of Pharmacy newsletter constitutes guidelines pharmacists must go by, correct?
A. Yes.

Q. Have you ever seen that in the South Carolina Pharmacy newsletter?
A. I've never seen where it said we had to go with every single interaction with them. I haven't seen that.

Q. If it does, you should follow that, shouldn't you?
A. If I saw it, I would. I would, yes.

Q. And you're required to look at that magazine, aren't you?
A. I am.

Q. You're required to know it, aren't you?
A. I'm required to look at it.

Q. Required to understand what it means?
A. Verbatim, no, but —

Q. I don't mean memorize it.
A. OK. Well, yes. Yes.

Brickman uses his knowledge of the law to get the answer he needs from the witness. He first gets the witness to admit that he is required to follow the guidance in the South Carolina Board of Pharmacy Newsletter. Then, he gets the witness to admit that if the Newsletter requires the counseling, he is required to understand the Newsletter and follow it. This is as good as an admission because the Newsletter does require it.

> **Practice Tip**
>
> To get an admission, use Brickman's technique:
>
> 1. Know the facts better than the witness.
>
> 2. Know the law better than the witness.
>
> 3. Repeat the question until the witness answers it.

Pharmacist had duty to put disease information into system

Brickman next asks the supervisor about his knowledge regarding the drugs he had given John multiple times in the past for his kidney disease.

Q. *But if you had dispensed this Renvela and you had known what it's used for, that it's used for kidney failure with people on dialysis, do you believe you then had a duty to put it in the system?*
A. No.

Q. *If the law says otherwise, do you agree you've violated your standard of care to John?*
A. Yes. If it says that I should have, then obviously, I have.

Once again, we see the value of knowing the case better than the witness. Brickman knows that if a pharmacist is aware that a patient has a disease, he should enter it into the computer. The pharmacist supervisor does not know that requirement. Because Brickman is so well prepared, he gets the admission.

Pay depends on number of prescriptions filled

Q. *Now, the pharmacist told us that they have certain formulas for determining bonuses of people.*
A. Um-hum.

Q. *And one of the factors for bonuses of pharmacists—one of the factors considered are the number of prescriptions filled; is that correct?*
A. Yes....

Q. *Does the pharmacist in charge also—his bonus—depend on the number of prescriptions filled?*
A. A lot more so.

Q. *OK.*
A. I get—I get the—I get the big—well, they would say I get the big bucks. I'm not sure that's what it is, but they say I get the big bucks. So I'm the one that actually has to make sure that—that the sales are met. Like I just had an evaluation, you know, and they'll tell me how far I'm below on my—on my expectations as far as sales go. I got an e-mail yesterday that—how I stood on midweek sales. So **I'm pretty constantly, you know, being told about how I stand on my sales.**

Q. *And when you say sales, are you referring to prescriptions?*
A. Yes.

Q. *So we live in a capitalist society. The pharmacy wants to make as much money as they can, correct?*
A. And everybody else.

———— ∞ ————

Q. *Are y'all always busy at this pharmacy?*

A. Yes. Now, that was another thing I disagree with Kay [Kimball]. Kay says, you know, we are usually busy but sometimes, and I'm like, I don't have it that way, because my—my downtime, I'm doing—I'm doing something that needs to be done, you know, all the time. **I can barely find time to do the managerial stuff.** I have a really hard time doing that, because I'm— it takes two people to—to fill the prescription, the volume that we have there. And like I've told people many times, I say, we never — **we literally never catch up.** I've never gotten—I don't think I can remember a time when we didn't have a bag sitting there that we had to check. **There's bags there all the time.** Even late in the afternoon there's bags. And most nights I have to stay down there and—and I'll check those bags before I go home. So it's—it's real busy.

> **Practice Tip**
>
> Listen for memorable phrases in answers that you can use later as leverage for settlement or when at trial. Here, the witness admits:
>
> 1. "There are bags all the time."
>
> 2. "We literally never catch up."
>
> 3. "I'm constantly told how I stand on sales."
>
> 4. "I barely can do managerial stuff."

Brickman not only gets needed admissions, he probes for the motivation that explains the pharmacy's failure to counsel patients on drug side effects. Here, Brickman gets the details about putting sales ahead of customer safety that explain the problem.

Violates Pharmacy Practice Act

The Pharmacy Practices Act requires the pharmacist to consult with customers about prescription side effects. Brickman inquires why the supervisor does not follow it.

Q. *Now, you mentioned earlier that one of the reasons you're not able to follow the Act [Pharmacy Practices Act] is because you just don't get the opportunity.*

Defense Counsel: Object to the form.

By Brickman:

Q. *Do you recall that?*

A. **I am given the opportunity. I could—I could do that.**

Q. *Could do that?*

A. **I could do that, but then no one would get their medicine.**

Q. *You wouldn't get your bonus either, would you?*

A. No, it's a matter of people. The bonus—I've told them before, I say, I don't really care about—much about the bonus, but **I got people screaming at me to get their medicines out.**

Q. *OK.*

A. **Their children are crying, you know, and they want their medicine. And they get**—in a lot of cases, they could care less whether I talk to them or not.

Q. *You need more pharmacists?*
A. Everybody does, I think.

Q. **Do you need more pharmacists at your store in order to be able to do your job properly according to the Act?**
A. **According to the Act, I do. Yes.**

Q. *Now, you said you don't know whether a medicine is being prescribed for its intended use according to the manufacturer or for some other use, correct?*
A. Correct.

Q. *And so as a result, you're not certain whether the dosage is for some off-label use or the intended purpose, correct?*
A. Yes.

Q. **How do you find out which it is so that you can determine whether the dosage is correct as a pharmacist?**
A. **I don't look into that. I assume that the professional takes care of that.**

Q. **You don't make any reasonable effort to find out?**
A. **It's all—it happens all the time. No, I don't.**

Q. *You don't make any effort, do you?*
A. If it's—not really. No.

> ### Practice Tip
>
> By confronting the witness with the law, Brickman forces the witness to admit he did not follow the Act. The witness cannot avoid answering two simple but devastating questions: 1) Should you follow the law? and 2) Did you follow the law?

 In another part of the deposition, the supervisor would even admit that the pharmacy won't change, so his proposed solution is that the laws regulating pharmacists should change.

Brickman has achieved complete victory. The supervisor admits he needs more pharmacists in order to comply with the Pharmacy Practices Act. He then admits that he makes no effort to determine if the dosage is correct because he is relying on the doctor. He "assumes" the doctor has checked the dosage. Unfortunately, John was the victim of several incorrect assumptions by his doctor and the pharmacy.

Dr. Smith assumed the dialysis clinic would monitor for Methotrexate toxicity, so he gave a prescription that was outside the manufacturer's guidelines. Then, when John went to pick up his medication from the pharmacy, the pharmacists assumed that Dr. Smith had given the correct prescription, even though it was contrary to the guidelines in the pharmacy's own materials for Methotrexate. The only reasonable assumption made was by John, although it was a mistake. John assumed that his doctor would give him a safe drug to treat his skin rash and the pharmacy would give him a prescription that was safe to take, given his kidney disease.

After these depositions, the case quickly settled. Let's quickly review why Brickman was so successful. First, he knew the guidelines for prescribing Methotrexate and its required monitoring better than the doctor whose job it was to prescribe the drug correctly and who makes a living doing it. Likewise, for the pharmacists, Brickman knew the requirements for pharmacists to counsel customers about the dangers of their prescriptions better than the pharmacists who practice their craft every day. Third, Brickman knew the weaknesses of the computer system better than the pharmacists. In short, as revealed throughout this section, Brickman displays litigation skills at the very highest level.

In addition to all the lessons Brickman's depositions have taught us, perhaps the greatest lesson is that if we don't sincerely care about our client and aren't willing to put in the maximum effort to be prepared, we shouldn't take the case.

13.7 CHAPTER CHECKLIST

Brickman's general advice

1. "I find that the best lawyers are not the smartest but they are the ones that are best prepared, work the hardest, and put in the time."

2. His guiding principle for handling a case is that you need to be on the right side of the case, and the case needs to be interesting.

3. "The day of discovery depositions is long gone. So, as much as you can, you prepare for depositions as if they're going to be presented to juries."

4. "The only lawyers that don't lose are those who don't try any cases."

Brickman's advice for preparing for the deposition

1. Get as many documents as you can before taking a deposition. But don't wait for all the documents. You don't want opposing counsel to "fully understand" your case. You need to take the deposition as soon as possible during the discovery period.

2. "You have a theory of what you are going to try to prove, what you're going to try to get out of this deposition, and what you need to convince a jury that you have a meritorious case."

3. In cases where expert witnesses are needed, make sure you have the best. It is time-consuming, but find one who is recognized by peers in his field and is interested in what you are doing.

4. Too many lawyers walk into a deposition with just a blank legal pad of paper. "I don't care how smart you are, you are not off the top of your head going to do a good job."

Brickman's deposition advice

1. Think about two things: 1) What do you want to get out of the witness to make your case? and 2) What areas do you need to avoid to prevent the witness from hurting your case?

2. To lay the trap, ask questions that prove that the witness either did something that was against the law or did not know the law.

3. If the witness lies during the deposition, you should impeach him if you think the case will likely settle. Otherwise, save the surprise for trial.

4. Brickman expects the witness to be respectful and honest. But when the witness strays, Brickman does not hesitate to show he is in control: 1) know the law and facts better than the witness, 2) show righteous indignation with your tone of voice, and 3) inform the witness that his testimony will be displayed before jury.

Lessons to learn from Brickman's depositions

1. Brickman asks precise and simple questions.

2. His meticulous preparation makes his depositions read like devastating cross-examinations at a trial.

3. He listens intently to make sure the witness answers his question and is not evasive.

4. Knowledge is power. Brickman knows the facts and law better than the witness.

5. Brickman does not accept at face value the answer, "I don't recall."

6. To get an admission, use Brickman's technique: Know the facts better than the witness, know the law better than the witness, and when the witness does not answer the question, start the next question with, "That was not my question," and then repeat the question until it is answered.

7. Listen for memorable phrases in answers that you can use later as leverage for settlement or when at trial. Brickman gets the pharmacist supervisor to admit: "There are [prescription] bags all the time," "We literally never catch up," "I'm constantly told how I stand on sales," and "I barely can do managerial stuff."

8. By confronting the witness with the law, Brickman forces the witness to admit he did not follow the Pharmacy Practices Act. The witness cannot avoid answering two simple but devastating questions: 1) Should you follow the law? and 2) Did you follow the law?

CHAPTER FOURTEEN

—⊶∞∞⊶—

Don Tittle

The Purpose Driven Deposition

Detective Thompson has still destroyed my life, and he's still out there working cases. I want him held accountable. I want him brought down.

— Olivia Lord, wrongfully arrested for murder

---

*D*on Tittle is a determined fighter who has taken a particular interest in those whose civil rights have been violated by the police or the prison system. Soon after graduating from the University of Texas School of Law with honors, Tittle became a prosecutor to get trial experience. He explained that unlike many prosecutors, he often felt compassion for the defendant in the courtroom. He realized that everyone makes mistakes, and the unforgiving mindset of numerous prosecutors did not fit with his outlook. He added that where prosecutors often only saw black and white, he saw grey. He felt uncomfortable with all the resources the prosecution had and how few the defendant had.

Tittle related that another problem for criminal defendants is that too much conduct has become criminalized by the justice system. Moreover, while society often presumes that the defendant is guilty of the crime before the trial ever begins, Tittle points out that it is not that simple, that there are many factors that should merit a closer look before someone is charged with a crime or found guilty. While he greatly respects the work of the police, he does not put on blinders and "back the blue" without reservation.

Tittle left the Dallas District Attorney's Office and began his own law practice that evolved from representing criminal defendants to one where he has now become a pre-eminent civil rights attorney.

CHAPTER HIGHLIGHTS
- Use depositions to create a turning point at trial
- Develop the right demeanor: polite but firm and direct
- Beat the evasive witness

In addition to outstanding trial skills, Tittle has the unique right to tell a client who has been abused by police power, "I know exactly how you feel." This empathy comes from an experience he had soon after opening his law practice. Tittle was falsely charged with tampering with evidence regarding a client he was representing for a hit-and-run accident.

Although the grand jury refused to indict Tittle, for six months he had to face the publicity of being charged with a crime he did not commit. The rush to judgment in his quick arrest was followed by an overly aggressive police investigation when the police desperately tried to build a case against him, even though Tittle provided statements from judges and prosecutors that exonerated him.

The abuse of power, lack of reasoning, and failure to search for the truth by the police in Tittle's own case is something he has seen repeated in many cases he has handled since then. Over the past two decades, he has served as lead counsel in some of the most highly publicized cases of police misconduct and civil rights violations in Texas. More recently, since 2010, he has had five cases among *Texas Lawyer's* annual list of Top Texas Verdicts & Settlements.

A sampling of his victories includes a case that involved a scheme where police planted fake drugs on illegal immigrants and arrested them for drug possession. Many of the immigrants spent months in jail before the scheme was uncovered. Tittle took on the civil rights case and sued the police department. The multi-million dollar settlement Tittle obtained showed how even the most helpless and disadvantaged can receive justice if they have a skilled lawyer who cares.

Tittle represented another underdog when he filed suit for a female inmate who was repeatedly raped in jail by a prison guard. She felt powerless and thought no one would ever believe her. Tittle did. His victory in that case proved that those who abuse their power can be held accountable, no matter how vulnerable and weak the victim may appear to be.

Based on all of his experiences, Tittle has developed these insights about a police officer's testimony, whether given in court or at deposition: "Police officers will almost never say, 'I don't know, or I don't recall.' When they're pressed on an important issue, they will avoid saying one of those two answers and, instead, make something up."

But Tittle points out that the police officer who is reluctant to admit a lack of knowledge is really no different than any other expert who testifies.

Furthermore, Tittle believes, "I think the majority of all witnesses are telling some truths and some untruths. Police officers are no different. It's just that what they are testifying about is generally much more important than the testimony of the average witness. They're testifying about matters that pertain to a person's liberty, and so when they start fudging or exaggerating the truth, the ramifications are much greater."

Although police officers are human like everyone else, jurors tend to presume they are always telling the truth. In fact, many courts try to overcome this presumption by specifically instructing jurors that they should not believe the testimony of a police officer just because he is one. But the problem of the jurors' favorable presumptions toward the police persists. Tittle concludes, "Officers are not used to having their authority challenged in court. They develop an 'us against them mentality' that other witnesses don't have. When they go to trial, their team is the prosecutors and other cops and forensic people. That's their team, and they're going to win." Let's turn to one of Tittle's most fascinating cases where he beat the opposing team.

> *Whenever you suggest in your questions that a police officer has cut a corner or should have done something better, the officer will often make up something to defend his position instead of simply saying, "I don't know."*
> — Don Tittle

14.1 INTRODUCTION TO *LORD V. CITY OF DALLAS*

In this case, you will see one of the most dramatic turning points in any trial, and it was only made possible by Tittle's skillful questioning at a deposition. Tittle represented Olivia Lord in a civil lawsuit following her arrest for the murder of her boyfriend, Michael Burnside. A year after her arrest, a grand jury refused to indict her. She then filed a lawsuit against the arresting officer, Detective Thompson, alleging he knowingly arrested her without probable cause.

Throughout the civil lawsuit and during the trial, Detective Thompson and his legal team continued to insist that Olivia had committed murder. But in the closing arguments, Thompson's lawyer completely changed his strategy and admitted to the jury the very point that Tittle had been trying to prove: Olivia was innocent of murder.

When the defense lawyer made the apology, you could have heard a pin drop, if not for Olivia's gasp and breaking down in tears. Many jurors mirrored her emotions.

It was the first time in the four-year battle since her arrest that anyone from the Dallas Police Department had apologized to her, or in any way, even hinted that she had a valid complaint. Perhaps the most shocking thing about the apology was that Thompson's lawyer himself made it, even though Thompson, who was sitting next to him at counsel table, had only moments before testified that he still believed Olivia was guilty. It is not hard to imagine the dismay Thompson must have felt at this moment, but when your own lawyer turns against you, you know the ship is sinking fast.

This rarest of apologies had its genesis in Tittle's devastating deposition of Detective Thompson before trial. To understand why this turning point in the closing argument occurred, we need to gain some background about why Olivia was arrested, and Tittle's strategy in Thompson's deposition. Then we can explore how the deposition had such a dramatic effect on the trial.

14.2 MICHAEL BURNSIDE'S DEATH AND OLIVIA LORD'S ARREST

According to the police, at 12:38 a.m. on May 9, 2010, Michael Burnside, age thirty, was shot and killed in his home by an acquaintance, Olivia Lord, age thirty-three. Michael was the co-owner of a business that made houses more energy efficient. Olivia was a loan officer at a mortgage company. Officers responded to Olivia's 911 call when she said that she had found her boyfriend lying on the kitchen floor with a gunshot to his head.

When the police arrived, Olivia told them that she and Michael had spent most of the evening together and that a close friend of theirs, Brian Jaffe, had also been there shortly before the shooting. Olivia stated that she and Michael had been arguing. Having dated him for almost a year, she was upset that he was planning to go to Las Vegas for a bachelor's party. She was also angry because Michael was making a lot of effort to plan a birthday party for a friend when he had not planned a party for her recent birthday. During the argument, Brian left. Olivia walked her dog and then returned, and her argument with Michael continued.

She then went into the bathroom to remove her mascara. She heard a noise that sounded like broken glass coming from the kitchen. She walked out of the bathroom and saw Michael lying on the kitchen floor. She was confused and immediately called Brian. When she got on her knees and used her hands to inspect what was wrong, she discovered that Michael had been shot in the head (as it turns out by a 9 mm Beretta handgun). She claimed she immediately called 911.

Detective Thompson was suspicious. Michael's body had been found on the kitchen floor, but a 9 mm Beretta was five feet from his body, too far for someone who had shot himself and fallen to the floor. There were also pools of blood on the floor that did not explain why Olivia had called Brian before calling 911, given how serious his injuries appeared to have been. There were also towels and bottles of cleaning solution on the kitchen floor. Finally, there were drops of blood trailing away from the kitchen floor into another room which were not consistent with a suicide in the kitchen.

Detective Thompson examined Olivia's hands, and there was no blood on them despite her saying that she had not washed her hands. Detective Thompson also noticed that her body smelled like bleach or cleaning solution, as if she had used it to wash herself. Detective Thompson looked at Olivia's cell phone and found that she had waited seven minutes to call 911 after calling Brian. Why would she wait seven minutes to call for help? Michael was barely alive when paramedics arrived but died shortly after he was taken to the hospital.

Although Olivia wanted to go the emergency room to be with her dying boyfriend, the police informed Olivia that she would need to come to the police station to give a statement. The police contacted Brian and told him he needed to also come to the station. Detective Thompson would learn from Brian and Michael's family that Michael had a love for life and would never commit suicide.

But many of the "facts" that initially led Detective Thompson to suspect Olivia would unravel. A day after the shooting, Thompson discovered that Olivia had immediately called 911 after calling Brian. There was no seven-minute delay. Months later, a prosecutor handling the case learned that a fireman who had responded to the scene admitted he may have accidentally kicked the gun while it was on the ground. Olivia would explain that the drops of blood leading away from the kitchen came from her clothing after she went to Michael's limp body and then tried to walk around the house to get reception as she frantically called 911 multiple times.

Finally, Brian and Olivia told police that the towels and cleaning solutions were on the kitchen floor because they had emptied them from under the sink as they tried to fix it earlier in the evening. The evidence would also show that there was blood on Olivia's fingernails and hands which was consistent with Olivia's version that she did not wash her hands.

Detective Thompson was nicknamed D-Train. His colleagues "liked to say that when he pursued a suspect, he was as unstoppable as a locomotive." At the beginning of his shift, he would cheerfully announce, "Let's solve some murders, my brothers" and "Let's make a bad thing right." He was not only popular on the police force but also became popular on TV. *The First 48* is a reality TV show on A&E that follows detectives as they solve crimes. Thompson was featured in an episode on which he solved a murder where no body was found. It was one of the series' most popular episodes with over 2.3 million viewers. Producers told him that he was so charismatic on TV when he interrogated suspects or befriended witnesses that audiences mistook him for an actor playing a detective. Detective Thompson trained officers at the local Police Academy and led seminars across the country. He was a big proponent of "victimology," which is an investigation style that looks at the victim's behavior and relationships to help solve a crime, instead of focusing solely on the suspects.

According to Thompson, his big break in the case came twenty-eight days after the shooting. Michael's father called Thompson and told him that one of Michael's neighbors said that he had heard that another neighbor, Sheida Rastegar, had information that would prove Olivia was the killer. Thompson went to Rastegar's home. Rastegar said that he had heard screaming at Michael's house. He went outside his home, which was across the street from Michael's, and he spoke to Olivia in Michael's front yard before the police arrived. Olivia was distraught. She told him in so many words that she did not mean to shoot him, it was an accident. Rastegar said that he had tried to tell the police that night about the conversation but was told to go back inside his house.

Lord's arrest and prosecution

Based on this information, a month after the shooting, Detective Thompson submitted an affidavit for an arrest warrant. In order for the police to arrest someone for a felony they have not witnessed, they must write a sworn statement that explains the facts which support their belief that a crime occurred. This affidavit is presented to a judge who then issues an arrest warrant if he determines there is probable cause that a crime occurred. Once a judge reviewed Detective Thompson's affidavit, an arrest warrant was issued for Olivia. Olivia spent nine days in jail before posting bond.

At a subsequent hearing to determine probable cause on August 10, 2010, Detective Thompson testified about many of the facts above, and a judge again found there was probable cause that Olivia had committed murder. The next step for the prosecution was to present evidence to a grand jury for an indictment.

In the ensuing nine months, Olivia's criminal defense attorney, Joe Shearin, presented evidence of Olivia's innocence to the prosecutor handling the case and eventually to a grand jury. On May 11, 2011, the grand jury decided not to indict Olivia.

The revenge

When Joe Shearin called Olivia with the good news, she was grateful but added, "Who cares? Thompson has still destroyed my life, and he's still out there working cases. I want him held accountable. I want him brought down."

What Olivia wanted is no easy task. Just because a grand jury decided not to indict her did not mean that she could automatically recover civil damages. She hired Tittle. Tittle is not a zealot who will challenge the police for any reason. He believes that most officers do admirable work, but he is not afraid to take a case when justice demands it. Tittle knew he had to prove with facts—not mere accusations—that Thompson had intentionally or recklessly made false statements to the court and prosecutors in order to arrest Olivia, or that he left out significant facts that would prove Olivia's innocence. Thompson would later state that without Rastegar's statement, he did not believe he had probable cause to arrest Olivia.

Below is the section from Thompson's arrest affidavit related to this one fact:

> On Wednesday, June 9, 2010, a witness came forward. This witness is an attorney who resides across the street from the complainant [Michael Burnside]. This witness provided a recorded statement. He stated that on the night of the offense, the suspect made an excited utterance to him inferring that she did not mean to shoot the complainant.

Olivia brought two claims in her lawsuit. The first was that Thompson violated her Constitutional right to be free from an arrest without probable cause. To prove this claim, Olivia needed to show Thompson was more than simply negligent when he presented his sworn affidavit to the judge that stated there was probable cause to arrest her for murder. She had to prove that Thompson intentionally or with reckless disregard for the truth failed to provide the judge with information critical to a finding of probable cause, or else, misrepresented a known fact.

Olivia's second claim was that after her arrest, Thompson initiated a malicious prosecution against her. To prove this claim, Olivia had to prove that Thompson acted with malice in providing information to prosecutors in order for a grand jury to indict her. Malice means ill will or gross indifference to the rights of others.

Throughout discovery and at trial, the defense maintained Detective Thompson had only the highest level of professionalism to ensure that justice was done. Given this confidence, it is not surprising that the defense never offered any money to settle the case.

Before turning to Detective Thompson's deposition, we need to take a closer look at Rastegar's conversations with the police. He gave two statements, one at his home and the other at police headquarters. Both are summarized below.

Rastegar's first statement to police at his home

In an interview at Rastegar's home, Thompson learned that immediately after the shooting, Olivia went outside Michael's house and told Rastegar—who had left his house to investigate the noise—that she did not mean to shoot him, it was an accident. Neither Thompson nor his partner, Detective Lundberg, took notes.

Rastegar's second statement at police station

After the interview, Thompson asked Rastegar to come to the police station to give a recorded statement. When he arrived later that day (June 9, 2010), he was interviewed by Thompson's partner, Detective Lundberg. The interview was videotaped, and excerpts can be seen at www.TurningPointsatTrial.com.

Rastegar said that he had been lying in bed and heard a scream, so he went out his front door. He saw a girl he had never seen before and a fire truck slowing down like it was looking for an address. Rastegar ran to the woman [Olivia] and asked if she was OK, and she fell on her knees and said something to the effect of, "He's dying." Rastegar repeatedly stated that these were his "impressions" and he did not remember her exact words. Another "impression" was that Michael had been "shot in the head."

Rastegar told Lundberg that he had the "impression" that there was not another person in the house. Rastegar said he could not swear that Olivia had told him that she "didn't mean to shoot him."

Rastegar denied that Olivia had said something like, "I shot him in the head, but it was an accident." Rastegar explained, "The rest is surmise, is what I'm saying because there's only two people in the house, and he got shot in the head. And it was an accident. And now, later on, I find out — that part is later on. Later on, I find out there is a shot in the back of the head, then I surmise the accident happened like this (demonstrating by pointing his finger to the back of his own head)."

Rastegar told Lundberg that his entire conversation with Olivia lasted five seconds. Near the end of the interview, Thompson came into the room. Rastegar uses his index finger and points at the back of his head to demonstrate to Thompson and Lundberg how he thinks Michael was shot. It was something Rastegar had shown Lundberg five previous times before Thompson arrived.

14.3 DEPOSITION STRATEGIES

Before starting a deposition, Tittle always knows the legal and factual elements he will need to prove at trial or survive a summary judgment motion filed by opposing counsel before trial. To get this information, he relies on the jury charge the court will use at trial.

I asked Tittle what he does when he knows an officer is not telling the truth in the deposition. Does he prove that fact by showing him a document that is inconsistent with his testimony, or does he save the surprise for trial? Tittle explained that in civil litigation it is hard to save a surprise for trial because everyone has the opportunity to review all the evidence and witness testimony before trial.

Consequently, he usually does not wait to surprise the witness. Instead, Tittle will confront the witness with whatever document he has that proves he is lying. However, you won't find Tittle screaming. Tittle describes his demeanor in the deposition as "polite but direct. I'm not afraid, but I'm not a jerk."

Finally, I asked Tittle's opinion on videotaping depositions. Tittle points out that in an ideal world, you would video all of them. "But let's be real here. Expenses are an issue. I owe it to my client to think about the expenses." Consequently, Tittle videos the important witnesses, but won't video all the depositions, particularly if he can force the witness to testify live at trial.

> *The police officer will always be the good guy at trial. The best way to prove otherwise is to show the jury that he intentionally lied under oath at his deposition. It doesn't even have to be about the main issue in the case. Every time I can show the jury he lied, the jury becomes less inclined to give the officer the benefit of the doubt.*
> — Don Tittle

14.4 THOMPSON'S DEPOSITION

Now, let's analyze why Tittle's deposition later causes the turning point at trial. Tittle's greatest fear was that Thompson's lawyers would argue that Thompson had been sloppy in his investigation and that he had simply not chosen his words carefully enough when he described the Rastegar interview in his affidavit. The defense knew that Tittle had to prove more than just negligence. Tittle had to demonstrate that Thompson's statements were intentional and reckless.

Consequently, the best defense would be for Thompson to admit that he had made some mistakes, he's not perfect, and he regretted that Olivia had been wrongfully arrested. In addition, Thompson could point out that he had no motive to lie in order to get Olivia arrested. For example, he had no prior encounters with her. The defense did not choose this strategy.

Tittle believes it is very difficult to prove that police officers have lied. First, most jurors are willing to give the police the benefit of the doubt. Second, police officers are extremely reluctant to criticize each other, much less admit that a fellow officer has done something wrong. Tittle knew from experience it would be very difficult to find any officer who would criticize Thompson's work.

Since Tittle knew that Thompson would never admit he had lied in the arrest affidavit, Tittle's strategy was to show that Thompson had made a number of other incorrect statements. The more mistakes Tittle could prove, the more likely jurors would believe that the mistakes in the affidavit weren't accidental but intentional or reckless. In essence, the more smoke Tittle could find, the more likely he could prove there was fire.

> *Many lawyers just ask questions because they are in the lawyers' outline. Questioning a witness without a purpose drives me crazy.*
> — Don Tittle

Most attorneys waste precious time at the beginning of a deposition on questions that have nothing to do with the case. Tittle, however, starts by focusing on the critical statement in the arrest affidavit where Thompson says that Rastegar gave a recorded interview and related that Olivia admitted to accidentally shooting Michael.

Thompson appears at end of Rastegar's second interview

Q1. Did you observe that interview (Detective Lundberg's video interview of Rastegar at police station)? Were you in a room monitoring it or observing it?
A. No.

Q2. At what point did you see the videotape of it?
A. It was probably a week later.

Q3. When did you learn that Rastegar was of the belief that Michael had been shot in the back of the head? On the porch [**at the first interview**] *was he making those comments?*
A. No. It was — it was when I **watched** the interview a week later between he and Detective Lundberg.

Q4. Prior to that you had never heard any reference by Rastegar indicating that he believed Michael had been shot in the back of the head?
A. No.

Q5. Did Lundberg tell you anything about the interview? I mean, I would assume he's a key — you considered him one of the key or if not the key witness in the case, right?
A. Yes.

Q6. After the interview I assume you had some conversations with Lundberg, right?
A. Yes.

Q7. And what did Lundberg say about the interview?
A. It wasn't a long conversation. **He just very briefly told me that he kind of wavered** and he didn't — I'm just kind of summarizing what I believe that conversation to be. He may not have used those exact words but he had **kind of wavered** on what he said initially on the front porch, that he wasn't as specific as he was on the front porch.

Here, Tittle sets up Thompson for some very dramatic moments later at trial. Immediately after the shooting, Thompson repeatedly told Michael's friends, including Michael's business partner, that Michael had been shot in the back of the head, despite the fact that there was a contact wound to the right temple. This was an important mistake because for a contact wound to occur, the muzzle of the gun must be pressed up against the flesh when the trigger is pulled.

While it might be possible that you could commit suicide by pointing a gun at the back of your head, it is improbable due to the fact that you would have to contort your hand and arm and then still have enough leverage to pull the trigger. In any event, when Detective Thompson told people Michael was shot in the back of the head, his mistake gave people the impression that Michael had been murdered.

> *I'll bet my career on it, that she did it.*
> —Detective Thompson commenting to fellow officers

This rumor that Thompson started for some unknown reason would make its way around the neighborhood and eventually be heard by Rastegar. When Rastegar heard this incorrect information, he believed it could not have been suicide and that someone else must have pulled the trigger, and the only other person in the house was Olivia.

If Thompson had followed a smart strategy of claiming mere negligence, he could claim that his only mistake was to characterize Rastegar's statement too strongly in the arrest affidavit, since there was a video of the Rastegar interview showing Thompson appearing as Rastegar points to the back of his head. But Thompson did not tell the truth as evidenced by the answer to Q4 where Thompson states that he did not know that Rastegar ever was under the impression that Michael had been shot in the back of his head.

Second, in Q7, Thompson denies that he spoke at length with Detective Lundberg after the interview. Instead, there was only a "very brief" conversation. Instead of admitting the truth, which would not have hurt his arrest affidavit, Thompson's testimony would be undercut at trial when Lundberg would testify that he spoke to Thompson at length about the interview as soon as it was over. Lundberg believed that although Rastegar had wavered, he still provided strong evidence of Olivia's guilt.

Q. *If you had learned the information that he—that Rastegar had wavered during the interview prior to presenting it to Judge Lollar, it being the affidavit, do you believe that you would have wanted to modify the affidavit in any way?*
A. No.

Another goal of a deposition is to get the witness to make an outrageous statement like the one above. An outrageous statement is one that does not have the ring of truth to it. It is as good as getting the witness to admit he made a mistake and actually is even better. First, a jury won't believe a ridiculous statement. Second, by making the ridiculous statement, the witness won't receive any forgiveness from the jury for making a mistake but, instead, will be hammered by it for not telling the truth.

Thompson should have just said that although Rastegar wavered for most of the interview, at the end, he finally said the same thing that he had said at the first interview. Consequently, Thompson could claim that the significance of Rastegar's waver might be open to interpretation in hindsight but, at the time, he did not think it was that significant.

But Thompson doubles down and makes an outrageous statement. Here, it makes no sense that *if* he believed the *key* witness in the case had wavered, he was not obligated to present that information to a judge.

Next, Tittle gets Thompson to admit that without Rastegar's statement, he did not have probable cause to arrest Olivia.

Q. *At some point you determined that you had — you thought anyway — you had probable cause to get a warrant for her for murder?*
A. That's correct.

Q. *All right. When did you come to that conclusion?*
A. 28 days after I talked to Ms. Lord.

Q. *28 days is what? What is — what happened on the 28th day?*
A. Mr. Rastegar.

Q. *The conversation on the porch?*
A. Yes.

Thompson writes affidavit before Rastegar gives statement to police

Q1. *Lundberg did the interview* [**at the police station**] *of Rastegar prior to the affidavit, right?*
A. No.

Q2. *He did it after the affidavit?*
A. I had prepared the affidavit **before** Lundberg had interviewed Mr. Rastegar.

Q3. *Meaning you had input the information for the affidavit prior to Lundberg's interview?*
A. Yes.

By listening carefully to the witness' answers, Tittle develops a devastating fact against Thompson. Tittle learns in the answers to Q1 and Q2 that Lundberg's interview, which was mentioned in Thompson's affidavit, was conducted *after* Thompson had written the affidavit. If Thompson's affidavit were true, the interview would had to have occurred before the affidavit had been written. The actual sequence of events contradicts Thompson's sworn statement. In Q3, Tittle confirms what Thompson had just said to make sure the witness cannot later say he misunderstood the question.

Thompson's views on contact wound

Tittle then asks Thompson why he did not put the fact that there was a contact wound in the arrest affidavit. This omission was significant because two months after submitting the arrest affidavit, Thompson testified at the probable cause hearing that a contact wound was "consistent" with suicide.

Q. *Why didn't you put down any information [in the arrest affidavit] that it was a contact wound to the right temple?*
A. Because it was irrelevant in regards to whether or not — **the contact wound doesn't mean that — it doesn't mean anything. It doesn't mean anything, so it was irrelevant in regards to my probable cause** that I had to take before a magistrate to show why I felt that she committed murder.

Q. *Isn't a contact wound to the right temple by a right-handed person at a slightly upward trajectory more consistent with a suicide than a homicide?*
A. No.

How would Thompson try to get out of this trap? Obviously, he knows that if the wound was consistent with suicide, he should have put that in the arrest affidavit. Watch what he does and see how persistent Tittle is.

Q. *Well, look, Officer, I'm giving you an opportunity to go through here and — this was sworn testimony* [**at the probable cause hearing**].
A. Right.

Q. *At a time when the woman was staring life in prison in the face.*
A. Right.

Q. *This was your sworn testimony. So you seem to be going through and changing a fair amount of it now.*
A. Well, you gave me the opportunity to do it.

Q. *I'm asking — **well, it doesn't mean your sworn testimony is just out the window.** I'm just asking you in what way would it be more complete, and I'm going to continue to give you that opportunity —*
A. Right.

Q. *How is it that on that question that you're asked in the examining trial about —*
A. Sir, I'm a human being just like anybody else. I'm not perfect. So because I testified this way on that date doesn't mean that it was perfect or that there was some words that I may have used that were inappropriate, and having said that on that question, you just said is it more consistent, and I would say no. **I should have said no that day, but I didn't.**

Q. *So what would your—if you were just completely going to get a do-over on that answer, how would you answer it today? Let's read the question that was asked.*

A. [**Thompson reads the question from the probable cause hearing**] "The question is, Because in a suicide it's more consistent with a suicide contact wound, correct, and I said, That is correct." **It's not correct.**

Tittle was in disbelief at the change in sworn testimony. Tittle now realized that Thompson would change his sworn testimony in an effort to support his arrest of Olivia. While Thompson thought he was helping his case, he actually was falling into Tittle's trap. The more he changed prior sworn testimony and the more outrageous statements he made, the more it would prove that his statement in the arrest affidavit was intentional or reckless. Thompson should have just said what is obvious to anyone whether you are a police officer or not: a contact wound is consistent with suicide.

Consequently, Thompson's better answer at the deposition would have been to admit that a contact wound could indicate suicide, but he was focused on the recent statement by Rastegar which linked Olivia to the murder. Because he was focused on the Rastegar statement, he probably should have mentioned the nature of the wound in the affidavit. Besides, just because it is a contact wound does not mean that Olivia could not have shot Michael at point blank range.

Tittle presses forward to confirm that Thompson was really changing his previous sworn testimony from the probable cause hearing.

Q. *And it is at least consistent with a suicide if the shot is to the right temple and is a contact wound, is it not?*

A. I just testified that—

Q. *You're saying that's not consistent?*

A. I just testified that it was not, and I find it offensive that you would ask me that question twice while I already previously testified that it's not.

Q. *I don't mean to offend you but I find—*

A. Well, I've just—I've answered it twice.

Q. *OK. I don't mean to offend you.*

A. OK. Thank you.

Q. *I'm—**but if you're offended by questions being asked twice, watch your interview of Ms. Lord**.*

A. Well, that's what I get paid to do.

As an aside, Tittle reminds Thompson of his interview with Olivia. In that interview, Thompson repeatedly accuses her of killing Michael. He yells

---

Practice Tip

You need to be firm in the deposition. You are in charge, not the witness.

at her, curses at her, and intimidates her. Olivia repeatedly sobs, claims her innocence, and says that she loved Michael. You can view excerpts of Olivia's interview at www.TurningPointsatTrial.com.

Tittle then asks Thompson a few questions about that interview, and Thompson gives another outrageous answer.

Q. You, on the very night of this incident, knowing that it was a contact wound to the temple, accused her of being the killer, right?
A. Yes, I did.

Q. Did you believe that at the time that you were saying that to her, did you believe that she was the killer?
A. I don't know.

Q. Can you amplify that answer at all?
A. No.

Q. So you — as of the time that you're interviewing her, you couldn't say that she was the killer even though you were accusing her of being the killer?
A. I don't know.

It is ridiculous for Thompson to answer, "I don't know." Either Thompson considered her a suspect or not. Those are the only two answers. In the interview, Thompson said, "I do believe you killed him. I believe it with all my heart." The lesson is that if you can get the witness to give an outrageous answer, it is better than a confession because it will just get the jury angrier, since the witness is not forthcoming.

Thompson's better answer at the deposition would have been to say that he thought she was the killer and that was why he was trying to intimidate her into a confession. That would have been believable. And although it may or may not have been a correct assumption, it did not mean he would intentionally mislead a judge with his arrest affidavit.

> **Practice Tip**
> Often a witness becomes defensive and, instead of answering truthfully, he gives a misleading answer he thinks will help him but actually hurts because a jury will punish the witness a lot more for lying than for admitting to a mistake.

Conversations about blood spatter evidence

Q. Is it true that you had a conversation with the medical examiner prior to doing the affidavit about the blowback bloodstain evidence?
A. I don't recall when I had a conversation with the medical examiner.

Q. Did you ever tell Dr. Quinton that the blow-back evidence had been tested and indicated that Ms. Lord had blow-back evidence on her?
A. I don't know.

Q. And it's—and during that conversation with the doctor, assuming that you had one, do you recall the conversation coming up about blow-back bloodstain evidence?
A. No.

Q. If the claim is made that you told him that the blow-back evidence had come back indicating that it was on Ms. Lord, and you told that to the medical examiner's office, would you deny having said that?
A. Yes, I would.

Q. Because the blow-back evidence hadn't even been tested, had it?
A. That's correct.

Blood spatter occurs when the pressure from the muzzle blast hits another body at close range and blows back the fluid from the body on to the hand or clothing of the person firing the gun. Usually, the blowback splatters small blood droplets that have traveled at a high velocity. It is a critical piece of evidence if it exists.

The medical examiner would testify at trial that on June 7, 2010—just two days before Thompson submitted his arrest affidavit—Thompson called him about his autopsy finding of "pending." Thompson described that there was now blood spatter evidence on Olivia's clothing which was *inconsistent* with Olivia's claim that she was in another room when the shooting occurred. The Medical Examiner said this was the main reason he changed his finding on the autopsy from "pending" to "homicide."

Nonetheless, Thompson at first indicates he does not know whether he had this conversation with the Medical Examiner. Tittle doesn't accept the vague answer, "I don't know." He forces Thompson to admit that he would remember having such a conversation if it had occurred.

Thompson tells prosecutors that Olivia fled to California

Aside from the arrest affidavit, Olivia also sued Thompson for malicious prosecution for the false statements he made in his prosecution report which he submitted to prosecutors after he arrested her. Prosecutors rely on a detective's prosecution report to decide whether or not to seek an indictment against someone. Let's examine how Tittle builds his case.

Q. Detective, in your prosecution report, you indicated that you discovered that the suspect had fled to Palmdale, California. Do you recall making that reference?
A. Yes.

Q. What led you to the conclusion that she had fled? Well, let me back up. The word "fled" would indicate someone who is trying to get away. Do we agree on that?
A. Yes.

Q. I mean, I'm — just so we don't have a semantic argument later, you're — that was put in here to indicate that she is trying to run from the situation or get way from the situation as opposed to simply going somewhere on a trip?
A. Yes.

Q. OK. What led you to the conclusion that she had fled to California?
A. The day before — the day before I obtained the probable cause affidavit for an arrest, I was back at [Michael's house] with crime scene technicians.... And it was a full-blown deal where there was a lot of [crime scene] vans and things. Well, I had received a phone call from Mr. Jaffe, and Mr. Jaffe had told me something along the lines that Ms. Lord had seen us there, and this is the day before I do the [affidavit] for arrest.... Mr. Jaffe had told me that — and I don't know how he came to know it, but that she was either on a plane or preparing to get on a plane to go to California or Florida.... That's why I put that in [the prosecution report].

∞∞ —

Q. You wouldn't dispute, would you, that placing the phrase that someone is trying to flee to California, that that creates a very strong — that creates an implication of guilt?
A. Yes.

— ∞∞ —

Q. You had come to learn that she had pre-paid tickets for a couple of weeks?
A. I don't know. I don't know what she had.

Q. Wouldn't it matter to you?
A. Not necessarily.

Q. So she was planning to flee with her — and she was traveling with nieces or nephews, wasn't she?
A. I don't know who she was traveling with.

Q. Would that matter to you?
A. No.

Thompson tries to create a presumption of guilt by suggesting that Olivia fled to California when she saw the police at Michael's house. Tittle undercuts this theory by questioning Thompson on the fact that Olivia had bought the plane tickets two weeks before the police even arrived at Michael's house. Also, she was traveling with children, hardly a way to escape without notice.

PARTIAL SUMMARY OF THOMPSON'S ADMISSIONS, CONTRADICTED STATEMENTS, AND OUTRAGEOUS STATEMENTS

Helpful admissions

1. Without Rastegar's statement, there was no probable cause for arrest. (Narrows issues for trial.)

2. Affidavit was written before Rastegar's recorded interview. (Affidavit states it was based on recorded interview.)

3. Admits he testified incorrectly at probable cause hearing about contact wound. (Shows mistaken testimony given under oath.).

Incorrect

4. Unaware that Rastegar believes Michael shot in back of head. (Video shows Thompson present for critical portion of interview.)

5. Detective Lundberg only briefly discussed Rastegar interview with Thompson. (Lundberg testified that he gave full debriefing to Thompson.)

6. Claims he did not tell Medical Examiner that the blood spatter evidence on Olivia's clothing indicated she shot the gun. (Medical Examiner would testify he clearly remembered this conversation, and that is why he changed autopsy finding from pending to homicide.)

Outrageous

7. A contact wound is not consistent with suicide.

8. If Rastegar had wavered, Thompson did not need to alert judge.

9. When asked whether he believed Olivia was the killer when he accused her in her interview, he said, "I don't know."

10. Thompson alleged that Olivia "fled" to California when she saw crime scene technicians come to Michael's house even though she had bought plane tickets to California 13 days earlier.

Thompson's failure to investigate Michael's financial problems

Q. Did you look into whether **[Michael]** *had any IRS issues or any problems with the IRS?*
A. No.

Q. Would — if he had, would you consider those to be financial difficulties?
A. I don't know.

Q. Well, if someone owed a substantial amount of money to the IRS do you — would that cut against what Michael's dad was telling you? [that Michael did not have any financial problems]
A. Not necessarily....

Detective Thompson believed that Michael was doing well in business, in part from his interview with Michael's parents. Why didn't Thompson just admit that if Michael had been in financial difficulty with the IRS, such a fact would have been important? If he had answered this way, it would be just an indication that Thompson was not thorough by failing to check with the IRS.

Tittle relates that Michael had received letters from the IRS demanding $50,000 for back taxes he owed. He also owed a rental car company money for a car he wrecked. Thompson's disingenuous answer of "not necessarily" helps Tittle prove that if Thompson cannot give a straight answer to a lot of simple questions, then he must have intentionally lied in the arrest affidavit.

Thompson does not believe Olivia is Michael's girlfriend

Q. To your knowledge, did Ms. Lord have any financial incentive for him to die?
A. I don't know.

Q. Well, that's a fairly common motive in a homicide, right?
A. (Nods head.)

Q. Something that you would investigate with regard to a situation like this, isn't it?
A. No.

Q. Did she stand to profit?
A. No.

Q. You wouldn't look at that?
A. Not in this case....

Q. OK. Why not?
A. Because she wasn't — she was — she wasn't anyone significant to him.

Q. They were about to move in together. Did anyone tell you that?
A. That's not true.

Q. It wasn't true?
A. No, that's not true. His family will tell you that that's not true.

Q. *Sounds like you placed a lot of emphasis on what the family of Michael Burnside told you?*

A. Well, when you conduct victimology, sir, you come to know who are close to the victims, who his primary relationships are, secondary relationships are, and through these people I learned that he and his father were very close.

Q. *What was Michael's relationship with Ms. Lord?*

A. She was just a girl to him. **She was just someone that he knew.**

Q. *Not a—well, from your investigation, did you determine that she was his girlfriend?*

A. Not necessarily.

Q. *Something that you would—you would not classify her relationship with Michael as that of a girlfriend?*

A. No.

Q. *What was it?*

A. I believe she wanted it to be more. That's what the argument was about that night is that she didn't feel that Michael was treating her like what she wanted to be. Where, in fact, Michael was just kind of enjoying himself.

When Thompson declared that Olivia was not Michael's girlfriend, Tittle knew that Thompson would say anything if he thought it would help him. Tittle said that everyone knew that Olivia was Michael's girlfriend. Perhaps Michael's mother and father did not want to admit it, but all of Michael's friends confirmed that they were practically living together. In particular, on the night of the shooting, Michael's friend since high school, Brian Jaffe, told Thompson that Olivia was Michael's girlfriend, and she was about to move in with him.

Thompson's belief that parents easily accept a child's suicide

Q. *Do you find that it's difficult often for parents to accept that their child might have committed suicide?*

A. No.

Q. *You don't?*

A. No, sir.

Q. *Because I notice when Junior Seau died recently, you know, they indicated that that was a suicide. Immediately I remember hearing the parents, they think there was foul play. I heard that many, many times. Would you say that my—my view on that subject is just way off?*

A. Yes....

Tittle gets Thompson to make another outrageous statement: It's easy for parents to accept that a child has committed suicide. He then relates the question to a current event that the jury will understand and remember when it views the deposition. Despite the comparison to the football player Junior Seau, Thompson still disagrees with Tittle.

Thompson does not know the legal limit for intoxication

Q. *During the **victimology**, did you learn anything about his drinking habits?*
A. I learned that he liked to enjoy a drink.

Q. *.20 in your blood when it was tested a number of hours after your death would indicate that it was at a very high level at the time of his death, wouldn't you agree?*
A. Not necessarily.

Q. *No. What would it indicate to you, that it was under the legal limit?*
A. That he was at home drinking.

Q. *.20 is, what, almost triple the legal limit?*
A. I don't know.

Q. You don't know what the legal limit is?
A. No.

Q. *Well, how much would it indicate — it — it has to mean something to you as a detective, doesn't it, that the guy who has a gunshot wound to his right temple is a .20?*
A. It meant to me that a man was in his home enjoying the fact that he had just closed a big business deal and that he was enjoying drinks. That's all that it meant.

Q. *Really? It didn't mean that he was extremely intoxicated?*
A. No.

Q. No. Well, if you had believed he was extremely intoxicated, would that have played any factor in your mind as to what happened?
A. Absolutely not.

Michael's previous incidents of playing with guns

Q. *Did you learn anything about his propensity to get a little reckless with guns when he'd been drinking? Did anyone make that comment to you?*
A. Not necessarily the way that you said it.

Q. *Well, in what way did someone say something along those lines?*
A. I questioned Jaffe, and I was the one that raised that line of questions. Because it was important to me to know.

Q. *And Jaffe confirmed that he did — that the guy —*
A. I hadn't finished answering the question.

Q. *OK. Go ahead.*
A. And Jaffe had said to me that he had to…basically get on him about the manner in which he was handling a gun…. I didn't interpret that to be where he said that there was multiple incidents of [Michael being] reckless with a handgun. I interpret that

as he told me that there was a specific incident, and I don't know whether it was that night or a previous night, that he was reckless with a handgun but, mind you, I raised that question. I interpret that as he told me that there was a specific incident, and I don't know whether it was that night or a previous night, that he was reckless with a handgun, but mind you, I raised that question.

Q. He being Michael Burnside?
A. Yes.

Thompson was very proud of his skills at solving murders through "victimology." Thompson believed that by studying the personality and relationships of the victim, he could learn who had killed the victim. Tittle jumped on Thompson's theory and challenged his conclusions. Tittle points out that a .20 blood alcohol level several hours after death is almost three times the legal limit of .08. Unbelievably, Thompson, who is an experienced detective, claims he does not know what the legal limit for alcohol is.

He then goes further out on a limb by claiming that .20 means that Michael was just at home enjoying a drink to celebrate a business deal. He then doubles down again and says that even if he thought Michael were extremely drunk, it would not have made any difference in his conclusion about what happened.

Given these two incredible answers, Tittle gives Thompson the chance to do it a third time, and he does. Thompson says that even though he had learned that Michael had been reckless with a handgun either the night of his death or a previous night, it was not a factor in his investigation.

Thompson testifies in this manner even though Jaffe had told him on the night of the incident that Michael had pulled out a gun while he had been drinking earlier in the evening. In addition, Jaffe told Thompson he had seen Michael playing with guns two or three times before, and one time Michael was pointing the gun recklessly as if he were certain it was unloaded without checking it.

Grand jury decision does not persuade Thompson

Q. As you sit here today, do you believe that Ms. Lord shot Michael?
A. Yes, I do.

Q. So you do not believe this was a self-inflicted gunshot wound?
A. No, sir.

Q. Since the date that the Dallas County grand jury no billed it, have you attempted to take it back to the grand jury?
A. No.

Q. It's just your ongoing opinion that she, in fact, killed him?
A. Yes.

Perhaps the most outrageous statement made in his deposition was Thompson's insistence that Olivia was still guilty of murder despite the grand jury's opposite conclusion—a no bill. A more reasonable defense would have been that Thompson agreed with the grand jury's conclusion or, at least, would respect its conclusion.

Thompson does not know definition of exculpatory evidence

Q. Do you have to include exculpatory information in an affidavit?
A. I'm sorry?

Q. Do you —
A. Simplify.

Q. —know what—exculpatory information is?
A. Would you simplify that for me?

Q. Any evidence that tends to negate the guilty or negates probable cause.
A. Now, your question again was?

Tittle's entire strategy has been to prove that since Thompson made so many inaccurate or outlandish statements during the investigation, he must have intentionally or with reckless disregard of the truth made a misleading statement about the Rastegar interview in his arrest affidavit. Here, Detective Thompson pretends not to know the definition of exculpatory evidence. Every rookie police officer knows its definition. We can only speculate why Thompson would make such a statement, but perhaps the best reason is that it fits in with his pattern of assuming that Olivia committed murder when he arrived on the scene on May 9, 2010. From then on, he believed the end justified the means. So, for this line of questions, he was going to fight Tittle on every question he asked.

14.5 SUMMARY OF TITTLE'S TACTICS

Tittle knew his case inside and out. Whenever he saw a chance to challenge Thompson with facts he knew that he could prove, he did. This forced Thompson to make up inaccurate or outrageous statements to defend his actions.

> *When a witness is highly defensive and hell-bent on not giving an inch, that mentality gets the witness in trouble quickly in a deposition.*
> —Don Tittle

Tittle also listened carefully for ridiculous answers and made it clear to Thompson, and later to the jury, that such answers were unbelievable. For example, what officer doesn't know the legal limit for alcohol or wouldn't accept a grand jury's decision not to indict. Finally, Tittle listened for helpful admissions which are listed below. Many attorneys get information from a deposition and don't know what to do with it. Tittle will use the admissions to narrow the issues for trial and focus his cross-examination.

FINAL SUMMARY OF THOMPSON'S ADMISSIONS, CONTRADICTED STATEMENTS, AND OUTRAGEOUS STATEMENTS

Helpful admissions

1. Without Rastegar's statement, there was no probable cause for arrest. (Narrows issues for trial.)

2. Affidavit was written before Rastegar's recorded interview. (Affidavit states it was based on recorded interview.)

3. Admits he testified incorrectly at probable cause hearing about contact wound. (Shows mistaken testimony given under oath.)

Contradicted statements

4. Unaware that Rastegar believes Michael was shot in back of head. (Video shows Thompson present for critical portion of interview.)

5. Detective Lundberg only briefly discussed Rastegar interview with Thompson. (Lundberg testified that he gave full debriefing to Thompson.)

6. Claims he did not tell Medical Examiner that the blood spatter evidence on Olivia's clothing indicated she shot the gun. (Medical Examiner would testify he clearly remembered this conversation, and that is why he changed autopsy finding from pending to homicide.)

7. Olivia was not Michael's girlfriend. (Multiple people said the opposite.)

Outrageous statements

8. A contact wound is not consistent with suicide.

9. If Rastegar had wavered, Thompson did not need to alert judge.

10. When asked whether he believed Olivia was the killer when he accused her in her interview, he said, "I don't know."

11. Thompson alleged that Olivia "fled" to California when she saw crime scene technicians come to Michael's house, even though she had bought plane tickets to California thirteen days before.

12. The fact that Michael owed $50,000 in back taxes to the IRS did "not necessarily" show that he had financial problems.

13. Does not find that it is difficult for parents to accept that their child may have committed suicide.

14. Does not know the legal limit for intoxication.

15. The fact that Michael had an alcohol level of .20 in his blood only meant he was enjoying a drink in his home.

16. The fact that Michael had been known to play with guns was not a factor in his investigation.

17. Olivia was guilty of murder despite grand jury's decision to the contrary.

18. Pretends not to know the definition of exculpatory evidence. (It is evidence that tends to prove someone's innocence, a definition any officer would know.)

14.6 THE CIVIL TRIAL

Now that we have reviewed Thompson's deposition, let's see how Tittle used it to set up the turning point at the trial. First, let's look at an excerpt of defense counsel's opening statement. Watch and see what tone she sets for the trial.

14.7 DEFENDANT'S OPENING STATEMENT

Defense Co-counsel: As you heard Mr. Tittle tell you, he believes the evidence will show that Detective Thompson intentionally, knowingly or with reckless disregard for the truth, committed acts that resulted in the deprivation of Ms. Lord's Constitutional rights.

Mr. Tittle also believes that Detective Thompson maliciously caused Olivia Lord to be prosecuted because no reasonable police officer could have believed that probable cause existed based on the information and facts known to Detective Thompson at the time. We believe that the evidence will show that Mr. Tittle is wrong.

Detective Thompson will tell you that contrary to Mr. Tittle's characterization of him, that **he's a conscientious detective**, that he was doing the best job that he could under a very stressful and difficult situation and that he investigated this case to the best of his abilities, and rather than being motivated by ill will or malice or bad motive, he was motivated by a desire to do the right thing, to get at the truth, to make sure and ensure that justice had occurred, not only for the victim, Michael Burnside, but also for Ms. Lord, to ensure that her civil liberties were not violated.

He will tell you that he's suffering as a result of this lawsuit, too, because it is his reputation that is on the line.

At the close of the evidence, we will ask that you return a verdict in favor of Detective Thompson and all the claims that Ms. Lord has brought against him.

We thank you for your service and the time that we know that you will give this case.

Thank you.

There is no explanation why defense counsel would make such an argument after Thompson's deposition. But her words would come to haunt her in closing arguments. It was a devastating mistake for counsel to tell the jury that Thompson was suffering as well as Olivia. There was no reason to think the facts would support such a claim at trial, and they did not. As mentioned at the beginning of this chapter, Thompson's lawyers would distance themselves as far as they could from Thompson's actions in closing argument. But before we get to that dramatic moment, let's watch how Tittle used the deposition against Thompson during his cross-examination.

14.8 CROSS-EXAMINATION OF DETECTIVE THOMPSON

Detective Thompson was called as a hostile witness by Tittle at trial. Although technically the excerpts below are from his direct examination by Tittle, it is really a cross-examination. When a party calls a hostile witness to the stand, the court allows the attorney to use leading questions — as you would do in a cross — to question the witness. Watch how Tittle uses Thompson's admissions, contradicted statements, and outrageous statements taken at Thompson's deposition to create a devastating cross-examination.

By Tittle:

Q1. *All right. Detective Thompson, we've been* [in trial] *since Thursday morning with evidence. You've now heard everything that has been testified to in this courtroom, correct?*

A. That's correct.

Q2. *You haven't done any further investigation into the death of Michael Burnside since July 2, 2012* [the date of his deposition], *have you?*

A. No, I have not.

Q3. *And with everything you've heard in this case, is it still your belief that Olivia Lord murdered Michael Burnside?*

A. Yes, it is.

Q4. *There hasn't been one bit of evidence in this case that has caused you to even — has caused you pause, in your opinion, that she murdered Michael?*

A. No, sir.

Q5. *Now, Detective, it's true, isn't it, that you've made a number of false statements under oath in this case?*

A. No, that's not true.

Tittle sets up Thompson for a devastating cross. In Q1, Tittle wants the jury to hear Thompson admit that he has heard all of the evidence at trial (He had been sitting at defense counsel table because he was the defendant). In Q2, he sets the trap for Q3. He wants to confirm that Thompson has not done any further investigation since his deposition on July 2, 2012. In his deposition, Thompson admitted that he believed Olivia was guilty of murder despite the grand jury's decision not to indict her.

In Q3, Tittle turns the focus to the evidence presented at trial. If Thompson answers that after hearing the evidence at trial, he now believes Olivia is innocent, the admission proves that she never should have been arrested because the evidence at trial consisted of information Thompson had known or should have known before he submitted the affidavit for her arrest. This is what Thompson should have done. It would have allowed the defense to argue that Thompson conducted a flawed investigation, but not one that rose to the level of making *intentional* misleading statements to get Olivia arrested.

But Tittle knew that Thompson was not reasonable and had made so many incredible statements in his deposition that he would answer that his opinion had not changed. His refusal to be open to changing his mind proved that, for whatever reason, he intentionally made misstatements in order to get Olivia arrested.

In Q4, Tittle highlights for the jury what he has already asked in Q3. He wants to emphasize that there is not one piece of evidence that has made Thompson reconsider his conclusion of Olivia's guilt.

In Q5, Tittle then pivots to his second topic: Thompson's lies. Thompson denies he has lied under oath in the past. Tittle knows he won't get Thompson to confess to lying, but wants to show the jury the past inaccurate statements by confronting Thompson with prior sworn statements that were made: 1) in his probable cause affidavit which was filed to get Olivia's arrest warrant, 2) at the preliminary hearing, 3) at his deposition, and 4) in a second affidavit he submitted with a response to a summary judgment motion filed by his lawyers in the civil lawsuit.

Q. *You have sworn under oath in a deposition that I took of you in this case, right?*
A. Yes, sir....

Q. *And every time you've given sworn testimony you've understood that you were under oath; is that right?*
A. That is correct.

Q. *And you understand the penalty involved for giving — for knowingly giving false testimony under oath, right?*
A. Yes, sir.

Tittle locks the witness in to the fact that his prior statements at his deposition were given under penalty of perjury.

Q. *You've heard testimony in this case—you've heard the recorded interviews. You heard Brian Jaffe* [**Michael's good friend**] *say it that night. You've heard Olivia say it. And it is your testimony, taking all of that into consideration, that you do not know what their relationship is, you can't say?*
A. That's correct.

Q. *You have actually denied under oath* [**in the deposition**] *that she was even his girl-friend, correct?*
A. **I did that for a reason....**

Q. **You testified under oath that she was not his girlfriend, right?** [**Tittle repeats question**]
A. **That's correct.**

Practice Tip When a witness does not answer a simple question, repeat it until he does.	Tittle gets Thompson to admit that at his deposition he denied that Olivia was Michael's girlfriend when that was not the evidence. When Thompson tries to wiggle out of answering the simple question, Tittle repeats it to force the witness to give a direct answer.

His deposition answer became even more incredible after Olivia had testified at trial. Anyone who watched her testimony would have seen that Olivia sincerely loved Michael, he loved her, and that they were practically living together. In addition, other witnesses confirmed this relationship.

Tittle then turned to the arrest affidavit.

Q. *And, in fact, you have testified that you did not believe you had probable cause in this case until the Rastegar statement, right?*
A. That's correct.

Q. *So to clarify, without Rastegar, no probable cause?*
A. Without Rastegar I wouldn't have filed a case, exactly.

This question was set up by Thompson's deposition testimony where Tittle locked Thompson into the position that his break in the case came 28 days after the shooting when he interviewed Rastegar on his porch. Without getting that critical information at the deposition, Tittle could not create this dramatic moment at trial which was now even more important because of what had happened earlier at trial.

Thompson's partner, Dale Lundberg, testified at trial that he had *fully* briefed Thompson on his interview with Rastegar immediately following the interview. In his deposition, Thompson had denied this had ever occurred. On

Tittle's cross-examination at trial, Thompson maintained that his only discussion with Lundberg was at the conclusion of the interview where Lundberg had told him in a *brief few seconds* that Rastegar had wavered a little bit.

Knowing Thompson's deposition inside and out, Tittle built on this fact to show that Thompson should not have relied on Rastegar in the arrest affidavit when he had wavered and was of low character.

> Q. *And, in fact, you even have testified that at the same time that Lundberg was telling you he wavered and we need to talk,* **you had already described Rastegar as a person of very low character; isn't that true? Those are your exact words in your deposition?**
>
> A. **That's right. I did say that**.... May I have the opportunity to explain that? The reason why I said he was of low character...is because when we went to Mr. Rastegar's home.... I made a critical mistake, I thought. I thought [since Rastegar was a criminal defense attorney], he would be a credible person.... I made a statement about low character, because I chastised him because he said, "I didn't want to come forward, and I didn't want to be involved." So, I was upset that here's this man that's supposed to be a criminal defense attorney and has had this information all of this time and did nothing with it.

But Tittle doesn't let Thompson get the last word in. He uses the deposition to hammer home his point.

> Q. **In your deposition, you stated after his interview with Lundberg, meaning Rastegar, "It was very obvious to me that he was a man with very low character." You said, "Not necessarily his credibility; he just had bad character." Now, that's what you knew before you went to the Judge with the affidavit to get her charged with murder, right?**
>
> A. **That's correct.**
>
> Q. *And Lundberg has told you he's wavered and we need to talk, right?*
>
> A. That's correct.

Rastegar's reliability given his mistaken impression about shooting

> Q. *Isn't it true that in your testimony, in your deposition, you testified that you were not even aware that Mr. Rastegar was under the belief that Michael had been shot in the back of the head until a week after the recorded interview?*
>
> A. One more time, please.
>
> Q. *You learned that Rastegar was of the belief that Michael had been shot in the back of the head when you watched* **[a week later]** *the interview between him and Lundberg, correct?*
>
> A. That is correct....
>
> Q. *Now, that, in fact, is a false statement, is it not? Because we have a photo of you in the room with Rastegar, and he's pointing at the back of his head?*
>
> A. [Witness does not answer question.]

Q. Well, how significant is it to you that Rastegar was under the belief that Mike had been shot in the back of the head?

A. **It had no significance** because I didn't know where he got that from. I didn't know where he got that from, but the mere fact that he believes that he was shot in the back of the head had nothing at all to do with what he's telling us, especially what he said on the front porch about what he was told....

Q. Doesn't it go toward his reliability?

A. Mr. Tittle, I've sat in this courtroom, and I've listened to a lot of people who's come up here and testified and has no credibility and completely lied right up here on this stand. I've been here for a whole week.... So, I'm not going to make any separation between Mr. Rastegar and any of the other criminal defense attorneys that I've heard here, because I've heard perjury in this courtroom. So I believe in what Mr. Rastegar said. And even though he may not have been absolute in regards to what he saw or what he heard, I believe that that night, Ms. Lord said what she said to him. Now, his ability to recall it and describe it, that's another thing. But I believe that he heard what he heard.

Q. We can agree on something. We can both agree we've heard perjury in this courtroom.

A. I can agree—I can say that I've heard perjury. And if you're saying that I'm committing perjury, I'm not about to go into any courtroom and put my 22 years on the police department on the line for anybody. I've never committed perjury, and I'm not going to commit perjury. I have a reputation, whether or not you believe that, one that I care about.

The outrageousness of the statement he made at his deposition is emphasized at trial. The fact that Rastegar was under the mistaken belief that Michael was shot in the back of his head is at the crux of Rastegar's conclusion that Michael was murdered and did not commit suicide. Since the only other fact he knows is that Olivia was the only other person in the house when Michael was shot, Rastegar naturally concludes that Olivia must have shot Michael.

It would also come out at trial that Thompson took a statement from another witness before the arrest affidavit who said that Rastegar had told him another version of what Olivia had said. In that version, Rastegar claimed that Olivia said she shot Michael because he had tried to kill her. The point is, before Thompson presented the arrest affidavit to the judge, he knew that Rastegar had given wildly inconsistent versions of what he had heard Olivia say.

Thompson no longer believes Olivia fled to California

In the earlier deposition excerpt, Thompson stated that the reason he believed Olivia fled to California was because Brian had said that Olivia had seen crime scene vans at Michael's house several weeks after the shooting and believed her arrest was imminent.

In a report Thompson prepared for prosecutors after Olivia's arrest, he stated that Olivia had fled to California. Tittle continued his attack on cross. Tittle showed the jury Thompson's informal investigative notes — which are different from a formal prosecution report — and they revealed that Thompson knew Olivia's plane tickets had been prepaid and not bought on the spur of the moment as he had implied in the prosecution report. After showing Thompson his notes, Tittle asked these questions:

Q. *I asked you whether — in the deposition if [the fact that it was a] prepaid ticket [was a factor] in your determination of whether she had fled, and you said, "No, that wouldn't matter to me." Is that right?*
A. That's correct.

Q. *And I asked you, "Well, would it matter if she had a prepaid ticket and she was traveling with a bunch of nieces and nephews?" And you said, "No, that wouldn't matter to me either in making that determination."*
A. That's correct.

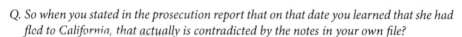

Q. *So when you stated in the prosecution report that on that date you learned that she had fled to California, that actually is contradicted by the notes in your own file?*
A. That's correct.

Q. *Even based on everything you've heard in this courtroom, you still believe that she fled to California?*
A. Well, I know now that she didn't flee to California.

Thompson explains contact wound

Q. *And so getting back to where we were a minute ago, you said [at trial] that that night [of the incident], when you left the room with Olivia, you had to give her the benefit of the doubt, maybe he killed himself. And I would ask you to turn to [page] 106, line 25 of the deposition. I asked you, in fact, in your deposition, "When you learned that it was a contact wound, did you consider the possibility that it might be a self-inflicted gunshot wound?" And you said, "No," right?*
A. Yes.

Q. *And then, in fact, I said, "Not at any time?" And you went on to explain that — and I'm reading from lines 9 through 14 — that after you had talked to her, because of things she said, you ruled that out as a possibility. Isn't that what you said in your deposition?*
A. That's correct.

Q. *But you're saying now that when you left that room, one of the things you thought to yourself, was, well, maybe he killed himself?*
A. That's correct.

Q. Again, what you testified to in your deposition would not be accurate, would it?
A. That's not necessarily true.

The outrageous comment that Thompson made at the deposition is a lot harder to make at trial with the jury present.

Thompson now knows the legal limit for alcohol in blood

Q. Isn't it true that you have stated under oath that whether Michael Burnside was intoxicated that night would not be of importance in this investigation?…
A. That's correct. That's correct.

Q. And, in fact, I asked you [page 100 line 8 of the deposition] what the legal limit was in Texas, and under oath you said, "I don't know."…And I said—after that I said, "You don't know what the legal limit is?" And you said?
A. "No."

Q. And you do not know what the legal limit is in Texas on alcohol? Is that your testimony?
A. I do now. I mean, at the time I didn't. I mean —

Q. What is it now? What do you know it to be now?
A. .08.

Q. And you've been an officer for how long?
A. 23 years.

Q. So at the time you gave your sworn testimony under oath, you'd been an officer for 22 years, roughly?
A. Yes.

Q. And you're saying you didn't know it up to that point, but since the date of the deposition, you have now learned that it's .08?
A. Yes. I'm not ashamed of that. I didn't know it.

Tittle then built on this incredibly claimed ignorance about intoxication to Thompson's statement in his deposition about Michael playing with guns.

Thompson admits Michael had been reckless with handguns

In his deposition, Thompson had testified that he had heard of only a single incident when Michael had been reckless with guns. Here is how Tittle used the deposition to undermine Thompson's credibility at trial.

Q. Now you learned from Brian Jaffe that there had been several instances in which Michael had been reckless with guns, correct?
A. Yes.

Q. But in your deposition, under oath, you claimed to me that, in fact, Jaffe only described a single incident; isn't that true?
A. If it's in my deposition, that would be true.

Q. *Now, the truth is that Brian Jaffe, in the recorded interview [he gave to police], told you that he had been reckless with guns on several occasions, not just a single incident, right?*

A. That would be correct.

Thompson denies he misled medical examiner

Q. *Now, there has been talk in this case by Dr. Quinton as to whether you misrepresented some information or incorrectly stated some information to him about the evidence of high-velocity blood, blowback or spatter on Ms. Lord's clothing. Do you remember that testimony [at trial] from Dr. Quinton?*

A. Yes.

Q. *Do you believe he is one of the individuals who has committed perjury in this court-room?*

A. No.

Q. *Do you believe that he was telling the truth?*

A. Yes.

Q. *Do you deny telling Dr. Quinton that [Olivia] had that high-velocity evidence on her clothing?*

A. That's not correct.

Q. *You didn't tell him that?*

A. That's not correct.

Q. *He testified that the clear implication, the clear understanding between you, the homicide detective, and him, the [medical examiner], was that you were telling him that she had high-velocity blowback bloodstains, blood spatter, whatever you want to call it, on her clothing, and that that was what you relayed to him, right? You heard him testify to that?*

A. Yeah. But I can't be accountable for his clear understanding of what I said to him. I can only be accountable for what I meant for him to get from that conversation.

Q. *You've heard the phrase — that type of evidence called blowback, right?*

A. Yes. But I can't testify to it. I've heard of it.

Q. *You can't testify to it because what?*

A. Well, I'm just not forensic — I don't have expertise in forensics.

Q. *You wouldn't even recognize it if you saw it, would you?*

A. Maybe, maybe not....

Q. *Detective, you surely are aware in cases in a homicide investigation, if a person shoots someone from close range, there is a distinct possibility that there's going to be a discharge of fluids back on them and it's going to spray them or their clothing [blowback evidence]? Isn't that true?*

A. Sir, I have no forensic background at all, none.

Q. *I'm not asking you that, whether you know how to do the testing. But you know the significance of the results, right?*

A. Not necessarily. [**Tittle then challenges this answer**]

Q. *Have you not testified in front of Dallas County criminal juries in homicide investigations that someone was guilty of murder because they have that type of evidence on them and that it would suggest they must have been at or near the location when the gun went off?*

A. A lot of time the Rule is in effect [**which does not allow witnesses to watch the trial they have testified in**], so when the crime scene folks are testifying to that, I'm not allowed to be in the courtroom. [**Thompson dodges the question**]

Q. *In [the probable cause hearing], page 17, line 21, Mr. Shearin [Olivia's lawyer] asked you, "And do you have an opinion as to whether or not there was blowback bloodstains on her clothing?" And you answered, "I don't have an opinion," right?*

A. Yes.

Q. *And then he asked, **"Well, do you think that might be important to have those clothes analyzed?" You said, "Yes, sir." And he said**—top of page 18, line 2—top of 18, line 2, **"If you believe that she was the shooter and there are bloodstains on her clothing, wouldn't it be important whether or not it was blowback?" And to that answer**—the answer to that question, you said?*

A. Yes.

Q. *"That is important. Yes, sir." So, in fact, contrary to what you're telling this jury, you do know the significance of the blowback evidence in a situation like this in placing someone — in connecting someone to the shooting, right?*

A. I never denied that it wasn't significant. [**Thompson indeed denied it was significant in his earlier answer.**]

Q. *Well, you never denied that it was significant?*

A. You just asked me a question —

Q. *No, no, no, no, no. That's what you just said to this jury under oath right there. You never denied it was significant, right?*

A. You just asked a question to me whether or not it was significant, and I just replied to your question that I didn't believe that — I didn't say that it wasn't significant. You just asked the question a few minutes ago.

A. I don't even know what you're saying. I really don't....

Q. *We'll look at your answer in the [probable cause hearing]. "If you believed that she was the shooter and there are bloodstains on her clothing, wouldn't it be important whether or not it was blowback?" And at that time you said, "That is important, yes, sir," right?*

A. OK.

Q. *Now, let's look at what you testified to at your deposition when I asked you — page 121, lines 10 through 14. "In your experience, or based on your experience that you had at the time of this incident, did you consider the blowback evidence to be significant in investigating a murder case?" And under oath, you answered what?*

A. "No."

Q. Would you agree that your statement in your [probable cause hearing] about blowback evidence and under oath in the deposition, those contradict each other?

A. Not necessarily. [**Tittle moves on to another topic**]

SUMMARY OF THOMPSON'S INCONSISTENT STATEMENTS ABOUT THE SIGNIFICANCE OF BLOWBACK EVIDENCE	
First statement at trial	Blowback evidence not significant
Probable cause hearing	Important to analyze clothing for blowback evidence
Deposition	Blowback evidence not significant
Second statement at trial	Denies that moments earlier he had told jury that blowback evidence was not significant

No witness is going to admit to lying under oath. But the jury has no doubt about what has just happened. Tittle backs Thompson into a corner from which there is no escape. First, Thompson testifies at trial that blowback evidence is not significant. Tittle then confronts him with his sworn testimony from the probable cause hearing where Thompson says it is significant. In order to reconcile these inconsistent statements, Thompson then denies that moments earlier in the trial he had ever testified that blowback evidence was not significant.

Tittle—knowing the jury was paying attention to the earlier statement in court—challenges him about his attempt to deny what he had just said in court. Then, to hammer home the point, Tittle uses the deposition to highlight that Thompson has given two opposite opinions about blowback evidence. The reason these inconsistencies are important is because the medical examiner had testified at trial that Thompson had told him that there was blowback evidence on Olivia which would be significant evidence–if true–because it would prove she had shot her boyfriend at close range.

Thompson admits affidavit written before Rastegar's second statement

*Q. Now, getting back to the recorded interview of Rastegar and how you characterized it in the probable cause affidavit. The truth is, Detective, that you—you actually prepared the affidavit **before the recorded interview** even occurred, right?*

A. That's correct.

Q. That's what you've sworn to, right?

A. That's correct.

*Q. So you've stated in the affidavit that it's based on the June 9th **recorded** interview, right? That's what the affidavit says; the plain language says, "Based on the June 9 interview".... That's what it says, right?*

A. That's what it says.

Q. You've stated and sworn in an affidavit that you have knowledge of a statement made during a recorded interview, but now you're telling us that you actually wrote that [affidavit] before the recorded interview even took place.

A. I wrote it before it took place, that's correct.

Q. Is that not on its face a false statement to the Judge?
A. No.

Q. Is it not a material misrepresentation to the Judge to indicate what was said in the recorded interview, that had not taken place?

A. No, that's not correct.

Tittle uses logic to win his point. Again, he knows that Thompson is not going to admit to making a false statement. But the logic of Tittle's questions proves that Thompson did. There is no way you can tell a judge that the affidavit is based on a recorded statement if the affidavit was written before the recorded statement was ever made.

Now, let's turn to the defendant's closing arguments and watch one of the most dramatic turning points at trial you will ever see. The defense counsel making the closing argument was a different lawyer from the one who made the opening statement. He is responding to Tittle who has already presented the first part of his closing argument (the summation).

14.9 DEFENDANT'S CLOSING ARGUMENT

Defense Counsel: May it please the Court, Counsel, Ladies and Gentlemen.

Good morning. We spent a week together now. You have been attentive and patient while we presented the evidence to you.

If I could, in the time allotted, I wanted to tell you what I believe the evidence shows, just like Mr. Tittle has. **I'm not going to be as loud and I'm not going to be throwing my hands around as much. I like to have a civilized adult conversation.**

I intend to show you the respect you are entitled by speaking directly and to the point. You're not going to hear a lot of flowery lawyerly talk from me. If you're looking for that, you're going to have to go to TV. You're not going to get it here.

I will start by telling you that Mr. Tittle and I know each other for years now, and I know him to be a great attorney, and I greatly respect him.

I tell you that it was no accident that the very first witnesses you heard from in this case were witnesses who were here to tell you how badly Ms. Lord was damaged by this, because his case is about emotional appeal and getting your anger up.

Now, this has been a really difficult, difficult, emotionally draining trial. We have watched witnesses become openly emotional. We don't blame them for that. I've watched you become very emotional and react to it. And that's why he did it, because it's about, to a large extent, pulling on your emotions.

And it is impossible not to feel sympathy for Ms. Lord in this situation. It's impossible. But the oath you jurors took was a solemn promise to follow the Court's and you told us that you would follow the Court's charge.

The instructions you are given are in the Court's charge to the jury. And one of the things that the Court tells you — and if you ever feel confused when you look at this charge, on page 6 of the charge, the Court tells you that in deciding the facts of this case, you must not be swayed — in deciding the facts of this case, you must not be swayed by bias, prejudice or any favor to any party. Sympathy must not factor into your decision about what happened. And that's what this case is all about, is what happened.

It's going to be tough — I know this — **but it is your duty** — as the Court tells you in the very first part of the charge, it is your duty to apply the law, as the Judge explained it to you, regardless of the consequences.

Defense counsel does some things well in his closing, but he does not start strong. His first comment to the jury is an attack on Tittle. He complains that Tittle has been "loud" and "throwing his arms around." In contrast, defense counsel says that he will have a "civilized adult conversation" with the jury. Not only did he mischaracterize Tittle's closing, his condescending tone demeans what Tittle has said and would anger jurors further who were sympathetic to Olivia.

He then goes on to say he has great respect for Tittle. The order of these arguments makes his second comment about respect seem insincere. His closing would have been much better if he had started by simply saying he respected Tittle as a lawyer and then said he was going to focus on the facts and not the emotions of the case.

Also, whenever you have to remind the jurors about the oath they took not to be swayed by emotions or sympathy, then you are admitting that you are scared you are going to lose. It is ridiculous to think that by reminding the jurors of their oath to be fair, that they are magically going to change their mindset and view the facts of the case differently. Every human being makes decisions based on emotions; a trial is no different despite a court's instruction or a lawyer's plea.

14.10 TURNING POINT IN CLOSING ARGUMENT

All of Tittle's strategy in the deposition and at trial led to the moment that follows.

> Now, when this trial started last Wednesday, [co-counsel] told you that what you were going to do in this courtroom is you were going to think this was a criminal trial where you'd have to decide whether she was guilty or not guilty. And [co-counsel] was spot-on about that. Practically every one of the witnesses that Mr. Tittle brought you in this trial bent over backwards to convince you that she did not kill Michael Burnside.
>
> But that's not the issue in this case. The issue in this case is whether there was probable cause to believe at the time Thompson submitted that affidavit to Judge Lollar, was there probable cause to believe.
>
> But since Mr. Tittle has made this case about whether she is guilty or not guilty, I will speak to that issue right now. [Co-counsel] and I have spent weeks, perhaps months, looking over every piece of paper that we could, photographs, watching videos, and there remained for us some unresolved questions. Those remaining unanswered questions aside, **I'm telling you, she didn't do it**.
>
> **I know you didn't do it** [counsel looks at Olivia]. **She didn't do it** [counsel looks at jury]. But that's not the issue in this trial.
>
> What it's about — what this trial is about is whether this detective had probable cause to believe that she did it at the time he acted. That's what it's about.
>
> There it is, folks. I don't agree with the detective. **He was asked if he believes it, and he told you on the witness stand he still believes it to this day.** That's his belief. He didn't lie to you. That's what he thinks. That's what Detective Lundberg still thinks. **I disagree with the detective. There it is.**
>
> But a belief is not a violation of the Constitution. You have to look at the facts. So let's talk about those facts.

> But Detective Thompson, God bless him, he didn't know [the facts that have come out at trial]. We can disagree with the manner and the means by which he tried to find it out. If you don't like the interview techniques [he used with Olivia], write to Chief David Brown of the Dallas Police Department and tell him you can't have this going on. But don't punish this man because he used every bit of knowledge he possibly knew, every trick

in the book, if you will, accusing her, seeing if she changes her baseline, rolling back, "explain it to me, give me options. Tell me. Help me."

It is an impossible and disingenuous argument to make when defense counsel says in effect, "My client thinks Olivia is still guilty of murder, but I don't. Even so, let me tell you why you can still reach a verdict for my client." When defense counsel looked at Olivia and told her she was innocent, Olivia broke down crying, and the jury had a visceral reaction. Given the mountain of evidence against Thompson, it was defense counsel's only choice.

The problem with the decision is that it came much too late. It was completely inconsistent with his co-counsel's opening statement when she told the jury that it should have sympathy for Detective Thompson because he was suffering from the false allegations. Moreover, throughout the trial, the defense lawyers challenged the plaintiff's witnesses at every turn in a vigorous effort to support Thompson's belief that Olivia was a murderer.

The turning point is even more dramatic because defense counsel says the reason he now thinks Olivia is innocent is because he has had the benefit of weeks and months in preparing for trial to review all the evidence in the case. He suggests that the luxury of time and the amount of information is something that Detective Thompson did not have.

But that argument is completely undercut when defense counsel then states that after hearing all this evidence at trial, Thompson and his partner Detective Lundberg still believe Olivia is guilty.

14.11 TITTLE'S REBUTTAL ARGUMENT

Tittle: Members of the Jury, [defense counsel] is not concerned about me, I can assure you. He's not concerned about me or my questions that I might ask or things I might say to you. He's concerned about the facts. That's why he's saying that stuff.

He doesn't think I've got some special ability as a lawyer to make something appear one way that it's not. **He knows what's happened in this courtroom.** And actions still speak louder than his words, because this case has been pending now for several years. Those words haven't been spoken by [defense counsel] in all of that time. There has been plenty of opportunities to say, "Olivia, you didn't do this." No way, haven't even come close to saying that.

But in closing statement, with a fear of what's coming, based on the facts, now he offers it.

You don't even have to go back years. You only have to go to the opening statement, four days, five days ago or a week ago. They didn't say it in opening statement. **They didn't stand up and tell you she was an**

innocent woman. No way. In fact, [defense co-counsel] said there are things that are very troubling about her conduct. They said there's blood spatter on her; that's what that's about.

And he mentioned you could write a letter to Chief Brown. You could. And you might hope that some assistant in his office opens it and maybe they'll read it and maybe they'll even tell Chief Brown. But I can think of a whole lot better way for you to get Chief Brown's attention, and I can guarantee you that's one he'll hear.

Notice how Tittle immediately pounces on defense counsel's best arguments. Tittle confronts the accusation that he was making up for a weak case by desperately trying to appeal to the jurors' sympathies. Tittle succinctly points out that the truth is that defense counsel is really afraid of the facts Tittle has on his side. The proof is in defense counsel's belated apology to Olivia. Tittle contrasts this delayed apology with the defendant's defiant opening statement that embraced Thompson's actions and sought the jurors' sympathy for a well-meaning officer who was wrongfully accused.

In addition, defense counsel had advised the jury in his closing that if they were upset with Thompson's tactics, they could write a letter to the Chief of Police. Tittle immediately points out how disingenuous that idea is. The Police Chief may never learn about the letter, but he will certainly hear a large verdict.

14.12 VERDICT

After deliberating for two days, Olivia won both her claims. The total award was $1.2 million, which included attorney's fees.

14.13 THE AFTERMATH

The question that may never be answered satisfactorily is why did Detective Thompson make the statements he did in his deposition. Tittle's theory is that when Detective Thompson arrived on the scene on the night of the killing, he was told—mistakenly—that Olivia had waited seven minutes to call 911 after discovering Michael lying on the kitchen floor. Even when he learned the following day that Olivia had called 911 immediately, Thompson made a series of assumptions that always favored murder no matter what the evidence was. He had a hunch, but nothing to support it. Then, when Rastegar allegedly told Thompson at his house that Olivia said she had accidentally shot Michael, it confirmed everything Thompson believed.

A reporter for a magazine pointed out that Thompson was interested in the victimology of Michael. Michael's father, a successful businessman, described

Michael as very positive and mentioned that Michael had called his mother earlier in the week to say he was coming over for lunch on Mother's Day, which was the day after the night of the shooting. Moreover, his best friend, Brian Jaffe, related that Michael's motto was, "I love life." Perhaps Detective Thompson could not accept that Michael killed himself, either accidentally or intentionally.

But there can be no doubt that Detective Thompson's rush to judgment can be seen in his interrogation of Olivia at the police station on the night of the shooting. (View the excerpts of the interrogation at www.TurningPointsatTrial.com.) A retired homicide detective who was an expert witness for Olivia testified at trial that Thompson's techniques were outlandish. He also corroborated Tittle's theory that Thompson had left out of the arrest warrant important evidence that proved Olivia's innocence.

Despite Thompson's testimony at his deposition and trial that he still believed Olivia committed the murder, the jury foreman said after the trial, "I had to cover my mouth I was so appalled. There was no way a person with an IQ above 65 could have concluded that Olivia had shot Michael."

After the trial, Thompson was placed on desk duty pending an investigation conducted by the Police Department. Despite the jury verdict, the Public Integrity Unit found that there was no evidence that Thompson misrepresented any facts on government documents or that there was any evidence of criminal wrongdoing. Detective Thompson remains active on the Dallas Police Department.

As for Olivia, she sobbed as she testified at trial about her love for Michael and that Thompson's interrogation of her was a "mental rape." Her days in jail were "torture." She lost her career because whenever she applies for a job, employers find her arrest on the Internet.

Now that the trial is over, she has only found work at a retail store for $14 an hour, a far cry from her previous job in the mortgage business. It is difficult for her to date because men eventually find out about her arrest. When she goes out in public, she perceives that people see her as the girl who killed her boyfriend.

Tittle and his team of investigators failed to find Rastegar before trial. After the trial, Rastegar appeared and told a reporter that he never told Thompson on his front porch that Olivia had admitted shooting Michael.

14.14 CHAPTER CHECKLIST 🖉

Tittle's deposition advice

1. "Police officers will almost never say, 'I don't know, or I don't recall.' When they're pressed on an important issue, they will avoid saying one of those two answers and, instead, make something up."

2. "I think the majority of all witnesses are telling some truths and some untruths."

3. Use the jury charge to prepare yourself at a deposition on what you need to know about the law in order to win your case.

4. Have the right mindset. Tittle describes his demeanor as "polite but direct. I'm not afraid, but I'm not a jerk."

5. If you can attack a witness at a deposition, do it. Don't save a surprise for trial.

6. Video a deposition if you can, but the reality is that the cost is a large factor you need to consider in making the decision.

7. "Many lawyers just ask questions because they are in the lawyers' outline. Questioning a witness without a purpose drives me crazy."

8. "When a witness is highly defensive and hell-bent on not giving an inch, that mentality gets the witness in trouble quickly in a deposition."

Tips from Tittle's deposition

1. Don't waste precious time at the beginning of a deposition asking the witness about educational and employment history. Cut right to the chase.

2. At the beginning of the deposition, watch your witness carefully to see if he is scared, evasive, combative, or telling the truth.

3. Listen to the answers carefully. If you don't, you will miss a unique opportunity to help your case.

4. You need to be firm in the deposition. You are in charge, not the witness.

5. Often witnesses get defensive and, instead of answering truthfully, they give a misleading answer they think will help them but actually hurts because it does not make sense to the jury at the time of the trial.

6. If the only truthful answer is "yes" or "no" and the witness answers "I don't know," that answer is as good as an admission because the jury won't believe the "I don't know answer."

7. Know your case inside and out before the deposition so you can recognize weaknesses in the witness' testimony.

8. If a witness is aware you are knowledgeable about the facts, he will either tell the truth because he knows you can prove the truth, or he will get very defensive and tell a lie to try to protect himself. Either answer gives you a victory: The truthful answer helps you, but you can also prove a false answer is wrong with other evidence at trial.

9. Tittle achieves three goals: the witness makes helpful admissions, inconsistent statements, and outrageous statements.

PART SEVEN

———— ∞∞∞ ————

Appellate Oral Argument

INTRODUCTION

*A*lthough this book focuses on turning points at trial, it would be naive to think that juries have the final say. Win or lose, an appeal to a higher court is in the back of every trial lawyer's mind. If the issue on appeal is a close one, the appellate court grants the attorneys a hearing to argue their case before a panel of appellate judges. This is known as oral argument. Whether you won or lost at trial, the appellate oral argument is the ultimate turning point that will decide your fate.

In this part, we are going to look at three brilliant lawyers who share the insights and strategies that make their oral arguments successful. The first attorney is Bryan Stevenson, whom we met in Chapter Three for opening statements. He is internationally known for his advocacy of death row inmates, juveniles in prison, and civil rights. We will look at two of his Supreme Court arguments.

Next, we will meet Lisa Blatt who holds the record for a woman for oral arguments before the U.S. Supreme Court and is referenced on the Supreme Court's website as the perfect example of an attorney who is well prepared for oral argument.

Finally, we will turn our attention from the arguments made at the United States Supreme Court to an argument made in a state supreme court. You will find that the strategies are different, and we will learn from one of the country's greatest appellate advocates, Alan Dershowitz. His meticulous preparation and brilliant advocacy skills overturned a murder conviction that had so much intrigue that it could have been a Hollywood movie.

CHAPTER FIFTEEN

Bryan Stevenson

Have a Conversation, Not an Argument, with the Court

I come from a world where we value redemption over revenge.

— Bryan Stevenson

---

*B*ryan Stevenson is one of the country's preeminent civil rights attorneys. He has received innumerable accolades for his legal work on behalf of indigent adults who are on death row, adults and children who have been wrongfully convicted, and adults and children who are suffering from cruel and unusual punishment in prison. He has also won historic rulings before the United States Supreme Court, including one which held that mandatory life-without-parole sentences for children 17 or younger are unconstitutional. Perhaps Desmond Tutu best summed up Stevenson's impact on society when he declared, "Bryan Stevenson is America's Nelson Mandela, a brilliant lawyer fighting with courage and conviction to guarantee justice for all."

Stevenson grew up on the eastern shore of the Delmarva Peninsula in Delaware, where he relates, "the racial history of this country casts a long shadow." His neighborhood was racially segregated and poor. He lived in a rural settlement where some lived in tiny shacks without indoor plumbing; the outdoor "playground" was shared with chickens and pigs. He remembers, "The black people around me were strong and determined but marginalized and excluded." His father could not attend high school because there was not one for black children. As an adult, his father worked in a food factory and did domestic work at beach rentals on the weekends. "It seemed we were all cloaked in an unwelcome garment of racial difference that constrained, confined, and restricted us."

CHAPTER HIGHLIGHTS

- Don't repeat what is in your brief
- Listen to what the judges need answered
- Evasive answers destroy your argument

His grandmother, who was born in the 1880s, was the daughter of slaves. She had a big influence on his life. She instilled in him a sense of identity and the belief that he could accomplish anything he set out to do.

After graduating from college with a degree in philosophy, Stevenson attended Harvard Law School and the Harvard School of Government. During law school, he felt disconnected from the theoretical teaching of the professors and the students who seemed more experienced and more certain of careers working at large successful law firms. While feeling lost at Harvard, he realized that "proximity to the condemned, to people unfairly judged — that was what guided me back to something that felt like home." It was a value his grandmother had instilled in him when he was a child. She repeated to him often, "You can't understand most of the important things from a distance, Bryan. You have to get close."

The turning point in Stevenson's legal career came when he took an internship during law school at the Southern Prisoners Defense Committee (SPDC). The SPDC helped prisoners on Georgia's death row. That internship would eventually lead him to the founding of the Equal Justice Initiative (EJI) in Montgomery, Alabama, which had its beginnings in 1989. EJI has many goals, including: 1) stop the death penalty, 2) help people on death row, 3) improve prison conditions, 4) correct excessive punishments, 5) free those who have been wrongfully convicted, 6) end racial bias in the criminal justice system, 7) prevent children from being put in adult prisons, 8) tackle abuses of power by police and prosecutors, and 9) increase awareness of racial history and injustice.

There is no shortage of statistics to show the daunting challenge Stevenson has undertaken. As Stevenson observes, the United States is "very different today" from what it was 40 years ago. In 1972, there were 300,000 people in prison. Today, there are 2.3 million. In 1980, there were 41,000 people in prison for drug offenses. Today, those numbers have swelled to 500,000. With those numbers, it is not surprising that the United States has the highest rate of incarceration in the world. But the problem does not end with incarceration. In the United States, there are also 7,000,000 people on probation and parole.

Stevenson points out that mass incarceration has fundamentally changed our country. One out of three black men between the ages of 18 and 30 is in prison, on probation, or on parole. In large cities, the figure is 50–60 percent. (In poor communities and communities of color, this mass incarceration has created a feeling of hopelessness.)

But the system creates injustices also for poor communities. Stevenson declared the following in his TED talk given in March 2012 (discussed in Chapter Three). "The system of justice treats you much better if you are rich and guilty than if you are poor and innocent. Wealth, not culpability, shapes outcomes. And yet we seem to be very comfortable. The politics of fear and anger have made us believe that these are problems that are not our problems."

Stevenson adds that skilled lawyers make a difference, but the poor do not have access to them. Also, there is a presumption of guilt that shadows young people of color. They get stopped by the police more often, and if they don't handle those confrontations well, they will get arrested. One in three black males and one in six Latinos born in 2001 are expected to go to jail during their lifetimes. There are 14 states that have no minimum age limit for trying a child as an adult. As a result, children are placed in adult prisons and targeted for abuse. Today, there are 10,000 children in adult prisons.

Statistics regarding the death penalty are also very troubling. For every nine people killed on death row, one has been exonerated. But Stevenson points out that we accept it. He further highlights that in the states of the Old South, you are 11 times more likely to get the death penalty if the victim is white and not black, 22 times more likely if the defendant is black and the victim is white. Fortunately, in his fight for justice, Stevenson has gotten 115 people off of death row.

Among his many accolades and achievements including 11 honorary doctorate degrees, here are just a few more: He has written a *New York Times* best-selling book, *Just Mercy*, which was honored by the *New York Times* as one of its 100 Notable Books of 2014. When he gave a TED talk to discuss his work at EJI, he received one of the longest ovations in its history. Moreover, his speech has been viewed over 2,321,000 times. (You can watch it at www.TurningPointsatTrial.com.) In 2010, the NAACP honored Stevenson with the William Robert Ming Advocacy Award for the spirit of financial and personal sacrifice displayed in his legal work.

Stevenson has a passion for making the justice system work fairly for everyone. We will examine two cases in detail where he did just that. But before we do, let's hear what Stevenson has to share regarding the challenges of his cases and oral argument. Three things were immediately apparent when I interviewed Stevenson: He is passionate, caring, and brilliant.

There were times during the interview that I felt as if I was listening to a religious leader instead of a lawyer. He never invoked specific Bible passages, but throughout our discussion there were the undercurrent themes of redemption, forgiveness, and compassion. He could also see all sides of an argument, instead of just forcefully arguing one position without giving credence to an opposing viewpoint. Despite all his accolades, he was self-deprecating, and his arguments were never made with anger, but rather, a kindness and optimism that one day others might see things the way he does.

15.1 ORAL ARGUMENT STRATEGIES

Listen

An unforgiveable mistake lawyers make at oral argument is that they fail to listen. Stevenson explains, "You can go into an appellate court and give a beautiful speech about why you think you win," instead of listening to the questions the court needs answered. If what the court is concerned about is some really peculiar, esoteric question about something procedural, you're not going to get their vote unless you resolve that question.

While the issues before a lower appellate court are simpler, at the Supreme Court the justices are "thinking about 100 things that have nothing to do with your case. They're thinking about the precedential implications. They're thinking about things like, 'How does this position me on other issues that I care deeply about, like state autonomy. Like who interprets the Constitution?'"

"There are all these other issues that they're thinking through that have nothing to do with what the right outcome is in your case, but the outcome in your case is going to be influenced by those concerns." No matter where you give an oral argument, listening is paramount.

Know your audience

Stevenson urges that is it important to know the judges' views on your panel, both from their previous decisions and how they act at oral argument. While at a lower appellate court, all the judges may be undecided on a particular issue, Stevenson explains that it would be naive to think that at an argument before the United States Supreme Court, all nine judges are undecided. "They've got very strong views about a lot of these topics that have been clearly articulated in prior decisions, and you can guess where they're going to end up. It doesn't mean that they've made a final judgment, but you know where they're coming from, and there is always going to be someone in the middle and sometimes on some issues where you don't have that kind of history, you really don't know. At lower courts, I think it's less clear because they don't deal with these kinds of issues as frequently."

In death penalty cases, Stevenson says, "There is a lot of pressure to affirm. Judges don't like to overturn these cases because they're high publicity and there is a lot of criticism that comes with it." No matter what his oral argument is, Stevenson always

> **Practice Tip**
>
> Stevenson reveals, "I always want to see the court in action before I give an argument. If I'm going to be the first argument on Tuesday but they've got arguments on Monday, I just want to get there on Monday and just watch that court."

talks to other lawyers to learn all he can about the judges whom he is going to appear in front of.

Answering difficult questions

Similarly to knowing your audience, knowing how to answer difficult questions is a must. For some judges, "If they ask you a question that has an answer of yes or no, if you don't start your answer with yes or no, they're done. They'll give up on you. They'll close the books, they're going to check out. They're just not going to follow, and you've got to know that about your court.

"But if you are engaged in a conversation, you can answer, 'Yes, but....' to candidly answer the question but also explain why the judge is incorrect. Another way to answer the question is to say, 'No, but it is only because in these circumstances the outcome would be different.'" No matter how you answer, Stevenson instructs you to start with a direct answer of yes or no. Stevenson adds, sometimes when it is impossible to answer yes and still win his argument, he will do the following: "I'll say, 'Justice Snow, I know you want me to say yes. I know that given the logic of your question the answer would be yes, and I know that my opponent is going to say yes, but I have to say yes, comma, blah, blah, blah.' You have to stay credible."

Stevenson explains that it is no different when you are in a conversation outside the courthouse. "When people talk to each other and somebody asks a really penetrating question, and they know the answer is yes but they don't want to reveal it, we'll do things that are non-verbal, and we'll do things that are verbally kind of active to get the person to not make a judgment based on that one word. You have to do that in appellate advocacy all the time."

I pointed out to Stevenson that he smiles a lot when he gets asked a difficult question. I interpreted his smiles as meaning, "I know what you want me to answer, but I'm going to persuade you differently." He agreed that it is all about engaging with the judges. "What you don't want to do is to make them believe you can't help them get to a different place on an issue."

Some lawyers advise that you should ignore the judges that are clearly against you and not waste your time responding to their questions. Stevenson strongly disagrees. Even with problematic personalities on the bench, you still have to treat the court as an institution that requires a certain amount of respect and deference. Stevenson believes that even for the judges that may rule against him, he never wants to offend them by suggesting that it would be immoral to do so. Such an attitude is only going to provoke people. "The judge who rules against you doesn't want to think that she is immoral. If you start loading things up and setting things up, it makes it very hard for them to engage you. They'll just want to fight you, and that's not what you want."

Do not rely on notes

Stevenson does not take a notebook full of tabs with cases and records up to the podium. At most, he takes a short outline. But he usually just takes a sheet of paper and a pen to make notes if the questioning gets so intense that he needs to keep track of who is asking what questions.

He has memorized an opening statement that answers the question that is the sticking point for the judges who are undecided. He knows he may be cut off at any moment, but he is prepared with an opening argument. In your opening statement, you need to know if the court is worried about setting an unacceptable precedent, disrupting the administration of law, or putting dangerous people back on the streets. "Whatever you think their concern is, that's what you want to address first."

Sometimes at lower courts (never the Supreme Court), you need to be prepared to speak for a long time without getting questions from the bench. The bench may be disinterested, and you need to fill the time. When the bench is quiet, it is called a "cold bench." On the other hand, some courts feel it is disrespectful to interrupt you and purposefully want to hear you give a presentation.

Stevenson adds that when you are reading your notes or a document, it makes the court want to check out. "They either want to get you away from your prepared document and engage you in conversation, or they'll just give up, and they'll just sit back and wait until you're done."

Finally, Stevenson states that your delivery cannot be monotonous. It must be "engaging and interesting," and it cannot be that if you are tied to your notes. "The brain is active; it wants to be engaged, and it wants to be stimulated," or it will go elsewhere. Notes make your presentation less interesting and less conversational. In short, Stevenson puts it this way: "They are a real liability."

Have a conversation with the court

Stevenson never wants to respond to the court with a disingenuous "canned answer." Instead, he wants to engage in a conversation that makes the judges feel comfortable in telling him what they really think about an issue. If they ask you a difficult question, Stevenson instructs that you can respond as follows: "I completely understand what you are saying, but if you think about it this [way], that issue is not really an issue." Stevenson says you won't uncover that judge's concern unless you listen and invite him to tell you what is troubling him. "I want a judge to feel like he can ask me anything. No question is stupid or offensive, or problematic or provocative. Ask me, because that's going to facilitate the conversation that might allow me to say something that changes his thinking about the issue." Stevenson wants to build his credibility by listening and being candid.

Stevenson adds, "I think an appellate judge is going to be really frustrated if people come in only prepared to say the things that they've prepared to say. That's really frustrating for a judge who has real questions, because then you have to hope that you could anticipate what his questions are so perfectly that every question is answered in what you prepared. That's just not likely—particularly in the Supreme Court, where you've got nine very distinct perspectives and divergent views about the Constitution and about the issues. There is no way."

> *I want to have a conversation with the court. I really don't want it to be an argument. I want them to feel like they can ask me anything and that they're going to get an honest answer.*
> —Bryan Stevenson

Know what you need to win

Stevenson instructs that one of the challenges in oral argument, particularly at the Supreme Court, "is understanding what's essential to win." It is very easy to get distracted by questioning from judges who have their own agenda. For example, you may get a question from a judge who you know is going to rule against you, and if the question is broad, you don't want to use precious time giving a long answer which won't persuade that judge no matter what you say.

You want to be "respectful and responsive, but you want to get those votes in the middle."

Never cut off the judge

Stevenson explains:

> You never cut the judge off ever, ever, ever. Whatever the judge has to say is always more important than what you have to say, and you stop immediately and don't cut a judge off. I think again you have to be prepared for a conversation, so don't get stuck in the text reading or in an outline where you can't make eye contact and engage someone.

Present your best self

One mistake Stevenson sees repeatedly, but makes no sense to him, is when lawyers don't put their best foot forward. He used an analogy to make his point:

> If you're trying to persuade someone to go out with you, most people have to think a lot about what they're going to say. They try to be charming. They try to do all these things that present their best self. I'm oftentimes seeing lawyers at an appellate argument that seem to be doing the opposite.

They are whiny. They seem angry and mad. They get offended by questions that suggest that the other side has a good point.

They seem hostile to their opponent for no good reason. Even before the opponent has said anything, they are mad and angry. They are bitter about something that the other party said, and I just think it's not very useful to present the worst parts of yourself when you are in that setting. I just think of it as if you're trying to get somebody to go out with you. If you are trying to get a court to rule in your favor, it's probably not a bad idea to think about presenting yourself in [the best] way. And that's one of those things that I'm surprised by, but I see it a lot.

Skillful advocacy versus evasive resistance

Perhaps one of the hardest challenges at oral argument is conceding a fact that hurts your case. It could be a mistake your client made or a line of cases that goes against the relief you need. Stevenson instructs that you cannot be in denial.

> *I think conceding things is something you have to be comfortable doing in oral argument. When you don't concede, the court just loses confidence that you are even looking at the law the way they're looking at the law.*
> — Bryan Stevenson

I think the line between skillful advocacy and evasive resistance to revealing something that you know exists that the court is asking about is sometimes a thin line, but sometimes it's a big line, and you cannot pretend that it's not a problem.

I want to persuade the judge that I read the law just like he does and my conclusion is "A," and he can trust that my conclusion is right because we read the law the same way. If you are not paying any attention to the fact that there are these 10 cases that go against you, you are just ignoring that, then you are not reading the law the way that judge has to read it. You have got to make it clear that you're aware of those things and that you are prepared to concede, but that there's precedent that suggests that this should be the right outcome.

Don't repeat what is in your brief

Stevenson points out that a big mistake many lawyers make is that they presume the court has not read their briefs. Consequently, lawyers just repeat what is in their briefs without any more clarity or adding any enhancements. Stevenson says with a laugh, "The judge just starts to tune out. It's like, 'I can think about where I'm going next week. I can think about what I'm going to have for lunch, and I won't miss anything because it is all in the brief.'" Stevenson pauses, and then says with emphasis, "But when you start saying things that are actually enhancing your arguments that you're presenting, or even altering them or framing them differently, then that would actually make the judge pay attention, and it's like any conversation."

Don't re-litigate a winning point

> I think sometimes when you've won a point, and it's clear from the argument of the other side that the point is in your favor, you don't need to keep re-litigating something you've already won because sometimes you can stir it again and this time you get a different outcome.
>
> Sometimes the court will pick up on something that helps you. That you haven't emphasized. You need to re-enforce that what they are thinking is what you think too. I think that's a really important thing.

Address the judges by name

Stevenson shares another secret: "I tend to be more personal. I call judges by their names." Noting that the Supreme Court has its own local rules, he gives an example of what he means in the lower courts by pretending that I am the judge.

> I'll say, "Justice Read, you wrote an opinion in 1999 that basically said that it ought to be ABC. I want to say that I agree with you, and if you apply that analysis here, the outcome would be what we are advocating."
>
> It can't hurt. It's not pandering as much as just engaging that judge, number one, but also reminding that judge that this is territory that he or she has covered before. That will be useful, and I think small things like that just show you have thought it out and are useful to do when you are arguing.

Moot court is a must

A big mistake lawyers make is that they don't moot their appellate argument. Stevenson gets a group of five smart critical lawyers to act as judges and go through a rehearsal of the oral argument. Stevenson instructs that the beauty of appellate advocacy is that the issues are framed by the briefs, so you can really "advance your preparation." Lawyers who don't moot their arguments are making a "terrible" mistake. Also, by going through the exercise of thinking of the strengths and weaknesses of all the arguments, the moot helps those who are playing the roles of the judges get ready for their next oral argument.

Know the record and case law

One challenge every appellate attorney has is deciding how much he needs to know about the facts and law before an oral argument. In lower courts, Stevenson believes you can get "closer to knowing it all." The reason is that those courts are bound by precedent, and there is a more finite universe of material to learn.

On the other hand, at the United States Supreme Court, it is tricky because you are often talking about issues that do not have a precedent. Instead, you are borrowing from different ideas, and the judges can borrow from different things, and the universe of case law is less defined. But as a general rule, he tries to know everything he can.

15.2 PARTICULAR CHALLENGES FOR DEATH PENALTY AND CRIMINAL APPEALS

In death penalty appeals, Stevenson has a very difficult challenge. We will learn how he overcame it in the Nelson case that follows. The main problem he has is that courts have made a priority out of finality over fairness. In essence, courts have said that the guilty verdict may be illegal, unfair, or even unconstitutional, but because the issue was not objected to at trial or raised in a timely manner on appeal, the appellate court is not going to disrupt the conviction or sentence. "The finality narrative has really shaped the death penalty and criminal litigation in very profound ways. There is also a lot of pressure from victims and the public not to overturn a conviction."

To reset the narrative on appeal, Stevenson tries to persuade the judges that he has complied with whatever procedural doctrine that the opposing side or the judges are asserting that blocks relief. But he also tries to get the judges to reflect "a little bit more about whether it's true that finality [of a conviction] always trumps fairness."

Watch how Stevenson accomplishes this. First, he knows what a judge must be thinking at his core. "I don't think a judge talking to a law audience could sell them on the idea that if something really unfair and illegal has happened to you, the judge doesn't care because you didn't do something in a certain period of time." Then, he points out to the court that the finality doctrine is really based on fairness. That is, it is not fair to the state to have to defend a conviction over an extended period of time. Stevenson then explains that if fairness really is the governing principle, we should not give deference to finality since we should ultimately care about correcting the problem. "You actually have to elevate fairness in a way that makes the judges uncomfortable with the outcome."

15.3 VIEWS ON THE DEATH PENALTY

I asked Stevenson how he responds to victims who complain that his representation of death row inmates delays the justice they deserve and increases their suffering. As always, Stevenson gave a thoughtful and compassionate response.

> I write [in *Just Mercy*] about when my grandfather was murdered when I was 16. I've had family members who've suffered horrific violence from violent crime. I never want to complicate a victim's family members' effort to respond or recover from violent crime. I've got to represent my clients, but I hate violence. I do. I really do. I hate it. If I had all power there would never be another human being ever murdered.
>
> It's because I hate violence so much that even the impulse to kill back is something that I'd like to protect people from, and I get that it's a little paternalistic. I get that, but I do. It's like when you have kids. One kid hits the other, your impulse is to not let the other kid back and then let it spiral, right? Ultimately, you want to do something. That's the sort of the way I feel about the death penalty. That's my own view. Not everybody has to agree with that. I get it. But that's why I'm not confounded by that. I am attentive to how we meet the needs of people who were the victims of violent crime, and I think we should be doing a whole lot more.

> *I don't think there's something redemptive in facilitating the death of another human being.*
> — Bryan Stevenson

> I think instead of promising people an execution, we ought to be providing people with counseling and services and money and a whole host of things that might actually help them recover, but we don't do that. What we do is to say if you really loved your husband, father, or son, brother, daughter, whomever, you've got to insist on the death penalty. Then we subject people to years of torture by making it seem like it's their personal responsibility to make sure there's an execution. I think that's cruel. I think that's horrific. I think it's abusive.
>
> Then what we do is create a whole new arena where we're going to value some victimization over others. So, 80 percent of the people on death row here [in Alabama] are on death row for crimes committed against people who are white and 65 percent of all murder victims in the state of Alabama are black. It becomes yet another way in which we create this stratification of whose lives matter through the death penalty, and it's so gratuitous. If you don't have the death penalty, that's one less thing we have to worry about in terms of making this point about which lives matter more than others. All of that feeds into it.

Stevenson then repeated for emphasis, "I think we don't help victims enough. I don't think we respond to victimization. I think we respond to it in cheap and easy ways, and the death penalty is a cheap, easy way to say we care about victims because it doesn't actually deal with all the complexities that are created when someone loses a father or husband or a child. That's complicated stuff."

In his book, *Just Mercy*, and in his TED talk, Stevenson challenges the belief that the death penalty is appropriate for capital murder. I asked him to provide some more details. He explained:

> I think too many of our opinions have been shaped around something like the death penalty by asking, "Does this person deserve to die for the crime that they've committed?" You can get to yes on that question and still not believe in the death penalty, if you ask these other questions: "Do we deserve to kill if we have a system that treats you better if you are rich and guilty than poor and innocent? If we have a system where race matters more than guilt? If we have a system that will frequently result in executing innocent people? If we have a system that is political where people with power get protection, and people without it don't?" Just those four things.
>
> If we are going to execute people because they are poor, because they're black, we are going to execute some innocent people, and it's political. Should we give to that system the right to kill? A lot of people who may think that…. someone like David Nelson [discussed below] deserves to die for his crime may nonetheless think, though, we don't deserve to kill if we're going to do it in this way. The integrity of the system is the only thing we have to allow us to decide whether David Nelson deserves to die or not.

I asked Stevenson if he could support the death penalty if the process could be perfected. He explained:

> *I actually think my extra honest answer is, if we lived in a world with no poverty and no racial bias and complete accuracy, I don't think we would want the death penalty. I don't think anybody would want the death penalty. We would be so evolved that the idea of killing people as a way of responding to bad acts would just be unimaginable.*
>
> — Bryan Stevenson

If we could live in a world where there's no race bias. Where there's no poverty. Where there's no bias against the poor and people of color. Where there's always accuracy and reliability, to be honest, my presumption is that I would still be against the death penalty because to me it doesn't make sense to kill someone to show that killing is wrong. There's something inherently illogical about that. To be extra honest, I don't really know because I've never lived in a world where there's no poverty. I've never lived in a world where there's no racial bias.

For me it's like saying, "If there were no race issues involved and there was no economic exploitation, could you imagine slavery ever being acceptable?" No, but I don't understand how you could have slavery in a world where you didn't have those kinds of distinctions being made between people. That's the way I feel about the death penalty. I just don't think it would have any value or purpose if it wasn't advancing some idea about the value of some lives versus others. There's no way to imagine that if we don't think about the ways in which we have this hierarchy of victimization. My clients on death row are some of the most victimized people on the planet.

If I take their histories, their childhood histories, their abuse histories, the amount of violence they've seen, the amount of violence they've experienced and the neglect, they could be anybody, any constellation of people you want to put together in terms of who's been victimized by crime. The problem is their victimization turned into the victimization of others, and they got labeled this way.

15.4 ARE CRIMINAL DEFENDANTS GUILTY?

I asked Stevenson about the American public's view that criminal defendants standing trial are guilty. This view is corroborated by the fact that the conviction rate in America hovers around 93 percent every year. Stevenson responds that he "profoundly" disagrees with that assumption. "I don't think there's been a time in American history where there were more innocent people in jails and prisons than today. Just looking at the death penalty, we've now had 153 exonerations of people who were convicted of capital murder and sentenced to death.

"The death penalty is the most refined, regulated, proceduralized, funded part of the criminal justice system, and yet, for every nine people we've executed, we've identified one innocent person on death row." Stevenson adds that the figure does not begin to take into account the large number of innocent people on death row who have not had their cases evaluated properly.

Stevenson explains that if the error rate is one out of nine, "Why do we think it's going to be lower for the rest of the system where there are fewer resources, less care, less scrutiny, less review and less engagement? It's going to be higher. That tells me that this number of innocent wrongly convicted people is in the thousands." He continues:

> I really think today that this idea that the police only arrest guilty people is a very misguided one, very misguided. Look, I've lived in communities where the police will come and arrest every young man of color between a certain age just for being in a certain spot. If you mean by "guilty," you mean guilty of being black. Guilty of being poor. Guilty of being out late at night. Guilty of not using good judgment. Guilty of something, but not guilty of crime. I strongly disagree with that. Look at…the stop and frisk stuff in New York, 90 percent of the people they stop and frisk, they don't arrest because they can't find anything that would substantiate a criminal charge.
>
> There was a time when anybody who got stopped got arrested. They weren't going to go through the time and effort of frisking you. They would

> *If 50 people are guilty of being in possession of marijuana, but only five are arrested and convicted, and you play that out over and over and over again, there comes a point where it becomes unjust to say these five are guilty and the other 45 are not, and that's what our drug policy has been.*
>
> — Bryan Stevenson

charge you and if you didn't show up as being guilty, that would be fine. They didn't care. The burden on the system got so great that there was an effort to try to do a little bit more before the arrest was made, but… if 90 percent of the people they're stopping who they suspect of crime are innocent based on what they conclude, then we have every reason to doubt that statistic isn't going to carry over at some high percentage for the people that they charge at arrest. I definitely don't think that most people arrested are guilty or all of them are guilty by certainly no means.

You can go to any major university in this country. If I was the Drug Czar, and I sent the DEA to Harvard and Yale and Texas and Alabama and Auburn and any school you can think of, we would find lots of kids illegally in possession of narcotics, of marijuana and other drugs, and we could arrest them and subject them to prison sentences under our laws. In fact, our laws would even mandate that, but society would not tolerate repeated DEA raids at Harvard and Yale and major colleges and universities in this country because the parents and the schools and the community wouldn't accept that.

What we do [instead] is…repeated targeted DEA raids at low-income housing projects and in low-income neighborhoods. We sometimes go into places, and we put up chicken wire and trap everybody inside. Then we go through from house to house to see who is in possession of drugs, and we arrest them. We say that these are guilty drug users, and we beat up on them. We send them to jail. We know that there are lots of people just like them [not being targeted]. So, even in that context, guilt is not synonymous with culpability, and culpability is not synonymous with justice, right?

Ultimately, it becomes unjust to only pick the five who were defined as guilty because of their age or their race or their something. In some ways, it's even more provocative than prosecution of innocent people in my mind. There [are] 50 houses all doing the same thing, but only the same five get prosecuted over and over again. That's going to create outrage because the knowledge of these others are the same and getting away with it actually makes what you're doing even more problematic which is why… the scale of justice is complicated for me.

15.5 *NELSON V. CAMPBELL* BACKGROUND

For most, David Nelson was far from a sympathetic client. In 1971, he was convicted of beating an 82-year-old man to death in a Birmingham, Alabama, parking deck. He was released after serving three years in prison. On New

Year's Eve in 1977, he was a passenger in James Cash's cab in Birmingham. He robbed him of $20, and then shot and killed him.

Later that evening, he was with his girlfriend of one month, Linda Vice. They were at Theo's Lounge in Birmingham where they met Wilson Thompson. Nelson introduced Vice as his sister.

Thompson and Nelson talked about having an orgy with Vice at Thompson's mobile home. They left the lounge at 1:30 a.m. and arrived at Thompson's home about 30 minutes later.

Everyone had some drinks, and then Nelson ordered Vice to remove her clothes. She was reluctant. Then, Thompson took off his clothes, and Nelson ordered Vice to take off her clothes and lie down on the bed, which she did. Nelson told Thompson he could have oral sex with Vice. Just as Thompson began to perform oral sex, Nelson shot him in the back of the neck at close range with a .38 caliber pistol. The bullet exited Thompson's neck and entered Vice's leg.

Thompson fell face forward on the bed, and Vice got up screaming, at which point Nelson shot at her twice, one bullet hitting her wrist and the other grazing her head. Vice fell to the floor. Nelson began ransacking the mobile home. When he returned to the bedroom to find Vice still alive, he pulled down his pants and told Vice to perform oral sex on him. She told him she was dying. He threw a blanket over her and left the room.

Vice ran out of the mobile home with the blanket around her bloodied body and went to a nearby house where she called 911. When the police arrived, Thompson was dead, and there was no sign of Nelson and Vice. The next day, Nelson was the passenger in a car that was stopped for driving erratically by Vice. When the police officer determined the car belonged to Thompson, Nelson was arrested. The car was searched and the .38 caliber pistol was found along with Thompson's belt, which Nelson was wearing.

At trial, the prosecution's theory was that after killing the cab driver, Nelson needed a car to get out of Birmingham. He lured Thompson at Theo's bar to meet Vice. Then, he convinced Thompson to invite Vice and himself to Thompson's home with the false promise of an orgy. Once there, he committed the murder, and he and Vice drove away with Thompson's car.

In a long procedural history that is unimportant for our discussion, Nelson was eventually convicted of both Thompson and Cash's murders and sentenced to death. He was granted a stay of execution in 1996 when a doctor stated that Nelson could provide a kidney for his ill brother. Doctors later determined the transplant would not work.

Nelson's execution was rescheduled for October 9, 2003. Three days before the execution, Stevenson filed a civil rights action against Donald Campbell, the commissioner of the Alabama Department of Corrections ("Prison"). The type of lawsuit Stevenson filed in federal district court is commonly referred to as a 1983 action because it refers to the number of the section of the Civil Rights Act of 1871 that provides relief for a prisoner.

Before getting to the merits of Nelson's appeal to the Supreme Court, I asked Stevenson if he had sympathy for Nelson and to explain why anyone should care about a three-time convicted murderer. Stevenson faced the question head on.

> I would certainly say that he had a criminal history that was not the kind of history that you want to use when making an argument about what the Constitution requires. We are going to test the Court's commitment. [Nelson was a] lifelong alcoholic that had used drugs. Prior criminal, had violent crime history etcetera. If you are looking for an attractive client to present to the Court around some Constitutional issue, this would not be the person you'd pick, but our point was that it's the integrity of the rest of us that's implicated when we start butchering people or cutting on people in a cruel way during an execution. It's not even about Nelson, it's about the character of the kind of society we want to live in.

He then added that we can't really know the truth about Nelson's crimes and any mitigating factors about his life.

> We don't really know what happened in that case because he didn't have the kind of defense lawyer who would develop the facts that you could actually have a contextualized narrative. My own view is that it was much more complicated than what it is reported as. But we never had the chance to talk about that because that door had been closed years earlier, and in-effective assistance of counsel was one of the issues. He lost on it, but you never know all of the things that were really going on, and you can't know until you have a good lawyer making a good defense.

Let's focus now on Nelson's appeal to the Supreme Court. Stevenson was not challenging Nelson's convictions, death sentence, or the method of execution (i.e., lethal injection versus electrocution). Instead, Stevenson argued that Alabama's use of a "cut-down" procedure (discussed in detail to follow) to access his veins for a lethal injection was cruel and unusual punishment under the Eighth Amendment to the Constitution. The Eighth Amendment prohibits the "unnecessary and wanton infliction of pain," and courts have long held that the Amendment protects prisoners from "the gratuitous infliction of suffering."

The Prison responded that Nelson's lawsuit should be dismissed on procedural grounds. Without getting too much into this issue, the Prison argued that Nelson's lawsuit was really a habeas corpus petition and should be dismissed. The reason is that courts have ruled that much of the relief a 1983 action provides must yield to the specific limitations of the federal habeas corpus statute. The habeas corpus statute allows a prisoner to challenge his conviction or the duration of his sentence.

Generally, a habeas corpus petition can only be filed one time after a prisoner meets strict requirements. Nelson had already filed one habeas corpus petition. A prisoner can only file a second habeas corpus petition if he first seeks permission from the appellate court before filing the lawsuit. Nelson never sought this permission. Consequently, the Prison's position was that Nelson had intentionally mislabeled his lawsuit as a 1983 action in order to avoid the prohibition of filing a second habeas corpus petition without the appellate court's permission.

The Eleventh Circuit agreed with the Prison and ruled that Nelson's 1983 claim in fact challenged the method of his execution and was the functional equivalent of a habeas corpus petition. Since he had already filed one, he was not allowed to file a second one.

Stevenson sought review from the United States Supreme Court. The issue before the Supreme Court was whether section 1983 could provide relief for a prisoner seeking a stay of his execution in order to claim that he was subject to cruel and unusual punishment as prohibited by the Eighth Amendment.

15.6 NELSON ORAL ARGUMENT

The quote in the box is one of Justice Scalia's searing questions at the oral argument detailed in the next section. It captures one of Stevenson's problems. Stevenson had the unenviable task of representing what some might call a reprehensible client before the Supreme Court and arguing that even a three-time convicted murderer deserved protection under the Constitution. Earlier that year, the Supreme Court had denied several last-minute requests to stay executions for prisoners who argued that a lethal injection was cruel

> *The crime was committed over a quarter of a century ago for which he was condemned [to execution]. And what he's really concerned about is an incision?*
> —Justice Antonin Scalia

and unusual punishment. In addition, Nelson was the second-longest serving inmate on Alabama's death row. Let's watch how Stevenson frames his argument and persuades the justices. (To listen to the oral argument, go to www.TurningPointsatTrial.com.) Here is how he began his argument:

Stevenson's opening argument

Stevenson: Mr. Chief Justice, and may it please the Court. Six days before petitioner's scheduled execution in this case, **an execution that he had sought and informally requested to be carried out as soon as possible,**

prison officials went to him and for the first time told him that to deal with a medical problem that both parties acknowledged exists, he would be subjected to a procedure that would be conducted by State officials, not necessarily medically trained, not necessarily licensed, where they were going to make a two-inch incision in his arm, cut through fat and tissue and muscle, until they had a vein that they could access for the purposes of inserting a catheter.

Court: Well, presumably at a much earlier date, the prisoner did know that he would be scheduled to be executed by lethal injection.

The Court immediately implies its impatience with last-minute appeals filed just before an execution. To deal with this recurring problem, Congress had passed the Prison Litigation Reform Act ("PLRA") in 1995 which, among other things, limited last-minute appeals that interfered with implementation of executions. Stevenson anticipates this concern. He mentions in his first sentence that Nelson wanted his execution to take place as soon as possible. He then responded to the Court's question as follows:

Stevenson: **Absolutely, Your Honor**.

Court: And he did know his veins were compromised.

Stevenson: **Absolutely**.

Court: So — so presumably in — well in advance, he could anticipate a problem.

Stevenson: Yes, Your Honor, and he did. He immediately began contacting the warden at Holman Prison…and informed [the warden] he had this condition, that they would need to create protocols necessary to deal with it.

The State admitted that they had never dealt with someone in this condition before and began offering all kinds of things that would accomplish this execution. Let him bring in a physician that can insert a catheter. Let's get some protocols established so that we don't have any problems. And for six weeks essentially, this effort was being made [by the prison].

He had been previously told that they were going to do this 24 hours in advance, that they weren't going to make this kind of two-inch incision, and even though he hadn't been assured there would be medical people, he was relatively comfortable with that. He did not file suit. **It's only six days before for the first time that the State announced they would have this kind of invasive procedure carried out by someone who was not necessarily medically trained.**

In his first two answers, Stevenson does not make the mistake that most lawyers do. He does not get defensive or evasive when answering a question that might hurt his case. Instead, he answers "absolutely." He bides his time, and then, when there is an opening, he explains why the lawsuit was filed at the last minute despite Nelson's knowledge that he had the pre-existing vein problem. (The vein problem was due to years of drug abuse, and previously prison personnel had difficulty gaining access to his veins for routine physicals. Obviously, access to his veins would be needed for the lethal injection.)

In fact, Stevenson turns the potentially devastating question around and points out that it is the Prison's actions which have caused the emergency before the Court. As Stevenson had stated in his written brief to the Court, the warden had originally told Nelson a month before the execution that prison personnel would cut a half-inch incision in Nelson's arm and catheterize a vein 24 hours before the scheduled execution. Nelson agreed with this procedure.

However, at a second meeting on Friday, October 3, 2003, just six days before the execution, the warden informed Nelson that prison personnel would now try a "cut-down" procedure, where prison personnel would make a two-inch incision in Nelson's arm or leg and that only local anesthesia would be used. In addition, there was no guarantee that a doctor would perform the procedure or even be present.

In the 1983 action, Stevenson asked the federal district court to delay the execution until the prison provided him with a protocol for dealing with the medical problem of gaining access to problematic veins and to develop a procedure consistent with contemporary standards of medical care.

Stevenson had submitted an affidavit from Dr. Mark Heath with his brief to the Supreme Court. Dr. Heath is a board certified anesthesiologist and assistant professor at Columbia University College of Physicians and Surgeons. He maintained that the Prison's proposed cut-down procedure was a dangerous and antiquated medical procedure that should be performed only by a doctor in a hospital environment with deep sedation. He declared, "[T]here is no comprehensible reason for the State of Alabama to be planning to employ the cut-down procedure to obtain intravenous access, unless there exists an intent to render the procedure more painful and risky than it otherwise needs to be." The doctor further described the procedure as one where a series of sharp incisions would be made through the skin, muscle, fat, and underlying tissue until a large vein could be reached. Given Nelson's compromised veins, this procedure would be pointless and could lead to complications of severe hemorrhage or heart attack.

Nonetheless, the Court's impatience with last-minute requests to stay an execution is evident with its further questions. Watch how Stevenson eases this concern.

> *Court: How long ago was the conviction for which he was condemned to death?*

> **Stevenson:** The conviction was 1978. The death sentence is 1994. He spent a lot of years on death row under an illegal death sentence that the Eleventh Circuit overturned in 1993.

> *Court: The crime was committed when?*

> Stevenson: In 1978. The death sentenced imposed here was committed in 1994, and it's worth noting that even then Mr. Nelson was very, very unsure about fighting a death sentence. **He told the judge he wanted a death sentence. No appeal briefs were filed in the Alabama appellate courts.**

Stevenson points out that this is not a case where Nelson is trying to overturn his death sentence. Instead, it concerns his Constitutional right to be free from cruel and unusual punishment in the execution of that sentence. Another undercurrent in the case was whether Stevenson was challenging the method of execution such as whether one is killed by lethal injection, electric chair, or some other manner. Those challenges must be brought in a habeas corpus petition, which Nelson had already filed and exhausted.

In the next section, the court asks Stevenson to distinguish his case from someone who challenges the combination of chemicals used in a lethal injection, which must be brought in a habeas corpus petition.

> Court: *Would you say — would you be making the same argument if his complaint was not this two-inch cut but the combination of chemicals?*

> Stevenson: No, Your Honor. I think that's a much — a much harder question because that does, it seems to me, get closer to the execution. **What's analogous to our claim** is a claim where the prison says a week before the execution that we're going to and effectively **shackle you to a hitching post and not give you any food for 72 hours. We contend that that kind of treatment would be in violation of the Constitution. What we'd be trying to block is that treatment, not the execution**. The reality is in this case —

> Court: *Well, I mean, you know, as you know, we've — we've turned down certiorari in — in these cases challenging the type of drug used. What — what is the difference between, you know, your using a drug that's — that's going to hurt me and your using a catheter procedure that's going to hurt me? I don't —*

> Stevenson: I think the primary difference, Justice Scalia, is that those are a method of execution cases. They are challenging the method of execution. Here we have a procedure that is not even unique to executions.

> Court: *Well, but they're not challenging the method of execution. **If you want to execute me by drugs, they're saying, that's perfectly fine, just don't use a drug that hurts me. And just as here,** you're saying if you want to execute me by lethal injection, that's fine, just don't use a manner of lethal injection that hurts me. I find it very difficult to separate the two—*

> Stevenson: Your Honor…, [h]ere we have a completely severable procedure. **We have something that is not in any [way] required by the execution. And — and the State is saying we want to do it this way, and there**

are 100 other ways that it can be done. And in fact, it's just the discretionary conduct of the State prison officials that puts us in this situation.

We have a battle of analogies. Justice Scalia suggests Stevenson should lose because his case is just like a prisoner who complains that a particular combination of chemicals used in a lethal injection hurts him. Stevenson disagrees and compares it to the treatment of the prisoner prior to the execution, either by making a large incision in the arm or the analogy of shackling someone to a post. Scalia challenges Stevenson one more time and Stevenson pushes back hard.

> *Court: This comes close because you say it's unconstitutional to proceed with lethal injection under these circumstances.*

> Stevenson: No. We tried really hard to not say that. What we say, it is unconstitutional to proceed with venous access in this manner, to conduct medical care in this manner. It violates recognized standards of medical care. And that's what we're saying you cannot do. We have no objection. Mr. Nelson doesn't object to lethal injection. He doesn't even object to venous access. What he objects to is some kind of inhumane cutting by people who are not qualified or competent to do that.

> And like any other condition of confinement, the fact that he is near an execution, the fact that he has been scheduled for an execution shouldn't exempt him from protection if the State at the last minute announces that this is what they intend to do. This has not historically been a big problem. There have been over 700 executions in this country involving lethal injections.

Stevenson reminds the Court that Nelson is not objecting to lethal injection, only the unnecessary and inhumane way being proposed by the prison to cut into Nelson's arm to find a vein.

The Court then presses Stevenson by making its best argument why Stevenson should lose.

> *Court: And—and the crime was committed over a quarter of a century ago for which he was—he was condemned. And—and what he's really concerned about is—is an incision? I find it difficult to contemplate that this constitutes cruel and unusual punishment.*

> Stevenson: Well, Your Honor, it's not our position that he is seeking and—and demanding the most advanced procedures. What I think he is objecting to is something that we regard as fairly barbaric, to have a correctional staff member come back with a scalpel, make a 2-inch cut in his arm, cut through fat and tissue to get to a vein with no assurances that that person knows what they're doing, violates the basic standards of medical decency.

> And it's not just a cruel and unusual punishment. This Court has created a line of cases under *Estelle v. Gamble* that talk about deliberate

> *Yes, he's on death row. Yes, he's forfeited some of his basic expectations, but he hasn't given them all away. He's still entitled to be treated with some regard.*
> — Bryan Stevenson, oral argument

indifference to serious medical needs. This is a medical care case. Yes, he's in prison. Yes, he's on death row. Yes, he's forfeited some of his basic expectations, but he hasn't given them all away. He's still entitled to be treated with some regard.

As he has done throughout his argument, Stevenson maintains credibility with the Court by not hedging when pressed about the weaknesses in his case. But he also never gives an inch when it comes to what his case is all about. In short, Stevenson points out that his client may not deserve to live in the Court's view, but he is still entitled to be treated fairly under the Constitution.

Prison's argument

Much of the Prison's argument involved the nuances of various procedural bars to Stevenson's ability to bring his client's case before federal courts and ultimately the Supreme Court. Below are just the highlights that respond to Stevenson's opening argument and that Stevenson will address in his rebuttal argument. Kevin Newsom argued for the Prison.

> *Court: You were going to — you were going to tell us that, you know, the sky is going to fall if we find that this is 1983 [a civil rights case].*
>
> Newsom: I think it will fall pretty hard, Justice Kennedy. I think that if this Court concludes that Nelson in this case can — can challenge this — this cut-down as a means of gaining venous access, then the lower courts will be inundated with challenges to all manner of State execution procedures just as this Court was inundated with challenges following —

Throughout his argument, Newsom emphasized that if the Court were to rule in Stevenson's favor, there would be a flood of prisoners challenging the method of their execution under section 1983.

The Court then asked Newsom a key question it would later cite in its decision.

> *Court: But was there — whatever labels you use, was there something else that they asked for that you were not willing to give?*
>
> Newsom: They — I'm sorry. Go ahead. I didn't mean to —
>
> *Court: Yes. I thought I understood from the briefs that there was the first step. Everybody agreed if they could do it that way, it would be OK. And then there was something else that the defendant said should have been done before you*

would ever get to the cut-down, and if you got to the cut-down, certainly you'd want to have proper medical personnel there to administer it.

Newsom: The point that I'm trying to make is that — that in fact those first two — what the plaintiff asked for in this case was indeed percutaneous central line placement. That's the label not that I'm giving it but that they gave it. That's the procedure that they wanted, and now I'm trying to tell the Court that — that percutaneous central line placement is a central line placement through the skin with options one and two, central line placement in the thigh, central line placement in the neck, are indeed both percutaneous central line placement. **So, no, there is — I think there is no disagreement here that percutaneous central line placement is the preferred method and will, in fact, be used, a cut-down to be used only if actually necessary.**

Newsom acknowledges that the Prison would follow what Nelson's doctor recommended. This was a turning point in the case and would be cited by the Court in its decision.

This acknowledgment to follow the recommendation of Nelson's doctor is quite different from what the Prison proposed when the 1983 action was first filed in the lower court. At that time, the Prison proposed attaching a direct intravenous line to the external carotid vein located in the neck. If this failed, it would make a two-inch incision in the front part of the arm in order to isolate and dissect the saphenous vein. As Stevenson pointed out in his brief to the Supreme Court, the problem with this solution was that humans do not have an external carotid vein in the neck, and it is common medical knowledge that the saphenous vein is located in the leg, not the arm.

15.7 REBUTTAL ARGUMENT

In the Prison's argument, Newsom had told the Court that Nelson had many remedies in Alabama state court that would have avoided the necessity of filing a 1983 action in federal court that would burden the Supreme Court with its ultimate review. Justice Sandra Day O'Connor asked Stevenson about this argument.

Court: We were told there were a couple of other methods besides rule 32.

Stevenson: There are none, Justice O'Connor. The only thing we could do is file a motion for a stay. At the point at which the stay motion was requested here, April of 2000, Mr. Nelson didn't want a stay. He doesn't want a stay of execution. He actually wants his execution to be carried out.

Court: Well, he did ask for a stay you said, in order that this could be resolved.

Stevenson: Absolutely.

Court: So, as I understand it, he does want a stay in order that this can be heard.

Stevenson: Well, he wants a stay to—he wants to enjoin the kind of conduct that we're talking about here, but filing a stay motion in the Alabama Supreme Court would not get him merits review where we could present the kind of facts that we're now presenting.

And I have to say that access to the federal courts in this case has really changed the State's position. Nothing that we've been talking here this afternoon about what they intend to do was ever presented to Mr. Nelson until he got in front of the federal judge....

They have never made that offer [of percutaneous line placement]. They're making it here today. It's because we're in court, and, of course, we can't get to court unless this Court recognizes our authority to bring a legitimate challenge that does not attempt to invalidate his conviction or sentence. There is a gap.

Court: Well, what we heard today, does that satisfy the prisoner's request that these—all of these other things be used first?

Stevenson: Well, if—if the State had then and would now concede that percutaneous line placement would be an acceptable method, then, yes. That's all we were seeking. But of course, without a remedy—

Court: Is that not what was said today?

Stevenson: Well, it's not said in a way that we can enforce, Your Honor. Until we can go to the district court, go to a court, and enforce any of these representations, we are at risk. And that's all we're asking. That's all Mr. Nelson asked in the first instance. And the irony, of course, is if it had been permitted to proceed, I think we would have resolved this. He'd already be executed. And I think their conduct today strengthens that position. And that's why we would urgently ask this Court to reverse the rule that the Eleventh Circuit is now applying which bars prisoners like Mr. Nelson from getting federal review. It's not asking a lot.

And I understand the fears, but I don't agree with Mr. Newsom that this is opening up anything. People can file complaints now. They could have done it for the last 20 years....

What this Court shouldn't do out of fear is to block prisoners like Mr. Nelson who have legitimate constitutional complaints from getting remedies that are precisely the kinds of claims that could and should be resolved in a manner that they've been discussed about—discussed today easily.

Stevenson told me that it wasn't until oral argument at the Supreme Court that the Prison ever offered to avoid using a cut-down procedure. Until the argument, the Prison's position had been that Nelson had exhausted all his appeals. Consequently, the Prison could administer the drugs in whatever way it deemed appropriate. The Prison's attitude was, "You're guilty of murder, and we get to do this any way we want to." Stevenson believes it was that callous attitude that helped achieve a unanimous opinion for his client.

15.8 SUPREME COURT'S DECISION

In a unanimous decision, the Court ruled that Nelson was entitled to challenge the State's proposed "cut-down" procedure in a 1983 action instead of a habeas corpus petition. It sent the case back to the district court to determine if the "cut-down" procedure was necessary. But given the State's concession at oral argument that it would use Nelson's recommendations, the Court predicted such a hearing would not be necessary.

Despite the Court's prediction, there was continued litigation in the lower courts. After being on death row for more than 27 years, Nelson died in prison on November 2, 2009, of natural causes before his method of execution could be resolved. He was 64 years old.

15.9 *MILLER V. ALABAMA*

The second case we are going to examine involved the question of whether it was cruel and unusual punishment under the Eighth Amendment to sentence a juvenile to a mandatory life sentence without parole.

Evan Miller was 14 years old when he committed his crime. He had lived a horrifically tragic life. His stepfather had abused him, and his mother suffered from drug and alcohol addiction. Consequently, he had been in and out of foster care his entire life. When he was only six years old, he tried to commit suicide, followed by three more attempts prior to age 14. Miller regularly drank alcohol and used illegal drugs.

One evening in 2003, he was at home with his friend Colby Smith. A neighbor, Cole Cannon, came over to buy drugs from Miller's mother. After the drug deal, Miller and Smith followed Cannon back to his trailer where all three smoked pot and played drinking games.

When Cannon passed out, Miller stole his wallet and split the $300 he found in it with Smith. But when Miller tried to put the wallet back in Cannon's pants, Cannon awoke and grabbed Miller's throat. When Smith saw this, he grabbed a baseball bat and began to strike Cannon with it. Cannon released his grip, and Miller took the bat from his friend and began to beat Cannon with it. Miller placed a sheet over Cannon's head and told him, "I am God, I've come to take your life," and hit Cannon one more time.

Miller and Smith returned to Miller's home and then after a period of time, they returned to Cannon's trailer to cover their tracks. They set the trailer on fire, and Cannon died from his injuries and smoke inhalation.

At first, Miller was charged as a juvenile, but Alabama law allowed the District Attorney to transfer the case to adult court, which he did. The court agreed to the transfer citing the nature of the crime, Miller's mental maturity, and his prior juvenile offenses for truancy and criminal mischief. Once in an adult court, the State charged Miller as an adult with murder in the course of arson, which carried a mandatory minimum punishment of life without parole. Miller was convicted.

At the United States Supreme Court, the issue was whether the Eighth Amendment to the Constitution prohibited a mandatory life sentence without parole for a juvenile because it is cruel and unusual punishment.

Stevenson points out that what often gets lost in juvenile cases is the context of the crime which mitigates what the juvenile has done. For example, what is missing from the summary of the facts above is the fact that Cannon gave gin and whiskey to Miller and Smith at his trailer and then sent the boys out to buy marijuana, so they could smoke it. If the police had intervened at that point, Cannon would have been charged with criminal offenses including predatory exploitation of children. "Nobody would have had an ounce of sympathy for that person." But after the fire, Cannon becomes the tragic victim of an arson murder.

Stevenson says the point is that there is a complicated narrative to the crime, and it is difficult to get the Court to understand the mitigating factors for his client because the end result of Cannon's death overshadows everything that preceded it. Consequently, sometimes it is better to argue to the Court on behalf of the community of clients—in this case all juveniles who are facing life without parole—than deal with the particulars of an individual case. Stevenson wanted the Court to understand that he was representing all children.

What made the oral argument extraordinarily unique is that the Supreme Court had decided to hear a companion case following the Miller oral argument, and Stevenson was the lawyer for that case as well. Consequently, Stevenson had back-to-back oral arguments. The second case involved a juvenile named Kuntrell Jackson, who was also 14 years old when he took part in the shooting and killing of a store clerk.

Stevenson knew that nothing he was going to say would change Justices Alito and Scalia, who had indicated from a past decision that they would vote against him. He knew that they were going to ask questions about originalism and big Constitutional questions. As Stevenson says, "You are not going to add anything to that debate, so you don't want to get stuck there."

It helps to understand the context of the Miller case. A lot of juveniles were executed between 1976 and 2005. In 2002, the Supreme Court banned the execution of adults with intellectual disabilities in *Atkins v. Virginia*. The analysis the Court used was that it was cruel to execute someone with a mental age of a teenager.

After that opinion, a lot of lawyers were trying to get the Court to extend the ban to actual teenagers, but the Court was reluctant to do that. On the other hand, many advocates felt that the Court should let the states decide whether teenagers could be executed. In 2005, the Supreme Court banned the execution of juveniles in *Roper v. Simmons*. One of the questions that came up during the oral argument was if juveniles are too young for the death penalty, why aren't they too young for life without parole?

In 2010, Stevenson argued a companion case at the Supreme Court, which resulted in its decision in *Graham v. Florida* that life without parole imposed on juveniles for non-homicides violated the Eighth Amendment. Unfortunately, the impact of *Graham* was not that profound, because of the 3,000 children serving sentences for life without parole, only a couple hundred were there for non-homicides.

In *Miller v. Alabama*, Stevenson was making back-to-back arguments before the Supreme Court. Both boys were 14 years old. Stevenson did not know how far the Court would go — if at all — to cover more children. There were lots of possibilities. One was not to extend *Graham* any further. Second, the Court could rule that mandatory life without parole sentences were not allowed, but a judge could impose the sentence as long as he had the discretion to choose another sentence. Third, the Court could have said that mandatory life without parole was acceptable in an intentional murder but not allowed in a murder that occurred in connection with a felony. Another possibility is that the Court could have drawn an arbitrary line and decided that teenagers of a certain age such as 14 and younger could not be sentenced to life without parole. If the court drew the line at 14 years of age, it would effect about 100 children, while a demarcation line of 17 years of age would effect more than 2,000 teenagers. Given all these possibilities, Stevenson felt it was crucial that he answer the questions but listen to find out where the votes were and which direction the Court was headed.

> *All oral arguments for me are listening exercises. What the court has to say is so much more important than what you have to say, because they get to decide.*
>
> —Bryan Stevenson

15.10 MILLER ORAL ARGUMENT

(The entire oral argument can be heard at www.TurningPointsatTrial.com.)

> **Stevenson:** Mr. Chief Justice, and may it please the Court: In *Graham v. Florida*, this Court recognized that children are inherently characterized by internal attributes and external circumstances that preclude a finding of a degree of culpability that would make a sentence of life imprisonment

without the possibility of parole constitutionally permissible under the Court's Eighth Amendment excessiveness analysis.

While the issue in *Graham* involved juveniles who were convicted of non-homicide offenses, these deficits in maturity and judgment and decision-making are not crime-specific. All children are encumbered with the same barriers that this Court has found to be constitutionally relevant before imposition of a sentence of life imprisonment without parole or the death penalty. In fact, in *Roper*, this Court acknowledged that these differences between children and adults exist even in the cases involving the most aggravated murders. These deficits, these differences, are even more pronounced in young children.

Justice Ginsburg: Mr. Stevenson, but in Roper, *the Court also made the point—when it ruled out the death penalty, it said, "To the extent the juvenile death penalty might have residual deterrent effect, it is worth noting that the punishment of life imprisonment without the possibility of parole is itself a severe sanction." So, the Court in* Roper *seemed to be anticipating this case and suggesting that—that it was all right, it was constitutional.*

Stevenson: There's no question, Justice Ginsburg, that the—the default sentence in *Roper* was life imprisonment without parole, but we actually think that, specifically with regard to that provision, there is no greater deterrent effect, and these deficits, that these problems that children experience, lend themselves to an analysis that is subject when the punishment is life imprisonment without parole. Like the death penalty—

Notice how Stevenson candidly and directly answers Ginsburg's question. He begins his answer by admitting, "There's no question." It is the perfect way to gain credibility with the Court. He reads the case law just as Ginsburg does, but he wants her to reach a different conclusion. But before he can explain, Justice Scalia interrupts him. Remember Stevenson's tip earlier in the chapter to "never interrupt the judge." Here he does not try to finish his argument but defers to Justice Scalia.

Justice Scalia: What about 50 years? Is that—is that too much?

Stevenson: What the Court held in—in Graham—

Justice Scalia: Well, you know, once—once you depart from the principle that we've enunciated that death is different, why is life without parole categorically different from 60 years or 70 years or—you know, you'd be back here next term with a 60-year sentence?

Stevenson: Justice Scalia, I think you're absolutely right, that there is a point at which a term-of-year sentence could constitute the same kind of judgment—

Justice Scalia: OK.

Stevenson: — as life imprisonment without parole.

Justice Scalia: Good.

Stevenson continues to admit when a justice is right, even when it is Justice Scalia who he knows will write a dissenting opinion. But after granting Justice Scalia a concession, he quickly pivots and explains why Justice Scalia is not completely right.

Stevenson: It's a challenge, and I — and I concede that. But I — and so, the first part of my answer would be that I think the easier rule to write would be that there is a categorical ban on all life without parole sentences for all children up until the age of 18, acknowledging —

Justice Scalia: How — how do I come to that decision? What do I — just consult my own preferences on this matter? Something like 39 States allow it. I mean, the American people, you know, have decided that that's the rule. They allow it. And the Federal Government allows it. So, I'm supposed to impose my — my judgment on — on what seems to be a consensus of the American people?

Stevenson: Well, at least in this case, you'd look to your precedent in *Roper* and in *Graham*, which drew that line.

Justice Scalia: Well, that's not going to help me, you know.

Stevenson: Well, I understand —

(Laughter.)

Stevenson: I understand, Justice Scalia, but I don't think you can draw much comfort in the fact that 39 jurisdictions make this theoretically possible. That same number existed in the *Graham* context. Most of those jurisdictions have not addressed a minimum age for life without parole.

Even while answering a question from one of his most ardent opponents, Justice Scalia, Stevenson creates laughter. He is engaging the Court. His goal is to have a conversation, not an argument. Stevenson concedes that the points he is making are not going to convince Scalia which creates the humorous moment. He respectfully disagrees with Scalia while hoping that his arguments will persuade those justices in the middle who are undecided.

Justice Kennedy: If we can focus on the mandatory aspect of the case, I think — I know you'd prefer a more general rule — it may be that we have to have your general rule. I'm not sure. If I'm the trial judge, and I have to determine whether or not I'm going to give life without parole, and it's discretionary, what — what do I look at? Are — can I get social scientists to come in and tell me what the chances of rehabilitation are? Are there — are there statistics? Now, we have some quite compelling stories of rehabilitation in this case. I don't know if they're isolated; I don't know where they are in the statistical universe of how often rehabilitation is — is demonstrated and is real. What do I look at? What's a judge supposed to do?

Stevenson: Well, I think one of the problems, Your Honor, with — with trying to make these judgments is that — that even psychologists say that we can't make good long-term judgments about the rehabilitation and transitory character of these young people. That's the reason why in *Graham* this Court didn't permit that kind of discretion. We know that —

Justice Scalia: Well, I thought that modern penology has abandoned that rehabilitation thing, and they — they no longer call prisons reformatories or whatever, and punishment is the — is the criterion now. Deserved punishment for crime.

Stevenson: Well —

Justice Scalia: Now, if that's the criterion, is everything that you say irrelevant?

Stevenson: I —

Justice Scalia: Let's assume I don't believe in rehabilitation, as I think sentencing authorities nowadays do not. Both at the federal and the state levels, it's been made clear.

Stevenson: Well, I — I — no. I think it would still be relevant, Justice Scalia, but — but I also don't think that correctional facilities have identified themselves as having no role to play in the rehabilitative process. I mean, one of the problems with this sentence of life imprisonment without parole is that it actually bans and shields this population from a whole range of services that are specifically designed to rehabilitate: education services, treatment services, anger management programs. All of these programs exist within prisons, including the federal prisons, because we do care how people perform when they are released. And so, correction is still very much the heart and soul of what we do.

Notice how twice Stevenson begins to answer, he is interrupted by Scalia, and he immediately stops and listens. Stevenson instructs that too many lawyers are focused on what they want to say instead of listening to the justices and trying to understand what they need to have answered in order to make a ruling. Stevenson listens and then challenges Scalia by arguing that prisons do provide rehabilitation and that his premise is wrong.

Justice Kennedy: Well, again, it seems you're just forcing us into a — a bipolar position. We're either going to say that you can't prevail at all or that everyone under 18 is — cannot get life without parole. I don't see this middle course —

Stevenson: Yes.

Justice Kennedy: —which you seem to have abandoned, and you can't tell me how a judge would apply it if we — if we chose not to abandon it.

Stevenson: Well, I — I don't intend to abandon it, Justice Kennedy. I mean, obviously, I'm arguing for this categorical ban, but I think the Court could obviously do something else. We think that there is a basis for concluding, unquestionably, that a child under the age of 15 should not be exposed to life without parole based on this Court's precedents and on the data presented. The Court could set a categorical line there and, at the same time, make a determination that subjecting any child under the age of 18 to life without parole where there is no ability to consider age is fundamentally at odds with what this Court has now constitutionally recognized in both *Roper* and *Graham*.

Notice how important it is for Stevenson to listen. He hears Justice Kennedy's concern that he might be forcing the Court to decide that there should be a complete prohibition of life without parole for juveniles and that there would not be enough votes to do that. Stevenson does not back off of his main goal but offers the court a middle ground. It was at this point that Stevenson sensed he would win at some level because Justice Kennedy was a key swing vote.

In this next excerpt, Justice Ginsburg asks a very specific question. Not only does Stevenson know the facts of the case very well, but he offers yet another reason why the sentence of mandatory life without parole is unfair.

Justice Ginsburg: Mr. Stevenson, may I ask you a case — a question specifically about the Miller case? There were two boys involved in this horrendous crime. The older one took a plea and got life with parole. Was the plea offered to Miller?

Stevenson: No plea was offered to Miller. The — what tends to happen, and there was some evidence of this that was developed earlier, is that the question was who was going to give a statement first, who was the most cooperative, whose lawyer is most effective at accomplishing that. There were some complaints. There's a post conviction [motion] pending now that makes some allegations about what the lawyer didn't do to facilitate a plea. But, no, there was no offer of life with parole made to Evan Miller.

And one of the difficulties, of course, in these cases is that, you know, the younger you are, the more vulnerable you are, the less experienced you are, the less capable you are of managing these dynamics in the criminal justice system that sometimes can be very outcome-determinative.

Rebuttal argument

In his four minutes of rebuttal argument, Stevenson succinctly addresses all the important questions that the justices have raised during his opponent's oral argument. In this excerpt, Stevenson clearly explains his positions.

> **Stevenson:** Thank you, Mr. Chief Justice. I just want to make clear that the rule we seek would not require states to impose the same sentence on juveniles convicted of homicides from juveniles convicted of non-homicides. The states would be free to do that if they chose to, but they could certainly create a regime where it's life with parole where there are different ages for eligibility. In fact, the State of Nevada makes you eligible for parole after 15 years if the crime is a non-homicide, 20 years if it's a homicide. The states would still have a great deal of flexibility to create, consistent with this Court's rule, a regime that makes these distinctions.
>
> Justice Kennedy, I did want to direct your attention to two amicus briefs that I think respond to two of the questions you've raised. There is an amicus brief submitted by criminologists in this case, and it looks specifically at the question of deterrence. And what they've found is life without parole has not had any measurable deterrent effect. The states that don't put juveniles — don't subject children to life without parole have actually experienced the same level of decrease in violent crime and homicide as the states that do. And, in fact, in some of those jurisdictions, the decrease is even more significant.
>
> I also want to address your question, Justice Scalia. There is — there are some studies that have established that juveniles are more likely or less likely to recidivate after an intervention than adults. Generally speaking, homicide offenders are categorically less likely to recidivate than many non-homicide offenders. Drug offenders and property crime offenders are much more likely to recidivate than — than homicide offenders. And so, there's a lot to support that a judgment rooted in these penological concerns would be well supported here.

15.11 SUPREME COURT'S RULING

In a 5–4 decision, the Supreme Court granted everything Stevenson asked for. It decided that mandatory life imprisonment without parole for those under the age of 18 at the time of their crimes violates the Eighth Amendment's prohibition on cruel and unusual punishments. Justice Kagan wrote the opinion, and she was joined by Justices Kennedy, Breyer, Ginsburg, and Sotomayor. Chief Justice Roberts filed a dissenting opinion in which Justices Scalia, Thomas, and Alito joined.

The majority concluded that the mandatory penalty scheme prevents the sentencer from taking into account a juvenile's age, that youths are typically less culpable than adults, that youths can be rehabilitated, and that the sentence may not deter other juveniles as it would adults. The Court concluded that "by subjecting a juvenile to the same life-without-parole sentence applicable to an adult—these laws prohibit a sentencing authority from assessing whether the law's harshest term of imprisonment proportionately punishes a juvenile offender.... [I]mposition of a State's most severe penalties on juvenile offenders cannot proceed as though they were not children."

In particular, the Court found that in Miller's case, no one can doubt that Miller deserved severe punishment for killing Cannon. That is "beyond question." But the sentencer needs to examine all the circumstances before concluding that life without any possibility of parole was the appropriate penalty. For example, the Court pointed out that "if ever a pathological background might have contributed to a 14-year-old's commission of a crime, it is here."

15.12 STEVENSON'S NEXT CHALLENGE FOR THE SUPREME COURT

The two cases we have examined won't be Stevenson's last trips to the Supreme Court. He shared with me his next two biggest challenges. First, he believes that there should be a minimum age for trying children as an adult. Today, there are 15 states that have no minimum age requirement. Consequently, Stevenson represents 9, 10, and 11-year-old children who face a long sentence in an adult prison if convicted. The fear of children serving a 30–40 year sentence in an adult prison forces children to take a plea to a crime that they would otherwise challenge at trial.

As Stevenson declares, "I think it's really cruel to imagine that we could put a nine year old in a prison with adults or make a judgment about a nine year old that says that he has to be in prison for 30 to 40 years. I just don't think what nine year olds do can be assigned the kind of culpability and autonomy that we assign to an adult."

Second, Stevenson states that no child should be housed in an adult prison. On any given day, there are 10,000 children being housed in an adult prison or jail. Although Congress passed the Prison Rape Elimination Act which prohibits housing children in adult prisons, there is no enforcement provision in the Act which would allow Stevenson to force a prison to comply. With a look of determination for the daunting task ahead, Stevenson concludes, "I feel like if we can get to the court on either of those claims, we've got a chance."

15.13 CHAPTER CHECKLIST ✏

Stevenson's oral argument strategies

1. One of the biggest mistakes lawyers make is that they fail to listen.

2. Know your audience.

3. When asked a difficult question, answer yes or no before giving your explanation.

4. Do not rely on notes.

5. Have a conversation with the court. Do not give canned answers.

6. Know what you need to win.

7. Never cut off the judge.

8. Present your best self.

9. Have the courage to concede a fact that hurts your case. Evasive answers destroy your credibility.

10. Don't repeat what is in your brief.

11. Don't re-litigate a winning point.

12. Address the judges by name.

13. Moot court is a must.

14. Know the record and case law.

Particular challenges for death penalty appeals

1. The biggest challenge is that courts have made a priority of finality over fairness.

2. There is pressure from victims and public on the court to uphold a conviction.

3. Your task is to reset the narrative for the judges.

4. Elevate fairness in a way that makes the judges uncomfortable with the outcome.

Stevenson's views on the death penalty

1. "I don't think there's something redemptive in facilitating the death of another human being."

2. "I think instead of promising people an execution, we ought to be providing people with counseling and services and money and a whole host of things that might actually help you recover, but we don't do that."

3. "Eighty percent of the people on death row in Alabama are on death row for crimes committed against people who are white, and 65 percent of all murder victims in the state of Alabama are black."

4. "I think too many of our opinions have been shaped around something like the death penalty by asking, 'Does this person deserve to die for the crime that they've committed?' You can get to yes on that question and still not believe in the death penalty, if you ask these other questions, 'Do we deserve to kill if we have a system that treats you better if you are rich and guilty than poor and innocent? If we have a system where race matters more than guilt? If we have a system that will frequently result in executing innocent people? If we have a system that is political where people with power get protection, and people without it don't?'"

Are criminal defendants guilty?

1. Conviction rate in America is 93 percent.

2. Stevenson profoundly disagrees that most defendants are guilty.

3. The death penalty is the most funded and regulated part of the criminal justice system, and the error rate is one out of nine.

4. The error rate must be significantly more for crimes that don't get the attention the death penalty does.

5. "If 90 percent of the people they're stopping who they suspect of crime are innocent based on what they conclude [and then release them], then we have every reason to doubt that the statistic isn't going to carry over at some high percentage for the people that they charge at arrest [and set a trial date for]." In other words, if the error rate is 90 percent for people they stop on the reasonable suspicion that they did something wrong, the error rate will also be high for those people they actually arrest for probable cause that they committed a crime.

6. If the police target minorities and the poor, that's going to create outrage. In those circumstances, guilt is not synonymous with culpability, and culpability is not synonymous with justice.

Tips to learn from Stevenson's oral arguments

1. Stevenson prepares a short opening argument that summarizes why he should win.

2. Stevenson candidly concedes questions when appropriate by saying, "absolutely."

3. Stevenson is never evasive when answering questions.

4. The only notes Stevenson has at podium is a blank sheet of paper to keep track of particular questions the judges ask.

5. Stevenson eases the judges' concerns by showing them how to arrive at the decision he wants and still follow the particular law the judge is questioning him about.

6. Stevenson uses analogies to make his point. In *Nelson*, he compared the cruelty of the incision conducted by a non-doctor to shackling someone to a hitching post and not giving him food for 72 hours.

7. Stevenson de-emphasizes the vicious crime by highlighting the mitigating facts of his client's history prior to the crime.

8. When the crime your client has committed is particularly vicious, it is better to argue how the outcome will affect a large class of people and not just your client.

9. Stevenson creates laughter with the court by engaging it in a conversation and being candid.

10. In rebuttal argument, Stevenson addresses all the important questions asked by the judges during his opponent's oral argument.

CHAPTER SIXTEEN

———∞∞∞———

Lisa Blatt

Channel Your Client

I definitely think of every case as war and someone is going to die here.... I don't want it to be me because there is clearly a winner and a loser.

— Lisa Blatt

---

*L*isa Blatt belongs to an elite group known as Supreme Court Specialists. But even among this specialized group, Blatt stands out. She holds the record for most oral arguments by a woman. She has made 33 appearances, winning 32 times.

But it is not just the number of her appearances and her winning record that make her exceptional. Perhaps the highest compliment any appellate lawyer could receive is to be cited by the United States Supreme Court itself as the model by which all attorneys should aspire for oral argument.

In the current Guide to Counsel written by the clerk of the Supreme Court, there is a section entitled, "Preparing Your Argument." The guide instructs:

> For an excellent example of a counsel who was intimately familiar with her client's business, see the transcript of argument in *United States v. Flores-Montano*, 541 U.S. 149 (2004). The case dealt with the searching of vehicle gas tanks by customs agents at an international border. Government counsel [Lisa Blatt] had a total grasp why and how

> **CHAPTER HIGHLIGHTS**
> - Bring energy and raise the temperature in the courtroom
> - Relying on case law is not enough
> - Only objective is to win, leaving all your credibility and professionalism intact

the agents conducted the searches and provided convincing explanations to all questions posed by the Court.

Blatt's success is no accident. After law school, she started her career at a prestigious law firm, Williams and Connolly, where she was a trial lawyer. She was drawn to appellate work and soon took a job with the Solicitor General's office where she argued before the Supreme Court 28 times. She now heads Arnold & Porter LLP's Appellate and Supreme Court practice.

16.1 MAKE THE CLIENT REAL

Blatt finds the key to victory on appeal to be very similar to that at trial. "You start thinking from the beginning what your story is going to be. You know you are going to have to write a brief and argue the case. From the very get go, it's what is the summation?…What is our theme, why do we win?"

When I asked Blatt how she makes the client real, she responded incredulously, "You learn who the client is." What seems so obvious to Blatt is far from clear to the vast majority of attorneys. Those attorneys only pay lip-service to the principle that you should know your client. Blatt applies the principle rigorously, and it pays off.

Most lawyers preparing for oral argument would study—with varying degrees of intensity—the facts, case law, and briefs submitted by both sides. It would not even occur to them to do what Lisa Blatt does. In order to make her clients come alive, she really gets to know them. In *United States v. Flores-Montano*, she traveled to a U.S. Customs Facility and spent an entire day taking apart a gas tank and learning about other tools that are used to search vehicles. Blatt does not believe that you can persuade judges by being professorial or having an attitude that "this is how the law should be." Instead, the "job of an advocate is to persuade someone, and to persuade someone, you need them to identify with you just like you would with a jury."

Unlike most lawyers who only learn the background of the case, Blatt wants to know it and make it real. As she explains, "It's not just that some case law says, 'I win,' it is that if I don't win, this is what happens. This is what actually is happening in the real world to this particular company or to a family trying to adopt a baby or…protecting the nation's border."

This practice of visiting the client and "channeling it" began when she first started out. When she worked at the Solicitor General's Office, she would shock government agencies that she represented by showing up at their offices to see how they operated; other appellate attorneys never made such visits.

Her practice continues today. In a recent case before the Supreme Court that involved a water dispute claim between Texas and Oklahoma, Blatt was able to correct opposing counsel's factual statements at oral argument about a particular river system because she had seen it for herself by visiting the disputed area on the Oklahoma border prior to oral argument. It is one thing to rely on maps in preparation for an argument, but what better way to make your case come alive than to relate to the Court what you have seen with your own eyes.

> *I'm a very big believer of channeling your client. Make the client real just like you would do with a jury.*
> — Lisa Blatt

16.2 DELIVERY

Blatt relates that she memorizes her "spiel," which is what she would say if she were to begin her argument and were never asked a question. It amounts to about two pages of words. Then, she memorizes the answers to anticipated questions. She realizes that most people would think her style is "crazy," because you need to be fluid, as the questions may be slightly different from those you anticipated. But for Blatt, the memorization relaxes her and gives her a sense of security.

I challenged Blatt as to why she thought that memorization is a good way to prepare for delivering an oral argument. I believe that if you are simply repeating memorized words, you cannot passionately convey your argument. You need to have a conversation with your audience, whether it be a jury or a panel of judges on appeal. But Blatt cleared up my concern immediately. She does not memorize words that she has written down. Instead, she explained, "When I say I memorize, I have orally talked through it so many times that what I memorize is oral speech."

Blatt reveals that her style before the justices is designed to "raise the temperature of the room." She brings energy to her arguments and is not afraid to say something provocative. She explains, "I definitely think of every case as war and someone is going to die here…. I don't want it to be me because there is clearly a winner and a loser." This philosophy also motivates her preparation. Others might think, "'Well, I'm just going to do the best job I can.' I can't think that way. That's not enough for me."

> *Your only objective is to win, leaving all your credibility and professionalism intact.*
> — Lisa Blatt

As you listen to Blatt's oral arguments cited in this section, you will find that nothing is stilted, bland, or "memorized" about her responses to the justices' questions. She carries on a very passionate conversation with the justices. She directly answers their questions. She makes it clear that both the law and common sense are on her side.

Another tip Blatt reveals is that you should not be constrained by case law. Most lawyers don't even realize that on appeal, you can change the law. Too many times lawyers get bogged down because they are not sure if the case law supports their position. Instead, lawyers should have the attitude that "if the rule makes sense, the case law will follow…. If something doesn't make sense, you should expect that justice and the law will catch up to common sense."

Also, just like the great trial lawyers profiled in this book, Blatt believes you need to simplify your case so that your argument is persuasive and understandable. She recently argued a case in the Ninth Circuit that had extremely complicated facts. Companies were required by the Clean Air Act for Regional Haze Pollution (CAARHP) to use retrofit technology to become compliant with EPA regulations. There was a choice between three regulatory pollution control options. The companies argued that the least restrictive option was the most cost effective; the environmental groups were pushing for the most restrictive option; and EPA chose the middle one.

Blatt wanted to cut through the mind-numbing details and clarify the arguments before the Court. She said the case was just like "Goldilocks and the Three Bears with each technology being Mama Bear, Papa Bear and Baby Bear, and the EPA was Goldilocks." Blatt explained that the EPA was acting as if it were Goldilocks by arguing that what the companies and environmental groups were pushing for was either too hot or too cold. The point that the parties were making was that Goldilocks was simply not acting reasonably by just arbitrarily picking the middle technology.

Her analogy not only got laughter from the court, but the judges picked up on the analogy and used it to ask questions of the EPA lawyer who followed Blatt. Her oral argument can be found at www.TurningPointsatTrial.com.

Blatt advises that you have less than 30 minutes to get your story across. "It's a very short window; unless it's very simple, you are just going to lose them."

It is one thing to be prepared for oral argument, but you also need to have confidence. You must believe not only in your client, but also in yourself. Blatt cautions, "Don't let them see you sweat; this is your chance."

Not surprisingly, Blatt believes that you should practice your argument in front of others prior to your oral argument. This practice is known as moot court. The key is to find colleagues who are motivated to help you by spending the time to read the briefs and ask you intelligent questions that will prepare you for oral argument. Blatt finds colleagues who are similarly situated who also do appellate arguments. Those colleagues will also call on her for help in their preparation for their arguments. Blatt finds that moot court is the perfect place to find out if your arguments work or fall flat.

16.3 MAINTAINING CREDIBILITY

Everyone fears being asked at oral argument a question he doesn't know the answer to. The question might relate to a fact that you have forgotten or neglected to learn.

Most lawyers will hem and haw, stutter, or pause trying to think of an answer. Blatt believes the opposite response is correct. If you don't know the answer,

"You quickly say, 'I don't know.' and say it with confidence...and move on." Any other response spells disaster because you are wasting everyone's time.

Blatt points out that other problems arise when a judge asks you questions such as "Did you waive that argument? Why didn't you cite this case? Or, what did you say in your brief?" Blatt tells the law students whom she teaches as an adjunct professor at Georgetown University to remember Kevin Spacey's line from *House of Cards*: "There is nothing more persuasive than the naked truth."

So, just tell the panel the truth as fast and as directly as you can. They won't know how to react because it happens so rarely, and they will move on. While it might seem hard to admit a mistake in your briefing in front of the court or when a case is going against you, it should not be.

Proof that this strategy works comes from a case while Blatt was working at the Solicitor General's Office. She knew the government had made a mistake and admitted it at oral argument but still won the case. Blatt points out, "It's the most persuasive advocacy because nobody knows what to do when you say to the panel, 'You are right.'"

> **Practice Tip**
>
> Blatt advises to be candid and admit bad facts. "The faster you get to the truth, the more time there is to make your argument."

Let's now turn our attention to Blatt's arguments in the gasoline tank search case mentioned briefly earlier and in the adoption of Baby Veronica case.

16.4 *UNITED STATES V. FLORES-MONTANO*

In *Flores-Montano*, United States Customs agents seized 81 pounds of marijuana from Manuel Flores-Montano's gas tank when he tried to enter the United States from Mexico at the Southern California border. The issue before the Supreme Court was whether the agents needed reasonable suspicion of wrongdoing to search a motorist's gas tank as he crossed into the United States.

The details of the seizure are as follows: Flores-Montano was driving a 1987 Ford Taurus station wagon. At the U.S. border checkpoint, a customs inspector told Flores-Montano to get out of the car. The car was then taken to a secondary inspection station.

At the secondary station, a second customs agent inspected the gas tank by tapping it and noted that the tank sounded solid. Then, the inspector asked a mechanic under contract with Customs to come to the border station to remove the tank. Within 20 to 30 minutes, the mechanic arrived. He raised the car on a hydraulic lift, loosened the straps and unscrewed the bolts holding the gas tank to the undercarriage of the car, and then disconnected some hoses and electrical connections. After the gas tank was removed, the inspector hammered off Bondo (a putty-like hardening substance that is used as an automotive body filler) from the top of the gas tank. The inspector opened an access plate underneath the Bondo and found 81 pounds of marijuana bricks. The process took 15 to 25 minutes.

Prior to trial, the judge ruled that the government could not use the seized marijuana as evidence at trial because it did not have a reasonable suspicion of wrong-doing when it searched the gas tank. The government appealed this pre-trial ruling, and Blatt argued for the government before the United States Supreme Court.

At oral argument, Blatt was bombarded with detailed questions about the way gas tank searches were conducted, how long they took, how much they cost, and how often they were done. She never failed to answer a question correctly. As mentioned earlier, the Supreme Court's Guide to Counsel refers lawyers to Blatt's oral argument as the model for preparing for oral argument. Let's look at some of her exchanges with the justices to see why she was so effective. The full transcript can be found at www.TurningPointsatTrial.com.

> Blatt: Twenty-five percent of all drug seizures along the Mexican border are hidden in gas tanks, we've not only found marijuana, cocaine, heroin, currency, methamphetamine, there have been weapons and ammunition —

Blatt makes her client, U.S. Customs, come alive. This is not just a case about 81 pounds of marijuana. It is about the right of agents to protect our country from the illegal entry of more serious drugs and even guns and ammunition.

> Court: *How much time does it take* [to remove a gas tank and put it back together]?

> Blatt: Well, in this case, once the —

> Court: *To take it off and put it back?*

> Blatt: Well, in this case it took under a half an hour, but, Justice O'Connor, I want to stress that in other cases, depending on the type of car, it might take an hour or two hours, and the last thing we want is our customs official to be on a Fourth Amendment stopwatch and telling the mechanic to rush. So they need — need —

> Court: *On the 25 percent figure, you say 25 percent of all seizures from vehicles? Does that include 25 percent of seizures where you search the person or?*

> Blatt: No, it's 20 —

> Court: *What's — the 25 percent is a percentage of what?*

> Blatt: Twenty-five percent of narcotics seizures in terms of amount of seizures along land borders. That doesn't include seaports —

Blatt not only knows how long it took to search the gas tank in this particular case, but she alerts the judges that it may take much longer depending on the type of car. She also has the exact answer regarding the 25 percent figure.

As Blatt always does, she has channeled her client and made the custom agents come alive. She alerts the judges that the agents doing the search should not be under additional scrutiny — "a Fourth Amendment stopwatch" — to do their job more quickly.

The justices then asked Blatt about the different means for determining if gas tanks contain contraband. For example, the case before the court involved a drug-sniffing dog who alerted the customs agent that something was suspicious. But Blatt knew not only the facts of her case, but every detail of custom searches throughout the country. Let's watch:

> **Court:** *Is the practice then to just go straight to that procedure* [disassembly of gas tank] *and skip the dog and the tapping* [on the tank]*, or do they go through the whole thing?*
>
> **Blatt:** Well, they have dogs at all the major ports of entry, but the dogs don't always alert, so I wouldn't say it's necessarily skipping, but the dog may not alert. They also at some of the facilities have what are known as fiber-optic scopes, which are extremely sophisticated and effective equipment. Unfortunately, 75 percent or higher of all tanks have, in the filler tube, have an anti-siphoning valve that blocks the entry of the scope into the tank, but they will try that if they have it. It's not always available. It's an extremely expensive piece of equipment. It costs $16,000 per unit. But if they have that, presumably they try that first, and if it's blocked, then they put the car up on a lift and unscrew the metal bolts that are holding them that — to the metal straps that are holding the tank and they'll remove the tank. And then from there on it's pretty straightforward on how to open up the tank.

> **Practice Tip**
> Know your client. Prior to the oral argument, Blatt took apart a gasoline tank. By having this hands-on experience, her argument carries the weight of authority as she precisely explains how the procedure works.

> **Court:** *I mean, let's say 1,000 cars cross the border point in an hour. What percentage of those will have their gas tanks removed?*
>
> **Blatt:** Not very many, Justice O'Connor. Let me give you these statistics. There have been 120 million vehicles that passed through this country's borders last year, and over the last four years, four years, there have been 8,000 gas tank disassemblies.

———— ∞∞∞ ————

> Court: Suppose — suppose you prevail. Are there any regulations or — or procedures under which you'll keep statistics and data, so that say over — suppose you prevail, then over the next five years we can — we can look back and see that there have been 10,000 searches and contraband has been discovered only 5 percent of the time or something?

> Blatt: Yes, they keep statistics on seizures of narcotics and what are known as positive and negative seizures. And in the last four years of the 8,000 gas tank seizures that have happened, 85 to 90 percent of those have been what are known as positive hits or there's been a presence of contraband, and so 10 to 15 percent of those have been so-called negative searches where the tank is reassembled and the motorist sent on their way, and I — we would expect that those statistics to continue, that they have limited resources and they conduct a search when they think it's appropriate and necessary.

The justices were concerned about the consequences if they ruled that the United States did not need a reason to search a gas tank. As a result, Blatt got asked a myriad of questions regarding such an outcome. She had answers for every question and thereby raised the comfort level for the Court to rule in her favor, giving the government the absolute right to search a car's gas tank upon entry at the border.

Not surprisingly, Blatt's knowledge of searches was not limited to gas tanks. She was familiar with all types of searches, and the justices took the argument in a direction for which only Blatt could be ready. The justices started asking about how intrusive and damaging agents' searches were when they were looking for drugs hidden in car seats. Let's watch this exchange and see how Blatt's intimate knowledge defuses the Court's concerns.

> Court: But your — your answer to my question about property is, as long as you're not wantonly destructive, you can — any — anything that's in the car as distinguished from a person?

> Blatt: That's our — that would be our position, but I'm saying it also involves a very distinct factor, and that is that there's a deprivation of a significant property interest if the item is going to be obliterated or its value is going to be destroyed, and that's not the contention made in this case or the type of deprivation of a privacy — of property interests you would have with a gas tank. But sure, if you took a vase and smashed it when you could have looked in it, or let me just say if you wanted to open up the trunk —

> Court: Well, but not just on the — the — if you smash it unnecessarily, but suppose the only way to get behind the fabric in say a seat cushion or something like that is to cut it open. It — does your policy apply to that situation too?

Blatt: Well—

Court: *Because I don't suppose [there is a] seamstress who sews up the seat right away.*

Blatt: Right. Well, you have to look at first what the type of deprivation is, and if it's a teeny little tear that can be easily repaired, maybe there's not a significant deprivation.

Court: *But suppose it's something that cannot be repaired.*

Blatt: Let's—

Court: *You have to cut up a seat—a seat cushion. What—what do you do?*

Blatt: Let's suppose that there's a significant deprivation. It would at least be reasonable for the court to look at what kinds of alternatives were available to the government. As a practical matter, Justice Stevens, we—customs officials have long, skinny metal probes which are like needles that they use to search upholstery, so if it's fabric you wouldn't even see it going in and out. If it's leather, you probably are going to get a tiny hole. Now, whether that would constitute a significant deprivation—

Court: *I see.*

Blatt: —might turn on the facts and circumstances, but these are wonderful pieces of equipment that customs officials use all the time to look inside places that are hard to see, and they use them exactly on seats.

But to be sure, Justice Stevens, customs gets complaints about upholstery. They let a dog into a car and the dog scratches the upholstery or the agent's going in there and searching and he steps on something.

These kinds of things happen at the border and customs have to—have a job to do and they've got to use whatever force is reasonably necessary. But I think these cases are separate because they involve some arguably significant deprivation of the owner's possessory interest in that piece of property. If it's a leather seat and it's torn, the value's gone down.

But the Ninth Circuit applies a rule that doesn't let customs officials open up a container even where they can put it back without damaging the tank, and so we think that case is quite distinct.

> *I trust you implicitly.*
> —Justice Scalia
> commenting on
> Blatt's answer

Blatt is always candid in her arguments and never loses her credibility. In the exchange above, she readily admits—without being asked—that custom agents can damage property inside a car during searches. In her rebuttal argument, Blatt continued to cite statistics to answer the justices' questions with facts and above all, candor. Too many attorneys become so biased in representing their clients that they forget that their argument will lose credibility if they lose the trust of the justices by failing to answer questions honestly.

16.5 *ADOPTIVE COUPLE V. BABY GIRL*

One of the most compelling cases the United States Supreme Court decided in the last several years was *Adoptive Couple v. Baby Girl, et al.*, better known as the Baby Veronica case. It garnered national headlines and sparked heated debates across the country regarding the rights of biological parents, rights of adoptive parents, and the best interests of a child. To see a video of the coverage that summarizes both families' struggles, go to www.TurningPointsatTrial.com.

The case would not have ever reached the Supreme Court but for a federal statute. In 1978, Congress passed The Indian Child Welfare Act (ICWA) to address the consequences of abusive child welfare practices that separated Indian children from their families and tribes through adoption or foster care placement, usually in non-Indian homes. Before the law's passage, as many as 30 percent of Indian children were being taken by the states from their Indian families and placed in non-Indian homes. The children were being taken for many reasons, including poverty, non-traditional child rearing, and the perceived neglect of Indian parents. The removal rate was much higher than for other races.

Concerned about the dwindling numbers in Indian Tribes, Congress established federal standards for state-court child custody proceedings involving Indian children (discussed in more detail below). In December 2008, Christinna Maldonado (who is predominantly Hispanic) and Dusten Brown (who is a member of the Cherokee Nation) became engaged. One month later, Maldonado told Brown, who lived about four hours away from her, that she was pregnant. After learning of the pregnancy, Brown asked Maldonado to move up the date of the wedding. He also refused to provide any financial support until after the two had married. The couple's relationship deteriorated, and Maldonado broke off the engagement in May 2009.

In June 2009, Maldonado sent Brown a text message asking if he would rather pay child support or relinquish his parental rights. Brown responded via text message that he relinquished his rights. Maldonado then decided to put her baby, Veronica, up for adoption.

Working through a private adoption agency, Maldonado selected Matt and Melanie Capobianco, non-Indians living in South Carolina, to adopt baby Veronica. The Capobiancos supported Christinna Maldonado both emotionally and financially throughout her pregnancy. The Capobiancos were present at Veronica's birth in Oklahoma on September 15, 2009, and Matt even cut the umbilical cord. It was determined later that Veronica is 1.2 percent Cherokee.

The next morning, Maldonado signed forms relinquishing her parental rights and consenting to the adoption. The Capobiancos initiated adoption proceedings in South Carolina a few days later and returned there with Veronica. After returning to South Carolina, the Capobiancos allowed Christinna Maldonado to visit and communicate with Veronica.

In contrast, during the pregnancy and the first four months after Veronica's birth, Brown provided no financial assistance to Maldonado or Veronica, even though he had the ability to do so.

Approximately four months after Veronica's birth, the Capobiancos served Brown with notice of the pending adoption. (This was the first notification that they had provided to Brown regarding the adoption proceeding.) Brown signed papers stating that he was "not contesting the adoption." But Brown later testified that, at the time he signed the papers, he thought that he was relinquishing his rights to Maldonado, not to the Capobiancos.

Brown contacted a lawyer the day after signing the papers, and subsequently requested a stay of the adoption proceedings. In the adoption proceedings, Brown sought custody and stated that he did not consent to Veronica's adoption. Brown also took a paternity test, which verified that he was Veronica's biological father.

A trial took place in the South Carolina Family Court in September 2011, by which time Veronica was two years old. If South Carolina law had applied, Brown would have lost since in South Carolina, the consent to an adoption by a biological father—who has no custodial rights—is not required. But the family court concluded that the Capobiancos had not carried the heightened burden under ICWA's section 1912(f) of proving that Veronica would suffer serious emotional or physical damage if Brown had custody. The family court, therefore, denied the Capobiancos' petition for adoption and awarded custody to Brown. On December 31, 2011, at the age of 27 months, Veronica was handed over to Brown, whom she had never met.

The South Carolina Supreme Court agreed with the family court, and the case was then appealed to the United States Supreme Court. At the time of the oral argument, Veronica was 3½ years old and had been living with her father for over a year. The Supreme Court would need to decide whether Veronica would have to change homes again for a second time and move halfway across the country to South Carolina.

The legal issues before the Supreme Court

There were many complicated issues before the Supreme Court involving statutory construction and the interplay between federal and state statutes. But an exhaustive attempt to understand all of them would distract us from this section's scope, which is to learn strategies for oral argument from one of the greatest appellate advocates in the country, Lisa Blatt.

In short, there are two main ICWA sections that the parties hotly disputed.[1] Congress declared that ICWA was passed in 1978 to deal with the alarming problem of Indian families being broken up through foster care or adoption to non-Indian homes. Section 1912(f) bars involuntary termination of a parent's rights in the absence of a heightened showing that serious harm to the Indian child is likely to result from the parent's "continued custody" of the child. Section 1912(d) conditions involuntary termination of parental rights with respect to an Indian child on a showing that remedial efforts have been made to prevent the "breakup of the Indian family." You will see in the arguments below, there is a heated debate on whether a biological father who does not have custody is a "parent" as defined under ICWA who has heightened rights when a child is adopted.

The South Carolina Supreme Court held that two separate ICWA provisions barred the termination of Brown's parental rights. First, the court concluded that the Capobiancos had not shown that Brown's custody of Veronica would result in serious emotional or physical harm to her beyond a reasonable doubt under section 1912(f). Second, the court held that the Capobiancos had not shown that active efforts had been made to provide remedial services and rehabilitative programs to the father, designed to prevent the breakup of the Indian family as required by section 1912(d).

16.6 BLATT'S ORAL ARGUMENT

Most lawyers go their whole careers without ever getting the chance to watch in person a Supreme Court argument, much less argue a case before it. The next best thing is listening to one (videos are not available). Here is your chance. Go to www.TurningPointsatTrial.com to hear the Baby Veronica oral argument.

Listening to the entire argument takes about an hour. You will get a unique chance to observe how well-prepared and articulate the lawyers are — particularly Lisa Blatt — and the opportunity to hear brilliant justices argue with one another and the lawyers. You will also hear another extremely well-known and respected Supreme Court lawyer, Paul Clement, who is a former United States Solicitor General.

---

[1] **(d) Remedial services and rehabilitative programs; preventive measures**

Any party seeking to effect a foster care placement of, or termination of parental rights to, an Indian child under state law shall satisfy the court that active efforts have been made to provide remedial services and rehabilitative programs designed to prevent the breakup of the Indian family and that these efforts have proved unsuccessful.

(f) Parental rights termination orders; evidence; determination of damage to child

No termination of parental rights may be ordered in such proceeding in the absence of a determination, supported by evidence beyond a reasonable doubt, including testimony of qualified expert witnesses, that the continued custody of the child by the parent or Indian custodian is likely to result in serious emotional or physical damage to the child.

Blatt had only finished one sentence before she was interrupted, and the battle began. The audio reveals that Blatt speaks with strong conviction and measured compassion.

> **Blatt:** Thank you, Mr. Chief Justice, and may it please the Court: All parties agree that even if the birth father is a parent under the Indian Child Welfare Act, the state court decision below awarding custody to the father must nonetheless be reversed unless Sections 1912(d) or (f) create custodial rights that the father concededly does not have under state law.

Blatt comes out firing and succinctly summarizes her argument in one sentence. One issue before the court was whether Brown—given his total lack of involvement with Veronica—could meet the definition of "parent" under ICWA. Blatt argues strongly that even if he were given the benefit of that doubt, he still would not win unless sections 1912(d) or (f) create new rights he would not have under South Carolina law because, under South Carolina law, a biological father—who has no custodial rights—has no rights to object to an adoption.

But just 29 seconds into her allotted time of 20 minutes for oral argument, Blatt was interrupted by Justice Sotomayor, who would later write the dissenting opinion against Blatt.

> *Justice Sotomayor: Are you suggesting…if it is a father who has visitation rights, and exercising all of his support obligations, is it your position that— that because that father's not a custodian, he has no protections whatsoever under (d) or (e)? The state can come and take the child away from an unfit mother or father if they're the ones with custody, and that responsible parent who only has visiting rights has no protections under (d), (e), or (f)?*

Justice Sotomayor would write in the dissent that the phrase "continued custody" in section 1912(f) could not be interpreted to contaminate the entire statute by limiting protection only to biological fathers who had physical or state-recognized legal custody of a child. For example, when the statute defines father as a parent under another section (section 1903(9)), there is no mention that the father has to have custody to be a parent. Moreover, Congress made express findings at the beginning of ICWA: "There is no resource that is more vital to the continued existence and integrity of Indian tribes than their children."

Blatt does not dodge the question but answers it directly.

> **Blatt:** Under state law, if you're paying child support and you bring a paternity action and sue for visitation rights, that's a petition for custody. So all a birth dad needs to do to protect himself is to acquire legal rights.
>
> This father had no legal rights whatsoever, parental or custodial, and the word "breakup," even the other side concedes, it's discontinuance of

an existing legal relationship. There was no **legal** relationship between this child and the birth father or his relatives.

—————⚬⚬⚬—————

What follows is one of the highlights of the oral argument. After Blatt makes her point, Justice Scalia succinctly sums up what will turn out to be the dissent's strongest argument, one which directly challenges Blatt's position.

> **Blatt:** What is so extraordinary about this case, particularly the United States' position, is that the adoptive parents' failure to remediate a dad meant that the dad got custody of the child. So if this dad had had a drug problem because there was no treatment of him the [lower] court held, well, that's a basis for giving the dad custody.
>
> But there's no language in the statute that even remotely suggests that it's a rights-creating provision. All of both of (d), (e), and (f) are protections that assume existing rights and then make it harder to terminate those rights.
>
> *Justice Scalia: Your—your argument assumes that the phrase in the statute "to prevent the breakup of the Indian family" only applies where—where the father has custody. I don't—**I don't know why that should be true.** If—if that's what Congress meant, they could have put it much more narrowly.* ***They had a very broad phrase, "to prevent the break up of an Indian family." And this guy is—is the father of the child—***

When you listen to Scalia's tone on the audio recording, you will understand how convincing his argument is. His words are said slowly, with sincerity and passion. His simple question goes to the very heart of the case. It is a question said with such feeling that Blatt must know there is no way to change his mind. But Blatt is not discouraged and she presses on.

> **Blatt:** So he—
>
> *Justice Scalia: —and they're taking the child away from him even though he wants it.*
>
> **Blatt:** OK. But when you—

> *They're taking the child away from him even though he wants it.... And that—that is not the breakup of—of an Indian family?*
>
> *—Justice Scalia*

Justice Scalia: And that—that is not the breakup of—of an Indian family?

Section (d) only allows the breakup of the Indian family if remedial measures have been taken and were unsuccessful. Here, no remedial efforts were ever made when Veronica was adopted. Blatt explains why that was not necessary under ICWA.

Blatt: The only relationship the dad had is one of biology. And, Justice Scalia, you cannot logically break up that biological relationship, nor can you provide remedial services to prevent the breakup of that biological relationship.

Justice Scalia: Oh, I see. You're reading—you're reading "Indian family" to mean something more than—than a biological relationship, right? You're going to hang a lot of—a lot of other ornaments on that phrase?

Once again, Scalia is unmoved. He asks incredulously in so many words, "How can the father not be considered a part of the family?" But Blatt does not give an inch and, instead, counters with two reasons why Scalia is wrong.

Blatt: Well, I'm hanging — I'm hanging a lot on two things.

Justice Scalia: I mean, it seems to me he's the father, the other woman's the mother, that's the — that's the Indian family, the father, the mother, and the kid.

Blatt: He has a biological link that under state law was equivalent to a sperm donor.

Justice Scalia: He's the father. He's the father.

Blatt: And so is a sperm donor under your definition. He's a biological father and nothing else in the eyes of state law. And under that view—

Justice Scalia: This isn't state law. This is a federal statute which uses an expansive phrase, "the breakup of the Indian family."

Blatt: Right. And there is no Indian family here. The only breakup—

Justice Sotomayor: What's the difference with a sperm donor? I mean, I know that you raise that in your brief. But going back to Justice Scalia's point, if the choice is between a mother, a biological father, or a stranger, and if the father's fit, why do you think that the federal statute requires that it be given to a stranger rather than to the biological father when the statute defines "parent" as the biological father?

Blatt: And assuming all biological fathers that are acknowledged or established are swept in, which would include any biological father, the only stranger in this case was the birth father, who expressly repudiated all parental rights and had no custodial rights. So again, the problem the other side has—

Justice Ginsburg: But he didn't. I mean, he — he said that he was prepared to surrender rights to the mother, but not to a stranger. And when the issue of adoption came up, he said, "Yes, I want to assert my parental rights."

Blatt: It was too late. There's not a single state law that lets a dad, birth dad, hold that kind of veto power over a woman.

Blatt's meticulous preparation is evident here. She is aware not only of the standard in South Carolina where this case originated, but the standard in all 50 states. Her preparation strengthens her argument as she disputes Justice Ginsburg's reasoning by declaring that not one state follows the justice's logic. She also shows the Court the impact of ruling against her client: absentee fathers can't be given the power to come out of nowhere and determine how a child is raised when they have shown no previous interest.

In the first ten minutes of her argument, Blatt has deftly answered questions from three of the four judges who would join in the dissent against her: Sotomayor, Scalia, and Ginsburg. Those strong answers will help persuade the other justices who will choose her side. Next up, the last dissenter, Justice Kagan.

> *Justice Kagan: But what's the point of labeling [the father] a parent if he gets no parental rights under the statute and if the termination provisions don't apply to him?*
>
> **Blatt:** Notice, right to counsel, and heightened consent requirements. So the mother here, the birth mother is a parent, so she had a right to notice, right to counsel, and heightened consent requirements.
>
> *Justice Kagan: But what is he supposed to —*
>
> **Blatt:** So those are very significant.
>
> *Justice Kagan: Well, how are they significant? I mean, I'm trying to understand this because if you get notice, but then you have nothing to say in the proceeding because the statute gives you no rights and the statute doesn't terminate those rights —*
>
> **Blatt:** Right.
>
> *Justice Kagan: — what are you supposed to do once you get notice?*
>
> **Blatt:** Justice Kagan, just because he's in the door as a parent, that doesn't mean the statute lets him leave out the back door with the child when there was no, no determination with respect to — I mean, any kind—it would be unprecedented to think that because you had a failure to remediate to prevent the breakup of an Indian family, that's a basis for awarding custody? And that's the United States' view, which is —
>
> *Justice Kagan: I think you're not answering the question of what's the point of labeling him a parent if he gets none of the protections that the Act provides to a parent?*
>
> **Blatt:** You're assuming that this entire Act was to make sure unwed dads who are Indian got more time than non-Indian dads to veto adoptions, and that had — that's not even remotely the purpose of [ICWA].

> *Justice Kagan, just because he's in the door as a parent, that doesn't mean the statute lets him leave out the back door with the child....*
>
> — Lisa Blatt, oral argument

The analogy of the house is perfect. Blatt reminds the justices not to let Brown sneak out the back door just because he is a biological parent when he has done nothing to assert his rights. Blatt continues:

> **Blatt:** So state law is you have to support the mother during pregnancy or at birth. So the cases are pretty clear that the father can't wait till he learns of the adoption.
>
> *Justice Kennedy: So the state law determines when his rights under the Federal Act end?*
>
> **Blatt:** No. State law determines just when you have parental rights to begin with. [There's] no question that this particular dad, had state law applied, the adoption would have gone forward and his rights would have been terminated by virtue of his lack of a right to — to object to the adoption.

The other side doesn't really have a definition of "custody" or "continue" that would sweep in a dad without any parental rights. And I do just want to say in terms of looking, taking one step back. This is not the case that Congress had in mind when it passed the Act to halt the depletion of the tribal population. This involves accretion and conscripting other people's children to grow the tribal population based solely on a biological link.

Justice Kagan: Ms. Blatt, continuing on the assumption that this man is a parent under the statutory definition, what your argument seems to be suggesting is that there are really two classes of parents under the statute, right, that everybody is labeled a parent, but then there are the parents who get the protections of — of the termination of rights provision and the parents who don't. And I'm just wondering why if this statute creates two classes of parents it didn't say that in a more upfront kind of way?

Blatt: Yes.

Justice Kagan: It seems a strange thing to read into a statute in this sort of backhanded way that there are really two kinds of parents.

Blatt: Well, I think it's rather completely upside down that this entire statute, with 20 or 24 references to removal, custody, return of child to the parent, is somehow being read to create rights. There is no language in this statute that creates custodial rights, and the birth father in this case because of an exhaustion failure under (d), walked off with the child without any best interest determination. If I could —

Chief Justice Roberts: Thank you, counsel.

Blatt argues that to get the benefits of ICWA, you have to do more than just be the biological father. Under section (d), there was no termination of family rights because Brown had failed to make any effort to establish his rights as a family member by seeking legal custody or providing support for the mother during pregnancy or birth as required by South Carolina law.

Guardian Ad Litem:

Paul Clement, the attorney appointed to represent the Guardian ad Litem for Baby Veronica, argued next. He said that the case should be returned to South Carolina so that the court could make a determination as to what was in the best interest of the child before awarding custody.

16.7 ORAL ARGUMENT OF ATTORNEY FOR DUSTEN BROWN

Charles Rothfeld represented the biological father, Dusten Brown. He argued that the Supreme Court of South Carolina decided the case correctly. Let's take a closer look at his argument.

> **Rothfeld:** Thank you, Mr. Chief Justice, and may it please the Court: It is simply false to say that this child's custody was transferred without a best interest determination as is apparent from any reading of the lower court decisions in this case. Both of the state courts here looked very closely at the situation here and they found, in their words, that the father here was a "fit, devoted, and loving father," and they said expressly and found expressly as a factual matter that it was in the best interest of this child.

Also, during the argument, it is clear how close this decision will be as seen from the following exchange as Rothfeld discusses whether the lower court applied the correct standard for determining custody:

> *Justice Sotomayor: Tell me why you are fighting Justice Breyer?...*
>
> **Rothfeld:** No. I—I think that that's right, and I certainly don't intend to fight *Justice Breyer. I—I think that—*
>
> *Justice Breyer: You should if I'm not right.*
>
> (Laughter.)
>
> **Rothfeld:** I don't—
>
> *Justice Ginsburg: But I think Justice Breyer is quite wrong because [a standard that considers the] serious emotional or physical damage to the child is far from a best interest standard.*
>
> *Justice Scalia: It sure is. And do you know of any state that—that applies best interest of the child standard to termination of parental rights as opposed to adoption?*

Rothfeld: Absolutely not. And—and I think I—I will try to agree with both Justice Breyer and Justice Ginsburg and Justice Scalia and say that—

Chief Justice Roberts: But not me, right?

(Laughter.)

Rothfeld: And Justice Sotomayor. And always—always the Chief Justice.

Justice Kagan: You might just have to pick—

Rothfeld: Which gets me to five, so.

Later in his argument, Rothfeld responded to one of Blatt's main arguments.

Rothfeld: And if I can turn to something which attracted some attention from Justice Scalia and Justice Sotomayor in their exchanges with Ms. Blatt, the application of Section 1912(d) and whether or not the parental rights of this—this father, who unquestionably satisfies the definition of parent in ICWA, Section 1912(d) says that parental rights cannot be terminated unless remedial efforts have been made, rehabilitative efforts have been made to fix a family that is broken in some respect. And Ms. Blatt suggests that that does not apply here because there was no Indian family. I think what Justice Scalia said was absolutely right. There unquestionably was a family here in the ordinary sense.

There was a mother, there was a father, there was their little girl, there were grandparents who very much wanted to be involved in the life of this child, who knit socks for her. There's no question—

Justice Scalia: Is my recollection correct that—that he had offered to—to marry the mother, and she rejected that?

Rothfeld: That—that is quite correct. I think that the genesis of this case, they were an engaged couple and the mother broke the engagement. The father wanted, very much wanted to marry the mother, wanted to—

Justice Ginsburg: I thought that there's some ambiguity there because one reason why he wanted to marry was that he would get more pay and allowances.

Rothfeld: Well, there—there are disputed facts as to what was going on, and so I don't want to hinge a lot on this. But I think it is quite clear the father—they were engaged, the father wanted to marry the mother.

The father's testimony—and the family court found, so we're not talking about simply, you know, assertions here. The family court found that the father was excited by the pregnancy, was looking forward to the birth of the child, that he wanted to marry the mother so that she would qualify for military health benefits. The father at the time—

Chief Justice Roberts: He was excited, but there is no doubt he paid nothing during the pregnancy and nothing at the time of the birth, right, to support the child or the mother?

Rothfeld: That—that is true. But I—I am—

Chief Justice Roberts: So he was excited by it, he just didn't want to take any responsibility.

(Laughter.)

Justice Scalia: Well, that—that was after she had rejected his offer to marry her, no?

Rothfeld: Yes. I mean—of parental traditional of parental interest of the child. That seems to me quite—

Justice Kennedy: Well, these—these considerations are why domestic relations pose the hardest problems for judges. Our domestic relations judges all by themselves every day have these difficult problems. If we could appoint King Solomon, who was the first domestic relations judge, as special master, we could do it. But we can't do it.

Rothfeld: That—that—that—

Justice Kennedy: But what we have—what we have here is a question of a federal statute which, as I must understand it, displaces the ordinary best interest determinations of the state courts.

Deputy Solicitor General

Edwin Kneedler argued for the United States which had filed a brief in support of the birth father. He began as follows:

> **Kneedler:** Mr. Chief Justice, and may it please the Court: I would like to start with the definition of "parent" under the Act because I think a lot flows from that. The Act provides that a parent—a parent of an Indian child is the—if it's the biological parent, except where the child—or where the parent—paternity has not been established or acknowledged.
>
> Here, the—the father's paternity was acknowledged and established, both courts below found. As a consequence, he has not simply a biological relationship to the child, he has a legal relationship to the child, created under federal law.

Later in the argument Kneedler passionately argued the following:

> **Kneedler:** Nothing could be more at the core of tribal self-determination and tribal survival than the determination of tribal membership and the care about what happens to Indian children.

16.8 BLATT'S REBUTTAL ARGUMENT

The appellant is always allowed time for rebuttal argument. Blatt had three minutes to make her final points. Before she began her rebuttal, she felt she had lost the case and that her clients were never going to see their daughter again. She thought to herself, "It's now or never." She always tells her clients, "You never go down without swinging."

She decided that "In addition to just answering their question, they need to hear what's going to happen if we lose. No one will adopt an Indian child. The game is over, and I'm not going to not tell that."

> *You are either going to win or die trying. You don't want to look back and think, "I should have said this."*
>
> — Lisa Blatt

Blatt: Thank you, Mr. Chief Justice, and may it please the Court: If you affirm below, you're basically banning the interracial adoption of abandoned Indian children. There's not a single adoptive parent in their right mind who is going to do what the court below said, which is go through these Kafkaesque hoops of making sure an absentee father's desire to be a parent has been stimulated. This is a private adoption. This is absurd that an adoptive parent would beg the family court to go provide parenting classes. And I wanted to —

Justice Sotomayor: Counsel, this Act, in terms of voluntary surrender of Indian children by parents, says that it's not final for an adoptive parent until the court does the adoption decree. It gives the mother the right — or father — to rescind the voluntary adoption till the very last minute. Has that stopped adopt — voluntary adoptions?

Blatt: No, but this — first of all — I mean, I love that about this case, the irony here. He had no — we didn't need his consent under state law, so the application of 1913, which allowed this withdrawal of consent, mandates the return of the child. Well, there was no way to return this child to anybody other than the mother.

And I want you to keep in mind about this case, is your decision is going to apply to the next case and to an apartment in New York City where a tribal member impregnates someone who's African-American or Jewish or Asian-Indian, and in that view, even though the father is a completely absentee father, you are rendering these women second-class citizens with inferior rights to direct their reproductive rights and their — who raises their child.

You are relegating adoptive parents to go to the back of the bus and wait in line if they can adopt. And you're basically relegating the child, the child to a piece of property with a sign that says, "Indian, keep off. Do not disturb." This case is going to affect any interracial adoption of children.

Justice Scalia: That was its intent.

Blatt: No.

Justice Scalia: You don't think that's what its intent was?

Blatt: No.

Justice Scalia: It only applies to children of—to tribal children. And—and the purpose was to establish much more difficult standards for the adoption of—of a child—

Blatt: No, no, Justice Scalia.

Notice how Blatt does not back up an inch. Not many advocates know how to spar with a Supreme Court Justice. But Blatt doesn't back down, nor does she offend Justice Scalia by pushing back too hard. Her tone on the audio is firm, passionate, but also respectful.

Justice Scalia: Now, maybe you—you disagree with that policy, but that's clearly a policy behind the law.

Blatt: No, I think the policy is fantastic. It was talking about Indian families who were being ripped away because of cultural biases and insensitivity. This case didn't involve cultural biases.

Justice Scalia: It didn't say that. It—its definition of—

Blatt: There's 30,000 pages of legislative history that's talking about the removal. That was its intent.

Justice Ginsburg: That, Ms. Blatt, is what provoked the Act that Indian children were being removed from their families, but the Act is written in much broader terms.

Blatt: I agree. [section] 1915 is extraordinary, if you read it the way the tribe does, which is—and the government does. And a little bit about the membership criteria. The tribe's view is any child born Indian is automatically a member. So even if the parents withdrew their tribal membership, this child would be covered.

Chief Justice Roberts: Thank you, counsel. The case is submitted.

16.9 COURT'S DECISION

Two and a half months later, the Supreme Court ruled 5-4 in favor of the Capobiancos. Justice Alito delivered the opinion in which Justice Roberts, Kennedy, Thomas, and Breyer joined. Justice Scalia wrote a dissenting opinion, and Justice Sotomayor wrote a dissenting opinion with whom Justice Ginsburg and Justice Kagan joined.

Justice Alito adopted Blatt's reasoning and started his opinion with this strong statement of his ruling:

> This case is about a little girl (Baby Girl) who is classified as an Indian because she is 1.2% (3/256) Cherokee. Because Baby Girl is classified in this way, the South Carolina Supreme Court held that certain revisions of the federal Indian Child Welfare Act of 1978 required her to be taken, at the age of 27 months, from the only parents she had ever known and handed over to her biological father, who had attempted to relinquish his parental rights and who had no prior contact with the child. The provisions of the federal statute at issue here do not demand this result.

Adoptive Couple v. Baby Girl, 133 S.Ct. 2552, 2556 (2013).

Justice Alito concluded his ruling by echoing Blatt's reasoning in her rebuttal argument that a non-involved biological father should not be allowed to veto an adoption. He declared that the ruling below had put certain Indian children at a great disadvantage. Under that ruling:

> A biological Indian father could abandon his child in utero and refuse any support for the birth mother—perhaps contributing to the mother's decision to put the child up for adoption—and then could play his ICWA trump card at the eleventh hour to override the mother's decision and the child's best interests. If this were possible, many prospective adoptive parents would surely pause before adopting any child who might possibly qualify as an Indian under the ICWA.

Id. at 2555.

To understand how divided the court was over this issue, Scalia's short dissent succinctly sums up his views: "Parents have their rights, no less than children do. This father wants to raise his daughter, and the statute amply protects his right to do so. There is no reason in law or policy to dilute that protection." *Id.* at 2572. Justice Sotomayor was no less troubled by the majority's decision: "In truth, however, the path from the text of [IWCA] to the result the Court reaches is anything but clear, and its result anything but right." *Id.*

On September 23, 2013, Dusten Brown turned custody of Baby Veronica over to the Capobiancos. The *Tulsa World* summarized Brown's emotional good-bye and the ecstatic reunion of the Capobiancos (Go to www.TurningPointsatTrial.com to see the full description and photos.)

Blatt told me that her analogies in her rebuttal of "adoptive parents at the back of the bus," "casual sex in a New York City apartment," and "sign around an Indian child's neck" shocked many of her colleagues who practice in front of the Supreme Court. They felt it wasn't very professorial and, even for Blatt's no-nonsense style, it was very, very direct. Given this response from her colleagues, I asked Blatt if she would have softened her rebuttal if given the chance to do it again. Not surprisingly, she said she would do it exactly the same way. She was going to go down swinging and, thankfully for her clients, she did.

16.10 CHAPTER CHECKLIST

Blatt's insights on oral argument

The first thing to do on appeal

1. As soon as you get the case on appeal, determine what your story is going to be.

2. Arguing to judges on appeal is similar to a jury argument: you must succinctly answer the question, "Why should you win?"

Channel your client

1. Blatt believes to win, you must "channel the client."

   — Get to know the details about your client's issue.

   — There is no substitute for seeing in person how your client's business operates.

2. To persuade judges, you need them to identify with you just like you would with a jury.

   — Relying on case law is not enough.

3. Unlike most lawyers who just learn the background of the case, Blatt wants to *know* it and make it real. "It's not just that some case law says, 'I win,' it is that if I don't win, this is what happens. This is what actually is happening in the real world to this particular company or a family trying to adopt a baby or…protecting the nation's border."

Delivery of oral argument

1. Memorize your "spiel," which is a summary of your argument (about two pages of words) in case you don't get any questions from the judges.

2. Memorize answers to anticipated questions.

   — Do this by orally repeating your answer until it feels natural.

3. Blatt brings energy into courtroom and "raises the temperature."

   — Don't be afraid to say something provocative.

4. Simply trying to do your best is not good enough.

5. Your attitude should be that every case is a war, and you don't want to be the one that dies.

6. "Your only objective is to win, leaving all your credibility and professionalism intact."

7. "Don't let them see you sweat." Have confidence in yourself.

8. Don't be constrained by the case law. Argue with common sense, and expect the law and justice to follow.

Simplify your case

1. You have less than 30 minutes to get your story across. Unless it is simple, you are going to lose them.

2. Remember Blatt's *Goldilocks and the Three Bears* analogy as an example of simplifying a complicated case.

Maintaining credibility

1. Most lawyers fear being asked questions they don't know the answer to.

2. Most lawyers will hem and haw or pause trying to think of an answer.

3. Don't hesitate. Instead, quickly say, "I don't know." Say it with confidence and move on.

4. When asked if you or your client has made a mistake, tell the panel the truth as fast and as directly as you can. They won't know how to react because it happens so rarely, and they will move on.

Rebuttal argument

1. Always go down swinging.

2. Never have the regret of failing to tell the court the consequences of its decision for your client.

Moot court

1. It is essential to practice your oral argument in front of colleagues who are motivated to read the briefs and ask you relevant questions.

2. Moot courts are the perfect time to see if your arguments and rhetoric succeed or fall flat.

CHAPTER SEVENTEEN

Alan Dershowitz

Meticulous Preparation Wins

When you do an appeal, your only advantage in that court-room is you know more than the judge does. They may know more about the law, but you know more about the facts. You have to be the master of the facts.

— Alan Dershowitz

$\mathcal{D}$ershowitz's bio was discussed in Chapter Six. Without repeating his accolades here, he is simply considered one of the best appellate lawyers in the country. He has also been a part of many famous cases, including the representation of O.J. Simpson, Bill Clinton, Mike Tyson, and Julian Assange. He is also a frequent legal analyst for CNN. In this chapter, we are going to look at one of his most dramatic appellate arguments.

17.1 TAILOR YOUR BRIEF TO THE ARGUMENT

Dershowitz points out that one mistake lawyers often make is that they "throw into their appellate brief canned arguments that they've made before and have been rejected." This lack of effort is detrimental to an appeal. Similarly, Dershowitz has noticed that some lawyers even have the nerve to find old briefs he has written that now appear in collections on the Internet. The lawyers then copy and paste sections of his old briefs and put them in their current briefs. These lifted sections don't fit but allow the lawyers to create a brief without putting in the necessary time and effort. Unfortunately, the clients are unaware of the sloppy representation they are receiving.

> **CHAPTER HIGHLIGHTS**
> - Be the master of the facts
> - Lay a trap for the other side
> - Fail-safe tips for delivering your argument

17.2 PREPARING FOR ORAL ARGUMENT

Not only do lawyers not put the necessary time into writing a quality appellate brief, but they also don't make the effort to know their case inside and out. Such a failure is inexcusable. Obviously, you need to know all the significant cases discussed in your brief and your opponent's brief. But you also need to know the facts from the trial. Dershowitz reviews the trial transcript multiple times until he knows it cold. He is determined to be supremely prepared every time he walks into the courtroom.

He related that he not only knows the trial transcript of the case he is arguing, but he also reviews the trial transcripts of the leading cases that are discussed in the briefs. Dershowitz relates that he was once arguing a double murder case before the United States Supreme Court, and "there was a very important precedent, and I had gone back and read the transcript of the precedent case, in addition to knowing the transcript in my case."

I countered that such a practice was almost unheard of. He responded:

> I mean you have to know more than the judges know. That's the key. You have to remember for you it's your only case, for judges it's one of three. You have the advantage of being able to know a little bit more about it. I go back, and I read the records of the most important cases as well, so I can say that in that case what really happened was A, B, C, and that's really important.

I was most surprised in my interviews with Dershowitz when I learned his views on moot court. Most lawyers swear by them. He doesn't use them and doesn't believe in them, in contrast to Bryan Stevenson and Lisa Blatt who are featured in this book. Instead he explains, "I think of the hardest possible questions that anybody could ask me. I then try to prepare answers, but I know more about the record of the case than a moot court judge would. I try to use my own moot court instead of having strangers coming and asking me questions. I find that's more effective." My advice is to try both approaches. There is a lot to gain from a moot court, but only if those on the court have put the necessary time and effort into the exercise. Oftentimes, they don't.

> *There's an enormous difference between winning an appellate argument and reversing a conviction; there's an equally significant difference between wanting to see a conviction reversed and finding a valid basis for reversal; all the hard work in the world cannot bring about a result if the facts and the law don't justify it.*
> —Alan Dershowitz

17.3 BIGGEST MISTAKE LAWYERS MAKE

I asked Dershowitz what is the biggest mistake lawyers make. He immediately answered, "Whenever I go and listen to arguments, other arguments, I'm shocked at the lack of preparation that some lawyers come to an oral argument with. It's just shocking to me sometimes how unprepared they are for the questions. That's why it's so important to be extremely well prepared. I can say this with pride, I'm not bragging, I'm just stating the facts, so please don't misinterpret it. I've argued probably 250 appeals over 50 years. I don't think I've ever been asked a question that I didn't know the answer to, that I, at least, couldn't provide an adequate answer to based on the record or based on the cases. I don't think I've ever been caught short on lack of preparation. I pride myself on that."

17.4 DELIVERY

Arguing before an appellate court should not be undertaken unless you are willing to master appellate advocacy skills. Dershowitz relates the story of an attorney who failed to do just that.

> I'll never forget a case. I argued a death penalty case in the Supreme Court. The case before me was also a death penalty case. The Texas public defender had rewarded some old retired lawyer, good guy, who had given up the commercial practice of law and had devoted his life to helping people on death row. Great, wonderful guy, didn't have a clue as to how to argue the case in the Supreme Court. Justice Scalia just walked him into every trap. At the end, he said to me, when we walked out after the arguments, he said, "I think Justice Scalia liked me." I was so tempted to say, "Of course he did. You gave him everything he wanted."

Let's look at the right way to deliver an oral argument. In the first minute of the oral argument, Dershowitz frames the argument by "insisting that this is the framework in which the court decides the case. Then, in almost every argument, I try to lay a trap for the other side. I give the court questions that I want them to ask my opponents. Either I'll say, 'I'm certain that my distinguished opponents will agree with me that,' or, 'Your Honors, this is the crucial question. I'm not sure if the record permits for a disagreement, but please ask my distinguished opponents whether they agree or disagree with....' I notice that the judges are all taking notes when I do that. I notice my opponents sitting there shocked, 'Oh my God.'"

"I try to discombobulate the other side a little bit by throwing them off their game. It's also another way of maintaining the control over the appeal. This is the agenda. This is the framework. This is the question I want you to ask. This is my appeal. That's what I try very hard to do."

Dershowitz conceded with a smile that there was one time his strategy did not work (out of about 250 appeals). "A judge said, 'Mr. Dershowitz, we'll decide what questions to ask the appellee in this case.' I said,

> *If you ask the right question, you're more likely to get the right answer than if you let the court just muse about it.*
> — Alan Dershowitz

'Thank you, Your Honor. I'm sure you'll ask excellent questions.' And, I just backed away from him." But Dershowitz's experience has taught him that usually the judge will ask the question Dershowitz suggests.

"I almost never start with a statement of facts in my oral argument. I almost always start with the conceptual way in which I think the issues are and how the court should approach deciding the issue. I try to give them a road map how to write their decision."

Dershowitz believes a significant mistake lawyers make is that they read their arguments. Dershowitz does not take a notebook to the podium. Instead, he not only argues without notes, but he tries to "include in my argument a few noteworthy phrases that the judges might want to borrow and put in their opinions. Judges love to have clever phrases in their opinions, so I try to feed them some of them. I noticed often they appear in the opinions."

I have found that some lawyers just keep speaking until the red light on the podium indicates that their time is up. I asked Dershowitz about his view on this issue. He immediately referenced one of his most famous appeals, the von Bülow case. He had argued 20 minutes in his initial argument and had saved 10 minutes for rebuttal. He was really "raring to go" in his rebuttal argument. But as he listened to his opponent, he suddenly realized, "I've won the case two-thirds of the way through the other side. I waive rebuttal. My client was shocked. The TV people were shocked, 'Why is he waiving rebuttal?' I couldn't have improved my situation right there. I didn't want to open myself up to questions that might have hurt my side, so I waived rebuttal."

Dershowitz cautions that he doesn't usually do that. Another tip he shared is that he likes to set aside more time for rebuttal than other lawyers. He prefers to divide his allotted time between his main argument and rebuttal if he can, but some courts won't let him. He will take as much time for the rebuttal as the court will allow. "I like to have the last word. I'm good on my feet, so I like to be able to say, 'All right, here's what our position is and here's what their position is. Here's the difference between us. Here's the place in the record that shows we're right.' The summation, the final argument, is often very important."

17.5 HOW TO ANSWER DIFFICULT QUESTIONS

Lawyers usually don't listen to the judge. Thus, they fail to adjust their argument accordingly. For example, Dershowitz often sees a lawyer give an argument, and then a judge will interrupt with a question, and the lawyer will respond, "'Your Honor, I'll get to that.' No, no, no. You have to answer it right there, and you have to turn it into an opportunity to make your argument stronger."

> *A question is your friend.*
> — Alan Dershowitz

Dershowitz explains further that the solution is not to answer "Yes, but…." Instead, he says, "You figure out a way of re-framing it or answering the question and then moving from the question. 'As Your Honor rightly pointed out, here….'" Dershowitz adds with emphasis, "The oral arguments I dread the most are when the court doesn't ask me any questions, when you have a cold bench. I'll try to deliberately provoke questions. 'Your Honor might be wondering whether….' You know, something. You have to get the court engaged in the oral arguments; otherwise it's just routine affirmance, affirmance, affirmance."

I asked Dershowitz how he handles perhaps the toughest question in any oral argument, "Won't you concede your client did something wrong?" It is a very difficult question when your client might be in the courtroom and has paid you to defend him on appeal. Dershowitz recalled a case where he had that issue in spades. He was representing a producer of Broadway shows. "It was a very complicated case where his wife adopted a child. He didn't want to adopt the child. He was divorcing his wife, but [a question was would] the adoption go through. I was making the argument in front of my client that this man would make an awful father because he doesn't want this child, and you don't want to force a man to adopt a child. In the middle of the argument, this guy was probably in his eighties at the time, he got up, 'I'd be a great father! My lawyer shouldn't be able to say that.' I said, 'Excuse me, sir. Let me make the argument.' We won the case, but…. You only have one audience, it's the judge. You have to work it out with your client later."

Dershowitz explained that a way to handle a similar situation in advance is to explain to your client that "This will cost you in the short term a little bit, your own dignity and credibility, but in the end I have to maintain my credibility to win this argument. You have to let me acknowledge that you're not an angel, but you shouldn't be convicted of this crime."

"You can't lose your credibility by disputing facts that are clearly not disputable. You have to argue around the hardest facts that are against you." Even at trial, you can't please your client by making an argument to the jury that is inconsistent with the evidence.

Dershowitz gave another example that came from a trial of the importance of maintaining your credibility. A good defense attorney "screwed it up by in the beginning, in his opening, saying, 'My client was not at the scene of the crime.' Then, when the evidence proved overwhelmingly that he was, he had to acknowledge that he was at the scene of the crime. That hurt a lot. He should have never said that in the opening. I think he didn't know what the evidence was going to show and how overwhelming it was…. He was caught a little off guard."

17.6 *TABISH AND MURPHY V. NEVADA*

Dershowitz relates that many of his murder cases have not been whodunits, but wasitduns. That is, was a crime committed? Such was the situation when he was asked to defend Sandra Murphy on appeal after her murder conviction. Murphy was the fiancée of Ted Binion. Binion was a celebrity in Las Vegas. His famous hotel, the Binion Horseshoe Casino, was also known for hosting the World Series of Poker. Murphy lived with him and was significantly younger. She also was an exotic dancer. In addition, Murphy had an equally young lover, Richard Tabish.

Murphy found Binion dead in his home on September 17, 1998. She called 911 and was so hysterical when the police arrived that she was taken to a hospital. The police immediately concluded Binion's death was a drug overdose. Binion was a heroin addict, and his drug supplier had sold Binion a large quantity of black tar heroin the day before his death. Heroin-smoking paraphernalia and traces of the drug were found in a bathroom near his body. Toxicology reports would later reveal the presence of heroin, Xanax, and Valium in Binion's body.

The medical examiner concluded that the cause of death was an overdose, but he could not decide whether the death was a suicide or an accident. But there were some other interesting circumstances that created intrigue in the cause of Binion's death. A few months before his death, Binion lost his gaming license to operate the casino. As a result, he took his large personal collection of silver coins and bars worth $8 million from the casino. In the summer of 1998, Binion hired Richard Tabish to build an underground vault for the silver on a vacant parcel of land near Binion's ranch. Tom Standish, one of Binion's lawyers, testified at trial that he heard Binion tell Tabish that if he died, Tabish should get the silver from the vault so that greedy Binion family members would not try to keep the silver from Binion's daughter, Bonnie.

On September 18, 1998, the day after Binion's death, Tabish called the Nye County Sheriff and told him about Binion's instructions and that he was going to follow them and remove the silver from the underground vault. But after Tabish and some hired men had loaded the silver into their trucks, the sheriff arrested Tabish.

A week after Binion's death, his family hired a private investigator. Six months later, the investigator took his findings to the medical examiner who changed his opinion about the cause of death to homicide.

One theory the prosecution had for the mode of killing was burking. Burking got its name from a series of murders that took place in Scotland in the early 1800s. William Burke and William Hare, two Northern Irish immigrants to Scotland, would find victims who typically were homeless, drunk, or very sick and would kill them by sitting on their chest or putting a knee on their chest with such force that they were suffocated. For example, with each breath the victim tried to take, the weight of the knee or body would push further down on the chest and compress it so much that the victim eventually could not expand his lungs to inhale any more air.

The advantage of "burking" was that there were no signs of strangulation, such as bruising or marks on the neck. Consequently, the deaths did not look like killings. Burke and Hare's motive was that they would then sell the bodies to doctors for use as cadavers. It was customary during the early 1800s for famous doctors in Scotland to conduct lectures in anatomy where they charged medical students and the public to attend. Sometimes hundreds would show up, but the doctors needed cadavers to make the anatomy lectures a success. Often, the doctors would use the cadavers of recently executed criminals, but such bodies were in short supply. Burke and Hare took advantage of the shortage and made a profit from their criminal enterprise.

At Murphy's trial, the prosecution had one of the world's leading pathologists, Dr. Michael Baden, testify that the cause of death was burking. He made his conclusion by examining various photographs of the body which showed a significant mark on Binion's chest consistent with burking. But the prosecution also provided another theory to the jury for the cause of death. It presented a medical expert who testified that Binion had been forced to swallow a deadly mixture of Valium, Xanax, and heroin.

The prosecution put on this testimony to overcome the initial conclusion of the police that Binion had died of a heroin overdose. He was a known heroin addict and had received a large delivery of black tar heroin just before his death.

The prosecution had another piece of damaging evidence. Binion's estate lawyer testified that the day before he died, Binion called him and said, "Take Sandy [Murphy] out of the will if she doesn't kill me tonight. If I'm dead, you'll know what happened." After eight days of deliberations, the jury found Murphy and Tabish guilty.

Dershowitz was retained for the appeal. He focused on two problems with the trial: the burking theory and the court's decision to allow the jury to hear the hearsay statement of Binion's estate lawyer. Dershowitz soon found out that the prosecution's burking theory was not so strong as it led the jury to believe.

Dr. Baden's trial testimony was that there was a bruise on Binion's chest that was consistent with his shirt button being pressed into it. Dershowitz got the photograph enlarged and used the most sophisticated technology to analyze it. Dershowitz presented it to one of the world's leading dermatologists who concluded that the mark was not a bruise but rather a benign skin tumor that had been present for years before his death. He added that the bruise could not have been caused by an external cause; he wrote that he had "never in my experience seen lesions such as this caused by pressure."

A second issue on appeal was the hearsay statement. The "safest and neatest," as Dershowitz explained, issue on appeal was the judge's decision to allow Binion's lawyer to testify that Murphy would be the killer if he were found dead. "This was a smoking gun that must have influenced the jury, since it was, in effect, testimony from the grave. The ghost of the dead man, as in Shakespeare's *Hamlet*, was pointing to his killer." Murphy had told Dershowitz that Binion's lawyer hated her and had made the statement up to ensure her conviction.

The problem for the defense at trial was that there was no way to cross-examine Binion as to whether he made the statement or not because he was dead. Given that fact, how could the jurors assess the credibility of the statement? The prosecution countered that the defense's complaint was the very reason the statement should have been allowed before the jury; the defendants had killed the very person the defense was now complaining about not being able to cross-examine.

A hearsay statement is in-court testimony by one person as to the out-of-court statement made by another. Usually, such statements are not allowed at trial. But there are several exceptions. One is if the statement is offered to show the state of mind of the speaker. In this case, the prosecution argued that Binion's alleged fear of death by Murphy proved his state of mind and that he was not suicidal. The problem with this argument was that the statement — if true — also showed the murderous state of mind of Murphy. Dershowitz pointed out that there was no way for the jury to limit its consideration of the statement to Binion and ignore the "explosive statement" about Murphy's state of mind.

> As lawyers like to argue: "When you throw a skunk in the jury box, you can't get rid of the smell even if you remove the skunk."
> — Alan Dershowitz

With this background in mind, let's turn to the oral argument.

17.7 ORAL ARGUMENT

Unlike the United States Supreme Court arguments that we examined in the previous two chapters, judges in lower appellate courts do not dominate the argument with questions and statements of opinions. Lawyers must adjust and be prepared to speak at length about their positions.

I asked Dershowitz why there was this difference and how to prepare for it. He explained that the United States Supreme Court "gets the most interesting cases. They're already interested; otherwise, they wouldn't have voted to grant review, whereas in the state Supreme Courts, in many states at least, in murder cases there's a mandatory appeal. Also, they have a much, much bigger docket. State Supreme Courts have many, many more cases than the United States Supreme Court.... When you're arguing at the state court, you have to be prepared for a cold bench or an inactive bench. I'm prepared to go all the way and just argue, but I'd much prefer if I could provoke them to asking me a question."

To fully appreciate Dershowitz's skills, you need to listen to his oral argument, which can be found at www.TurningPointsatTrial.com. Dershowitz embodies the three attributes of all great public speakers: credibility, logic, and passion. For example, whenever judges ask him a question, he never hesitates in giving a direct answer. Second, his arguments are easy to follow and are supported by references to the record on appeal or to important cases. But what is most indicative of Dershowitz's skill is his passion. He emphasizes key words in most sentences to drive his point home to the judges. He also will pause for dramatic effect. Furthermore, he never speaks at the same pace. He always varies it.

I asked Dershowitz if he ever tried to teach his speaking style to others. He replied that he is not aware of his style. "I don't even notice that. What I teach my students is to be yourself. You know, if you're quiet and unassuming, you shouldn't be trying to be different at oral argument. You have to be as conversational and as who you are as best you can. That, to me, is the key. You have to project with authenticity in your argument. You just can't be somebody else."

> *People ask me all the time, "How can we be more like you?" I say, "Don't be more like me, be more like you. Figure out what you do best and make the argument fit your particular strengths and personality."*
> — Alan Dershowitz

After listening to his argument, no one could doubt that Dershowitz believes 110 percent in his case. The reason he is very effective is that if someone presents a very logical argument with passion, it becomes difficult to disagree with him or her. Notice how Dershowitz builds crescendos into most of his sentences. This vocal technique, combined with the others mentioned above, makes for a very compelling argument that is interesting to listen to both for its content and its drama. Although I agree with Dershowitz's conclusion that you have to "be yourself," I would add that we can all become better public speakers by incorporating techniques used by the best public speakers, such as Dershowitz.

Dershowitz raised two main points at oral argument: the prosecution had inconsistent theories about the cause of death that were improper to submit to the jury, and the court allowed Binion's hearsay statement that was prejudicial to Murphy.

Prosecution's inconsistent theories of cause of death

May it please the court. My name is Alan Dershowitz, and I'm here on behalf of appellant Sandra Murphy. I'd like to reserve five minutes. I'd like to apologize to the court for the hoarseness of my voice. I have a flu. This is an unusual case in which each of the State's two expert witnesses testified in effect that there was a reasonable medical doubt about the other State's witness's conclusion concerning the cause of death. Dr. Simms, who performed the autopsy, testified that the cause of death was a combination of heroin and Xanax. Dr. Baden, the State's other expert witness, categorically rejected that proposition. The State called these witnesses and vouched for them both.

Dershowitz concisely sets forth the first issue he wants to discuss in his oral argument. There is no wind up and long summary of the facts. He gets right to the point and argues that the contradictory testimony is fatal to the prosecution's conviction.

Under the law of this jurisdiction, the prosecution cannot ask the fact finder to accept the conclusion regarding a cause of death in a murder case after it has introduced an expert witness who categorically rejects that cause of death. In the leading case of Azbill versus State, the burning bed case, 84 Nevada 345, the prosecution tried to argue death by fire, but the court ruled that "The state who undertook to present the evidence closed the door to death by fire in offering the testimony of Dr. Grayson who had testified that in his medical opinion fire had not caused the death," so too here.

Dr. Simms' testimony closed the door on the prosecution's burking theory by creating a reasonable doubt about Dr. Baden's alleged cause of death. Well, Dr. Baden's testimony closed the door on its drug theory by creating a reasonable doubt about Dr. Simms's alleged cause of death. The prosecution told the jury that the twelve of you need not be unanimous as to the cause of death.

[T]his is surely the kind of verdict by fragmentation rather than by unanimity that this Court and the Supreme Court has condemned. Now, although this Court has held and the Supreme Court has held that there need not be unanimity in regard to "the preliminary factual issues which underlie the verdict," there must be unanimity in the case I'm quoting where there is a genuine possibility of jury confusion or that a conviction may occur as a result of different jurors concluding that a defendant committed, and here's the keyword, conceptually distinct acts.

If several of the jurors, for example, believed that no drugs were forced into Binion, and several of the jurors thought that the combination of drugs rather than suffocation was the cause of death, the end result could be a verdict which left open the realistic possibility that the cause of death was not criminal at all or, at least, that there was a reasonable doubt about whether the cause of death was criminal.

Dershowitz next focuses the court's attention on whether the prosecution ever established a criminal cause of death through Dr. Simms's testimony.

The government in its brief says, "Our position." It's a very interesting word. "Our position is," and they said this in the summation, "that the cause of death may have been," they quoted one possible theory, "may have been that they administered the drugs, made him weaker, expected he would die of the drugs and saw the gardener outside and decided to burke him to speed up the process."

There's only one problem. They never submitted that hypothesis to either of their experts. There's nothing in the record of this case to demonstrate that it is possible to create a cocktail of Xanax, Valium, heroin, make them soluble in water, make them palatable enough to drink. There is simply no expert testimony as to how they conceivably could have got him to drink the drugs as you know you can't put drugs in somebody through their mouth when they're dead or unconscious to swallow. Reflex has to be in existence. What they have is a position without any evidence to support it.

> *What they have is a position without any evidence to support it.*
> — Alan Dershowitz, oral argument

Dershowitz's last sentence, "What they have is a position without any evidence to support it," is a wonderfully simply phrased sentence that you can use in your next argument.

Justice Leavitt: Didn't the State present expert testimony that he was suffocated?

Dershowitz: The State presented Dr. Baden, who said that as the diagnosis of exclusion, "I have concluded alone among the six experts, I have concluded that he was burked," and of course, if he's burked, it's homicide. There's no data that he burked himself. There's no data about that. The problem is that it was the diagnosis of exclusion and the State itself, I think if they're pressed, they will have to acknowledge that would not have been sufficient evidence to take this case to the jury. At least, they would never have presented this case to the jury. If they would have, why didn't they? They would have had a clear and simple path; present one witness.

They knew that neither witness standing alone was enough. They made their bed and they have to sleep in it. They could have presented one witness. They could have made this a one witness case and then tried to persuade you on appeal if they want. Unlikely that Dr. Baden's testimony, a diagnosis of exclusion standing against five of the witnesses. One of them was the State's own witness.

Justice Leavitt: Well, couldn't the jury decide which one of the witnesses they want to believe?

Dershowitz: No. No, Your Honor. Not when the State presents two. Not under Azbill because under Azbill, the same situation prevailed. You had two witnesses, but one doctor presented by the State and vouched for by the State said, "She could not have died from the flames." This court said that closed the door. The State cannot be in the position of presenting mutually exclusive contradictory witnesses and then say, "Ladies and gentlemen of the jury, pick and choose. Pick and choose." When one witness creates a reasonable doubt about the other witness, and the other witness creates a reasonable doubt about the first witness, that is a reasonable doubt.

Again, Dershowitz answers the judge's question directly. He says "no," and then lends credibility to his answer by succinctly explaining why. His answer becomes more authoritative when he cites the Azbill case that is precedent in Nevada. Dershowitz then turns to his second argument.

Hearsay evidence

Your Honor, the other crucial piece of evidence that was submitted, and it was a dynamite piece of evidence, if I were a prosecutor, you'd die for this piece of evidence, the decedent on the night before he dies says to his lawyer that "If I'm dead you'll know what happened. Take Sandy out of the will if she doesn't kill me tonight."

The State has the unbelievable arrogance to argue to this Court that it used that evidence only to show the state of mind of the decedent and that it was not trying to prove that the decedent believed that Murphy intended to kill him. They acknowledged that if that's the way they used it, it would be an improper issue. You can't use hearsay to prove the state of mind of somebody else.

Now, just listen to the closing argument and conclude whether you believe that they used it in this way. Here's the closing argument. "Take Sandy out of the will if she doesn't kill me tonight. If I'm dead, you'll know what happened." This is the prosecutor. **"Truer words were never spoken."** In other words, taken for its truth, not state of mind. **"Truer words were never spoken. Less than 24 hours later, Ted Binion was murdered in his house. He was murdered by people that presumably he trusted. He was murdered by his former girlfriend and her newfound lover."**

Let them explain to you how this statement which was the apex of their closing argument deals with his state of mind, the victim's, rather than clearly a prediction like in the Shepherd case. "She's going to kill me." That's the way it was used.

Justice Leavitt: Didn't the defense set forth the theory of suicide?

Dershowitz: Yes. We concede right here today—

Justice Leavitt: Didn't the State have to offset that?

Dershowitz: Right, but it can't use it this way. Here's what it could say: It could say first of all it has to first overcome a burden. Just because you entered a suicide [evidence] doesn't mean the State can introduce any hearsay statement. It has to show that the statement is inconsistent with a suicidal state of mind....

If you believe that the State really introduced it only for that reason, **then you must challenge them why did they use it in this fashion. Why did they use it to show it was a prediction that was going to come true?** Even if it's true that they had a narrow basis for introducing it, they clearly misused it, and the judge should have seen that coming as they were told to see it coming in the preliminary.

We see another example of Dershowitz directly answering a question from a judge instead of sidestepping the issue when he says, "we concede." Second, at the beginning of this chapter, Dershowitz stated that he liked to use phrases in his argument that the judges might use in writing their opinion. Here, he cites the prosecutor's closing argument where the prosecutor says, "Truer words were never spoken." Now let's turn to the court's opinion delivered after oral arguments.

The court decided that the hearsay statement should not have been allowed into evidence at trial and that such a mistake warranted a new trial. The court concluded that the State's evidence was highly circumstantial and the "statement is akin to testimony from Binion after his death. Without a limiting instruction, the risk was unacceptable that the jury would improperly consider the statement as evidence of appellants' intent or conduct during its eight days of deliberation, particularly in light of the State's closing argument that 'truer words were never spoken.'" The court's opinion tracked Dershowitz's argument perfectly and even used the exact phrase he recited to the judges in his oral argument.

Finally, notice in the above excerpt that Dershowitz suggests to the court to "challenge" the government attorney why the prosecution wanted the statement admitted. As Dershowitz said in our interview, he wants to provide the court with important questions to ask opposing counsel so he can frame the argument. Although the court did not ask this specific question, but rather others that Dershowitz suggested (see below), the "challenge" certainly highlights the weakness of the government's position which is reflected in the court's written opinion reversing the verdict.

Government's oral argument

Within the first minute of the government's oral argument presented by David Wall, the court interrupts Wall and echoes the argument Dershowitz asserted.

> **The Court:** *These experts were presented by the State. Both of them were presented by the State with apparently inconsistent theories.*
>
> **David Wall:** Correct.
>
> **The Court:** *Now, the Azbill case says that that's improper.*

In another exchange, the court tracks Dershowitz's argument in framing a question for the government.

> **The Court:** *Why doesn't Mr. Dershowitz's argument that that's a logical extension of Azbill apply here?*
>
> **David Wall:** Because for one thing, we can't always tell how defendants kill their victims.

17.8 AFTERMATH

Getting the appellate court to grant a new trial based on the trial court's error in allowing the jury to hear Binion's hearsay statement was no easy feat for Dershowitz. Hearsay law is not clear-cut, particularly on this issue. After the oral argument, a judge on the panel told a friend of Dershowitz's that Dershowitz's argument on hearsay was the best one he had ever heard.

But Dershowitz did not simply want to get a new trial. He wanted to ensure an acquittal if he were successful on appeal. Consequently, he had an expert already lined up who could prove that the prosecution's main theory of burking was premised on a false fact.

In the second trial, the prosecution was at a huge disadvantage due to Dershowitz's advocacy. It could not use Binion's hearsay statement, and its scientific theory was completely undercut by Dershowitz's expert witness. Not surprisingly, the jury rejected the prosecution's theory that Binion died from either burking or a deadly cocktail mix. Instead, the jury concluded it was a suicide. Murphy now operates an art gallery in California.

17.9 CHAPTER CHECKLIST ✎

Dershowitz's 20 tips for appellate advocacy

1. Don't put canned arguments into your brief.

2. Sloppy briefs that are not tailored to your specific appeal harm your chances.

3. Know the trial transcript of your case *and* the transcripts of the other leading cases at issue in the briefs.

4. "When you do an appeal, your only advantage in that courtroom is you know more than the judge does. They may know more about the law, but you know more about the facts. You have to be the master of the facts."

5. Instead of doing a moot court, "I think of the hardest possible questions that anybody could ask me. I then try to prepare answers, but I know more about the record of the case than a moot court judge would."

6. Never write out your oral argument.

7. In the first minute of your oral argument, frame the issue for the court by insisting that your framework is how the court should decide the case.

8. Try to lay a trap for the other side by suggesting to the court questions it should ask your opponent during her oral argument. For example, you can say, "I'm sure my opponent will agree that…." or "Your Honors, this is the crucial question. I'm not sure if the record permits for a disagreement, but please ask my distinguished opponents whether they agree or disagree with…."

9. "I try to give them a road map how to write their decision."

10. One of the biggest mistakes lawyers make is that they read their oral arguments.

11. Do not take notes to the podium.

12. Dershowitz tries to "include in my argument a few noteworthy phrases that the judges might want to borrow and put in their opinions."

13. If the court will allow it, split your time between your opening argument and rebuttal. Dershowitz likes to save as much time for rebuttal as the court will allow.

14. In rebuttal, Dershowitz likes to tell the court, "All right, here's what our position is, and here's what their position is. Here's the difference between us. Here's the place in the record that shows we're right."

15. A big mistake lawyers make is that they don't listen to the judge and thus fail to adjust their argument accordingly.

16. "A question [from the judge] is your friend."

17. When there is a cold bench, "I'll try to deliberately provoke questions. 'Your Honor might be wondering whether….'"

18. "You can't lose your credibility by disputing facts that are clearly not disputable."

19. When the court forces you to concede a bad fact against your client, you have to realize that "you only have one audience, it's the judge. You have to work it out with your client later."

20. "All the hard work in the world cannot bring about a result if the facts and the law don't justify it."

Q & A WITH THE AUTHOR

Q. What's the most important piece of advice you feel that this book offers to lawyers?

A. Be true to yourself and apply only the techniques used by the great lawyers that fit with your personality and litigation style. As Oscar Wilde said, "Be yourself: everyone else is already taken." I could not agree more. Litigation is more an art than a science.

Q. What made you decide to write a book like this?

A. Although many famous lawyers have written memoirs, none of those memoirs had the purpose to teach specific trial skills to lawyers. I wanted to bridge the gap from the many memoirs written by outstanding lawyers to the trial textbooks currently on the market that use hypotheticals and do not examine actual trials.

Q. What surprised you the most while your were conducting these interviews?

A. I was surprised how genuinely open each lawyer was about sharing his and her secrets. There was never any concern that an opponent might read the lawyer's chapter and be better prepared for a future trial. It is a risk all the lawyers took, but they had an overriding desire to help all lawyers become better. It was a generosity of spirit that continued to amaze me with each interview I conducted.

Q. How can a lawyer improve his or her litigation skills?

A. I am a big believer that the only way to learn to become a great trial lawyer is to study actual trials and get courtroom experience. Unfortunately, trial textbooks do not examine actual trials but use contrived fictional cases as the springboard to teach trial skills. Such a starting point is not realistic and doomed for failure. Once you learn the correct principles of trial advocacy, you need to find a way to get to the courthouse. If your current caseload does not look promising, volunteer as a criminal defense attorney or get involved in pro bono cases that are likely to go to trial.

Q. In the Introduction, you mentioned the process of how you wrote this book. Could you elaborate more on it?

A. I asked each lawyer what skill they wanted to teach my readers. After that, I spent countless hours reading thousands of pages of transcripts and editing them for each chapter. Then, I would meet the lawyer being profiled to discuss their general strategies and then the specific skill they wanted to focus on from the edited transcripts.

Q. What do you think makes a particular case a good teaching tool or example?

A. This is a great question. First, the case has to be interesting. It also cannot be too complicated. If it takes forever to summarize the facts, the reader is going to lose interest. Finally, to be a good teaching tool, the examples need to be memorable. Readers are very unlikely to forget McClain's use of leading questions to get his client to tell how working in the popcorn plant caused his horrific lung problems or Lanier's use of unforgettable analogies such as a boy scout's compass or watermelons being dropped off the roof of a building to discuss Merck's negligence regarding its drug Vioxx.

AFTERWORD

I strongly believe that the best way to learn litigation and trial skills is by studying transcripts from real cases. There is simply no way to learn such skills from the current textbooks that use contrived examples based on hypotheticals. That conviction led to the writing of *Turning Points at Trial*. Now that you have read this book, I hope you will agree that this learning process is more effective, practical, and memorable than the conventional method used in other books.

As I was writing this book, I was often asked, "What do great trial lawyers have in common?" My answer has three parts. First, each lawyer I interviewed was the best prepared and most knowledgeable person in the room, whether he was in a conference room for a deposition, a courtroom, or a court of appeals. *Turning Points at Trial* reinforces the time honored truth that success takes a lot of hard work.

Second, each lawyer framed his or her case in simple terms that would connect with the audience, whether the audience was a jury or a panel of appellate judges. I am sure everyone remembers Mark Lanier encouraging the jury to think about Merck money when it was considering damages, or Bryan Stevenson's strategy to talk about our collective identity when trying to persuade others on hotly disputed topics such as the death penalty or the fairness of the criminal justice system.

Third, each lawyer was passionate. Lisa Blatt said, "Your only objective is to win, leaving all your credibility and professionalism intact." Each lawyer described his or her passion in a slightly different way, but all were consistent in their love for their craft and their fervent desire to help their clients.

Finally, the revered Supreme Court Justice Benjamin Cardozo was once asked how he got all the interesting cases. He said, "Are you kidding? They are the most boring cases in the world until I get them, and I make them interesting." Use the secrets shared by the lawyers in this book and make your next case the most interesting one possible. It will make all the difference.

WORKS CONSULTED

*T*o avoid use of distracting footnotes within the chapters themselves, listed below are the sources for material that I consulted in addition to my interviews and the sources cited in the chapters.

CHAPTER ONE

Berenson, Alex. "Vioxx Verdict Raises Profile of Texas Lawyer." *New York Times,* August 22, 2005.

"Japan's Takeda Pharmaceutical Hit with $6bn Actos Damages Bill." BBC News, April 8, 2014.

Parloff, Roger. "Stark Choices at the First Vioxx Trial." *Fortune,* July 15, 2005.

Tigar, Michael and Angela Davis. *Trial Stories.* New York: Foundation Press, 2008.

CHAPTER TWO

Gallo, Carmine. *Talk Like TED.* New York: St. Martin's Press, 2014.

CHAPTER EIGHT

Bennett, Robert S. *In the Ring.* New York: Three Rivers Press, 2008.

CHAPTER TEN

Berenson, Alex. "Vioxx Verdict Raises Profile of Texas Lawyer." *New York Times,* August 22, 2005.

Feeley, Jeff and Kanoko Matsuyama. "Takeda, Lilly Jury Awards $9 Billion Over Actos Risks." *Bloomberg,* April 8, 2014.

Levine, Daniel and Edmund Klamann. "Japan drugmaker Takeda to fight $6 billion damages awarded by U.S. jury." Reuters, April 8, 2014. http://www.reuters.com/article/us-takeda-pharm-actos-verdict-idUSBREA3708F20140408

CHAPTER ELEVEN

The summary of the Stowe case was edited for length and clarity from Plaintiff's Opposition to Defendant's Motion for Summary Judgment.

CHAPTER FOURTEEN

Hollandsworth, Skip. "A Shooting on Spring Grove Avenue." *Texas Monthly,* November, 2014. Accessed on January 15, 2015. http://www.texasmonthly.com/the-culture/a-shooting-on-spring-grove-avenue/.

CHAPTER FIFTEEN

Stevenson, Bryan. *Just Mercy.* New York: Spiegel and Grau, 2014; TED talk given in March 2012. Accessed on June 2, 2015. www.Ted.com/talk.

CHAPTER SIXTEEN

Clerk of the Supreme Court, *Guide for Counsel,* 7 (2013). Accessed on January 15, 2015. http://www.supremecourt.gov/oral_arguments/guideforcounsel.pdf.

ACKNOWLEDGMENTS

*O*bviously, the book could not have been written without the generosity of the lawyers I interviewed. But the book required the help of many others who are too numerous to mention such as the editors, proofreaders, and many others involved with the production of the book.

Nonetheless, I cannot fail to specifically thank Caroline, Gloria, Jenna, and Will who were so instrumental in this book's success. I also want to thank Brian Stoltz and Bradley Clark for their insightful comments. Also, thanks to John Parker and Steve Fahey for providing me a wonderful career at the U.S. Attorney's Office and their support.

But the person I need to mention the most is my wife, Linda, whose faith in me caused me to write this book. This book was only an idea I had thought about for several years but never prioritized or believed was possible to write. When a door had closed on a project, Linda urged me to finally make this book happen.

After deciding to write this book, the excitement of writing it was often countered by countless roadblocks along the way, and many of them seemed insurmountable. These obstacles were all the more daunting because I was trying to write a unique textbook that many doubted could be done.

No matter the obstacle or how long it lasted, Linda always provided a compassionate and thoughtful sounding board, a solution, and just the right dose of humor. There were also the many sacrifices of time my family, and primarily Linda, made in order to allow me to write this book during countless nights, weekends and vacations.

Ralph Waldo Emerson once said, "Nothing great was ever achieved without enthusiasm." It was Linda's enthusiasm for me, her belief in my writing skills, and her unwavering passion that others would benefit from my teaching that made *Turning Points at Trial* a reality.

ABOUT THE AUTHOR

*S*hane Read is a nationally recognized expert who has helped thousands of attorneys throughout the USA and Europe transform their deposition, trial, and oral advocacy skills through his consultations, training programs, and keynote speeches.

He is the author of bestselling litigation textbooks that include Turning Points at Trial, Winning at Cross-Examination, Winning at Persuasion for Lawyers, and Winning at Deposition. Two of his textbooks have won the Association of Continuing Legal Education's top honor for Professional Excellence. He is the only author to win this award twice. His textbooks have been adopted in law schools across the country and critically acclaimed by publications such as Bar Journals and Kirkus Reviews. In addition, his textbooks have been endorsed by judges, professors, a former U.S. Attorney General, a former

U.S. Solicitor General, and past presidents of city, state and national trial lawyers' organizations such as IATL and ABOTA.

He has been an adjunct professor in trial advocacy since 1999 at Southern Methodist University's Dedman School of Law. He has also taught new and experienced lawyers throughout the United States, including training programs at national law firms, the National Institute of Trial Advocacy's headquarters, the Department of Justice's National Advocacy Center, and state bars around the country.

He is a graduate of Yale University and the University of Texas School of Law. He began his legal career in 1989 at Akin Gump in Dallas, before joining the

U.S. Attorney's Office in Washington, D.C., from 1992 to 1998. Since 1998, he has worked at the U.S. Attorney's Office in Dallas in both the civil and criminal sections. He has tried over 100 trials to verdict over the past 30 years and has served as lead counsel for 22 oral arguments before appellate courts.

For more information go to www.shaneread.com.

---

[1] T1The views expressed in this book are solely those of the author and do not reflect the views of the Department of Justice.

INDEX

leading questions in, 161, 226
length of, 155, 257
in *Lord v. City of Dallas,* 414–424
mistakes in, 173
notes in, 156, 178–179, 254
"pay dirt" endpoint in, 176
pitfalls of, 149
principles, 225–229
setting up of, during opening statement, 223–225
in *Simo v. Mitsubishi,* 257–268
strategies, 152–153, 254–257
to support case, 239–240, 246
theme in, 187, 225, 258–259
in *United States v. W.R. Grace & Co.,* 184–211
witness preparation for, 124–125

D

Damages
in closing argument, 293–298, 306–307, 320, 349–350
deposition and, 378
emotional, 112–114
instructions from judge for, 293–294
pain and suffering and, 112–114, 322–323
punitive, 290–293, 293–298, 320, 349–350, 378
range for, 349
strategies, 294–298
"Data dump," 97
Death penalty cases, in appellate oral argument, 446–449
Declaratory statements, in cross-examination, 161
Delivery
of appellate oral argument, 475–476, 501–502
of closing argument, 307
of cross-examination, 156
emphasis in, 76–77, 80, 507
of opening statement, 13–14, 38–39, 72–73
of winning argument, 72–73
word choice and, 82–83
Demeanor, 6
Demonstrative exhibit, 13. *See also* Exhibit(s)
Deposition(s)
case theory and, 361
credibility and, 420–421
cross-examination and, 176, 240

N

O

Z

Made in the USA
Coppell, TX
22 August 2024

36310979R20308